The Sabres of Paradise

The Sabres of Paradise

LESLEY BLANCH

Carroll & Graf Publishers, Inc.
New York

Published by arrangement with Viking Penguin, Inc.

First Carroll & Graf edition 1984

Carroll & Graf Publishers, Inc.
260 Fifth Avenue
New York, N.Y. 10001

ISBN: 0-88184-042-4

Manufactured in the United States of America

For
Edna and Marston Fleming
with love

Contents

Illustrations

Acknowledgements

I am indebted to many people for their generous help during the writing of this book. First, the descendants of the Imam Shamyl whose unique sources were so warmly shared. Count Hilarion Woronzov-Daschkov gave me much valuable material, especially concerning his ancestors, three of whom were Viceroys of the Caucasus. Prince Alexis Scherbatow (whose mother, Princess Anne Bariatinsky, was the Field-Marshal's great-niece) generously lent me family papers and an unpublished portrait of his great-great-uncle, Prince Bariatinsky.

So many people were generous of their time and patience, answering my questions, remembering, and pointing the way: my thanks are due in particular to Monsieur and Madame Resat Nuri Darago; Monsieur Jacques Vimont; and Colonel Serge Obolensky. To Madame Lucia Davidova I owe more than I can ever express for her guidance and companionship as I wandered through the Caucasian maze. To my husband, Romain Gary, I owe an especial debt for his enthusiasm and understanding during the years I was absorbed in Caucasian research.

I thank Countess Alexandra Tolstoy for sparing time from her work at the Tolstoy Foundation to talk of her father's life in the Caucasus, as I thank Monsieur Constantine de Grunwald, the historian, for so much encouragement and indulgent help and Monsieur André Malraux for his lively interest and views on how best to illustrate the book. This brings me to Prince Gargarin's wonderful drawings made during a tour of duty in the Caucasus. These have a strange quality, at once factual and romanticized; thus we see, in the portrait of Hadji Mourad, not only the awe-inspiring landscape, but 'the Red Devil' himself, drawn from life.

Most of the sources of the Murid Wars are in Russian; a few Arabic or Turkish: therefore I want to thank all those who worked with me on the intricacies of translation or interpreting, especially Monsieur Nikolai Gubsky, Monsieur Mahommed Ali Issik and Madame Neclâ Tonak, as well as Mr. Hugh Brooke for his valuable assistance in assembling my material. Above all, Mrs. Osyth Leeston who so devotedly worked with me to produce order from the chaos of my original manuscript.

I also wish to express my appreciation of the patience and co-operation shown by various governmental departments—of the Embassies of the U.S.S.R. in London and Paris and the Turkish Embassy in Paris, where I am especially indebted to Monsieur Barhaten Ornekohl, as I am to all departments of Turkish officialdom in Istanbul. The Bibliothèque Nationale, Columbia University, the New York Public Library, the New York Society Library, H.M. Foreign Office Library, and that of the Royal Geographical Society were all infinitely helpful; and especially, the London Library. Here, I wish to acknowledge my deep debt to the late J. F. Baddeley. Long before I ever approached the mountains, his *Conquest of the Caucasus* stirred my interest; but when I began my own researches I discovered, at the London Library, The Baddeley Bequest. This comprises the Russian sources he had amassed during his life in Russia, at the turn of the century, together with his notes and index. Through this material I was able to form my own estimates of many events and characters, and to reassess a number of basic sources which otherwise could only have been obtained by many months of work in the libraries and archives of the U.S.S.R.—this being a cherished project which I was not able to realize at the time I was writing the book.

I must also say how grateful I am to Mademoiselle Hadduc Daghestanli for her generosity in passing on some of the sources and material for her forthcoming biography of her father, General Mahommed Fazil Daghestanli Pasha. This book, to be published in Turkey, is one which all who are interested in the Caucasus await impatiently.

Lastly I want to thank Monsieur Samuelian, of Paris, in whose Librarie Orientale (an Aladdin's cave for bibliophiles) I spent so many rewarding hours, founding my own collection of Caucasiana, and but for whose advice and help I might never have succeeded in finding Shamyl's descendants.

I am indebted to the following publishers for permission to quote from these works:

Ivan Ilych, Hadji Murad and Other Stories by Leo Tolstoy (World's Classics Series), translated by Louise and Aylmer Maude. Oxford University Press. pp. 72, 276-7. *A Hero of Our Times* by Mikhail Lermontov. George Allen & Unwin Ltd. p. 193. *My Past Thoughts* by Alexander Herzen, translated by Constance Garnett. Chatto & Windus Ltd. pp. 159, 160, 184, 240-1. *The Russian Conquest of the Caucasus* by J. F. Baddeley. Longmans, Green & Co. Ltd. pp. 233, 300, 409. *Eternels Compagnons de Route* by D. Merejkovsky. Éditions Albin Michel. pp. 194-5. *La Sainte Russie*, French translation by Henri Troyat. Éditions Bernard Grasset. p. 195. *Nicholas I* by Constantin de Grunwald, translated by Bridget Patmore. MacGibbon & Kee and Douglas Saunders. pp. 360, 362. *Dead Souls* by Gogol. Benn's Essex Library, edited by Edward G. Hawke with an introduction by Stephen Graham. pp. 145-6.

The Sabres
of Paradise

I know how to use a dagger—
I was born in the Caucasus.

ALEXANDER PUSHKIN

Introduction

The Caucasians wrote love-poems to their daggers, as to a mistress, and went to battle, as to a rendezvous. Fighting was life itself to these darkly beautiful people—the most beautiful people in the world, it was said. They lived and died by the dagger. Battle-thrusts were the pulse of the race. Vengeance was their creed, violence their climate. 'I am at my eleventh head', boasted a Caucasian princeling, a twelve-year-old, who spoke French with a Parisian accent which won the admiration of Alexander Dumas and who coveted his father's bag of twenty-four rebel heads, severed as contribution to the pacification of the province. The baby prince Georghi Melikov, at an age when he might have been sucking his thumb, was running it over the blade of his *kindjal*, or two-edged dagger, lisping that it had been made for him by Mourtazali the celebrated armourer. When Agha Mahommed, 'the Persian Eunuch', took Tiflis in 1795, his troops raped all the women they fancied, and as a memento of their victory they ham-strung the right leg of every virgin taken. But the women, too, knew how to fight, for they were believed to descend from the Amazons. Beneath their veils they wore a dagger. When the inhabitants of Akhulgo were besieged by the invading Russian army in 1837, women fought beside men; when their ammunition had gone, they flung down rocks on the oncoming troops; when there were no more rocks, the men hurled themselves to death, on the bayonets below. And when the men were gone, the women flung down their children, as living missiles, and leapt after them. Such was their desperate resistance. Such was this climate of violence.

Severed enemy heads or hands were always good coinage in the Caucasus. A Tousheen girl's dowry was reckoned in these trophies. The more dashing a young Caucasian *delikan*, or brave, the more severed hands dangled from his saddle-bow. Right hands, of course; left hands hardly counted, and the loss of one never stopped a Caucasian from fighting. Sliced-off ears, a less cumbersome method of indicating the number of heads taken, were usually strung along the whip thong. When one Tchetchen chieftain found his son dead of wounds, he cut his body into sixty pieces, and sent out horsemen across the mountains and valleys, each with a fragment, to be given to his kinsmen and vassals. For each piece, an enemy head was returned. Thus was his son's death avenged. Vengeance, vendetta or *kanly*, was often pursued through three or four generations, decimating whole families, till there was no one left. A household was only reckoned poor, only pitied, when there was no one fit to fight.

Vengeance and violence; such was the Caucasus throughout its dark history, reaching its apogee during the first half of the nineteenth century, when the invading Russian armies marched eastwards acquiring their Asiatic and near-Eastern provinces, and met their first check among the Caucasian mountains. All the warring Moslem tribes now banded together in one terrible force, and under one man, Shamyl, the Avar, their Prophet and Warrior. In 1834 he sprang on to the scene in a flash of steel, a clap of thunder, like some flamboyant Prince of Darkness, the dramatic nature of his legend and his black banners matched by his back-cloth of towering mountains, perpendicular rock cliffs topped by eagle's-nest *aôuls*, or fortified villages, hung over ravines slit so deep no light ever penetrated the abyss where torrents raged, and a never-ceasing wind howled down the passes. This was his birth-place— the wild mountains of Daghestan, an almost unmapped rock waste, set between Black Sea and Caspian.

Only the Caucasus—only Shamyl's will—barred the Russians' overland route to India, and their long-cherished dreams of colonial expansion—eastwards. Every mile their armies marched east, every village taken, every Cossack frontier post established, was watched apprehensively by the rest of Europe, from Westminster to the Porte, by way of the Hofburg and the Vatican. Baron Meyerdorff, as the Tzar Nicholas I's mouthpiece, spoke of Russia's salutary influence upon Western Asia. But Countess Nesselrode, wife of the Russian statesman, spoke for future generations, and other continents too, when she wrote: 'Europe could not reconcile itself to the flagrant lack of delicacy in the simple fact of Russia being a great power.'

The story of Shamyl's life and times is, therefore, in part the history of Russian colonial expansion, and in particular that era known as the Murid Wars, 'The Time of the Shariat' as it was sometimes called; the time when Shamyl revived and enforced Mahommed's laws, using them as an arm against Russian conquest; the time when his warriors fought a holy war, for Allah and liberty, and their sabres were, to them, the keys to Paradise.

*   *   *

In 1801, the kingdom of Georgia had been peacefully annexed by Russia. Imeretia and Mingrelia followed suit in 1803 and 1804. But to the north, in the mountains of Daghestan, a resistance began which was to flame into a terrible war lasting until 1861. These campaigns, the Murid Wars, took their name from Shamyl's warriors, the Moslem tribesmen whom he welded into an army of fanatics—fighting monks known as Murids, their leaders, Naibs. No Naib was ever taken alive.

Whoever writes of the Caucasus writes of extremes, and whoever writes of Russia—of the essential Russian temperament—writes of excess. On the battlefields of the Caucasus these were met together with terrible consequences.

The invading Russians, all the might of the Tzar's Armies of the South, were dwarfed by the forbidding mountains, which stood like a great wall, separating the Christian and Moslem world. These mountains seemed the boundary of Europe. Beyond, all was legend and fable. From afar, the Caucasus had appeared a voluptuous Oriental dream. 'Colchis, land of the Golden Fleece, the soft-breathing south', the sweetmeat childish oriental world where the dancers of Shemakha undulated, their braceleted and hennaed feet stirring the gold-laden dust of Asia. But the mirage proved to have a core of bloodshed and fury; for gold, there was steel; for love, hatred.

Three sounds echoed through the mountains: the sound of drums calling the people to war, or beating out the savage rhythms of the *lesghinka*, the sound of the wind howling down the passes, and the sound of a flute played by a shepherd.

Such was the Caucasus in the first half of the nineteenth century. Everywhere, extremes; tigers roaming the tropic, eastern lowlands; eagles soaring above the gaunt uplands. Gigantic mountains straddling the land. The White Mountains, the Black Mountains; 'ravines where the bat flies by day, and night adds little to their gloom.' Aôuls—mountain villages—from which the women and children had been banished, and where only warriors lived, and from which they galloped out, to raid and die, chanting their death-songs and fighting some last-stand battle bound together, a living rampart against the Russians' fire. Even the word aôul has an onomatopaeic harshness: a sinister ring conjuring desolation and doom. All around were arid regions where nothing lived, where only the wind raged, never ceasing. Ridged rocks where no mule could climb, yet straining lines of Russian soldiers hauled their guns into position. 'Can a dog go there? Where a dog can go, a Russian soldier can go too,' said General Grabbé, as the Tzar's Army of the South fought desperately to subdue and conquer the cruel Caucasus, key-position of their colonial expansion.

Yet, some landscapes, like some nations and people, reveal a second side, or other face. The Caucasus is such a land, at once harsh and exotic, forbidding and compelling. And Shamyl, the embodiment of his land, was at once warrior and mystic, ogre and saint, foxy and innocent, chivalrous and ruthless. Beneath the heroic overtones of both man and land elegiac murmurs were sometimes to be heard. Shamyl the Avar, the dread Chieftain, could love his wife with such a passion that he forgot everything—his battles, his men, his cause—to reach her bedside when she lay dying.

And down in Tiflis, in the glowing lowlands, beyond the shadows of the mountains and the battles' periphery, there was an atmosphere of seduction, voluptuous adventures and political intrigue. Vineyards and orange groves, bazaars piled with silks and spices, Persian jewellers weighing turquoises by the pound, and Caucasian armourers working on the beautiful damascened blades for which they were celebrated throughout the world. From the Tartar mosques, the chants of the Faithful rose at evening to mingle with the singing of bearded monks in the Armenian churches. Ramshackle, fretted balconies overhung the river Koura, where, in the twilight, the sound of *târ* and *zurna* accompanied the plaintive songs of Georgia. Yet this southern softness was never that 'dew-dropping south of love-whispering woods and lute-resounding waves'. The land, like the people, retained a savagery behind the beauty.

Everywhere in Tiflis at this time, black-veiled crones, all limping, an oddly regimented step: they were the survivors of those virgins whom Agha Mahommed's Persian troops had raped and ham-strung so long ago, and whose children looked now to Russia to protect them against the threat of Moslem domination, Persian, Turkish, or tribal.

On the roof-tops, at evening, the long-nosed, doe-eyed Georgian beauties took the air, fanned themselves, and eyed the swaggering warriors who prowled round, cat-like, in their soft leather boots: wooing, fighting men, dark demoniac figures in their pointed black lamb-skin caps and shaggy goat's-hair *bourkas*, the all-enveloping cloak of the Caucasus, worn by the Georgian peasant and noble, by the Russian officers and by the tribesmen from the mountains.

'I saw one of them, today,' writes a Tiflis visitor, recording his first glimpse of the dreaded mountaineers. 'He was riding a steed as fiery as himself. They flew away together like the wind and the clouds, and seemed but one . . . a stream of silvery light, for the horse was grey, and the man's clothes glittered with chain mail, his arms silver and steel. . . .'

In the surrounding country, and north along the banks of the Valerik —the River of Death—Cossack outposts, where a race of flat-faced, snub-nosed, burly men lived: 'Cossacks of the Line'. They had been bred to hold the line of Russian fortifications, those frontiers which thrust year by year farther south—and east. Here the Cossacks lived and died, raided and were raided by the 'Tartars' as they loosely called the agglomeration of Caucasian tribes who all united to resist their Russian invaders.

Stretching across the narrow span of the Caucasus, from Caspian to Black Sea, and bordered north by the Russian steppes and south by the

Turkish and Persian frontiers, was a handful of dusty little garrison towns such as Khassif Yourt, Poti, or Temir-Khan-Shura: bases from which men went out to die; where water-buffalo snorted in dried-up streams, where bad champagne, tattered packs of cards and easy women were the only distractions for the young Russian officers quartered there (Tolstoy and Lermontov among them). They were generally a breed of raffish St. Petersburg *jeunesse dorée* exiled to the Caucasus by debts, duelling, unhappy love affairs, or liberal opinions too freely expressed.

Farther to the north, cradled among gigantic peaks, were the newly built mineral spas where St. Petersburg society found all that it interpreted as exoticism and danger. Handsome, savage princes; eternal snows; tropic vegetation and romantic ruins. Kisslovodsk and Piatigorsk, where the waters were considered particularly effective against the ravages of syphilis, and where the more degenerate Russian aristocracy congregated hopefully in an atmosphere of scandal and luxury; where a duel to the death—such as Lermontov's—was held to have been well worth engineering, if it provided distraction from the ennui of provincial life. This highly seasoned environment made even the most celebrated Don Juans look to their laurels. The visiting ladies hankered after mountaineers or brigands. Nothing else would do.

Wounded Russian officers sent to recuperate at Kisslovodsk were much in demand, as they strolled, pale and intriguing, beneath the avenues of eucalyptus; but what the ladies craved, what they had really come to seek, was a local noble, a Shamkal, an Emir, or Khan. Even an untitled, lawless Lesghien, such as they had discovered in Bestoujev's torrid tales, would do. Suddenly the salons of St. Petersburg had become stultifying. The marble perspectives and winter-gardens had begun to pall. They packed and left for the Caucasus.

Until Shamyl captured the two Princesses, ladies-in-waiting to the Tzarina, in 1854, of which I shall tell later, it had been secretly every woman's dream to be seized, flung over the saddle of a pure-bred Kabarda steed, and forced to submit to the advances of some darkling mountaineer.

Indeed, Madame Hommaire de Hell recounts the case of a Russian lady who had been abducted by the Lesghiens and was later rescued, after great difficulties, by a detachment of General Grabbé's men, but who fled back to the mountains again, so gallant had she found the tribesmen.

*   *   *

In this climate of drama, where vengeance was the first principle, weapons were personified, taking on a character, an entity of their own.

I was made for Ammalet Beg, says one blade. *I will help thee by day and by night* (both legally and illegally), says another. *I am slow to offend, quick to avenge*, says a gold and ivory inlaid kindjal. *May thy kindjal rust* was a malediction. They were not the sickle-shaped scimitars of the romanticized east, but straight and heavy. The kindjal was a two-foot dagger, fluted and double edged; the *shashka*, a huge sabre, barely curved and very weighty. No Caucasian man was properly dressed without his kindjal, and women, too, wore a smaller, but scarcely less formidable dagger, thrust through their waist-belt. The kindjal was used slashingly. 'The cut' was *de rigueur*. To kill with the point lacked artistry. Weapons were a cult, as dear as honour itself.

Everywhere, at all times, the Caucasian people fought. Battle thrusts were the pulse of the people. They fought among themselves, or against the invaders, with an equal fury. Successive waves of would-be conquerors had found them a terrible foe; Roman legions, Arabs, Attila, Genghis Khan, Tamerlane—and the Persians, who called the Caucasus 'Seddi Iskender'—the barrier of Alexander. The mighty conqueror had set out to possess the world, and met his first check here. Legends of Caucasian impregnability lingered on in Persia, where there was a saying: 'When a Shah is a fool, he attacks Daghestan.' Some invaders were not even considered worthy of a pitched battle by the Caucasians. Nadir Shah, having conquered India and its many fiery kingdoms, next decided to subdue Daghestan and the Caucasian provinces. But he was met, and defeated, by a raging army of Amazons. The men had not thought it worth while turning out themselves.

'When shall blood cease to flow in the mountains?' runs a local proverb. 'When sugar canes grow in the snows', comes the answer.

Aloof, yet dominating this violent land, stood the mountains, majestic and unchanging through the centuries. They were the 'frosty Caucasus' of which Shakespeare sung. The Mountain of Stars, where the Djinn Padishah, the mighty chief of the Furies, lives; Kazbek, where legend has it Prometheus was chained; Elbruz, highest peak of the Black Mountains, 'which no man may scale without God's leave', and where, in the hollow between its twin peaks, they tell you the Ark rested on its way to Ararat. The first person known to have climbed Elbruz was a young Englishman, Douglas Freshfield, who took time off from his studies at Oxford in 1861. He made the ascent without much fuss; the local guides were not believed when they first returned to the aôuls far below, telling of the victorious ascent.

These were the mighty ranges that dwarfed the Alps, and were to inspire Tolstoy and change his whole concept of life. 'But the mountains! the mountains!' he cried, galloping towards their vast horizons, there to find the inspiration for what Turgeniev described as his finest work, *The Cossacks*. They came to obsess him; through them he discovered that elemental simplicity for which he longed, and for which he was to strive all the rest of his life. The fountain-head of his regeneration was formed here ... 'from that moment, all assumed the new, sternly majestic character of the mountains. . . . "Now life begins," seemed to be sounded in his ear by some solemn voice.'

To Shamyl, who straddled these mountains like a legendary giant, they were his birthright, his kingdom. From their shadows he first unfurled his black standard. In the name of Ghazavat! Holy War! he wielded the dissenting mountain tribes into the implacable army of fanatics whose private feuds were submerged in their common hatred of the Infidel invaders. For twenty-five years, he dominated both land and people. For twenty-five years, the Caucasians accepted lives of bleak abnegation and hardship—for Shamyl. His Murids revolved around his dark presence with the slow set circling of planetary forces. In life and death his word was law. All of them were vowed to resist Russia to the death. His four wives bowed before him in love and submission. His little son was sacrificed to the cause of freedom. His sister flung herself into a raging torrent, six hundred feet below, to die on his command. His mother lay at his feet, beaten unconscious on his orders when she pleaded mercy for a defaulting tribe.

Yet this terrible figure could be seen, by those few who ever came to know him in later life, laughing with childish pleasure at the antics of a cheap conjurer and confessing he found the beauty and plunging décolletées of the Russian ladies quite overpowering. Though that was in his more mellowed, older days. At the height of his power, he was often to be seen sitting cross-legged at a low table, opposite his favourite cat, a large, very plain black and white creature who was a capricious eater, and for whom Shamyl ordered special dishes.

But then, tenderness is in the tradition of tyrants. The Tzar Nicholas I, Shamyl's life-long enemy and, like him, a tyrant, could walk bare-headed, with brimming eyes, at a pauper's funeral. The odious Ali Pasha of Janina always wept copiously and asked pardon of the flowers he picked. Nor did he hesitate to drown his sons' wives, and even insured that his sons should be watching, from afar, when this macabre boating-party set out across the lake in carefully riddled barques; the shrieking victims sank within seconds, dragged under by the weight of their wide velvet trousers, their jewels and finery. Soon the rippled surface of the lake was still once more; only a gauze turban floated among the water-lilies. . . . Yet Ali Pasha was known to have waded into that lake, beard high, to rescue a pair of giddy butterflies.

Not that there could be any true comparison between Ali Pasha and Shamyl. Violence apart, they were men of a very different kidney. Shamyl's love for his children—for all children and animals—was returned lavishly. Yet he was to sacrifice his adored son, Djemmal-

Eddin, whom the Russians forced him to surrender as a hostage during a series of bitter reversals in 1839. Shamyl the father made the sacrifice for Shamyl the warrior. *The Caucasus must be freed!* But from that moment, the fury of his leadership was rendered even more fanatic by the rage of a father robbed of his first-born. He waited for the moment when he might obtain hostages of enough consequence to enable him to bargain for the return of Djemmal-Eddin.

That day was to come.

The son's pathetic destiny, and his part in this drama, have been overshadowed by the sweep of Caucasian history, and the place occupied by his father. We trace, among many interwoven threads, these two lives, one so full of Olympian thunders, the other, an elegiac melody, soon stilled.

Part One

I

The Time

Europe could not reconcile itself to the flagrant lack of delicacy in the simple fact of Russia being a great power.   COUNTESS NESSELRODE

Today, the name of Shamyl means little outside Russia and the Near East, though there are exiled Caucasian families living in Turkey (among them some of Shamyl's descendants) who still hang his portrait on their walls with all the reverence accorded to an ikon. There is an old house overlooking the Bosphorus, where a lamp burns before his portrait by night and a vase of fresh flowers is placed there every day.

A hundred years or more ago, leading European newspapers devoted columns to his exploits: questions were asked in the House of Commons as to Britain's commitments in the Caucasus, his bravery was extolled from public platforms, and English ladies were sewing an elaborate piece of bunting designed to become his flag. Shamyl's heroic stand was interpreted with gratification as a deliberate check to Tzarist designs on India. The Caucasus barred the overland route to Delhi: it was clear, this man was an ally, 'a really splendid type who stood up to tyrants . . . and deeply religious, even if he did have several wives . . .' Thus the ladies of the parish sewing circle, fortified by tea and pound cake, as they stitched away at an appliqué of scarlet stars on a white ground and dreamed of it fluttering from some dark Caucasian peak.

There was no doubt Shamyl had captured England's imagination. Enterprising music-publishers were selling *The Circassians' March* (adapted for the pianoforte), while *The Shamyl Schottische*, with a richly coloured cover, depicted a land of mountain ranges where eagle-faced warriors flourished swords or fondled Arab chargers. Curiously, the English public seems to have been far more aware of Shamyl during his early years than the Russians. To them he was at first merely represented as a rolling-eyed Tartar ogre, in the terms of crude woodcuts sold at village fairs to girls whose sweethearts had been marched off to fight against him.

While Russia, as a whole, was only waking slowly to the significance of Shamyl in the gathering momentum of their colonial expansion, Britain, a practised hand at colonial conquest, was suffering the liveliest apprehension over Russia's designs in the Caucasus and east- wards. 'The Caucasian Isthmus and Circassia is the key to all the pro- jected enterprises of Russia in the East', wrote an impassioned political columnist in the early 'forties. 'To Great Britain in particular the success of the Circassian cause must be held of first-rate importance to the security of her Indian domains, and the maintenance of that high position she has held, and ought to support in Central Asia. The mere presence of a British fleet in the Black Sea would be a signal for the Turks, Persians and those Crimean Tartars that now acknowledge Russian authority to arm, simultaneously, and the result would probably be the retreat of Russia to her own snowy steppes.' Sounding that irrepressible tutorial note, not unmixed with business acumen familiar to students of British colonial development, the writer continues: 'It is our *duty*, our obligation, by our rank and influence among nations, to procure, for the sake of humanity, a cessation of hostilities in Circassia. We should also endeavour to enlighten be- nighted inhabitants of that portion of the globe by imparting to them our laws and institutions which, however imperfect, are founded in wisdom, tested by experience, and have, confessedly, a direct tendency to propel man onward in the path of civilization.' (Not that there was much cause for complacency in England in the 'fifties; when thirty-six thousand people escaped intolerable poverty by emigration in 1851 alone; when fifty thousand women worked for less than sixpence a day; and when the vast majority of what was described as 'the Lower Orders' still meekly remained in that uncomfortable station of life in which it had pleased their masters to leave them.) The writer adds, naïvely enough: 'This civilization and enlightenment will be best insured by establishing [with Circassia] *commercial relations* which would answer a two-fold purpose of enriching them, and as they advance in industry and wealth, of rendering the barrier still more formidable against the inroads of the only European power [Russia] which seeks through its wanton aggression and insatiable ambition, to disturb the harmony of nations.'

Echoes of these encouraging opinions must have reached Shamyl, who, at all times, seems to have been comparatively well-informed of the outside world, being a subscriber to newspapers and journals from St. Petersburg, which were read to him, often on the march between battles, by his interpreters who trotted beside his stirrup, gasping out the news—some weeks late, but still bringing echoes of life in London, Vienna, Baden-Baden and Paris. Of politics, *le beau monde*, the Bourse. . . . With what joy must Shamyl's women have fallen on these news- papers, have smoothed out the crumpled sheets covered with what seemed to them unintelligible hieroglyphics. They only knew some Arabic, or their own Ma'aroumat or Avar tongue: but how eagerly they must have studied the fashion page adorned with Monsieur Worth's monstrous crinolines and feathered bonnets. In the late 'fifties the legend of the crinoline had penetrated even the Caucasian strongholds, and one traveller recounts meeting a swarthy brigand figure, galloping along, heavily armed, but carrying the huge cage of a crinoline purchased in Tiflis for his bride's delight and the astonishment of the whole village.

Shamyl presently became convinced of England's sympathy, and lost no time in announcing this powerful ally to his chiefs. There was the case of Captain Bell where something more than sympathy had been apparent. The Captain's vessel, *The Vixen*, had been captured off the coast of Circassia by a Russian man o'war, and created a diplomatic incident of the first magnitude. The British stoutly maintained the cargo was salt—just salt; but the Russians insisted they found large quantities of arms—destined to aid Shamyl and his men.

Soon, Shamyl began addressing Queen Victoria personally, in a series of appeals, ruler to ruler, asking her support in his struggle against Russian tyranny and religious persecution. His letters, formed in the graceful Turco-Tartar script, and signed by all the most venerable and respected cäids and mollahs of Daghestan, were arriving regularly in London, though there is no telling if they ever reached Buckingham Palace. Mollahs, and even Imams, did not receive quite the same sympathetic consideration which Victorian England accorded magistrates, curates and bishops. But Victoria, shrewd and well-informed, must have realized Shamyl's significance in near-Eastern and Eastern power politics. In the early 'forties H.M. Foreign Office messengers were hurrying between St. Petersburg, Delhi, London and the Porte with dispatches telling of his every move. Caucasian independence, as such, was not of great matter to the big powers: but anyone who might oppose Russia was of note. As early as 1827 Lord Palmerston was writing to his brother, Sir William Temple: 'Metternich must be an idiot if he does not see that Russia is the windward quarter of the heavens, and that his dirty weather must come from thence, and therefore that he should look for some shelter westward.'

Any man, and any land, standing between Russia and India was of consequence to England, as the Afghan wars were to prove.

'The English fear the Russians' war in the Caucasus may threaten their possessions in India', wrote an impartial observer.... 'Persia becomes almost a Russian province: Russia could threaten Lahore, the Peri of precious stones. The Sikhs, trained to war by the French, would become invincible were they supported by the Russians. Were the Russian army to declare it wished, not to subdue, but to *liberate* India from English domination, they would see all India come under its standard, led by the different princes. Tartary, the nursery of invaders, could, if roused by Russia, in a year of bad pasturage, throw huge masses of warriors into India. How could the Bengal army resist such a tide?'

Even the smallest aspects of Caucasian inter-tribal warfare had now become of interest to Britain.

II

Russia had, from time immemorial, been an object of speculation and mistrust to Western Europe. There had always been an Iron Curtain. Russia had always been a world of its own, something remote and improbable, lying behind natural geographic barriers and those other man-made barriers of a police state—of Tzarist Russia.

When Dr. Johnson stated that the uses of travel were to regulate the imagination by reality, he spoke at a time when travel was interpreted as the Grand Tour, France, Italy and the Alps. . . . The mere thought of Russia exceeded most imaginations. The language was unmanageable; the calendar was twelve days back; the journey took all of three weeks over abominable roads which caused the post-chaises to disintegrate *en route*.

Even after the advent of railways the journey was a considerable undertaking. Old Princess de Lieven, who had spent most of her life hurrying from one European Embassy to another meddling on an international scale, still preferred her own carriage, and declared that anyone who could be cooped up with heaven knows who in a railway compartment lost not only their dignity, but their independence too. Few people went to Russia, except diplomats, opera singers or merchants. Fewer people still, in proportion to the population, ever left it. Its natural barriers of snow, mud, dust and distance were reinforced by the striped black and white frontier posts and guard-houses, which demanded passports, police permits, bribes, and, in the case of the aristocracy or wealthy few, a special permission from the Tzar himself before they could take either themselves or their fortunes out of the country. The bulk of the nation remained behind these frontiers all their lives, gripped in a thrall of mechanical difficulties and a certain Oriental inertia, or fatalism. De Custine described the Russians as blond Arabs, Orientals, 'who, in their former migrations, lost their road, and whose chiefs, by mistake, led towards the North, a people born to live in the sun'. 'The contour of their manners,' said another traveller, 'is purely Asiatic.'

Lord Palmerston was a most pronounced Russophobe. His views were shared by three men who held positions of great importance in near-Eastern politics, and their combined suspicions were fostered by the more jingoistic sections of the press, so that at last Russia could do no right. Lord Ponsonby and Stratford Canning, afterwards Lord Stratford de Redcliffe—'the Great Elchi', or Ambassador—had been Britain's successive representatives to the Porte between the years 1832–58. David Urquhart, a sensation-seeking journalist and, for a while, secretary of Embassy at Constantinople, was equally fanatic in his hatred of Russia. Moreover, Dr. John McNeil, British Minister to Teheran in 1836, was also the author of a war-mongering treatise on Russia's increasing power in the East. All these Russophobes spent their time fomenting public opinion against the common bogey. Calmer voices, such as Lord Melbourne's, were drowned in the uproar. Richard Cobden, who had lately returned from a visit to Russia, wrote a pamphlet maintaining that it was not Britain's place to interfere in Russian colonial expansion—particularly in her relations to the Porte (which the extremists wished England to defend as if it had been Dover). Cobden even claimed that Russian trade with Turkey—conducted through the Black Sea ports, and an open, Free-Trade Bosphorus—would be harmless, since British merchandise was vastly superior to any the Moscovites could offer. Nevertheless, Russia's every move was watched with suspicion and resentment, and when the Caucasus rose in rebellion, and their resistance assumed the character of a holy war, every inter-tribal feud, every sortie, assault or siege was followed closely.

Not only the British, but the Sultan and the Pope, were opposed to a Russian occupation of the Caucasus. Under the cloak of religion, there had been other movements and leaders who disputed this territory. Towards the end of the eighteenth century, a most powerful political influence was wielded by a mysterious character known as Elisha Mansour—Mansour Bey.

His real name is not known. In the guise of a Dervish he led the Circassians in open revolt against Russia, while encouraging the Daghestan chieftains to persecute the Christian Georgians. He was, in fact, the first to preach religious unity as a means of opposing Russian expansion. There were the most romantic stories of his origin; some say he was a Tartar, who studied Sufism in Bokhara; but it is also said, 'in view of archives preserved in the Vatican', that he was a Genoese priest, first sent to the Near East by the Pope, as a Jesuit missionary, to counteract the influence of the Greek Orthodox church at Erzerum. But after some years in the Caucasian frontier country (where he led a most dissipated life), he was converted to Mahommedanism. He next appears as an agent for the Sultan of Turkey, who sent him to Circassia to work against the Russian ascendancy over the tribes of the Black Sea (the Krim Tartars having been, for centuries, tributary vassals to the Porte). But in 1791, at the battle of Tartar-Toub, Mansour Bey was taken prisoner by Potemkin's troops and dispatched to the frozen twilight lands of Northern Russia where, at the dread Solovetzki monastery on an island in the White Sea, he pined and died.

III

To understand the alarm with which Europe, and England in particular, viewed Russia, it is necessary to recall something of Slav colonial expansion during the eighteenth and nineteenth centuries.

Although both Ivan the Terrible and Peter the Great had continually enlarged their frontiers, and were ever conscious of the strategic importance of acquiring territories and ports in Asia Minor, Russian colonial expansion had begun in earnest around the middle of the eighteenth century, in quite another region, when that private enterprise known as the Promyshlenik sailed into San Francisco harbour in rough wooden boats and began trading Chinese silks and precious stones from the Urals against sea-otter pelts and fruit.

Nevertheless the undertaking did not prosper. From the accession of Nicholas I in 1825, it was clear they could hope for no support from the Crown. Nicholas disliked the whole venture. Anything in the nature of liberalism, or individual enterprise, aroused his fury. The prospect that a Russian Empire might grow up so far from the surveillance of St. Petersburg—and so close to Mexico, too, where Independence had been proclaimed in 1823—riled Nicholas, who was already warming up to his self-appointed rôle as 'the policeman of Europe', the guardian of Thrones. He would have preferred *no* Russian Empire to a free, liberal one. 'I would rather fall back as far as China, than ever adopt a Constitution,' he told the Marquis de Custine in 1839. But in spite of Royal disapproval, the Russian-Californian Company lingered on, a handful of men and a small fort, declining year by year until, in 1841, Government backing was withdrawn and the whole place was sold up to a Swiss adventurer, Johannes Sutter.

However, Russian expansion south and east was under rather better auspices, though the price was heavy in lives. Each year the armies pushed back the Asiatic frontiers a little more. The conquest of the Caucasus, an undertaking begun in the seventeenth century as a trifling campaign, was to last, waxing and waning, until 1864. Peter the Great had marched his men to the Caspian and, eyeing the fruitful valleys and ports, installed himself at Derbend and decided to wrest this splendid prize from Persia.

Inland the mountains of Daghestan seemed less inviting. The great chain loomed gigantic and menacing above the invaders. Local legends held that they were made of solid gold: but their peaks proved inaccessible fortresses held by intractable tribes. Even so energetic an

optimist as Peter the Great decided against a mountain campaign. . . .
Content to settle for the lowlands, he next concluded a treaty with the
Persians, who concealed their joy at being relieved of so unmanageable
and unprofitable a territory. A Russian governor was installed, with a
token force to keep order.

But no order could be kept. The Asiatic chieftains were indifferent
to their so-called rulers. Shah or Tzar—it was the same to them. They
went their own way, and a short way it was with anyone who interfered. During Peter the Great's expedition they had flayed one of his
generals, Prince Bekovitch, and used his skin for a drum. The Khans
and Princes of Georgia, Azerbijan and Daghestan decided that the
Russian soldiers made splendid game, and they sometimes went out
after them in hunting parties, with jewelled weapons and cheetahs
crouched across their saddle-bow, trained to leap on the quarry. Soon
Russia was thankful to withdraw her decimated ranks by a series of
elaborate diplomatic moves through which the Caucasian provinces
were returned to Persia. There followed a lull in Russia's imperialistic
designs until, during the reign of Catherine the Great, the gargantuan
Potemkin set about building an empire worthy of his adored mistress.

His designs were no sooner put into practice than they were questioned and impeded by other powers. Russia was already too strong for
the liking of Britain, France and Austria. The French Ambassador at
St. Petersburg, reporting a conversation which he had with Potemkin
in 1786, stated that he had remonstrated against Russian regiments
being sent to the Caucasus, 'that barrier placed by Nature between two
Empires' (Russian and Ottoman). In a dispatch to his government,
Ségur, the Ambassador, held that the Empress had been most unwise
to embroil herself in the quarrels and feuds of the Caucasian peoples.
By taking Georgia under her wing, she was paying too heavily—twelve
thousand or more men annually; as well as expenditure of time, money
and energy were required to protect this small independent kingdom
from the threats of Persia and the assaults of neighbouring tribes. He
concluded, cynically, that from the point of view of Russia's enemies,
perhaps their designs for Caucasian conquest should be observed with
satisfaction, since they harassed and decimated the armies, both by
battle and the ravages of the climate.

When the second Russo-Turkish war broke out in 1787, the Russian
army was not strong enough to continue the Caucasian campaigns
simultaneously, and they withdrew their forces, hoping, too, that this
would mollify the Persians, who were also showing resentment at
Russia's expansion eastward. At the end of the war in 1791, the Treaty
of Jassy insured that the Sultan should in no way hold or influence the
Georgians, or those neighbouring provinces under his rule. Thus
Russia could now turn her attention elsewhere. Dreams of Caucasian

mountain victories must wait. First, Potemkin envisaged an outlet on
the Black Sea, foreseeing its strategic value, sensing, too, that once
conquered it would represent a better bargain than the turbulent
Caucasian provinces. Both geographically and temperamentally, it was
more suited to conquest.

IV

The Khans of the Crimea, the Krim Khans, were the last fragments
of the great Mongolian Empire left in Europe. They were the descendants of Genghis Khan, but like the palaces and gardens of their capital,
Baktchiserai, they had degenerated in a most melancholy fashion. However, they still lived nobly, though simply, for to accumulate riches was
against their creed, and one suit, one sword, one horse, was considered
enough for the Khan, while his daughters were always married off to the
bravest, most distinguished, but generally the *poorest* nobles, who were
thus enriched by their bride's dowry. The legacy of the Mongol hordes
was still apparent in the system of *docus-docus-lemé*, or nine times nine,
which always applied to the dowry. (Nine was a sacred number.) Nine
times nine furs, nine times nine robes, nine times nine mattresses, nine
times nine pillows, richly embroidered in gold and silver, nine times
nine Chinese silk coverlets, and nine times nine fur coverlets. Thus
the dowry very sensibly seems to have been largely made up of
bedding.

The luxury of the Khan's palaces were not so much dependent on
riches as on the voluptuous beauty of their setting. At Baktchiserai
nightingales sang in the flowering trees; there were pearl-shell fountains and an insidious mixture of sacred and profane love, of harem and
mosque. The tombs of the Khans still stand, breathing an atmosphere of
gentle gloom: that heady draught of romanticized melancholy which
only the East knows how to distil, and which, once tasted by the West,
is forever craved. The town of Baktchiserai appears suddenly. You
come on it over the brow of the hill, a straggling, long street, lined with
seedy bazaars and booths, and dominated by the Khan's palace. Sacred
and profane love: beside the tombs, the ghostly echoing gardens where
the odalisques languished. During the Crimean War, the Palace became
a hospital: but it is remembered more for the legend which inspired
Pushkin's poem *The Fountain of Baktchiserai*, the story of a Polish
Countess and her lover, a Tartar Khan.

There are several versions of this romantic episode, and the love
stories of at least three Christian women, captives, and cherished wives
of the Khans, are by now interwoven and generally confused. Their
basic similarity lies in the religious fervour of each lady and the tolerance
displayed by their Mongol lovers. In each case, however wild, these

Krim Khans appear to have made the most devoted husbands, particularly susceptible to the religious scruples of their wives. One member of the Khanate family even went so far as to embrace the Presbyterian faith during a stay in Scotland, when visiting the relatives of his Scottish bride. He had been entirely subjugated by the blonde beauty of a Miss Neilson whom he had encountered in the Crimea. History does not tell us what she was doing there; perhaps, like the pretty young Miss Lyon who had been engaged by Catherine the Great to act as nurse to her Imperial grandson, the future Emperor Nicholas I, Miss Neilson, too, had brought her affectionate common sense to bear in some baby Khan's nursery. I like to imagine her Tartar bridegroom, set down in a Highland glen, striding the heather with that supple Asiatic grace, a splendid, if incongruous, figure, with long Chinese-style moustachios, a diamond aigrette glittering in his turban, his brocaded caftan glowing out beside the more sober tartans of the ghillies. Or taking tea and instruction at the Manse, seated between his rosy bride and the Minister, discussing some scriptural point pertaining to his conversion. This seemingly ill-assorted pair returned to the Crimea where they lived in a palace beside the Black Sea, in monogamous unity, happy ever afterwards.

At Baktchiserai, the ghost of another Tartar's Christian bride lingers among the nightingales and roses. Deliareh Bekeh's grave is marked by a handsome octagonal marble mausoleum: a faded gold inscription reads:

> This is the tomb of Deliareh Bekeh, beloved wife of Khan Sahin Ghirei. Died 1753. She was a Christian.

Nearby stands a fountain—the Fountain of Baktchiserai—the fountain of tears; its elaborate shell-form, tier upon tier, is now chipped and arid. Once, the shells brimmed over, drop by drop, heavy and slow as the bitter tears they commemorated—tears shed by a grief-stricken Khan for his departed Christian wife. Deliareh Bekeh had been a Georgian slave in the Khan's harem before winning his undying love. When she became his wife, she was tormented by religious scruples. In vain the Khan offered her freedom of worship; she could not reconcile herself to their marriage. Evidently she was the stuff of martyrs, for she caused a Cross to be carved on the wall, surmounting the Crescent which adorned her bedroom. This mute but ever-present reminder of her defection cast a blight on their bliss, and it is not surprising to learn that she pined and died, fading from life and love in the flower of her beauty, leaving her husband quite distracted by his loss. However, there seems to be some doubt as to whether the fountain was in fact erected in memory of Deliareh Bekeh, or another, equally adored Christian woman, Marie Potocka; the Khans were a lesson to bereaved husbands everywhere, being inconsolable in their grief, and poetic in their monuments. Small wonder that Baktchiserai is still pervaded with an overwhelming sense of melancholy. Such romantic sorrows have left their mark, indelibly.

Although for many centuries the Krim Khans had declined in stature, they displayed the sacred six-horse-tailed standards which all Asia revered, and the Turks treated them with great consideration, for they represented a powerful bastion against the possible threat of Russian invasion. All the same, these Tartar Princes felt their decay keenly, and were inclined to be touchy, like poor relations. Upon the occasion of a state visit by one of the Ghirei, Khan Devlet, to the Sultan in Constantinople, he had been asked what he would like as a mark of special esteem. With one foot in the stirrup, his cortège forming behind him for their leave-taking, the Khan demanded the Grand Vizier's head. There was nothing for it but to comply. A scimitar sent the turbaned head rolling towards the visitor on the instant, and honour was satisfied all round.

*   *   *

But by 1777 such exigencies were doomed. Field-Marshal Suvorov led his troops out of Moscow—southwards. In 1783 the whole Crimea was annexed by Russia, and Potemkin was able to lay the Khan's vasselage and the beautiful vine-wreathed shores of the Black Sea at the feet of his Empress.

Now Catherine's imperialistic appetite was whetted. Having acquired the Crimea she began to eye further conquests. Why not the Caucasus? After a series of distracting young lovers (who never absorbed her to the exclusion of her Empire), she selected her youngest and last favourite, Count Platon Zubov, twenty-five to her seventy. Together they planned a revival of the Greek empire—under Russian control. Constantinople, and perhaps India, should be seized. The Cross would rise above the Crescent! Thus they schemed, this odd pair, nested down in the tiny, glass-lined Alcôve Room at Tzarskoe-Selo. Catherine had contrived it as a folly, a retreat, during her amorous hey-day. Only here, in all the immensity of the Palace, could she feel herself a woman rather than Empress, a state which she believed she preferred. The Alcôve Room was still there, much as she left it, before the second world war: its fragile violet glass pillars were set between two magnificent salons, and was no more than a mirrored niche, the length of the bed which was its purpose and sole content. I remember how its violet depths reflected a stream of curious tourists, crowding and peering, trying to catch some shadowy *scène galante*.

We, too, peer closer, seeing another scene: the overblown, but still sumptuous Empress, 'Semeramis of the North', and the dandiprat. There is a samovar beside them: they are drinking tea in crystal glasses. Catherine puts a spoonful of cherry-jam in her saucer, peasant fashion. The sable coverlet is spread with maps and papers. The pampered greyhounds jump up to lick Catherine's face, scuffling the papers. A large-scale map of the Caucasus is gummed across one of the looking-glasses. Catherine stabs at it with a plump heavily ringed finger. Zubov's eyes flash, a melting blend of adoration and patriotic fervour. They will storm the Caucasus! Tiflis will be the Viceregal headquarters! Persia must be subdued! . . . They will take the Porte. . . . And so, control the East. Cross over Crescent. . . . Catherine nods happily. . . . She is delighted with this audacious boy's Imperialism.

Presently, Platon's younger brother, Valerian, a baby-faced youth who, nevertheless, had distinguished himself in the Polish and Turkish campaigns under Marshal Suvorov, was dispatched at the head of an army to reconquer the Persian provinces of the Caucasus and become its first Viceroy. With a flourish of trumpets the young general marched south. He was received kindly, even patronizingly, by the tribal rulers and Khans of the Caucasus, and the frontier provinces that marched with Persia. They had never seen his kind before. Come to subdue them? That whey-faced boy? They laughed derisively, speaking among themselves in that mysterious tongue, Chakobsa, 'the Hunting Language', which the rulers and Princes used when they wished to converse in secret, and of which no more than a few words have been discovered. They were in a good humour, for they anticipated some excellent sport ahead. Human game . . . worth waiting for.

Derbend, once more Persian territory, and the Russians' first objective as a key port, offered little resistance, and farther south Baku also fell to the Russian guns. All the same the Persians mustered a considerable army, and at one point put no less than eighty elephants in their line of attack. Soon, however, they withdrew to a discreet distance, preferring to come to terms. They had learned in the past what it meant to cross swords with Russia, and what it meant to try to hold the Caucasus too. But before young Zubov had realized the magnitude of the task before him, or how, night by night, his ranks were thinned by an invisible army, those pouncing Caucasian tribes with whom he could never come to grips, a benign fate intervened. The Empress died, and her son, Paul I, beginning as he meant to go on by persecuting or dispossessing all his mother's favourites, recalled Valerian. The would-be Generalissimo-Viceroy left on the hour. His army were to follow, to make their get-away as best they could. The tribesmen swept down from the mountains, Avars, Lesghiens, Tchetchens and Kabardians, a terrible pack, who set on the Russians. Once again all thought of Caucasian conquest was put aside.

V

Throughout its history the Caucasus has been the cradle and tomb of many races. Its name derives from the Sanscrit, and signifies white or snowy mountains. The giant peaks of Elbruz, Kazbek and Adai-Khokh rise glittering white above the range of lesser mountains which stretch across the whole Caucasian isthmus, forming a fortress, a natural barrier against invasion. The tracks winding across these peaks and through the valleys below were the route followed by all the successive waves of invaders, defeated armies, nomad tribes and migrations which beat against these mountains. Some crossed, some died, some stayed: but each of them left their imprint. Their echoes are still found, in a dialect, a place-name, a creed, a legend, a piece of armour, a strain of fair-haired people, like the Khevsours.

At last no man could unravel the merging of peoples; of Scythians, Medes and Persians, Genoese, Greek and Mongol: Koumoukh, Kurd, Armenian, Turcoman, Ossete and many more. It was said that seventy different languages were heard in the market-place of Tiflis, while Pliny tells us the Romans employed a hundred and thirty-four different interpreters to conduct their affairs in the Caucasus. It was not until the tenth century that the Slav invasion began in earnest. Led by Sviato-slav, the Muscovy princes and their armies occupied the whole country between the Caspian and Don. But they were superseded by another wave of Arabs; they in turn being ousted by Tamerlane who marched on the Caucasus in 1387, when all the races and rulers fell back before him. Thus the tides of battle, until, in the sixteenth century, the struggle narrowed down to Persian Sofi, Turkish Sultan and Russian Tzar. Even so, the many tribes each pursued their various ways of life, observing or participating in the struggle, but basically still aloof and independent in spirit. Only in the nineteenth century, under Shamyl's sway, did they all band together as one Moslem force, the issue to be decided between Tzar and Imam—between Cross and Crescent.

After Valerian Zubov's ignominious retreat, no more definite action was taken to subdue the Caucasus, until Catherine the Great's grand-son, the Emperor Alexander I, decided on further colonial expansion. His father, Paul I, whose megalomania knew no bounds, had planned to seize and share the Ottoman Empire with Napoleon, whom he admired passionately: he had already vowed the Don Cossacks to his project. They were to invade India as a first step to total domination of the East: however, his death, strangled by his courtiers, put an end to such schemes. His son Alexander was far more level-headed, and did not set his sights so high. He would be content with the Caucasus and in consolidating Russia's position in the lately annexed Georgia.

He had returned to Russia at the head of his armies after leading them to victory over Napoleon, and the Allied occupation of Paris in 1814 (where his troops left the city a lasting souvenir of their presence in the word *bistro*—in Russian, 'hurry', 'quick'; the big bear-like Slav soldiers would harass the restaurants and street booths with demands for food, quickly—*bistro*! So the word passed into French usage, applying to any unpretentious, quick-serving little restaurant).

After such epic victories as Borodino, the Tzar and his generals did not anticipate much trouble in conquering the Caucasus: it was necessary to the completion of the Empire: it would round off the years of conquest; for the professional soldier it would be a rather agreeable form of postscript to the campaigns, a last jaunt.

Yet, once again, Russia found herself faced with an intractable enemy, master of partisan tactics, and aided by a terrain composed of perpendicular mountain gorges and impenetrable forests. Baulked, the Russian generals decided on a ruthless system of reprisals. The native population must be broken, crops and villages razed, wells choked, orchards cut down, vineyards trampled. They must be brought to heel. No quarter must be given—not that any was ever asked by the fighters —and the campaign must be brought to a close without further delay. Great God! They were becoming positively insolent, these Tartars! Thus, General Yermolov, the Titan figure who dominated the Caucasian scene when in 1816 he was first appointed Commander-in-Chief of the Army of the South. To the Caucasians he was the Moscow Shàitan —the Muscovy Devil. They feared and admired him, as his troops adored him. To the latter he was Batioushka—little father. Yermolov's gigantic stature, roaring voice and violent nature was the personification of those mythical heroes of Russian legend, the Bogatyri, giants mounted on colossal horses, who rose up from the steppes and marshes and engaged in epic battles, their weapons clashing with thunderous force, their voices making the very earth tremble.

Mikhail Yermolov had the same legendary aura. He was born in 1777, fought under Suvorov, rose to become a colonel at Austerlitz, fought with the Austrian army against the French, and served with brilliance throughout the Napoleonic Wars. In 1814, at the Allied occupation of Paris, he was in command of the Russian and Prussian guards. The Emperor Alexander I recognized his stature, and two years later, in 1816, appointed him over the heads of a jealous clique of high-ranking courtier-generals to become Commander-in-Chief in the Caucasus, and Ambassador Extraordinary to the Persian Court of Fatih Ali Shah. His appointment was taken as a personal insult by the entire military caste surrounding the Emperor. From that moment Yermolov was engaged on two fronts: he fought his country's enemies wherever he found them, and at home his own enemies fought him by every means. Generally he ignored them, brushing them off like so many gnats. Sometimes he rumbled, terrible ogre thunders, lashing out at them with a huge paw, so that they subsided, for a while. He had no use for the foreign element around the throne. He was all Russia, as national a figure as the Bogatyri, or any of the moujik recruits who loved him, and for whom he always had time to stop and talk, or pause by their camp-fire, sharing their cauldron of *stchii*, sour cabbage soup. The St. Petersburg courtiers felt the sharp side of his tongue: when the Tzar asked what favour he would like, as a reward for his services, he replied: 'To be born a German, for then I shall be able to get all I want', a remark which has a timeless irony about it, and, a century and a half later, still rings oddly true.

Experience had taught Yermolov that to be respected by the Asiatics, he must show an equal cruelty and force to all who did not co-operate. For all his brutalities, he was inspired first by loyalty to his Emperor and devotion to his country. He fought for Russia, not for personal aggrandizement, in spite of the accusations of his enemies at Court who claimed that he meant to raise his own standard in the Caucasus and, supported by his army, defy the Tzar. When, some years earlier, Alexander I's humanitarian principles had been outraged by accounts of Yermolov's methods of conquest, the Titan had replied, 'I desire that the terror of my name shall guard our frontiers more potently than chains or fortresses.' And he continued to drive ramrods through his prisoner's ears, auction off the women of the defaulting villages (keeping and marrying one beauty himself) and generally to apply ruthless Asiatic standards of conquest to the mountaineers. ('Humble thyself O Caucasus, for Yermolov is coming', wrote Pushkin, sharing the national enthusiasm for conquest.) Yermolov suppressed lingering Persian influences and consolidated Russian acquisitions by his own means. He was entirely single-minded, fighting the Caucasians on their own terms. 'Condescension is to the Asiatics a sign of weakness,' he said. 'I am inflexibly severe out of motives of humanity. One execution saves hundreds of Russian lives.' All the same, Alexander I recoiled from Yermolov's brutalities. The Tzar had been influenced by Laharpe, whom Catherine the Great had appointed as her grandson's tutor; he would, she felt, introduce a more liberal European influence, to counter Romanov absolutism. The gentle, already mystically inclined Alexander was rather half-hearted in his desire for colonial conquest: he remained a prey to doubts, and counselled mercy to his Viceroy.

But neither ruthlessness nor mercy prevailed. When the Emperor

Alexander died in mysterious circumstances in the south, at Taganrog on the sea of Azov, leaving no son, his heir and brother, the Grand Duke Constantine, Viceroy of Poland, had abdicated in favour of the youngest brother, Nicholas, who had reluctantly accepted what he regarded as his sacred trust. He was proclaimed Emperor early in December 1825. The news did not reach the Caucasian provinces till some weeks later, so that Yermolov, then in command, quite understandably had made his army swear allegiance to Constantine. But, to Nicholas, this was proof of his arrogance and anarchistic designs. Nicholas would brook no arguments, though there were few among the courtiers who attempted to defend Yermolov's mistake. It was obvious the brute meant to raise his own standard in the Caucasus and set up to rule the south for himself, just as once each Cossack hetman had tried to prove himself independent of the Crown. The sooner he was recalled the better: in any case, for all his roaring, he had not succeeded in bringing the tribesmen to their knees. On the contrary, Daghestan was now in open revolt. If he could not impose the Tzar's will, then there were others who would. Already Nicholas was envisaging a triumphal tour of the south with a conqueror's welcome in Tiflis. It was most frustrating to be told so often that the moment was not ripe. He took it as a personal affront.

In March 1827, Nicholas I invested Count Paskiévitch with supreme power in the Caucasus, and Yermolov was relieved of his command in a manner at once unjust and venomous. But Nicholas was never one to show generosity to those he disliked personally, particularly those he suspected of democratic views. The old lion might be, as he claimed, a descendant of Genghis Khan—but he was altogether too popular with his troops. He did not keep them at a distance: indeed, at times he seemed one with them. His simplicity and direct moujik's force was something which was utterly alien to Nicholas, as rigidly encased in his Germanic rectitude, as tight as his uniform, unbending only to the sleek, military sycophants who knew how to bolster his autocracy.

Yermolov left the Caucasus, the scene of his greatest glory, in a hired carriage. No one bothered to furnish him with anything better. He was of no account now to the authorities. Only his troops felt themselves abandoned, resenting the treatment of their commander to the point of mutiny. Tears streamed down their faces as they watched him go. He accepted his fate stoically, sitting wrapped in the shabby old cloak he generally wore, and in which he slept, too. (No beds, no coverlets, for him—even at his zenith.) The carriage rattled out of Tiflis and headed north, along the great Georgian Military Highway that Yermolov himself had constructed. Not even a squadron of Cossacks accompanied him: not one of the forts he had built fired a salute as he passed.

The officers had received their orders: Paskiévitch was the Commander-in-Chief now. Yermolov was recalled, discredited. He no longer existed. He was a shade, driving into the shadows. The mountains retreated, dwindling like his glory. The carriage disappeared into empty horizons. Ahead lay nothingness, all the triumphs and dramas of his Caucasian life were narrowing to a pin-point—Orel, a small provincial town where he was to live on, a forgotten exile. He did not bother to defend himself. Perhaps he knew that, for posterity, he would become one of the mightiest names in Russian history. He was to outlive both the Tzar Nicholas and the hostility of his critics: his last days were lit by a golden glow of recognition, of adulation even. He died in Moscow in 1861, one with the Bogatyri legend to the last.

He had been the first to subdue, even in part, the Caucasus; to build the chain of forts and open up the Georgian Military Highway; the first to incorporate Persian and Tartar Khanates into Russian territory. But there is no doubt his methods—his arrogance and cruelty did enormous harm: they precipitated the Persian war of 1826, and were directly responsible for the revival of Muridism and the fanatic antagonism of Daghestan and the Tchetchen provinces. His Caucasian achievements are summed up by the military historian J. F. Baddeley in the following terms:

> Yermolov's supreme merit, in Russian eyes, was that he recognized from the beginning the necessity of extending Russian dominion over the whole of the Caucasus, including the independent and semi-independent States and communities up to the borders of Persia proper, and the northern limit of Turkey in Asia. But the means he adopted to attain this end were, at least, questionable.

But neither Yermolov's might nor the overwhelming forces of his successors were to conquer the Caucasus so soon.

2

The Setting

Il ne faut pas parler des Asiatiques en moraliste.   GOBINEAU

The historian Froude wrote: 'History must be studied in all its length, all its breadth, and in all its depth: nothing else gives us the necessary perspective.' Thus, in writing of Shamyl we must place him first in his time—the first half of the nineteenth century, and then in his place—the mountains—and then, in turn, we must place those mountains in their frame. To the north, the vast Russian steppes; to the west, the lowlands of Georgia, bordered by the shores of the Black Sea. To the east, the oily grey Caspian; and to the south-east, all the arid wastes of Persian and Turkish border country—Asia Minor, a landscape of desolation and dust, of cruelty, sophistication and barbarism, an area in which Great Britain, Napoleonic France and Russia were all out-manœuvring each other during the years of Shamyl's childhood, so that from the Caucasus, the nations' struggle for power was clearly seen.

Since part of Shamyl's southern frontiers merged with the Persian boundaries, and the whole Caucasus was bound up with, if not imprinted by Persian proximity, let us observe the Persian scene more closely.

Early nineteenth-century Persia was focused round one man—the Shah Fatih Ali. He had been known as Baba Khan and was chief claimant to the Peacock Throne, then occupied by his uncle, the abhorred Agha Mahommed. When the Agha was murdered by two slaves he had condemned to death (but whose sentence he had not yet bothered to put into execution), Baba Khan acted with dispatch, and warned by the fatal consequence of his uncle's inertia, he liquidated overnight all the rival claimants, including his brother, and succeeded, himself, to the Peacock Throne, being thereafter known as Fatih Ali Shah, Shah-in-Shah—King of Kings. He was a remarkable personality, at once enlightened and barbarous, vigorous and languid, generous and cruel.

Although a self-indulgent monarch, he was the first to bring his

27

country into the orbit of both European politics and advancement. His uncle, the Agha Mahommed, had ruled by terror alone. He had been the Eunuch chief of the Kadja tribe; these Kadjas were not Persian by origin, but Turkish, from the forest regions of Mazandaran. In the eighteenth century they replaced the worn-out Sophi dynasty, one of degenerate exquisites, and the Kadjas assumed Persian nationality, much as the house of Hanover became the ruling English dynasty. Agha Mahommed was a brilliant military strategist, but of a blood-thirsty nature. He liked nothing better than to open a battle (rather in the manner of distinguished personages opening a ball by dancing the first waltz before the dazzled assembly) by personally bayoneting the first prisoners brought in triumph to his tent. This repulsive individual knew no misgivings. On one occasion, we are told that, being occupied in counting the numbers of gouged-out eyes he had ordered to be brought to him as gauge of a victory, his faithful Vizier Mirza Sheffi ventured to remonstrate with him. 'Does your Majesty think it possible that Allah may not be pleased with this?'

Agha Mahommed slowly raised his head, carefully keeping his dagger between the filmy heaps in the order in which he was counting them, and replied: 'Sir, by my head, if there should be one eye too few, I myself will make up the number with yours.' It was an unanswerable argument.

His frightful treatment of Tiflis when he occupied it, in 1795, was directly responsible for the Georgian acceptance of Russian protection later. The shuffling old women who had limped about with that curiously regimented step had been the virgins his troops had raped and ham-strung as a souvenir of their victory—and it had not been forgotten by their fathers and brothers. The Georgians loyally supported the Russians, their co-religionists, and fought beside them in the Russo-Persian war of 1826 and throughout their long struggle against Shamyl and the Moslem Caucasian tribes.

II

In 1800, when George XII, last monarch of Georgia and head of the Royal House of Bagration, on Batonishvili, lay dying of dropsy in his palace in Tiflis, he took the decisive step and dispatched a deputation to St. Petersburg, offering the crown of Georgia to the Emperor Paul I. He knew that his vacillating, undisciplined people would be better off, absorbed into the Russian Empire; he believed Russian rule would prove enlightened; were they not co-religionists, too? The Shah and many of the neighbouring Khans or Shamkals were all fanatic Moslems.

(These views were not shared by his brother, however. Prince

Alexander accused him of being a traitor, and, in dudgeon, withdrew first to the mountains of Daghestan, and then to Persia, from
where, living a desperate, fugitive's life, he was forever intriguing against
Russia, rousing Persian and tribal opposition, and stirring up local
revolts.)

The Emperor Paul accepted the Georgian Crown in December 1800.
Barely ten days later, King George XII was dead. His had been a
vigorous and enlightened rule. He had been a beloved monarch, a
valorous warrior, a devout Christian, an astute statesman, steering his
country away from the dread Persian grip, into the orbit of Russian
protection. His private life, too, was one of considerable achievement.
He had contrived to maintain a balance of power between all the
various ramifications of the royal house, and he had sired, by his two
wives, no less than twenty-two children, one of whom bore the poetic
name of Zlataoust, or Golden-Tongued.

It was an age of incredible fecundity, and the most irrepressible
family urges. Uncles were often twenty years younger than their nieces,
daughters older than a new step-grandmother; the patriarchal monarchs remarried, and married again, gathering momentum as they
aged, spring-boarding, as it were, off the coffin of one deceased wife
into the marriage-bed of the next, scarcely a year between the successive waves of offspring. Invention in names seems to have given out
early in the game, and there are double and treble crops of Salomés,
Vakhtangs, Davids and Alexanders, most confusing to the historian.
King George XII's father, King Herakli II, had, by his three wives, no
less than twenty-eight children.

Under the dense shade of such a family tree, all kinds of intrigues
flourished. Brother opposed brother; sisters loved half-brothers, mothers
vied with step-children, or slew rivals who threatened their bed or
inheritance. When King George XII's widow, Queen Maria, realized
the full implications of her late husband's abdication, she resisted as
fiercely as her brother-in-law, Prince Alexander Batonishvili, had done.
She had that essentially feminine sense of possession, which is exercised
indiscriminately over people, property and position. The Queen clung
to everything. No matter that she and her children stood to lose more
by resisting a Russian protectorate, and presently being seized, once
again, by Persia. She was not prepared to give up anything. *Everything*
must be held, for herself and her children: she saw things in terms of a
family feud, and feared the covetous eye which all the legion of half-
brothers and uncles now cast on her own brood. She was determined
that either she or her children were to reign, to live in the Palace, and
wear the regalia. Her intrigues became so energetic that she succeeded
in undermining much of the lately established Russian administration.
General Tzitzianov, Georgian by birth, and one of her distant relatives

but wholly Russian by upbringing and sympathies, had been appointed Governor-General. It was a wise choice, for he was both gifted and high-minded, and, knowing the land and the people, dealt ably with both the Christians and the Moslems. At last even his forbearance was tried too hard by the Queen's intrigues. He decided on her arrest, and early one morning sent General Lazareff to fetch her from the Palace. The Queen feigned illness, remained in bed, and flatly refused to move. The General left the room, intending to order her removal by force—if necessary, to transport the whole carved and gilded bed from which she defied him. But at that moment her son and daughter drew their daggers and fell on the officer left to guard the royal prisoner.

Hearing the uproar, the General rushed back, demanding that the Queen call off her children, who were now hacking the unfortunate officer to pieces as he lay at their feet in a pool of blood. Queen Maria was watching the slaughter unmoved; but when the General approached her bedside she struck, viper-quick, and stabbed him to death with a dagger which she had kept concealed (perhaps for the purpose of her own suicide) beneath the embroidered silk coverlets.

For this act she was deported to Russia among a convoy of common criminals, the once magnificent Queen trudging the endless steppes for many weeks, chained to the next prisoner, eating the black bread of bitterness. Her long life was spent in expiation of her crime: first immured in a convent, and later in honourable captivity in Moscow. The Emperor Nicholas found it more expedient to display magnanimity towards the Georgian princess, in view of maintaining harmonious relations with her homeland.

Towards the end of her life she was pardoned, and even patronized, and was brought to St. Petersburg, where as late as 1850, in her eighties, she was sometimes to be seen at Court functions, a darkly brooding matriarch among the dowagers.

III

For a hundred years, Russia and Persia had parried and thrust across the frontier country of Azerbijan and the key ports of the Caspian. Both countries claimed the intermediary zones of the Caucasus and Georgia. But the Russians had no intention of merely subduing an aggressive neighbour. Their own desire for colonial acquisitions made it essential for them to control zones beyond their present frontiers. This, in its simplest reduction, was their policy. They were determined to obtain all those areas abutting and beyond their own (which in this case they regarded as the farthest borders of Caucasia). Thus in the event of attack, or indeed under any circumstances, these territories would lie, like an outer bastion, a girdle of buffer states, between Russia proper and any enemy. The Persian Khanates of Erivan and Shirvan, with the port of Baku, served their purpose admirably, and so presently did a slice of Turkish border country, the Pachalik of Kars, of Bayazit, and to the north-west, Akhaltsik, with its port of Batoum, on the Black Sea, won by the Russo-Turkish war of 1828.

Whether these territorial gains were all part of a sinister policy to obtain supremacy in India, as the British had decided to believe, has never been proved. The Tzar was always deeply wounded at such aspersions and denied them with passion. 'I do not want an inch of Turkish territory,' he told Lord Palmerston during his visit to England in 1844, 'but I will never allow any other powers to seize it.' The English statesman listened in bland silence, giving nothing away. But: 'One is denying the teaching of history if one believes that Russia is not thinking of extending to the south,' he noted. 'All governments, especially absolute governments, think of increasing their territories, for political, rather than economic, reasons.'

The Emperor Nicholas admitted to a cherished hope that the Cross might supersede the Crescent. His dream was to see Jerusalem restored entirely to Christian hands. He had *no* designs on India, he said: but he detested Turkey openly, detested and opposed the Sultan's oppression of the Christian minorities. Just as his father, the Tzar Paul I, had accepted the submission of Georgia and protected the Christian Georgians against Persian abuse, so he, Nicholas, was ever ready to protect (and absorb) the Christian minorities of Asia Minor. The Armenians, for example, were being persecuted and massacred daily by the Turks, so that when his religious connections were combined with territorial gains, it was altogether a most convenient arrangement.

'Russia', Lord Palmerston was wont to say, 'was just a great humbug.' The Turkish campaign of 1829 following immediately on the Persian war of 1826–8 left Russia master of those border states she had coveted so long. Footholds in the Caucasus were ceded by the Treaty of Adrianople, and at last Russia's position in Asia Minor seemed secured. The object of two hundred years of intermittent fighting appeared to be won. The vast Empire was now firmly established: south to the Crimea, ruled by the docile Krim Khans; west to the Austro-Hungarian Empire, with Poland as a border province held, if uneasily, by the Russian-imposed Viceroy; north and east to the Chinese boundaries of the Amur, where Nogai-Tartars, Kalmuks, Buriat-Mongolians, and a hundred other races gave little organized resistance, and the whole immensity of Siberia and outer Mongolia were bastion enough. . . . Madame Nesselrode was right. Indelicate it might be, but there was no denying the fact that Russia was a very great power.

Only the Caucasus, only the mountains of Daghestan, those dark and menacing peaks, remained unconquered, showed signs of renewed hostility, and open revolt, as the tribes gathered to repudiate the Treaty. Neither force nor persuasion nor cunning won them over. The Russians had yet to realize that they were pitted, not only against a national resistance, but against a fanatic religious movement—which was to grow until every village was a fortress, every man a fighting monk, and the whole country led, in battle, as in prayer, by an Imam who preached resistance with fire and sword.

IV

The Shah Fatih Ali was well aware that his court was the setting for a violent collision of European politics, and he appears to have savoured his singular position, playing with first one mission and then another, in majestic enjoyment. First the English sent Captain, later Sir John, Malcolm, whose mission was, in his own words, 'to form an alliance with Fatih Ali Shah, who, by his puissance, held not only the means to check the Afghans, who ever threatened to invade India, but likewise to repel the ambitious view of France'. (And perhaps, Russia?)

Napoleon countered this by dispatching Marshal Joubert who succeeded in establishing a treaty, which was ratified by Napoleon himself, at Tilsit, where the newly accredited Persian envoy was received in state. General Gardanne was next dispatched to Teheran, accompanied by seventy officers, to reform the Persian army; at this point, England had fallen out of favour, and British emissaries were unable to set foot there. But by 1801 the French were discredited, and English influence (largely owing to the pro-English sentiments of Abbas Mirza, the heir apparent) once more paramount.

*   *   *

Sir John Malcolm had been instructed to persuade the Shah to sign political and commercial treaties neutralizing French influences, and he had achieved this end: moreover his whole conduct and charm won the esteem of the Persians. His graceful manner, at once courteous and firm, had particularly impressed the Shah. There was, for example, that interesting conversation on the question of monogamy, a subject the Shah found as fascinating as the West found polygamy. The Shah lost no time in sounding out the Englishman.

'I have heard a report which I can scarcely believe,' he said. 'It seems that your King has but one wife.'

'No Christian prince may have more,' replied the Ambassador.

'O, I am well aware of that,' said the Shah, 'but he may have a little lady, I believe?'

'Our gracious King George III is an example to his subjects in both morality and restraint, in this respect, as in every other,' was Sir John's lofty response.

To which the Shah rejoined that such a state might be very right, but he certainly would not want to be the king of such a country.

When the Shah asked if the French were not a very powerful people, Sir John replied: 'Certainly: otherwise they would not deserve to be mentioned as enemies of England.'

Such a man was revered throughout Persia; his mere presence at the Court stiffened the whole nation against threats of aggression from other nations. But alas, a short-sighted British Government recalled him as soon as his immediate mission was accomplished so that for some while no British representative was left in Teheran, a state of affairs which Napoleon did not overlook. He now began to make a series of elaborate overtures. By 1806, having declared war on Russia, and being confident of the outcome, he offered to restore Georgia to Persia and subsidize the Shah, who, in return, was to support a French invasion of India. 'Bonaparte planned to chain the bear of Russia and the lion of Persia to his chariot, and so to drive in triumph over the rich plains of India,' wrote Sir John Malcolm, watching events from the bow-window of his club in St. James's, and no longer in a position to intervene, or even advise.

Fatih Ali was not so favourably impressed by the French envoys, and on receiving Napoleon's offers, he still hesitated, recalling the agreeable society of Malcolm and his suite, all of whom had been, the Shah felt, an especially sustaining and reliable group: men of action—of honour, too. If only they could have stayed on. . . . He sent urgent appeals for British support, and played for time, putting off the French envoys with evasive answers. But the British were strangely indeterminate; no positive policy was forthcoming, nor was any emissary. Thus at last the Shah was compelled to sign a treaty with France, something he was loth to do, in spite of the Georgian prize dangled before him so temptingly. But Persia was only a small pawn in the great game Napoleon played. Presently, he signed peace terms with the Emperor Alexander I, and no more was heard of returning Georgia to the Shah of Shahs. In Britain talk of French designs on India was superseded by speculations as to Russian intentions, and more missions, chiefly of a military nature, were hurriedly dispatched to Persia. In the early years of the century Russia had held the Persian border provinces of Baku, Shirvan and Karabagh, as well as some Turkish pachaliks along the Black Sea. Under the wise administration of General Tzitzianov, there had been no trouble, but after his death (by treachery) in 1806, discontent grew, and the Persians invaded and re-took Karabagh and other frontier zones.

A large force was led by the exiled Georgian Prince Alexander, who could count on hordes of Daghestan tribesmen whenever Russia was attacked. But even this formidable army was defeated, at Aslandouz, when ten thousand of them fell before the Russians, whose losses were slight. Thus encouraged, the Russians now crossed the dread, serpent-ridden steppes of the Moughan and besieged Lenkoran, a Persian fortress designed by English military engineers. It fell after a desperate resistance which lasted five days, and enraged the Russians. In the words of a Russian general-in-command: 'The extreme exasperation of my soldiers at the obstinacy of the defence caused them to bayonet every one of the four thousand Persian garrison. Not one man or officer escaped death.'

This carnage was watched by all the Caucasian tribes. It would be their turn next. But unlike Persia, they could not count on British aid which, though it did not stave off ultimate defeat, at least prolonged the struggle. The tribes knew that the Russians had lately captured eleven cannons, of British make, inscribed: 'From the King of Kings to the Shah of Shahs'. Later, in his dispatches to the Tzar Nicholas I, Paskiévitch, the conqueror of Erivan, wrote: 'If the English have enormous influences in the East, it is because they have constantly and warmly taken to heart the interests of those who have sought their protection, politically. . . . It was a matter of offence to us [the Russians] that Abbas Mirza failed to prefer ourselves, who refused him even the title of heir to this father's throne, solemnly guaranteed to him by the treaty, to a nation which supplied him with money and arms, and with officers to drill his troops.' And to die beside them, he might have added.

In 1814, British influence being stronger than ever at the Persian court, a third Anglo-Persian treaty was concluded, by which 'the limits of Russia and Persia shall be determined according to the admissions of Great Britain'—and, of course, the two powers primarily concerned. But since a situation of tension, and even bitterness, soon arose over the question of subsidies, the British Government presently withdrew their military support, though Colonel D'Arcy and Captain Hart, of the Royal Artillery, remained on to occupy positions of extraordinary confidence in Persia. Hart was a martinet; he compelled the royal princes to serve a term in the ranks, but they bore him no grudge. To Captain Hart, Persia had become his adopted country; as Generalissimo of the toy army of Azerbijan, he raised a regiment known as Shaggogies, as well as commanding a battalion of grenadiers, most of them Russian deserters from posts on the northern frontiers, officered by Georgians who had not been able to stomach Russian rule. Hart died in Persia of cholera, in 1830, and was greatly mourned.

Yet for all the pride Hart took in his regiments, for all the devotion and drill he and other British (and French) officers had lavished on the Persians, they were never able to make them a first-class army by

European standards. For all the elephants, and camels, and hordes of furious fighters, they lacked discipline; their artillery was poor; their tactics, too, were usually determined by the impetuous masses who fought, or fled, on a whim. Moreover, regular troops were hard to come by: after a few months in the ranks, they were likely to desert, to return to their families and farms (even though being soaked in oil and set alight was an accepted punishment for desertion or insubordination in the Persian army). They had no *esprit de corps*, said the European officers. Persian cavalry, on the other hand, were a formidable foe, the horses being trained to fight under their rider. Stallions were generally employed: it was a custom dating from Xenophon. 'The tremendous noise of horses fighting among themselves is known to all travellers in the East,' says Ker-Porter. 'They seize, bite and kick each other with the most determined fury. Even in skirmishes between the natives, their horses take part in the fray, tearing at each other with their teeth, while their masters are at similar close quarters upon their backs.'

After the second Russo-Persian war in 1828, the Shah came to realize not only Russia's terrible qualities as an enemy, but the uneasiness she inspired as a neighbour (even after he had surrendered). He could not forgive the enormous indemnity they had asked at Turkmentchai: *sole* rights of navigation on the Caspian and twenty million roubles indemnity, the free exit of Armenians from Persian to Russian territory. Adding the numbers of Armenians, ninety thousand or thereabouts, to the massed exodus of Tartars from Azerbijan, who had aided the Russians and claimed to be oppressed by Persian rule, the Shah felt some anxiety over his depleted population. Then, too, the conduct of Field-Marshal Count Paskiévitch had rankled. Not so much his victories, as the manner in which he had celebrated them: occupying the Palace of the Sirdars at Erivan, his top-booted officers strutting through the shimmering mirrored halls which had been designed for softer music. And then, seizing all those priceless manuscripts from the library of the mosque at Ardebil, saying that Senovsky, the eminent Orientalist at St. Petersburg, wanted to copy them! As if they would even be returned! (And, indeed, they never were.) Taking Tamerlane's sword away from the captured Persian General Hassan—and then presenting it to the Emperor: not content with that, seizing his—the Shah of Shah's—own battle-tent as a trophy! When Paskiévitch at last retired from the Army, as Prince of Warsaw, with the name of Erivansky added to his own by order of the Tzar, he withdrew to the vast castle of Gomel, in Poland, also given him by his grateful monarch. Here, in the lofty hall, the Shah's battle-tent was erected as a permanent monument to his victories. Its plumed magnificence was still to be seen, until the Russian revolution. I have been told, by one who played among its grandeurs as a child, that it was embroidered in huge jewels, slabs of uncut rubies and emeralds, its ropes tasselled with pearls, its stanchions, solid gold, its echoes, those of the Peacock Throne. The adoption of the title 'Prince of Erivansky' especially enraged the Shah. But whatever his own emotions, it was clear that Russia, as an empire, could no longer be opposed. The awful weight of Russian displeasure had convinced Fatih Ali Shah of the wisdom—of the positive necessity—of inactivity. However, the Shah was no Sardanapalus, dying theatrically when dethroned, and spending his last moments in an orgy of destruction while his Court and women dutifully perished round him. On the contrary, Fatih Ali Shah merely exchanged power-politics for chess and dalliance among his favourites.

V

So we see Fatih Ali, transfixed, a jewelled set piece in a land of blue dalliance, seated on his Peacock Throne, resigned with truly Oriental fatalism to letting Fate take its course with only the minimum of plotting. But let this enforced interlude be, at least, as agreeable as Persian tradition and imagination can make it. The houris of the Imperial harem (or *anderoun*) numbered around eight hundred—a mere bagatelle beside the Khan of Khokand's three thousand—most of whom were indeed, as well as name, his wives or concubines. Court portraits represent the Persian charmers as a beetle-browed, posturing band, at once graceful and grotesque; they are often depicted like tumblers, standing on their hands, their hennaed feet in the air; or juggling with dishes of pomegranates, turquoise and gold sherbet ewers, or a single, perfect rose.

The Court sit beside fountains, in formal, walled gardens, beneath almond or poplar trees. They seem a hermaphroditic band, princes, eunuchs, men, women and boys—those 'Ganymede boys' in spangled turbans, who so impressed Sir Dodmore Cotton's mission when they arrived in Persia in 1626. The sexes appear indistinguishable in their flowing robes, love-locks snaking down each painted moon-like cheek. They eye each other with languid, sidelong glances, all passion spent, as they fondle each others' bosoms, or the baby boars, tusky nestlings, which they regarded as love-tokens. Persian Court portraiture is strictly conventionalized; there are canons of grace and beauty, symbols of love and power; and a tradition for representing Europeans, too. Though their faces are represented in the same full-moon manner, with almond eyes, diplomats are generally recognized by their red stockings, which custom decreed they must wear for royal audiences. English ladies are first recognized by the little dog they carry, a woolly pet of unknown breed, which the Persians had observed was ever their inseparable companion.

Fatih Ali Shah had many pleasures. We read of scorpion hunting by candlelight, the local breed being a particularly venomous and snouted kind. Horse-racing, too, was conducted, if not on Newmarket lines, still with great enthusiasm, and a number of English jockeys appeared on the track. The English were always favourably regarded by the Persians. The Shah felt a strong personal affection for a young Mr. Strachey, a celebrated Adonis, whose quite sensational good-looks were as much value to British prestige as whole companies of men-at-arms. The Shah was so partial to Istarji, as the Persians pronounced Mr. Strachey's name, so dazzled by him, that he had a number of portraits painted to adorn his various residences, ever to remind him, if his friend were absent, of his classic profile, his blooming cheek and melting eye. Indeed, the Shah addressed an ode to this ubiquitous gentleman which became so celebrated throughout the East, that on the occasion of the Afghan prince, Dost Mahommed, being introduced to another Mr. Strachey, he at once burst into Fatih Ali's panegyric.

And then there were the ladies. In his country residence at Gulhek, there was a large tank, or pool. 'The Shah liked to sit beside it, while his harem came sliding down from an upper gallery, shrieking joyously, and slithering down the chute in a state of nudity. The Shah caught them, one by one, and flung the luscious armfuls into the tank.' Well might Sir John Chardin write: 'A Seraglio wipes out every inconvenience in the world.'

The Shah's heirs were abundant. In 1826, according to conservative estimates, he had sixty-eight sons, one hundred and twenty-four senior grandsons, and fifty-three married daughters who had one hundred and thirty-five sons between them. The Shah's total male offspring, to the second generation, were reckoned at three hundred and twenty-seven, while in his seventies, his progeny, to the third and fourth generation, amounted to some thousands.

However patriarchal Fatih Ali Shah may have been in fact, his portraits do not convey Abraham so much as Nebuchadnezzar, in his more magnificent, pre-vegetarian days. The Shah has something Assyrian in his black-bearded majesty: he is altogether too foppish and dissipated to be classed as a family man. The portraits reveal a splendid figure, sitting rigid as a chess-man in a caftan of crimson velvet sewn with enormous pearls and diamonds, diapered close, a chain mail of jewels.

Precious stones are, to the Oriental, a voluptuous delight rather than an adornment, or an investment, as to the Westerner. They spend many hours contemplating them, caressing them, with the same deep sense of satisfaction displayed by the British towards their pets, or the Americans towards their automobiles. Every aspect of domestic life (among the wealthy) reflected this obsession with jewels. Bird-cages were gold-barred, and studded with precious stones, coffee cups were moulded from huge flawed emeralds. The Shah's library was furnished with a terrestrial globe supported by a solid gold frame; the seas were of studded emeralds, the countries of various precious stones. The Persian lover likened his mistress' charms to jewels, while poems of a martial nature abounded in similes such as this Moghul war song:

> The air was cut by purpled sabres,
> Into solid ruby the blades were turned.

We are told that Fatih Ali's jewelled costume weighed one and a half hundredweight. He is portrayed wearing a *tespyeh*, or *tazbikh*, the Persian name for the Moslem rosary, long as a skipping-rope, all enormous emeralds and pearls. His tall, pointed astrakhan *papakh*, or bonnet, shimmers with a sweeping diamond aigrette backed by black heron plumes, their tips bent by the weight of immense pearl drops. His feet are thrust into turn-up-toed, high-heeled jewelled slippers; his arms are encircled, above the elbow, with the wide jewelled *bazubands*, or bracelets of state. His face is painted with the abandon of a Matisse canvas, bold effects of scarlet, white and black. His eyes glitter from between great sweeps of khol; his eyebrows meet, like two jet scimitars. The vivid patches of rouge on his sallow cheeks are invaded by the high-mounting black beard, the finest in all the kingdom, it was said, and as black, as densely curled as his astrakhan bonnet. But sitting there rigid among the jewelled bolsters, the crystal goblets and the narghilyes, even though surrounded by his sons, massed in ninepin-like rows, it is not a family scene.

The Persian sense of elegant formality, expressed in their art, and gardens, is also found in their approach to corporal punishment. When a delinquent provincial governor was sentenced to be bastinadoed in the main square at Tabriz, sentence was carried out on a fine Shiraz rug. When one of the Shah's cousins suffered the same punishment, for having lost a campaign against the Russians, his humiliation and pain was softened by the presence of the Shah himself, and, in homage to his rank, the Shah's next-of-kin Abbas Mirza struck the first blow. Lord Bloomfield quotes a dispatch from Persia, received while he was at St. Petersburg, stating that the Shah had just invented a new punishment for political offenders. Their teeth were drawn out and then hammered into their own skulls in the presence of the whole government.

On New Year's day it was customary for the Shah to appear before his subjects, on the Palace balcony, and receive their homage. On one such occasion, we learn that the wife of the British Minister, Colonel Shiel, planned to witness their picturesque ceremony, where, she had been told, the Shah's mood was indicated by the colour of his robe; green, the Prophet's own colour, indicating a holy detachment, blue, good will, and so on. But Lady Shiel was unavoidably detained at home that day; perhaps it was just as well, for the Shah appeared before his prostrated people and Ministers, garbed in scarlet—indicating displeasure. At a given signal, fifty wretched prisoners were dragged forward, bound hand and foot, and in a slash of steel, fifty scimitars were raised and fifty heads rolled in the dust. The Shah inclined majestically and withdrew.

In Afghanistan, until well on into the 1920's, executions by cannon were regarded as very *recherché* spectacles, and the government and members of the Corps Diplomatique were regularly invited to attend, in full dress and decorations. The custom was only abandoned after several pieces of flying flesh hit one Western Ambassador full in the face. This occurrence, which might be described as a miscarriage of justice, produced so many protests from the Corps Diplomatique that the practice was discontinued, or confined to purely national audiences.

*   *   *

But however appalling or autocratic the Persian rulers appeared, they never succeeded in intimidating the Russian envoys. Yermolov had met them, as later he was to meet the Caucasians, on their own terms of brutality and cunning. When envoy of the Tzar, he had flatly declined to remove his boots and don the long scarlet stockings which Persian Court etiquette prescribed for those about to enter the Shah's presence. The British had been far more pliant: they did all that was requested, wore the red stockings and remained standing throughout their audiences. So did the French. When told that General Gardanne had made no objection to the red stockings, Yermolov snorted: 'After the red cap of liberty, the red socks of servitude!' He himself had kicked aside the Court officials, stamped into the Royal presence in his topboots, gone right up to the Peacock Throne, and sat heavily down beside it. It had the oddest, most salutory effect on the Shah of Shahs. Besides, Yermolov was not only an Ambassador, but Commander-in-Chief of all the Russian Armies of the South. 'When I spoke, the Persians seemed to hear not my voice alone, but the voices of a hundred thousand men.' His claim to be the descendant of Genghis Khan greatly impressed the Shah, and Yermolov never allowed him to forget it.

Altogether, the impact of his personality, like his violent, roaring voice, was overwhelming. 'I relied on my wild-beast's muzzle, my gigantic and terrifying figure and limitless voice: they were convinced that anybody who could shout so vociferously had good reasons to be obeyed.' Sometimes, when things were not going his way, he feigned madness, a mighty madness to match his Herculean frame: or he would sob, unrestrainedly, assuring the Shah that he was thus affected by mere contemplation of the Shah's perfections. It was an almost irresistible mixture of bombast, arrogance and flattery. After Persia had been brought low by the war of 1828 it always showed a proper respect for Russia, and never aided its Moslem brothers in their struggle for Caucasian independence, however much the Prince Alexander Batonishvili, in his self-imposed exile at Abbas Mirza's court, in Tabriz, still urged them to action, still raged for revenge, for power to oust the Russian interlopers from his own Georgian lands.

VI

Not only Russia's soldiers but her diplomats, too, paid their dues to that limitless quality of savagery, of excess, that is the abiding climate of the Near East. The curious affair of Griboyedov's death exemplifies this. It was to be the last gesture of Persian defiance, and it seems to have had its roots in both religious superstition and harem etiquette: unless—as sometimes whispered—it was instigated by the British. In any case, to the Caucasians watching intently from afar, it was yet one more example of Russian arrogance.

Griboyedov had been appointed Minister to Persia in 1828. He knew the country and the people, and the Court. Ten years earlier he had been Diplomatic Secretary to General Yermolov. But, if the General was a raging lion, Griboyedov was an owlish figure, a secretary bird, peering at life through his huge horn-rimmed glasses, at once remote and quizzical. He was a typical *chinovnik*—a civil servant—conforming to the pattern of his particular class. There had always been a tradition of literature among the civil servants: Griboyedov was one of the first. Pushkin and Gogol were to follow: and like them, what he wrote was considered impudent, too liberal, if not downright seditious. During the stifling hot nights of a summer's leave spent in Tiflis in 1821, he wrote his immortal comedy: *Woe through Wit; or the misfortunes of being clever.* But in St. Petersburg it was rejected by the censors; it was a biting satire on Russian society, on the chinovnik or class system in particular, and naturally unacceptable to the very gentlemen who were called upon to license or withdraw it. 'A piece of impudence'. 'Subversive', they said, and Griboyedov had to be content to read it to a small circle of friends.

After the Dekabrist Revolt, in 1825, Griboyedov was caught up in the wave of general alarm and arrested as a dangerous liberal; but he was released and sent to serve under Yermolov in the Persian campaigns. At the end of the war, he was dispatched to negotiate the peace treaty of Turkmentchai. On establishing the terms he returned to St. Petersburg to have the treaty ratified. By now, the years of exile, of wandering, of the East, had become part of himself. The North was alien. He had just married a Georgian beauty, the fifteen-year-old Princess Nina Tchavtchavadzé, whose younger brother, Prince David, then a boy playing unconcernedly on the family estates at Tzinondali near Tiflis, was later to marry that Princess Anna of Georgia, who, with her sister Varvara, was to become known throughout Russia and Europe for the dark drama they lived as prisoners of Shamyl. But this lay more than twenty years ahead. Meantime Griboyedov's own drama was yet to be played out.

In St. Petersburg, while awaiting the Foreign Office ratification of the treaty, Griboyedov felt himself enmeshed in a way of life he had come to detest. Looking out on the grey slushed streets, he began to write a nostalgic romance, *A Georgian Night*. . . . But it was never finished. Abruptly, he was sent back to Persia, as Minister Plenipotentiary, to supervise the execution of the treaty. Suddenly the sun shone again. Persia was his life now; whatever its faults he adored this arid region, and he would work for better understanding between it and his native land.

His government post-chaise crossed the Caucasian mountain passes, came down into the verdant valleys, and rattled on, eastward, to the desolation of the Persian frontier lands, where only the almond trees softened the biscuit-coloured hills. On the outskirts of Teheran, he was met as a conqueror, with a conqueror's retinue. A procession of sumptuously dressed figures in brocaded caftans lined with sable, their turbans heavy with jewels, stood beside kneeling elephants and leashed lions backed by cavalry in chain mail with fluttering pennons. Beside them, a throng of strangely draped, blood-stained figures. It was the month of Moukharrem, the month in which Al Hussein the Prophet's grandson had been killed. For the Faithful, the followers and members of his sect, it was a time devoted to gloomy revels, when they slashed themselves with their swords, wore their own shrouds mottled with their own blood, poured red-hot ashes on their bowed heads and wailed ceaselessly, working themselves into morbid ecstasies. They stood there, behind the official deputation, watchful and resentful of this Infidel come among them as conqueror.

At that moment there occurred one of those unforeseen trifles which sometimes lead to gigantic consequences. Griboyedov, riding towards the gates of Teheran and the assembled multitudes, found his own chestnut horse lamed, and changed to another. One of the guard supplied him with a fine black stallion: it caracoled forward, bearing Griboyedov to his fate. How could Griboyedov know the chance changing of his mount would be taken as an evil presage—that Ibn Sa'ad of accursed memory, the slayer of Imam Hussein, had ridden a black stallion too?

The wailing and the cheering ceased. There was silence, suddenly pierced by a yell. *Ya Hussein!* The Faithful surged forward with cries and imprecations, closing round him. The black stallion reared, and the crowd fell back. The soldiers drove them off, and they retreated, muttering, to follow the state procession, wailing again, and tearing at their mottled shrouds. When the high wooden doors of the Russian Legation crashed shut on Griboyedov, they took up their places outside, a silent picket of hatred. All Teheran talked of it by nightfall. It would end disastrously. Death to the Infidel Dog! Enough of Russian might! Dzhakhat! Holy War! The wind of mob violence fanned round the city and centred itself on the Russian Legation, where Griboyedov and his bride were living in uneasy reunion. The temper of the people quickened as they spoke of the treaty. Dzhakhat! The ugly cries were heard again, as the followers of Hussein began stabbing themselves, in protest, outside the walls of the Legation.

Presently the Shah left his capital for a change of air at one of his summer palaces. He was followed by most of the Court, his sons, and the moon-faced beauties of his harem. Dr. McNeil, the Englishman who had such a restraining influence on Persian impetuosity, soon followed the Shah to his country retreat. Everyone knew what horrors came of Holy wars. . . . In the name of the Prophet, all was permitted to the Faithful.

But Griboyedov stayed on. The treaty had to be put into execution. Perhaps he was optimistic: or fatalistic: perhaps he sensed that his death, like his life, lay in and through Persia. But presently he sent his young wife away: she was pregnant. She would be better out of the unhealthy city air, he said. She went, docile, protesting, queasy, loving. . . . She never saw him again.

Now the darkness closed round. Now Griboyedov was alone, and knew himself doomed. Over a harem intrigue, all the stifled hatreds were released. By the terms of the Turkmentchai treaty, all those Armenians who chose to return to their native land, now under Russian protection, were to be allowed free passage. Mirza Yakoub, a eunuch from the Shah's harem, an Armenian by birth, demanded his right to leave Persia forthwith. Griboyedov agreed to his taking up his quarters in the Legation. But the Shah was incensed to the point of madness that one of his own servants, one of those persons who had access to the inviolable privacy of the Imperial anderoun, or harem, had now dared to leave—to *live* outside those sacred precincts! (for those who had beheld the splendours either died, or were dispatched—they did not live to tell). Was he now to be established and protected by the Infidels?

This was altogether something beyond the Shah's endurance.

He insisted on the return of his eunuch, together with two Armenian

women who had been living placidly in the harem of a Persian nobleman, but who had been mysteriously abducted, and reappeared as
refugees in the Russian Legation. Griboyedov refused. It was madness.
No diplomacy, no force, could set up against the ethics and intrigues of
the harem. It was said the Shah had instigated the whole thing.
Matters went from bad to worse. The women had been sent to the
Legation for purposes of identification, some said: others, that they
might be kept there, in safety, till they could be repatriated to Russian
Armenia. In any case, once there, they stayed. Griboyedov was stubborn. His sense of duty hardened to blind folly. He refused to return
either the eunuch or the women. The whole matter, he insisted, must
be referred to Count Nesselrode, the Minister for Foreign Affairs in
St. Petersburg.

Now all classes of Persians were roused to fury: the Shah, the Hus-
seinites, the fanatics, the people. . . . Every man saw himself threatened,
his harem violated. Griboyedov represented not only a political and
religious affront, but a domestic menace too. Only Griboyedov seemed
unmoved by the uproar. He was firm. The issue must now be decided
by St. Petersburg. But the issue had been decided long ago, on that day
when he rode into Teheran on the black stallion.

Ya Hussein! A mob of ten thousand stormed the Legation, and soon
overcame the desperate resistance of the small Cossack guard.
Griboyedov was trapped, and retreated, sword in hand, from court to
court, room to room, till the last guards lay slaughtered round him and
there was no more ammunition left. The mob broke down the last
barricade and stabbed him to death before they dragged his body into
the streets for all to rejoice. A shashlik vendor cut off his head and stuck
it, spectacles and all, on a spike above his meat-stall. The Unbeliever's
head! He did a brisk trade, that night, and all Teheran came to stare.
Griboyedov's right arm was hacked off at the elbow—for there was a
fine diamond ring on one finger; what was left of his body was tied to
a string of dead cats and dogs and trailed round the city by the Faithful,
before they flung it on a dung heap, where it rotted and was forgotten.
The Russians in Tiflis sent furious representations in the name of the
Tzar. On the Shah's orders, what remained of Griboyedov was collected from the dung heap, stealthily, by lantern-light (for it would not
do, even now, to appear too submissive towards Russia), and placed in
a coffin to lie in an Armenian church during a week of sanctifying
masses, sung day and night by the bearded monks and the *sargarvarg*,
one of that specialized race of Eastern mourners who watch and wail
by the body in frenzies of professional grief. Then, one night, a lumbering ox-cart set out on its slow plodding way to Tiflis, where Russian
authorities and the prostrated widow waited.

On the road north the great rock plateaux narrowed to gorges, and a solitary horseman came galloping out of the desolation: he reined up, for it was a full day's ride since he had encountered a living soul. He was a swarthy-looking young man, slight, his woolly black curls almost as shaggy as the bourka he wore over European riding clothes. His eyes were dark blue, peculiarly brilliant, lively and enquiring. It was Alexander Pushkin, the poet, on his way to spend some time among his friends, the exiled Dekabrist officers, now serving with the Army of the South, engaged in the Turkish campaign before Erzerum.

'Where are you from?' he asked the old peasant driver, and smiled his wide, impish grin.

'Teheran,' was the reply given dourly, with a scowl.

Pushkin glanced at the clumsy wooden crate which jolted as the cart moved.

'And what have you got there?' he asked idly.

'Griboyedov,' said the old man, tugging at the reins. 'They killed him like a dog.' The oxen strained forward and the cart creaked on its way.

Pushkin reined back, bared his head, and watched the cart out of sight. The incident moved him profoundly: he was to write of it in letters and notes. 'I know of nothing happier, or more enviable, than the last days of his storm-filled life. Death, coming to him in the heat of a brave and unequal battle, was neither terrible nor wearisome, but, on the contrary, sudden and beautiful.'

It was as if Pushkin envied him his release, the nobility of his death, as opposed to the futilities of life which were already choking Pushkin. Perhaps he was aware, even then, intuitively, that ten years later another such rough wooden coffin would be lying in the back of another cart, or sleigh—for it would be a winter's dusk, in the north, near the Sviatigorsk monastery—where another stranger would accost the driver, idly enough, to ask what he carried.

'Pushkin—some poet fellow, killed in a duel. . . . They are burying him like a dog.'

3

Shamyl

It is in the mountains that the eagles
dwell.   TOLSTOY

For most of the details of Shamyl's earlier life and battles, there is only
one known local source: *The Chronicles of Mahommed Tahir of Karahi*. As
Shamyl's devoted follower, Tahir acted as his secretary during the early
fifties, and much of his material is from the Imam's own dictation,
during his captivity. The Chronicles were written in Arabic and after
Tahir's death in 1882 his son Habibullah continued the work, amassing
more eye-witness accounts of the Murid wars. It is from this chronicle,
together with certain family sources, that I have tried to weigh up the
conflicting accounts of Shamyl's life, his victories and defeats. Sometimes both Russian military sources and the Arabic chronicle tally: but
sometimes they are diametrically opposed. However, in purely bio-
graphical material, the Chronicles are probably exact, for they agree
with Shamyl's own accounts, given, in his last years, to his son Khazi
Mahommed, from whose grandchildren I obtained much of my
material.

Shamyl's birthplace was the aôul of Ghimri, in north-eastern
Daghestan. It was typical of its kind, a rock fortress, rather than a
village, cornered by tall, stone watch-towers: as forbidding and savage
as the surrounding landscape. Its terraced, flat-roofed houses were
piled one upon the other, and were often honeycombed into the solid
rock of the mountain-side, hanging perilously above ravines, and overcast by towering snow-peaks. Although such aôuls were generally terraced towards the south, so that the scorching summer sun could ripen
the few laboriously cultivated vineyards or peach trees, it was, before
all else, a landscape of desolation, an apocalyptic scene. Stones,
savage wastes, slit defiles which revealed, five thousand feet below,
rivers raging over the rocks. Heavy clouds clung to the mountains most
of the year, and seemed to close in on them in a menacing, possessive
manner. Sometimes a narrow ledge, clinging to the cliff face, led to a
tree-shrine—one of those stunted thorn bushes, or some skeletal growth

45

where Caucasian tradition decreed the pious should attach a rag, a fragment of their clothing, as a testimony of prayers offered for the soul of whichever Mollah or holy man the tree represented. A never ceasing wind moaned round the mountains, fluttering the rags, a greying, melancholy vegetation which knew no spring.

It was this austere scene, in the last years of the eighteenth century, which cradled the little Shamyl. There are no records of his birth, but it is believed to have been about 1796. His father, Dengau, was an Avar nobleman; his mother, Bahou-Messadou, was of equally noble birth. Nine generations of high-bred Avars lay behind them; but Shamyl has no need of ancestors. Like Napoleon, he could have said, '*Ma noblesse date de moi.*' There was a local belief that he was, in reality, the child of that Prince Alexander Batonishvili who had opposed his brother, from ceding his Georgian kingdom to Russia in 1801. Before settling in Persia, the Prince had fled to the mountains of Daghestan, where he lived a fugitive's life for some years, Russia's implacable enemy, and a hero among the local population. Since Shamyl's handsome eagle-features bore a marked resemblance to the Bagratid family type, and he always moved with a particular air of majesty, the belief that he was, in fact, the Prince's son became widespread. Although no doubt apocryphal, such a legend fits well with his subsequent lifelong struggle against Russian domination. Certainly, the following account of the Prince, given by Sir Robert Ker-Porter, who encountered him in Tabriz in 1819, might have applied to Shamyl defying all the Russias from his mountain fastness. 'It was impossible to look on this intrepid Prince,' he wrote, 'however wild and obdurate, without interest; without that sort of pity and admiration with which a man might view the royal lion hunted from his hereditary wastes, yet still returning to hover near, and roar in proud loneliness his ceaseless threatenings to the human strangers who had disturbed his reign.'

As a baby, Shamyl had been named Ali, but being of a sickly cast, it was decided to change his name, this being a Caucasian custom said to deflect the malign spirits centred round children. And so it was: no sooner had the little Ali been re-named Shamyl (or Samuel) than he throve. By nature he was moody, intractable, a silent little creature, who seemed lost in dreams and held himself aloof from his only sister and most of his companions; although he had one especial friend, or 'kounak', an Avar boy, a few years his senior, who was to become celebrated as Khazi Mollah, Imam of Daghestan, the first to preach resistance to Russia. It was from this companion that Shamyl would eventually inherit the spiritual and absolute rulership of Daghestan, to become its third Imam. But while the elder boy was already marked for the mosque, spending many hours in prayer and the study of Sufi doctrines, the younger boy lived in a world of legends, peopled by mythological creatures, djinns, and fabled monsters, which in his imagination inhabited a nearby plateau set among the desolate rock wastes, a region feared throughout Daghestan. No villager would venture near after dusk: but the young Shamyl was in the habit of spending whole nights there, sharing, said the villagers, some kind of sinister secret with these djinns, almas and peris whose *Walpurgis Nacht* revels were lit by jets of flame which could be seen from afar, blazing up into the sky, curiously livid flames, flickering, falling, and blazing up again.

Naphtha sources abound in this area, both in the mountains and along the Caspian shore, and even flare up from the depths of the sea. The Zoroastrian fire-worshippers based their mystical beliefs on these flames, and came from far away to worship at the tempal of Guebres. There were many local legends of fiery beings, fire-birds, and lovely, crowned, winged women-birds that soared from the flames. Such flames are the principal theme, expressed in the stylized, geometric forms which signify both prayer and legend in the beautiful old Soumakh, Shirvan and Baku rugs from these regions.

In the dark mountain landscape of Ghimri, where the nights were lit by tongues of flame, there were also sudden, terrible storms and rushing winds that sounded like the beating of giant wings. To the people it was the passing of Simurg, the gigantic white bird of Solomon, who looks with one eye at the past, and with the other at the future, and who lives forever in Kafdagh, and who flies through the night to visit the peaks of Ghimri, there to hold his awful revels. But such legends did not alarm the young Shamyl. Whether he was already sustained by a sense of invested sanctity—or whether he sought, in this mythological court, that majesty of which he dreamed, to which he felt himself born, and which he did not find in the aôul, we do not know. It is recorded that even as a child his pride knew no bounds, and he moved and lived as if he were a being set apart. Unfortunately he was still a rather fragile boy, without the physique to enforce his majesty. And his pride suffered from the undeniable fact that his father was a drunkard. After trying many times to turn him from liquor, Shamyl vowed he would stab himself to death—die on his own kindjal—if his father continued in his ways. This produced the desired effect, for Dengau loved his son, and knew him capable of dying for a principle. From that moment he lived sober. It was Shamyl's first victory over self-indulgence, easy living, and the flesh—all things against which he was to thunder later.

At last Shamyl's arrogance reached such a degree, and so enraged the other village boys, that they banded together to teach him a lesson. He was ambushed as he returned from an all-night absence in the mountains. Setting on him, they beat him senseless and, having knifed him in the stomach, left him for dead. Returning to consciousness Shamyl's first instinct was to hide from both taunts and sympathy. He dragged himself back to the mountains, contrived to bind up his own wounds and obtain those herbal concoctions for which the mountaineers were famous. The methods used for treating wounds with herbs (a skill which was given plenty of opportunities to perfect itself in this part of the world) were known and respected by even the Russian army surgeons. Sometimes the village doctors succeeded in clamping shut the torn arteries by means of applying a large, ferocious species of local ant. Once the pincer-like mandibles had fastened on the arteries, the rest of the ant's body was snipped off—the pincers remained in place. The gaping wound was bound up, herbs were applied, and no blood-poisoning followed.

The tradition of the people was not only stoic, but fatalistic. It was in God's hands. *God hath pre-ordained five things on his servants, the duration of life, their actions, their dwelling places, their travels and their portions.* If it was written that they were to live, to fight again—for to live was to fight—they would recover, however shattered their bodies. They lay there, mangled, pierced, and bled white: they drank the herbal brews, submitted to torturing treatments—and generally recovered. The Russians found them a most stubborn enemy. Killed—or so it seemed— they still lived. One Murid, or holy warrior, would rush out of a beleaguered aôul brandishing his shashka in one hand, a pistol in the other, his kindjal between his teeth, and hurl himself on the astounded Russians, firing rapidly in all directions, then, dropping his gun, begin to thrust and slash with his steel, so that five or six enemy were accounted for before he too fell; and even in the dying he would usually contrive another deadly thrust. 'They don't seem to know when they ought to die, sir,' says a Russian soldier in one of Lermontov's Caucasian tales. 'Indeed, sir, these villains can hardly ever be killed. They are a people without the slightest idea of propriety.'

So the stoical young Shamyl hid his wounds and his humiliation, and did not return to Ghimri until he was not only recovered, but toughened by an implacable, self-imposed regime of physical culture. From that moment on, he forced himself to feats of endurance, changing himself into a lean, iron-hard athlete. His great height—he stood six feet three inches—topped by a towering black lambskin *papakh*, or cap, made him appear a giant. (But then the principal protagonists of the coming struggle were all giant figures: Shamyl and his sons were each well over six feet; so were Field-Marshal Bariatinsky and Hadji Mourad; while both the Tzar Nicholas and his son, Alexander II, shared the Romanov stature.)

Shamyl could out-fight, out-ride, out-swim and out-run all the rest of the mountain people; just as they had their own methods of curing wounds, so they had their jealously guarded methods of training and hardening both themselves and their horses (usually bred in the plains, or from Kabarda) to be able to cover the enormous distances and endure the violent changes of climate their raiding tactics and the country demanded. And likewise, the *djighits*, *delikans* or Caucasian braves, the dashing young mountaineers, trained themselves to an extraordinary stamina. They were, by breed, a slim wiry lot, generally considered the world's most handsome people; tall, dark, eagle-faced, with narrow, beautifully formed hands and feet, and wasp-waists (partially induced by binding them tightly with the still-warm skin of a freshly slaughtered sheep). Over all, they had an indefinable air of elegance—of breeding. They ate very sparingly, as a race, but the fighting men ate least of all: thus, in the Caucasian wars, they were better able to withstand the rigours of long marches in barren country, unfettered by the cumbersome supply-wagons which hampered Russian columns on the move and included such unmanageable objects as five-foot-high brass samovars, to hold fifty gallons of tea, without which the humblest recruit would have mutinied. Wine was forbidden the mountaineers by their religion, and although the country produced fine vineyards, which were laboriously cultivated wherever a patch of earth clung to a southern, or lower, slope of the mountains, as a race the Caucasians drank little, regarding it as an indulgence to be reserved for special occasions. There was nothing Mediterranean in their approach to life, however many strains of Greek and Roman were crossed in their remote ancestry. Meat was a rarity at their tables, and then only lamb, goat or chicken. Their magnificent physique was generally maintained on a few cakes of rough-ground millet, and a little goats' cheese. During a campaign, these virile creatures were often seen to eat, and appear well nourished by a few leaves, or even flowers—rhododendrons being considered particularly sustaining. They trained themselves to run great distances, swiftly, at a level speed, without panting, by carrying a bullet, or a pebble, in their mouths. Their lives were a mixture of personal austerity and heroic excess.

Shamyl lashed himself to their strenuous pattern until, at twenty, he was famous for his feats. He could sever the butt of a rifle with one blow of his kindjal, and was once seen to cleave a Cossack horseman almost to the saddle in one cut. He could clear a seven-foot wall at a leap, or, as they said in local idiom, 'stride a Khevsour'. (This tribe, strangely blond giants, were believed to be descendants of the Crusaders; they wore chain mail decorated with Maltese crosses, while their swords, handed down from father to son, often bore the Crusaders' device: *Ave Mater Dei*. They were celebrated for their great height. Carpet-dealers in the bazaar in Tiflis have always measured their rugs against the nearest Khevsour.)

Even among such a centaur-race as the Caucasians, Shamyl's horsemanship was remarkable. The mountaineers' equestrian acrobatics had the same brilliance as the Arabs'. Perhaps it was a legacy from their Arab conquerors in the eighth century. At any rate Caucasian *djighitovkas* —festivals of horsemanship and daring—were similar, and equal to, the Arab fantasia and made even the Cossack riders seem inept by comparison; trick-riding, circus stuff, all of it in daily use in their violent raiding warfare. Shamyl was speaking to the people in a language they understood best when he flung himself into the saddle at one bound, cleared the high gates of the aôul in another, and scorning the path, leapt a precipice, hanging head-downwards under his horse's belly, swinging up the other side to stand in the saddle and, at the gallop, shoot a coin spun high in the air. Later, when he called them to battle, when he preached the Shariat—the Law, and the Tarikat—the Way, they knew the mettle of their new leader, and followed blindly. Perhaps, when the young Shamyl was outpacing the fieriest djighits, he was, even unconsciously fostering his legend, the legend that surrounded him by both circumstance and design all his life, and which was, even in its more theatrical aspects, to strengthen his other, mystical aura of leadership.

II

This quality of tinsel, of glittering heroics, invests some of the greatest figures, tyrants, heroes, kings. They appeal to popular imagination and they are represented popularly. But is there not, perhaps, something basically meretricious, or tinselled, in their nature, too? Are they not a judicious, rather than accidental, mixture of braggadocio and grandeur? We are told that Socrates' epileptic fits, whether genuine or simulated, greatly enhanced his legend: the historian Gibbon dwells on the dangerous effects of 'a conscience that slumbers in a mixed state, between self-illusion and voluntary fraud'. Heroes of this kind, who kindled a flame that has never died, often have, in their bravery, a certain bravura, a certain calculated attitudinizing: their flamboyance lends itself to popular legend, to broad-sheets, ballads and barn-storming troupes. Many such characters are immortalized in the crude prints, known as Mr. Pollock's Penny Plain and Twopence Coloured Theatrical Prints, which in nineteenth-century England were everyday fare, and are now collectors' items. It was through these images— theatrical prints, *Mr. Kemble as Timour the Tartar*, broad-sheets, with wood-cuts illustrating *Hannibal crossing the Alps*, Saladin, and even Aladdin, and Harlequin too (for heroic drama overlapped with pantomime)—that the nineteenth-century West envisaged the East; in particular, Asiatic heroes, such as those of De Quincey's *Revolt of the Tartars*.

The world of those earlier illustrations is a simplified one: the issues are clear; good and bad; saint and villain; robber, parson; pacha, pauper. Mountains are perpendicular, needle-peaked: forests are sombre masses of impenetrable vegetation. Sunsets are as orange and geometrically rayed as the Japanese flag. Women are ethereal beings, whether celebrated ballerinas, mothers of conquerors, or Oriental houris. This is the nineteenth-century concept of woman. The pure oval of her face is always framed by sleek tresses; her dove-like glance is limpid, trusting, silly, recalling Byron's melting heroine, Mazeppa's love,

> Like saints that at the stake expire
> And lift their raptured looks on high,
> As though it were a joy to die . . .

She is born to be betrayed, a poor, weak plaything for man. Men are seen in a firmer mould. (This too was a nineteenth-century concept.) They are strutting heroes, hirsute and agile. They strike commanding attitudes, and though often encased in chain mail topped by cumbersome plumed helmets, or turbans, they do battle, scale Gothic castles a size too small for them, roll their eyes, brandish swords, and generally behave heroically. It was in such terms, then, that Europe envisaged Genghis Khan, Timur the Tartar, Alexander the Great, Sulieman the Magnificent, and also Shamyl. My first acquaintance with Shamyl was such a chance encounter: a crudely coloured engraving, iconic in character, found in an old scrapbook among embossed Valentines and silhouettes. 'SHAMYL THE LION OF DAGHESTAN' I read, but was no wiser. The haughty glance, the splendid moustachios, and the brandished scimitar belonged to the Penny Plain and Twopence Coloured world of Mr. Pollock's Theatrical Prints, upon which my childish imagination had been nourished. Among them, did I once come across a print of Shamyl and his gallant band of Murids? (Robin Hood and his Merry, Merry Men in the Pollock idiom, pitted against the ogre Tzar and all the Russian villains would have been in the proper tradition.)

Many years later, in Kiev, when I passed along a quiet street lined with porticoed wooden houses shabbily elegant, set behind high fences, where lilac and sun-flowers sprawled, I was told that Shamyl, in exile, had lived in one.

'He fought for freedom. . . . The Tzar kept him in a cage. . . .' The echoes stirred; there was a brief half-formed image of a lemon-coloured glove closed over a scimitar, and a pointed Tartar cap. SHAMYL THE LION OF DAGHESTAN . . . That proud hero in a cage?

It was many more years before Caucasian history began to come into focus for me, along the shores of the Black Sea, and in the villages of

Asia Minor where Shamyl's dark splendours still shone. There I was to hear legends and facts, memories and echoes, of the man and his epic battles, his ideals, triumphs, and tragedies, all interwoven; family tales told beside the Bosphorus, hearsay mumbled by an old woman sunning herself under a vine at Diabekir; or scraps of history recalled by sleeping minds, stirred to recapture the forgotten past.

III

Shamyl, as a young man, was supremely elegant; his natural distinction gave him a princely air, apart from the severe elegance of his clothes. These were of the finest, and of black or white only.

He wore the classic costume of the Caucasus—perhaps the most dashing ever devised. A *tcherkesska*, or long, full-skirted, wasp-waisted cloth tunic was barred across the chest by double rows of silver cartridge-cases. Over this, a shaggy black goat's-hair cloak—the bourka. Usually, the Caucasians wore a heavy lambskin cap, the papakh; but Shamyl, when he assumed power, enhanced this by a gigantic red-tasselled turban. It was the head-dress of a religious leader.

Perhaps the most subtly elegant of his accoutrements were those supple, glove-thin, soft black leather boots, so typical of the Caucasians, which seem moulded to the ankle, as their saddle and bridle seemed moulded to the horse. He rode only thoroughbreds—Kabarda stallions.

His beard, and the palms of his hands, were stained the dark orange of henna (Moslems consider henna to be one of the trees of Paradise), making the extreme pallor of his face even more startling.

Shamyl knew how to maintain his legend, his aura of leadership, before the people. 'Throughout the East', says Sir Richard Burton, 'a badly dressed man is a pauper, and a pauper—unless he belongs to an order having a right to be poor—is a scoundrel.' But Shamyl was neither of these; he was a noble, and though austerity was the first tenet of his faith, he never abandoned the fastidious standards of his caste.

And here he recalls Tolstoy, who ultimately attained an almost extravagant austerity, exchanging the Moscow salons, champagne suppers and smart tailoring, for the simplest food grown on his lands. He liked to wear a *roubashka* (the peasant's shirt) woven for him by his own peasants from the finest linen or lambs' wool. It was a state of mind based on surfeit and sophistication. To him, simplicity was the greatest luxury. And if, as his daughter, the Countess Alexandra Tolstoy, recalled when we discussed degrees of luxury, there was no running water at Yasniya Poliyana, it was not Tolstoy who fetched the buckets from the well. For unfortunately, simplicity is a state which is mostly achieved only through great difficulty, or the complicity of others.

When a Caucasian boy attained his majority—generally at the age of seventeen or thereabout—he was expected to have proved himself, first of all in battle: if not in some inter-tribal fight, at least one of the local vendettas. As a horseman and swordsman he must be above reproach; his scholarship must include, beside his own language, some knowledge of Arabic, and an ability to improvise the chants by which each community handed down its histories and battles.

When the elders agreed that the boy was worthy of manhood—and a place among the delikans or djighits—a celebration was held in which the whole aôul participated. The young djighit was presented with splendid arms—the finest his family could afford; sometimes these were handed down, from one generation to another, and inscribed with the name of the maker, and original owner, many centuries before when numbers of Italian armourers had settled in the Caucasus. A whole lore surrounded weapons; for good luck, the kindjal was used to slash a cross, skywards, when the new moon appeared. Weapons were used symbolically, too; rival claimants for a mistress' favours would each try to cast a spell of impotence on the other. This was done by half unsheathing the kindjal, three times; or half withdrawing the cartridge from the <i>ghizir</i>, its breast pocket case. Together with a ritual imprecation, this was considered enough to daunt the fieriest lover.

At the celebrations held for a young djighit, a feast was held in which the whole aôul participated. Sheep were roasted whole, bowls of yoghourt and honey lined the tables and a local wine flowed. This, having been boiled, or passed through fire, was considered purified, and thus permitted by Moslem canons, though frowned upon, in principle. It was a potent brew, and had the most enflaming effects. Yoghourt was an especial delicacy: it was held that Allah himself had taught the Patriarch Abraham how to make it. Songs were sung and strolling players recounted heroic legends, or those interminable sagas of the Caucasus which always tell of epic battles, and whose refrains are always dirges for fallen heroes, mystical figures, or those about to win Paradise by dying in battle against the Infidel. The Song of Hamzad is typical:

How hot the day; only our swords to shade us!
How thick the smoke, how dark the night.
Only our guns to light us!
Oh birds, fly homeward! Give our last greeting to our sisters.
Tell them our only mourners will be ravens:
Our only dirge, the howling hungry wolves.
Tell them we died, sword in hand, in the land of the Giaour,
Where the ravens pick out our eyes, and the wolves tear our flesh.

The Caucasian people luxuriated in sombre similies, and their songs, if generally holy, scarcely sounded that cheerful note which sustained Marvell's seamen in the English boat. Yet this was the music of the people, sung to the accompaniment of *duduks*, thin, reedy pipes, the *târ*, or the *pandour*, a three-stringed cithern, minor harmonies, plaintive as an autumn evening. But to them, it represented festivity, and, as such, had its place on every ceremonial occasion.

Their dances were less lugubrious: they were the expression of a race at once fiery and sensual; those beautiful undulating steps which are a sort of stylized courtship, pursuit and retreat, languorous and slow. Or the stamping, leaping, wild sword-dances performed by the warriors, spun to the insistent beat of a drum, or *dohol*. This angry pulse beats through all the music of Asia Minor, monotonous, hypnotic, and galvanic, too; accompanying pantomimes of combat, of convulsive death-throes, and victory. The drums dominate both traditional Caucasian folk-music, and much of the work of the contemporary composer Aram Katchaturian. It is, essentially, the music of a warrior people.

The *lesghinka*, the national dance of the Lesghiens, is begun by the women, with slow, almost imperceptible steps, sidling, trembling, sipping paces. The dancers' long flowing sleeves shield their faces. Gradually the rhythm quickens to a furious stamping beaten out by drums, as the women are joined by the men, who circle round them, hem them in, advancing, before each fresh retreat. It is a dance of conquest, of mating.

Some of these dances represent prayers, and begin with the slow postures of worship. But gradually they quicken to the mesmeric frenzies of dervish dances; such as the Nakshibandyiés' ritual gyrations, which Shamyl, when later he headed one order of this sect, must have known, and used, to enflame his followers.

The more secular dances of the djighitovka were generally performed by torchlight, the dancers weaving in and out of the shadows, the flames glinting on the weapons stuck in their belts, the daggers and pistols which they never removed, even in the dance; torchlight flickering on swarthy faces, catching the curve of a lean cheek, the flash of black eyes, brilliant beneath the towering black sheepskin caps, as they darted love and daring at a veiled girl. Then, as the firelight flickered lower, the djighits would plan the next day's delights: contests of wild rams, wrestling, spectacular feats of marksmanship and the daring and acrobatics of the djighitovka.

IV

Shamyl's spiritual teacher was the Mollah Jamul u'din, a descendant of the Prophet, and a man of profound piety and learning, who loved the strange, violent, yet dreamy young man who in turn came to love and trust him implicitly, obeying his commands long after he had become the imperious ruler who would brook no word of criticism else-where. With his tutor, Shamyl was from the first disciplined and studious. He learned Arabic, and studied Arabic literature, philosophy and theology, progressing towards the complicated Sufi doctrines, which, since religious evolution is a fundamental principle of Sufism, included a comparative study of Adam, Abraham, Moses, Jesus and Mahommed. It was apparent that this was no ordinary student, and Jamul u'din sought to prepare his charge for that great destiny which, according to some, was already written on his brow.

Both Shamyl and his friend, Khazi Mollah, were presently marked for the priesthood. Both believed themselves to be sanctified by Divine promptings; and soon, both were studying Sufism at Yaraghl, the centre of Muridism, where this religious revival was to develop into the politico-military movement known as the Murid Wars, from which the figure of Shamyl emerged and dominated all others. Intemperance seems to have obsessed Khazi Mollah too, for on one occasion he insisted that Shamyl should give him forty lashes, in public, for the sin of having tasted wine before he realized its terrible evil. Shamyl, in turn, submitted to the same chastisement as a proof of his own sincerity.

At Yaraghl, the celebrated Mollah Mahommed preached Muridism, and here the two young men became initiates. Here Khazi Mollah first began to exhort, in the guise of Divine inspiration, resistance to the Infidel, freedom from Russia's rule. The mystic and political aspects of the struggle were becoming one—Ghazavat—Holy War. But Jamul u'din was opposed to violence, no matter to what end, and he forbade Shamyl to have any part in a war, holy or otherwise. Since his authority over Shamyl was still absolute, the young man returned to Ghimri to continue his studies with his tutor. Perhaps there was another inducement besides the Prophet's doctrines: he had already encountered the beautiful young girl who was to become his first wife, whom he loved with a consuming passion. Fatimat was the daughter of Abdul Aziz, celebrated throughout the Caucasus as the best surgeon. The family lived at Ountsoukoul, an aôul which lay across the moun-tains, to the east of Ghimri. Fatimat possessed that mysterious charm, that dark delicately boned beauty of the Caucasian women:

> She had the Asiatic eye . . .
> Dark as above us is the sky . . .
> All love, half languor and half fire . . .

But from whatever motives, whether out of obedience to the Mollah Jamul u'din, or for love of Fatimat's dark eyes, Shamyl remained at Ghimri for some years, while Khazi Mollah went about the countryside preaching the new militant Muridism and rousing the tribes to resist their Infidel invaders. Although energetic and brave, he does not appear to have been a prepossessing man: he was short, with beady eyes, a straggling beard, and a long face pitted with small-pox. Moreover he nagged. The people were forever being told they must stir themselves to further efforts. 'The Moslem may keep the Shariat, but all his giving of alms, all his prayers and ablutions, all his pilgrimages to Mecca, are as nothing, if a Muscovite eye looks on them. . . . Your marriages are unlawful, your children are bastards, while there is one Muscovite left in your land,' he thundered.

'Death to the Giaour! Ghazavat!' echoed the people dutifully: but all the same they ventured to remind him that to resist the yellow-haired Infidel dogs was more than a matter of drawing their swords; the Russians held their chiefs and wives as hostages, controlled the valley pasture lands of their cattle, surrounded them on all sides, and used the slightest excuse to bring down a terrible retribution on their heads, burning their villages and confiscating their crops, so that ruin and starvation ensued. But according to Khazi Mollah this suffering should be offered upon the altar of renunciation. No good could come of this world—or the next, either. Renunciation was all. It seems to have been a singularly bleak creed. Even Mahommed promised houris in his Paradise.

Not so Khazi Mollah. He preferred his Murids to be unmarried men, or such as had renounced their wives. To become attuned to God, life must be lived in abnegation. Joy must have no part in man's scheme: the perusal of religious exercises, meditation, or battle, resistance to the Infidel, were the only indulgences he approved. Nor must there be any hope of immediate salvation. Only by a long series of reincarnations, each one progressing painfully towards an ultimate and total self-abnegation could man hope to approach his stern Deity. Indeed his zeal was carried to such lengths that, in a few harried villages, he became known as Tazi (dog) Mollah.

Thus Khazi Mollah, going from province to province, exhorting the people to the new Faith. 'The Day of Deliverance is at hand,' he told them. 'Soon the Infidels will be driven out of your land forever: it is written! Be strong. Prepare your weapons, fortify your aôuls, mortify your flesh, as soon you will mortify the flesh of your enemies. We will nail their hands to our gates, and their heads shall roll down the mountainside, even as their blood colours our rivers.' It was indeed a stimulating prospect. No Caucasian could ask for better than a sanctified war, although Khazi Mollah demanded that each village he visited should destroy their hard-won vintage. The great jars of wine were shattered in the market-place, with ceremony, as gauge of their faith, and the renunciations to follow. As the wine cascaded down the narrow streets, spreading in a dark, blood-like stain, Khazi Mollah and his attendant Murids would march on towards their next objective, chanting: 'This world is a carcass and he who seeks it a dog'. However rough and long the mountain track, Khazi Mollah never rode: humility and mortification at all cost. Yet in spite of his force, his dedication, he had none of the magnetism, or that compelling majesty, which Shamyl's great warrior soul was to radiate. But Shamyl's hour had not yet struck, and for some years he was to remain at Ghimri, immersed not only in the purely doctrinal aspects of Muridism, but in the practices of his Dervish sect—the Nakshibandyié. This noviciate was particularly severe, and included a thousand and one days as a lay servitor; for one lapse, the whole period was begun afresh.

*   *   *

Basically, Muridism and Sufism are one. The Sufi doctrines were probably first established in the Caucasus by the Arab conquerors in the eighth century. They were most firmly entrenched in the eastern coastal regions, round Baku, or Shemakha, where villages with such names as Arab-Shamli and Arab-Kadim, continue the trade of camel-breeding, and the particularly swarthy skins of the population all tell of an Arab legacy. Such links abound in the Caucasus: in Daghestan in particular.

According to the Sufi mystics, Islam consists of three separate, but linked parts: Shariat, the Law, Tarikat, the Path, and Hakikat, the Truth. Like much else of Moslem mysticism, it is eminently practical. The Shariat is the whole body of Moslem law for the guidance of the community: the Tarikat and the Hakikat are for the progressive spiritual development of those who aspire higher. The Hakikat is only for the few, perfected initiates. Once this state of grace is achieved, man is only a step from God. Now he is capable of achieving unity with the Divine Spirit: this is known as Maarifat, when, during his ecstatic visions he will become, himself, divine. This condition of ecstasy is called by the Sufis, *Kh'al*. It is known to mystics in many religions. The state of meditation is brought to such a degree of abstraction, that the spirit is entirely freed from the flesh, and the personal self is temporarily liberated from all terrestrial limitations of time and space. This degree of beatitude, of illumination, although not sustained, changes the recipient for ever. Having known Infinity, having merged with the Divine Spirit, the mystic has become one with them. Man's limitations have no further meaning for him: he knows no more doubts or fears, nor even good or evil: he is, in himself, part of the Divine Spirit. Nor does he even retain any distinctions of race or creed. *Whosoever does not acknowledge that it is immaterial whether he is a Moslem or a Christian has not achieved the truth and knows not the essence of Being.*

Thus, in its origins, Muridism was not war-like in character,

however much it came, during the nineteenth century, to be identified
with the Caucasian Wars of Independence. The Russians spoke of
the 'Murid Wars', for they preferred to believe their motives were to
establish and protect Christian minorities, and small mention was ever
made of the underlying stimulus of territorial gains. To the Caucasians,
few of whom had attained the holy detachment of Maarifat or Kh'al,
the war was one of defiance and defence—but also conveniently seen in
terms of religion. Ghazavat! Death to the Infidel dog—but, perhaps not
so much because he was an Infidel, as because he threatened their
liberty and invaded their land. Thus each force, respectively sustained
by the banners of their righteousness, were occupied for thirty years
interpreting the teachings of Jesus and Mahommed in a welter of blood
and suffering.

Originally Muridism had been a movement incorporating different
sects which all followed the same basic principle. Each sect was headed
by a Murshid, while the members of the sect were known as Murids.
(Murshid, one who shows or leads: Murid, one who seeks or follows.)
Muridism had declined in power over a long period of time, to become
at last an almost forgotten doctrine, inscribed in the libraries of a few
mosques and medressahs, or religious colleges, though having no more
bearing on the life of the people. But at the end of the eighteenth
century Ismael Effendi of Shirvan revived its teachings in all its
degrees, Shariat the Law, Tarikat the Path, and Hakikat the Truth.
The movement had an immediate response: it gripped the people, took
root and began spreading as a religio-political movement, threatening
the Russians who were in uneasy control of this area, having lately
acquired it in a victory over the Persians. They acted swiftly. Ismael
Effendi was exiled to Turkey, while his sect, the Nakshibandyié, were
dispersed, some Murshids being sent to languish in northern Russian
provinces. And, for a time, no more was heard of Muridism.

Like most faiths, it throve on persecution. Suddenly, around 1827, it
sprang up, refreshed, in Yaraghl, brought to the mountain fastnesses of
Daghestan by one of Ismael Effendi's lesser followers. The impact was
immediate. There, in the secret valleys and inaccessible aôuls, it took
root and penetrated the country before the Russians were aware of its
revival. At Yaraghl, the Mollah Mahommed was expounding the
revived doctrines, and the tribes were now coming from all over the
Caucasus to crowd his mosque. Among them, two young theological
students, Khazi Mollah and Shamyl.

Muridism was a heady brew of mystic and absolute power, though
even after it had become, to the Russians, synonymous with resistance,
it was variously interpreted: there were the Murids of the Tarikat who
never took up arms, as opposed to the Murids of the Ghazavat who
fought a Holy War fanatically. To these last there was no other inter-

pretation of the Prophet's teachings. If to live in peace meant submitting to the Infidel rule, there could be no peace. While the Tarikat abhorred violence and, in the face of force, counselled a withdrawal to some inner spiritual sanctuary, this was not a doctrine which came easily to the fiery Caucasian tribes. Most of them felt that, in this issue, the Tarikat must be modified, or adapted, to meet the more bellicose tenets of the Koran, which promised short shrift to an Infidel foe. Even without Khazi Mollah's exhortations, the Caucasians were now ready for battle.

Presently the Russians realized that resistance had, once more, hardened in the mountain core of the country. A struggle which they had regarded as over, was reopening as an issue of mystical significance, threatening to absorb the whole population, and turn each Believer into a fanatic warrior, defending Islam.

Since the Mollah Mahommed remained a Murid of the Tarikat, in that he never actually fought, leadership was presently transferred to his disciple, Khazi Mollah, who, in 1830, became known as the first Imam of Daghestan. But he was to fall under Russian bullets, and his successor, Hamzad Beg, to die of a hundred Caucasian dagger-thrusts, before, in 1834, Shamyl succeeded them both as third Imam and imposed the Shariat on the whole Caucasus.

4

The Holy War

*To make war—to kill, without being killed,
is an illusion.*   DRAGOMIROV

While Khazi Mollah went proselytizing from aôul to aôul, Shamyl remained at Ghimri occupied with Sufi doctrines. Presently, however, he began to leave his theological studies for battle sorties, and accompanied the Murids on their more desperate missions. The time for action had come.

Islamic philosophers divide man's perfected life into three—a time for learning, a time for action, a time for contemplation. Shamyl's life followed this pattern.

Khazi Mollah had now abandoned proselytism for battle, and although, throughout his brief hey-day, he showed a sense of generalship only second to his oratory, he never obtained that mastery of military tactics, nor that compelling force possessed by Shamyl, and it was against the latter's advice that he now embarked on a series of campaigns to undermine Russian authority. Shamyl considered this was too soon; that the whole Caucasus must be won over to the Murid cause, before they could grapple with the Russians—who were a highly disciplined and well-equipped army. Their first victory must be over the various hostile tribes. There were still defections which could lead to disaster. Shamyl counselled a further period of proselytizing, a further lashing and scourging of the waverers. But Khazi Mollah was impatient for his Holy War: if not yet against the Infidels, then against the waverers, or those tribes who had ceded to the Russians. They *must* be converted, by faith, or fire and sword.

So he dispatched messengers to Pakkou-Bekkhé, Khanum, or ruler of Avaria, demanding her pledge of support against the invading Infidels: but Pakkou-Bekkhé refused. This strong-minded woman, widow of the Khan, acted as regent for her three sons. Her husband had ceded his territory to the Russians some years earlier, and she held this in fief for them and received a subsidy, which made Khounzak, her capital, one of the most prosperous centres in the Caucasus. It was a large aôul,

60

comprising more than seven hundred houses; like all the rest it was a piled-up rock structure, heavily fortified against marauding tribes, and indeed, until the advent of cannons, like most of the other aôuls, it was an impregnable fortress. Its harshness was tempered by terraced gardens along the southern ramparts, where vines and silk-worms were cultivated, and orchards clung precariously to the bluffs. The aôul was cornered by the usual watch-towers which dominated the surrounding country, the ravines and river-bed lying some five thousand feet below. It appeared invincible, and such Pakkou-Bekkhé thought it to be.

Although most of Avaria had joined forces with Khazi Mollah in a sweep of religious fervour which the Khanum could not stem, the inhabitants of Khounzak had remained unmoved. They were satisfied with their present way of life. Salvation could go. Neither Khazi Mollah's denunciations nor his threats moved them. But while Pakkou-Bekkhé was inspired by loyalty to her husband's treaties, her people preferred to remain under the more easy-going Russian rule for other reasons. A large number of them were desperate characters, cut-throat fugitives from tribal justice, who had fled their own districts to take refuge in Khounzak, where, safe from vengeance, they were accepted and protected under Russian domination. Thus Khounzak defied Khazi Mollah, and awaited any further developments with complacency.

In May 1830 Khazi Mollah marched against them with eight thousand men, attacking in two columns, one headed by himself, the other by Shamyl. Such was the Murid's dread reputation, that, as they were sighted in the ravine, far below, a wave of apprehension swept through Khounzak, and before a blow was dealt, the citizens began to waver. As the Murid's columns converged on the aôul, their dirge-like battle hymns echoing across the rocks, panic seized the Khounzaki, and they laid down their arms. The Russians were less to be feared as an enemy. Undoubtedly it would be wiser to accept Khazi Mollah's terms, and go over to his camp without bloodshed.

Not so Pakkou-Bekkhé. She was determined to maintain her treaty with the Tzar. She went about the fortifications, inspecting the defences, rallying the people, and ordered them to defend Khounzak to the last. But, on the first attack, the Khounzaki retreated to the second line of defence. The assault was overwhelming. Now Pakkou-Bekkhé, sword in hand, rounded on her troops, calling them cowards, unworthy of their arms, a lily-livered lot. The age-old Amazonian note sounded: 'If you are afraid, then give the women your swords, and hide behind our skirts while we fight.'

This had the desired effect. The men flung themselves on to the Murids in desperation, and taking them by surprise as they were about to enter what they believed to be a surrendered city, fought with such fury that they drove them off with severe losses, taking many prisoners.

The various Caucasian tribes which had joined the Murids, now saw these invincible warriors routed by a woman, many of their ranks led off as prisoners, and the ravines strewn with dead, their blood wet on the abandoned banners. Khounzak, the city they had regarded as an easy victory, had shown a totally unexpected resolution. The Murids were compelled to retreat in confusion. There was nothing for Khazi Mollah to do but accept a temporary check: he withdrew to Ghimri to brood, while Shamyl, having narrowly escaped death at the hands of his humiliated troops, presently joined him. In public the two leaders attributed defeat to a lack of faith on the part of their followers, Allah's punishment on a still too pleasure-loving luxurious, irreligious people. But in private together, in the low white-washed cell occupied by Shamyl in the medressah, a theological school attached to the mosque, there were reproaches and bitter arguments.

As Khazi Mollah and Shamyl talked together, the coral or amber beads of their *tespyehs* sliding through their fingers endlessly, the sunlight slanted across the small barred windows, latticing the straw-matted floor. As in most Eastern houses, the windows were set very low, almost at ground level, to suit the eye of those who sat on the floor, rather than in chairs. In the deep embrasures of these windows, a few parchment scrolls; on the inlaid cedarwood book-stand, a massive volume, the Koran, or the doctrines of some Persian mystic. No cushions, no *tchibouques* or dalliance here. It was the stern setting for stern-purposed men.

They had been rash, said Shamyl. It was not yet the hour Allah had ordained for battle. If such defeats could be inflicted by the Khounzaki, how could Khazi Mollah hope to prevail against the Russian armies? Victory could never be his until all of the Caucasus was united as one force, fighting for one faith. Only through Islam could they ever break the Infidels' creeping, insidious hold. Only religious fervour would prevail over back-sliding and bribery. The war might be, basically, for independence, but to be fought whole-heartedly, it must be in Allah's name—for Islam—and fought by the whole Caucasus to a man.

*   *   *

For a few months Khazi Mollah restrained himself, but by mid-summer he had overridden Shamyl, and embarked on a series of new and successful sorties against the Russians. In May he had marched on the fortress of Vnezapnaya, but was unable to storm it. Reinforcements from Russian headquarters arrived to harass his rear-guard, so he craftily withdrew into the forests, drawing not only the reinforcements, but half the garrison after him.

In the profound forests where jungle vegetation coiled round the gigantic trees, and a world of twilight terrors closed on the Russian troops, Khazi Mollah's men were at home. This was as much their terrain as the mountains and ravines. The Russians, used to cavalry charges in open country, used to fighting in line or square formations, had not yet acquired the rudiments of guerilla warfare. 'As a soldier, the Russian is most strong in all the staying qualities. . . . He goes into battle singing his national hymn lustily, with no thought as to his fate. He is at first dull and slow in initiative and self-reliance', writes a military observer. 'It is only after he has passed through several battles that he learns by terrible experience the knack of looking out for himself. He instinctively looks for orders and obeys them with blind instinct: left on his own he is almost helpless, and will often get killed from standing still and waiting for a command, when everyone who has the right to give an order is dead. . . .'

'Deprived of their officers, a body of Russian troops may degenerate into a helpless, immobile mass, being slaughtered by their very cohesion. But they will never take panic.' Such, went on the observer, was the regrettable tendency of the French soldier, 'whose imagination sometimes serves to destroy his discipline, turning everything to wild panic'. In the early part of the nineteenth century, military observers were particularly partial to making such obnoxious comparisons. They had been following the French campaigns against Abd-el-Kadir in North Africa closely, and a number of these experts now hurried to the Caucasus, to follow the latest wars of another savage and resistant people.

Although it has never been established that Shamyl made a first pilgrimage to Mecca about this time, there is little doubt that he did do so, and that he met there Abd-el-Kadir, the fanatic Arab Chieftain, who performed the Hadj in 1828-9. Together these two probably planned their resistance to the Infidel invaders, as part of a widespread Pan-Islamic movement. In 1834, the French invasion of North Africa was opposed by Abd-el-Kadir: and in 1834, Shamyl emerged, to lead the Murids in their Holy War to defend the Caucasus from Russian invaders. 'Paradise lies in the shadow of our sabres!' cried Arab and Murid alike as they went into battle against the Infidels.

However superficial the judgements of the detached military observers might seem, an element of truth remained: the Russians were fatalists. Crying '*Ss' Bogom!* With God!' they went into battle almost indifferent to their own lives. At first, and for many years, they were no match for the Caucasians who, although equally fatalistic as to the expenditure of their lives, fought for the freedom of their homes, as well as their beliefs. The Russians fought for God and Tzar (the two being indivisible, to them); in the case of the moujiks, because they were recruited; in the case of the officers, often because they were profoundly bored and sought the stimulus of battle; but for neither of them was it for personal issues. Among the Caucasians, each man fought for his soul's salvation, on his own terrain. Now, in the forests, they inflicted terrible losses, and the battles went to Khazi Mollah, who was quick to profit by it.

Neither the Turks nor the British, watching from outside the battles' periphery, nor even the Russians, ever realized the full significance of Muridism. The Ghazavat—Holy War—was a fanatic means of self-purification, a form of martyrdom, a path to Mahommed's Paradise. To repel the invaders was of primary importance to Shamyl, and he used the Murid creed to further his aims: battle, suffering, death—for Allah—for freedom—were now subtly interwoven by Shamyl so that, while, to the Russians, the Murid wars were basically for conquest, to the mountaineers, they became Holy Wars, of resistance to their Infidel invaders, for their souls' salvation. Thus the Tzar's muskets were met with the sabres of Paradise.

In August the people of Tabassaran requested leadership against the Infidels. Khazi Mollah accepted, though, once again, Shamyl counselled prudence. This campaign was not wholly successful, except in harassing the Russians, and cutting their supply lines. But by November Khazi Mollah had won several more minor engagements, all turned, with an equal address, to his profit.

He was wont to halt, on the march, and crouching on the ground, his little foxy eyes closed, appear to be listening intently to some far-off sound, imperceptible to the rest. . . . When questioned, he would reply that he fancied he could hear the clanking of chains—the chains of the Russian Generals, now being led towards him as captives. It was a picturesque technique for keeping alight the interest and hopes of his Murids, and they moved forward with redoubled force. By November, emboldened by a further series of minor victories, he made a most audacious raid on Kizliar, sacked the aôul, looted it, and made off with several hundred prisoners, largely the more comely women, which would suggest that even his austerity sometimes conceded certain sweets to the victor. The Russians were exasperated by such daring: they were finding the Caucasians much more than their match in this unfamiliar guerilla warfare. In December 1831 General Rosen was writing: 'I arrived here at a time of great disturbance. Never were the mountain tribes so insolent, or so persistent in their undertakings. . . . If Khazi Mollah was not killed at Tchoumkeskent, as it is rumoured, they will be on the move again next Spring.'

And, in the spring of 1832, Khazi Mollah reappeared, more menacing than ever. Emboldened by his triumphs, bolstered by a growing support (for in the mountains, as elsewhere, nothing succeeded like success), he was raring to go.

Meanwhile, a winter's inactivity, snowed up at Ghimri, had permitted Shamyl to taste the sweets of love with the beautiful Fatimat, to whom he was now married; but Khazi Mollah was consumed by other fires. For him, no woman, no child, nothing, could turn him, for one hour, from his fanaticism. After a preliminary series of skirmishes with the Cossacks of the Line, north, on the Russian boundaries, he decided to thrust right at the heart of the lately acquired Russian territories. By besieging the fortress of Nazran, he threatened Vladikavkaz itself.

At Nazran the Russians felt themselves to be masters of all they surveyed. The little town was of a strategic importance altogether disproportionate to its size. It was the gateway to the Caucasus, the link between Europe and Asia. Those who held it controlled the sole road east—the celebrated Georgian Military Highway which had been hacked through the mountains, a direct route from Vladikavkaz down to Tiflis and the rich Georgian lowlands. It wound through sombre defiles, past forts and ruined castles such as Darial, where legend tells us, the voluptuous Queen Tamara held her awful revels. (But then in Georgia, the alleged scenes of her debauches are as many as the beds in which Queen Elizabeth is said to have slept, in England.) The Georgian Highway descends and mounts, clinging to the rock face, and winding beside the furious waters of the Terek, until, climbing the pass of Krestovaia—of the Cross—it is dominated by a huge cross planted there by Yermolov, like some defiant challenge to the original Moslem inhabitants of the region. The road had taken five years of Titanic struggle to build, but General Yermolov had directed the labour himself and allowed nothing to stand in his way—neither men, money, nor nature. Once achieved, its upkeep was almost as laborious, for avalanches often broke its surface or blocked it for months at a time. When Nicholas I was asked to defray some further expenditure on it, he remarked that it had already cost as much as if it had been paved with silver roubles. He did not mention the lives, the blood. His troops were expendable.

II

Vladikavkaz was a typical town of its time and place. An overlay of Europe was imposed on an Asiatic village. Potemkin had founded it, foreseeing its value not only as a military base, but as a commercial centre, a trading post between Northern Russia, the Caucasus and the Trans-Caspian provinces. The bazaars displayed fine rugs, with all the beautiful, strange and bright imagery of the nomad Caucasian tribes: there were weapons inlaid with silver and ivory, sheepskins and Persian silks, saddles and spices, and shaggy Bactrian camels grouped in groaning concourse beside the Kabardian horses which were prized above all others by both Russians and tribesmen. There were steam baths, Persian and Russian, Tartar mosques and an Orthodox church: later additions were the bank, the *bureau de poste*, and a little park laid out in style, where a military band played in the evenings. The tree-shaded boulevards followed a geometric pattern—north and south, east and west: here a few indifferent restaurants and inns were found, beside the Merchant's Club, and a number of comparatively new houses, low and one-storeyed, where the visitors from the capital established themselves with their own servants and belongings to continue the idling pattern of their days. Fading northern belles came to Vladikavkaz husband-hunting: so did enterprising match-making mothers. There was less competition here, than at the more elegant spas such as Kisslovodsk or Piatigorsk. And some of the young officers were splendid catches, scions of the noblest houses, their names inscribed in the celebrated *Livre de Velours*, to which the hierocratic instincts of the Russian was so profoundly sensible. The bluest blood, the greatest names were now to be found concentrated in the Caucasus, like some miraculous, accessible well from which ambitious matchmakers might hope to hook a golden fish.

III

Although, in Russia, all members of the same princely families went by the title of prince, there being, about this time, a hundred and fifty Prince Galitzins, some of the nobles considered themselves finer than others, and indeed were so. The Galitzins were established in Moscow in 1408. The Dolgoroukys, Narischkins and Voronzovs vied with the Troubetskoys, the Shouvalovs, Sheremetievs or the Bariatinskys, who were connnected with the house of Romanov. The Narischkins were a princely family which had originated in Bohemia, and settled in Russia in the thirteenth century. One ancestress, the Tzarina Natalia Narischkin, was the mother of Peter the Great. Two others perished in the Kremlin for their part in the Strelitzi revolt. Like the Voronzovs they were a family whose roots were entwined with those of their country. (These Narischkins should not be confused with others of the same name, who emerged from the Crimea in the late eighteenth century. The two families were distinguished, rather unkindly, by Petersburg society, as *les bons et les mauvais Narischkins.*

The late-coming Baltic Barons were despised by the original Boyard families, or the descendants of Rurik; so were the Polish families who had been incorporated into the ranks of Russian nobility when Catherine II became Queen of Poland. As for the legion of Georgian and Armenian princes—the majority of them were self-styled, profiting by the confusion and lack of records at the moment when Russia acquired the Eastern provinces and dispatched small government clerks to sort and classify the local gentry. There were said to be three thousand Armenian 'princes', while the Georgians were scarcely less ennobled. There were, however, a few families from these regions whose beginnings were lost in antiquity, whose blood equalled any Romanov, and who were created Princes of the Russian Empire too.

There were three princely Armenian families—the Argoutinskys, the Abamaleks, and the Beboutovs; while in Georgia, the great feudal families numbered eight or ten. The blazon of the Batonishvilis, or Bagrations, the last ruling house, comprised among other things, the sling that killed Goliath, David's harp, the lion of Solomon's throne, and our Lord's seamless coat. The Imeritinskys, Gouriellis, Dedichkelianis and Mingrelskys were scarcely less noble. Among the proud names of the *Livre de Velour* were some which derived from very far afield: the Orbelianis claimed Chinese blood; the Abachidzes, Abyssinian. A strong Tartar strain was represented by the Youssoupovs, Kotchoubeys and Tarkovskys. The Ghireis descended from Genghis Khan; the Dondoukovs from Kalmuck nomads (though among the Kalmucks, anyone owning a flock of sheep was called prince). The Vassiltchikovs had been Grand Dukes of Lithuania, and accordingly snubbed all the Baltic barons, while the Davidovs and Eristovs, descending from Seldjuk dynasties and King David, considered everyone else very small fry. And all of them banded together to patronize those of foreign origin, like the O'Briens, Learmonts, Hamiltons, or Reads, to say nothing of a legion of German names, generally concentrated in the Army lists, such as Totleben or Klugenau; families who had only been a generation or two in Russia, arriving there as soldiers of fortune or hunted exiles. But any of the scions of the nobility, any of the *jeunesse dorée* who were garrisoned at Vladikavkaz, found themselves the object of considerable social manœuvring. Since ennui and spleen were both *à la mode*, the young nobleman found it easy enough to support the tenor of life in the little town: it was not nearly so boring as it was fashionable to find it; and there were always hearts to break, in the manner made so romantic by Pushkin's Oniegin.

IV

Above the town, dominating it, and set at a little distance away, was the Governor's house, centre of military life and social hopes, and the focal point of unspoken Moslem hatred, though this undercurrent of hate was generally ignored, or underestimated, by the visitors. But, abruptly, the easy, idling life was ended. There was no more time for spleen. Two Cossacks from an outpost farther south galloped into town with the news that Khazi Mollah was reported heading north with a large rebel force, and already skirmishing with Russian troops *en route*. They—for to the Russians, whether civil or military, the Caucasian tribes were always referred to with a mixture of apprehension and admiration as *they*—were heading towards Vladikavkaz. The audacity of it all! The inconvenience, too. The small garrison was inadequate and short of supplies; a token force. Carriages or saddle-horses stood at every door. The visitors packed desperately, piling their belongings into calf-skin trunks, their servants loading hat-boxes, bedding, and the samovars without which no Russian, princely or humble, ever travelled. There was no more talk of romantic scenery, of picnics along the banks of the Terek; another ten years of bloodshed were to pass before Lermontov was to write of it as the River of Death; but Pushkin's description of Vladikavkaz as being the point where 'the Caucasus takes one into its sanctuary' was now quoted with irony.

No news reached Vladikavkaz. Scouts sent out to reconnoitre either did not return, or came back with little positive information. On the third day, a fearful cannon-fire gave place to stillness. Thick white fog blanketed the foothills. The snow peaks were hidden; nothing stirred. The Russians waited in anguish. Nazran was known to be short of supplies, and undermanned: without reinforcements it could never hold out. But had the reinforcements got through? Or were they defeated? Vladikavkaz had emptied but for a handful of staff-officers, some wounded who could not be moved, and such of the city folk from the north who had not yet found transport. They were short of horses, of arms. The handsome inlaid silver daggers and pistols which had been bought as tourist trophies were now being primed or sharpened. Astute peasants from the hills were bringing unbroken horses and selling them at huge profits to buyers who never even succeeded in saddling them: after a time, they kicked down the stable door and dashed away to freedom. There was nothing to be done now but await developments, and the Russians sat sipping local champagne in an atmosphere charged with apprehension. Fearful stories of treachery, and the Tchetchens' way with prisoners, had been circulated long ago: they had added piquancy to the even tenor of life in Vladikavkaz. Now they were revived. They did not need any embellishments. The prison pits, where Russian soldiers literally rotted, were recalled, so were the Lesghiens' methods of running horse-hairs through their prisoners' heels. The threads festered, caused agonies of pain, and rendered every step torture: such methods were very effective against any attempts at escape. Women? It was better not to think of their fate. . . . As dusk fell, the third evening, it was decided to sent out a party of neutral Ossetine tribesmen, who, for a considerable sum—in gold—agreed to reconnoitre. Early next morning they galloped back to report that Nazran was still holding out. At first the heavy bombardment had not turned Khazi

Mollah's attack, and he had seemed to be winning the day, but he was suddenly attacked in the rear by a large body of Ingoushi, who were a tribe hostile to him. Choosing their moment with cunning, they inflicted fearful losses and slaughtered his wounded as they lay there, helpless. Khazi Mollah had been forced to retreat, leaving his dead; this, to Caucasian tribes, was an outrage against their most sacred laws.

Khazi Mollah fought without an acquired technique. He had never read Clausewitz; nor had he heard of Dragomirov, first tactician of the Russian army, a disciple of Suvorov, who was categoric: 'Never sound the retreat. Never. Warn the men that if they hear it, it is only a ruse on the part of the enemy.' But the Caucasians, fighting without any tactical knowledge, meeting each fresh situation as it developed, were less conventional, more supple. Pride could give way to necessity. They retreated as they attacked, as part of the battle's ebb and flow. On one point they were in accord with Dragomirov, who thought the rifle, however perfected, of secondary importance. 'It can', he wrote, 'only prepare the terrain for the principal element—man.' And he continued, much as Khazi Mollah or Shamyl might have done: 'Give me soldiers prepared to fight to the death, and I will look after the tactics. Men, men, and again men. Always men—they are the first and best instrument of battle. . . . We must never forget that our mission, as soldiers, is to kill, even though being killed ourselves. We must not shut our eyes to this fact. To make war—to kill without being killed is an illusion. To fight—to be killed without killing—that is clumsy, inept. One must know how to kill while being ready to be killed oneself. The man who is dedicated to death is terrible. Nothing can stop him if he is not shot down on his way.'

Such beliefs actuated both the Russians and Caucasians. Small wonder that the struggle was so long, so terrible.

5

'The Time of the Shariat'

Ho! the Chosen of God; there is no fear upon them,
nor do they grieve.   KORAN, X. 63

By the autumn of 1832, Khazi Mollah and Shamyl were falling back steadily. It was now evident that the Russians meant to wipe out Caucasian resistance once and for all, and, by razing the land, seizing the cattle and destroying the aôuls, to break the civilian resistance. Tchetchen spies brought the news that General Veliaminov was preparing to attack Daghestan with intent to capture Khazi Mollah alive or dead. Together, Shamyl and the Imam selected Ghimri as the best place in which to make their last stand. It was, too, their birthplace, the setting of their childhood friendship. They would die there together, accounting for as many of the Infidels as possible, before they fell themselves. The bare rock face towered up from the valley in unbroken slabs of limestone. There were no trees, no foothold anywhere. The mountaineers leapt from ridge to ridge, jumped chasms, or where even their horses, bred to such hazards, shied from the brink, they muffled the animals' heads in a cloak, and took them over at a gallop.

Ghimri was considered impregnable; only one road, and that a precipitous track, clinging to the cliff face, with a sheer drop below, wound down and across the stony wastes, towards Temir Khan Shura, the Russian headquarters, about twenty-four miles east. This track road narrowed to the width of a man, as it ran between gullies at the base of the mountains directly below Ghimri. The valley lay one mile below— one mile as the eagle swooped; but there were thirteen miles of zigzagging paths for man and beast. Any body of men passing through were obliged to go in single file; here, a whole regiment could be held at bay by a handful of sharp-shooters. It was by this path that the Russians must approach, argued the rebels. The only other way was a goat-track over the peaks towering above Ghimri, so that, high as the village was, it seemed dwarfed, menaced by these jagged summits which, for much of the year, were snow-capped and shut out the sun entirely.

70

This goat-track was seldom used, even by the villagers themselves. It descended on the village in a series of almost perpendicular turns and was plainly impossible for troops carrying equipment and guns. Yet it was on the existence of this very path that General Veliaminov based his attack. 'Could a dog pass? Then that's enough. Where a dog can go, so can a Russian soldier,' he said, outlining his plan to the harassed staff-officers. Dividing his forces, the general sent some across the heights, to surprise the village from above, while his main body of men were to attack from beneath.

Khazi Mollah had constructed several strong lines of defence, rising in tiers, commanding the ravines and valleys below. These formed natural fortifications; and in the type of warfare to which the tribes were accustomed, with short-range rifles and hand-to-hand fighting, Ghimri appeared unassailable to its garrison. The Russians had guns: cumbersome artillery, almost impossible to manœuvre, but if once brought up to their lines, capable of destroying all Khazi Mollah's defences in a few rounds. The Murids had not reckoned on the Russians being able to haul their big guns into range, in such a region. But then, neither side had yet fully understood the quality of their opponent. Khazi Mollah was known to be a dangerous and daring commander: but the Russians were as yet unaware even of the existence of Shamyl, his lieutenant. As to the Russians, the tribesmen thought them a stiff, pasty-faced lot: they had not yet gauged the temper of such commanders as Klugenau, or Veliaminov. These men were less spectacular figures than the old Muscovy Shäitan, Yermolov, who roared and fought them in their own manner.

Both Klugenau and Veliaminov were cool customers. Kluke von Klugenau, a stolid-looking figure of German origin, was seldom seen without a cigar, and once fought through a whole engagement, hacking his way out when surprised and surrounded by two thousand rebels in a forest ambush, without ever removing the cigar from his lips. Veliaminov was particularly noted for his sang-froid, often delaying an action so that his men might finish their dinner comfortably (arguing that they would fight better on a satisfied stomach), while the less phlegmatic Tchetchens waited in a state of suspended ardour which preyed on their nerves.

Sitting on a drum, before Ghimri, telescope to eye, Veliaminov was soon observed by the rebels, who directed a storm of bullets at him. As they spat around him, he complained that his staff officers were falling against him, jerking the telescope. 'Gentlemen, I suggest you fall elsewhere.' When Dadiani, the Prince of Mingrelia, commanding the Erivanski regiment, begged him to take cover, the General replied: 'Yes, Prince. I agree—this is a very dangerous spot, so will your Highness be so good as to lead your regiment against the line of defences on the right?' This tradition of military politeness recalls a passage in one of Tolstoy's stories of Caucasian warfare.

'"Charming!" said the Major, watching (a cavalry charge). He approached the General.

'"Really a pleasure, fighting in such beautiful country!"

'"Above all, in such good company," replied the General speaking in French and smiling graciously.

'The Major bowed.'

Some of the officers showed the courage of despair. Captain All-brandt, a young man consumed by an unhappy love affair, had joined the Caucasian armies to end his miseries. He displayed a most reckless bravery, and courted death again and again, often volunteering for suicidal missions, yet always emerging unscathed. During the battle for Ghimri he was hit over the heart, but the bullet was deflected by a brass ikon he was wearing. However, since no aura of mystical fanaticism was attached to Captain Allbrandt, none of his escapes were attributed to miraculous intervention—as in the case of Shamyl. He was just a very desperate young man; and a lucky one, too, for at last, having covered himself in glory and survived years of Caucasian campaigns, his beloved softened, and accepted him as her husband. Though here his luck changed, the marriage being said to be an unhappy one.

The battle of Ghimri began in earnest on October 17, after several days of preliminary skirmishing. It opened with desperate fighting on both sides. The sappers blasted a foothold for the guns: inch by inch the Russians dragged their heavy artillery into range, and set about demolishing the fortifications which Khazi Mollah had so laboriously constructed. They were harassed by small bands of fighters who sprang on them, apparently from nowhere, cutting them to pieces as they reached for their weapons: but when the troops who had been deployed to cross the mountains by 'the dog's path' surprised the aôul by opening fire, the Murids knew the battle lost. They had counted on Hamzad Beg, one of their Naibs, to lead his men against the Russians and hold them, on the mountain top. But he had withdrawn, leaving the way open. Cunning rather than valour was his mark: subsequent events proved him to be not only cowardly, but treacherous.

Now, in the doomed aôul, the Murids stood firm, beginning their wailing death-chants, calmly waiting till the enemy should come within sword reach. Some of them fastened themselves leg to leg, by their sword belts, forming a living bastion of bodies, lashed one to the other. This was one of their traditions, a last stand where they fought and died as one. Others waited, crouched behind the rocks, ready to spring.

As the Russians closed in, puzzled by this sudden immobility, the Murids leapt on them, and a series of desperate hand-to-hand combats raged along the walls. No quarter was asked; none was given. At one

point of the outer defences, a battalion of the 41st Rifle Regiment
drove the rebels on to a ledge from where there was no escape: they
could only die, sword in hand, or fling themselves over the rocks to
certain destruction. 'The Murids fought wildly: more than sixty were
killed on the spot, and the rest hurled themselves down and were
dashed to pieces.' Thus one eye-witness. Another states that the
Russians, fighting with the same fury as the Murids, fought hand to
hand, flung the wounded rebels over the precipice, or hurled themselves
down with their foe, still fighting as they spun through space, locked in
mortal combat.

At dusk, all the outer lines of defence had been taken. Only the
village itself remained to be occupied. Sixty years later, an eye-witness
was to describe the scene inside the stronghold. 'Five hundred Murids
were surrounded by ten thousand Russians,' said an old man encountered by J. F. Baddeley, as he rode about the Caucasus. The old
man had been a boy at Ghimri, but he remembered it well. 'When
Khazi Mollah called the last roll-call, only twenty of us were left to
answer him.' The Russians advanced, to find that two stone guard-
houses, at the entrance, remained unsubdued, and were firing on them
with deadly precision, picking them off, man by man, as they advanced.
Veliaminov ordered these guard-houses to be cleared, and, after a few
rounds of artillery fire, the crumbling, burning walls revealed a band
of Murids, fifty or more, who had retired to die fighting. Among them,
Shamyl. They came out to meet their enemy singly, or in pairs, sword
in hand, stepping forward with slow deliberation, and then, suddenly
violent, slashing right and left, accounting, at close quarters, for two or
three Russians apiece, before they fell. There was a ritual assurance in
their bearing. They died for Allah: their swords were His: it was written.
Already, above the din of battle, the siren songs of the promised houris
were sounding in their ears.

> The Houris of Paradise look down on us from their heavenly
> casements.
> They wonder, whose shall they be? And she who falls to the bravest
> will vaunt her lot.

Only two Murids escaped death; one of these was Shamyl. This first
spectacular escape from what appeared certain death, and the manner
in which he fought and vanished, have passed into Caucasian history.
It was the beginning of his legendary invincibility, the legend of his
miraculous preservation. This is how one Russian officer recalled the
scene:

> It was dark: by the light of the burning thatch we saw a man
> standing in the doorway of the saklia, which stood on raised ground,
> rather above us. This man, who was very tall and powerfully built,

stood quite still, as if giving us time to take aim. Then, suddenly, with the spring of a wild beast, he leapt clean over the heads of the very line of soldiers about to fire on him, and landing behind them, whirling his sword in his left hand [Shamyl, it will be recalled, was left-handed] he cut down three of them, but was bayoneted by the fourth, the steel plunging deep into his chest. His face still extraordinary in its immobility, he seized the bayonet, pulled it out of his own flesh, cut down the man and, with another superhuman leap, cleared the wall and vanished into the darkness. We were left absolutely dumbfounded. The whole business had taken, perhaps, a minute and a half.

When, next morning, in the raw, misty October dawn, the Russians went about the village reckoning the dead, the body of one particularly impressive-looking Murid was noticed among the corpses heaped before the doors of the saklia. This body seemed petrified in the ritual Moslem attitude of prayer, kneeling, one hand raised, pointing to heaven, the other holding his dark beard. It was Khazi Mollah, first Imam of Daghestan, who had fallen among his faithful Murids. The Russians were overjoyed. Allah's chosen, felled by *Russian* bullets! This would undoubtedly put a stop to Caucasian fanaticism. Without a leader the tribes would soon quieten down, soon abandon their mystical fervour. Khazi Mollah's body was too valuable a piece of propaganda to leave at Ghimri. It was taken in triumph to Tarkou—capital of the Shamkal of Tarkou's territory. He was one of the native rulers who had been unswerving in his loyalty to Russia, to whom he had ceded amicably some years earlier, and it was considered by the Russian commanders to be a mark of particular esteem that they entrusted the rebel Imam's body to his care. After exposing it in the market-place of Tarkou, for several days, as a proof of Russia's victory, the Shamkal ordered it to be buried at Bournaya, in the mountains nearby.

Meanwhile, Ghimri, deserted, ruined, sacked, had fallen to the Russians. The Imam was dead, his Murids slaughtered. Shamyl (then unrecognized as a potential successor), gone to earth, and probably dead of wounds. Now the Russians congratulated themselves that the fight was over, the Caucasus won.

The fact that it was not, that it was to resist for another twenty-five years, lay in the force of one man's will—in Shamyl's unshakable belief in his divine right, in his mission, as Allah's chosen mouthpiece on earth—his Prophet and Warrior.

6

The Tzar

*His Majesty is sovereign and autocrat. He is accountable
to no one in the world.*
PETER THE GREAT'S MILITARY STATUTES

Now two men, destined to become mortal enemies, unknowingly faced
each other across the length of Russia, Shamyl the Avar, and the Tzar
Nicholas I. Each was sustained by religious conviction, each actuated
by an inflexible personal pride. Beyond the fact that both were despots,
no more violently contrasted characters could be imagined, and their
struggle gradually assumed a personal nature, embittering both men,
and rendering all possibilities of a peaceful settlement hopeless. Had
Nicholas died sooner, had his son, the benign, though woolly minded,
Alexander II succeeded earlier, the Caucasus might have been spared
its agony.

If landscape affects character, and gives to the inhabitants of a
region something of its own characteristics, no two men reflected better
their environment. The icy marble regularity and magnificence of St.
Petersburg was embodied in Nicholas I; while Shamyl's violent nature,
at once exotic and harsh, was reflected in the mountains and valleys of
the Caucasus. No more extreme contrast could be imagined, than
between the towering chain of mountains rising from lush valleys, and
those leaden swamps over which Peter the Great's capital sprawled.
Between the huddled stone dwellings of Daghestan and the gigantic
Russian palaces lay centuries. These palaces, with their glittering
chandeliers, and vast perspectives of parquet reflecting mammoth
malachite urns and gilded French furniture, were sumptuously Slav
versions of baroque and rococo, translated by Italian architects
Rastrelli, or Tressini, into terms of rose-pink granite, lapis lazuli and
malachite, larger, brighter, more magnificent than their Italian inspiration, to meet that excessive quality so admired by Russian natures. In
the words of Madame de Staël, 'in Russia, if they do not attain their
objective they always go past it'.

The Emperor Nicholas' fetish love for uniforms was such that almost every rank, or *tchin* of the Civil Services, besides the Army and Government, had their own uniforms and degree of gold lace, giving the city an air of being some massed Army manœuvre. Politics and protocol came before prayer in St. Petersburg. It was very far away from the Murids, intoning and swaying in the austere white-washed mosques of Daghestan.

II

The Caucasus was something apart. And yet, it was to pass into the the blood-stream of Russian life, inspiring its writers and musicians and bringing, through them, its impact to the whole nation. Behind every phrase of Russian music, even behind the artless shrilling of peasant songs, the noisy recitative of the *chastoustchki*, there is a minor echo, or cadence, of those Mongol musicians who rode up out of the steppes with Genghis Khan. It is an age-old heritage, like the Mongol cast that so often lies beneath the Slav mask. But in the nineteenth century, after the conquest of the Caucasus, another note sounded, more insidiously Oriental, which was to weave itself forever into the texture of Russian music, largely through the inspiration of Balakirev. He was the first to fire Rimsky-Korsakoff, Borodin, and Moussorgsky with those Asiatic rhythms which are woven into their themes and which, in their purest form, are found in Balakirev's own music. Mili Balakirev was born in 1836, in Nijni Novgorod, a city steeped in Tartar legends. In 1862, he spent a holiday in the Caucasus, and from these weeks stem his Oriental idioms.

Caucasian and Oriental music had its own particular pulse, a *saccadé* rhythm of drum beats, the insistent, fevered wildness of sword-dances, fire-dances, and scorpion dances, those ritual steps danced by men, telling of battle or hunting. They are still to be seen in the remote villages of Asia Minor. Interwoven with these drum-beat rhythms are voluptuous, plaintive melodies, the music of dancers whose hennaed feet scarcely move, and seem only to tremble, as their serpentine arms undulate, enticingly. . . . The Dancers of Shemakha, celebrated throughout the Caucasus. But these fierce or voluptuous rhythms, like Lermontov's evocations of the Caucasus, and the Caucasian stories of Tolstoy and Bestoujev-Marlinsky had not yet become part of Russian consciousness. For most people, the Caucasus was still only a faraway battlefield, a distant graveyard for the legion of recruits who were levied by force from the villages. To the dandified staff-officers at the War Office, it was a poorly mapped mountainous area, pin-pointed by unpronounceable names: a theatre of operations which neither that old savage, Yermolov, or his successor, Paskiévitch, had yet succeeded in conquering.

To the Emperor Nicholas it represented failure—humiliation. His most cherished dreams were thwarted. He was quite at a loss to understand how a chain of mountains and a few wild tribes could have withstood his might for years. It was insufferable.

Across all the Russias the Tzar ruled so autocratically, he turned his 'pewter stare' on the Caucasus with displeasure. These rebels had defied him too long. No matter which General was sent to finish off the campaign quickly, the fact remained, it dragged on in a most inexplicable fashion. The Emperor sat in his study in the Winter Palace, a sombre, green-walled room overlooking the Neva, where the distant needle-spire of the fortress of Peter and Paul pierced the mists, reminding and reassuring him that there, at least, those who had defied him were languishing in mildewed cells, imprisoned for life. Even now, as he sat facing this symbol of his authority, his staff-officers were waiting outside for an audience, in which they begged to submit the latest Caucasian dispatches, and in particular General Grabbés' recommendations concerning the new rebel leader, the Imam Shamyl; it was vital that his influence over the whole region should not be underestimated, wrote the General; that the Emperor should realize he was now faced with a most redoubtable foe, whose personal magnetism had galvanized whole provinces, and hardened the entire Caucasus to a new degree of resistance.

III

The Emperor Nicholas I was an absolute monarch, a polished aristocrat, whose marble rigidity encased the very incarnation of tyranny and reaction. His own curious brand of idealism (incorporated in the Holy Alliance) was expressed pedantically, and imposed ruthlessly. He was the product of German tutors and a German mother. His attention to detail was thoroughly German, like his penchant for uniforms. There was little of the Romanov in his nature. He disliked to be reminded of such ancestors as Ivan the Terrible or even Peter the Great. As to his grandmother, the Empress Catherine, she was, he said, a fine *Emperor*, implying she was not the sort of *woman* he admired. Those few of her courtiers still alive were seldom invited to the Winter Palace, and the summer-houses which dotted the park at Tzarskoe-Selo, temples of love, like the purple-glassed Alcôve Room, were kept shut. The Emperor and his wife Charlotte, a self-effacing German Princess, lived for the most part in the Winter Palace, or at Gatchina, a morose, *faux-Gothique*, château outside St. Petersburg. As a parent he was oppressive: his sons were forbidden to smoke—indeed his hatred of the weed was such that he tried to impose a ban on smoking throughout the capital. Card-playing and horse-racing, too, were condemned; but his efforts to found a temperance league were, as might be imagined, in this vodka-steeped land, doomed to failure. 'Look at the Russian,' says Radistchev, in his sermon (or plea), *A Journey from St. Petersburg to Moscow*. 'Look at him, and you will find melancholy. If he wants to shake off his misery, there is only vodka.' The Empress Catherine did not brook such remarks: Radistchev was sentenced to death, but later sent to expiate his outspokenness in Siberia.

Everywhere Nicholas' despotic grip was apparent. It took hold that December day of his accession, when he rode out from the Winter Palace to quell the ill-organized idealism of the Dekabristi gathered on the Senate Square. 'The Revolution that stood and waited' was a tragic instance of high-minded ineffectiveness.

The Dekabristi—so named from the fact that their revolt took place in December—were a group of cultivated and liberal young army officers, devoted to reform the liberation of the serfs and above all to the formation of a constitutional government. Their very idealism, in its purity, made them incapable of carrying out their revolt against the tyranny which Nicholas embodied. Their abortive stand was a heroic madness, embodying the whole of nineteenth-century Slav psychology. The time was not ripe: the people were not ready; the idealists stood alone, and fell alone. Alexander Herzen was to write of them with love and anguish, throughout his Memoirs:

> Between 1812 and 1825, there appeared a perfect galaxy of brilliant talent, independent character, and chivalrous valour, a combination quite new to Russia. These men had absorbed everything of Western culture, the introduction of which had been forbidden . . . They were its latest blooms, and, in spite of the fatal scythe that mowed them down at once, their influence can be traced, flowing far into the gloomy Russia of Nicholas, like the Volga into the sea.

The merciless manner in which the new Tzar suppressed, not only the Dekabristi, but every personal freedom or liberal measure, kept the country cowed throughout his reign, and made him the embodiment of that tyranny which the Dekabristi sought to destroy. 'The only tumults possible in Russia are those caused by the struggles of the flatterers surrounding the Throne,' wrote the Marquis de Custine, the Frenchman whose findings on a journey through Russia in 1839—fourteen years after the Dekabrist revolt—remain a classic, but are not altogether objective. During part of the journey, he was accompanied by a Polish friend, and much of the book was written in the house of Polish exiles who no doubt imposed purely Polish interpretations on de Custine's observations.

Nicholas was to hold Russia in this cruel grip until the day he died.

Significantly his last words to his son were: 'Hold all.' Perhaps the dark background of his father's end had formed this ruthless vein: he had been too young, at the time, to participate in the drama, but his elder brothers, the Tzarevitch Alexander, and the Grand Duke Constantine ten years his senior, had been, though unwilling conspirators, still, in a sense, party to the crime. Nicholas' father, the mad Tzar Paul I, had been strangled by a band of conspirator-patriot-courtiers, determined on his abdication.

Paul I's reign had been one of terror and injustice: no one was safe; sentries were flogged to death for a missing button. Ministers were flung in dungeons on a whisper; a Lieutenant Akimov was exiled to Siberia after his tongue had been cut out for composing an impudent epigram on the newly built Isaaki Cathedral. In matters of state, a similarly unpredictable tone prevailed. Policies were reversed; generals were recalled from their command overnight, as we have seen in the case of Count Valerian Zubov. Chaos deepened, as Paul's arrogance strengthened. He was Tzar: no one else counted. 'The man to whom I speak is ennobled—just so long as I speak with him', he said, sweeping aside every other person's lesser claims to authority, privilege or responsibility. All the same, he once proposed an admirably practical scheme which would certainly have brought wars to an end, if generally adopted. In a moment of acute diplomatic tension between England and Russia, he suggested that he and the British monarch should fight things out, man to man, as champions of their respective countries, without involving anyone else. Unfortunately the offer was not taken up, nor, in the century and a half since it was made, have any inflamed rulers ever carried their convictions to such personal lengths. 'We are all in this together' is not always enough to sustain millions of unwitting, unwilling victims of planned warfare.

If the Emperor Paul caused his subjects to live in terror, he too was terrorized. Only eight years before, the mob had guillotined Louis XVI. He believed his Minister and friend, Count Pahlen, planned to dethrone him: his own wife, he believed, was in agreement. Paul never forgot or forgave his mother, Catherine the Great, for her *coup* when she turned against her young husband, Peter III, to seize the crown and accede, over his dead body. Would his wife do likewise, Paul wondered? His pale, starting eyes were forever searching for danger: everyone around him was suspect. He lived barricaded into a small suite of rooms reached by one corridor in a wing of the gloomy Mihailovsky palace. This was newly built: the stone walls sweated damp, the chimneys smoked. Here, Paul lived alone with his fears. Even his favourite, the Countess Lopoukhine, whose rooms above communicated by a tiny stone staircase, could not dispel his terrors.

At last his exigencies menaced the whole country, and his abdication became a necessity of state. The conspirators had decided that the Emperor must sign the act of abdication, or die. 'What if he refuses?' asked one. Pahlen shrugged: 'One cannot make an omelette without breaking eggs.'

The Tzarevitch Alexander was young and idealistic, adored by the army, the Court and the people: he had at last allowed himself to be persuaded that his father's abdication would be for the good of the country. But there must be no violence. Pahlen and his band did not bother to discuss their plans with him. He was still a queasy boy.

Alexander waited in his suite, in another wing, far removed from his father's room. It was too late to draw back now, and he suffered agonies of remorse. Suddenly the conspirators burst in, flushed with wine and triumph. They had run the Emperor to death in his bedroom, hardly waiting for his refusal to sign the abdication before striking him down and strangling him. The Tzar had tried to hide in a chimney: they had pulled him out by one leg: a silk scarf choked him, and a gold snuff-box bashed in his head. He was finished off by some eager conspirator jumping on his stomach. Apoplexy, said the death certificate signed by Sir James Wylie, the Court physician; but it was whispered that several doctors worked the rest of the night to get the corpse fit for Sir James to see.

When the conspirators bowed low before Alexander, calling him Tzar, he recoiled from them. 'I have murdered my own father!' he cried, and fainted away.

He was never to forget that terrible night. Horror and remorse pursued him all the rest of his life. He was never allowed to forget, nor were his brothers: their mother, the widowed Empress, saw to that. Her murdered husband's blood-stained clothes were arranged meticulously, as if ready for use, in the antechamber leading to her rooms. Every time her sons came to visit her they were obliged to pass through this morbid exhibition. Although Nicholas was only a child at the time of his father's assassination, his whole boyhood and youth were shadowed by the affair. It was probably responsible for his elder brother Constantine's decision to abdicate, on the death of Alexander, in 1823.

IV

As to Alexander, a strongly mystical strain in his nature developed into a melancholy neurosis: he seemed racked by the earthly glories he had not wished to inherit by violence: and the more glories his reign gathered—even the defeat of Napoleon, and the ever enlarging frontiers of his country, only seemed to oppress him increasingly. He relegated more and more power to his close companion, the sinister Arakchiev, who held all Russia in a reactionary grip. The glorious morning of Alexander's reign faded into a gloomy twilight, made even more obscure by the mystical miasmas which Madame de Krudener generated so energetically from the alcôve where she received the infatuated Tzar.

This remarkable woman exercised a considerable influence on European politics at this time. She was of Russian birth, elegant and seductive; a romantic pietist, who had arrived at a formidable blend of flesh and spirit; mind, too, for she had some literary pretensions. Her close friendship with Queen Hortense had opened the doors of Parisian society, and, soon, her mystically inclined conversation, combined with a series of Lady Hamilton-like attitudes, and a shawl dance, had so intrigued *le tout Paris*, that many who came to mock, stayed to pray. Benjamin Constant and Chateaubriand were regular visitors, and when, presently, the Emperor Alexander was included in this eclectic band, Madame de Krudener's salon was crowned. The Emperor fell under her sway at once.

It seems to have been an ambiguous relationship. In his letters, he asks her to pray for him to resist the temptations of Paris. She speaks of the sacrifices she has made 'in submitting, yet again, to the painful and humiliating ordeal of an earthly affection'. Her tone was one of teacher to pupil: 'If you could continue to progress without me, I would go away . . . but . . .' She stayed; they continued to meet, and 'from their alcôve came the first project of the Holy Alliance. Madame de Krudener was received everywhere with full diplomatic honours, as if an Ambassadress from Heaven.' But at last her influence began to wane; and she fades from view around 1822.

Not that the circumstances of her departure were without drama. She had struck up a friendship with two other eccentric ladies, the Princess Galitzin, and a mysterious French émigrée known as Madame Guacher, who had succeeded in rousing the Emperor's interest. Courtiers were apt to hint at a dark past, but the Emperor defended her with the utmost chivalry. When these three ladies banded together to form a sort of lay sisterhood, given over to good works and political intrigues, their influence became such that at last the Emperor was persuaded to order their removal to the south, to the Crimea. Dressed in flowing grey robes, they left St. Petersburg in September 1822, mocked by the Court, but mourned by the poor, by whom they were beloved for their generosity.

On arrival in Taganrog, they set about proselytizing, but without much success. Holding open-air prayer-meetings for the puzzled Tartars soon took its toll of Madame de Krudener's health, already undermined by the fervours of her apostolic vocation, and she died a year later.

Princess Galitzin was of sterner stuff. No sooner was her friend buried, than she cast off her robes and installed herself at Koreis, where a small court soon centred round her.

The third lady was even more remarkable, if we are to believe certain contemporary sources, she too, like Madame de Krudener, had once swayed thrones: she had, in fact, contributed to the overthrow of the French monarchy, for she was none other than the Countess de la Motte, whose part in *l'affaire du collier* needs no recapitulation. After escaping French justice, she had lived in London, where she was supposed to have died. But, soon after, she appeared in Russia as Madame Guacher. She, too, after the death of Madame de Krudener, abandoned proselytizing, exchanging her nun's robes for Amazonian attire, and the life of an eccentric recluse. She preferred to walk, or ride, in stormy weather, and could often be seen galloping through torrential rains, 'as if pursued by Satan himself'. One evening, during a particularly fearful storm, she took shelter in the house of a neighbour, Colonel Ivanov.

> Without uttering a word, or honouring me with a single look, or caring for the water which streamed from her clothes, she sank down on the divan, and remained lost in thought. She wore an Amazonian petticoat, a green cloth coat, a broad-brimmed felt hat, with a pair of pistols in her belt, and carried a tortoise in her hand, which animal she addressed as Dushinka, or 'little soul'.

The tortoise was a present from the Emperor Alexander. 'And as long as I have it near me, I shall not utterly despair of my destiny,' she said. The Colonel, a true romantic, believed her to be the illegitimate offspring of some Royal amour. He had observed that she often received dispatches from St. Petersburg, and seemed 'notwithstanding her exile to have retained a certain influence over the Tzar'. Madame Guacher became more and more eccentric. Suddenly, in the autumn of 1823, she died.

As soon as the Emperor learned of this he appeared greatly agitated, and sent a Cossack courier to the Crimea, to obtain a certain casket, which, with the aid of the Chief of Police, was found hidden in the house. Two weeks later the sealed casket was delivered to the Emperor, who, we are told, was so impatient to obtain its contents, that he had the lock broken, there and then, in the presence of some of his more intimate circle. Inside lay a pair of scissors, which can hardly have been the reason for Alexander sending his courier four thousand miles at the gallop. I have always wondered what became of the tortoise.

Two years later, in 1825, the Tzar died at Taganrog, not far from the place of exile of his three strange friends. Mystery shrouded his death too. There was a popular belief that, following a carefully laid plan, the corpse of an unknown man was sealed in the Royal coffin. The Tzar himself was thus enabled to disappear, by the complicity of his doctor, the Tzarina, and one trusted aide-de-camp, to live out a long life of expiation as the monk, Father Feodor Kouzmitch, a strange and venerated figure whose true history has never been divulged. That there was some secret concerning the Emperor's death is admitted, just as there is a mystery surrounding the life of Feodor Kouzmitch. It is said that when the Emperor Alexander III opened the coffin of Alexander I, an alabaster mask covered the face, and the Emperor, refusing to have it removed, ordered the coffin to be re-sealed. And when the Soviet Government opened the coffin, it was found to be empty. No explanation has ever been forthcoming.

V

It was surrounded by these sombre shades, and on this note of doubt, that Nicholas succeeded, after his elder brother Constantine's rejection of the Crown. Perhaps his tyrannies are thus explained, though they cannot be condoned, for his reign was one long agony of suppression, cruelty and reaction. 'The whole art of Russian government is in the use of violence', wrote an Austrian diplomat in 1840. (Yet the Austrian Government, headed by the Emperor, and sustained by the Court, did not hesitate to call on Russia, on Nicholas, 'the policeman of Europe', to bring the might of his Cossacks to suppress, so terribly, the Hungarian patriots' rising of 1848.)

On the accession of Nicholas, in 1825, the pendulum swung from Alexander's humanity back again to the insane despotism of Paul. There was, in Nicholas' marble rigidity, something almost more terrible. Yet he, too, sometimes displayed that lack of balance which was so characteristic of all his forebears. While mercy was almost unknown to him, he could, on occasions, mystify every one by the extravagant benefits he would lavish on the families of his victims, lavished, as if to salve his conscience, with a sort of self-indulgent gusto.

After suppressing the Dekabrist Rising of 1825, this reaction was particularly apparent. At the execution of the five ringleaders, bungling inefficiency reached its apotheosis, the ropes breaking, so that the hangings had to begin all over again. 'Unhappy country, where they do not even know how to *hang* you', said Ryliev, as he was strung up for the second time. But the Tzar, who had been waiting at the Winter Palace, torn between impatience and anguish, at once displayed a most tactless magnanimity towards Ryliev's widow, who was urged 'to make use' of the Tzar at all times, for any needs. Colonel Pestel, the ringleader, left a younger brother who was instantly promoted to be the Tzar's aide-de-camp. We can imagine with what horror the boy attended on the man who had signed his brother's death warrant. Often the Tzar seemed to be performing some private act of expiation, stifling his conscience rather than acting mercifully.

* * *

The Emperor Nicholas I was seen by most of Europe as a *chevalier sans peur et sans reproche*; a devoted husband and father, the father of his people, a noble figure whose classic perfection of features mirrored an equally noble soul, and whose 'flashing, Jupiter glance', as one lady-in-waiting described it, had a dazzling effect on the beholder. Alexander Herzen was harsher in his judgement. 'I know nothing so terrible,' he wrote: 'nothing which could so banish hope as those colourless, cold pewter eyes.' Yet Nicholas could, when he chose, appear irresistible. His manners were perfect, he possessed a magnetic charm, and most dangerous, persuasive powers, which he could apply at will. Such were his powers—or such was the Russian inclination to recant, that we have, in many instances, notably in his interviews with the Dekabristi and Alexander Pushkin, examples of his magnetic powers. Most of these courageous, convinced liberals succumbed to the power of his majesty: they appear to have been stupefied by him, admitting their guilt, embracing their sins, and almost begging for punishment—which, having won their confidence, the Tzar meted out implacably.

According to the historian Constantine de Grunwald, we may be touching here on a fundamental aspect of the Russian character: these orgies of self-accusation are traced throughout their history, and are not the product of any one age or rule. I am reminded of the boyar who was condemned to the rack by Ivan the Terrible and who, between each groan, cried: 'Lord God! I beseech you to bless tyrants!' Radistchev, the liberal, and would-be reformer, after serving a term of imprisonment during the reign of Paul I, returned to what he dared to hope might be a newer, freer Russia, under Alexander I. He offered his services and advice to the young Emperor, who accepted them in the good faith in which they were made. But no sooner had he begun to work out his proposed legislative reforms than he was overcome by strange doubts—with horror at his own blasphemous temerity towards Holy Russia and the Tzar, and, pouring himself a glass of sulphuric acid, gulped it down and died in agony. Even here, in this tragic end, we see the national vein of excess. Most suicides would have been content to blow their brains out, hang themselves, open a vein, or take some unobtrusive poison. But Radistchev took sulphuric acid.

Perhaps the only truly Slav quality which Nicholas I shared with his people was this strain of excess. His unbending rectitude, his love of

order, punctuality, industry, discipline and orthodoxy, were all carried
to excessive lengths. Sometimes, behind the clockwork metronome of
duty which was his heart-beat, we see the violent reactions of Ivan the
Terrible—the same imposition of his own will, over all else, that
characterized his father.

In his home life, too, the Emperor was a domestic martinet, his
whole family standing trembling before him. Although considered the
most handsome man of his time, the portraitist Horace Vernet found
his the harshest face he had ever painted, and the young Queen
Victoria, after receiving him at Windsor Castle, on the occasion of his
state visit in 1844, wrote: 'The expression of his eyes is terrible.' (The
flashing, Jupiter glance had not impressed her.) 'I have never seen anything like them; he is severe and gloomy, imbued with principles
nothing on earth could change. . . . Politics and the army—those are the
only subjects that interest him.' Nevertheless he had worked havoc, as a
young prince, among the languishing princesses of the lesser German
courts, from among which the latter-day Romanovs were wont to
choose their brides. Nor was his spell cast solely over princesses, for one
positively human touch is detected in his love of masquerades and the
liberties which his Haroun al Raschid expeditions to the public *bals
masqués* of St. Petersburg permitted him. 'For women, the *tchin*' (the
rigidly graded system of fourteen class distinctions) 'does not exist . . .
especially at a masquerade,' he used to say, profiting by the numbers of
pretty women from all walks of life with whom he could flirt and talk,
and from whom he learned much that was going on in his capital. This
towering, elegant stranger intrigued the women: he had the great
height which characterized all the Romanov men, and his features
were classic. Sometimes he was recognized, but generally he liked to
think he remained incognito. On one occasion a gushing charmer had
ventured to tell him he was the most handsome man alive. 'Madame,
that is a matter which concerns my wife alone,' was the rather dampening reply. There were still many years to go before he was openly
entranced with Pushkin's giddy young wife, or, later still, had persuaded
the discreet Mademoiselle Nelidov, one of his wife's ladies-in-waiting,
to become his mistress. By then his happiness was too late to have a
mellowing effect, and he died, as he had lived, a tyrant.

'There does not exist on the earth, at present,' wrote de Custine, 'not
in Turkey, not even in China, a single man who enjoys and exercises such
power as the Emperor. Let the reader figure to himself all the skilfulness
and experience of our modern governments, perfected as they are by
centuries of practice, put into exercise in a still young and uncivilized
society. . . . The administrations of the West, aiding the despotism of the
East; European discipline supporting the tyranny of Asia; the police
employed in concealing barbarism, in order not to destroy, but to

perpetuate it . . . Let him conceive the idea of a half-savage people who have been enlisted and drilled, without being civilized, and he will be able to understand the social and moral state of the Russian nation. . . .' He went on to say that the reigns of both Catherine the Great and Alexander I only prolonged the systematic, the deliberate infancy of the nation. Catherine, he says, merely instituted schools to please the French philosophers, whose approbation her vanity sought. Writing to the Governor of Moscow, one of her ex-favourites who had complained that attendance at schools was low, the Empress replied in a most cynical vein: 'My dear Prince, do not distress yourself because the Russians have no desire for knowledge. If I institute schools, is it not for ourselves, but for Europe, in whose estimation we must maintain our standing.' And, continuing on a note at once prophetic and realist, she added: 'If our peasants should really seek to become enlightened, neither you nor I could continue in our places.'

No doubt the Emperor shared his grandmother's views. The people must keep their place, or he could not keep his—an eventuality too dreadful to contemplate.

Although Nicholas I always displayed a terrible severity towards his own people, political offenders especially, he was generally magnanimous towards conquered nations, though the Poles became an exception. Their nationalistic fervours always exasperated the Russians, and Nicholas, with his meticulous attention to detail, used to warn his generals during the Polish campaigns against the seductions of Polish women. The Poles would be better suppressed entirely (though press-ganged into the Russian army, they could still serve some useful purpose. . . .)

But whether, Poland apart, the Tzar's general magnanimity was due entirely to the dictates of his conscience, or inspired, in part, by a wish to disarm, or reassure, other spectator nations as to the purely local limits of his activities, we do not know. In any case, after the moderation which he displayed to the Persians in 1828, when he might have made crippling demands, and even occupied Teheran, the Tzar was seen by the rest of Europe and the near-eastern and Balkan rulers as a glorious figure, whose magnanimity and power were equal. Emissaries of lesser powers now began circling round him in a sort of *contredanse* of flattery and awe infinitely agreeable to Nicholas. The Emir of Bokhara rendered homage; Montenegro established an Embassy in St. Petersburg. The Afghans were respectful, the Persians subdued. Alas! the Sultan, while rendering homage, remained unmoved by the Tzar's suggestion that he might consider being converted to Christianity, the better to represent what Nicholas now described as 'the great number of his subjects'. But this circuitous approach to the problem of Christian minorities on Moslem soil was to remain unacknowledged for many years. As to the great powers, Britain, France, or Austria, they appeared cordiality it-self, and if they kept an ever-watchful eye trained on the Russian Empire, no gleam of anxiety was permitted to show. The senior execu-tants of the *contredanse* moved to a stately measure, bowing, but not scraping.

VI

Even within his own frontiers, among his own oppressed peoples, Nicholas enjoyed an extraordinary degree of reverential love. It was as if those people required, or craved, an absolute monarch; as if his tyrannic grip appealed to some fundamental craving for submission, deeply ingrained in the whole nation, a basic strain to be traced throughout their history, and which remains in their blood-stream, under whatever sway. The Emperor Nicholas appears to have exercised a hold over his nation, comparable to, but less understandable than, that wielded by Shamyl in the Caucasus. No matter that he was harsh, obstinate, bigoted, hypocritical, ruthless and self-satisfied: he was con-vinced of his divine mission, of the divinity of kings, and this conviction he was able to impose on the people, from the courtiers, by way of the merchants and peasants, to the serfs. Most of the convicts, marching painfully towards Siberia, bore him no grudge; to them, as to himself, he seemed above criticism.

We read of the Tzarevitch, Nicholas' eldest son, returning from a State tour to the battlefield of Borodino, meeting with a Siberian convict convoy, singing their melancholy religious chants as they stumbled onwards—to hell. The Tzarevitch stopped his traineau and spoke to the chief guard, an old police sergeant who had made the journey thirty or more times, and who was so overcome by the dazzling Presence, that he could only stutter and salute like a marionette. There was also a German doctor who had voluntarily accompanied several such convoys, though whether from humanitarian motives, or that curious preoccupation with cruelty so often existing and encouraged in the Germans, we do not know. His information regarding the convoy much interested the Tzarevitch. The prisoners, said the doctor, except for two incendiaries and two assassins who were chained one to the other and kept in close custody, showed no regret at their lot. They were all planning, he said, to build up their fortunes in Siberia by work-ing in the gold mines. (They were petty thieves, or serfs, sentenced by their owners for excessive laziness or drunkenness.) A whole new life was opening before them, said the doctor, with some ambiguity. . . . The Tzarevitch requested the doctor to ask them if they were well and lacked anything.

We can imagine the scene: the empty expanses of snow and lowering

winter skies . . . a thin streak of light yellowing towards the horizon, as
the short winter day ended. Seated in his scarlet traineau, the handsome, genuinely kindly young Tzarevitch, the sea-otter collar of his fur-
lined pelisse turned up to shelter him from the bitter wind, his out-
riders and equerries gathered round obsequiously: the doctor striding
back, along the rutted tracks, towards the group of forgotten men; we
can imagine how the guards closed round them when the royal question
was asked. Which among them would dare do otherwise than bow and
cheer? . . . Back came the doctor with this answer: all of them replied
they were in excellent health and spirits, and lacked for nothing, he
said. . . . Even so, the Tzarevitch's gentle, slightly bulging eyes looked
doubtful . . . 'Mon Prince,' said the German doctor, 'the moment is not
far distant when deportation to Siberia will be no longer a punishment.
Every day fresh letters arrive from those already there, finding their lot
marvellous, and urging their friends to join them. . . .' It was after this
encouraging conversation that the German doctor presently obtained a
decoration, with the splendid title, 'General of the Condemned Deportees of the Province of Moscow', a title and post to which only Gogol's
pen could do justice, and only the Germans, with their passion for
long-winded titles for any grade and shade of occupation, could savour
fully.

Such Siberian deportees worked, burrowed together, in fetid caverns,
lit only by a dim lantern placed before an ikon of the Virgin. They went
barefooted, or with their feet wrapped in rags or straw; their boots were
long ago worn out on those months of marching to their doom. They
slept in the outer caverns, slimy and damp and dirty. Sometimes they fell
where they worked, and were only roused by the *nagaiikas*—the flailing
whips of the Cossack guard. Or else they were dragged out dead. They
were forbidden to talk to each other, and no man might ever say for
what reason he had been deported. In this half-world of darkness and
suffering, the passing hours were beaten out to the sound of chisels and
hammers, as they quarried for veins of lapis lazuli, or amethyst. The
chips of stone formed a wounding hail, and more than half of the convicts soon lost an eye. Few escaped, and fewer still lived out their
sentence. Only the lice flourished.

These were the conditions which were to inspire some of the greatest
writing of Dostoievsky and Gorki. But, until the Revolution, the
Siberian mines were generally celebrated first as a source for all those
semi-precious substances from which malachite urns and lapis lazuli
pillars derived: in particular, the source from which Carl Fabergé's
exquisitely complicated bibelots sprang. Today they are collector's
items, coming rarely under the auctioneer's hammer; glimpsed,
occasionally, in the pawn-shops and jewellers of Monte Carlo, where,

in winter, a few, very few, old Russians still creep from their pensions to warm themselves in the sun, or to haunt the Casino, spectres at a feast which must, by an earlier, remembered hey-day, now seem strictly rationed.

Carl Fabergé devised the fabulous playthings of a vanished world. Easter eggs in gold and amethyst and enamel, thimble-sized, which opened to present lesser eggs, and lesser still, each one revealing a royal face framed in pearls; or parasol handles, cigarette boxes and holders; all kinds of *fanfreluches* with the Imperial cypher in first-water diamonds; love tokens from a Grand Duke to a ballerina; tokens of Imperial esteem, bestowed on courtiers or statesmen; delightful little family jokes translated into terms of onyx and jade, blue-john, rose quartz, tourmaline and beryl.

They were soon to become tombstones—glittering little tombstones, memorials to both the prisoners in the mines, and that aristocracy for which the mines were worked.

7

The Warriors

They don't seem to know when they ought to die—
indeed these villains can hardly ever be killed.
They are a people without the slightest idea of
propriety.   LERMONTOV

Although Nazran was saved, and Ghimri had fallen, the Russians
realized that only by the acquisition of an entirely new technique of
warfare could they hope to subdue the rebels. Their guns and equipment served to hamper rather than help them, for they were either
being hauled up almost vertical mountain paths, or forcing a passage
through impenetrable forests. In the campaigns of 1823 General
Yermolov had succeeded in clearing a path through the Forest of
Göiten—a wide path, as much to protect his men from sharp-shooters
as for transport. But it had not been kept cleared, and by 1832 it was
once again choked, shoulder-high in vegetation. All nature, here,
seemed hostile to the Russians. The burning summer sun skinned them
as it beat down, day after day. They suffered sunstroke and thirst: in
winter the snow and ice hampered their movements, or froze them to
death as they slept, when bivouacked in the forest, often without fires
for fear of betraying their whereabouts. And the torrential rains and
chill mists of both spring and autumn penetrated their bones, bringing
rheumatic fevers and pneumonia. They were not, for many years,
properly equipped for such extremes of climate—extremes, moreover,
which could be met with, all in one area, within the space of a day's
march between tropic forests, coast swamps or mountain passes.
Except for the adoption of bourkas, the goat's hair capes, tent-
like in cut, worn by the Caucasians which could be spread out to
protect both rider and horse, the Russians wore an unsuitable uniform
just as, for many years, they fought with an obsolete type of flintlock,
since the Tzar opposed changing them, as well as so many other
reforms. He detested change. Cold steel had been good enough for
his ancestors: he had no faith in innovations, whether a new type
of gun, or a more practical uniform. As to a new Legislation—a

Constitution—his face darkened with fury at the mere hint of such a possibility.

In spite of engagements of the most violent and sanguinary nature, the Russians soon discovered a certain monotony in Caucasian warfare. Sometimes, for months on end, they never saw their enemy. Yet no day closed without losses. General Tornau wrote that 'fighting went on from beginning to end of each march: men fell, but no enemy was seen. Puffs of smoke in the jungle alone betrayed their lurking places, and our soldiers, having nothing else to guide them, took aim by that. . . . Our sharpshooters, who went in pairs (later the number was raised to ten, and even twenty), often lost sight of each other in the forest, and strayed from the main column. Then, the Tchetchens would arise, as it were, out of the ground, and spring on the isolated men, and hack them to pieces before their comrades could come to their rescue.' Such harassing tactics were particularly dreaded by the Russians when retreating with their wounded.

'The Tchetchens had a way of handling their weapons only at the last moment. They would charge on the enemy at tremendous speed; at twenty paces they would fire, holding the reins in their teeth; then, swinging back their guns, they would rush right on to the Russians, whirling their shashkas over their heads, slashing with fearful strength.'

In the beginning, the Russian troops used, generally, to fire without taking particular aim, in a manner considered 'very proper against a regular line, but not effective against the scattered Caucasians'. Therefore specially trained Finnish tirailleurs were sent to join the Army of the South, and the Russian technique of firing much improved, though still, in the opinion of one military observer, 'inferior to the French, English and Prussians, in this respect'.

But in the matter of cold steel, there was no denying the Caucasians were masters of the field. They soon learned to defend themselves against the bayonet, but the Russians were not so able at warding off the slashing thrusts of the shashka. Both Russian swordmanship and weapons were inferior to those of the mountaineers. To the Caucasians, their arms were their most valued possessions, preserved and handed down from generation to generation: some of the weapons dated from the Crusaders who had passed that way; they bore Italian or Latin inscriptions, telling of their maker and first owner. Some of these swords were so tempered that they were known to have cut through the barrel of a Russian musket at one stroke.

Like the Arnauts (Albanian mercenaries), Caucasian tribesmen enjoyed not only fighting, but the noise of battle, and sometimes copied their habit of notching the bullets, in order to make them sing louder. They fought with relish. 'Among themselves they sabre each other in the way of friendship,' says Lermontov. And again: ' "I've seen a man beaten to pulp with the butt end of our muskets," ' says a Russian soldier, 'and having been pierced with a bayonet and riddled like a colander, still waving his shashka round his shameless head, and shooting like a madman. . . . They don't seem to know when they *ought* to die—indeed these villains can hardly ever be killed. They are a people without the slightest idea of propriety.'

Here is General Tornau's description of a typical day's campaigning:

After a march the troops camped for a day or so, the time being determined by the number of aôuls to be destroyed in that particular region. Small columns were sent out to ravage the rebels' houses and fields: crops were destroyed, aôuls set ablaze, and the resistant tribes shot down. . . . At evening, our wounded and dead are brought back to camp. Our Tartars (those of the tribes who have gone over to the Russians) ride in with severed heads dangling from their saddle bows. There are no prisoners, the men ask for no quarter. Their women and children are generally hidden before our approach, in hide-outs where no one would care to risk seeking them. Now the head of a column comes into camp. It has been out on a night-raid. The rear is not yet in sight: it is still fighting its way through the forest. The nearer it comes to the edge of the forest—to open space and safety, the quicker grows the firing. The rebels are making the most of their chances. We can hear their yells, as they surround and press on the rearguard from all sides; they rush in, flourishing their swords, driving our men onward, towards the last clearing, where the rebel sharp-shooters await them with a deadly hail of bullets. We are obliged to rush back a fresh battalion and several guns, to disengage the rearguard, if they are to be saved without useless sacrifice. . . . Communications are generally kept up by means of horns, signal numbers being given to the detached bodies of troops rear, front or flank, and these numbers constantly changed before the enemy can learn to distinguish them. . . . In camp men are sent out to cut grass for fodder. (Often the horses cannot be protected unless picketed inside our lines, where, perhaps, there is no pasturage.) At once a fresh fight begins. Fuel for cooking purposes or for the bivouac fires is only obtained by further fighting. If there is brushwood or any semblance of a watering place, it must be covered by half a battalion and artillery, otherwise the horses will be shot down or driven off into the forest. One day is like another; yesterday's happenings will be repeated to-morrow—everywhere, the mountains, everywhere, the forests, and the Tchetchens are a ferocious tireless enemy.

II

In describing their adversaries specifically as Tchetchens, General Tornau is being exceptionally precise. Just as Shamyl was generally referred to as 'He'—the god-like, awesome pronoun being used by Russians, the renegade tribesmen who acted as their spies or guides, and the Caucasians themselves—so the Caucasian tribes, in all their complicated ancestry and racial distinctions, were simplified by the Russians, one and all being generally known as Tartars. So that when the Russians were reminded of Napoleon's remark: 'Scratch a Russian and you will find a Tartar', they considered it most offensive. They felt themselves remote from Tartary. Although, to the rest of Europe, they might appear as Asiatics, they themselves drew a very sharp distinction. Accepted standards of beauty had to be 'purely Russian'; the blond, broad-faced, grey-eyed beauty of the north. Anything slant-eyed, of an exotic cast, was denigrated. 'The least tinge of the Tartar taint is as difficult to efface as that of Africa: the elongated eye, the spreading nostril, the unhealthy, jaundiced hue, are sure to be revealed,' wrote one Western traveller, secure in his classic profile and general pinkness and whiteness.

As to the Tartars—mediaeval Russian legends and *skazki* were full of Tartar ogres felled by simple-simon Ivans. Even the heroic Ilya Mourametz was overwhelmed by the 'Tartar odour' of his foes. Though here, we may reflect on national or personal reactions to various odours. Differently pigmented skins are each held to be insupportable, or at any rate, very marked, to the other. Tolstoy, as a Russian, speaks of the curious unmistakable smell, acrid and leathery, which clung to the Caucasian warriors. But the Moslem Murids shuddered at the smell of the pork-fed Christians. The anonymous English author of *Revelations of Russia in 1846* remarks the distinctive smell of the Russians: 'strange, tallowy, insupportable', he says, 'deriving, no doubt, from Muscovite habits'. He claims that the steam baths, so much part of the Russian life, from noble to moujik, 'having a temperature enough to cook fish, induces a copious perspiration, which is kept up by drinking inconceivable quantities of hot water tinged with tea. Since the bulk of their food is fermented cabbage, sour black bread, and enormous quantities of rank hemp-seed oil, used for cooking, all the essences of these things seem to stream through their pores.' Another Western traveller, likewise nose-in-air, visiting the ancient harem of the Sirdars of Erivan, then occupied by General Paskiévitch's troops, wrote: 'And here, where formerly Persian odalisques rested among perfumes and flowers, the Russian soldiers emit that odour peculiar to them.'

Generals of the Tartar hordes allotted a ration of musk and ambergris and strange spices to their warriors before a battle. (Herodotus tells us that some of the most highly prized scents were derived from a sticky substance, found in the beards of billy-goats browsing on thornbushes along the Arabian coast.) The Tartars issued their perfumed ration, rather as later troops were issued a tot of rum, to brace and embolden. Though the Tartar practice might be interpreted otherwise: perhaps the perfumes were used, not so much to fortify the wearers, as, like rounds of ammunition, to overcome their enemies: a primitive example of chemical warfare.

III

The Tchetchens were to play a particularly significant part in the Murid wars. They were a beautiful, bold, independent people, the élite of Shamyl's army, their independence fostered by the fact that their territory was the fertile lowlands where cattle, fruit, grain and forests abounded. They had conserved little or nothing of their origins, for their Arab conquerors had substituted the Koran for their own legends and history, but they are thought to have originated in Europe rather than in Asia, as the Avars and mountain tribes of Daghestan had done. Without their supplies of grain, cattle, fodder and fuel, Shamyl would not have been able to continue his fight so long: it took the Russians some time to realize this, but having done so, they still found it impossible to wrest the prize from him until the middle fifties.

In camp, among the Russian officers, a special code of conduct prevailed. It was considered extremely bad style to show any interest in the enemies' fire, as it whistled overhead. 'Although bullets fell right and left in the interior of the camp square, conversation must continue, as we ate, or sat around the camp fire, without the least show of emotion. Anyone whose voice faltered was the object of general ridicule. It was *de rigueur* to remain seated, and never, under any circumstances, to duck.' One newcomer who tried to conceal his involuntary recoil by a sneeze was obliged to keep up an elaborate pretence of a head-cold until he had steadied his nerves. This tradition of sang-froid was, for the soldiers of this time, often all they had with which to meet the challenge of pain; amputations or primitive field surgery were generally performed without opiates; even a dose of laudanum was little help against the surgeon's hack-saw. I am reminded of Lord Uxbridge, who, after the battle of Waterloo, supported the removal of a leg with the utmost coolness, merely remarking that the saw seemed rather blunt; and another officer, at the same battle, who, having watched the surgeon amputate his hand, called back the orderly who was removing it from the room, saying: 'Not so fast! I'll have my rings back if you don't mind.'

Owing to the nature of the country, uneven ground, forests, swamps and rocky defiles, a column on the march could seldom be sure it would not be taken by surprise, any more than a camp could be sure of a night's repose.

Our camp was always disposed in a square, infantry and artillery on the outside, and cavalry and transport in the middle. By night the number of sharp-shooters was increased: the reserves were advanced, and in front in danger spots, secret pickets were set after nightfall, when the enemy could not know their whereabouts. Absolute silence was the rule. The pickets were not allowed to challenge anyone except by whistling, and they had strict orders to open fire at the smallest sound, the least rustle in the darkness. On each face of the square, pickets were detailed to reinforce the guard in case of real attack. These men lay on the ground beside their guns and ammunition, watching, waiting. The rest, soldiers and officers, slept inside the square, generally undressed, and troubled themselves little over the bullets with which the Tchetchens favoured us every night, creeping, cat-like, right up to the camp, in spite of all our precautions.

Yet we have some curious side-lights on the Caucasian campaigns as a whole from memoirs left by various officers, Count Constantin Benckendorff and Colonel George Vlastov among them. The latter tells us that while the Russian troops generally sounded the reveille at half-past five, breakfast and the morning's work was seldom interrupted before ten o'clock, as the rebels, 'who like their leisure', rarely gave any signs of life before then. Vlastov's Caucasian service was in the latter part of Shamyl's reign—in the 'fifties, and it is probable that the Imam kept his Murid troops, whenever possible, at prayer and pious ritual for several hours, each day: he never forgot that Caucasian unity, the strength of his forces, depended first on the degree of Moslem fervour which was sustained.

For the Russians there were certain distractions which were permitted, and even encouraged, under the most trying circumstances. We read of one sybarite who, at garrison headquarters, succeeded in imparting an air of luxury to his quarters by making his orderly wash the floorboards in champagne. Another, who had a bugler call him at 6 a.m., for the especial pleasure of turning over and sleeping on again till his regular reveille, at 8. Variously, the officers succeeded in maintaining individual standards of comfort and relaxation. Some kept a mistress, one of the exotic dancers from Shemakha, perhaps, who had been bribed away from her vocation, from her almost religious devotion to these ritual posturings, to rage or droop, in an atmosphere heavy with cigar-smoke and military banter. Some studied astronomy, geology and botany, unlikely subjects which their remote situation and the intermittent nature of the campaigns gave them the leisure and desire to study. The officers of one regiment sported red-topped boots, signifying they had fought knee-deep in blood. Some obtained a vicarious excitement from retailing the latest scandals from St. Petersburg, though they were sadly out of date by the time they reached the

Caucasus, since letters, like books and newspapers, often took two months en route. There were amateur theatricals (Griboyedov's *Woe Through Wit* being first performed by a band of Yermolov's officers, at the time when Griboyedov himself was Russian Minister to Persia). There were concerts—for where there are Russians, there will always be music—beautiful harmonies, sung by those deep-toned voices which seem to be part of some centrifugal force, as if issuing from the earth itself—voices which even at their most inexpert recall Chaliapin, sharing something of his curiously veiled, or smoky tone, something peculiarly national.

Sometimes there were horse-races, the officers' splendid mounts pitted against a local breed, a smaller, unprepossessing-looking animal, but which, with a Cossack rider up, usually led the field. Occasionally there was a ball where those few officers' wives who were in the Caucasus could preen it over the local ladies. But the dancers of Shemakha were not invited. These sort of evenings were consecrated to the *valse* rather than their more inviting undulations. Occasionally some young bloods might stamp through the fiery rhythms of a Polish *oberek*, or a *lesghinka*; but it was, before all else, a ladies' evening. . . .

IV

Apart from a straggle of camp-followers, women were a rarity. Those few officers' families who were hardy enough to install themselves in the Caucasus, around the military bases, were generally born and bred to the country, daughters of Terek or Grebensky Cossack officers, perhaps children of the garrison, to the second or third generation. Few of them had ever travelled farther afield than Tiflis, and knew nothing of the world lying north of the mountains. But they were remarkably well educated, having acquired both learning, and even *savoir-faire*, from the exiles, known as *les malheureux*, often young men of the most brilliant birth and background, sent to the south to serve a sentence for duelling or liberalism. Degraded to the ranks, with no money or position, these unfortunates were traditionally welcomed in the officers' mess of every garrison, were still invited to the General's table, and free to earn a few roubles acting as tutors to the children of the local society. Count Benckendorff, whose memoirs reek with arrogance—with an odious, overbearing patronage and self-aggrandizement, speaks of them with exasperation; *les malheureux*, he says, were thoroughly spoiled; they were of no use, and merely a heavy responsibility and expense to their commanding officers. Yet however sharply the aristocrat courtier Benckendorff dismissed them, there were, among their ranks, many brilliant figures. Another writer tells us. 'These men being outwardly *très comme il faut* (whatever their private life) and ever *très gentilhomme* towards the garrison families, the majority of young girls grew up to absorb the style, conversation, and *tenue* of a St. Petersburg belle. Thus, at a ball such as the officers sometimes gave, at Grosnia or Hassif Yurt, one remarked little difference between garrison society and that of the capital.'

Parties and picnics, amateur theatricals and waltzing were distractions which were, naturally, only possible during a lull in the fighting, to celebrate some triumphant engagement, or to restore morale, after some humiliating defeat. But routine manœuvres, or expeditions to cut wood, often assumed the aspect of a picnic, where the regimental cooks devised unexpected delicacies, and the officers, stretched out on Caucasian carpets, drank the excellent local wines, recited verses, and no one spoke of war. Occasionally such expeditions were accompanied by the more available ladies—some of that small band of exiled Western women, Viennese, or French, perhaps, who found themselves, by intent or accident, living precariously as milliners, pastry-cooks, café-singers, or *filles galantes*, in these backwaters of Asiatic Russia. Then the scene assumed the aspect of a *fête champêtre*: larger rugs and softer cushions were spread out under the trees; bottles of champagne put to cool in the icy mountain torrent, and when the soldiers were marched off into the green glades, and their axes rang out, faraway and muffled, the ladies untied their bonnet-strings, fanning themselves languidly, voluptuously sinking back against an epauletted shoulder, murmuring the most intoxicating promises, while some soft voiced tenor strummed his guitar and sang the traditional melodies of Russia, so nostalgic, so obsessive.... *Peterskaya Street*—the coachman's song; or *Evening Bells*:

> The haunting sound of evening bells
> That bring me back my youth,
> That ring me back my childish hopes
> Again, again . . .
> O! bring me back my youthful dreams,
> My childhood's home once more.
> Ring me my love—my love again,
> And then, no more, no more.

As the song died on an echo, the ladies and their artful coquetries were forgotten, as each man saw again the vast plains of Russia, the slow rivers and limitless horizons of their homeland. 'Golden headed Moscow', its thousand cupolas glittering amid the snows, the spice-laden dusk settling over the Fair booths at Nijni Novgorod; a samovar purring in the lamplight of a northern winter's day: to each exile—home.

Not one of these picnics, no song, no charmer, no detail of the Russians' life in camp, that was not reported in meticulous detail to

Shamyl by his spies. He believed in studying his enemy thoroughly: beside, he was curious as to the altogether unimaginable ways of the West.... New-fangled weapons, and big cannon which the mountaineers held in dread, calling them 'the Father of Guns' or 'the Tzar's Pistols'.... All the Russians' possessions, habits, every detail was noted. Even their indulgencies, breakfasts of mutton cutlets washed down by a pint of porter, or enormous quantities of cigars and cigarettes, were incomprehensible debauches to the puritan Murids, who were still compelled to admit that none of it prevented their fighting furiously.... Strange opponents, these gold-laced officers from the north, dancing, clasped to their half-naked women, drinking, and smoking—even in battle.... Shamyl and his Murids could not fathom their opponents.

So, while the picnic parties enjoyed a few hours of respite, hidden nearby, cat-footed and silent, the Lesghien spies were all around them, creeping through the forest undergrowth, crouched in the tree-tops, earthed in fox-holes, but always there, waiting, watching, with the hunter's stillness, with his unblinking stare.

V

There was from the beginning, from the first disastrous campaigns, a solidarity in this Army of the South which amounted to a family attachment, and was apparent between even the lumpish recruits and the more arrogant officers, to whom their men were *rebiata*—boys; while the men addressed their commanders as *batioushka*—little father. This was in marked contrast to the rigid sense of protocol, the reverence for rank which was instilled in the Guards' regiments, and those station-ed in the north, around Moscow or St. Petersburg. Here Generals were addressed—if addressed at all—as 'Most High Excellency'; Princes and Counts, apart from their army rank, were 'Your Illustriousness'; while less lordly, lower-grade officers were 'Your Nobility'. Since it was generally held that the army was the only honourable career open to a young aristocrat, the officers were, usually, heavy with titles, often deeply conscious of their rank, and unwilling to forgo the smallest mark of privilege and respect to which they considered their birth entitled them. Their troops, besides mastering the army grades, had also to be acquainted with the finer shades of ennoblement. It could have been a flogging matter to address an 'Illustrious' Captain as a 'High Noble Colonel'. Even the up-graded army rank would be no sop to an outraged princeling. Yet, in contradiction to these niceties, it was customary for every officer, from general to subaltern, to address his men as brothers, the traditional morning salute being: 'Good morn-ing, brothers.' This is said to derive from Peter the Great's address to his troops on the eve of the battle of Poltava: 'Brothers! Know that in to-morrow's battle your Tzar fights among you and watches you, but that the life of Peter, like your own, is as nothing compared with the welfare of the country which we serve in common.'

During the reign of Alexander I, a system of military colonies had been established, whereby the men were at once soldiers and land-workers; peasant-settlers and guards. Large, meticulously planned settlements were built in various provinces, with barracks, churches, officers' quarters and married quarters. The men were encouraged, or even commanded, to marry, their sons being integrated into the service from the age of seven. One hundred and forty-two thousand soldiers and three hundred and seventy-four thousand peasants made up the military colonies towards the end of Alexander I's reign, all of them seething with discontent, but helpless in the grip of an implacabe military administration. In 1819, the settlements in Novgorod resisted, but were quelled, like the soldiers of the Semenovski regiment, a few years later. Even the serf's bondage did not irk or humiliate the people as did this tyrannic militarism.

Ever since the young officers, who had defeated Napoleon in the 1812–14 campaign, had returned from their triumphant occupation of Paris, they had seen their fatherland in a very different light. The young Tzar Alexander whom they had adored, in whom they had believed so implicitly, was hardening, his idealism giving place to a kind of mystical despotism. The officers had absorbed the new currents of thought in Western Europe, but on their return they found a growing reaction, brutality and oppression awaiting them. This was the lot of the armies who had fought, they believed, for Liberty. 'They de-manded the fulfilment of promises. But they were given chains and prison cells.' So wrote Kalhovski, from his cell in the Fortress of St. Peter and Paul. So thought a legion of disillusioned army officers, who set about forming a number of secret societies, each vowed to freedom. The Society of the South, the Union of Public Welfare, or the Society of the United Slavs, were all forerunners of that last idealistic crystallization—the Dekabristi Society which, by 1825, was to pay so terribly for its aspirations, and to lie, crushed forever, at the feet of Nicholas I.

The abusive system of soldiers' settlements—the Cantonist ranks, was to continue for many years, and it was from among them that some of the troops in the Army of the South originated. The twenty-five-year term of service of the Cantonists was found here, too—some men had spent their whole lives campaigning, sent to the Caucasus when young, and remaining on, grizzled and hardy, to welcome their sons, sent to fight beside them as young recruits. Thus they often formed families, or clans, rather than regiments.

Beside the regular Orthodox priests who accompanied the regiments, each division had a Catholic chaplain and a Protestant pastor, for those who were of such faiths. Every campaign opened with the benediction of the Church. The massed forces were drawn up in a square formation, column on column; in the centre stood a group of priests who conducted mass, and then walked down the lines, sprinkling the troops with holy water. A roll of drums ended the ceremony, and set the army on the march, while the curious tumblers, buffoons and singers, attached to each company, marched alongside, beginning their leaps and grimaces, their strange grotesque music of tambourines, triangles and penny-whistles, interspersed with bawdy songs, by which they kept the men's spirits high. 'Ah! we went marching gaily then,' says a veteran, recalling his first Caucasian campaigns.

But presently, as they penetrated deeper into the dreaded wastes of Daghestan, no tumblers' antics, no bawdy songs could cheer them. However savage the campaigns in Tchetchen country, where sharp-shooters lurked behind every tree, and Russian losses were terrible, the land itself was not hostile. There were trees, grass, streams: it was a world they knew. Dying, there, the men still felt themselves among friends. Not so in Daghestan, where nothing lived: where an endless labyrinth of precipices and gigantic phantasmagoric peaks formed an accursed desolation—a hell, which they had reached before death.

Whether in the forests, or mountains, the regimental surgeons were an over-worked lot. Fevers and frost-bites augmented the wounded who were their charge. The surgeons shared the ardours of the campaigns, often fighting beside the troops. In such a terrain, transport to base hospitals was generally impracticable, so that the surgeons worked on the battlefield or in field wagons, as the troops advanced or retreated.

A good deal of ill-feeling was occasioned in 1848 among the army doctors and their families by a play, put on in St. Petersburg, which presented one of the most heroic sieges of the wars in circus terms, with the General's beautiful daughter bandaging the wounded on the ramparts, under heavy fire, while the doctor was portrayed as a comic, poltroon character. The Tzarevitch Alexander's personal physician, Henochin, took this as an insult to his profession, and complained in the most vigorous terms to the Emperor Nicholas. The monarch ordered the play to be withdrawn, or altered, immediately; and so awful was his displeasure, that the same night St. Petersburg audiences saw the doctor transformed, sabre in hand, stemming single-handed a whole Lesghien assault, while the comic coward's role was transplanted on to a Jewish vivandier.

In 1819, before the Murid Wars took shape, the permanent Russian force in the Caucasus numbered around fifty thousand men, divided into eight infantry, four chasseurs, two grenadiers, and one carbineer regiment; but later in the year, the Tzar Alexander, under pressure from Yermolov who foresaw the coming struggle, raised the number to about seventy-five thousand men, organized and dispersed in a manner calculated to hold down the restless natives without necessarily resorting to arms. The army of occupation was expected to live off the land, and to be entirely self-supporting; married companies in permanent garrison towns were 'to develop and steadily improve the domestic economy' of the garrison. The soldiers were expected to build their own forts and homes; to haul timber, quarry stone, plough, sow and reap, and be their own carpenters, bootmakers and tailors; it was an extension of the Cantonist system. A small garrison of three hundred men would be given its own team of bullocks, ploughs, troikas and horses, as part of its equipment, so that the earlier generations of Russian soldiers in the Caucasus were settlers as well as warriors.

Only twenty years later, with Shamyl's rise, it became necessary to pour in fresh regiments, guns and cannon, and more and more men whose sole business was to fight, to live or die under conditions of extreme hardship, living off the land in the terms of an army on the march rather than a garrison on settlement. Fighting in such a terrain, ill-equipped and scarcely trained, huge numbers of men had been levied from the provinces throughout Russia, from prison settlements, or from Poland (the latter losing no time in deserting to the mountaineers). These raw recruits often died before they had learned how to hold their bayonets. Fever and the general conditions killed off many of them. It was reckoned that 200,000 men were needed, each year, to replace the losses by battle and disease. A lack of organization, the loss of supply wagons, insufficient warm clothing, no boots and, at times, no weapons, reduced their ranks terribly. Against the furious Caucasians, whose whole life was dedicated to steel, they could not, at first, make much of a stand. It was only under pressure from his generals that Nicholas at last gave way, grudgingly, in this matter, and quantities of new guns and cannon had been dispatched across the whole length of Russia, the ox-wagons lumbering through the Gorge of Dariel, and down into Tiflis, many months later. But there was plenty of time, as, fortunately, there were plenty of men; war was to continue for another twenty-five years, demanding more, and ever more, in blood, and steel, and obedience, and faith.

'The force of the Russian army', wrote one observer, 'has ever been their profound love of country. Their belief in their military duty is woven together with their faith. Profoundly religious, the Russian soldier never separates, in his innermost thoughts, his country, his Tzar and his God. It is with this knowledge that the Russian generals, on the eve of battle, before pitting their men against death, speak to them of God. This might seem puerile in any other country, but here it produces an extraordinary effect. 'For the Russian soldier,' says Benckendorff, 'war is something sacred. He goes into battle as one entering a church, crossing himself and whispering a prayer.' 'God in our midst', said the soldiers of the ikon which each company carried with them.

Napoleon gauged the Russian soldier's mettle, their qualities of stoicism, and dedication: '*Pour vaincre le soldat russe, il ne suffit pas de le tuer, il faut le renverser,*' he wrote in bitter admiration. As fighters they were brave without bravura, they fought with cold conviction, but were never exalted as were their more volatile adversaries. Shamyl early recognized their qualities, and was often to hold them (and the French) up as examples to his own troops: hard words for his devoted Murids to accept. 'I would give all of you—such as you are— for only one of these regiments of which the Tzar has so many: with a body of Russian soldiers, I would have the whole world at my feet, and all would bow down before Allah, the only God, whose only prophet is Mahommed, whose chosen is none other than I—your Imam,' he stormed, after the defeat of Akhulgo in 1837. Shamyl was a born general: he fought with tactical brilliance and lion-like courage. He was quick to recognize the superiority of disciplined, manœuvrable troops over his more impetuous partisans. His own men were fanatic— the Russians were stoic: between these two poles, he believed, lay the highly trained professional armies of France: it was this model he wished to follow.

Yermolov was the first of the Russian generals to practise the *razzia*, or raid; he obtained the system from the Cossacks, who learned it themselves from their constant skirmishes with the tribes. But Yermolov's successors were more classical in their methods. It was to take several more years of fighting to acquire the new techniques. Meanwhile the Russian soldiers fought on, stubborn and devoted, under conditions which were terrible and strange to them. Lord Stratford de Redcliffe, watching from the British Embassy in Constantinople, described them as 'a million of soldiers trained to implicit obedience, selected from sixty million of ignorant and fanatical slaves'.

There was a touching humility in these simple souls. They seldom grumbled, and lived as they died, stoically. For country, God, and Tzar, all was accepted. Perhaps the lives they left did not offer much either. They were serfs, born to hardship and injustice, working their whole lives through for the enrichment of others, living and dying in darkness and superstition, in mud and snow, their only solace vodka. Whether soldiers or serfs they were born to serve their masters unquestioningly.

However, there were exceptions: occasionally they felt a sharp resentment. Tolstoy tells us that when, in the 'fifties, Prince Simon

Voronzov, son of the Viceroy of the Caucasus, a most privileged young officer, was joined in camp by his wife, the beautiful Princess Marie Vassilievna, the men were embittered. This accomplished coquette was the daughter of one of Alexander I's A.D.C's, Prince Vassili Troubetskoy. Her mother was the daughter of the Chief of Police in Vilno—'the greatest beauty of her age'; her daughter inherited her blonde loveliness. She was as indiscreet as her husband was indifferent. That Prince Bariatinsky, commander of the Left Flank, was her lover, was known to the whole Army of the South—her husband included. Petersburg goings-on, the men called it, and called her hard names, too, when she swept into their midst, her crinolines trailing the muddy fields, her aura of seduction, of perfumes and graces soon hidden under the tent-flap, from where a glow of candle-light, and the sound of popping champagne-corks and soft laughter could be heard in the still evening air. All through the night, while the jackals howled and yelped eerily in the hills, the soldiers were sent out, in pickets, to scour the countryside, to intercept any marauding Tartar bands, that the Princess might spend her nights comfortably. And when, as it often happened, there was a skirmish or ambush in the hills, and the men returned carrying the wounded or dead, they called the Princess a whore, a murderess, and spat as they passed her tent. But they knew their place. They did not rebel openly. Their forbearance and humility was only equalled by their courage.

These simple men made superb soldiers, unquestioning, stoic, and some foreign military observers appreciated them fully. 'The Russian trooper is very economic of his cartridges, for he has a superstitious feeling they belong to the Tzar.' 'Our powder belongs to the Crown,' they say, sharpening their bayonets cheerfully? And Dragomirov (from tactical rather than economic motives) stated that 'thirty cartridges should serve a good soldier for even the fiercest engagement'. The men scarcely thought to put a price on their own lives, these Ivans and Selifans and Kozmas, who were the essential fibre of the Russian army. The Caucasians, who fought for their liberty, for Allah, and for Allah's prophet, Shamyl, showed an almost greater degree of humility and endurance. They were able to withstand any climatic extremes, to fight with sabres when their guns had gone, and with daggers and javelins when their swords too were gone, and live and march whole days and nights on a handful of flour. So, while both sides were slowly reforming their system of warfare, the partisans becoming more disciplined, the Russians more supple, they were still well-matched adversaries.

8

The Cossacks

The Cossacks are the eye of the army.   SUVOROV

Above all, it was from the observation and practice of Cossack fighting that the Russian Army of the South learned to resist the Caucasian tribes. The Cossacks of the Line—'the advance guard of the advance guard' as they were called—were born and bred to the Caucasus. They were the Terek or Grebentsky Cossacks, and came of generations of frontiersmen, often interbred with the Caucasian women whom they had taken when raiding the mountain villages along the natural frontier formed by the river Terek. Sometimes their raids penetrated far into Kabarda or Tchetchen territory, unprovoked sorties or return raids to settle some mountaineers' foray. Circumstances had compelled them to compete on equal terms if they wished to survive. Therefore they fought and met the Caucasian guerilla tactics in kind. They rode like centaurs, on the small, vigorous horses of the steppes, performed all the vaunted feats of the Caucasian riders, lived off the land, and were the equal of the rebels in forest fighting. Since their communities had been long exempt from military service in the Russian army, on condition that they manned the frontier posts, they knew little of drill or formation fighting, but had evolved their own methods to hold the line. When border skirmishes passed into open warfare, and numbers of Russian regiments poured in from the north, it was seen that one Cossack outpost gave a better account of itself than a whole company of regulars. These untried northerners found that, unless they could force a battle on open ground, they had little chance of routing the mountaineers, who employed every ruse to lure them into rock or forest country, there to annihilate them, as Khazi Mollah had done after the siege of Vnezapnaya.

The Cossacks were more than regiments bred to guard the ever-thrusting frontiers of the Russian Empire. The Cossacks of the Line were only one section of a whole people, with their own way of life and traditions, reflecting their racial types and the region where they had first been imposed as a soldier settlement. However much they intermarried with the local population and absorbed the various regional characteristics, they remained apart, never wholly absorbed: they were, first of all, Cossacks—an unassimilating strain. The name 'Cossack' derives from 'Kazak', which, in Tartar, signifies vagabond.

While the Ukrainian Cossacks were rigidly Orthodox, those of the Don and the Volga were Sectarians, Raskolniki, or Old Believers, who resisted both Infidel and Orthodox, until at last they were defeated by Peter the Great at Poltava. They were a particularly stubborn lot, and adhered to various rituals which did not conform with the Muscovite clergy: for such seemingly trivial details as crossing themselves with two fingers, a special observance of the sacraments, and a reversal of Orthodox movements, anti-sun-wise around the high altar, they stoically accepted exile and persecution. There were, besides the Don Cossacks, the Cossacks of the Kuban, the Ural Cossacks and others, settled by the Russians all along their newly acquired frontiers, from the Black Sea to Siberia. Thus those guarding the lines of the trans-Baikal or Mongolian frontiers had an infusion of Turkic and Mongol blood, while the Terek, Grebentsky and Kuban Cossacks, crossed with a Circassian or Tartar strain, acquired something of the mountaineers' eagle-dark, aquiline beauty. All these widely different racial types were grafted on to the original blond, rather flat-faced, Slav type which is said to have originated in the nomadic tribes roving the steppes, marauding bands, driving their booty, cattle and women before them as they went. They first appear as rooted agricultural communities in Western Muscovy and Little Russia around the twelfth century. They were violent and stubborn, brooking no authority, spiritual or temporal, though eventually they professed Christianity, the Orthodox faith, and came to swear allegiance to the Princess of Muscovy.

As time went by they split into separate communities, their numbers increased by bands of desperadoes, 'outlaws or banished men' as two English traders of the Russian Company described them in 1573. They were men who had fled the law, runaway serfs, recruits escaping the regular military levies, or those who had fled religious persecution: hunted, desperate men, all of them, adventurers who had nothing to lose, but who found it best to keep on the move, to become one of a powerful group who could live beyond the reach of authority. Thus the Cossack camps, or *tabr*, began to assume the aspect of purely masculine, or even monastic, institutions; their inmates fighting celibates—not by choice, however, and they remedied their celibate state wherever possible, by making off with the women of the town they pillaged. Sometimes they carried them with them, more often they left them at a base against their occasional returns to the region.

Their leaders were known by the name of Hetman in the Ukraine, and in other regions as Ataman. Bogdan Chmielnicki and Mazeppa were celebrated figures in the hierarchy of Ukrainian Cossacks, while Platoff, Ataman of the Don Cossacks, took up arms against Napoleon. Another celebrated Cossack, Emilian Pugachov, was from the Volga-Ural regions. His revolt 'for Land and Liberty' cost him his life. But whether Hetman or Ataman, the Cossack chiefs had absolute power of life and death over their followers, living by their own strictly observed laws and codes of honour. Tarass Bulba—the Hetman round whom Gogol wove his marvellous tale—was impelled to kill his own son for disloyalty: something which Gogol's critics denounced as theatrical—exaggerated. But although Tarass Bulba is an imaginary character, he is the prototype of his kind. Not only did his code demand that he kill his own son, but that he stand among the crowd to watch another son tortured by the enemy; and to stand there to the end, proud witness of the boy's courage. At last, to die at the stake himself, having avenged his son's death and accomplished the whole savage pattern of his breed.

Tarass Bulba was a Zaporozhitz Cossack. Of all the Cossacks these were the wildest. Their name derives from the Russian word *porojzhi*—river falls. Their *Sietch*, or base camp, lay beyond the rapids of the Dnieper, one of the many islands that were strewn about the ever widening expanses of the river. As it flowed onwards it became a vast inland sea, surrounded by desolate marsh country, horizons of coarse grass and reeds, or sedge, where only the wild geese stirred, and where no plough had ever turned the earth. Here the Cossacks lived out their violent lives, alternating between plundering forays or punitive raids against their Polish persecutors, the Jewish money-lenders who were their traditional enemies, or the threats of Sultan or Tzar. It was a rhythm of epic battles and brutish delights. Here they built and repaired their wagons; brought their wounded after a battle: traded with the Jews or Armenians whose avarice overcame fear and led them, again and again, to the dangers of the Sietch, as goldsmiths, tanners, tailors, armourers, or money-lenders.

The Cossacks considered themselves the equal of any man. 'The Cossack does not doff his cap—even to the Tzar' was a cherished saying among them. They had their own standards of splendour; their boots were often heeled in silver plates which gave a metallic beat to their bounding Gopak dances, and to the squatting, kicking leaps of the *prisiadka*. Their baggy velvet trousers 'wide as the Black Sea' were generally daubed with tar—this being intended to show their indifference to fine materials; and every shaven head was adorned with a long scalp-lock, often two feet in length.

At the Sietch they practised their marksmanship, learned to swim the Dnieper against the current, hunted for game, gambled and drank, enjoying gargantuan feasts in keeping with their roaring appetites.

Drunkenness was considered almost a tribal rite. Here this apparently undisciplined, yet actually rigidly controlled, republic of adventurers lived by their own laws. Thieving among their own people was punished by death. The culprit was bound to the Pillar of Shame, a heavy club beside him. Each passer-by was bound to deal him a blow, until he died. A murderer's end was hideous. He was placed alive in an open grave, the body of his victim, in a coffin, laid on top of him, and the earth was shovelled over both of them, stamped down by the silver-heeled boots of the whole camp. No novice was considered a true Cossack until he had reached the Sietch by swimming the Dnieper (the great, flat-bottomed ferry-boats were for proven men, traders, and horses) and by killing at least one Moslem. Here, to the Sietch, they brought the prisoners and spoils: here they bred their celebrated horses, those small, narrow-headed, deep-chested, shaggy animals which were capable of such fabled speed and endurance. Of such a breed was the wild horse that galloped over the steppes with Mazeppa bound to his back. Much later, the Cossack horses changed in breed; Arab blood was introduced by Count Orloff (Catherine the Great's favourite), who bred them at Tambov. Here he produced a strain which came to be celebrated all over the world, as the Orloff Blacks.

Across the centuries, homeric bursts of laughter still sound; the shouting, belching, stamping and cries, like the smell of fresh blood and stale sweat that seems to rise from the marshes to hang in a miasma of savagery. Lit by the tongues of flame that flicker and sink among the charred ruins of a sacked village, we see them roasting an ox whole, stirring a giant cauldron of '*slava*', or '*glory*', a fiery brew composed of vodka, red wine and honey seasoned with pepper. Great, shaven-headed, hugely moustachioed men; weasel-faced rats, slit-eyed, or gap-toothed, slashed and scarred in a hundred fights. Men wearing ragged furs, red fox or wolf, over their bare bodies: wearing towering turbans sliced from a dying Turk's head; velvet caftans laced in gold, filched from a tembling boyar, and pearls ripped from some shrieking girl: Mandarin's robes, broad swords and chain mail—plunder by which they lived and had their being.

It was Potemkin, a figure whose gigantic animal force shared something of the Cossacks' own qualities of violence, who was to set about annihilating the Zaporozhitz Cossacks. The Empress Catherine believed they were be oming altogether too powerful, too daring. She ordered her favourite to subdue them. Their island headquarters, the Sietch, had for centuries seemed impregnable: but after a series of terrible struggles Potemkin's armies succeeded in routing them. Some fled to Turkish territory, and others were presently reorganized as the Black Sea Cossacks, centred on the Eastern shores of the Sea of Azov, where, their exuberance curbed, they were set to guard the newly acquired territories against attack. Thus they joined the rest of the Cossack settlements as a kind of living rampart against the enemy who lurked, ever-ready to spring, all the length of this vast empire. It was a triumph of colonization. In a letter dated April 25, 1785, the Empress Catherine writes: 'The Russian Empire cannot be destroyed, for we love and seek, and find, and establish order everywhere. It takes root, and I defy anyone to destroy it.'

II

The Grebentsky Cossacks were the first to penetrate the Caucasus, and eventually, to hold the Line. They were said to have originated in Riazan; but being goaded beyond endurance by the domination of the Tzar Ivan III, they decided to remove themselves farther afield. Thus they moved southwards, building powerful rafts, on which they, their families, herds and horses, were enabled to float down the Don, until, reaching the Volga, they followed its course to the Caspian, finally reaching the Terek and the shelter of the mountains. Here they settled and prospered, even coming to terms with the Caucasian tribes, who did not show themselves particularly hostile unless threatened. The Terek, stretching from one side of the Caucasus to the other, formed a natural boundary, and although the Cossacks were, in the main, tolerated by the tribes, they generally lived on the northern side of the river, making both forays and trading sorties into the mountaineers' country, southwards.

They considered themselves superior to both the 'savage' Tchetchens and the 'effete' Russians: no man could match them in battle, they boasted; and presently they began to regard themselves as a warrior caste, delegating all agricultural work to the women, or else hiring Nogai Tartars as labourers. These were the last degenerated remains of the once mighty Jewish Empire that had ruled from the steppes of the Volga to the Caspian. They had sunk apathetically, to become those tired, melancholy creatures who worked for the Cossacks. In appearance they rather resembled their flocks, with long, vacant faces. Traces of their Jewish past were to be found in their predilection for weeping, and the women met regularly to enjoy wailing parties, often weeping for events that had occurred a century ago. They explained their decline by saying they had achieved all that a race could: that God Himself no longer tolerated them, and that their hour had struck —they must go.

The Cossacks, either working themselves, or employing the Nogai Tartars, soon adapted themselves to the lands they held. In the Caucasus, along the Terek, they assumed many aspects of Caucasian life, besides their methods of fighting and riding. They copied the Kabarda and Tchetchen weapons, using the shashka rather than their own lance, and their women were often drawn from among the Kabardians or Tcherkess tribes. One of Ivan the Terrible's wives was a Tcherkess princess, with whom the Grebentsky Cossacks were on particularly good terms, and it was owing to her intervention that these outlaws were at last recognized by the Tzar. But in return he stipulated that they should build him a fortress at the mouth of the Soundja on the Black Sea, and hold it, in the name of Muscovy. Thus, fort by fort, frontier by frontier, man by man, the Cossacks came to defend Russia in heroic terms. But, by the middle of the nineteenth century, and on until the Revolution, they had come to represent the reactionary force and brutality by which they were used to impose the Tzarist regime. At last all the glowing adventure of their name became synonymous with pogroms, and unarmed workers falling under the nagaika, or Cossack whip. Only with the Revolution did they once again band together as an independent force—now opposing the Reds, now escaping to Turkey, now part of those marauding bands, fighting nomads, who roved the steppes of Outer Mongolia, harrying the Chinese. 'Our frontiers are across the saddle of a Cossack horse,' said the Chinese generals, falling back before the Cossack thrusts during the post-revolutionary era of Asiatic conflict. Later, more of the Cossacks who had remained in the Don and Kuban territories were absorbed into the Red army, fighting magnificently against the Nazis. The renowned Marshal Budenny was a Cossack from the Kuban, his picturesque, rather florid appearance, hugely moustached, his fur papakh set at a jaunty angle, his whole air at once ruffianly and heroic, was in the direct tradition of his Cossack ancestry.

During the eighteenth century Russia's demands had become increasingly heavy. The Cossacks were expected to provide food and quarters for the troops, fodder for their horses, to scout for them and act as spies and interpreters, repair the roads and bridges, and continue to cultivate the land as well as insuring the free passage of the government couriers. Soon, the Cossacks found themselves part of Russia's military organization, which, while resenting, they yet accepted. Each man had to furnish his own horse and weapons: each family had to supply one man towards the formation of a Cossack regiment, which absolved them from supplying recruits to the regular Russian regiments, and gave them a communal ownership of rich lands taken from the Caucasians. These were generous rewards— but no more than the just deserts of such fighters as the Cossacks; without them the Caucasus could never have been taken, and it was particularly bitter for Shamyl and the mountaineers to find those very Cossack settlers with whom they had lived in comparative harmony, with whom they had, as it were, enjoyed the exchange of plundering forays, now turned against them in earnest, aiding the hated Infidel invaders.

As the war in the Caucasus hardened into a life and death struggle, Cossack reinforcements had to be dispatched from the farthest Don and Ural settlements. But they came very unwillingly, for they had never been threatened by the Caucasians: yet when defending Russia against an outside enemy—such as the French or Turkish armies—they fought superbly. They had arrived at a state of absolute submission to Russian militarism; fighting had become their trade and their pride. They were mercenaries.

Everywhere, all along the line, the Cossack *stanitzas*, or settlements, showed a profound piety. As soon as one was built, even if it were the crudest log stockade, a five-domed church would be added. Long before this was completed, the Cossacks would have arranged a fine peal of bronze bells, often strung on posts, or from a tree, like some strange fruit, and sounding soft and deep across the wilderness. They had a truly Russian passion for bells: sleigh bells, church bells, bells on their cattle, bells hung on the hoop of wood, the *douga*, which curves over every cart or carriage horse; bells on the camels that ploughed the green fields along the Amur, bells at morning, bells at evening, sounding across the silky stillness of Lake Baikal, bells sounding from a legion of Cossack outposts, in the plains and mountains and valleys hemmed with enemies; bells which spoke to them of the thousand belfries that boomed and pealed and clanged and hummed over Mother Moscow, Golden-Headed Moscow, heart of Russia, from which they were excluded, yet which they lived and died to defend.

The Cossack *kreposts*, or small forts, were admirably organized, models of practical planning, economic of men and material, and suited to the country they dominated. They were always small, often inhabited by only half a dozen men, never far from the next post, usually within gunshot, so that a system of alarm signals could be exchanged, and if necessary, mutual help could be obtained quickly. Each krepost had its watch-tower and alarm bell: the fortifications were often only a rough clay-walled square with slit windows, as in the forts established by the Americans, in Indian territory. Every stanitza and krepost had its guard post, a primitive contraption of four stout poles, twenty or more feet in height, hammered firmly into the earth, which had on top a sort of cross-barred seat reached by a ladder. Here the look-out man sat, much as the whalers' look-out man perched high on the mast-head, scanning the horizon. Here, by day and by night, he watched and listened. A rustle in the reeds down by the river, a glint of light in the valley, spelt danger. All around, seemingly empty, yet menacing wastes, silent steppes, vast distances where, as the sun sank behind the darkening mountains, no man knew if he would live to see the morning.

At a given signal, the whole chain of forts could communicate, sounding an alarm, or lighting a beacon which concentrated large relief forces within a matter of hours. But battles here were often a matter of minutes only. And as the Murid Wars took shape, and flamed into all their terrible force, the relieving troop would sometimes come on a blackened, still smoking ruin, with no living soul to tell what had happened. Then, before the blood had dried on the ground, a little graveyard would spring up; spears stuck in the ground marked the graves of the tribesmen, and a rough wooden cross, that of the Cossacks. Generally, the mountaineers were punctilious in collecting their dead. A truce was always called by the Russian commanders for this purpose; but in certain isolated skirmishes, or after some over-whelming engagement where the dead lay in huge numbers, they were buried beside their enemies, Moslem and Pagan and Christian, quiet, at last, in the dark Caucasian earth.

9

The Struggle

When will blood cease to flow in the mountains?
When sugar-canes grow in the snows.

CAUCASIAN PROVERB

Although Shamyl was convinced of his mission, of Allah's divine promptings, he was not, by nature, personally ambitious. He did not seek power or aggrandizement except as a means to an end—the execution of Allah's will. He would have served humbly under any leader he believed capable of restoring Muridism and Caucasian independence. Where these two ends were concerned, he was ruthless. If it were expeditious to destroy those who stood between him and fulfilment, whether friend or foe, they must perish. The Russians had killed Khazi Mollah, and, often as the two friends had disagreed over tactics, in matters of their faith and loyalty they were united. They had never come to a real issue over the conduct of the war. Yet Khazi Mollah's death may have spared them a final rupture. He lacked Shamyl's qualities of leadership. The day would probably have come when Shamyl could no longer serve under him, or the people themselves would have turned, instinctively, towards the younger man, recognizing his stature. But before that day, before Shamyl's election as third Imam and accession to absolute power, there was still one more drama to be played out by the rise and fall of Hamzad Beg, who succeeded Khazi Mollah as second Imam.

His reign was brief and ignoble: his end violent and deserved, brought about by his own treachery. Hamzad Beg was, first of all, an *abrek*, or outlaw, his whole life lived by violence and cunning. He changed his colours to suit his gains, and was unstable, dangerous and daring. He was born in Avaria in 1789. His childhood was indulged, his education excellent; he spoke Georgian, Arabic and Persian. His father had been of *Djanka* origin: the Djankas were children of mixed marriages—noble on one side, common stock on the other; sometimes they were the children of Khans by morganatic marriages, but they never assumed the rank of their noble parent. Hamzad Beg's father had gained riches and privilege through valour. He had been attached to the court of Akhmet, Khan of Avaria, at Khounzak, and in recognition of his services to her husband, the widowed Khanum Pakkou-Bekkhé, whose heroic defence of her capital had already been told, adopted the young Hamzad as a member of her household, treating him as one of her sons, a generosity he was to repay later, with treachery.

After some years of life at the Khan's court, he returned to his home town, a spoiled, self-centred good-for-nothing, leading a life of dissipation and hard drinking. But suddenly, with that curious pattern followed by certain mystics, who step overnight into grace from debauch, he cast aside all the habits of his youth, and flung himself into religious studies under Khazi Mollah at Ghimri. He rose quickly in the hierarchy of the medrassah, to become one of the inner circle of Murids, who, however much they planned action, a holy war, still drew their spiritual inspiration from the Sufi teachings of the old Jamul u'din.

When the campaigns of 1831-2 broke out, Hamzad Beg led a force of men to engage the Russians, and defend the Djar provinces. But he was defeated overnight, and the country was annexed by Russia; at which, sailing with the wind, he pressed to offer his submission. In many cases, the submission of a prince or powerful Khan, such as Pakkou-Bekkhé's husband had been, was well worth the cost of a pension to the Russians, particularly when the prince in question sided openly with them against Muridism. But here, Hamzad Beg appeared exactly what he was—a treacherous creature, a poor fighter, a greedy worthless man. When he arrived at the Russian headquarters at Tiflis to discuss the delicate matter of the pension, he was treated with scorn, and even arrested.

That he was presently freed was due to a matter of private vengeance, approached in that elliptical fashion so typical of the Orient.

His release was brought about through the intercession of Aslan, Khan of Kazi-Koumouk, a ruler who had proved his loyalty to Russia, and who now answered for Hamzad Beg's good conduct. The motives beneath his moves to free Hamzad were very simple. He saw in him a means of revenge—not on the Russians, but on Pakkou-Bekkhé.

Aslan was a man who burned with a sense of injury; he lived to avenge himself. His hatred was that of the scorned and rejected suitor. He had been promised Pakkou-Bekkhé's daughter Sultanetta. But, suddenly, that stern matriarch had broken off the marriage, preferring an alliance with the Shamkal of Tarkou's son. Aslan had been passionately in love with Sultanetta, and now he planned Pakkou-Bekkhé's downfall with a deliberate cruelty. No matter if it should take years to bring about. There was time. . . . But he would get his revenge, and enjoy it. He had found it impossible to turn the Russians against Pakkou-Bekkhé. She had continued loyal to her husband's obligations and treaties, as we have seen, proving herself both in the heroic defence of Khounzak, and afterwards. Her sons, too, were determined to resist Muridism and stand beside the Russians. So Aslan bided his time, until, in Hamzad Beg, he saw an instrument of vengeance. Thus, from the hatred of a slighted lover, grew terrible consequences which were to change the whole face of the Caucasian wars.

He set about poisoning Hamzad's mind against the Khanum. He dwelt on her wealth, her power over her people; the necessity of removing her. He who did so would ingratiate himself with the Murids, and, with her downfall, the whole of Avaria could be brought under their black banners . . . He was speaking disinterestedly, as a friend . . . His only loyalties lay with Russia, of course. . . . But if Hamzad Beg felt himself rejected by them. . . . If he felt that, after all, his place was at Ghimri, among the Murids, what better token of devotion, of leadership, than to win over Khounzak, and all Avaria, to the cause? Whoever achieved this would become a hero, a liberator, a great figure in the Murid ranks, respected alike by the tribes and the Russians. Thus he played on Hamzad's pride.

Inexplicably, in this land where weakness was never condoned, and treachery was punished by death, Hamzad Beg presently reappeared at Ghimri, to become, once more, a trusted member of the Murid ranks. Why his ignominious submission to Russia was overlooked, we do not know: nor do we know by what means he succeeded in convincing both Khazi Mollah and Shamyl of his sincerity, but, in any case, he was once again beside them at the mosque, and on the battlefield, one of the inner circle of Murids who occupied positions of trust.

After the fall of Ghimri, when his cowardly retreat from the mountain-top also seems to have been overlooked, he ventured to return among the shattered Murid ranks, as they began to reform, in secret, though without a leader, after Khazi Mollah's death and Shamyl's disappearance. Shamyl had made his escape from the ruins of the beleaguered watch-tower in the spectacular fashion already described (with a tiger-spring over the heads of the Russians, in a slashing one-man battle), but he was known to be terribly wounded, pierced by a dozen sword-thrusts. He had vanished into the darkness with another of those tiger-leaps, like a wild beast, to die alone somewhere in the wastes. His body had never been found, either by the Russians or the Murids, though both had searched the surrounding country. No one doubted that he had died of wounds, and already his memory began to assume a legendary quality.

The Murids needed a new leader: there was no one to rally them. In their dispersed and shattered condition, they cannot be blamed for taking Hamzad Beg as their second Imam. He accepted the honours and responsibilities without hesitation. For him, they were a means to personal aggrandizement. He immediately gathered some Russian deserters whom he formed into a corps, commanded by their own officers, to fight beside the Caucasians. In some cases they were Poles, conscripted into the Russian army as so much cannon-fodder. Their hatred of the Russians was extreme; so that Hamzad Beg felt himself safe to make them his personal body-guard: but this scheme did not prove altogether successful, since the highly-drilled Western troops could not fight successfully beside such independent, guerilla fighters as the Caucasians.

During the first eighteen months of his rule, Hamzad Beg was largely preoccupied with mustering his army, and arousing the people's interest and sympathy by a display of fanatic zeal. First of all he set about castigating them, imposing even further denial and prayer. Then he sentenced himself (for his defeat in battle) to a hundred and one blows.

It was a blood sacrifice, and also an impressive theatrical spectacle for the people, whom he realized, shrewdly enough, must be kept enthralled. They had few pleasures left now. Muridism saw to that. Djighitovkas and marriage feasts were curtailed. Music and dancing were forbidden: indeed, so austere was the tenor of life now, that some tribes (particularly the Suanetians) used to order and participate in their own funeral feasts, after which there seemed little left to look forward to.

Hamzad Beg allowed no memory of his own unregenerate youth to temper the sentences he passed on defaulters. Even minor indulgences such as smoking or drinking were severely penalized. Soon his piety and divine inspiration were unquestioned: his power became absolute. Now he could relax. Now he could turn his thoughts to more personal issues. At last he could begin to plan the overthrow of Pakkou-Bekkhé. This was the way to bring all Avaria under his rule, and to reappear before the Russians as a redoubtable enemy. Aslan Khan had been right: besides, it would be a suitable way to repay Aslan's good offices in obtaining his freedom from the Russians. Aslan himself contrived to walk a tight-rope between the Russians and the tribes, remaining on good terms with both. Occasionally he goaded Hamzad Beg by reference to Pakkou-Bekkhé's apparent invincibility. She still stood, he said, sword in hand, between her people and Muridism, which all the Caucasus now craved. Any gratitude towards Pakkou-Bekkhé, any remembrance of her generosity to him in his youth, does not seem to have entered Hamzad Beg's head. But before he could put his designs into practice, Shamyl was to re-enter his life, to reappear at Ghimri among the Murids, like some shade returned from the dead.

II

All these months Shamyl had lain in hiding in the mountains, not far from Ghimri. His lungs had been pierced, his flesh slashed with innumerable sword-thrusts, several ribs were broken, and two bullets remained in his body. He had been found by some shepherds who had escaped the taking of Ghimri; they had known him as a boy, for their saklias, or huts, lay on his nightly path towards the mountain-tops, those dread regions where no one dared to follow him. The shepherds had sheltered and cared for him, fetching his father-in-law, Abdul Aziz, the celebrated surgeon, to save him. Moreover, they had brought Fatimat, his wife, to him, without revealing his whereabouts or, indeed, his existence to anyone else. It was found that Shamyl's wife had disappeared from the hiding place where the mountaineers had placed their women and children before the battle began. It was believed that she had gone to search for her husband's body, and fallen into Russian hands.

After a while Fatimat was forgotten: women were of little consequence, to the Faithful. They were chattels, scarcely held to have souls. Yet Shamyl loved his wife with so consuming a passion that once, during a battle, learning she lay at death's door, he abandoned everything to go to her.

Now she came to him. These months in hiding were perhaps the only quiet they had ever known, their only life lived together in love and stillness. For ever after, there were Shamyl's constant preoccupations with his life as a Murid, as Prophet and Warrior, in which Fatimat had no part. But now they were alone together in the little saklia, and for a while, until his wounds healed and until the world pressed urgently upon them, they could think only of each other. No news from the outside reached them. The shepherds had heard there was a price on Shamyl's head, set by the Russians who were unconvinced of his death. But they had soon given up the search. These mountain devils were impossible to track. . . . If he still lived, he had gone to earth, and it was useless to hunt for him, said the staff officers. They did not think him of great consequence, anyhow: the price only amounted to three hundred roubles—a very small sum. There was other work to be done: provinces to be occupied, pockets of resistance to be cleared up, forts to be built and held, aôuls still to be stormed. No one thought of a handful of huts high on the ridges above Ghimri. The saklias lay beyond the range of either Murids or Russians. A few ramshackle stone shelters. What use were they? Who lived there? Some old shepherds and their wives: besides, the whole region was accursed: let them be.

In some of the mountain country, whole villages of saklias were hidden, burrowed into the rocks, troglodyte fashion, so that a rider could pass over the roofs without being aware of their existence. Others were shacks, above ground, but wretched quarters, even for the hardy Caucasians. They are traditionally constructed of rough stones piled one on another, the chinks between them are rarely filled up with clay, but remain open to the wind and rain. At night the light of the fires glows out from between the uneven stones and the smoke seeps through to mingle with the damp eddies of mist and cloud which generally hang about the mountain-tops. In Shamyl's day the shepherds seldom came down to the aôuls except for some special needs; to repair a weapon, to purchase some rare luxury, tobacco, a flute, or a new bourka. Their women spun cloth from rough sheep's wool: they cobbled their shoes together from crudely dressed buckskin, and lived chiefly on a rough millet bread, sour milk and goats' cheese, which they patted into large rounds and set to weather on the roofs. These roofs were generally roughly thatched over with twigs and boughs dragged up from the scrub-covered lower slopes. There were no trees, no vegetation of any kind in the highlands: it was a phantasmagoric landscape of rocks, crags, stones, peaks and glaciers.

Alongside the cheeses spread on the roof there was usually an array of flat, mud-like bricks, composed of dried cattle dung, straw and water, trodden down to a tight-packed substance known as *kourpitch*, and used for fuel. According to the length of time this mixture is stored and dried, so is the degree of heat which it gives out. Well-packed kourpitch burns fiercely and glows like coal. Food cooked on it has a special, not unpleasant flavour, a smoky-sour tang which, to those who have tasted it, always evokes the Caucasus: a flavour which at once conjures up the towering peaks, the rock wastes, the chill uplands, and tart smoke-filled atmosphere of any saklia. Here, crouched on sheepskins, barely sheltered by the walls (bleached with wind and sun and rain outside, and blackened to a gleaming oily darkness by the dense smoke within), the traveller, not yet wholly ensnared by the strange obsessive fascination of the Caucasus, thinks longingly of the comparative comfort of any ordinary aôul—these being, in themselves, of a bleakness unimaginable to most of the pampered West.

To Shamyl and Fatimat, the shepherd's saklia must have represented paradise. They would not have missed the rugs or cushions or few comforts which made up the simple furnishings of their home at Ghimri. The Caucasian people are by nature austere; besides Shamyl had long practised a monkish detachment from the world and the flesh. Only Fatimat, with her beauty, her womanly grace, could have still held him to earthly delights. It was, no doubt, for her sake he had continued a traditional domestic pattern. He did not share Khazi

Mollah's whole-hearted belief in renunciation, nor believe he had out-raged a jealous God by being happy with her. Did not the Koran say, 'Woman is thy field, go then to thy field and till it'? (although it also said: 'Woman is the camel to help man through the desert of existence.)'

As often as his life of battle and endeavour permitted, in these early days, Shamyl must have returned to Fatimat's side—playing with his little son Djemmal-Eddin and the cats he loved; stretched on cushions beside the glowing brazier, his weapons laid aside, the beads of his amber tespyh sliding through his fingers endlessly, we imagine him watching Fatimat moving about the room, padding softly, her feet thrust into embroidered red leather slippers, the heavy silver bracelets clinking on her fine-boned wrists as she served him the millet cakes, rice and honey which were his usual meal. She wore the costume of her race and rank, that of a Daghestani gentlewoman: loose, flowered silk trousers almost hidden by a full-skirted, tight-waisted surcoat with wide, flowing sleeves and elaborate silver-braided fastenings. A great many gold and silver coins hung from the end of the long black braids, four or five of them, into which her hair was divided. Fine muslin veils and coloured silk kerchiefs were wound round her head and across her face when she left the privacy of her quarters; and on gala occasions she wore a tall pointed cap or head-dress, from which more veils flowed. In summer, she went barefooted; in winter her slippers were protected from the mud and snow by high wooden clogs or pattens. Instead of the bourka which men wore against the piercing Cacuasian winters, she was wrapped in an embroidered felt cloak lined with fox skins, or sables even.

A certain luxury prevailed among the mountain nobles, for it was customary to raid the merchants' caravans as they filed through the pass of Dariel. Here the caravans could be trapped easily enough; their guards shot down, and the haughty, groaning camels and pack mules unloaded. Here, between the rocks which rose to such im-probable heights, a handful of 'Tartars' could swoop and scatter even a well-armed military escort, making off with the spoils before rein-forcements could arrive. Thus, both the merchandise of Tiflis and the East, brocades, silks, tea, spices, jade, and fine furs were intercepted as they were transported northwards, while baggage trains of goods coming south to Tiflis and the spas, laden with goods from Moscow and St. Petersburg, gold watches, china, Tula silver, French laces, snuff, ribbons and bales of fine materials from Manchester cloth mills were likewise seized, and found their way into the more prosperous aôuls, such as Ghimri had been before its fall, before the Murids' renunciatory creed had taken hold.

At her waist, the delicate, supple waist for which her race was famed, Fatimat wore a gold and ivory handled dagger which was no mere ornament, for every woman was taught how to use one, for defence or attack. Pushkin sounded the heart-beat of the people when he wrote: 'I know how to use a dagger, I was born in the Caucasus.'

Like all Caucasian women, Fatimat was very slim and graceful. Even on the rare occasions when a traveller records seeing a plain face in the mountains, he invariably goes on to remark exceptional grace of carriage and movement.

It was the custom for Caucasian girls to be laced into a tight corselet of deerskin which constricted and formed their narrow bodies (and was said to induce lung disorders) but undoubtedly accounted for much of their attenuated grace. This corselet was put on, with cere-mony, around the age of eight, and it was never removed until their marriage, generally at the age of fourteen, or thereabouts, when it was the bridegroom's privilege to rip open the seams with his kindjal. As a refinement of *volupté*, in some marriage cermonials, along with the token rape or abduction of the bride found all over the near East, the bridegroom was expected to untie, knot by knot, the long line of leather thongs which laced his bride's corselet. This complicated undertaking was designed both to heighten the fever of desire and to prove the bridegroom's control, or self-mastery. A too impatient or bungling lover lost all respect in the eyes of both his bride and the community.

Fatimat, during her brief life, must have found Muridism a rival more powerful, more possessive than any woman. Shamyl was not as others; he was a dedicated being set apart, and no one, not even she, his adored wife, the mother of his first-born son (the Eastern woman's proudest boast), could ever encroach on his life as Allah's mouthpiece. She must have learned to put away all considerations of personal happiness, submerging herself, knowing herself to be of little moment beside the goal of Murid faith and Caucasian independence.

That is why, at last being together in the faraway saklia, with nothing left but each other, they must have been able—for the space of Shamyl's recovery—to live in that magic, self-centred vacuum of all lovers.

Even so, there were intrusions. Shamyl's sister descended on the saklia, filling the air with reproaches and lamentations. Her brother's stubborn adherence to the Shariat had reduced the family—and all the survivors of Ghimri—to misery. Was her brother badly wounded; or was he perhaps malingering, or did he simply long to be with Fatimat? Wounded, yes—but enjoying himself too—that must not be, not while Ghimri lay in ashes, its people living in fox-holes or caves: not while she, his sister, was there to remind him where his duty lay.

We are told that Shamyl was lying on a heap of straw, his face as expressionless under the lash of her tongue as in the heat of battle. Fatimat crouched beside him, silent before the invading fury. Her sister-in-law's voice rose and fell like the huge shadows cast by the flickering wood fire. As she gesticulated and rent her veils in the traditional way, her bracelets jangled, the firelight sparking off the beaten gold and rough-cut stones. She had contrived to save some of her treasures when Ghimri fell and saw nothing incongruous in wearing them now. As she continued her recital of the people's plight, the magnitude of defeat, and Russia's might, Shamyl's fever mounted. When at last she was persuaded to leave, he suffered a relapse, and his wounds reopened.

Later, when Shamyl insisted on miraculous powers and divine support, he used to declare his wounds had reopened in a protest directed by Allah against his sister's jewels, against her wanton display of earthly treasures wholly unacceptable to the Lord. And there was no one who cared to dispute it.

III

When at last Shamyl reappeared among the Murids, he never spoke of his escape or his life in the saklia, nor did he allow anyone to question either himself or Fatimat. He had returned. That was all. Was he loth to tell of those months of weakness; or was a strain of theatricality asserting itself again? Was he once more fostering, deliberately, his miraculous legend—that of a marked being—supernaturally preserved, to continue Allah's work? In any case, it is proof of his disciplined nature, his lack of personal ambition, that he at once became Hamzad Beg's most devoted lieutenant, serving under him loyally.

Together they ranged the country, establishing the Tarikat, organizing bands of armed men sworn to resist Russian authority by force. Avaria seemed a rich prize, its people now only held back from integration into the Murid ranks by Pakkou-Bekkhé's will. Pakkou-Bekkhé played for time, and dispatched her second son Omar to Tiflis, to ask for Russian support against Hamzad Beg's threats. The young Khan Omar was accompanied by his foster-brother, Hadji Mourad. We shall hear more of him later, for he became famous throughout the Caucasus, his legend, like his might, only second to that of Shamyl, whose most powerful ally and dangerous rival he became. And his death fired Tolstoy to write a masterpiece.

When they rode into Tiflis, they found Baron Rosen, the Commander-in-Chief, had no time for them. He sent some of his elegant aides-de-camp who distracted them with cards, wine, and women. In the words of Hadji Mourad, who was not caught by their wiles: 'Omar's body was as strong as a bull, and he was brave as a lion, but his soul was weak as water. . . . He would have gambled away his last horses and weapons if I had not made him leave.'

The Russians' indifference turned the two young men against them, and on their return, they advised Pakkou-Bekkhé to accept Muridism. When Hamzad and his Murids stood before the city, they sent their emissaries to meet him, saying they would join the Ghazavat, if the Imam would send a learned man to explain it to them. 'But Hamzad shaved off our Elders' beards, pierced their nostrils, and hung cakes from their noses, like buffoons, and sent them back to us, saying they would send us a sheik to teach us the principles of the Ghazavat—but only if Pakkou-Bekkhé sent her youngest son, Boulatch, as hostage.'

The Khanum was a most determined woman. She still held to her pact with the Russians. But now, as Muridism flamed and spread through the land, she knew she could no longer restrain her people. She therefore agreed to adopt Muridism—but refused the Ghazavat. She would not take up arms against her late allies. On this point she was adamant. But, as a token of her good faith, she sent Prince Boulatch, a child of eight, to Hamzad Beg's camp, as the hostage he demanded. Still Hamzad was not satisfied, and demanded that her eldest sons, Abou Noutzal Khan and Omar Khan, should be sent to negotiate a treaty.

Omar rode out alone, but after some hours had passed, without news of him, the distracted mother ordered her remaining son Abou Noutzal to go to his rescue. The Prince guessed the fate that awaited him—he sensed Hamzad Beg's treachery—and he refused to walk into the trap. Pakkou-Bekkhé flew into one of her redoubtable rages and taunted him with cowardice.

'You are prepared then, to lose your last son!' said Abou Noutzal. 'So be it. I will go.' And he flung himself into the saddle and galloped towards Hamzad Beg's camp, followed by a small company of *noukkers*, or pages—among them, Hadji Mourad. Arriving at the Murid camp he was received with honours and conducted to the tent where his brothers were lodged. But as soon as the tent-flaps had fallen behind him, Hamzad Beg's men sprang on the noukkers, butchering them where they stood. Hearing the firing and the cries, Omar rushed from the tent, and was himself cut down. Abou Noutzal drew his sword and dagger and went out to avenge his brother's death. According to Hadji Mourad, one of his cheeks had been hacked off, and hung down. He held it with one hand, and with the other fought off all who came near him with his dagger. 'Springing on them like a raging lion, he killed right and left, accounting for more than twenty Murids before he died of wounds, himself.' The little Boulatch was dragged shrieking from the tent by Hamzad Beg. Hadji Mourad (on his own admission) was suddenly seized with terror, for the first and last time in his life, and leaping on a horse he made his get-away, escaping the rain of spears the Murids flung after him. So ended the Khounzakis' resistance to Hamzad Beg.

The two Murid chiefs had been quite unmoved by the slaughter. For Hamzad it was the execution of a long-cherished plan: the payment of an old debt. For Shamyl, an action purely incidental to battle, something essential to the conquest of Avaria. Together they now returned to the capital, where, having at last cornered the Khanum, the Amazon Pakkou-Bekkhé, torn the sword from her grasp, and beheaded her with it, Hamzad Beg proclaimed himself Khan of all Avaria: moreover he so far forgot his Murid vows of abnegation and self-denial as to install himself in the palace in a most ungodly luxury.

When the news of this victory reached Aslan Khan, that foxy prince was overjoyed. He dispatched a runner with two letters for Hamzad Beg: one, designed to save his face with the Russians, upbraided Hamzad for his cruelty and threatened him with vengeance. The other, hidden in a fine gold watch from the Tiflis goldsmiths, was flowery with compliments. 'O Faithful Hamzad! Henceforth you are my son. Together we will purge the country of unbelievers.'

IV

In the Caucasus, *kanly*—vendetta—was the whole creed of these people, often pursued through three or four generations. Sometimes whole families were destroyed, fighting for days and nights, till the last man or boy fell. Others, known as 'poor' families, those who had no fighters left, no more blood to spill, were immured for the rest of their lives, old men, weaklings and women, in some lonely watch-tower. They never dared to venture out, for they were disgraced and menaced. Food and water were left for them by pitying friends, but as they could not fight, they had no place in the community. Occasionally pale faces could be glimpsed, ghost-like, at the window, only to draw back sharply, fearing to be seen by their traditional foes, who prowled and waited, year upon year, to finish the fight. One step outside the door, and it would all be over. Such traditions decimated the population. Shamyl had always been opposed to them, and upon becoming Imam he tried to stamp out the whole tradition of kanly. The Russians, on the contrary, encouraged it, cynically. It was a practical method of wiping out the more explosive elements of the tribes. With a population regularly reduced by violence, whether inter-tribal, inter-family or regular warfare, the Caucasians first wish was for sons—to carry on the fight. Everywhere, widows were expected to remarry within a few months of their bereavement. Some tribes, such as the Ingoush, adopted curious measures. Any woman, single or widowed, could lie down across her threshold at night, her face veiled, and the man who accepted this invitation was performing a ritual duty. If a child was born of the union it was the charge of the whole community, and brought up in love and honour.

Vengeance being the order of the land, the murder of Pakkou-Bekkhé and her sons was presently to be avenged by two brothers, Osman and Hadji Mourad—he whose name was to ring through the Caucasus, second only to Shamyl in his heroic stature and legendary qualities, and of whom Tolstoy has left us his wonderful description.

At the moment of which I write, however, the moment of Hamzad Beg's approaching doom, Hadji Mourad was still one of the younger, lesser Murid hierarchy. He had been closely allied to Pakkou-Bekkhé's children, for his own father had been chosen, in the traditional Caucasian way, as the Prince Omar's foster-father, and Hadji Mourad and his brother had spent much of their youth at the Khan's palace. They now determined to avenge the slaughter. Their plans were known to several other Murids, and were probably suspected by a large number of the community, to whom it had been apparent for some while that their Imam was not the inspired and holy figure they had once imagined. Perhaps it was as well if he should now meet a martyr's death. They whispered among themselves, and began to take sides. One of Hamzad's lieutenants warned him of the conspiracy, but he dismissed him with fatalism. 'Who can turn away the Angels of Death when they come for my soul? What Allah has decreed must be.'

Next day, Friday, the Moslem day of prayer, a strange stillness hung over Khounzak. It was a pale September morning, the mountain peaks hidden by low clouds: at noon the muezzin sounded faintly, as if muffled by the mists. Hamzad Beg and twelve of his Murids went slowly through the deserted streets towards the mosque. The dark, cloaked figures walked majestically: they were wrapped from head to foot in their bourkas, their shaggy sheepskin caps shadowing their faces, their soft leather boots making no sound on the cobbles. They stepped delicately towards their doom.

The mosque at Khounzak was a low, grey-walled building, ill-lit and bare. It had none of the wordly magnificence of the Sulimanyé, or the gilded richness of the mosques at Tlemcen, or Cairo. In its austerity it was typical of the Caucasus, where houses, landscape, men and mosques, too, reflect the harshness of life.

Hamzad Beg entered the mosque and, taking up his place, began to pray, his followers beside him. Suddenly in the dark depths of the building, something stirred—the shadows thickened, shifted, and emerged as men—a group of crouching figures who advanced swiftly on the Imam. They were led by Osman and his brother Hadji Mourad, who flung back their bourkas, revealing their weapons. Before anyone could intervene, they had fired on Hamzad Beg and stabbed him, too. A Murid sprang on Osman and killed him, and conspirators and

Murids now engaged in a desperate fight, the population crowding in from without to join in the slaughter, till the prayer-rugs were sodden with blood and the walls and pillars spattered with shot.

Shamyl was absent from Khounzak, but when the news reached him, some days later, he wasted no time. His hour had struck . . . Enough of blood-feuds and vengeance—now all must be concentrated in one vast united force, fighting Russia together, their private enmities submerged in their submission to Allah's will. He rallied his men, marched on the aôul of Gotsak where Hamzad Beg's treasury was guarded, and where the little Prince Boulatch had languished in prison since the murder of his brothers. Shamyl was always to show himself ruthless where the execution of his duty, as he saw it, lay. Now he was determined to have no more intrigues, no pretenders, such as the princeling might become, in the hands of his enemies. Nothing, now, must turn him from his goal. Ghazavat! Holy War on the infidel Invaders. He seized the treasury, loaded it on mules, and ordered Boulatch to be strangled, his body flung down a ravine. This being done, he had himself proclaimed third Imam of Daghestan, and turned his horse towards Ghimri.

It was a terrible beginning to a reign at once terrible and glorious. Under his sway the whole Caucasus became a fortress, its disunited tribes forged together in mystic exaltation, yet gripped by an implacable administrative system. Their new leader was to enforce the Shariat, like his own laws, with fire and sword, so that this moment passed into local history as 'The Time of the Shariat'—Shamyl's Time.

10

The Imam

*Mahommed is Allah's First Prophet, and Shamyl
his Second.* THE MURID CREED

Shamyl's early years of absolute rulership as third Imam were concentrated on four things. First, the unification of the whole Caucasus.
Next, the constant harassing of Russian troops, rather than any pitched
battles, until he had strengthened and perfected his own armies. Then,
the establishment of a new law and order throughout Daghestan.
Lastly, and most important, the recognition of his divine mission and of
his place as Allah's mouthpiece upon earth. When he reappeared after
the defeat of Ghimri, as one raised from the dead, it was obvious to the
Daghestani that he was indeed Allah's chosen, and they rallied to this
miraculous revenant, their new chieftain, crying 'Mahommed is Allah's
First Prophet, and Shamyl his Second!' But, with the rest of his programme, Shamyl was to encounter varying degrees of opposition. His
first check was in the matter of unification. Shamyl wished to unite the
Caucasians, from Black Sea to Caspian. But a constant inter-tribal
feuding often flared up, costing lives, and turning them from their true
interest—freedom from the Infidel.

In the lowlands Shamyl was received with honour by the Tcherkess
chieftains, but they refused to commit themselves. Among the people,
his appeals fell on deaf ears, since no common tongue prevailed. Only
the mollahs and chieftains understood his Arabic, so he was obliged to
address the crowds in Turco-Tartar, the *lingua franca* of the Caucasus.
But it robbed him of that fiery eloquence for which he was so famous
in Daghestan. At last, believing that the Tcherkess were not to be won
over, and would at best do no more than fight their own battles against
the Russians, Shamyl returned to his own Daghestani mountains,
where he established his headquarters at Akhulgo, a name dark with
drama and bloodshed.

In the Tartar language, Akhulgo signifies 'a meeting place in time of
danger'. The aôul was well-named; it was an eyrie perched on the
summit of an isolated, conical peak rising sheer six hundred feet above

125

the river Kōisu which serpented round three sides of its base. All around lay desolation: bare rocks and gorges, the only approach a razor-edged path zig-zagging up the peak. Local tradition held that it was the Devil's handiwork, that Shaitan had, with Allah's permission, built it for his lair. It was a natural fortress, and as such, Shamyl's choice for his headquarters. Here he set about reforming the Murid ranks, and reorganizing the administration of the country. Here he built himself a small house where he installed his family: Fatimat, the little Djemmal-Eddin, and now, another son, Khazi Mahommed, named after Shamyl's kounak, the first Imam. There was also Shamyl's mother, Bahou-Messadou, lately widowed. The house was a simple one, but it had the distinction of being two stories high—something of a rarity in the Caucasus: it was built for him by Russian prisoners on the lines of a northern house, and he regarded it with pride. It was his palace, Akhulgo his capital, and Daghestan his kingdom—under Allah.

Shamyl had already proved himself to the Caucasians as a warrior. Now he was to prove himself as a legislator, the founder of permanent institutions and an established judicial system imposed on the Adats, or traditional statutes. Fines for failure to obey the laws of the Shariat went, along with raiding-booty, to swell the revenue: some of this was redistributed in the form of pensions for the wounded Murids and their families. Some was used, wisely by Oriental standards, to bribe the complicity of wavering tribes; some to purchase war-materials, and even to cast a simple silver medal which was the award of outstanding bravery. At his zenith, Shamyl was often accused of being rapacious, of laying up treasure upon earth, and stocking caches of gold and jewels in the forests of Itchkeria. But this was unjust. Shamyl was the least grasping of men; his personal life was one of austerity and self-discipline. If he held large stocks of valuables in reserve, it was because he knew the cost of war, the continued needs, when pitting his strength against the inexhaustible coffers of the Tzar. Yet, when fighting for booty broke out among his chieftains, he flung his treasure into the depths of a mountain lake, rather than have it destroy the unity of his troops. And, to this day, the villagers of Andi still believe that somewhere below the glassy surface of a nearby tarn, there lie gold dishes, ruby-studded sabre scabbards, great ankle-bracelets set with emeralds, and coral and amber drinking cups, all the loot of a Caucasian raid, flung to the fishes that unity might remain.

Among Shamyl's many innovations was that of express couriers, a system he had admired, as employed by the Russians posting along their military highways. But Shamyl did better by using a relay system across country, as the crow flies, or as the Avar gallops, where no foreigner could go, through swamps and forests, over mountains, and even those glaciers from which the five hundred snow peaks of the Caucasus rose so majestically. By employing the resilient, specially hardened and trained Caucasian horses who knew the country as did their riders, Shamyl succeeded in forming a chain of communication by which news travelled with incredible speed. Each aôul had to supply, and keep in readiness, their fastest horses, standing saddled and ready for the messenger who might gallop in at any moment on an exhausted mount. If the rider fell ill, or arrived wounded, his life was in the charge of the aôul which must furnish, on the instant, another rider to carry on the messages. Caucasians rode, as they fought, desperately, in snow-storms, in torrid heat, through raging torrents, and clinging to perilous paths overhanging chasms; they rode by starlight and in blanketing rain-storms, by day and night, carrying dispatches which told of every Russian move; of reinforcements; of Cossack raids; of staff changes at Russian headquarters; of a ball at the commandant's; of the arrival of supply-wagons; of an artillery officer stabbed to death by one of the dancers of Shemakha; of cannons being unloaded at Poti; of *pourparlers* with some local Khan. . . . Thus Shamyl became far better informed than his enemies, who often found themselves isolated, their lines of communication cut, their bribed spies, like their renegade allies, bringing false information; and all news arriving late, since their couriers were obliged to use the open road.

Shamyl imposed the death penalty for murder or treachery, and in many cases for disobedience, since he expected absolute submission to his will. Cowardice, regarded by the Caucasians with horror, was punished remorselessly. Cowards who had fled in battle were compelled to wear a piece of felt sewn to their back; they were forbidden any more communication with their families, nor could anyone ever speak to them again. And at the next battle, they were sent to the forefront, the quicker to accustom themselves to cold steel. There were, however, very few cowards among the Caucasians, fighting being their life, their whole concept of honour; and since death was viewed with Oriental fatalism, few men failed in their first duty as warriors.

II

The organization of Shamyl's army was based on the decimal system. First came a hundred Naibs, his highest ranking officers, then, lower ranking Naibs (sometimes known as Murshids), who numbered about a thousand. They obtained this envied rank, as bodyguard or special troops, only by rigorous testing in loyalty and strength. They were required to remain unmarried, or if already married, to cut themselves off from both their wives and homes during their term of service. In this, they were sharing the same sacrifices imposed on those accused of cowardice; but then, let no one imagine the Murid way of life to have been easy for either its followers, or those who faltered. Having vowed away their families, the Naibs were also vowed to lives of abstinence and denial regarding the food they ate, and the quarters in which they slept. Upon a Naib being appointed to command an area, he lived at the principal aôul's expense, was invested with powers of life and death over the people, and was answerable only to Shamyl. As with the rank and file of Murids, the slightest insubordination was punished by death.

The Murids, who made up the bulk of Shamyl's army, were sub-divided into tens and hundreds and five hundreds, under leaders of corresponding rank and power. They wore the Caucasian tunic, or tcherkesska, the men in brown, their officers in black: some wore the green turban of the Hadjis, and all were wrapped in shaggy black bourkas. When a body of Murid horsemen were seen approaching, they struck terror into the beholder, for they were a raven-like band, black-clad, with black banners: that saturnine colour-scheme being, perhaps, all part of Shamyl's sense of drama.

In time of need, the Naibs were supplemented by a levy of one man from each household; while in cases of emergency, every man in the aôul or district was under arms. Those who had sworn on the Koran to die for Shamyl received two bags of flour a month, and wore a small tab of green felt sewn to their sheepskin caps. The Naibs were a band of fanatically devoted men. In peace or war they were vowed by the sacred, ten-fold, Murid oath, to live and die for Shamyl, their Imam. Yet they were not merely heroic figures; they were also men of judge-ment and intellect, trained, like their leader, in the doctrines of Sufism and sworn to the spreading of both Shariat and Tarikat. They were at once Shamyl's bodyguard, his caïds, judges, apostles, picked troops and secret police. A Russian prisoner who had occasion, during his long captivity, to observe their workings, described them as 'the mortar binding together the stones from which Shamyl raised the fortifications of his power'.

It was an age and a land of picturesque similies. When Shamyl spoke of his warriors' swords as the sabres of Paradise, fighting a holy war, the Russian generals sent out proclamations throughout the Caucasus warning them that resistance was vain; were the heavens to fall, they told them, Russian bayonets would prop them up again. They described their armies as being more numerous than the grains of sand on the sea-shore. To which Shamyl, in a counter proclamation, asserted that his Murid hosts were as the waves of the ocean which swept away those sands. He further castigated the Russians as 'poisonous as the snakes that crawl in the steppe of Moughan'.

These steppes, which were in the coastal regions between Persia and the Caucasus, were dreaded from earliest times, for they were infested by deadly serpents, fatal to both man and horse. Plutarch speaks of Pompey being forced to abandon his design to march on the Caucasus, because of this multitude. Every spring, countless thousands writhed across the Arax, from Persia, into the Moughan, where they executed their sinister matings, circling and darting in hissing concourse, and no human being dared approach. In 1800, when Count Valerian Zubov besieged Salian, which was only separated from the Moughan by the river Koura, his soldiers, digging emplacements for their winter camp, found thousands of serpents numbed by the intense cold.

Thus when Shamyl employed such vivid similes, he roused the people against the Infidels in the language they best understood. And when the Russians employed the argument so much favoured by later dictators, that they were producing order from chaos and improving the lamentable state of the roads (these echoes merging with twentieth century talk of auto-bahns and Italian trains that ran on time), Shamyl had his answer ready. 'You say my roads are bad and my country impassable. It is well: that is the reason why the powerful White Tzar and all his armies who march on me ceaselessly can still do nothing against me. I do not venture to compare myself to great sovereigns. I am Shamyl—an ordinary Avar. But my bad roads, my forests and mountains, make me stronger than many monarchs. I should anoint my trees with oil, and mix my mud with fragrant honey, and garland my rocks with laurel and bay, so much do they aid me in my battle for Caucasian freedom.'

No wonder that Shamyl's blend of magnetism and eloquence had so powerful an effect. In the words of Bersek Bey, another adept in the use of florid metaphors, 'flames darted from his eyes and flowers fell from his lips'. Then, too, it must be remembered that he was a past-master at turning the most unlikely events into dramatic situations which fostered his own legend. From this distance it is impossible to estimate just how much Shamyl's magnetism, and that luminous, spiritual force, so often remarked by those who knew him, particularly in later life, was genuine, and how much, in the beginning at any rate, was deliberately contrived or presented with calculation. *As they beheld they became.* Perhaps he achieved his true spiritual stature through beginnings based on counterfeit, coming to grace through posturing, to the golden throne by way of tinsel. One thing seems evident, Shamyl dramatized himself, turning to his own advantage events which, less imaginatively treated, would have spelled disaster.

III

For an example of Shamyl's dramatic exaltation we must go forward in time to the year 1843 when the tribes of the Great and Little

Tchetchnia were hemmed-in by the Russians. Shamyl's troops were fighting, hard-pressed on other fronts, and could send no aid. The Tchetchens were without further means of continuing the fight, their houses razed, their crops burnt, their situation desperate. If no help was forthcoming they would be forced to offer their submission to Russia. Even so, they feared Shamyl's awful wrath; the thought of his reprisals made them decide to send a deputation to Dargo, then his headquarters, begging his permission to lay down their arms. But no one, neither warrior nor chieftain, could be found to undertake this mission. Although they were not, as a people, so fanatic as the Avars or Lesghiens, no one dared to breathe the word submission. All knew they risked their tongues being cut out, or their skulls split open, in this world, before facing Allah's wrath in the next.

At last a plan was devised. Tepi Mollah, a learned elder, reminded them that Shamyl's mother was known to exercise a considerable influence over her son; he revered her, and often confided in her as he had confided in no other member of his family except Fatimat, the beloved. A deputation would go to Dargo and lay matters before her, along with a handsome present to be distributed among the needy. Perhaps she could thus be persuaded to intercede with the Imam on their behalf. After all, this request was not based on cowardice. Were they to stand there and die, shot down, or starved to death? For the Murids, having taken the ten-fold oath, this was an accepted end, but many of the Tchetchens were not sustained by so positive a faith; there were limits to their docility.

Arrived at Dargo, the deputation went first to the house of one Hassim Mollah, who was on good terms with Bahou-Messadou. But this crafty individual recoiled from the whole idea. It was ignoble, dishonourable, he said; cowardly, unworthy of any True Believer. Submission to the Giaour? Had his ears heard aright? However his scruples were at last overcome by the chink of gold. The Tchetchens had collected three hundred gold pieces to offer Shamyl's mother; seventy-five of these were now offered to Hassim Mollah who, after haggling for another twenty-five pieces, agreed to approach his friend. The remaining two hundred pieces would amply suffice, he said. He would answer for it personally. . . . Say no more. . . . Locking away his own hundred gold pieces, he hurried off.

Although Bahou-Messadou was a wise and much respected figure in the Murid hierarchy, she had at times been heard to criticize her son's fanaticism as too harsh, too inhuman an imposition on the people. She never failed to counsel mercy and moderation: in short, in a world where woman's submission was absolute, she maintained a singularly independent attitude. She listened attentively to the Tchetchen's plea, and agreed to intercede with her son on their behalf. Over the veil that muffled half her face, her wise old eyes stared out, mournful, yet keen. It would be difficult; very difficult—dangerous, even: but she would try. . . . Muttering into her shawls, she disappeared into the harem.

That same night she asked an audience of Shamyl who, being occupied with the Naibs in planning a raid behind the Russian lines, and a further series of inflammatory speeches designed to rouse the less co-operative Tcherkess tribes, was in no mood to be interrupted by talk of submission. However, he remained closeted with his mother until midnight, when, leaving the room, his face inscrutable, he stalked through the ranks of waiting Naibs, and gaining the mosque, remained there alone for the rest of the night. Next morning the Khanum sent for Hassim Mollah. Pale, tear-stained and trembling, she told him that the Imam did not dare to answer such a request as the Tchetchens'. It was for Allah to decide, he said. Shamyl had therefore gone to the mosque, where, with prayer and fasting, he would await Allah's command. He next sent word that the entire population of Dargo was to collect before the mosque in readiness for the Divine decision. For three days and nights Shamyl remained inside, while, outside, the people waited, wailing and praying, sleepless and hungry. All life seemed suspended; a silence hung over the aôul, the streets and roof-tops were empty; only the dogs prowled, and, occasionally, a child's cry pierced the dirge-like chants of the kneeling crowds.

Suddenly the doors of the Mosque were flung open and Shamyl appeared, livid pale, his half-closed cat's eyes glinting beneath the huge chalma. He stood before them, as if turned to stone. The prayers and lamentations died away and, in absolute stillness, the people awaited his command. No flicker of expression was seen on his face, as two Murids led forward Bahou-Messadou, who knelt humbly before her son. Shamyl raised his left hand: 'Mighty Prophet, Thy will be done! Thy words are law to thy servant Shamyl.' Then, addressing the now prostrated crowds, he said: 'Inhabitants of Dargo! I bring you black news. Your brothers, the Tchetchens, have spoken shamefully of submission to the Giaour. But they knew their audacity, their lack of faith, their dishonour: they did not dare to face me, themselves, but used my mother, through her womanly weakness, to approach me. For love of her, as proof of her persuasions, I laid their request before Mahommed, Allah's prophet. For three days and nights I have sought the Prophet's judgement. And now, at last, he has deigned to answer my prayers . . . It is Allah's will that the first person who spoke to me of submission should be punished by a hundred lashes! *And this first person is my mother!*'

The effect of this speech was dramatic in the extreme. Bahou-Messadou uttered a piercing cry and fell at her son's feet. The people, at first thunderstruck, set up a wailing that echoed across the mountains. The boldest Murids prostrated themselves before Shamyl in silent supplication. But he remained inexorable. His mother was bound, and Shamyl himself seizing the whip from the executioners, began to lash the shrieking woman. At the fifth blow she lost consciousness, at which he flung himself across her body, sobbing uncontrollably. But suddenly, with that force and grace so often remarked in his movements, he sprang to his feet, his face now radiant, his eyes 'darting flames'.

'Allah is great!' he cried. 'Mahommed is his first Prophet, and I am his second! My prayer is answered! He allows me to take upon myself the remainder of the punishment to which my wretched mother was condemned. I accept with joy! I welcome the lash! It is the sign of your favour, O Prophet!' He tore off his tcherkesska and ripped open his shirt, and ordering the Naibs to continue the rest of the ninety-five lashes upon his own back, threatening them with death if they did not strike hard enough. As the whip flailed down Shamyl remained impassive, kneeling beside the unconscious woman. No grief or pain or even exaltation showed on his face as the flesh was torn from his bleeding shoulders. At the ninety-fifth stroke, he rose to his feet, put on his shirt, and advanced among the people, who remained kneeling, rooted with terror.

'Where are the Tchetchen traitors? Where is the deputation who brought this punishment upon my mother?' he asked, in his usual calm and measured tone. The unhappy Tchetchens, together with Hassim Mollah, were dragged forward, while the Naibs had already drawn their shashkas, ready to execute the sentence as soon as it was pronounced. The Tchetchens lay with their faces in the dust, whispering their last prayers. They did not even beg for mercy.

But the drama was not yet over: the *coup de théâtre* was yet to come. Stepping forward, Shamyl raised the grovelling Tchetchens and, telling them to take heart, to have courage and faith, he said: 'Return to your homes. Tell your people what you have seen and heard here. Depart in peace. Hold fast to the rope of God. Farewell.'

Naturally, such a drama was recounted throughout the Caucasus, having a most salutary effect on doubters. No further talk of submission was heard. By his sense of psychology, of theatre, Shamyl had contrived, first of all, to quell all talk of submission: then, to strengthen his mystical aura, as being in direct communication with Allah, the executant of His will; and lastly, to punish his mother: this was a double strategy, for, first of all, it reproved Bahou-Messadou herself, for meddling; then, it was a fearful lesson to the people, for in the Caucasus, as elsewhere in Moslem communities, parents and the aged were held sacrosanct. That he had, on God's command, raised his hand against his own mother spoke to the people as nothing else would have done. It was eloquent of the degree of God's wrath at the Tchetchens' proposals. Above all, his totally unexpected mercy towards the deputation amazed and impressed them. There could be no doubt, after such happenings, that Shamyl was indeed Allah's prophet upon earth. His word was, and must be, law. Their fate was to live or die for the black banners of Muridism.

IV

To return to the year 1837: after a number of sanguinary combats, and notably the storming, by the Russians, of the aôuls of Ashilta and Tilitl, the rebels were at last forced to retreat amid scenes of terror and butchery. General Fesé, the Russian commander, a most cruel and vain character, reported that Shamyl was at last routed, Akhulgo sacked, the Murids in flight, and all organized resistance at an end. Moreover, said the General's dispatch, written with a consummate sense of personal aggrandizement, Shamyl had been compelled to sue for peace, and he, Fesé, had agreed to an armistice. Although this was true in essence, it was, in fact, otherwise, for neither side was acting with entire good faith, and both sides regarded it as a merely temporary expedient; Shamyl to gain time, Fesé to gain glory.

Shamyl was finding the unification of the Caucasus took far longer than he had planned. There were many obstinate pockets of resistance left. Sometimes he seemed less of a leader than a conqueror, and many of the villagers found little to choose between Murids and Russians: both were menacing, both now enforced their will with terror. Indeed, Shamyl had taken to descending on the more unco-operative aôuls like a clap of thunder, an avenging majesty, who stalked through the awe-struck crowds, accompanied, in the manner of Asiatic tyrants, by his executioner, a tall figure dressed in black, carrying a long-handled axe, and followed by two sword-bearers who carried a number of freshly-sharpened shashkas, so that, however many sentences Shamyl imposed, there would be no delay in carrying them out. Hands were cut off at the least hint of disloyalty. Heads rolled in the dust right and left. Shamyl intended to be obeyed. He was Allah's mouthpiece; born to execute His will; his task to destroy the Infidel. No mercy, no weakness must impede his ultimate goal of a united, free Caucasia. The impassive face stared ahead, livid and chiselled, framed in the dark hennaed beard and overhanging sheepskin cap. The greenish eyes remained half-closed as, with a gesture of his left hand (the Imam was left-handed, and signalled men to death, as he clove open their skulls, with a single sweeping movement) he indicated the guilty. There was no appeal. According to their degree of guilt, the doomed men either seated themselves on the ground and bowed their heads to receive the fatal blow, or they were bound to a block. In any case they were soon dispatched. In Shamyl's realm, there was no room for waverers.

All the same, this personal attention to the problem of back-sliders took time, and demanded that Shamyl was constantly on the move, and prevented him concentrating on engagements with the enemy. He foresaw that time was still needed: time was his ally; it weakened his enemies, thinning their ranks by those bouts of typhoid and dysentery which attacked them wherever they went (the average life-span of a soldier in the Army of the South was three years). But that same passing time strengthened his own forces, giving them longer to equip and train, to lure the enemy deeper into unfamiliar, murderous terrain, and, above all, to impose his creed on the *whole* people, bringing them all under one standard—his own Murid banner. Therefore he decided to play for time and, after discussion with his Naibs, dispatched the following letter to Russian headquarters:

> From Shamyl Imam, Tashoff Hadji, Kibit Mahommet Abdourrahman of Karakhee, Mahomet-Omar-Ogli, and other honorable and learned men of Daghestan. Giving hostages, we conclude a peace with the Russian Emperor which none of us will break, on condition, however, that neither side should do the slightest wrong to the other. If either side breaks its promises, it will be considered as treacherous, and traitors are held accursed before God and the people. This letter will explain the complete exactitude and fairness of our intentions.

Having concluded the treaty, Shamyl returned to the mountains, his intention being to observe his bond, as he had said, just as long as the Russians observed theirs. And during this period, which he foresaw with perfect clarity could only be regarded as an interlude, he strengthened his position and repaired those aôuls most badly damaged in the late fighting—in particular, Akhulgo. He did not feel that he had in any way lost face by treating for peace after he had thundered so long for victory or death. He did not feel his honour involved, as he would have done by any oath taken on the Koran. He could give his word, and yet break it, since no True Believer found himself bound to an Infidel. It was a most convenient belief: and, oddly enough, the same argument seems to have inspired the Russians, who felt a promise given to such savages was not binding as a treaty made with one of the great powers. Therefore Fesé had no compunction, on returning to Temir-Khan-Shoura, to go by way of Ashilta and leave it a charred and sacked ruin, its crops devastated, its citizens homeless. It was to be a reminder of his might, a lesson to the other aôuls.

Heading homewards, from the lowlands where he had been, as always, preaching the Shariat, Shamyl was unaware of Fesé's last treacherous gesture. But on reaching the high mountain country, approaching Akhulgo, a messenger brought word of Ashilta's ruin, and Shamyl proceeded there in rage and hatred. When he and his Murids galloped up the rock defiles, their black banners flying, they found nothing but desolation and ruin where the aôul had stood. Ashilta was laid low, its five hundred houses reduced to rubble, its vines trampled, its wells choked, the cattle slaughtered, its inhabitants dead or taken captive. Even the mosque where, three years earlier, Shamyl had been consecrated Imam now lay in smouldering dust. This was the Russians' way of establishing their supremacy. Was it for this that he Shamyl, Imam of Daghestan, had bent his proud head and written words of peace? He sat his horse, immobile as ever, surveying the ruins. But he said nothing. His mind was made up. He wheeled his horse eastwards —to Akhulgo. At a gallop his Murids streamed after him across the mountains. There was no more talk of peace among them.

V

During the next few months Shamyl remained strangely quiet: was he, the Russians wondered, truly subdued? Fesé congratulated himself that the sack of Ashilta had had a most salutary effect on the Imam. In St. Petersburg, the Tzar decided to make his long-awaited triumphal tour of the Caucasus. He would receive Shamyl's submission—perhaps during his stay at Tiflis. It could be made a most picturesque and impressive occasion: he sent his orders to General Fesé, and began to anticipate his tour with some complacency.

It was premature. Even as the Royal orders were being written, in the green-walled study in the Winter Palace, Shamyl was completing the transformation of Akhulgo into an immense stronghold, a fortress, barracks and arsenal, from where he planned, presently, to launch a full-scale attack on the Russians. Akhulgo had been, before the advent of Russian heavy artillery, considered an impregnable fortress, but gun-fire and cannon-shot raked the outer walls and sent the watch-towers toppling, burying the defenders as they fell. Now Shamyl changed the whole system of defence. With a group of Poles who, having been con-scripted into the Russian army, lost no time in deserting to Shamyl's camp, he constructed a series of sunken defences, trenches, breast-works, earthen parapets, covered ways, underground stables and barracks, blasted in the rock. The saklias were converted into guard houses, look-out posts and small forts. Here, he amassed large supplies of provisions and ammunition, and made quarters for the families of some Naibs and Murid elect, as well as the hostages who were, on both sides, a regular part of Caucasian warfare.

Akhulgo was divided into two parts, Old Akhulgo and New. These two sections were dominated, like the bleak landscape, the endless horizons of emptiness, by an old watch-tower known as Sourkhaiz Tower. It had escaped the last battles, and Shamyl left it standing; its sharp silhouette was a landmark for many miles. Week by week, more men and supplies poured into Akhulgo. The flower of the Murid army were gathered there, some mounted, some on foot, all stood under his orders; it was a huge military camp, blasted into the rock.

When the Tartar spies who operated for the Russians began to arrive at Temir-Khan-Shura with news of this concentration, the staff officers were uneasy. Surely, Fesé had been both imprudent and unduly optimistic? Now he had raised the Emperor's hopes, who dared to dash them? Who now would care to try and persuade Shamyl to offer his submission at Tiflis? But the Tzar was due there in October—was already heading south. Less than a month was left before the ceremony of surrender must take place. Fesé, on operations in Southern Daghestan, sent General Kluke von Klugenau north to conduct the negotiations. His choice of emissary was good, for Klugenau was well acquainted with the mountaineers, known and respected by them as a brave and honourable warrior. If anyone could succeed, it would be he. Klugenau had no illusions as to the hopeless nature of his mission, but he wrote demanding a meeting with the Imam Shamyl, entrusting the letter to the Bek of Karani, chieftain of a neighbouring neutral tribe.

Shamyl appointed a meeting place perfectly suited to the occasion, and expressing, once again, his instinctive sense of drama. Throughout his life, this quality is to be seen, not only in his actions, manners and dress, but even in his choice of locale. The chosen spot was a narrow ledge of rock, beside a spring, between two towering cliffs; a dark gully, where the sun seldom penetrated, and the wind howled ceaselessly, winter and summer. On this chill autumn day (September 18), for autumn came early to the mountains and the winter snows were threatening by October, a lowering sky heavy with rain clouds made the morning seem twilight. Klugenau rode into the rock gully, accompanied only by Yevdokimov, his aide-de-camp, an escort of fifteen Don Cossacks, and a dozen of the Karani natives.

Shamyl was waiting for them. He sat his black stallion, wrapped in a bourka, surrounded by three hundred of his bodyguard, and Naibs, their banners darkening the shadowed gully. As the Russians appeared, they ceased the wailing chants which had been echoing mournfully, to raise one of their wild and terrible cries, part prayer, part battle cry, a wolfish howl, blood-curdling to northern ears. But twenty years of Caucasian service had accustomed Klugenau to the war cries, the cold steel, and the nature of these Caucasians. He rode on stolidly. Only the startled ravens circled overhead in shrieking discord, their wings flapping noisily.

Klugenau, who was a hugely built man, brusque, but courageous, and wholly sincere, now advanced alone, save for one interpreter. He took up his station on a little mound of rocks in the centre of the gully. Shamyl, too, rode forward alone, the only time he was ever seen, after his accession as Imam, without being surrounded by his bodyguard. In silence the two men came face to face. In silence they dismounted; the interpreter spread a bourka on the ground, and they sat down for the pourparler. Of their followers, not a man moved.

The two leaders' talk continued for several hours, Klugenau restraining his impatience in every effort to persuade the Imam. Shamyl listened, with his usual impassivity, but he refused to commit himself on a single point until he had consulted with his Naibs. Klugenau was becoming irritated and hungry by now: and having finished his supply of those cigars without which he could neither fight nor negotiate, he rose to his feet, indicating that the interview was over. He held out his hand to the Imam. Shamyl, leaping up like an uncoiled steel spring, with that peculiar force and grace for which he was celebrated, stretched out his hand towards the General, when, suddenly, the whole atmosphere of restrained hostility changed to one of fury. A Naib flung himself forward out of the waiting ranks and on to Shamyl, whose arm he seized. It was Sourkhai Khan, one of the most fanatic of Shamyl's followers. Furiously, he declared it unthinkable that their Imam, 'Allah's own Prophet', should touch the hand of an Infidel.

'Giaour!' he spat the insult at Klugenau, who, being already exasperated by his failure, now flew into a rage. Striking out with the crutch he was compelled to use since one foot had been shattered in battle, he tried to knock off Sourkhai Khan's turban. In the East this is considered the most deadly insult, the most calamitous happening the Moslem mind could conceive. Klugenau and his men would have paid with their lives, had not Shamyl acted quickly and with chivalry. Seizing the crutch with one hand, and holding back Sourkhai Khan, whose kindjal was already brandished an inch from Klugenau's throat, he ordered the rest of his band, who were closing round, to fall back and sheathe their swords. His voice could be heard, dominating the clamour and entreating Klugenau to withdraw quietly.

But Klugenau was now beside himself with rage: he stood there, bellowing a stream of Russian oaths, unmoved by threats or persuasion. At this moment Yevdokimov rushed forward, dragged him off by force, and at last persuaded him to remount and return to General Headquarters at Temir-Khan-Shura. Klugenau rode slowly off, looking neither to right nor left, growling, his face still thunderous. He was watched out of sight by Shamyl and his Murids: then they, too, mounted and rode off towards Ghimri, chanting as they rode, their bourkas pearled with the fine rain that now began to fall.

Silence invaded the gully once more. A mist crept down from the mountains; by four o'clock it was almost dusk. The bats came swooping out of hiding. From far away could be heard the melancholy cry of the jackals. It had been a dark day. Had the two chiefs been able to come to an understanding, many thousands of lives might have been saved, and rivers of blood and tears remained unshed. Above all, Akhulgo need never have fallen, and in its falling, bring about the tragic destiny of Shamyl's son, Djemmal-Eddin.

II

Tiflis

The sweetmeat, childish Oriental world.

In the autumn of 1837 it was announced in Tiflis that the Tzar would make a state visit to the Georgian capital. The whole city was in a ferment. The first local newspaper, *Tsiscari* (*The Dawn*), had only lately been started, and was considered a milestone on the road to enlightenment; this journal now devoted whole issues to the forthcoming honour. But the city, as a whole, had no need of the printed word, for Tiflis was first of all Oriental. The news spread from one quarter to the next before the newspaper was even distributed. The old city of Tiblissi, to give it its Georgian name, was a series of villages, citadels and bazaars all huddled together, swarming up and down the cliffs and conical hills, its narrow labyrinthine ways divided by the gorge of the river Koura. On one side, Nari-Kala, the Persian citadel, with its Armenian quarter; across the river, Avlabar, the Georgian town, with its fortress, and the church built by Vakhtang Gourgastan, the founder of Tiflis. In the centre, on the low ground, the newly constructed Russian or Europeanized quarter, administrative buildings, the theatre, the Nobles' Club, public gardens and restaurants, and a few shops stocking such Western luxuries as eau de Cologne, corsets, fans, kid gloves, and French novels. Towards the north, the town straggled out into dusty wastes, and a *mahallah*, or gypsy quarter, where handsome scowling creatures lolled in the sun. Beyond lay an agglomeration of Russian army tents, newly built barracks, stables, a hospital and the quarters inhabited by the staff officers, all painted that oppressive, dark blood-red which betokened Imperial property.

This now presented a scene of pulsating activity, with dispatch-riders coming and going at the gallop, while lamps burned all night in the General's rooms.

In a month—in a week—tomorrow—the Tzar would be here! The news fanned across the square of the Maidan, to the Tartar bazaars, where Persian jewellers weighed turquoises by the pound; it reached the fruit-vendors squatting beside their mounds of gigantic tiger-striped

139

melons, and was relayed to the dark booths of the Armenian armourers where they hammered the fine gold and silver damascened weapons for which they were so justly celebrated. It swept down the new boulevards, tree-lined and spacious, to gain the roof-tops and fretted balconies, where, under wreathing vines, the long-nosed, sloe-eyed Georgian beauties sat together in the limpid twilight, accompanying their languid chants with tambourine and lute.

The aristocracy of Georgia felt themselves very close to the Imperial family. Just as Georgia was regarded by Russia as a protectorate, so the high-born Georgians regarded themselves as god-children, or wards, of the Tzar. He watched over them *personally*, they felt; he had their good at heart. (This view was not shared by some members of the ex-monarchy, who had been dispatched to Moscow and held there, against the danger of possible intrigues. Their lands had been confiscated, and a long-promised indemnity only materializing in a grotesquely reduced form, although some were lodged in a house containing no less than a hundred and ten rooms.) But those who were less distinguished, less likely to be troublesome or expensive to the Russian government, looked forward to the Tzar's visit with emotion. They sadly missed the focal point of a Court: his visit would not only provide the longed-for panoply and protocol, but it would, surely, herald the final suppression of Muridism—removing, at last, the awful threat of Shamyl's domination.

By 1839, three generations (by precocious, prolific Georgian standards) had grown up and been educated in the military schools and Cadet Corps of St. Petersburg, and believed themselves *plus Russes que les Russes*. The princely Georgians were treated as Royal protégés, flattered and indulged, so that, wearing the Tzar's epaulettes, they did not feel them to be the yoke of slavery. The young girls were sent to convents and schools which the Empress inaugurated in the Caucasus; or they were received into the Smolny Institute at St. Petersburg where, in the worldly setting of a palace-like convent originally built by the Tzarina Elizabeth for the daughters of noblemen, they were educated under the Tzarina's eye. Their curriculum included weekly drives about the capital, to concerts, military reviews, or Court functions. The pupils were driven in closed carriages belonging to the Royal stables, and their eager faces peering out at the world were a familiar sight in St. Petersburg. Some of the girls were appointed *demoiselles d'honneur* to the Tzarina, or one of the elder Grand Duchesses, who held their own Court apart from the Winter Palace. The Emperor was always careful to select a number of his pages and aides-de-camp from among the Georgian princes, showing them an avuncular warmth seldom bestowed elsewhere.

Now that the Emperor was at last coming to Tiflis, things would go

better said the Georgians. They had become violently hostile to anything which opposed Russian influence in the Caucasus. Moreover, their
Christian faith abhorred the Moslem tribes whom they regarded as
brigands—*savages*—better wiped from the face of the earth. Shamyl's
rise had caused them the darkest of forebodings, for they knew the
country, the man, the tribes, and the fanatic nature of their enemy.
Those Georgians who were not already serving with the Russian army,
kept up a sort of running warfare of their own, the princes and land-
owners going out at the head of a troop of their own men, whom they
had trained and equipped, to engage in private battle-sorties. Although
Tiflis lay beyond the general periphery of the Murid wars, it was
accustomed to the sound of gunfire, the clatter of steel, or the sight of a
raiding-party galloping through the steep streets, their dead and
wounded slung across their saddles. Sometimes a severed Tartar head
or hand dangled from the lance of some triumphant princeling. A bag
of twenty-two Tartar heads had won the Tzar's special commendation,
and been rewarded by a fine diamond ring bearing the Imperial cypher.

All the same, it was generally felt that a certain restraint, or caution,
should mark the Royal visit; there had been a rather awkward moment
during the visit of a Grand Duke, not so long before . . . such things
could seem uncivilized—*barbaric* even. . . . It had been a particularly
festive occasion, with a supper party followed by a ball. But the evening
had ended on an unfortunate note, by the finding of a severed head—
only a Tartar head, of course—on a bench, under the ladies' wraps and
shawls. It had caused a great sensation among the visitors from St.
Petersburg. Some of the belles had to be revived with smelling-salts and
eau-de-vie. It had needed quite a lot of explaining. . . . Yet it had all been
so simple, really. Prince Badriz, a dashing young Georgian, had arrived
late: he had been conducting his own war, skirmishing in the foothills of
Gori (later to become celebrated as Stalin's birthplace). But the rebels
put up a stiff fight. When at last Badriz drove them back with losses, he
had missed the polonaise which, following the custom of Court Balls at
the Winter Palace, always opened the festivities in Tiflis society, too.
While the Prince was changing out of his battle-stained clothes, his
bodyguard, who were in charge of the trophy head, had become so
entranced by the spectacle of the brilliantly-lit ballroom with the
waltzing charmers in their pale satins and gauzes that they had put the
head down in a dark corner, where, unnoticed, it had been soon
covered by scarves and pelisses, and so remained, until its discovery
broke up the evening in confusion.

Such a contretemps must be avoided during the Tzar's visit. At all
costs order, grace and protocol must prevail.

The ladies spent hours closeted with their *couturières*, preparing new
toilettes worthy of the occasion, and calculated to arouse those tender

sentiments which, it was said, lurked beneath the Emperor's marble façade. There was a lot of tight-lacing and pomading of dark curls. The flamboyant *maquillage* of the Georgian beauties was employed in positively Impressionistic terms. Rouge was worn in large scarlet ovals on each cheek; dark eyes were richly outlined in khol, the eyebrows meeting across in that one sooty sweep so much admired in the Near East. Perfumes of the most overpowering nature, attar of roses and stephanotis distilled in the bazaar and bottled in delicate gold-engraved phials, were used drenchingly, while couriers were galloping, by day and night, to Vienna, to procure the sternest whale-bone corsets.

Meanwhile the older ladies, who were obliged to fall back on their conversational assets, now hurriedly read the novels of Sir Walter Scott, which, along with those of Paul de Kock (though these no lady could own to having read), were known to be the Emperor's favourites. Georgian cooks, grown fat and complacent preparing the staple local dishes, *tzartzavi* or *hatchapouri*, now practised making soufflés and sauces to rival the culinary flights of the French chefs in St. Petersburg, while the great land-owning families, such as the Davidovs and Djordjadzes, prepared their houses and estates to receive the Tzar in a style worthy of the descendants of King David.

The Tzar had specifically ordered that no foreigners were to be admitted to Tiflis during his visit, but one traveller, an Englishman, Captain Wilbraham, had already crossed the frontier coming in from Persia before the edict was enforced, and so arrived on the eve of the Royal visit. He found the Georgians extremely hospitable, going to all lengths to make their visitor feel at home. He was constantly being regaled with hot-buttered toast, a most delicate attention which he particularly appreciated after some time supping on the road with Persian caravanserais. The Georgians' *souplesse* is exemplified by the different ways they set about pleasing their various guests—buttered toast for Captain Wilbraham, and *bayadères* and skirmishes with bandits for Alexander Dumas who, nearly twenty years later, was visiting Georgia in search of the most vivid local colour, and who was not allowed to be disappointed.

Toast or no, Captain Wilbraham seems to have been rather carping: he had none of Dumas' childish sense of wonder. He complained of a lack of culture in Georgian society. The ladies were too painted—it gave them a bold look; waltzing was all the rage—they waltzed their time away. He blamed it all on the too rapid Westernization of the province.

Here sounds that sermonizing note so often found in mid-nineteenth-century travel books. The author's findings are, as it were, oiled over by a gloss of combined moral tone, piety and patronage. There was not enough local colour, or there was too much: if 'the natives' were too pressing, they were familiar; if they were not forthcoming, they were cold. If they received their guests in style, they were ostentatious; if casual, like the Sultan who received Motraye lying on the ground, they were accused of conducting themselves 'like the meanest Tartars'.

At General Headquarters, the Army was tense. The troops were kept drilling and polishing up their kit, to satisfy the Emperor's obsession with military detail. The senior staff-officers rehearsed their explanation, if not excuses, for the fact the war still raged. Some of the officers, those who had been reduced to the ranks, or exiled to the Caucasus, to serve an indefinite term in the Army of the South, on the Tzar's own orders, were very uneasy. They dreaded catching the monarch's eye. The Imperial memory was long. Every face, every failing, every case was recalled. One wretched young man, then stationed near Tiflis, had particular cause to dread the Royal visit. He had been the officer on night duty at one of the St. Petersburg guard posts, on a night of blizzard and snow, and thought it safe to retire to bed, leaving the sergeant in charge. Unfortunately the Tzar, driving about the city, stopped at the post, and did not find the officer on watch. The young man woke to the horrors of the Imperial Presence standing beside the bed.

'Come with me,' said the Emperor, ominously quiet. 'Come just as you are.' The unhappy officer took his place in the open sleigh, beside the Tzar, clad only in his nightshirt. Arrived at the Winter Palace, half dead with fear and cold, he was told to wait in the guard-house for the rest of the night. Next day he was dispatched to serve in the Caucasus, making the entire journey (by the Tzar's orders) wearing only his nightshirt. Miraculously he survived, to serve many years in the ranks, before being pardoned by way of a transfer to Hungary, where he died fighting with the Russian regiments rushed there to suppress the Hungarian rising of 1848.

II

When the Emperor Nicholas, 'Tzar of All the Russias', left St. Petersburg to travel about his vast realm, he was in the habit of using a small fast carriage which could be driven at breakneck speed. Relays of horses were kept ready all along the route, for the slightest delay made him irritable. His staff were left panting; they complained there was no time to eat or sleep. On such tours the Tzar was always accompanied by Count Adlerberg, a life-long friend and confidant, who knew better than to counsel even a half-hour's halt. Wrapped in a grey military overcoat, a bearskin rug across his knees, where a large-scale ordnance map fluttered in the icy wind, the Tzar was to be seen at the various posting-houses, staring round him with his usual pewter gaze. At this time, the roads were little more than wheel-tracks.

Every day the Tzar raced onwards, into the endless horizons. Vast steppes, forever over-reaching themselves, leading onwards into nothingness again, the versts computed by striped black and white guard-houses, topped by the Imperial eagles.

There were so many Russias. . . . Sombre forests dappled with mush-rooms, where, in the greenish twilight, the peasants went 'hunting bear with scarlet shot', as the songs told: desolate little villages where the landowners' porticoed mansion dominated a muddy track lined with hovels, where the serfs toiled out their lives. An ill-lit *traktir*, or drinking-house, offering escape to the moujiks who sat, or snored, or spat on the huge tiled stove; while others drank vodka and forgot the hopelessness of their lives.

The great provinces sprawled through seas of wheat, to further uninhabited steppes. East to Jaroslav or Kazan; west to Vitebsk and the Polish frontier, by way of the Pale, the Jewish settlements of mud, filth and oppression; south, beyond Moscow, to Koursk, Kharkov and Kiev. Crossing and re-crossing the great rivers, the carriage wheels alternately sparked by frost, sunk axle-deep in mud, or lost in a cloud of dust.

All the Russias . . . Bielo Rosso, White Russia, Veliki, or Great Russia, Tchervonyia, or Red Russia ('tchervonyia' being old Slav for red, and having no political significance), Malo, or Little Russia. . . . So many Russias; all of them in the Emperor's iron grip. Along the glassy grey stillness of the great rivers, the provincial towns were reflected. The same blue and gold cupolas of the church and monastery; the same yellow and white stucco court house with its double-headed Imperial eagle. The same bone-shaking, wooden-wheeled tarantass standing before the posting-house; the same white fences bordered with giant sun-flowers. The same avenue of silver birches, where, in summer, a woman walking under a pink parasol became a rosy glow on the still waters; in winter a sleigh racing over the snow became a dark streak across the polished surface of the ice.

The life reflected there was one of emptiness. Visiting, waltzing, dozing, gossiping, overeating—all the petty protocol of provincial society thirsting for the echoes of the capital, living out empty lives of frustration and pretension. The doctor, the lawyer, the retired major, and the overblown coquette; sly village priests, sure of their strangle-hold, the clergy Leskov has portrayed: this was the society which Gogol immortalized in *Dead Souls*, and which he happened to be writing in 1837 (when Dickens was writing *Oliver Twist*, and Stendhal, *La Chartreuse de Parme*), and the Tzar was dashing across his domains, south, towards the Caucasus.

III

For the Russian, speed was a form of intoxication, a childish yet profound craving, found in all ranks. At the fair grounds, as in the gardens of the Royal Palaces, Grand Dukes or moujiks, shrieking joyously in the downward rush of the *Montagnes russes*: toboggan-rides, troika-races to the islands, along the quays of St. Petersburg, at dusk. Everywhere, speed for speed's sake. Russian literature and popular songs reflect this intoxication: so does their folk art. Painted tin trunks and Palekh work, the beautiful traditional papier-mâché cigarette boxes and tea caddies, show us a world where brilliant coloured groups of peasants stand in their troikas, whipping on the plunging horses, as they race across the snows under black skies. Or we see the fabulous flowering of a Moscow street scene—the gilded onion domes and cupolas of Vassilli Blagennoie as a background to tiny gnat-like sleighs skimming about the snowy expanses of the Red Square. There, sleighs and troikas are never at a standstill: the horses never trot, they are always racing; *Paiidi!* Make way—shout the drivers, plunging onwards, sparks flying from their horses' hooves as great plumes of snow are flung backward in the dash.

Generally the Russian people detested exercise. They were, by inclination, supine, a passive race ('blond Arabs, a people meant to live in the sun', as de Custine says). 'They lived', says another traveller, speaking of the St. Petersburg nobility, 'from arm-chair to carriage or sledge: their bodies submitted *passively* to movement.' But speed, they adored and craved. They had *le vertige de la vitesse*. Passive speed, again. Being sped across the land in a sleigh, or *traineau*, behind very fast horses, troika racing, or the rushing descent of the Montagne Russe.

Perhaps this national passion for speed derives from the vastness of the land. The only thing to be done with such empty horizons was to gulp them at a gallop. When Gogol wrote his great passage on the troika speeding across the steppes, he likened it to Russia itself, advancing across the earth. The Emperor Nicholas had long ago identified himself with the country. Like another monarch's *'L'Etat c'est Moi'*, he saw himself as the embodiment of its history and referred to the weather as 'my climate'. While he was dashing south, perhaps he shared, in some half-formed reverie, some auto-intoxication of pride and pace, something of Gogol's nationalistic ecstasy.

Ah! the troika—the bird troika [wrote Gogol], who invented thee
But thou couldst only have had thy birth among a dashing people?
—in that land which has extended smoothly, glidingly over half the
earth . . . Is it not thus, like the bold troika which cannot be overtaken, that thou art dashing long, O Russia, my country? The roads
smoke beneath thee. . . . Ah, horses, horses, Russian horses! What

horses you are! Doth the whirlwind sit upon your manes? . . . O Russia, whither art thou dashing? Reply! But she replies not; the horse-bells break into a wondrous sound, the shattered air becomes a tempest and the thunder growls. Russia flies past everything else upon earth: other people, kingdoms, and empires gaze askance as they stand aside to make way for her!

IV

On October 21, the Emperor Nicholas arrived in Tiflis. It had been pouring with rain for several days, so that the brilliance of his entry, escorted by a bevy of twenty-four Georgian princes, their splendidly picturesque costumes spattered with mud, lost much of its effect. Rain fell in such torrents that the crowds soon dispersed, leaving only a few determined sight-seers, standing ankle-deep in mud, their cheers echoing thinly as the Imperial cortège passed. The Tzar was suffering from the effects of his long journey. In Mingrelia, fleas had not respected the royal person, and the icy autumn winds had inflamed his face, so he was short-tempered and swollen, and did not radiate his usual dazzling charm.

Shamyl's spies reported unfavourably on the Russian Sultan. They found Nicholas' Germanic type unsympathetic, his movements wooden, and his pale puffed features without true majesty. But rain or not, the city, as a whole, gave him a splendid welcome. The narrow streets of the old quarter were decorated with garlands of jasmine and laurel, looped from one overhanging balcony to the next. Every house, rich or poor, hung out its finest carpets in a glowing, if sodden display. The new boulevards were lined with troops, their muskets crashing on the pavé as they presented arms. Over all sounded the bells, every church pealing its welcome to the Defender of the Faith, the White Tzar, their protector. The chimes floated across the misty river, along the steep banks where the bridge built by Alexander the Great still stood, on and up into the forests which concealed the comings and goings of innumerable Tartar spies, Shamyl's men, watching, listening, sniping, raiding; biding their time, but never slackening in their ultimate plan to encompass Russia's defeat in the Caucasus.

At night, while lights blazed in Tiflis, a thousand wax tapers lighting the cathedral, or reflected in the glittering parquet perspectives of the Governor's ballroom, while illuminations glowed among the acacias and eucalyptus trees of the parks, high on the hills above the city, fire-fly flames could be seen flickering in the darkness. They were Shamyl's signal fires, a chain of communications, spreading across the mountains which he still held.

At staff headquarters, the Russian generals were now faced with a most disagreeable obligation. Someone must break it to the Emperor that there would be no ceremony of Shamyl's submission. Shamyl had refused Klugenau's parley, and also a subsequent letter, couched in the most generous terms, which had once again urged him to capitulate. Two days before the Tzar's arrival, a Tchetchen runner brought his last word on the subject.

> From the humble writer of this letter, Shamyl, who leaves all things in the hand of Allah. This is to tell you I am determined not to go to Tiflis; even though I be cut into pieces for refusing, for I have oft-times met your treachery, and this all men know.

When the Emperor was shown this letter, the Imperial displeasure deepened. He had not been satisfied with a number of army matters he had investigated en route for Tiflis: he found much to criticize in the conduct of the war. In fact he found the whole situation inexplicable. Why did the war drag on year after year? Why were more and more men required? Why was more and more equipment poured into the struggle? These Asiatics had become altogether too arrogant. Things would have to change. Having told his staff exactly what he thought of them, he soothed his feelings by dismissing Baron Rosen, the Commander-in-Chief, and then, during a ceremonial parade, without the least warning, tore off Dadiani, the Prince of Mingrelia's epaulettes, degrading him to the ranks, while awaiting a court martial. The painful scene was witnessed not only by the massed troops, but the flower of Georgian society, including the Prince's young wife, his family, and all his in-laws. The Prince Dadiani was Colonel of the Grenadiers of Georgia, son-in-law of the Governor, and an aide-de-camp to the Emperor. He was charged with graft, and employing large numbers of his regiment in his own private concerns. Complaints had reached the Emperor as soon as he arrived, and he was not slow to vent his rage on the unfortunate Dadiani.

An eye-witness to the scene on the parade ground remarks: 'This example, which proves no amount of interest can screen an offender, naturally alarmed the officers commanding the various regiments: peculation is so general that there are few, if any, whose conduct would stand close investigation.' The Emperor, seeing the distress his temper had caused the poor old Baron Rosen, announced to him, by way of consolation, that he was naming his eldest son one of his aides-de-camp. But even this sop could not dispel the atmosphere of apprehension which now prevailed, and the staff officers surrounding the Emperor kept a close watch for any would-be petitioners, who might expose further abuses.

Next night there was a State Ball, at which all the Georgian beauties and local rulers wore their national costume, and blazed with barbaric splendours. The Emperor opened the ball by pacing through a polonaise with a Georgian Princess of the Blood Royal, a squat and decidedly passé figure. The mother and sisters of Prince Dadiani's wife were present, trying to present a brave front, but, we read: 'Their assumed gaiety was sadly contradicted by their eyes, still red from weeping, in spite of a heavy application of khol.' The Dadiani's poor little wife of a few months had remained at home, crying unrestrainedly—crying for her lost happiness—for more misery to come. Being reduced to serve in the ranks, the wretched Prince Dadiani soon committed suicide.

The Emperor now turned his attention to international affairs, and upon meeting the Emir-i-Nizam, a high-ranking Persian, come to Tiflis to pay his respects, he attacked him, head on, over the matter of the Russian battalions, which had deserted to Persia many years earlier during the Russo-Persian war, and whom the Shah had most obstinately refused to hand back. Nicholas had long felt this to be not only a blow to his pride, but a matter of principle too. Russians—*Christians*—beside Mahommedans! It was an insult to both Cross and Crown. If the men were not returned at once, he told the Emir-i-Nizam, he would break off diplomatic relations. Such a frontal attack outraged every tradition of Oriental diplomacy. But it succeeded where all the efforts of Yermolov and Paskiévitch had failed, for later, the death-seeking Captain Allbrandt was selected to go to Persia; and, after nearly a year, he succeeded in winning over the deserters. In 1839, he brought them back in triumph, with colours flying and the regimental band playing. Alas! During their years in Persia the men had become very strongly influenced by their surroundings. Nourished on pilaff and sherbet, the bandsmen had gradually dropped from their repertoire all those briskly martial strains which they had played when salted herring and pickled pork had been their lot. Now, the drums and fifes executed *mélopées* which, melancholy or savage, were, first of all, voluptuously Oriental. And poor marching music it must have seemed, as the battalion faced northwards, and the dust of a column on the move eddied round the hennaed feet of their Persian women who ran beside them, wailing beneath their veils.

V

In Tiflis, the reception committee made the most feverish efforts to provide a programme worthy of the Emperor. His Imperial Majesty must be distracted, said his equerries, quailing, like the rest of the world, before the flashing Jupiter glance. In vain did the Patriarch of the Georgian church personally conduct the Tzar to the Cathedral of Sion for a Thanksgiving Mass. In vain did the nobility give sumptuous dinners, balls and receptions. In vain did the *kinto*, or street-corner wags, perform (rather purified) versions of their traditional entertainments, which, to this very day, are an integral part of daily life in Tiflis. In vain did the Georgian beauties don their national dress, with its flowing veils, tiny round, coin-hung cap, and trailing fur-trimmed *katiba*, or dolman, to posture and undulate before the Emperor in their national dances. The monarch was plainly distrait, if not downright disagreeable. 'I have no eyes but for my army,' he admitted.

In vain did the Tzar's hosts offer him the distractions of a Turkish bath—the hot steam baths for which Tiflis was famous; or present the local luminaries, and the most celebrated toper—Georgians were prodigious drinkers. In vain did the Tchavtchavadzé family offer him the hospitality of their beautiful estates at Tzinondali, which fifteen years later were to lie in blackened ruins, sacked, the servants killed, and the Princess Anna and her household abducted, to be held prisoner in Shamyl's aôul. And when the children of a newly organized orphanage (under Royal patronage) recited a thousand strophes of *The Knight in the Tiger Skin*, Georgia's epic poem by their greatest poet, Shota Rustaveli, dead seven hundred years, but the country's eternal glory, the Tzar remained restive, glum.

VI

Shota Rustaveli was born in the twelfth century, the classic period of Georgian literature. He received his education in Greece, and returned to Tiflis to become Treasurer to the celebrated Queen Tamara, for whom he nourished a hopeless passion. He was a brilliant scholar who studied Homer, Plato and the Persian mystics; yet he could not declare his love. At last he withdrew from her Court, and ended his days in a monastery at Jerusalem, where, in the eighteenth century, another Georgian, the Metropolitan Timofei, discovered his tomb together with his portrait in the church of the Holy Cross which had been founded by the kings of Georgia.

There was a long tradition of monastic scholars and poets in Georgia. Literature and religion were the two passions of the mediaeval Georgian princes. The Katholicos Antony, son of Jassei, the Mahommedan king, composed the first grammar of the Georgian language, and translated Aristotle. Vakhoucht, son of the King Vakhtang VI, went to Moscow, there to print a complete edition of the Bible in Georgian; while, in the seventeenth century, the Prince Orbeliani, or Brother Saba Soulkhan, travelled as far as Rome and Paris, where he was received by Louis XIV, and met La Fontaine.

In 1083, two more princely monks, the Vakouriani brothers, left Georgia and travelled on foot to Bulgaria, there to found the remote

and mysterious monastery of Batchkovo. It still retains a strongly
Caucasian quality, due, partly, to its withdrawn, forbidding air, and
partly to its setting, beside a racing river-bed, and surrounded by
towering, impenetrably wooded hills and rocks. But then, Bulgaria is
full of Caucasian echoes, in character, landscape and music. Large
numbers of Caucasians took refuge in Bulgaria when, at last, Shamyl
capitulated. Many strange pockets of little-known Moslem tribes have
remained in the hills, settled there by Bulgaria's Turkish overlords
when the Caucasus emptied before the Russian conquest.

VII

Although the Tzar's visit could not be said to have been a success
socially, it bore some fruits from the military point of view. The
Monarch now saw how impossible it was for him to direct, personally,
from the Winter Palace, every phase of the campaigns. He now realized
the necessity of deputizing. Much as he disliked such a course, he gave
more power, more freedom to Baron Rosen's successor, General
Golovine, while stating with icy precision what he expected the General
to accomplish before the next year was out. First, a descent on the
Black Sea forts held by hostile tribes; next, a cleaning up, or final
campaign, in the upper Samour regions; lastly, the conquest of
Tchetchnia and Daghestan—this to include Shamyl's capture, or
death. It was a formidable programme, and the General set about
planning the three campaigns, with three separate armies. While the
first two projects were put into action, becoming protracted, indecisive
campaigns which lasted many years and were fought and re-fought by
a succession of generals, the third project—that of defeating Shamyl
and subduing the Tchetchens and Daghestani was, actually, the key
campaign, and the one which most concerns us here. Count Grabbé
was placed in command, and received the Emperor's good wishes for
the campaign. Perhaps some inkling of the task he had imposed struck
the Emperor. Perhaps, though dimly, he now perceived something of
the nature of these Caucasian wars, for, as he took leave of his troops,
standing among his generals and Staff Officers, wrapped in his great-
coat, and ready to step into his carriage, he sounded a note of praise.
With that smile which he knew how to put on, like a mask, as one of his
detractors observed, he turned towards the Commander-in-Chief, the
Governor and the Mayor of Tiflis; his gloved hand made a graceful
gesture, part salute, part comprehensive, possessive sweep which took
in the sprawling city, lying in its cradle of hills, cut through by its
splendid new boulevards, dominated by the newly-built Governor's
Palace and the Administrative buildings towering above the old,

Asiatic huddle. . . . 'Now,' said the Tzar, 'I know the meaning of the words in Genesis "Let there be light, and there was light".' And so, having identified himself with the Almighty, he stepped into his carriage and was driven off at the gallop.

Part Two

12

Excess

In Russia, if they do not attain their objective, they always go past it.   MADAME DE STAËL

It has been said that Russia is not a state, but a whole world—a whole world where everything is on another scale: where excess prevails. Extravagance is the Russians' predominant characteristic. The tempo of their everyday lives seems, to other less extravagant peoples, a compound of violence and inertia, both carried to extremes, in love or war, politics, human relationships, architecture, or anything else. The Murid Wars brought two extremes together. The limitless wide horizons of Russia were abruptly halted by the almost equally limitless high peaks of the mountains. The horizontal clashed with the perpendicular. Russian fought Tartar, Christian fought Moslem; the man from the plains faced the mountaineer. North invaded South. Both were violent —compromise was unknown to either in this issue. The Tzar's inflexible pride, his iron discipline, and love of power for power's sake, was paid in blood and anguish, as was Shamyl's fanaticism. It was a duel of extremists.

We have seen how the Caucasians lived and died by extremes. In Russia, the same quality of excess is to be observed in both life and fiction; and contemporary Russian political giants are nothing if not extremists. 'Russia will never be protestant, will never be the *juste milieu*,' wrote Alexander Herzen in his mid-nineteenth century essay, *Russia and the Socialist Revolution*. All through the literature of Russia, we trace violent emotions and excessive actions. Some of Dostoievsky's characters appear almost incomprehensible to the more restrained West. Goncharov's Oblomov carried his inertia to such violent lengths that he lolled away his whole life on the sofa. In real life we see many similarly excessive gestures: Peter the Great executing an unfaithful mistress Mrs. Hamilton—though nothing remarkable here, in history's long procession of tyrannic royal lovers—but the Tzar went so far as to preserve her head in spirits, awful reminder to her successors, a pickled *gage d'amour* which must have been singularly dampening to the ardours of the alcôve.

Continuing the excessive, or emphatic vein, we find Count Bes-
borodko, a keen whist player, causing a cannon to be fired every time
his partner revoked. Another ardent gentleman, wooing the lady of his
choice, on being repeatedly put off, throughout spring and summer,
with her promise to give him an answer 'when the snows came', could
wait no longer; and so, during one dark night, he ordered hundreds of
tons of salt to be spread over the landscape surrounding his lady-love's
house. Next day, he called: 'Give me my answer; the snows are here,'
he said, and we are not surprised to learn the lady was at last won.
Alexander Pushkin's family, both the pure-bred Russian stock, and
those which descended from Hannibal, the Abyssinian protégé of Peter
the Great, were, in all things, excessive; even going so far as to hang an
erring tutor in the courtyard.

*   *   *

Mighty Potemkin was the apotheosis, the embodiment, of all Russian
excess, with his unappeased appetites, furious energies, limitless resolves
and inconsequent oddities. 'I am God's spoiled child,' he would say.
Having gratified every whim, he married the Empress, established her
empire, accumulated colossal fortunes, made love to a hundred women,
'talked divinity to his generals and tactics to his bishops'; and his nails
bitten to the quick, he would sit, covered in magnificent diamond
orders, gnawing raw turnips, his brow furrowed, thinking intently—
thinking of that vast Russian Empire he was building for his Catherine.
Or he would sit brooding over a collection of caskets, each crammed
with precious stones, which he would sort, arrange and rearrange,
voluptuously, though absently, as he planned some flamboyant
coup.

Even on the march, and at his camp, Potemkin liked to create the
same sumptuous atmosphere as Tzarskoe-Selo around him. His silken
tents were adorned with gilt mirrors and malachite urns. Sometimes he
was dressed with equal splendour, pomaded and perfumed, his coat
glittering with diamonds, while he worked on State papers with such
savage energy, that he reduced relays of secretaries to fainting point.
Sometimes, for days on end, he would not bother to dress, and would
even arrive at State receptions, or a ball, wrapped in a tattered (though
ermine-lined) dressing-gown spotted with ink and grease, a crumpled
nightshirt dragging below, from which appeared his bare, hairy legs,
and feet thrust into Turkish slippers. After calling for as many as
fifteen (golden) beakers of cabbage soup, at intervals of a few minutes,
he would roar for coffee. And when it was brought, turn away, tears
welling from his one Cyclops eye. 'Take it away. . . . I only wanted to
long for something. You have done me out of my pleasure. . . .'

God's spoiled child was extravagant to the end. Far from his beloved Empress, death overtook him, in the south, near Jassy, as he was heading homewards. He ordered his great gilded travelling coach to stop. 'Lift me out. I want to die in a field,' he said. 'He lived on gold, but he died on grass,' said his Cossacks, watching by the huge body. No golden coin could be found to close his one eye; but a copper kopek-piece served well enough. It was in keeping with this Russian giant, whose life had always swung from one extreme to the other.

II

Excess—and its offshoot, eccentricity: how it colours the sombre Russian landscape! Countess Saltikov's favourite hair-dresser kept in a cage, lest he should be tempted to work for anyone else; Ivan the Terrible's Italian architect, who was blinded after he had completed the church of Vassilli Blagennoie: it was to be unique. Wicked land-owners were known to have forced serf mothers to abandon their babies, the better to nourish litters of pure-bred greyhound puppies at the breast. Fabulously wealthy nobles sent their bailiffs as far afield as Dresden, or Sèvres, to purchase five-hundred-piece dinner services, which were then laboriously transferred, by wagon, to Moscow, or Riazan, or any other province, where, in one splendidly extravagant debauch, after being loaded with a gargantuan feast, sucking pig, stuffed carp, and sturgeon, were next used as targets for a shooting contest.

Count Skavronsky, an enthusiastic musician, compelled his entire household to address him, and each other, in recitative. Another noble-man never risked the ennuis of travel without being accompanied by a cow to provide fresh milk, and twenty carriages (lined with sable) loaded with actors and musicians, busy tuning their fiddles, and re-hearsing their lines, ready for the next halt.

The Empress Elizabeth's fifteen thousand dresses show an equal extravagance, while her habit of cutting out the tongues of anyone who lied to her contradicted her absolute refusal (on humanitarian grounds) to sign a single death warrant.

Just as the great Russian houses were staffed by an excessive number of servants (Countess Orlov, with eight hundred, complained she could never get a glass of tea when she wanted one) so prodigious numbers of house-guests were forever arriving, but seldom leaving. Time and distance were differently computed in Russia; yet, in a sense, they were interdependent. If, to visit friends, it was necessary to travel a thousand or more miles, by carriage or sleigh, people were apt to pack up and move in for a whole season. Time seemed as measureless as the land. Some visitors came for a summer and stayed for ten years. Some lived in a remote wing of the house, and, we are told, never found their way to the dining-room or met their host, but just settled down among other guests: poor relations, tutors, *dames de compaignie* and French governesses whose stay had outlived their usefulness. There they remained, embalmed in this universe of emptiness, the vacuum of their days occasionally broken by the sound of carriage wheels, or bells; a sudden stir of life, telling of the arrival or departure of the family that had forgotten their existence, or—carrying even vagueness to excess—had never remarked their presence.

The Russian army, too, reflected this quality of excess. During the reign of Paul I (perhaps the most extreme of all the Russians), men were marched off the parade ground and headed north, in chains, for the matter of a missing button. The officers took to stuffing their pockets with all their available bank-notes, thus, if victimized without warning, they would at least have some ready cash to aid them in their exile. Even in their attitude of blind devotion to the Crown, the Russian military caste showed excess. We read of that guardsman who, as late as the beginning of this century, was walking along the Nevski Prospekt, and encountered a band of drunken agitators who spat on him. Having returned to the barracks and finished his duties for the day, he blew out his brains, leaving a letter stating that, since the Tzar's uniform had been dishonoured by rabble spittle while *he* was wearing it, no other course was open to him. And everyone agreed, it was a worthy end.

Russian Grand Dukes could usually be relied on to behave with the most spectacular excess, gambling at Baden-Baden, or duelling in the Bois de Boulogne over some celebrated *poule de luxe*. Occasionally a Grand Duke persuaded some such lady to visit his Russian estates. She was as much a sensation in Russia as he had been in Paris, appearing at bear hunts in *toilettes* from the Rue de la Paix, distracting the beaters as well as the guns. She would return home decked with splendid jewels and telling stories of sleighs festooned with emeralds, or snows strewn with parma violets rushed from Grasse to prove the ducal lover had not forgotten his *innamorata's* favourite flower.

During the nineteenth century, Rome had plenty of opportunities to observe the extravagant Slav nature. Many of the wealthy Russian emigrés gravitated there, centring round the Volkonsky family, who are still remembered by the Villa, and Via Volkonsky. Princess Sophie dreaded a timber shortage, a lack of firewood, after her vast Russian estates where an infinity of forests stretched to the north, and she mistrusted Europe's resources, always travelling with a huge trunk filled with logs. Another Princess, Zenëide Volkonsky, who had been converted to Catholicism and was adored by the Roman poor for her unbridled generosity, died as a result of her extravagant kindness. She had noticed a beggar-woman shivering in a doorway, and tore off her own warm petticoats to protect her. She herself went home sneezing, and died of exposure, extravagant even in death.

'*Fu una Principessa Roussa,*' said the poor of Rome, as they followed her coffin, wailing. They could not foresee that it was to be a dirge for all her kind—that legion of flamboyant Russian nobles who have now vanished forever. If they still linger on, more modestly, they have learned that what passed for the spectacular and the picturesque when they were rich, is merely regarded as ridiculous or undisciplined now that they are poor.

III

Among the classic, nineteenth-century Russian idealists and political dreamers, men like Herzen, Bakounin and Ogarev, the scarlet thread of excess showed itself strong and clear, against the sombre texture of their existence. Whole lives were dissipated in conversation; in interminable political discussions, in needless journeys undertaken on the spur of the moment—such as one cited by Herzen: its object, vaguely formed, 'to see what was going on in the Caucasus'. The Russian exiles followed Shamyl's campaigns avidly. He opposed Tzarist reactionary force—he was their ally!

The scene is London, a house at Paddington Green, where Alexander Bakounin was then living. Although he had become a revolutionary of world fame, he continued the pattern of life much as he had lived when a student in Moscow.

Here is Herzen describing Bakounin's ambiance:

He used to receive anyone, at all times, everywhere. Often he would be asleep, or tossing on his bed, which creaked under him, while two or three Slavs would be in his bedroom, smoking desperately; he would get up, souse himself with water, and at the same moment, proceed to instruct them . . . telling them they must try to find Garibaldi, to be received by Mazzini, to reach Kossuth. . . . He was not too much given to weighing every circumstance, looking only toward the ultimate goal, and took the second month of pregnancy for the ninth. He carried us away, not by his arguments, but by his hopes. . . .

In the middle of all his arguments, lectures, arrangements and shouted orders, this leonine figure would rush to his writing table,

clear a little space among the cigarette ash, and begin to write a number of letters, to Semipalatinsk, or Arad, Belgrade, Constantinople or Bessarabia. . . . His activity, his laziness, his appetite, his titanic stature, and the everlasting perspiration he was in, everything about him was on a super-human scale.

—was, in fact, excessive.

Herzen goes on to describe the arrival of a young Russian officer burning for the Cause—for Liberty—who had succeeded in escaping from
Russia, and whose goal was to meet Bakounin. He had only arrived
the night before, but a friend undertook to bring them together.

'I'm sure you won't refuse to do something for the common
cause,' says Bakounin.

'Of course not.'

'There is nothing that detains you here?'

'Nothing; I have only just arrived, I . . .'

'Then, can you take this letter to Jassy, at once? From there you
must make your way to the Caucasus. We particularly need a
trustworthy man there.'

*   *   *

The extravagant Slav temperament was to be traced in all classes
of society, and was never more marked than in the whole nation's
positively abandoned attitude towards suffering. *Toska*, a sort of inner
misery, a neuralgia of the soul, a compound of *cafard* and spleen,
permeated the nineteenth-century Russian nature (but is, even now,
the hall-mark of the émigré, and not yet entirely subdued by collective
living, calesthenics, and five-year plans of contemporary U.S.S.R.).
Dousha—the soul, ever a matter for introspective discussion among the
classic Russians, as portrayed in their literature, was generally held to
represent the *suffering* soul. This occupied a special place, becoming a
national attribute, almost a matter of pride—like sex to the French.

Russian peasants in particular were partial to songs which dwelt on
their suffering—not of the body, as might have been expected, but of
the soul. It was born of their hopeless condition. For the middle classes,
it derived from the stultification of their lives; while satiety and egotism
bred it even stronger, in the aristocracy. There was a whole tradition
of these suffering songs beloved by the villagers (and still sung by
collective farm-workers), their shrill harmonies accompanied by bala-
laika and accordion, echoing over the rolling wheat fields and steppes,
heard at dusk across the sun-flower plantations of the Ukraine, along
the sandy flats of the great rivers. Tikhii Don . . . Quiet Don, and
Mother Volga.

> Grisha! thy soul suffers for me! Go! Suffer for another,
> My soul suffers for Vadim,
> My tears are shed for him.

They were lusty in their grief, savouring it to the full.

Even the wealthy merchants and privileged nobility subscribed to
this cult, and enjoyed nothing more than to spend whole nights of
expensively fostered misery, listening to the gypsy choirs who knew that
for every wild drinking chorus, every bacchanal, their audiences really

craved some melancholic soul-song. The gypsies sat on benches round the walls of some stark private room of a restaurant or inn, the men shaggy and sullen, the women bunched in shawls and buttoned into uninteresting dresses, many of them the most unprepossessing-looking matrons. They stared straight before them, their black, untamed stare piercing the haze of smoke and the fumes of vodka, singing their haunting airs while their listeners became maddened and intoxicated by misery, transported by the obsessive quality of singers and songs, of sadness and suffering souls alike. Whereas in England, the old-wives' panacea has ever been 'a good cry', the Slavs went further, and were apt to nationalize their grief. Dostoievsky's Lizaveta Prokofvyvna points to Myshkin, saying: 'I've had a real *Russian* cry over him.'

The suffering soul was not confined within the frontiers of Russia alone; the nineteenth century Russians took it with them into political exile, along with their samovars and ikons, and were to be seen, sitting in cafés, discussing the state of their souls as earnestly as any constructive programme. They were a strange blend of despair and optimism, grandiose schemes, futility and petty bickerings. As the century progressed, anarchists and terrorists superseded the first idealists, but even they sometimes stopped experimenting with a new bomb formula to luxuriate in discussions about the miseries of the soul. Man cannot live by bombs alone.

Today, the Russian peoples, while retaining a certain Oriental fatalism, have learned to replace futility by purpose, and to sublimate the emotions which ravaged Herzen and his circle. These earlier idealists irradiated the last glow of purely personal sufferings. Party took the place of person, and Communism was formed. Seething emotionalism was canalized into one collective whole, where action, five-year plans, and superhuman efforts had the effect of occupational therapy, and overcame the last faint echoes of *toska*.

Yet excess remains: it is the core of the Russian peoples, their strength and weakness, at once their comic relief (to the outside observer) and their glory. It is the key to both their past and their present, and it must mould their future too. It is often incomprehensible to the West, puzzling and frightening, like the force of nature which, at heart, it is. Anyone who has known and lived among the Russian people, anyone who is steeped in their literature, and studies their history, becomes aware of this quality, or elemental force—excess. Thus we see, in the history of Russia, that it sweeps on its way, like the symbolic troika of which Gogol wrote, thundering forward, once centuries behind the West, but suddenly outpacing the rest of the world in its furious forward dash, over and across every obstacle, over lives and ideologies, but ever onwards towards its own goal, 'and sometimes', as Madame de Staël observed, 'when not attaining its objective, going past it'.

13

Hostage

*Ah! is the Supreme Name of God: it was put on earth
to help the suffering people take breath.* SARI SAQATI

The second siege and fall of Akhulgo, in 1839, may be considered the turning point of the Murid Wars. What happened there hardened Shamyl's resolve so that nothing could deflect him from his vengeance. Now he waged a war intensified by personal hatred and revenge.

In May Shamyl had withdrawn to Akhulgo, there to await the inevitable Russian attack with fatalism. It was with God! He had done all he could to prepare the fort, and it was, by nature, almost impregnable, being surrounded on three sides by a loop of the river Andi Koisou, and set among perpendicular mountain peaks and gullies. The whole rock formation was divided into a sort of double plateau, to which the aôuls of Old and New Akhulgo clung; the bluffs rose sheer, sometimes overhanging the gorges of the river below. The two sections of the aôul were divided by a fearful chasm, through which ran a smaller river, the Ashilta, a tributary of the Koisou. The only means of access, from one aôul to the other, was a narrow plank bridge, seventy feet above the river. Until the advent of heavy artillery fire, such a fortress could not be stormed. Thus Shamyl took his stand there, awaiting the attack, if not with complacency, with calm.

All his family were gathered round him; his mother, his sister, his wife Fatimat and Djemmal-Eddin, and now, another wife, Djavarat, with her two months' old baby, Säid. Nothing is known about Djavarat. She was not, like one of Shamyl's later wives, Zaïdate, married for political motives: nor had she been a captive, as Shouanete. When we consider Shamyl's overwhelming love for Fatimat, and his basic austerity of character, it seems probable that this marriage was impelled chiefly by the warrior's wish for sons—for fighters, to carry on his battles.

The unexpected arrival of a large number of civilians, women and children, fleeing from a Russian advance, did not shake his faith. When his Naibs pointed out that there would now be a thousand or more extra mouths to feed, he showed no misgivings. All things were with

God. Having looked to his defences, he withdrew to the mosque, to meditate and pray. At dusk, he would usually appear on the flat roof and lead the assembled garrison in 'Shamyl's Psalm', which he had composed some time earlier, and which was designed to replace the traditional songs of the Daghestani. It was a sombre chant, and one not calculated to raise the spirits of the garrison.

> Preserve us from backsliding
> Bring us the longed-for end.

However, even in this harsh land there were sometimes the most surprising distractions: barrel-organs, whether playing a recognizable tune, or merely jangling brokenly, were much appreciated in the aôuls, 'which, it seems, are the ultimate destination of all these musical instruments when worn out by hard service in Europe', writes one astonished traveller.

*   *   *

On June 29, at dawn, the Russians attacked. The summer sky was dotted with cotton-wool puffs of smoke from their guns, and rising columns of fire crackled round the wooden supports of the Murid defences. By mid-morning, two Russian batteries took up their stations at the foot of the rock, which towered above them. Their commanders called for volunteers; their duty was to scale the bluffs and make a breach in the walls of Akhulgo.

It was an impossible order for the Russian soldiers to execute, for they were defenceless against the hail of stones and burning logs which the Murids flung down on them. Each time they tried to gain a foothold in the smooth cliff face, or succeeded in reaching some ledge, by climbing on each other's shoulders, they drew the fire of Shamyl's flank watch-towers (though, at this stage of the battle, the Murids generally preferred to hold their fire, relying on javelins and daggers, skilfully aimed from above). By nightfall three hundred and fifty Russians had been killed, and the cliff face was stained red with their blood. But even the most desperate bravery was of no avail, and the Russians were forced to retire.

In the fortress Shamyl had lost some of his finest fighters. After a lull of four days, the Russians reopened the attack. Field guns and ammunition arrived from Temir-Khan-Shura, and a new, better-placed battery was dragged up the rocks east of the fort, out of reach of the Murid muskets; this now blasted the main walls of Akhulgo to a mass of debris, under which many of the Murids were buried alive. But Akhulgo continued to defend itself, with unabated fury. Every time the Russian generals were convinced the fortress had fallen, and had sent in their men to occupy the ruins, they were met with a terrible resistance at close quarters. Presently, it was seen that only the outer defences had suffered. The fortress lived and fought back, from the depths of the rock, as yet almost untouched. There was no way of coming to grips with the garrison. Their food supplies were large. They had wells, and so could hold out indefinitely, picking off the Russians, one by one, as they tried vainly to scale the bluffs. On July 12, more Russian reinforcements arrived, but, having made a forced march from Southern Daghestan, were in no state to fight at once, and joined the ever growing mass of men and supplies that were accumulating in the valley below Akhulgo rock.

However many troops stood ready to attack, whatever number of sharp-shooters set out under cover of darkness, few returned, and the rock remained unassailable. It was now decided that before any fresh assault could be launched, there must be scaling-ladders, ropes to haul the guns, and a system of baskets and tackle by which both men and guns could negotiate a profound ravine which lay between them and the least precipitous approach. These being obtained, the Russians began, under a hail of bullets, to manoeuvre into positions from which they could, once again, attempt to penetrate Shamyl's stronghold. Their losses were terrible, but after another week of steady bombardment, by day and night, General Grabbé began to believe the reports of his spies—the renegade tribesmen—who were positive the end was near. Shamyl's losses, they said, had been heavier than supposed.

The outer and inner bastions were now destroyed: food supplies were getting low, as the main stores had been hit. There were no cattle to fall back on, for there was no fodder. The people were becoming exhausted by the ceaseless bombardment. Moreover, they were now surrounded by unburied dead. This was crucial, for the stench sickened the Murid garrison, and was even wafted, in horrible waves, on to the Russians far below. The torrid midsummer sun flailed down on dead and dying, and the flies tormented the living, while the vultures flocked from miles around, and sat brooding among the ruins. The water was contaminated and, most important of all, there was nowhere to bury the dead. It is curious to reflect that, however lightly the Moslem tribesmen held death, none would ever leave their dead unburied on the field of battle; and now, while they would willingly fling themselves over the ramparts, not one of them would dispose of their dead in this manner. So the bodies lay piled there, only partially covered by rubble, in dreadful disorder.

When Count Grabbé was told—quite incorrectly—that Shamyl was preparing to flee, he decided it was time to launch a final attack. Three columns were sent out; the first making their way along a narrow ridge, in single file, carrying the scaling ladders and equipment, and covered by the batteries on the opposite hills. But from what appeared to be a blank cliff face, a deadly fire was poured upon them. Against this fire they struggled to reach a broad ledge, or platform, from where they hoped to gain the now shattered topmost walls. Seen from below through the staff officers' telescopes this platform had seemed an excellent springboard for the assault. But on reaching it, those troops who had survived the Murid bullets, found themselves swept by cross-fire from two block-houses concealed in the rock, and unseen from the Russian positions.

Now, six hundred Russians, half of them wounded or dying, were all herded together on this platform, a precipice on either side, a sheer rock face rising above them, and their only line of retreat under heavy fire. It was a slaughter-house. The men staggered and reeled in their blood, and slipping, crashed down the precipice; presently, every one of the officers had been picked off by the Murids, who could now afford to take aim in a leisurely fashion, selecting the officers first and sparing their ammunition where the men were concerned. They knew that weakness, exposure, and the ravine, would finish off most of them by morning. The second column, approaching by another route, was soon accounted for by a number of huge boulders that were hurled down on them, so that they were crushed to death, the rocks and their remains blocking up the narrow path through the gorge and adding to Akhulgo's natural defences.

The third column, approaching from another quarter, contrived to reach some of the outer defences unopposed; but then, on a ledge overhanging a precipice, they were here suddenly met by a wave of women and children who sprang on them from the ruins above. The women were dressed in men's clothing (to mislead the Russians as to the numbers of troops), and in the tradition of their Amazonian ancestors, they rushed on the enemy with drawn swords, while the children, brandishing daggers, one in each hand, crawled under the Russian bayonets, to rip up the soldiers' bellies; when they themselves fell, their mothers seized their bodies and flung them down on the approaching enemy, or sprang like furies on the rifles, leaping with them over the cliff, dying, that there might be one less gun to fire on Akhulgo. Once again the Russian commanders were forced to retreat; to re-form and plan another attack.

Inside the aôul, things were by no means so black as the Tartar spies had pictured. Shamyl had now managed to evacuate most of his wounded, by night, across the river Koisou, and to gain reinforcements from other aôuls. Fresh supplies of ammunition and provisions were reaching Akhulgo, under the nose of the Russian sharp-shooters. Meanwhile, Shamyl's men were descending the cliffs at night, by means of ropes, and fetching river water to replace that of the contaminated well. In such circumstances, the siege could very well continue through-out the winter, that cruel snowy winter of the Caucasian mountains, which wreaked such havoc on the Russian troops.

During a lull in the fighting, while each side re-appraised the other, Shamyl and his Naibs returned to their prayers and meditation, spending their time in the mosque which still stood, though its minaret had been demolished by the Russian mortars. Meanwhile the women began to issue forth from the caves and ruins. They immediately set about imposing domesticity on drama, contriving little clay ovens, in which to bake bread, sorting and tidying the rubble, polishing the swinging brass lamps of the mosque, shaking out the beautiful prayer rugs, which even Shamyl's stern purpose had not denied the mosque in his fortress. The women gathered together, their swords laid aside, to mend their torn and battle-stained clothing or to cobble together the shoes and slashed *tcherkesskas* of the warriors. The surviving children played in sheltered corners, frisking and sunning themselves, like little animals escaped from the darkness of the caves. Those of them who were more than five or six years old were practising javelin throwing, or expertly sharpening their kindjals.

Among these children could be seen a boy of eight, Shamyl's eldest son, Djemmal-Eddin, who was to play so significant a part in the Murid Wars. He was a thin, thoughtful-looking little creature, very pale, with the enormous, black, slanted eyes of his mother, and a singularly sweet smile. He carried himself proudly, followed his father everywhere, and was already an accomplished horseman and marksman, and had been beside Shamyl in several raiding sorties, wielding a kindjal that seemed too heavy for him. This was not unusual in the Caucasus, where a boy of twelve was already reckoned a warrior. The Suanetian boys, who were nourished by relays of wet-nurses until the age of ten, acquired gigantic stature, and were able to account for themselves in battle from the age of seven onwards. Throughout the siege Djemmal-Eddin was to be seen, standing a pace behind his father, on the battlements, in the mosque, or at the Murid councils of war.

*   *   *

In the Russian tents, Count Grabbé and his staff were holding a series of conferences. Smoking large cigars, meerschaum pipes, and the more delicate local *papirosses* (or cigarettes), they drank glass after glass of tea, the orderlies attending to the big brass sam vars which hummed softly, a *leit-motif*, reminder of peace and home, b hind all the barked-out orders, and voices talking of battle, death and destruction.

Akhulgo could never be taken, they decided, unless they could succeed in cutting off every supply line, and surrounding it completely, by rebuilding the ruined bridges across the Koisou, and so gaining the country behind the fort—the route used by Shamyl's relief forces. A whole month was now spent concentrating on this project. A bridge was at last built, in spite of furious opposition from the Murids, who, however, could not withstand Russian artillery on open ground. More Russian reinforcements arrived by way of Ghimri, which, being Shamyl's birthplace, he had supposed would remain loyal to him and oppose the common enemy. But Ghimri made no move, and the Russian columns were allowed to pass unchallenged, something Shamyl never forgave. Heavy field guns were established in fresh positions. In such country it sometimes took a week to move a gun, the men dragging it into position themselves, up paths where no horse or mule could go. ('Can a dog go there? Where a dog goes, a Russian soldier can go.') Two battalions were detached from the siege to spread out over the surrounding country and intercept any rebels trying to relieve Akhulgo.

Meanwhile, a brilliant feat of military engineering was achieved by a dandified young officer, Count Nirod, who, at staff headquarters, had won a reputation for keeping five Persian houris for his exclusive enjoyment. Confronted by an even sterner challenge, he now devised a long covered wooden gallery which, slung on ropes, dangled over an almost perpendicular cliff face, and sheltered numbers of men from the Murid bullets, who were thus able to reach positions from where they could leap the remaining chasms and hope to scale the last overhanging rocks. This daring enterprise took several weeks to construct and place. It was twice dashed to pieces by the Murids, who climbed down during the night and severed the ropes, so that at last chains had to be used. The whole operation took place under fire: losses were heavy, and any man detailed to work on it regarded himself as doomed. However, Count Nirod, who was beside his men during the whole period, survived without so much as a scratch. (He was a very handsome, rich and seductive young man, so perhaps the prayers of his Persian harem were added to the good offices of that benign providence which so obviously watched over him.)

Those who survived the Caucasian wars without a scratch were rare. In the casualty lists, there are, besides the usual entries, killed, wounded and missing, large numbers listed as 'contused'. This describes the injuries, often fatal, but ranging from abrasions to being crushed to pulp, obtained largely by the nature of the country; from stones hurled as weapons; from rolling boulders, and falls down chasms and the mountainside.

By the middle of August, Grabbé congratulated himself that Akhulgo was entirely surrounded and cut off, and now only remained to be taken. If the fierce summer sun had worked havoc among his own men, half the force being down with typhoid, in the besieged aôul, conditions were now desperate. The well had dried up; there was no food left, no fuel, and the wounded could no longer be evacuated. Nor was there any timber. Wood, for both fuel and construction purposes, was one of the Murids' most precious commodities; and this mountain country was above the timber line. The Russian guns pounded the rocks by day and night, and were gradually blasting out the subterranean defences and hiding-places the Imam had built with so much labour and pride.

Shamyl at last knew himself trapped. Only a handful of his garrison remained alive; half the women and children were dead, and the ammunition was almost gone. Some time before, the chieftain, or Starshina of Tchirkei, a nearby aôul, had proffered his services to Grabbé, as intermediary, but Grabbé had told him he would accept nothing but Shamyl's surrender to the Russian Government, moreover, his son, Djemmal-Eddin, must be given up, as a hostage, as gauge of his good intentions during negotiations. To these terms, Shamyl would not, at first, agree, and he sent back his Naib Younouss with a very haughty answer, 'something it ill-befitted a Russian General to receive'. But all Shamyl had left, now, was his pride; his proud spirit raged against the humiliations and bitterness of defeat; nor could he bring himself to give up Djemmal-Eddin. After another week of futile raiding, sharp-shooting forays, losses by fever and exhaustion, both sides were even further weakened, but the Russians were no nearer gaining Akhulgo, nor was Shamyl in any better position to prolong his fight. By now, his remaining warriors were so exhausted that many of them openly prayed for death. Only Shamyl's terrible pride, his will, continued to resist. The sun-scorched rock was covered with corpses, and the carrion crows swooped low, as the emaciated survivors, now mostly women, tried to keep them off the dying.

On August 18, Shamyl raised a white flag, and, in bitterness and grief, agreed to give up the little Djemmal-Eddin as a hostage to the abhorred Infidels. The child did not cry; his father and mother had both told him to conduct himself proudly before the enemy: it would not be for long—only as long as the negotiations were in progress. He must go—he must submit, they explained to him, for only that way could he save Akhulgo, and so enable his father to live and fight another day. He must not use his kindjal on his captors, said Shamyl. He must conduct himself honourably, with courage and patience. The time would come when he could use it in battle—and a shashka, too—fighting once more beside his father. Fatimat dressed him in a white tcherkesska and a towering white lambskin papakh, telling him never to forget he was the son of Shamyl the Avar, Imam of Daghestan, Allah's Prophet upon Earth.

She was never to see him again.

Escorted by three of his father's most honoured Naibs, Younouss, Talgik and Eski Naib, the little boy left Akhulgo for the Russian lines. The Naibs carried their Murid banners; from their shadow, the child walked forward, alone. Half-way down the winding ledged path, now, for the first time free of a raking cross-fire, a group of Russian staff officers awaited their hostage. They smiled, and held out their hands kindly enough, but the child turned away, his eyes filling with tears. He forced them back, knowing he must not cry; he had cried once before, when the siege began, and he had gone to Akhulgo, leaving his Tartar pony in the valley. His father had been displeased. Tears were not for an Avar boy; not for any Avar, man, woman, or child, he said sternly. Tears were weakness, something to which no Avar could own. 'An Avar is a man from his cradle.'

The Naibs lowered their banners in a last salute, and the child was led off towards General Grabbé's tents. As he went, he looked upwards, to the ruined aôul where his mother was weeping. He searched in vain for her, for the flutter of her veils, among the faces which were crowded on the crumbling battlements. But he could still see his father, standing a little apart, like a figure turned to stone.

Shamyl waited till the little boy was lost in the masses of men and horses and tents, far below. As night fell, the lights of the camp could be seen like glow-worms, dotted about the plain. Sometimes a bugle rang out, and there came the sound of singing, camp-fire songs, and laughter. The troops were celebrating the cease-fire, and the capture of so important a hostage. At last the siege was won, they said, lapping up the extra ration of vodka with which they had been issued.

But the stone figure on the ramparts above was still there, in the darkness, watching them, and planning his terrible vengeance, a vengeance that was to take sixteen years to consummate; which was, for the second time, to involve Djemmal-Eddin.

All that night Shamyl brooded and raged. He would never surrender in person. His fortress might fall, his son be given up as a hostage—both were surrendered in Allah's name. Allah would aid him, and he would win them back—in time. Next day he would have to negotiate.

General Pullo and his staff were admitted to the fortress, where, in a rubble-choked cave, surrounded by the putrefying bodies of his fallen Murids, Shamyl received them with his usual haughty impassivity. He would surrender on two conditions, he said: that he was permitted to live in his native Daghestan, and that his son remained nearby, at Tchirkei, in the custody of the Starshina, or village head-man. General Pullo returned to the Commander-in-Chief with this news, and an uneasy quiet fell over the mountains and valleys. Negotiations continued for several days, but finally, General Grabbé found the Imam as uncompromising and stubborn as General Klugenau had found him when they met in the ravine. His tone, said Grabbé, was intolerable. Insolence, on top of such a resistance! He, Grabbé, would humble him yet. He sent back a curt refusal. Shamyl must live wherever the Tzar decreed; as to the child—he had already been dispatched to St. Petersburg, where the Government would decide what to do with him. This act, on the part of the Russians, was one of the most cynical treachery. It was an abduction, a betrayal of all those standards of warfare which they prided themselves made them superior to their enemy. In seizing his son, they treated Shamyl as a bandit, a savage rather than a warrior.

The message reached Shamyl like a thunderbolt. His answer was a furious burst of fire, flinging defiance at the Russians below. He had not imagined they would act so swiftly, or with such wanton cruelty, as to send Djemmal-Eddin away, so far away, to the unimaginable north of the Tzar's capital, without even informing his father. There was nothing he could do now to regain possession of the child. There were no terms, now, which would restore him. The Russians would use him as their most powerful weapon. Shamyl's only hope now lay in escape. Akhulgo might be lost—but Muridism must live on, to fight back—for Caucasian independence, and for Djemmal-Eddin, too.

Next day, when the Russians renewed the attack, expecting to be met with a return fire, an ominous silence prevailed. They advanced, and still meeting no resistance, swarmed into the fortress of New Akhulgo. Absolute stillness reigned. Only the carrion still flapped greedily about the terrible heaps of dead. As the invaders rounded a corner of the deserted aôul, they could see, across the chasm dividing New Akhulgo from Old, large numbers of the garrison now fleeing, climbing the opposite cliff, or crowded along the goat-track path leading to the narrow bridge spanning the ravine. As the Russian soldiers watched them, they were suddenly set upon by a mob of villagers, chanting Shamyl's Psalm, determined not so much to defend their aôul as to die for Allah.

General Milioutine, then a young officer, has left his account of the scene. 'A desperate fight followed: the women defended themselves as furiously as the men and hurled themselves, unarmed, against whole rows of bayonets.' But they were overpowered, and the Russians now concentrated on Old Akhulgo, where the remnants of the Murid garrison were making their last stand. Even now, they refused to surrender, and having the Russians at close range, fought with the utmost savagery, so that fighting continued for a week or more.

Every stone hut, every saklia or cave, had to be taken by force [writes Milioutine]. Women and children, with stones or kindjals in their hands, threw themselves on our bayonets, or in despair, hurled themselves over the cliffs to certain death; among them, Shamyl's sister. It is difficult to imagine the scenes of this ghastly battle: mothers killed their children with their own hands, so that they should not fall to the Russians; whole families perished under the ruins of their saklias. Some of the Murids, though exhausted by terrible wounds, sold their lives dearly by pretending to give up their arms, but treacherously stabbing those about to take them.

Enormous difficulties were experienced in driving the rebels out of the caverns in the cliffs overhanging the Koisou.

We had to lower soldiers by means of ropes. Our troops were almost overcome by the stench of the numberless corpses. In the chasm between the two Akhulgos, the guard had to be changed every few hours. More than a thousand bodies were counted; large numbers were swept downstream, or lay bloated on the rocks. Nine hundred prisoners were taken alive, mostly women, children and old men; but, in spite of their wounds and exhaustion, even these did not surrender easily. Some gathered up their last force, and snatching the bayonets from their guards, killed themselves, preferring death to captivity. The weeping and wailing of the few children left alive, and the sufferings of the wounded and dying completed the tragic scene.

On August 29, the siege was over. It had lasted eighty days, and cost the Russians half their forces. But victory turned to dust in the Russians' hands, for Shamyl had vanished. Every cavern was ransacked, every saklia, all the rubble-heaps were uncovered; the putrefying bodies were examined and re-examined. He was nowhere to be found; none of his people could, or would, shed any light on the mystery, and the thwarted Grabbé had to admit that, once again, Shamyl had effected an escape as legendary as that when he leapt over the heads of his captors at Ghimri.

For a long while the truth was not known, appearing to be yet another miraculous episode, but at last it was pieced together. It seems that on the night of August 21, after Shamyl had been told of Djemmal-Eddin's being dispatched to St. Petersburg, he had planned and executed his daring escape. It was a dark, overcast night, and Shamyl, accompanied by Fatimat and Khazi Mahommed, their younger son, a small band of devoted Naibs, and Shamyl's second wife Djavarat, carrying her baby Säid, who was only a few months old, all set out on their desperate venture.

Fatimat could not keep up with them as they crawled and clung to the cliff face. She was eight months gone with child; it was decided she should try to follow more slowly, and join them at the river, far below. Younouss stayed behind, to help her while the rest pushed on. For a day, the little party hid in a cavern, half-way down the cliff face, without daring to move, or look for Fatimat. Next night, again under cover of darkness they succeeded in crossing the ravine by means of a tree-trunk balanced perilously across the chasm. Shamyl carried Khazi Mahommed on his back, his shoes in his mouth, and had reached the opposite cliff safely, when he saw that Fatimat had joined the Naibs and was about to cross. In spite of her condition, and the yawning depths below, where the furious waters raged over the rocks, she, too, crossed safely. Djavarat was about to follow her, carrying the baby Säid, when a Russian picket, from the cliff top, opened fire, and both she and the baby were killed outright. The rest of the band could do nothing. It was useless to go back, across the death-trap tree trunk, to bury her. Moreover, they were now themselves threatened by the Russians' fire. Once again it was decided to go on. They destroyed the log bridge, so that no pursuers could follow them, and after hiding among the rocks until the Russian sharp-shooters gave up their watch, the little band crept down the side of the gully, and reached the river. Here, they lashed logs together to form a raft, on which they piled straw-stuffed dummies calculated to draw the Russians' fire, when, in the morning, they sent it on its course. In the dawn, the raft was launched, and as it was carried along by the current, the Russian pickets began firing on it, pursuing it downstream. Shamyl and his followers seized their chance, and waded upstream, hugging the cliff, until they reached a ravine which cut inland, and by which they hoped to gain some mountain sanctuary. But here, by ill-luck, they encountered another Russian picket, and a desperate fight ensued. Shamyl was wounded—one Naib was killed, while a Russian bayonet ripped through the little Khazi Mahommed's leg. But Shamyl's shashka accounted for the Russian lieutenant, and the picket, left leaderless, fled ignominiously.

All that day they crept inland, through the boulder-strewn ravines and dark gulleys of Tchechnia, crossing and recrossing the winding rivers, and climbing the sandstone bluffs to gain the upper, seldom traversed mountain lands. They had had nothing to eat since leaving Akhulgo—Khazi Mahommed could no longer bear the pain of his bayoneted leg and begged for water, for food; but there was none. Fatimat was deadly pale, and it seemed as if she, too, could go no farther. At noon they halted to rest, but they were seen and recognized from afar by a group of scouts from Ghimri, who had gone over to the Russians, and were reconnoitring for them. The Ghimrians opened fire, but their aim was poor, and their bullets spattered off the boulders. Shamyl recognized them for the traitors they were, and rising to his feet, regardless of the fact he presented a splendid target, he cursed them and, invoking Allah to be his witness, shouted that he would have his vengeance. 'We shall meet again, men of Ghimri,' he thundered, as he turned to follow his Naibs up the mountainside. A large burst of firing came from the Ghimrians, spattering round the fugitives once more, though they were not pursued. Perhaps even now Shamyl inspired them with fear. A bullet zinged by him but missed its mark. That night as they slept, flung down, too exhausted now to be on their guard, the treacherous Akhmet Khan, heading a band of renegade tribesmen, passed within a few feet of their hiding-place. He had obtained permission from the Russians to hunt down the Imam. But, in the words of the Chronicle, 'Allah diverted their eyes'; they did not discover their quarry, and returned to the Russian base. Once more Shamyl had escaped miraculously.

Muridism would continue; the battle was not over. But Akhulgo had cost Shamyl very dear. Djavarat and the baby; his son Djemmal-Eddin; his fortress, his pride, more than nine-tenths of his Murids, and Khazi Mahommed wounded—perhaps lamed. As to Fatimat and her unborn child, he did not believe that either could survive this desperate flight.

Now, it seemed that only the life of a hunted outlaw lay before him. But 'man is immortal till his work is done'. Shamyl's work was not done; and he went forward to meet his destiny, and to become the scourge and glory of the Caucasus.

*   *   *

With Shamyl once more gone to earth, the Russians were again congratulating themselves on victory. There remained some minor engagements, the suppression of the last, unruly tribes—mopping-up operations, they believed, but no more. As to Shamyl, Grabbé offered a small reward for his head, but did not trouble himself unduly over his enemy, and returned to Temir-Khan-Shura in a puff of triumph, while, in St. Petersburg, the Tzar celebrated the fall of Akhulgo by ordering a medal to be cast, and distributed among his victorious Army of the South. No one knew where Shamyl was: his flight was described as disgraceful by those officers who had hoped to make him their prisoner; but it was still not generally realized that, in escaping, Shamyl had escaped *with his arms*—and therefore, with his honour.

The Caucasian warriors preferred death to being disarmed. The enormous significance of weapons—the mystique of the sword, in the Caucasus, was not yet perceived by the Russians. As long as Shamyl was free, sword in hand, there had been no defeat. Russia had taken possession of a conical rock, at great cost; the Imam had lost much, but he had lost neither freedom, nor honour. To the Russians, however, he appeared a hunted fugitive, of whom Grabbé wrote: 'His shameful flight, and the terrible lesson read to all those tribes which supported him, have deprived him of all influence, and reduced him to such a condition that, wandering alone in the mountains, he must think only of the means of subsistence, and his own personal safety. The Murid sect has fallen with all its followers and adherents.' General Grabbé was very sure of himself. He went on to say that any future expeditionary force would meet with no resistance, and that a series of forts could now be built without meeting any opposition. 'No unrest, no risings, need be feared.'

'Excellent,' wrote the Tzar Nicholas, on the margin of Grabbé's report. 'So far so good: but a pity Shamyl escaped. I fear fresh intrigues on his part, in spite of his having lost the greater part of his means and influence.'

But in Daghestan, to his own people and the remnants of his Murid forces scattered throughout the mountains, nothing was changed. He remained their Prophet and Leader, and they awaited his next move.

From the moment when the little Djemmal-Eddin was surrendered, the dark shadow of Akhulgo—of revenge—began to fall on a number of unsuspecting persons, whose destiny, sixteen years later, came to be bound up with that of Shamyl. A terrible reckoning was exacted. And in the end, the one who paid the most was Djemmal-Eddin himself.

14

Crowns and Cupolas

*All the Russias . . . that land which has extended
smoothly, glidingly, over half the earth.*   GOGOL

From the Caucasus to St. Petersburg: a thousand miles across 'all the
Russias'; a three weeks' journey from one world to another for Djemmal-Eddin. From the Russian camp below the bluffs, he had been
bundled into a carriage, jammed between two large, cigar-smoking
staff-officers who had talked over his head in a tongue he could not
understand. But they had been kind enough, offering him apples and
sweetmeats, and showing him their pistols. He had refused all their
overtures, sitting there, rigid. But when the carriage had jolted to a
standstill outside the Commander-in-Chief's headquarters, at Temir-
Khan-Shura, he had refused to get out; he had kicked and struggled,
breaking away from his captors like a little wild animal. The big good-
natured tow-haired sentries soon caught him, disarmed him, for he was
brandishing his kindjal, and carried him inside, to where a group
of staff-officers, and generals with native interpreters, were gathered
round a roughly marked map. Among the group was a tall swaggering
black-bearded man, wearing a bemedalled Russian uniform, but with
a turban in place of a cap. This was Daniel Beg, Sultan of Elisou, ruler
of part of Southern Daghestan, who had for many years been a loyal
vassal of the Tzar's, who held the rank of major-general in the Russian
army, and whose wife and family lived very much *à la Russe*, in Tiflis.
Speaking Ma'arul-matz, the Avar language, which was all Djemmal-
Eddin knew, he tried to calm the furious child.

For the first time since he had left Akhulgo, Djemmal-Eddin could
understand something that was said. Daniel Beg told him to be brave,
to trust his new friends, and to try and understand that nothing bad
would befall him. In being torn away from his family, the worst had
already befallen; but that was done on Grabbé's orders: now, the child
was to be sent north, to the Tzar. Daniel Beg tried his best to reconcile
the child to his fate. He told him of the long, long journey he would
make, of the great city he would live in, and how he would see the

mighty Sultan of the North. The child did not know who the bearded general was, although he had heard Daniel Beg reviled often enough, as a traitor, by his father's Murids. Had he known who spoke to him now, he would no doubt have tried to rush at him with his bare fists. He stood mutinous and silent among the hated Russians, his father's enemies, a little trapped animal, while they talked and smoked and laughed among themselves, and, after staring curiously at their valuable hostage, forgot he existed. Presently a young staff officer who had been watching the boy thoughtfully, went up to him with a smiling yet grave manner and, bowing ceremoniously, returned the child's kindjal to him. It was a gesture of imaginative tact and classic chivalry; it was perfectly understood by the child who had been brought up among Shamyl's warriors. He was a prisoner of war, but he was trusted and honoured by his captors. For the first time since his capture, a faint smile crossed his face, and the enormous dark eyes looked less wildly. It was the first step towards that understanding and admiration which, at last, was to become so strong a bond between Djemmal-Eddin and the Russians. Long after he had grown up, he remembered the young officer's gesture; but he never discovered his name; perhaps it was Passek, or Loris-Melikov, then gaining their first taste of Caucasian warfare.

Now, he was bundled into a tarantass, wedged between two more cigar-smoking officers, to head north. The long journey had begun. The great mountains, Beshtau, Maikop and Kazbek, loomed over the dark defiles: through the gorge of Darial they reached the open steppe country. There were no roads until Kharkov; the tarantass rolled and pitched about the seas of grass. It was a bone-shaker affair—unsprung, its occupant sitting on a heap of sheepskins or straw: but it was strong and could rattle across four thousand miles of mud and dust, stones and snow before it needed repair; for the passengers it was another matter.

Now it rattled north, by day and night: Rostov, its gilded domes reflected shimmering in the broad waters of the Don. Kharkov, Koursk, Orel, Toula, provincial towns, garrison towns, market towns—all threaded on the endless versts of emptiness. They were carrying dispatches to the Tzar, some wolf-hounds and an escort of Cossacks accompanied them. Sometimes they stopped to sleep a few hours at a *korchma*, or wayside inn, where they changed horses: or they would come to a military post where their guard, too, would be changed. No one had time for the little boy. Besides there was no one who could speak to him in his own language. But they had given him back his kindjal, and so he understood that they trusted him neither to use it, nor try to escape. He sat quietly, watching everything around him in this new strange way of life.

To the child who had known only the bare, flat-cushioned rooms of his father's house in the aôul, these korchmas appeared marvellous. He did not see their squalor, their dirt, the greasy table-cloths and bug-infested walls. The lamplight, something he had never seen before, shone over yellow wood tables and chairs, the rows of bottles, the huge tureens of cabbage soup, the mounds of buckwheat *blinii* and the inevitable brass samovar. The waiters, in their grubby linen roubashkas, scurried about, waiting on the officers with an alacrity that told of fear as well as respect. After supper, while the child nodded in his chair, or curled up on the warm shelf above the big tiled stove, the officers generally found time for a game of cards and a bottle of brandy, before the tarantass started out again. Generally, the child was so soundly asleep that he only woke with the morning light on his face, as they sped northwards once more.

One day, nearly three weeks after they had left Temir-Khan-Shura, the spires and domes and cupolas of Moscow rose abruptly before them. The setting sun slanted across the plains, and glittered on the double-headed golden eagle topping the Spasski gate of the Kremlin. They drove beside the towering walls of the Kitai Gorod, or Chinese City—the merchants' quarter—and were in the labyrinthine heart of Moscow. All around them, bells pealed, and tolled, clashed and hummed, in the evening air. Djemmal-Eddin peered round, fearful and amazed. This was the big city of which Daniel Beg had told him! He had never imagined anything like it. Such gigantic houses, such streets and shops, and carriages, and people, such noise, such a bustle. . . . Fat long-haired merchants, soldiers, women—unveiled women with bright coloured dresses and feathered bonnets. Uniforms, so many different uniforms: here, as in the provinces, priests long-bearded, long-haired, black-robed figures. Everywhere, street-vendors crying their wares, selling little hot pies, *piroshki*, apples, and religious prints.

As they drove deeper into the labyrinth, the September evening fell to a lilac twilight. The street lights shone out, amazing and new to the child from the Caucasus. One by one, lights appeared in the houses, revealing new worlds inside. Families gathered around a samovar, children's faces pressed to the window-panes. In one house, between the damask curtains, he could see an enormous, brilliantly lit room, crowded with people, all laughing, talking and eating. Some of the carriages which brought the guests were lumbering old family coaches, large as houses on wheels, painted and gilded and elaborately cushioned, and each coach accompanied by a pair of scarlet-liveried, turbaned guards—heyduks, still used by the old-fashioned Muscovite families.

When at last they reached the red palace that was the Governor-General's residence, the child was still gaping. He climbed down from the carriage, and stood there, a lonely figure, in his Caucasian costume and jaunty lambskin cap. The officers motioned him to follow them, and he climbed the great sweep of marble stairs that led to the Governor-General's suite. Stairs: such flights of stairs as he could not believe. At home, there were no stairs: ledges were cut in the rocks, between one terrace of the aôul and another; and the two-storeyed house Shamyl had commanded the Russian deserters to build for him had, it is true, a rough, exterior stone staircase, leading to the upper rooms; but he had never seen anything like this great curved sweep of marble which seemed to coil upwards into the sky, three, four stories high, and all flooded with the brilliance of an enormous crystal chandelier. The Governor-General did not have much time to spare for the little hostage, however much he represented, to Russia, a signal of victory. He patted him on the head, and instructed one of his secretaries to see he was fed and put to bed. The secretary handed him over to a footman, who in turn gave him in charge of a housekeeper.

On the following morning, very early, he was wedged into a fast carriage (a *britchka*) between the same cigar-smoking pair, and they proceeded on their journey. The route between Moscow and St. Petersburg was the best in the realm: six hundred and seventy-seven versts of smooth, well-kept road, over which the britchka seemed to fly. This road had first been planned in 1816. Before then, only tracks had existed—tracks worn by generations of cartwheels and weary feet. With the accession of Nicholas I, the principal routes began to be constructed, mostly by convict labour, linking the cities and provinces. There were still no railways; the first railroad ran between St. Petersburg and Tzarskoe-Selo. It had been constructed in 1840, and though the government next undertook a line to Moscow, this was only completed in 1852. At the time of Djemmal-Eddin's arrival, Russia still travelled by britchka, the bone-shaking tarantass, troika, or sleigh.

If Moscow—an Asiatic huddle to most sophisticated visitors from the West—had appeared marvellous and strange to Shamyl's son, how much more extraordinary must St. Petersburg have seemed. This westernized city spread its superb Italianate perspectives on all sides: waterways, canals spanned by delicate iron balustrades, and the stretches of the Neva, widening from Kronstadt to the northern oceans, were all fabulous to the child who had never seen the sea, and who had only lived among arid rock plateaux. The Nevsky Prospekt, the palaces of Milliyonnaiya, the Admiralty, the Opera House, the mammoth cathedrals, granite monoliths, and the vast Senate Square, were all conceived gigantically. Above all, the Winter Palace, its quarter-mile length of pillars and porticos, ornate windows, sentry-boxes and echoing courts, seemed to be the habitation of some giant, or ogre, as indeed it was. The original building had been destroyed by fire, in 1837, but in accordance with Nicholas' command, it had been rebuilt within a year.

'The mighty result of human will applying human physical powers in a struggle with the laws of nature' [wrote de Custine, standing before its grandeurs two years later, and, as usual, moralizing]. The interior works were continued during the great frosts, he tells us. 6000 workmen were continually employed; a considerable number died daily, but the victims were instantly replaceable by others, brought forward, to perish in their turn in this inglorious breach. 'And the sole end of all these sacrifices was to gratify the caprice of one man! . . . During the frosts, when the thermometer was at 25 or 30 degrees below zero, 6000 obscure martyrs—martyrs without merit, for their obedience was involuntary—were shut up in halls heated to a temperature of 30 degrees of Reaumur, in order that the walls might dry out quicker; thus these miserable beings had to endure a difference of 50 or 60 degrees of temperature, on entering or leaving this abode of death which was designed to become, by virtue of their sacrifice, the abode of vanity, magnificence and pleasure.'

Now, behind the gigantic façade, within the courts and quadrangles, the Emperor Nicholas, 'The White Tzar', was awaiting the arrival of his little captive with a mixture of complacency and interest. Nicholas was well aware of the prestige such a hostage would give him—Nicholas —in the eyes of the Caucasians. He expected it would shorten the war by inducing Shamyl to surrender. He was fond of children, in a remote and dignified manner. He unbent, occasionally, and was an affectionate, if stern, parent; he very much enjoyed exercising his celebrated charm on the children of his courtiers, magnetizing them into his way of thought, leading them towards that reactionary pattern he held to be indivisible with loyalty. The army was the only suitable career for any young noble: to die for his country—for God and Tzar—the finest death. The Caucasus provided a splendid testing-ground, and as the cadets graduated from the Corps des Pages, or the various military schools which he personally supervised, Nicholas invited them to the Winter Palace, where, in the malachite drawing-room, almost over-come by emotion, he congratulated each one of them on the fortunate destiny which now gave them a chance to serve and die on the Caucasian front.

II

When Djemmal-Eddin was brought to the Winter Palace, the Tzar showed him a genuine warmth; he felt sorry for the lost child and he saw in him, too, a potential ally. This child could be trained into becoming a powerful instrument for taming the Caucasus. His trust and respect—his love, even, must be won. He turned the full battery of his charms on the unsmiling little boy, and through the interpreter, spoke to him kindly, without the least trace of that arrogance which was so often to be observed in his manner. He welcomed the child, spoke to him of the respect and admiration he, personally, felt, and all his generals felt, for the Imam Shamyl. He hoped, he believed, Djemmal-Eddin's captivity would not last too long. . . . Meanwhile, and here he smiled with that grace which so many of his subjects found irresistible, he wished Djemmal-Eddin to conduct himself honourably—as his father's son—to profit by his sojourn in Russia, to learn Russian, to benefit by all the blessings which the West could bestow. In a little while, he would perhaps enter the Corps des Pages, so that he could live close to the Emperor; he would study at the Military Academy, and the Tzar would see to it that he had a horse of his own; he could go and pick one out, from the Royal *manège*, said the Tzar, genuinely paternal. The youngest Grand Duke should accompany him. Meantime, with a comprehension that was unexpected, he arranged that the child should be placed in the household of one of his courtiers. 'He needs a home, other children round him—a nianyia,' said the Autocrat, suddenly turned human.

Next day, Djemmal-Eddin's wanderings were over. He found himself in a large, comfortable town house, where he shared the nursery with the younger children. A round-faced peasant nianyia took him to her heart, and soon he was able to smile, and to speak a few words of Russian. But for a long time he did not forget. At night, tucked in bed, with the red winking light of the lamp swinging before the ikon, a dark blur in the shadowy corner of the room, he remembered his mother and father, and those terrible last days of fighting at Akhulgo. Gradually, the fighting he had seen, the bloodshed and violence surrounding his childhood faded, passing into a half-world of memories and dreams, less real now than his life at St. Petersburg.

The Tzar appointed himself his guardian, watching over him with solicitude. He met all the expenses for the child's upbringing from his own purse, had him brought to the Winter Palace several times a week, and saw to it that he was, within the limits of his exiled condition, well and happy. On one point, however, he was adamant. No one must now speak to him of his past, of the Caucasus, or his father; nor must he, at present, encounter any of those Circassian and Caucasian princes who, having sworn allegiance to Russia, were being received at Court in increasing numbers, entering the Guards' regiments, or being appointed as aides-de-camp to the various Grand Dukes. These 'furious eagles', as they were called, filled St. Petersburg with a mixture of terror and delight. They worked havoc with the ladies, high and low, who granted them melting looks as, wearing their native dress, they paraded about the streets, 'with that eagle glance, that light, half-floating step peculiar to them'. They were greatly indulged by the Tzar, who realized they were not to be coerced. Their loyalty was invaluable— and flattering, too. But they were grown princelings, tried fighters; they could only be won, and kept, by indulgence and favouritism. Djemmal-Eddin was another matter. He was young enough to be transformed wholly: given time, the Tzar felt confident he would become as malleable, as devoted as could be wished—another son. Perhaps, one day, he might even be made Viceroy of the Caucasus—Regent under God and Tzar.

Meantime, these 'furious eagles' sometimes tried the Tzar's forbearance to breaking point. One Circassian Guards'-officer plunged his kindjal into the heart of a droshky driver over the matter of an exorbitant fare. At manœuvres, they sometimes ignored their commanding officer, galloping their horses, standing in the stirrups, the reins held in their teeth, flourishing a kindjal and shashka in each hand, leaping to the ground, on to the horse's back again, at the gallop. Wonderful feats of horsemanship, but in defiance of the command— *thoroughly* undisciplined. Yet what could the Tzar do? At all costs, he needed their loyalty, so he donned his smiling mask, stroked his silky moustaches, and bowed gracefully, as they thundered up to the very carriage where the Tzarina and her daughters sat watching the review in trembling delight.

It was not always possible to keep Djemmal-Eddin away from the echoes of his past. These reviews, for example, which were a regular part of Court life, and which all the Royal family attended, could only revive memories of djighitovkas he had watched, by his father's side in Daghestan. Then, too, the old widowed Queen Maria of Georgia, now pardoned, was sometimes commanded to attend State functions. On these occasions, she had a most unfortunate way of searching out Djemmal-Eddin, who was generally standing quietly behind the aides-de-camp, his diminutive figure dressed in the Court tailor's version of the Caucasian tcherkesska, and swallowed up among the crowd of Chevalier Gardes and Gardes à Cheval, Chamberlains and Gentlemen-in-Waiting who surrounded the Tzar. The old Queen always talked to him in some dialect that no one else, even the official interpreters, seemed to know. It was most annoying. What was she saying to the child? But it would not do to keep them apart too ostentatiously. . . . No one seemed to have realized that the old lady knew better than anyone else the feelings of the child whose exile was only just beginning.

The Marquis de Custine, writing of a Court Ball he attended in St. Petersburg about this time, was quite overcome by the luxury and elegance of the scene. How then must it have seemed to the wondering eyes of Djemmal-Eddin? De Custine speaks of the myriad wax tapers (no other lighting was ever used for fêtes at the Winter Palace), of the supper tables set with silver dishes, festooned in garlands of hothouse flowers, of the guests, all ablaze with gold lace and diamonds, their glitter reflected in the gigantic pier-glasses which lined the walls between the marble colonnades. Such marbles, glowing gold, veined with rose, sulphur yellow from the Urals, the deep crimson of *onyx rouge*, *Brocatelle violette du Jura*, massive urns of malachite and lapis lazuli; riotously gilded furniture, upholstered in shimmering Lyons silks—one, in particular, of interwoven gold and silver pheasants and ferns, had been designed by Philippe de Lasalle, whose beautiful design of bunched lilies adorned Marie Antoinette's bedroom in her heyday.

The uniforms of the Court officials, the various regiments, the Oriental princes, and even the less exotic guests, were all of a superlative magnificence. The Emperor wore the white and gold uniform of the Hussars, trimmed with black sable. The ladies, from the Empress down, wore their traditional Court dress, dark, rich-coloured velvets with ermine-trimmed trains, festooned with the most barbaric and splendid jewels to match the velvet—parures of rubies for crimson velvet, sapphires for blue, and so on; their heads literally bowed down by the weight of the enormous stones which adorned their head-dress— the *kokoshnik*, from which a long gauze veil floated gracefully. These costumes recalled the splendours of Muscovy, where the mediaeval Tzars held court in the low, vaulted halls of the Kremlin. 'In France', wrote de Custine, 'the balls are disfigured by the sombre attire of the men, whereas the varied and brilliant uniforms of the Russian officers give an extreme brilliance to the salons of St. Petersburg.' (An English visitor remarks that here even the wildest fantasies of a military tailor's brain were realized, the uniforms ranging the spectrum, and even including pink and violet.)

De Custine goes on to note the various Oriental potentates at the Winter Palace, whose presence, as declining powers, reminded him of the triumphal pomps of Rome. Among these Mongol and Asiatic princes, he mentions the Khan of the Khirgiz. This tributary vassal had come to St. Petersburg with his twelve-year-old son, hoping to gain the Tzar's interest, and eventually to place the child among the Royal pages, thus securing for him Russia's benevolence in his future reign. De Custine also mentions Djemmal-Eddin's comforter as 'an old Queen of Georgia who had been dethroned thirty years earlier. The poor woman languished unhonoured at the court of her conquerors. Her face was tanned like that of a man used to the fatigues of the camp, and her costume was ridiculous.' But she was the single discordant note amid all the glories. Everything else claimed de Custine's superlatives. Fabulous, fantastic, magic fête! We read of fountains set in groves of

lemon and banana trees 'where the northern dancers seemed transported by enchantment to the forests of the tropics. Here was not
merely luxury, but poetry, too . . .' And harmony. 'Several orchestras
were executing military symphonies, and responding to each other with
a harmony that was admirable.' No doubt they played a selection from
Glinkas' opera, *A Life for the Tzar*: it had become almost a national
anthem, and expressed so exactly the Tzar's own sentiments about the
sacrosanctity of his office, even if a carping critic did describe it as
'coachmen's tunes'.

The Empress Marie-Feodorovna had been Princess Charlotte,
daughter of the lovely Queen Louise of Prussia, and married the Grand
Duke Nicholas in 1816, when both were romantic adolescents. It had
been a love-match. All the strength of her domestic German sentiment
had been centred round her handsome young husband. When he
succeeded to the throne, unexpectedly, upon his brother's abdication,
she had been plunged overnight into limelight, drama and terror. The
bloodshed of the Dekabrist Rising had been a fatal beginning to their
reign, and she had never recovered from the shock. Her head shook,
aspen-like, upon her slender, graceful neck. She became emaciated and
livid, slept little and was a prey to nerves for the rest of her life. But a
certain inbred elegance and softness remained to charm all those who
knew her. She took a special motherly interest in Djemmal-Eddin; she
did not share her husband's dreams of Caucasian conquest; to her, war
represented nothing but suffering; the child was no pawn, no political
emissary, but only a lonely little boy. Sometimes she would have him
brought to the English cottage she had built in the park at Peterhof; it
was an unpretentious little house in the Gothic style so fashionable in
England. Here, the Empress said, she could rest her eyes from the glare
of all the gold in the Winter Palace and Tzarskoe-Selo. At the cottage,
she and the Tzar believed they were leading simple lives, as the
courtiers stood back, for a few hours, and there were no sentries presenting arms every time they walked in the garden. Here, in her
gemütlich little study, 'my small world', she must have won Djemmal-
Eddin's heart, teaching him how to build card-houses, feeding him the
Apfelstrudels of her childhood, and telling him German fairy stories
where Rumpelstilzchen and Snow-White merged, in the child's mind,
with legends of Simurg, the giant white bird of Kafdagh, and all the
peris and almas of the Caucasian mountains. After a while, when he
had begun to speak some Russian (French and German were the
languages of the Court, Russian being seldom heard there, except in the
presence of the Tzar, who commanded it to be spoken, as a gesture of
nationalism), he was placed in the Cadet Corps School. Although the
youngest pupil there, it is not surprising to learn that he showed a

remarkable degree of proficiency in riding, cavalry charges, sword
play, and general military demeanour.

At the yearly fête, held in honour of the Empress, it was the custom,
among other festivities, to hold a review of the Cadet Corps, the Empress
being present on the parade ground, in her calèche, and the Tzar
taking the salute as his embryo generals marched past. The all-seeing
de Custine was present on one such occasion:

> After several manœuvres had been perfectly executed, His Majesty
> appeared satisfied. He took the hand of one of the youngest cadets,
> led him forth from the ranks to the Empress, and then, raising the
> child in his arms, to the height of his head, that is—above the head
> of everybody else—he kissed him publicly. What object had the
> Emperor in showing himself so good-natured on this day, before the
> public? I asked the people around me who was the happy father
> of the model cadet, thus caressed by the sovereign, but no one
> satisfied my curiosity. In Russia, everything is turned to mystery.

Perhaps the mystery might have been solved if he had known of
Djemmal-Eddin, the youngest cadet, once Shamyl's pupil on the field
of battle, now the Tzar's protégé and pawn.

III

Alexander Herzen, in exile, was determined to shatter the sycophan-
tic silence which shrouded so many evils of Nicholas' reign. He had
much to say on the subject of Siberia, the military colonists, prison
conditions and other abuses. The Tzar's high-handed methods of pressing all the infant aristocracy into his Guards regiments was as nothing
beside his practice of conscripting thousands of small boys, serf children
from the villages, or children from the ghettos, all seized and marched
off for military or naval service. Herzen describes meeting one such
Jewish convoy. It had been raining heavily, the children were coughing
—those who were left, that is; about a third were already dead,
en route.

'Not half will reach their destination,' said the officer in charge.

'Have there been epidemics?' I asked.

'No . . . but they just die off like flies. A Jew boy, you know, is such a
frail, weakly creature . . . he is not used to tramping in the mud for ten
hours a day, and eating dry bread—then, being among strangers, no
father or mother, nor petting; they just cough and cough, until they
cough themselves dead . . . And I ask you—what use is it to the State?
What can they do with such little boys? . . . Well, we must be off. . . .
Hey! sergeant! Tell the small fry to form up.'

'They brought out the children,' continues Herzen: 'it was one of the most awful sights I have ever seen. . . . Boys of twelve or thirteen might somehow have survived it, but little fellows of eight and ten. . . . Pale, exhausted, with frightened faces, they stood in thick clumsy soldiers' overcoats with stand-up collars, fixing helpless, pitiful eyes on the garrison soldiers who were roughly getting them into ranks. The white lips, the blue rings under their eyes looked like fever or chill. And these sick children, without care or kindness, exposed to the icy wind that blows straight from the Arctic Ocean, were going to their graves.

'What monstrous crimes are secretly buried in the archives of the infamous reign of Nicholas, noiselessly sunk in the silent bogs of officialdom or shrouded by police censorship!'

And he ends: 'May the reign of Nicholas be damned for ever and ever. Amen.' It was his life's prayer.

IV

After the disaster of Akhulgo, Shamyl and his forlorn band had found sanctuary in the high mountain country where few Russian troops had yet penetrated. Here, at the aôul of Garashkiti, 'Shamyl the great Imam lived like a cast-off rag'. Here, Khazi Mahommed's leg was healed. Nearby, five weeks after their arrival, Fatimat gave birth to a third son, Mahommed Sheffi. Here, Shamyl and the eight Naibs that were left set about planning how best to re-form his scattered and broken forces. Here, Shamyl meditated and prayed, and soon, his reputation for wisdom and holiness began to spread abroad. Now numbers of mountaineers came to Garashkiti to seek him out, asking his leadership. The Mollah of Shouaïb and Djevat Khan—both powerful local chieftains—Avars, like Shamyl, supported him loyally. Six months after his flight from Akhulgo, he accepted the rulership of the Lesser Tchetchnia, and set out, to ride from aôul to aôul, inspecting his new territory, and preaching the Shariat once more.

Neither the Chronicles of Tahir, nor the Russians are able to explain the astonishing fact that within one year of the Akhulgo disaster, Shamyl had risen to power again. Within eighteen months he had once more put an army into the field; within three years defeated Grabbé; four years later, all Daghestan was reconquered, the Russian garrisons of the Tchetchnia destroyed or under siege, and once more, Muridism the rallying point for innumerable tribes. But so it was.

Shamyl reached the zenith of his powers between 1845 and 1850. Although greater numbers of troops were now concentrated against him, this was the gauge of his power; and a greater number of mountaineers now rallied to his standard. Although no absolute victory was obtained for either Russians or Caucasians with the ebb and flow of battle crowning first one side and then the other, it seemed at last as if only death could vanquish him, and the mighty Russian generals were compelled to admit they could do no more than hold him at bay. They could obtain no lasting foothold in the Caucasus: as soon as a province submitted, or was taken, it slipped from their grasp again. The very nature of the land opposed them, was Shamyl's ally, like the climate, which, winter by winter, forced them to stagnate in winter quarters, and in summer, brought its dread train of fevers and drought. Across the giant chess-board of mountains and valleys, hung a curious atmosphere of hopelessness; both armies were stalemated, remaining sometimes for months at a time, without any apparent action. But casualty lists told something of what it cost the Russians even to remain there: told something, but not everything.

Men were cheap in Russia; reserves were endless; men were levied, and often not even listed, from such sources as the prisons and the mines; the serfs could be mustered from Siberia to the Polish frontier. The Sarmatians, a Polish minority whose predilection for fighting was only equalled by the Tartars, were generally found in the Uhlan regiments of the Russian army, and came largely from the Shliakhta, the small impoverished nobility who, having lost fortune and estate, lived only to fight and, like true mercenaries, often forgot for what they fought in the pure love of fighting.

Just as Nicholas was to rely, cynically, in the Crimean War, on what he described as Generals January and February, to reduce the enemy ranks, so now there was General Manpower. On paper the numbers were never accurately reckoned although half a million Russians are believed to have perished in the Caucasian campaigns of 1834–59. (Shamyl's losses always remained unknown.) Organization was faulty, distances enormous, and the voices of the levied men silenced by the guns. They were rounded up, marched off, equipped or not equipped, trained or not, according to how urgently they were needed on the battlefield. Often, being issued with a bayonet, they were merely ordered to fight. (Though, naturally, this state of affairs did not apply to the disciplined, devoted body of regular troops, for whom, as we have seen, it was enough to die for God and Tzar.) Yet all of them, trained or untrained, fired by patriotism or pressed into service, raw recruits, or the flower of the army, faced the enemy side by side; died bravely, died horribly, died of thirst, of frostbite, of wounds, slashed to ribbons by a dozen shashkas; died of fevers, of scurvy, dysentery, or cholera; of privations and dirt and homesickness; of despair, too, when, as prisoners, recaptured trying to escape, their eyes were put out, and they lay hoping for death in Shamyl's prison pits. This was war: horrible wanton war. Glorious war, said those who directed it, who sent the men out to meet death.

All the while that Shamyl fought, every battle, every raid, every prisoner taken, was scrutinized by him in relation to obtaining Djemmal-Eddin's release. But however many daring raids his Naibs made, however many Chieftains and Begs rallied to him, whatever number of Russian prisoners were herded into his camp—even when so important a captive as Colonel Prince Ellico Orbeliani was held in chains—he was no nearer obtaining a bargaining point, on which to negotiate his son's return. Only an absolute victory over Russia as a whole—something to which even Shamyl's ambitions did not aspire, only the Tzar's death (for his heir, the future Alexander II, was known to be far less obsessed by dreams of Caucasian conquest) or the aid of some powerful independent country, such as Britain, could change matters. Or, less remote, though entirely improbable, the capture of some member of the Tzar's family. . . . A Grand Duke, perhaps, one of the Romanov princelings sent about the country to inspect barracks and monasteries, to review troops and flatter provincial administrators. But the Caucasian theatre of war having become a desperate issue, the young Grand Dukes were kept at a safe distance.

If only the Tzar would make another of his state visits to Tiflis. . . . If only he—Shamyl—could capture the great White Tzar! In 1838, he had not been powerful enough. Now things were different. He saw the Tzar dragged before him in fetters; saw the pomaded head bowed in submission; saw the plump, ringed hand forced to sign an order for Djemmal-Eddin's immediate release. . . . Thus Shamyl, luxuriating in thoughts of vengeance, his eyes narrowed to scimitar-curved slits, glittering with hatred. But the abhorred monarch remained in his capital, sending more, and ever more, waves of men to the Caucasus. Dragomirov's dictum echoes down the years: 'Men, men, and again men. Always men—they are the first and best instrument of battle.'

For all Shamyl's admirably organized system of intelligence, for all the prisoners he took, and the St. Petersburg journals and newspapers he had read to him by interpreters, he never obtained any direct news of Djemmal-Eddin, save that he was brought up at Court, as the Tzar's protégé. But, in 1845, he learned that his son was a pupil at the Corps des Pages, among the other young scions of nobility; this, while soothing his pride, did not reassure him, for the gazette went on to say that the young Avar was soon to enter the Cadet Corps, there to further his military studies, with the intent of obtaining a commission in one of the Guards regiments. The idea that his own son could enter the Russian army, even, at last, to fight against him, had never occurred to Shamyl, and it struck to his heart like the thrust of a kindjal. But it brought him no nearer submission. They had invaded his country, devastated its crops and aôuls, slaughtered its people, imposed their hated rule wherever they could; taken his son, and now—were rearing him to fight against his own father. The fight would go on, to the end. He would never surrender: he fought for Allah, freedom, and his own terrible pride.

15

Shadows on the Mountains

*I know not who could behold the Caucasus and not
feel the spirit of its sublime solitude awing his soul.*
SIR ROBERT KER-PORTER

Between 1830 and 1850 many remarkable figures appeared on the
Caucasian scene; some played great rôles before they vanished; some
stood shadowed in the wings of history, awaiting a cue which never
came. Some flitted across the immense landscape, and were silhouetted
for an hour, or a day, against the towering peaks, and then they, too,
were gone. Some found themselves there by chance; some, because of
Shamyl; others, in spite of him. Some had never heard of him, and
lived out a brief Caucasian episode, unaware of his thunders. Some, like
Lermontov and Tolstoy, fought against him, and in so doing, discovered
the Caucasus 'the exotic revelation', to many northerners. Some, like
Alexander Dumas, saw it as rich material for yet another book of
travel. He sweeps the reader along with him, breathless and marvelling.

He will visit the fair at Nijni Novgorod, float down the Volga, and
at last reach the Caucasus, 'where we shall visit Shamyl's camp:
Shamyl the Titan, who struggles from his lair, against the Tzar of all the
Russias. . . . Will he know our name?' asks Dumas, assuming the
majestic plural. 'Will he allow us to sleep a night in his tents?' But it
seems that the irresistible old rogue never encountered the Lion of
Daghestan: at any rate, an invitation to the mountain lair was not
forthcoming. Yet it is through Dumas—through a romantic epitaph he
wrote while in the Caucasus, that we are reminded of one of the most
celebrated Russian writers of the Caucasian scene. Alexander Bestoujev
is now as seldom read as Dumas; but in his day, under the pseudonym
of Marlinsky, his richly coloured Caucasian tales enjoyed enormous
popularity.

Bestoujev and his brother had been, like so many of their generation
and milieu, involved in the Dekabrist rising. His brother was hung, but
he was spared, and sentenced to hard labour in Siberia. After some
years, he was transferred to the Caucasus to serve in the ranks. (He had

been a Captain of Dragoons, but now was only so much cannon fodder.) In the south, he obtained the material for such tales as *Ammalet Beg*, which were published in many languages, and were equally admired beyond the Russian frontiers.

Bestoujev's fate was not forgotten by his fellow-writers. Mickiewicz, the great Polish poet, travelling in the Caucasus, encountered him in a Caucasian garrison town. 'The hand which Bestoujev held out to me had been torn from his sword and pen and attached by the Tzar to a convict's cart,' he wrote with indignation: he was described as 'a new Prometheus, chained there by Northern Jupiter', and the historian Ivan Golovine echoed these denunciations, and dedicated his book on the Caucasus to the memory of his friend.

But all of these tributes paled beside that of Olga Nesterov, who loved him, and offered her young life as proof. It was a melancholy and unnecessary episode, in keeping with the romantic traditions of the age. Moreover, it catered to that neurotic craving found in so many Slav natures, whereby they flourish and have their being only through the dramas and emotional demands they can inspire, or impose around them, on less resilient natures. Olga Nesterov was young, melting and beautiful; she loved the embittered poet wholeheartedly, and for a while they were happy together. But Bestoujev had lost the habit of happiness: perhaps he never had it. In any case, his craving for the absolute—for the ultimate, in love or suffering goaded him on towards disaster. At a dinner among his close army friends, he vaunted her fidelity. Until that moment, it had been unquestioned. Now, in the cynical fashion of the age and the messroom, someone idly questioned his boast. Bestoujev did not react in the classic manner, by naming his seconds. Instead, he seemed amused, and wagers were exchanged on the matter.

Next day, the unsuspecting girl went, as usual, to her lover's rooms. No one ever knew what happened. There was a shot, a cry, and Bestoujev rushed out distraught. His mistress lay on the floor in a pool of blood, shot through the lungs. But she was still conscious and sent for a priest. Later, under oath, the priest said she told him it was an accident—while trying to get the pistol away from Bestoujev (who, we may suppose, having made her suffer to the point of madness, was overcome with shame at his own conduct, and, seizing a pistol, aimed it at his own head). But it had gone off as she grappled for it. She died in her lover's arms. An enquiry was held, and only the priest's deposition saved Bestoujev.

But from that moment he sank into a sombre lethargy, which varied with outbursts of furious energy, when he galloped across the mountains, day and night, as if pursued. He sought danger, and seemed hungry for death. But, like his friend the desperate Captain Allbrandt, who also sought to still an unhappy love, he bore a charmed life. Together, these two haunted men sought every danger battle could bring. At last, during an action against the Abazertzky tribe, and outnumbered five to one, Bestoujev disappeared, swallowed up in the forest. Had he been killed? Had he killed himself? Had he simply lain down to die, having had enough of his life? We shall never know.

But the senseless end which his love imposed on Olga Nesterov will be remembered as long as her tombstone stands in the graveyard at Derbend. It is a simple black marble monolith, bearing on one side her name and the date of her birth and death, 1814–33. On the other side a single rose is carved—falling from its stem, symbolically wilted and broken. Below, one word, *Soudba*—fate.

There was a postscript; when, in the 'sixties, Alexander Dumas was visiting the Caucasus, he reached the wind-swept little cemetery overlooking the Caspian, and heard the tragic story of Olga Nesterov's love. He was moved to write these charming, often quoted, lines, which were later inscribed on her tomb:

> Elle atteignait vingt ans; elle aimait, était belle.
> Un soir, elle tomba, rose effeuillée aux vents.
> O terre de la mort, ne pèse pas sur elle;
> Elle a si peu pesé sur celle des vivants.

Thus, while Bestoujev is almost forgotten, Olga Nesterov's memory is kept green, far beyond Russian frontiers, through Dumas' pen.

The Frenchman had found the Caucasus most rewarding, the *excessive* quality of Russia particularly suited to his own temperament. He wallowed in local colour, violence, space, size; races where ten thousand wild horses swam the Volga, life in aôul and palace, *bayadères* and blood feuds. . . . At the Princess Mathilde's weekly dinners (she called him her Jumping Jack) he often recounted his Russian adventures, and the Goncourts fixed him for posterity, across the Napoleonic gold plate and silver of the Princess' table.

> A giant figure with hair turned pepper and salt, and the tiny, clear, sly eyes of a hippopotamus, ever observant, even when lowered. . . . With Dumas there is an indefinable something of both a side-show barker's hawking wonders, and a travelling salesman from the Arabian nights. . . .

II

Writers, gun-runners, adventurers, travellers, and scientists, the Caucasus overshadowed all of them: some, such as David Urquhart and Captain Bell lived dangerously, shipping in arms, to bolster the tribes against a Russian victory, playing a tricky game between British

Government, Tzar, Shamyl, and Sultan. Others, like Xavier Hommaire de Hell, scientist and geologist, went about the mountains, magnifying glass to nose, and seldom observed anything beyond its perimeter. For him the Caucasus was so much soil that came under his lens. His young wife Adèle kept a meticulous record of all his findings, and glancing aside found plenty more to note; in particular, the graft, waste and corruption of the Russian Army Commissariat, something her French sense of thrift had observed keenly. 'Official robbery', she called it, boiling with indignation at the neglected troops, the luxury of the officers' tables, and the cupidity of some officers, merchants and contractors, lining their pockets while the men perished from malnutrition or scurvy. Although gossip held that Madame Hommaire de Hell was becoming restive, being set aside for scientific findings, and had consoled herself with the poet Lermontov's advances, it is doubtful if they ever even met, since in 1841, Lermontov was still in St. Petersburg, living his dandy's life, cosseted by his grandmother. His poems to *l'ardente française* are evidently not addressed to her, and so, a legend fades: only a lesser legend, however; for Lermontov remains one of the most obsessive figures of the Caucasian scene.

III

Mikhail Yurvievitch Lermontov was the personification of Russia in the Caucasus, the prototype of all those splenetic, raffish young officers to whom the land came as a revelation. And he was much more: he was a great writer, who brought the Caucasus before the Russian people. To them, he remains 'The Poet of the Caucasus'; his name and the legends which surround his brief, doomed life and dramatic death, are forever linked with the land.

For the brilliant generation of men who first went to the Caucasus during the Murid Wars, the country's impact was overwhelming. It was at once heroic and exotic, and the mixture fired the imagination. But while Pushkin wrote largely of its romantic aspects, as in his *Prisoner of the Caucasus*, and Tolstoy was obsessed by the psychological impact of nature on man set down in such a scene, Lermontov revels in a sensuous unity with the land itself. He is one with *genius loci*. Poems such as *Mtzieri* with its wonderful evocations of nature—of glowing valleys and menacing mountain ranges—bring the Caucasus round us with a sense of anguish and joy, as if we saw it for the first time, or the last time, like Mtzieri the escaped monk—or like Lermontov himself. All his evocations of the Caucasus have that anguished clarity, that sharpened perception, which a first or last look bestows, and which resembles, perhaps, that intensity of vision experienced by the takers of mescaline or peyote. Lermontov had hardly begun to savour the

Caucasus with his voluptuous, painter's eye, before he was killed in a senseless duel. He had started to write his Caucasian tales and poems the moment he reached the mountains; he wrote furiously, as if he felt his time was running out. He saw the land both objectively and subjectively, the exotic and the sordid. He discarded the Byronic cast, that which was Childe Harold's—the stylized world of perfumed scarves and scimitars—for a more faithful landscape. And then, in *Taman*, a stark story, he caught the sinister aspect of men and scene in a manner quite new. When, in his old age, Tolstoy was asked which Russian story he thought immortal, he chose *Taman*; and Gogol, in a letter to a friend, wrote: 'No one among us has yet written a prose so perfect, so beautiful, so full of flavour.'

Lermontov's verses could be as voluptuous as his prose could be harsh. The whole sweep of the Caucasian scene starts from his pages.

Below the serene skies, Kisslovodsk or Piatigorsk, and the mighty Beshtau, its five snow peaks dwarfing the petty passions of Russian society gathered below. Idle conversations; threats, confessions, whispers of love, he caught it all. Valerik—the River of Death—with its dying men, Russians and Tartars, their blood staining its course. Scenes: a caravan, with its train of camels and noisy mountaineers; wedding celebrations in the house of a Circassian chieftain; a wayside inn. . . . Above all, landscapes—the whole sweep of the Caucasus beneath his pen, coming to life and invested with his own sense of wonder.

In the East, a glimmer of dawn edged the dark purple dome of the sky, and the steep snow-covered mountain slopes revealed themselves in the growing dawn. To right and left hung sombre, gloomy, mysterious abysses; among the crevasses and gullies of the nearest rocks, wreathes of mist crept and writhed serpent-like, as if aware of, and dreading, the approach of day. Everything was quiet. Both in the heavens, and on earth, as in a man's heart at the hour of morning prayer; only now and then a chill breeze blew from the East, ruffling the horses' manes. . . .

And an evening piece:

The sun was just dipping behind the snowy ridges when I entered the Koyshaursky valley. The driver, an Ossete, whipped up his horses, for he was anxious to cross the pass over the mountain before night. He was singing at the top of his voice. It was a glorious place, that valley. Mountains all around; inaccessible reddish cliffs, hung with ivy and crowned with clumps of giant plane trees; yellow slopes streaked with ravines; and, far above, the gilded fringe of the snows; while, far below, lay the Aragva thundering out from a black gorge, now filled with mist, to become a silvery thread glittering like the scales of a snake's skin.

Lermontov's landscapes are not Turgeniev's landscapes with figures, where the seasons rise from the pages, with the smell of wood-smoke in autumn, and the summer's air heavy with the scent of limes; nor does he share Tolstoy's unity with the earth—the soil itself. But he sees, and loves, passionately, the *Caucasus*, in its essence—its lonely grandeur and voluptuousness. The texture of the land, the world around him dazzled him, intoxicated him, so that we sense in his verses, a sort of drunken joy in an *earthly* paradise seen by an exile: something which he could not possess, but which he craved, like Mtzieri the hero of his poem, the novice who escapes the monastery for one glorious moment of freedom, of living, of seeing for the first time the world around him—the world of the Caucasus.

Bodenstedt, heavy, Germanic, but thorough, who spent years collecting data for his study of the Caucasus, wrote: 'Show me one book among the mass of thick geographic, historical and other works on the Caucasus, which would give one a better and more lively idea of the character of these mountains and their inhabitants than any of Lermontov's poems.'

The Russian writer Merejkovsky taking a more romantic view, writing of Lermontov's profound love of nature, describes it as *l'amour extra-terrestre pour la terre*. He develops his theme—that Lermontov was not all man: that he was part angel, part devil, a wandering, dispossessed soul, who craved some earthly anchor, who knew himself doomed to centuries of past and future disembodied wanderings—tormented by some sort of pre-natal memory, a vision, or remembrance of eternity. . . . 'I have lost count of my years,' wrote Lermontov, at fifteen, posing romantically. But was it entirely a fashionable pose? Again and again, in his writings, he returns to this theme, to those shadowy mysterious remembrances of another existence, of some immemorial past from which he would like to escape, forever, into the world of positive horizons. He puts into the mouth of his Demon his own longings for the anchorage, or shelter, of a four-square unknowing body:

I love the realism of your world, where everything is exact, formulated, geometric; whereas with us, we must content ourselves with I don't know what in the way of indefinite equations. . . . Here, on earth, I adopt all your customs: I enjoy myself at the Bains de Commerce. I love to sit there, stewing and stifling myself among the merchants and priests. . . . My dream is to be incarnated—without return—in the person of some obese merchant. . . .

Merejkovsky recalls the gnostic legend of which Dante speaks in the *Divine Comedy*. It established a link between the celestial world and our own.

The angels who have made their choice between the two camps have no need to be born. Time cannot change their decision, taken for all eternity. But for those who hesitate, who cannot choose between light and shadow, God has accorded a grace—that of being born into the world, so that they can make, in man's time, the choice they could not make, in God eternity. These angels are the souls of the newborn. The same grace which brought them to birth, hides from them the eternal past, so that their hesitations and doubts in the past do not influence, or determine, in advance, their decisions during that earthly sojourn in which they must decide their salvation or perdition in the eternal future to which they will return. That is why it seems natural, to us, to think of what will happen to us after our death—while we do not, and cannot, know what we were before our birth. We forget where we came from—trying to recall *towards what* we go. Such is the general rule, and experience of this mystical belief. Exceptions are rare. Very rare, the souls for whom a corner of the terrible curtain is raised, revealing some glimpse of the pre-terrestial mystery. One of these souls was Lermontov . . . If the dead continue to love the earth, it is probable that their love is like his (Lermontov's) a feeling of irreparable loss. This heavenly nostalgia for the earth is the exact opposite to the earthly longing for some heavenly paradise which the Christians crave.

Neither Lermontov, nor his Demon, nor Mtzieri, can accept a Christian paradise—they have found paradise on earth—in nature.

> Que me fait la clarté divine
> Que me fait le saint paradis?
> Toutes mes passions terrestres,
> Je les emporterai là-bas.[1]

wrote Lermontov in 1840, perhaps already sensing how short a time he had left to savour this world.

There are many translations of *Angel*—one of his loveliest and most loved poems. It tells of the midnight angel bearing a soul to its birth, a soul that ever afterwards strives to remember the angel's song. However, such poems do not translate. Their sense is rendered but their music is lost.

Lermontov was the first of the Russian writers to occupy himself with the question of Evil; chiefly of demonism. Its theatrical aspects intrigued him; it was fashionable, too, to dabble in the occult. And, besides, the whole pattern of his life seemed overcast by some sense of predestination, of fatality. He was described as the anti-Christ, part devil, part angel, part cheap seducer, part divine poet, who indulged in banalities and boredom, to prove to himself that he was all human.

---

[1] French translation by Henri Troyat (*Le Sainte Russie*).

Poor Lermontov! So pathetic, so dashing; so eager, so bored; so glorious, so silly, so young, and so sublimely poetic.

He lived a lonely, orphaned childhood in Moscow, brought up by his wealthy grandmother. At nineteen he had sprung into fame with a savage poem on the death of Pushkin, brought low by Court intrigues. Lermontov attacked the Tzar's tyranny, and spoke of lost liberties. Siberia would have been his lot, had not powerful friends intervened to have his sentence softened to exile with the Army of the South; and so, the young Hussar moved towards his destiny, to become the poet of the Caucasus, and to find fame and death among its mountains. Had he been sent to Siberia, would he have found inspiration? Would he have proved as receptive, as intuitive, to any other scene? It is unlikely. Lermontov was destined to immortalize, and be immortalized by the Caucasus. The seeming chance of a sentence transported from Siberia to the south was the pattern by which his destiny was fulfilled. His arrival at Piatigorsk, already surrounded by a dazzling aura of wickedness, persecution and poetry, set the town in a ferment. On sight, the ladies were in a taking, the gentlemen suspicious and jealous. But, in the measure in which he was detested, he was also loved by some of his companion-in-arms, who recognized, beneath the childish façade of spleen and bravura, the *bon enfant*. His troops adored him for the simplicity and warmth he showed them. With them, there was no need to pose.

Many of the veteran fighters—men who had been with the Army of the South for ten or twenty years, the remnants of Yermolov's men— Cossacks, and Tartar renegades—were, at that time, often operating on their own, in small partisan bands, scarcely attached to the army proper. They conducted their own private war, and welcomed the most dangerous missions. They were a ruffianly lot, who scorned the use of firearms, preferring to fight hand to hand with the shashka. Their uniforms left much to be desired, and they remained unshaven on principle. Lermontov, detached from the Tenguinski regiment, was given one such band to command. It was a tough assignment. But their theatrical appearance, their violence and daring, delighted him, and he flung himself into their life. Thus we see him, wearing a grubby red shirt, and no epaulettes. 'At the moment of attack, he cocked his cap over one ear and rushed, at the gallop, towards the Tchetchen outposts. . . .' Such heroics irked the more sober staff-officers. 'Ridiculous! One does not charge at fortifications,' said the classicists.

He was very much criticized by his superior officers for dressing the part. Few of them could understand the childish poseur who lingered within the embittered poet. The staff officers reported that he looked like a tzigane, his face blackened with dust and gunpowder. But his troops followed him blindly, and his missions were triumphantly successful; he was twice mentioned in dispatches, and recommended for valour, being proposed for the order of St. Vladimir; but in the Tzar's eyes, and in the eyes of the War Ministry, he was a dangerous poet, in disgrace. There must be no talk of bravery, or medals.

To the Tzar and his surrounding sycophants the bravery of such a rebel was only bravura. *Not granted* was written across the margin in the royal handwriting. There was nothing more to be said: the Tzar considered himself the embodiment of Peter the Great's military statutes, 'Sovereign and Autocrat accountable to no one on earth . . .' 'I cannot permit that one single person should dare to defy my wishes, the moment he has been made aware of them,' was another of his marginalia, written during the first part of his reign.

Even Lermontov's fighting exploits were interpreted as insubordination. He was to rot at the front, as Pushkin had been made to rot at the Court.

Thus he had to content himself with the frittering, flirting life of Piatigorsk, of card-playing and quarrelling, of love-making, of dancing till dawn, but always writing—writing the divine poetry which flowed from him with such abandon. In the tradition of so many of the nineteenth century writers, he was, besides, an excellent draughtsman. Pushkin, Victor Hugo, de Musset, and many more, drew with effortless ease; organically, with a mastery that was remarkable. They left caricatures and sketches, through which we see the life and times, the images of their mind.

Lermontov had a painter's eye: he wrote as one: his verses shimmer, incandescent with colour and light. His paintings (an aspect of his genius almost unknown outside Russia) place him far beyond the range of his contemporaries, with their talented sketches. We see beautiful, ambitious and satisfying landscapes; some of the canvases are quite large, and they are in another category, or degree of skill, beside his drawings. It is as if, confronted by the Caucasian scene, it sparked another aspect of his genius, drawing from him unsuspected powers to record it in paint, as well as ink. Once again we sense his ravishment and wonder; his power to interpret the *genius loci*. His landscapes have that peculiar quality which includes, or lures, the beholder into some mysterious depth or other dimension. We walk forward into a summer's evening among the pinkish rock cliffs and rosy afterglow surrounding the summit of Elbruz. Or, in the blaze of noon, we follow a limpid river where a train of camels thread through tropic groves, and far away on the horizon, we see a lilac line of hills, sharpening, as the sun declines; a promised land . . . We are lost . . . drawn into the reality of the scene, into the depths of the landscape. Lermontov has cast his spell again. *A memory of the Caucasus* shows us two warriors, Shamyl's men, we suppose; hooded figures, silhouetted against a streaked sunset, mounted on stocky little Tartar horses, ride over the darkening hills towards some hiding-place in the mountains. The picture has a sinister urgency about it. We are instantly involved in this drama, concerned with the rider's fate. . . In short, it is the perfect illustration to one of his romantic tales. The reproduction of this painting, and many more, in colour, have been used in a beautiful edition of Lermontov's collected works, published in Russia in 1955 by the Akademir Naouk USSR. There are, besides, several portraits of Lermontov as he was, in the Caucasus. His Hussar's uniform is almost eclipsed by a particularly shaggy bourka: his childish, haunting face stares out, delicate, peevish, and yet with a certain sweetness in the round brown eyes. The high, domed brow is decorated by a fashionably unruly lock of hair; the upper lip is pencilled by a faint moustache. Lermontov was short and unimpressive-looking at first glance; his flamboyance and attitudinizing were all part of his efforts to overcome this insignificant façade. He had, besides, the short man's overweening arrogance. He loved to torment, to deflate the pomposity of the courtiers and high-ranking officials, or to write inflammatory verses on freedom, much as Pushkin had done. And, like Pushkin, it had earned him deadly enemies, who at last encompassed his death. Twice within seven years, it was the Russian people's fate to lose their greatest poets, killed in duels which could have been prevented, but which the authorities took care to ignore.

The parallel between these two men, Pushkin and Lermontov, is a curious one. Both were great poets; both men were exiled; both lived lives of storm and neglect, and were loved and feared in the measure of their stature. Both wrote poems or tales which foreshadowed the manner of their own death. Both were obsessed by duelling. Both died in a duel, killed by favoured nobodies. Both were accorded a furtive funeral, and were recognized and mourned too late. Pushkin was mortally wounded at the Black Brook, on the Islands, at St. Petersburg, while his adversary, Danthés, the fatuous faced pet of the Court, lived on, almost unshadowed. In his old age, he was photographed, looking as fatuous as ever, grown paunchy, in a frock coat (no trace, now, of the dashing Horse Guard). But he basked, still, in the reflected glory of having killed Pushkin. Lermontov was shot dead by Martynov, on the slopes of Mashuk. Martynov was a worthless fellow officer, rich, spiteful and jealous, who was glad to foster some trumped-up quarrel, till it became a matter for pistols. Lermontov had fired in the air (a fact which was suppressed at the enquiry) but Martynov aimed at his opponent's heart. At first, for form's sake, he had been exiled to Kiev, under the surveillance of the Church. But as Goethe says, the Church has a good digestion. The Holy Synod soon found him fit to be pardoned. He lived on, preening it over provincial society, constantly reminding them, lest they forgot, that he had been compelled to challenge Lermontov. It had been a question of his sister's honour, he said.

Duels were an expression of the age: men duelled over nothing more concrete than an imagined slight. It was in the romantic tradition, too, to be tired of life—to risk everything on a card or a bullet; to shrug off life, or death, with the same air of boredom. Pushkin's hero, Evgueni Oniegin, reveals the young Pushkin's splenetic moods. The poet lived his dramas more than once, though fundamentally, Oniegin is closer to the character of Lermontov, than Pushkin. No doubt the younger man's admiration for Pushkin's work came to influence his character, besides his art, and he lived, as well as wrote, in the Pushkinian tradition. Petchorin in *A Hero of Our Own Times* has much of Oniegin in him, but he is largely a self-portrait. Lermontov explained him as being a composite portrait—as people saw him, as he saw himself. This was in the Oniegin vein. When Lermontov describes Petchorin's infamous duel with Grushnitsky, he is prophetic, foreseeing his own fatal meeting with Martynov.

As in the story, the real duel took place on a precipitous ledge, high on the slopes of Mashuk, above Piatigorsk. Lermontov had ridden slowly to the meeting-place, lingering, savouring that nature he loved so passionately, looking, sensing it all, as if for the first time, or the last: watching the light reflected through the arc of a waterfall, sun dappling the stones of a river-bed, the flight of a bird, the dew on a leaf, snow on the mountains. . . . His friends remarked that he seemed to be taking leave of it all. He is said to have possessed second sight: perhaps he knew that he would fire in the air, and Martynov would not. As the seconds primed the pistols, and paced their men, a fearful thunderstorm broke suddenly. Dark clouds rolled round the peaks, and the skies were ripped apart by lightning. Lermontov fell dead—murdered. Pushkin has said that Moscow, golden-headed Moscow, should be the birth-place of every genius: There could be no finer setting for a great poet's death than a thunderstorm on a Caucasian mountain.

At first the Orthodox Church refused him Christian burial. To them, a duel was a suicide. The black-robed, long-haired monks and clergy barred the monastery doors, and were adamant. But, at last, one of General Grabbé's staff officers persuaded them to say a few prayers, at dusk. It was a lovely summer's evening, the mountains silhouetted against the yellowing sky. A large number of Lermontov's brother officers came to pay their last homage—too late. The funeral service was gabbled to its end; the monks went back to their cells, the officers to their mess-room. It was all over. Darkness fell on the deserted graveyard, with its hump of newly turned earth strewn with waxy flowers.

But Lermontov had no need for a tombstone. Only the highest peaks of the Caucasus can serve as a fitting memorial to his tragic genius.

IV

Meanwhile, the character of the Caucasian wars was changing. The regular Army of the South, and those men who had fought beside them, as exiles, or mercenaries, or to escape some private grief, or even to pass the time, were now joined by a number of brilliant younger men from the Guards' regiments, who were to have a profound effect on the conduct of the war. Owing to the Emperor Nicholas' preoccupation with all the panoply of militarism, he had fostered several Cadet Corps schools, in which he intended the aristocracy to enrol their sons. The products of this system—a remarkable group of young army officers—now began to arrive in the Caucasus for their first taste of battle. They were exchanging the dandies' life of the Chevaliers Gardes, and the Gardes à Cheval, and other crack regiments, for the savagery of the Caucasus. The malachite salons of the Winter Palace, where they spent a good deal of time in attendance at Court functions, the magnificence of the Tauride Palace, with its ballroom built by Potemkin to receive Catherine the Great, their clubs and mess-rooms, the restaurants, shops, cafés and drawing-rooms of the capital, saw them no more. They had gone to war. Although Tolstoy was not one of this military clique, he also went to fight in the Caucasus, in 1851, as a debt-ridden young nobleman seeking to escape from urban temptations; but he spoke for all the Russian aristocracy when he wrote of their innate sense of frustration, 'of that everlasting ennui, bred in the bone, which descends from generation to generation, consciously, too, with the conviction that it is inevitable'. Like them, he felt that in the Caucasus, he would find himself, or lose himself, perhaps; at any rate 'with the aid of a cannon, assist in destroying the predatory and turbulent Asiatics'.

At first these newcomers were hotly resented by the old timers; but once tempered by battle, they proved to be some of the finest soldiers the Russian army has ever known. Among them, Prince Bariatinsky, handsome, wealthy, privileged, scion of the only noble family directly related to the Romanovs, a childhood companion of the Tzarievitch, and the object of his sister, the Grand Duchess Olga's, girlish love. Almost all Bariatinsky's years of military service were passed in the Caucasus, his name becoming synonymous with victory, above all, linked with that of Shamyl.

The Guards' officers brought with them an atmosphere of luxury and dissipation most misleading to those who judged them as tailors' dummies. Before, a sort of reckless, picnic gaiety had sufficed the officers behind the lines. Provincial distractions had seemed dazzling; and there were always the dancers of Shemakha. . . .

But this new crop of officers were eclectic in all things. The regimental tailors, who had previously turned out excellent uniforms, were considered quite impossible. The newcomers favoured a St. Petersburg cut, with a good deal of gold lace: they wore kid gloves and had their winter overcoats lined with sea-otter. They eschewed the dancers of Shemakha for intrigues with other people's wives. (Bariatinsky, according to Tolstoy, becoming at one time the lover of the young Countess Simon Voronzov, daughter-in-law of Prince Voronzov, the Viceroy, thus continuing his habit of loving in very high places.) They larded their talk with French or English phrases, always addressing each other as *Mon cher*, and drank only imported wines; none of the local stuff for them, though Chikhir, either red, or of a marked greenish colour, was palatable enough.

These late-comers to the Caucasus not only supped on champagne and lived in tents that were hung with pictures and mirrors, rode thoroughbreds, and loaded the pack-mules with ivory-backed hairbrushes, pomades and eau de Cologne, but some also brought their own domestics along. Colonel Count Benckendorff, who was frequently accompanied to the brink of battle by his chef and valet, also expected his batman to lie down and warm up the ground, before he himself sank to rest.

But to begin with, these sybarites despised, and were despised by the regular Army of the South; in particular, they exasperated General Veliaminov, one of the greatest generals, although 'a blood-sucking vampire', careless of his men's lives, according to his critics. He had spent his whole life campaigning; he was gazetted sub-lieutenant at fourteen, and was for twenty consecutive years bivouacked in the Caucasus. He had a particularly austere concept of a soldier's life, frowning on the presence of women within miles of his armies; no *vivandières*, no camp followers, no lights of love, or spoils of war. His dedication was positively Muridic. Like Yermolov, he had distinguished himself at Borodino; and he was in Paris in 1814, during the allied occupation. When Yermolov was appointed Commander-in-Chief in the Caucasus, he made Veliaminov his Chief of Staff. As early as 1828, he drew up his commentary and proposals for the conduct of the Caucasian wars, and these may be said to have laid the foundations of Russia's ultimate victory. 'Whenever the principles of Veliaminov, so eloquently advocated and so brilliantly put into practice, were departed from, disaster dogged the heels of his successors.' He was absolute in his conviction that only force of arms would prevail against the mountaineers. Like Shamyl, he knew the respect which strength commanded. The rebels' resistance, like their raids, might succeed temporarily, but they must be convinced of Russia's might, of her limitless reserves. They did not understand moderation. Once they realized that conciliation or generosity were not necessarily proof of weakness, and were backed up by a fearful striking power, then, and then only, could they come to terms.

'The Caucasus', wrote Veliaminov, 'may be likened to a mighty fortress, marvellously strong by nature, artificially protected by military works and defended by a numerous garrison. *Only thoughtless men* would attempt to escalade such a stronghold.' It took the long sequence of assaults, sieges, blunders and heroic sacrifices, thirty years of them, before the whole truth of Veliaminov's words were realized. Meanwhile, scowling, wrapped in a bourka, and content to eat from his soldier's canteen, Veliaminov observed the Guardees settling themselves around him so sybaritically.

However luxurious the outward tenor of their lives at the start, however much they cultivated the fashionable attitude of ennui, they were all imbued with a profound loyalty towards their Tzar, and a passionate, unquestioning belief in his god-like attributes. Like him, they saw this war as a crusade—the Cross over the Crescent, and, equally holy, Russia, Holy Russia, enlarged and supreme, ruling from the confines of China to Turkey. They expressed their fervour in picturesque terms, imposing an heroic or chevalresque flavour to the campaigns, by going into battle with songs and drums, and charging to well-rehearsed 'Hurrahs!' The highest-ranking officers and their staff, partly to be distinguished in camp, or battle, but largely in accordance with the new spirit of dramatized warfare, now devised their separate banners and emblems. Young General Passek's flag was white, with a silver cross, 'emblem of love and Hope', embroidered for him by the lady of his heart. The Commander-in-Chief's was crimson and gold, with the horse-tail standards of a six-tailed Bashaw, thus imparting an added note of Asiatic exoticism to the camp. General Lüders, commander of the 3rd Army Corps, displayed a banner of red and black, like the ribbon of St. Vladimir, which he wore. General Gourko, Chief of the General Staff, chose scarlet. Some banners were golden, some royal blue; none were green, for that was Mahommed's colour. When the pennons of the generals fluttered from their escorts' lances, or over their tents, the whole field shimmered with colour, in joyous contrast to the Murid's black banners which were sometimes to be glimpsed from afar, alternating with flashes of steel, light and shadow, as Shamyl's army wound through the dense forests or across the mountains. Then the newcomers were glued to their telescopes, straining their eyes to catch a glimpse of their legendary adversaries.

Tolstoy writes of a column leaving their fort at night for an expedition into enemy terrain. He describes the darkness, the ominous hush, broken by the croaking of frogs; the gallop of a horse, an order, curtly given. The column, at a trot, goes through the silent streets and shuttered houses of the town, from which, faint on the night air, drift snatches of a street-organ playing some forgotten German tune, the *Aurora-Waltzer* or *The Winds Blow*, a melancholy Ukrainian song. The men whisper among themselves, tense and awed. Over all, hangs the mysterious presence of Shamyl. The newcomer speaks to the Tartar guide riding beside him:

'Have you ever seen Shamyl?'
'No—we ordinary ones don't see *him* . . . There are a hundred, three hundred, a thousand troops, and Shamyl in the middle,' said the Tarter in an obsequious tone. 'Shamyl sends out his Naibs. . . . He remains on the highest mountains and watches through his telescope.'
'Is he far?'
'No . . . Over to the left. . . . Perhaps twelve versts away.'

So they whispered in the dark, before dawn, and, in the hills, the jackals could be heard, their despairing cries and wild laughter mingled with the soft sounds of the night. And, over everything, Shamyl's legend seemed to brood, dark as his banners.

V

Although Tolstoy was never, as was Lermontov, primarily associated with the Caucasus, still some of his finest work derives from the first, overwhelming impact of the mountains. The young Count Leo Tolstoy had left Moscow in 1851, to accompany his brother Nicolai, then returning to service in the south. The journey was begun, chiefly to rid himself of card debts that weighed on him in the city; he had left almost on an impulse; he was becoming restive in the degenerated sophistication of Moscow society; he might as easily have headed north, for when another brother was leaving for Siberia, the impulsive Leo jumped into the carriage beside him, and was only persuaded to remain behind when it was pointed out that he had no baggage—not even a hat. But had he gone north, he would probably have found that same freedom and truth he was to find in the Caucasus. He had a rendezvous with nature: he could have kept it north, or south. But only in the Caucasus could he have heard those first thunders of battle which, swelling to the bombardment of Sebastopol, were to lead him towards his masterpiece, *War and Peace*.

Meanwhile, dawdling in Moscow, entering up his diary, fuming over petty vanities—was one side of his moustache less luxuriant than the other?—did a certain beauty favour him?—he decided on a jaunt to the Caucasus. It would pass the time. Many of his friends were setting forth to take a few pot-shots at the rebel tribes. It was a quick way to

obtain decorations—glory, said the cynics. (But these were not the
military exaltés of whom I wrote earlier.) Besides, it was good hunting,
and Tolstoy loved hunting. Until now, he had been a splenetic idler,
much given to ponderous self-examination and fits of theatrical remorse.
His aunt was urging him, for the better formation of his character,
towards a *serious* liaison with some married women . . . '*Rien ne forme un
jeune homme comme une liaison avec une femme comme il faut,*' she wrote,
doting and worldly. But Tolstoy was to find wider horizons, larger
formative influences in the Caucasus. It was the impact of the mountains, of the mountain people, of life and death in the Caucasian
campaigns that were to change him forever.

In *The Cossacks*, writing of Olyenin's first sight of the mountains (but,
in fact, writing a purely auto-biographical passage), he says: 'From
that moment, all that he had seen or thought, or felt, assumed for him
the new, sternly majestic character of the mountains. All his recollections of Moscow, his shame and repentance, all his former illusions
about the Caucasus—all disappeared and never returned again. "Now
life begins", seemed to be sounded in his ear by some solemn voice.' It
was his first conscious contact with natural forces. He was to interpret
them, and all they stood for, to the more complicated West he was even
then learning to despise. Some of his finest work derives from these
sources. *Hadji Mourad*, Tolstoy's recollections of Shamyl's first Naib,
published posthumously, or *The Cossacks*, which Turgeniev considered
to be the most perfect writing in the Russian language. Tolstoy himself
selected Lermontov's *Taman*, so that these masterpieces were each
inspired by the Caucasus. In Tolstoy's *Cossacks*, and through his
experiences of Caucasian warfare, we can, perhaps, trace the seeds of
War and Peace. If the first stirrings of that conscience which pervades his
masterpiece were engendered in the Caucasus, Tolstoy found there, too,
that fundamental simplicity which came to obsess him, and for which
he was to strive for the rest of his life. On his last flight from complica-
tion—from that civilization he believed to be sick—the old giant who
lay dying in the station-master's house at Astapovo had been thinking
of returning to the Caucasus: he had spoken of this to his daughter
Alexandra, as one of his deepest wishes. But perhaps death, coming to
him there in the north, by liberating his spirit brought it back, at last,
to the Caucasian mountains—the fountain-head of his regeneration.
. . . ' "*Now life begins*" seemed to be sounded in his ear by some solemn
voice. . . .'

VI

Some of the men fighting in the Caucasus were activated by a pure
love of adventure, or a particular personal hatred of one side or another

—or any other reason which has, from time immemorial, lured man to battle. Large numbers of Poles and Sarmatians shared with the Caucasians an enthusiasm for fighting, *tout court*. Some were members of the Uhlan Corps of the Russian army; but once arrived in the Caucasus, they were apt to recall the basic hatred which existed between Russian and Pole, and repaying centuries of oppression and mistrust, they would go over to Shamyl's ranks. A few English mercenaries, fighting with Shamyl, found him strangely incurious. When British artillery officers began arriving, in twos and threes, overland from India, with offers to help train his men, no questions were ever asked. Cases of Russians deserting to the Murids were rare. As to the renegade tribesmen who had joined the Russians, they lived in terror of Shamyl's reprisals, should they fall into his hands. The Russians soon became used to the severed heads of their 'Tartar' spies being pitched over the stockade. Night after night, disfigured and bloody, they were flung down and rolled to a standstill to disclose a message scrawled across their brow: 'Thus perish the friends of Russia.'

Sometimes a foreigner fought under the Russian colours for purely personal motives. One young Frenchman, Michel Brousset, was remarked by some Russian officers on their rounds. He was painting a tent with huge figures—a bearded and turbaned mountaineer, impaled on the bayonet of a Russian soldier.

'I did it—that's me,' said the boy proudly. 'That's me, capturing Shamyl.'

He went on to say he was French; his father, a colonel in Napoleon's army, had married a Russian heiress. The boy had been born in France, and grew up on tales of his inheritance, of land and gold in Russia—all his, if a scheming uncle did not intervene.

'But, as a foreigner, I cannot inherit,' he went on. 'That's why I'm here, and so hard-pressed to kill Shamyl. For then, I shall win my officer's epaulettes, and the rest will be easy. I shall become a Russian, and then the inheritance will be mine.' He smiled confidently, as the officers wished him luck. But a few months later he was killed, storming an aôul. The wicked uncle had won.

So the shadows came and went across the Caucasian scene; and above them loomed the abiding contours of the mountains.

16

Loyalties

*O ye who have received the Scriptures, exceed not the
just bounds of your religion.*

CUFIC INSCRIPTION IN THE
MOSQUE OF OMAR, AT JERUSALEM

Although at first glance, it seems unlikely there was any similarity
between the people of mid-Victorian England and those of the
Caucasus, yet it is to be traced in their approach to religion—to
suffering, which, in each case, was offered up with relish. Caucasians,
both the exalted mystics and the people, were sustained by a stoic
discipline, and humility, feeling themselves part of some Divine pattern which nullified individual anguish. They offered up their sufferings almost impersonally, with a sense of fatality, for Allah! And,
however violent their sufferings, whatever sacrifices Shamyl, in the
name of Mahommed, demanded or imposed, they retained a certain
austerity, unlike the noisy, self-indulgent mid-Victorian expressions of
Christianity.

The pious English of this moment were more egotistic, and actuated
by a conviction of their own worth, which made them sometimes refer
to God with a proprietory air, rather as a faithful retainer, always there,
to sustain them when needed. Their Christianity was an exclusive raft,
saving, first, the classes, then the masses; but saving, first of all, those
who suffered most.

The nation, from Queen Victoria down to the most insignificant
schoolgirl, expressed this conviction in their letters and journals. Religion was part of daily life, as it was not in either the materialistic
eighteenth, nor the scientific twentieth century. Sunday school, Scriptural readings, family prayers, collective hymn singing, an exchange
of tracts, were part of every-day life: while letters dwelling on an interpretation of the Scriptures often passed between schoolboys, or that
strange and wholly sincere race of military mystics who are among the
heroic phenomenon of the age.

The young military mystics—men like Connolly, Nicholson and

Napier, Lawrence, or 'Chinese' Gordon, lived lives of asceticism and valour on the plains of India, in Afghanistan, or wherever the Empire called them. They corresponded on theology, or the meaning of the Scriptures regularly, in camp, or on the battlefield, as they had done at school. Engaged couples, in Victorian England, constantly assured each other, in their letters, of the long nights of prayer they would be able to enjoy together during their honeymoon, and after. These young Christians muscled into denials like athletic feats, all God's flesh quivering under the lash until, at last, the force with which they prayed, and suffered, and sang hymns, turned them into a kind of lay brotherhood, not unlike the people of the Caucasus who, under Shamyl, also offered up their lives on the altars of abnegation and suffering: or in the words of mid-Victorian England, 'Sanctified affliction'.

Sanctified affliction! The phrase which, here, has an unctuous ring, describes, perfectly, Shamyl's stern attitude towards the chastisements of his people. Only in this case, God was not, *personally*, afflicting His special favourites, as a mark of *personal* regard, so much as receiving, in the spirit in which they were offered, the abnegations of His Faithful. It was a harsher, more humble belief, but perhaps the sufferings were the same, either way, east or west. Down the ages and across the world, the cries and lamentations echo mournfully, sounding in desert and cities, in Wahabite mosques and Baptist chapels alike, over the mountains and along the rivers, Tigris and Thames and Don: everywhere suffering. 'Man is born to sorrow as the sparks fly upward,' says the Bible; and in 867 B.C. the Baghdad mystic Sari Saquati wrote: ' *"Ah!"* is the supreme name of God. He put this cry on earth to help the suffering people take breath.'

II

For a man to win a reputation for cruelty in the Caucasus betokens a degree of savagery quite unimaginable to the West. Yet, the Russian General Pullo had achieved this distinction. He was in command of a number of punitive raids throughout Avaria and Tchetchnia in the months following the disappearance of Shamyl. He was unscrupulous and brutal, and loathed by the Tchetchens. But when, holding down a rising province with too few men, he appointed the renegade Tartars as pro-consuls or officers, he was playing directly into Shamyl's hands. These renegades treated the mountaineers with terrible cruelty and injustice. There was no redress—nowhere to appeal: but when it was rumoured that the Caucasian provinces were to be disarmed and converted into peasant communities, on the rural Russian pattern, subject to the same taxes, serfdom and conscription, the whole Caucasus arose, blazing with revolt, and once again Shamyl appeared, as a revenant, to rally the tribesmen round his black standard. Since his escape from

Akhulgo, he had remained hidden in the mountains, preaching the Shariat, praying, fasting and meditating. But now the time was ripe, and once more he sprang on to the centre of the stage, as warrior and chieftain; a terrible foe.

'This troublesome man,' wrote the Tzar, in a memorandum to his generals, exhorting them to finish off the war quickly. For him, Shamyl still remained a bandit—a most unworthy enemy to be holding his great armies at bay. He simply could not understand the nature of war, nor the difficulties which beset his commanders.

For the next ten years, Shamyl was to continue at the zenith of his powers, a magnificent and savage figure, dominating the Caucasus, straddling the mountain-passes like some giant. Yet, awesome as was his name, he never obtained that reputation for barbarism which surrounded some chieftains; Shaté, the Tchetchen, for example, whose name struck fear into every heart. It is recorded that on one occasion a crying child exasperated its mother; she told him to hush and, as he continued, she shut him out on the doorstep, saying: 'Shaté! Shaté! come and silence my child!' By some cruel chance, Shaté himself was passing through the aôul, returning from a raid, and hiding from his pursuers in the shadows of this very woman's house. The mother heard a strangled shriek of fear, and rushed to the door. Shaté had taken her at her word, and cut out the child's tongue. Bounding on to his horse, he galloped off, and was lost in the mists on the mountain-top, before the alarm could be given.

On such ruthlessness was his legend fostered; but it was a degree of savagery unknown to Shamyl who, while displaying the utmost severity towards his enemies, and who neither asked, nor gave, any quarter, nor ever hesitated to destroy anyone such as the youthful Prince Boulatch, who could have been used, by the Russians, to weaken him, or threaten his power, still displayed certain standards of chivalrous conduct, and seldom showed himself other than doting towards children. His treatment of prisoners—of Russian prisoners in particular, was very harsh; many of them were kept in pits, under fearful conditions; but here again, it must be remembered that just as he had no barracks, or regular military headquarters, living and fighting in partisan fashion, so he had no regular prisons in which to house his captives.

There were degrees of cruelty in the East which were unfathomable to the West; in all their harshness, neither Shamyl, nor any of the Caucasians, approached the fanatic and deliberate cruelties practised on prisoners in Bokhara. In 1843, the brave and mystic figure of Captain Connolly, of the Indian army, stood beside Colonel Stoddart, facing the Emir of Bokhara, two men alone, deserted by their country, and left to meet their slow death in a dungeon pit, the flesh gnawed off their bones by vermin. It was the Afghan custom to keep rats and enormous sheep ticks specially trained for this torture, by feeding them meat, so that they should be particularly voracious when, from time to time, human victims were obtained. Quite late in the nineteenth century, a French traveller, Monsieur Moser, was kept under lock and key for some weeks in Bokhara (his papers not being in order), and he writes of the long dull hours spent at his window. 'By way of distraction, I used to watch, on bazaar days, what appeared to be large parcels flung from the top of the Minar Kalan . . .' These packets, turning in the air as they fell, were condemned prisoners, trussed like fowls, and flung down, their execution being reserved for market-days, as entertainment for the crowds. At the foot of the Minar Kalan, or Tower of the Executions, there was, says the Frenchman, a sinister hollow, or depression, in the dusty, stony wastes surrounding it. It was caused by the falling prisoners, year after year, century after century. Bokhara seemed to spread a blood-red shadow over Central Asia, a fetid darkness beside which the Caucasus breathed an air at once vigorous and pure, a climate of violence, but of a certain heroic innocence, too. Here, there was none of the degeneracy, vice, squalor and disease in which Bokhara wallowed.

To the Caucasians, cruelty was incidental, part of the price they paid to maintain those stern standards of justice and revenge, without which there was no honour. (And if there was no honour, there was no life, to a Caucasian.) Their history and legends always centre round these two themes, justice, vengeance. Cruelty, suffering, as a price, hardly counted.

The story of Kholchar is typical. Kholchar the Robber was the terror and pride of mediaeval Daghestan: at last he was captured by the Khan of the Avars, and condemned to be burned alive. At the stake, he asked one last favour, to sing his farewell song. His bonds were loosened and he was given a lute. But his last words, like his last deeds, avenged him as no sword could have done. He began to sing of his life—of the women he had widowed, the children he had orphaned, the virgins he had dishonoured . . . and these he called by name, so that they blushed beneath their veils and their fathers and brothers raged. 'Ye virgins of Khounzakh who look down on me, through your lattices. . . . Now look your last. You will not forget me. I have kissed the white breast of each of you, my doxies, even as I have stolen the trousers of the Khan's favourite wife!' So saying, he tore a crimson sash from his waist and waved it in the faces of the crowd, who saw, indeed, that it was a silk pantaloon.

Revenge! Even now, with his funeral pyre beginning to smoke round him, Kholchar was tasting his sweets. His voice rose above the crackling of the flames, the shouts of the crowd. 'Now hear my last song! . . . Sweet is my voice. . . . Sweetly it lured away your women! Your children too. . . . Like this!' And he leapt into the crowd, where the two young sons of the Khan were listening, rapt. Before any one could make a move he seized them, one under each arm and leapt back into the heart of the flames; he was seen to fling them into the burning heart of the pyre, and spring after them, himself. Above the shrieks and groans, and the fearful silence that followed, he was heard once more: 'Be silent, ye children of a whore.—I made you so. I burn with you! Avars and Khan! Go, tell my mother how I died, how, in my death, I took revenge.' The smoke thickened round the pyre, and he was seen and heard no more. But his name has remained, a cherished symbol of vengeance. Cruelty was of no account, beside the ultimate achievement.

The Caucasians were both a pastoral and bandit people, who lived, or died, by certain standards, who were wounded, or lost a hand in the traditional vendettas, but over whom the wind of freedom always blew, and who were savage, yet brave and chivalrous, with something of the grandeur of their mountains.

Shamyl was their prototype; and when he put his prisoners to death, it was by fire or sword, in anger—but not for pleasure. He always opposed any renegade Russians who had joined him being placed in a position of authority over Russian prisoners. One Russian officer, Kouznetzov, who had deserted over a reprimand regarding his artillery fire, burned with a sense of injustice and revenge, and was forever plaguing Shamyl to give him charge of the prisoners. But Shamyl refused. At last Kouznetzov discovered a message to some prisoners, smuggled in by way of a honeycomb. This was sent from Prince Voronzov's headquarters, and told of a plan to rescue them, urging them to keep up their spirits, as help was at hand. Kouznetzov was delighted: he reported the matter to Shamyl, who, forewarned, was able to set a trap for the would-be rescuers. As a reward, Kouznetzov asked permission to deal with the prisoners as he thought fit. Shamyl agreed, little knowing that Kouznetzov's spirit of vengeance would not be satisfied till he had hung all twenty-two of them. After that, Shamyl never again entrusted the deserters with any administrative responsibility, using them only as fighters, engineers, interpreters, or to build him the semi-European houses he favoured.

III

Behind the shrieks and groans and battle-cries which made up the fabric of the Caucasian wars, an idyllic note was sometimes to be heard, below the gunfire. Such an interlude was provided by the love story of Shouanete an Armenian captive, who, after Fatimat's death, was to become Shamyl's favourite wife.

During the middle forties, one of his principal Naibs, Akhverdi

Mahoma, descending on Tchetchnia in a series of daring raids, pushed as far north as Mozdok, a small town on the Cossack line. Although it was heavily fortified, he succeeded in carrying off a number of hostages. Among them, a beautiful girl of sixteen, Shouanete, of Armenian stock. Thinking the gift of such a beauty would endear him to the Imam, he presented her to Shamyl. Shouanete was a captive—a Christian, abducted from her home. She was alone, in the aôul of this savage Moslem chieftain—but she loved him on sight, as he loved her. She was more than twenty-five years younger, and of another faith. But now, at the height of his success, when the Khans and Naibs bowed before him, when he could take as many women as he chose, Shouanete became his favourite, and remained his companion and solace, all the rest of his days. He called her 'the Pearl'. She was tall, round-faced, blue-eyed and fair-haired, with an air of radiant softness. She lived and breathed for Shamyl. The hard life in the aôul—a particularly barbaric one after her well-to-do background of a Mozdok merchant's household—all was forgotten, in the happiness of being beside Shamyl. At last she forswore her former religion and adhered rigidly to all the customs prescribed for a Moslem wife, wearing the veil, holding no communication with her Christian family, and willingly accepted her place in Shamyl's harem.

In all, Shamyl had five wives. First, Fatimat the adored. Then, Djavarat, who died at Akhulgo. Next came Zaïdate, who considered herself the first and most important wife, because, through her father, the Mollah Jamul u'din, she was descended from the Prophet. Shouanete the Christian, was not elevated to wife's status for some while after her capture. Lastly, came Aminette, who was finally divorced for the unpardonable fault of sterility.

Of all these, save Fatimat, the loved and lost, Shouanete was closest to him. When, some years after her capture, her relatives tried to buy her back, by offering a large ransom, she refused to return to them, while Shamyl said he would not part with her for any sum of gold. Their love endured in spite of the machinations and jealousy of Zaïdate, who took first place in the harem, and allowed no one to forget it. But Shouanete, happy in her adoration of Shamyl, asked no more than his love, and always stepped aside, playing a subservient rôle, to keep an atmosphere of harmony around Shamyl on the few occasions he was at home.

Here the great warrior was to be seen, seated on the ground, in his apartments, beside a very large, plain black and white cat called Vaska-Nourman, who had been given to him by a Russian deserter. Shamyl was devoted to this animal, and always refused to eat anything which the cat could not also enjoy. Mouthful by mouthful, they shared their meal, Shamyl sitting cross-legged on his cushions, Vaska-

Nourman opposite him, purring lustily; between them, a low table, with a few copper dishes containing pilaff, yoghourt and shish-kebab, this latter generally ordered expressly for the cat, since Shamyl ate little or no meat. In his fondness for cats, the Imam recalls Mahommed, who, at the hour of prayer, finding a cat asleep beside him, on the skirt of his caftan, chopped the garment short rather than disturb the sleeping animal.

Early in 1853, when Shamyl was absent for some months, fighting in the mountains, poor Vaska-Nourman pined, refusing all food. In vain the choicest morsels were prepared for him, the household hanging over him solicitously: in vain Khazi Mahommed moved into his father's rooms trying to feed the cat by hand—it was inconsolable and at last died. The whole aôul was becalmed in grief. Khazi Mahommed assembled all the available Murid dignitaries to honour his father's pet, giving it a special burial and a funeral ovation worthy of a Naib. But no one dared inform Shamyl of the tragedy. 'Now it will go badly with me,' he said, hearing at last of his loss. To him, Vaska-Nourman must have been mascot and companion, someone who shared the days of his glory, and who returned his love unquestioningly, and made even less demands than the gentle Shouanete.

IV

In general, Shamyl's headquarters were now at the aôul of Vedin, to which he returned between battles. He named it Dargo-Vedin to commemorate that other aôul of dark memory, where Khazi Mollah had perished. It was designed to be an inaccessible retreat, and was only reached by fearful ascents along precipitous mountain paths. It was surrounded by an atmosphere of awe, and the people spoke of it as 'the Great Aôul'. We have an interesting account of it left by Atarov, a cousin of Shouanete, an Armenian merchant from Mozdok. In 1850 he decided to brave the Murids and to ask permission to visit his cousin. After protracted negotiations with spies, go-betweens, the Russian army and Shamyl's emissaries, the Mozdok merchant set out. 'Ss' Bogom!'— 'with God!' said the Russian sentries, watching him ride off into the hills. They never expected to see him again. *They* would not have done that for any cousin, they said, and crossed themselves, and spat.

At a certain spot in the foothills, at a given signal, a single Murid horseman rode up out of the woods to meet the merchant. He was one of Shamyl's Naibs, and he was followed by a band of twenty riders, Tchetchens, savage-looking men, though merry, too, said the merchant. The journey, which took a week, proved to be quite an undertaking. After each day's hard riding, always climbing, in fearful heat, the party stopped for a few hours to eat and sleep. The way became progressively harder, until they were faced with a series of almost perpendicular crags up which the lithe Tchetchens swarmed easily, leading their horses and half-dragging, half-carrying, the unhappy Mozdok merchant, whose sedentary life had not fitted him for these acrobatics. The Murids never seemed to tire, or grow breathless, like lesser mortals. They sang incessantly, a loud strident hymn called *La Allah illa Allahi!* The merchant was by now too exhausted to be awed by the fearsome company in which he found himself.

At last they came in sight of Dargo-Vedin, from which a cavalcade of wild horsemen streamed out to meet them. Shamyl's castle lay on a high plateau ringed by mountains, pierced by one narrow defile, or gap, in the sheer rock face. Behind it lay densely wooded slopes; in front, a terrible ravine where, far below, the unbridged river Chilo raged across the boulders. The fortress was surrounded by a stockade—two rows of heavy stakes bound together by clay. There was only one entrance and this was defended by block-houses, a watch-tower which dominated the whole countryside, and one large gun of European make. A little to the side lay a small settlement of saklias, and a mosque: here some Murids and a few chosen Naibs lived in attendance on the Imam. A powder-magazine, heavily guarded by day and night, and a storehouse for provisions, were beside a large water-tank fed from a mountain stream, which had been further diverted to fill an immense stone pool where both men and horses bathed. Shamyl's own house was set in the middle of the inner fortress, guarded by picked Murids without whom he never walked abroad, and who surrounded him with their drawn swords.

A mosque adjoined his own quarters which, though small, had the distinction of being two-storied. From the flat roof-top he could survey the whole sweep of the mountain. Outside the gates, a small colony of artisans were kept busy, shoeing the horses, mending saddles and bridles, making the glove-soft leather boots the mountaineers wore and, above all, tempering steel for their weapons. There was also a watch-maker, repairing a number of clocks and watches, working with great skill, says our Armenian observer. Timepieces were always considered the most desirable form of booty, and in any raid, the mountaineers prized them more than jewellery. They were also the classic gift, between Murid dignitaries, local rulers, or Turkish emissaries. The Russians, too, usually presented co-operative local chiefs with gold repeaters. So that from afar we seem to hear a multiple ticking rising from the mighty landscape, like some tiny but rhythmic insect hum.

The Mozdok merchant found his cousin whom he had known as Anna Uluhanova remarkably well and happy. She received him in her own quarters which were decorated in the Turkish style, with fine carpets, and a takhtar, or cushioned divan, running round two sides of the room. She was veiled, and only consented to remove her veil when they were quite alone. She also indicated that their conversation must be carried on in the Kumyk dialect, rather than their native Armenian, lest the watchers—for every move was observed, every word overheard —should think they spoke of the Imam, or his secrets.

Shouanete began by questioning her cousin about her family, when suddenly the door opened, and Shamyl stood on the threshold. Shouanete was overcome with confusion, blushed, stammered and hurriedly veiled herself, for behind him stood some of his bodyguards. But the Imam, whom we are told was an impressive, scarlet-bearded figure, with sleepy hazel eyes, was at his most sociable. He sat down beside his guest and began complimenting him on his courage and tenacity in coming to Dargo-Vedin. Atarov replied by thanking him for the permission. 'I would give it to some others,' replied Shamyl, with a sudden smile, 'but no one dares, or cares, to make the journey.' He enquired after 'our' family; it appeared he now regarded Shouanete's relatives as his own. (The fact that she had been first captured in a raid and presented to him as an addition to his harem, something which still rankled in Mozdok, had been quite forgotten by both Shamyl and Shouanete, who basked in perfect married bliss.) After Russian tea and excellent little cakes made by Shouanete, the Imam asked some very pertinent questions about France, Hungary, and the state of the Russian army; he then consented to receive a present from his guest— a handsome chronometer and chain, and a gold watch for Shouanete. He seemed pleased, but would not take it direct from Christian hands: Shouanete placed it beside him on the takhta, explaining that he must not be defiled by contact with the Giaour. She herself had long ago become a Moslem. Once again, Shouanete's cousin repeated the offers of her family, to buy her back with large sums of gold; but once again Shouanete refused, happily. She was a woman in love. The Imam merely smiled.

Next day, the Armenian left, receiving a fine horse as a parting gift. The Naib who had conducted him to Dargo-Vedin again accompanied him with an escort of thirty Murids. 'If any of my men ask if you have seen the Imam, deny it—only tell that you saw your cousin,' the Naib told him.

Atarov asked if the Murids would laugh at him—would disbelieve him. 'No one would laugh,' replied the Naib sombrely. 'They would kill you—like that!' He ran his finger across his throat. 'For,' he said, 'you must know, Shamyl, to us, is a supreme Being, Allah's Prophet, and he does not eat at the same table or speak with Giaours. Now you understand. Keep a bridle on your tongue.'

From that moment, no one from the outside world ever saw Shamyl face to face again, until Madame Drancy and the Russian Princesses were brought as hostages to his aôul.

V

With Shamyl's triumphant reappearance in 1840, a year after the disaster of Akhulgo, an era of the most desperate fighting began. No more compromise was possible, either for the Russians, with their sly talk of reforms, or benevolent rule, or for those mountaineers, who had once hung back from allying themselves wholeheartedly with the Murids. Now they surged round Shamyl, and he flung them, in living waves of defiance, against the Russian forces. Fanaticism was met with heroism. Shamyl rallied around him a number of powerful local chieftains, and under his leadership in Tchetchnia they now practised a system of jungle warfare, where his men crept and crawled, and climbed, cat-like, around the bewildered invaders, who could not advance without felling the trees and clearing a path through the undergrowth that blocked their every step, and held up the transport of both guns and supply wagons. He drew them farther and farther into the green, overcast jungles, and slaughtered them there.

A series of raids and sieges had lately occurred along the Black Sea coast, south of Anapa, where the Tcherkess tribesmen had been uniformly triumphant, although the Russians perished in circumstances of the utmost heroism. One after another, their forts were taken by the tribesmen, their garrisons massacred to a man, while the dread plagues and swamp fevers, which abounded in this region (causing it to be used as a military penal settlement, a sort of Slav Devil's Island), carried off whole companies in a few months. The weakened men fought bravely, but they were in no condition to stand a siege. Fort Lazareff, Fort Veliaminov, Fort Nicholas and Fort Mikhailovsky, all fell within three months of each other. It was a crushing blow to Russian prestige.

The revolt of these coastal areas was said to have been secretly organized by England, in order to make all communications between the Caucasian provinces and the Persian frontier more difficult: not so much to participate in Caucasian struggles, as to hinder any possibilities of a Russian force participating in the Afghan wars. Whether this was true or not, remains uncertain, though the activities of Captain Bell and his agents, up and down the coast, between the Crimea and the Turkish frontier, were unquestionable. At one point, in 1839, a strong force of Ubiques fell on five thousand Russians: the Ubiques were led by Captain Bell in person. 'A violent combat ensued, but the deadly fire of the Russian battleships, which came in shore to aid the troops, decimated the rebel ranks, and they were forced, at last, to withdraw into the hills. . . .' Russia now set itself to build a line of coastal forts which could ensure harbours and communications, independent of the tribesmen. And, as they built their forts, the mountaineers fought them, step by step. The Russian general, Raievsky, issued a proclamation couched in terms of Oriental hyperbole:

> Our sublime Emperor, whose armies are innumerable, has charged me to take possession of Toups, Shupliqua and Semez . . . to construct forts and arsenals, for his mighty fleet. I shall build roads and ports. Let all fall back peacefully! Our Sublime, all-puissant Emperor has ordered us, in spite of our might, to try, first, the way of peace and conciliation. Obey! If not prepare to receive a lesson. Listen O deserters, renegades and rebels! For five years, you have spoken in vain, of the promises and forthcoming help of the Queen of England, the King of France, and the Sultan. But our Emperor is at peace with these noble personages. They were our allies when we fought Bonaparte. They will do nothing for you now. . . . Do not believe in your false prophets any more than I believe the suspects that come to me (seemingly sent by you). Send me men of intelligence, of honour, and I will get on with them. If you wish for peace, I will be your friend. I do not wish for war, but do not force my hand.

The Tcherkess were unanimous in their fury. A proud and most menacing reply (signed in blood) was returned:

> For 12 years you have boasted of being masters and conquerors of our country. You lie! General Raievsky, you must know that all your forts are, for us, so many tombs, in our forests. They do us neither good nor ill. We will *never* become your subjects. We shall resist to the last man. You tell us that for years we have been the dupe of the English. We do not believe less in them, for your words. Try marching out, one hour from your fortress, and you will find out what we are. If you wish, truly, to be our friend, then write to your Emperor, tell him to recall his troops, to dismantle his forts, from Anapa to Karotchas. Then we could settle our affairs. Without that, nothing can be done.

But the Russians were too arrogant. They refused to parley with the Tcherkess (or Circassian) mountain chiefs who, not unnaturally, had demanded their intentions when the Russian fleet anchored, and began unloading war-materials in one of the crescent-shaped little bays of the Circassian coast. A suspension of hostilities had been called; but, while the tribesmen observed the pact, and laid down their muskets, the Russians went on unloading their supplies, without deigning to parley. At last the enraged chieftains raised their standards once more and, followed by the whole population of the coastal areas, now inflamed by their mollahs, and convinced as to the Holy nature of the war, they descended on the Russians in terrible force. As soon as they had inflicted a severe defeat, they withdrew, to fling themselves on the garrison of Navaginsky, who had imprudently left their fort, and rushed out trying to save the crew and valuables of several ships which had been, only the day before, flung on to the rocks by a violent storm. The Tcherkess closed in on them, circling round them, driving them, step by step, into the water, where they butchered them in the shallows, among the wreckage of the ships. Only a hundred men escaped.

This victory mounted like wine, to 'the rebels' ' heads. When General Grabbé called on them to lay down their arms, they defied him. 'The Tcherkess will never surrender to Muscovite domination as long as one warrior lives,' they wrote, and they sharpened their shashkas, and prayed in the mosques, and prepared to join Shamyl wherever he led them.

When news of Shamyl's continued ascendancy reached the Tzar, Imperial dispatches were sent racing southward, and the General Staff writhed under the lash of his pen.

Throughout the summer and autumn of 1840, furious fighting continued across the whole Caucasus. The Russians were now outnumbered, but succeeded, in September, owing to the daring of General von Klugenau, in surprising the aôul of Ghimri, descending by the precipitous five-hundred-foot goat-path, from above, as once before, in 1832, when Khazi Mollah had defended it to the death and Shamyl had made his legendary leap to freedom, over the heads of the Russian guns. But this, the second loss of Ghimri, hardly weakened Shamyl's prestige. Overall his campaigns were brilliantly successful. When, in January 1841, Klugenau dispatched a force of two thousand men against Hadji Mourad, Shamyl's first Naib, the expedition was led by no less a personage than General Bakounin, Commander-in-Chief of the Imperial Russian Artillery, who happened to be in the Caucasus on a tour of inspection, and, thirsting for the taste of battle, and confident that he would cut a fine figure commanding an engagement, insisted on taking over. But, in the storming of a mountain fort he was killed; the renegade militia attached to the Russians held back, and would not fight at the crucial moment; thus the Russians, having lost a third of their men, were forced to retreat. Month by month, Shamyl gained in strength till, by midsummer, Golovine was writing: 'We have never had an enemy so savage or dangerous as Shamyl . . . his power has acquired a religio-military character, such as, at the beginnings of Islam, was used by Mahommed to shake three-quarters of the globe . . . Hostages are killed without mercy . . . The rulers he has imposed are his slaves; death awaits all who are suspected of the faintest infringement of his rule. . . . The suppression of this terrible despotism must be our first care.' But the Russian High Command, equally despotic, was now weakened by a series of bitter intrigues and quarrels by which the various generals feuded among themselves, and jockeyed for favour with the Tzar. While they were bickering, Shamyl swooped on Kazi-Koumoukh and carried off the chieftain and his entire family, as well as the Russian Resident and his Cossack guard.

Next, General Grabbé's pig-headedness brought about a major disaster. Contrary to all counsels, he insisted on marching on Dargo, and was planning to subdue Boumbet and Andi too. It was useless to argue with him, his staff officers found. Useless to point out that, by abandoning Prince Argoutinsky's small division, then holding the flank, whole tracts of country were left at the mercy of Shamyl's raiders.

In Daghestan, the Russian forces were then concentrated in small groups, holding many poorly-fortified centres scattered over vast tracts of a difficult terrain which chafed under Russian rule. But Grabbé waved aside all objections, speaking of decisive action, and might. Collecting a force of no less than ten thousand men, he set out with colours flying. This is General Golovine's description of the disaster which followed:

> The very magnitude of the force he had amassed served to impair the efficiency of the expedition. He had with him a large number of military stores and provisions, a large number of carts, and some 3000 horses. On the march, this baggage train, owing to the difficult nature of the roads, stretched out several versts, and to protect it, even by a sparse line of soldiers, took nearly half the column. With a couple of battalions told off for the advance guard, and as many for the rear, and the rest broken up to form the protective lines on each side, or to help the train along, the whole force became extremely weak, having no men free to support the various units; besides which, it had to overcome the very great difficulties presented not only by Nature, but by the efforts of the mountaineers, who perfectly understood that this march through the deep forests gave them their unique chance of success, and that once the columns emerged from the difficult defile, they would have lost their best chance to destroy them. . . .
>
> The 30th May, the column made only 7 versts, though no enemy was encountered. Rain fell all that night, making the roads worse, and delaying progress to such an extent that up to the evening of the 31st, after a cruel 15 hours' march, fighting all the way, harassed continually by a hidden enemy, the column had made only 12 versts more, and was forced to bivouac for the night on a waterless plain. Next day the number of the enemy had increased, though according to trustworthy accounts, it reached less than 2000, owing to the main forces being with Shamyl, at Kazi-Koumoukh. The road became more difficult; barricades (hurriedly erected by the mountaineers) more frequent, and for the second day, the troops were without water. There were several hundred wounded and the general confusion increased hourly. The column had made only 25 versts in three days, and, at last, General Grabbé realized it was impossible to continue the advance. . . .

There was no more heroic talk. On the evening of June 1, he

abandoned his enterprise and gave orders to retreat by the same road. 'If the advance was unfortunate, the retirement was infinitely more so,' wrote Golovine.

We can imagine the despair of these men, trapped in the choking jungles which were alive with sharp-shooters. The Murid troops took up their places, at one point, in some gigantic beech trees, each tree sheltering thirty to forty men, who poured their fire on the approaching Russians. 'But the volleys of whole battalions failed to dislodge the garrisons from their improvised towers of defence.'

'Basically, the Russian people have no love for fighting,' says a German military observer, who followed the Caucasian campaigns closely. 'They seldom wear arms, or enjoy combats of beasts, as known to the Romans and Spaniards.' They did not display the swaggering militarism and brutality inherent in the German race; nor did they share the Caucasian tribes' passion for raiding, for cold steel, for 'sabring each other in the way of friendship', as Lermontov puts it.

At last, on June 4, the remnants of the Tchetchen expedition got back to Gherzel aôul, having lost two thousand men, and nearly all the provisions and stores. But Grabbé was a personal friend of the Tzar, in whose eyes he could do no wrong. Again and again, during his command, from 1839 to 1842, his blunders were overlooked. Besides, Nicholas fancied himself as a strategist: he liked to dabble in the war, to advise, and command from afar. Generals such as Yermolov, who had insisted on making decisions on the spot, had been replaced by others, more pliant. But the war dragged on, in a most unsatisfactory way. At last, in December, General Grabbé, aware of his increasing unpopularity with the army, and the total failure of his command, asked to be recalled, and was replaced by General Neidhardt.

This appointment was hailed with some misgiving by those young and brilliant officers from the north, already grown restive under the inept command of men such as Grabbé. While their immediate superiors, Passek, 'whose name was worth battalions', Major-General Prince Argoutinsky-Dolgoruky, Freitag, and many more, were all tried by years of Caucasian warfare, the final command, the overall conduct of the war had been, for many years, in the hands of men who proved themselves no match for either the Caucasus, or Shamyl. General Neidhardt prolonged the series of disasters and blunders which had so dispirited the Russian army under Grabbé's command. He was stupid, pedantic and slow, and no one has ever explained why the Tzar chose him as Supreme Commander.

Soon after his appointment, he issued a proclamation, stating that whoever would bring him Shamyl's head, should receive its weight in gold. On learning this, Shamyl sent a letter to the General, expressing his gratitude for the great compliment His Excellency paid him by setting so high a value on his head. For his part, wrote the Imam, he regretted he could not return the compliment, and must assure His Excellency that he would not offer a straw to anyone who delivered up General Neidhardt's head to him. A Tartar messenger galloped right into Temir-Khan-Shura, to the very gates of Neidhardt's quarters, to hand over the letter. His white teeth grinned out of a cloud of dust, as he reined up his plunging black stallion; the horse snorted and caracoled defiantly, before the astonished sentries. Then, with a thunder of hooves, and the Tartar war-cry, '*Ourouss! Ourouss!*' the rider was gone, leaping the barriers at the outskirts of town, and disappearing into the mountains, from where he had sprung.

*   *   *

Meanwhile, Shamyl continued to harass the Russians, moving so fast about the country that reports of his movements were not believed at Staff Headquarters. On August 16, Klugenau reported that all was quiet in Daghestan: but, on the 27th, Shamyl set out from Dilim, leading an army which, less than twenty-four hours later, appeared at Ountsoukoul, fifty miles away. He was joined by two of his most powerful Naibs, Kibit Mahoma and Hadji Mourad, each heading a big force, so that between them, Shamyl's army numbered ten thousand men. 'The rapidity of this long march over a mountainous country, the precision of the combined operation, and above all, the fact that it was prepared and carried out under Klugenau's very eyes, without his even suspecting it, entitle Shamyl to rank as something more than a guerilla leader, even of the highest class,' writes one military historian.

Sometimes Shamyl's ferocity nearly cost him his life; and, in the end, it came to weigh against him, causing the tribes to turn to the Russians, who by then had replaced Pullo's diabolic cruelties by Bariatinsky's more chivalrous methods; but first, there were many years of suffering and terror, imposed on the Caucasian people as a whole, who were shuttled helplessly between two tyrannic forces. Shamyl's belief that mercy would be construed as weakness sometimes led him to terrible actions. When his kounak, or sworn-friend, Shouaib, was killed, in the aôul of Tsonterii, owing to a blood-feud, or private vendetta, Shamyl sent two hundred of his Murids to arrest the leading citizens, for having failed to prevent the murder. But kanly—vendetta—was an accepted tribal law in the Caucasus, a matter concerning only the families involved, and it had not occurred to the citizens to interfere, just because Shouaib was Shamyl's kounak. They resisted the Murids violently and a pitched battle followed. Learning of this, Shamyl rode to the aôul, and in his finest rhetorical vein, he spoke a funeral oration over Shouaib's grave. After which he ordered their massacre, 'every living soul in the aôul, men, women and children, one hundred families in all'. And, satisfied that his kounak's death was properly avenged— that no other of his own friends would ever lack the support of fellow citizens in moments of danger—he rode back to his headquarters for the period of meditation, prayer and fasting in the Mosque.

Rarely, very rarely, a victim struck back before perishing. There was an aôul in Ingoush territory which the Murids knew to be hesitating between Russian and Murid pressure. The village elder, Goubish, held two Tchetchen spies and was, according to Shamyl's informers, about to give them up to the Russians, as a gesture of good-will. Shamyl intercepted the message and struck, with his usual lightning force, swooping on the village at the head of a troop of horsemen. Goubish was seized, and one eye gouged out, before he was bound and flung into a prison pit. That night, with the help of his family, Goubish escaped from the pit, managed to reach Shamyl's tent and overcome the sentry. Maddened with pain and hatred he fell on the sleeping Shamyl, wounding him severely. But Shamyl, who was unarmed, defended himself by seizing the man's head between his hands, tearing at his face with his teeth, until the man fainted, and was dragged off by the guards.

Although Shamyl was by now weak from loss of blood, he was not too weak to avenge himself still further. As always, he believed any show of mercy would be construed as weakness. The wretched Goubish had been killed outright. It was not enough. His two brothers who had aided him were cut to pieces, while the rest of his family, eight of them, were locked in their saklia and burnt alive. Shamyl's wounds were bound up, and he was carried to the mosque, there to give thanks for his miraculous preservation. He passed along silent streets, the people prostrated before him, not even daring to wail. Not one among them now, who dared to question their lot. They must live and die for Shamyl. He was Allah's chosen, their ruler under Allah. Mektoub! It was written. In blood.

17

Voronzov Glories

It was said of Prince Voronzov that through the whole of South Russia you could talk to no man for half an hour without hearing his name, and never without a blessing.   SYDNEY HERBERT

He was a finished courtier . . . he did not understand life without power and submission.   TOLSTOY

Sometimes, drinking tea from a cup that is painted, under its blue glaze, with a landscape that recalls the improbable beauties of the Crimea, I stare, nostalgic and rapt, remembering Aloupkha, and the man who built it, Count Michael Voronzov, whose name is forever one with the Caucasus. He was absolute ruler of southern Russia, Viceroy and Commander-in-Chief of the Armies of the South and, for ten years, Shamyl's deadliest enemy. But there is no trace, in these porcelain perspectives, of the Titan's struggle: only waterfalls and distant peaks, and palaces of a Gothic-Oriental cast, starting from bosky groves where odalisques pluck lutes, and turbaned cavaliers leap chasms. This is the legendary East as conceived by eighteenth- and nineteenth-century English porcelain manufacturers.

While Worcester and Staffordshire dinner-services often dwelt on pig-sticking, whole services being devoted to big game hunting with Maharajas on elephants, slaughtering noble tigers in bamboo thickets, gory scenes which cannot have encouraged the appetite, tea-services were in a gentler vein, suited to the ladies who sipped and chattered. A tea pot's curved flank reveals the most romantic scenes, shepherds pining beside ruins, or leading curiously formed camels to kneel before Zenobia. Gulping my tea, I peer deep into this microcosm, recalling Crimean shores, where Aloupkha was among 'the many Gotho-Moorish style Palaces, Turkish palaces, and Italianate villas which mingled with the simple Tartar huts and were the fruits of Count Voronzov's refining influence in that region'. Thus an early traveller, who wrote during the Count's rule, and therefore lacked the perspective which later placed the Count's architectural innovations on a lower scale than his political, agricultural or military achievements.

Count Michael Voronzov (he was not created Prince until 1845) bore one of the noblest names in Russia, descending from the first Boyar families. Their title was listed third in the hierarchy of Counts of the Russian Empire. Contrary to the belief that Russia was peppered with titles, the aristocracy was, for so vast an Empire, extremely restrained. There were not more than fifty princely families, and only about half that number of countal families, and of these only some twelve or fifteen who, as Boyars, were first ennobled by the Tzars, the rest stemming from Rurik and the feudal overlords.

Behind the Voronzovs lay a great tradition of service to the state. Through many reigns they had been beside the throne, and they considered themselves the equals of any Tzar. Their allegiance had made and destroyed many kingdoms, and they boasted that they were the only one of the noble families which had never been sent to Siberia. Four Voronzov ladies had worn the scarlet ribbon and star, the Order of St. Catherine, 1st Class, which was generally the prerogative of the reigning Empress and Grand Duchesses alone. Anna Voronzov had been given it by her cousin the Empress Elizabeth: the Tzar Peter III gave it to Elizabeth Voronzov, as his fiancée. Catherine the Great gave it to the redoubtable Princess Dashkov who, born a Voronzov, had played so conspicuous a part in the coup which placed Catherine on the throne. And when, much later, Count Michael Voronzov became Viceroy of the Caucasus, his wife, as Vicereine, displayed the order too. But none of them wore their decorations without having earned them by the dedicated loyalty of their whole lives. They were Russian nobles who let nothing, not even their Tzar, turn them from what they believed their duty towards their country and their high estate.

Count Michael, Shamyl's adversary, was the Voronzov apotheosis. It was as if many generations were all embodied or crystallized in this arrogant, astute, ruthless, yet high-principled man. He was an enigmatic figure, coldly handsome, a great milord in the English manner, haughty and reserved. He seldom smiled, and never lost his air of bland calm. No one knew him well; he was respected and feared (his cold rages were terrible), but he was not loved. As much warmth as he was able to show was reserved for the Georgians and those Tartars and Caucasians over whom he ruled absolutely; so absolutely, indeed, that he seldom consulted or informed the Tzar of his policies, acting entirely on his own responsibility, often subsidizing his developments from his private fortune.

He was born in St. Petersburg, in 1782. His father, Count Simon, had been Catherine the Great's Ambassador to London, and the young Count Michael had been brought up in England, retaining, to the end of his days, markedly Anglophile tendencies. Upon the accession of Catherine's son, the Emperor Paul I, Count Simon was recalled from the Court of St. James, to become his Grand Chancellor. But the Count, disliking all that he knew of the Emperor's character and policies, refused the office. This incensed the Emperor who at once confiscated the Voronzov estates, withheld their revenues and revoked the Ambassadorship. Count Simon still refused to return to Russia, preferring to live out his years of exile in London. Nevertheless, the Tzar offered, and he accepted, his daughter's designation as *demoiselle d'honneur*; a singular mark of esteem, since it was never given to anyone who lived outside Russia. The Ambassador wrote to his friend Count Stroganov on the subject, and expressed himself in his usual trenchant manner.

'If this favour had been offered during the past reign (that of Catherine II) I should have declined it, for I would have preferred to see my daughter anywhere but at a Court where Prince Potemkin's nieces were brought to bed regularly, without however losing their titles of *demoiselles d'honneur*.'

During his years of voluntary exile in London, the ex-Ambassador remained in dismal financial straits, for his fortune and revenues were locked up in Russia. However, his popularity among the English made him as welcome, in his disgrace, as in his hey-day, and his daughter, without a penny of dowry, contracted a brilliant marriage, becoming the second wife of the eleventh Earl of Pembroke (and it was her son, Sir Sidney Herbert, later Lord Herbert of Lea, who was to labour beside Florence Nightingale, to better the lot of the British soldiers fighting the Russians, in the Crimea). Just before his death, the Emperor Paul had contemplated trying once more to lure the obstinate Count Simon to return, this time as guardian, or chief tutor to the young Grand Duke Nicholas—later Nicholas I. But once again, Voronzov recoiled from any contact with the Tzar Paul.

With the accession of Alexander I, the pendulum swung once more in favour of the Voronzovs, and Count Simon returned to St. Petersburg in 1801 to occupy a position of trust close to the new young Emperor. His son lingered on in London, one of the *beau monde* who were gathered round the Prince Regent, racing on Epsom Downs, eyeing Harriette Wilson and her Paphian sisters, living the life of a young Regency buck. His popularity and good looks were such that his portrait, by Sir Thomas Lawrence—magnificently, flamboyantly handsome—was the sensation of the Royal Academy, and was, in fact, the portrait which won Lawrence his Academician. But, presently, the Tzar recalled him to be one of his Gentlemen of the Bedchamber, a post and a Court which the young man found stifling. Thus he joined the troops in the Caucasus and also served under General Kutuzov against the Turks, distinguishing himself from the first. As the Napoleonic wars gathered momentum, he was transferred to serve with the Allied armies, and to cover himself with glory. In 1813, we find him a major-general, at thirty-one, fighting under Blücher, and, at one point, at the battle of Craonne, opposed to (with an army of only eighteen thousand men) no less than Napoleon himself, with thirty thousand, in a most obstinate struggle lasting for more than eight hours. 'When at last, on the repeated orders of Blücher, he withdrew, it was without abandoning a single trophy to the enemy.'

The older Voronzov had not allowed age or infirmity to impede his sense of duty. When, in 1807, the Emperor Alexander met with Napoleon, at Tilsit, he had accompanied the Tzar, and was determined to turn him, if possible, from too fervent an acceptance of Napoleon, whom he abhorred. The meeting was held on a flag-decked raft on the Nieman, expressly designed to be beyond the range of eavesdroppers. But the old Voronzov was determined to know what passed. In the light of archives lately discovered by Soviet historians, it seems that some hours before the meeting, he contrived to have himself rowed out, and to crawl between the piles and beams supporting the raft: here he lay concealed, his legs dangling in the chilly current, while, as a reward for his daring and discomfort, he was able to overhear the entire discussion. And he did not hesitate to pass on to the British government certain passages which he considered likely to prove helpful to them, and to his cherished dreams of an Anglo-Russian alliance. While the cunning old statesman eavesdropped, the rest of the world, all the princes and generals, paced the shores anxiously, and the King of Prussia, whose fate was then being decided, was in such a ferment that he was repeatedly seen to urge his horse into the water, as if about to make for the raft: then, overcome by awe and timidity, he would rein up and return to shore, looking sheepish. Old Voronzov, crouched below the raft, carried himself with infinitely more majesty. Like all his family, he made his own laws, acting for the interests of Russia, as he saw them.

In 1815, at the end of the Napoleonic wars, his son Count Michael was appointed Commanding Officer of the Russian troops then occupying Paris. When, in 1818, the troops were withdrawn, he took it upon himself to settle, out of his own pocket, the debts incurred by his officers. He wished the Russian army to leave Paris as nobly as they had entered it. But even his wealth and generosity faltered before the sums of money this splendid gesture involved. The debts were settled; but the spendthrift officers found their commander wholly unsympathetic towards card-playing and dalliance on the long march home. He next accompanied the Tzar Alexander to the Congress of Aix la Chapelle, and was, for some years, alternatively soldier and diplomat. In 1823, the Tzar was determined to obtain his services in another field, and he appointed him a member of the Council of Empire, and Governor

General of New Russia and Bessarabia, where he established himself in magnificent state at Odessa.

At once his brilliant powers as an administrator were recognized. Yet, in spite of all his triumphs Count Voronzov had his sorrows. A Bessarabian gypsy foretold that his whole family would die out, and the property pass into other hands. His son and heir died childless— his other sons died young—his daughter bore no sons. At last, by the end of the century only one grand-daughter remained, to inherit the Voronzov glories. By 1918 she was an exile, and all the estates and properties were taken over by the Bolsheviks, thus fulfilling the gypsy's predictions.

Count Michael Voronzov married the Countess Elizabeth Branizky. She was, if not strictly beautiful, full of grace, charm and *joie de vivre*, and considered the most seductive woman of her day. She was born towards the end of the eighteenth century, and was perhaps the child of Prince Potemkin by his favourite niece, Alexandra Englehardt. (All of his four nieces had been his mistresses, a sort of ambulant harem, often accompanying their lusty uncle on his travels.) Alexandra married the Polish Count Xavier Branizky, a vastly wealthy man, who accepted the baby Eliza as his own. In any case, Potemkin bequeathed most of his vast fortune to Alexandra and the Empress continued to shower her with favours till her dying day, the Countess occupying a suite of rooms at the Winter Palace, directly adjoining those of the Empress, who watched over the baby Eliza tenderly.

When Potemkin lay dying by the wayside in Nicolaiev, it was Alexandra he asked for, she who rushed to him, driving across Russia by day and night, to hold him in her arms when he breathed his last. He left her everything—his jewels, properties, palaces. When her daughter Elizabeth Branizky married Voronzov, her dot was computed at thirty million roubles and the historic Potemkin diamonds, besides two hundred thousand serfs, innumerable salt mines and a number of almost limitless estates scattered throughout Russia, each commanded by a chateau stuffed with treasures. But beyond all this wealth, she was endowed with a curiously magnetic charm, an easy wit and grace. At Odessa, she was always surrounded by a crowd of admirers who sighed for her.

In 1823, Alexander Pushkin, then a young, impoverished, but already acclaimed poet, arrived in Odessa from St. Petersburg, exiled for some seditious verses, and attached to Voronzov's staff, he at once fell under the Countess Elizabeth's spell. Of all the many women in his life, she was something apart. She is held by some Pushkinists to have inspired his loveliest heroine, Tatiana, in *Evgueni Oniegin*. The haughty husband who had not deigned to notice the innumerable admirers who always circled round his wife, now evinced the liveliest jealousy. That Pushkin, a penniless underling, attached to his Chancellry, should add to the crime of liberalism, that of unconventionality, impecuniosity, untidiness, and a visibly passionate love for the Countess Voronzov, was intolerable. Voronzov had little sympathy for poets as a race, describing Byron as 'a writer whose usefulness may be said to be very slight'.

Pushkin was in no position to retaliate openly against Voronzov's condescension, but presently an impudent quatrain was being circulated all around Odessa, and the whole town sniggered at the lines:

Half-hero, and half-ignoramus
Let's add half-villain to this toll.
However, there is still a hope
That he will presently be whole.

Voronzov, too proud to admit he knew or cared that Pushkin dared aspire to, or win, his wife's favours, bided his time. Presently the poet was found to be corresponding with an old Scottish doctor on the subject of atheism, and Voronzov struck. It was a time of religious obscurantism; all Russia bowed before the Holy Synod which, supported by the Tzar, proclaimed free-thinking as dangerous as liberalism. Pushkin was banished from Odessa. There was nothing he could do against Voronzov's order. The husband was able, with a stroke of the Governor's pen, rather than the duellist's sword, to remove his rival. The Countess gave Pushkin a ring—some romantic Oriental talisman, which he cherished for the rest of his life; but they never met again. Writing later of Voronzov, Pushkin described him as 'a vandal, court cad, and petty egoist, who saw me as a collegiate secretary'. But here speaks not only the slighted poet, but the dispossessed lover.

That he and the Countess Eliza were lovers is no longer disputed. Indeed, with the Voronzov descendants it is, understandably, a matter of pride, unlike the prudish attitude of the Duchess of Alba's descendants, who were so determined to deny the Duchess had posed for Goya's Naked Maja, that they are said to have had her coffin exhumed, to prove her bone-structure was of quite another kind to that which the luscious flesh of Goya's canvas indicates. The love-letters of Pushkin and the Countess have lately been discovered in Russia, and are now glass-case exhibits over which earnest crowds of sight-seers pore as they tramp through the palatial halls where once Voronzov reigned supreme, answerable only to God.

Voronzov's brilliant administrative powers were first truly gauged by the manner in which he created a new Russian colony from what had been, however lush, a wilderness. At Odessa, he established commerce, built harbours, colleges, hospitals, an opera house, fine streets, and gathered round him an aristocratic circle who were appointed to administer the province. His policies gradually repopulated the desolate steppe country north of the Black Sea. He introduced steam navigation, on the Black Sea, imported English cattle and caused numbers of French vini-culturists to stock and supervise the new Crimean vineyards.

Voronzov's cynicism, like his method, and particular brand of sound, if arrogant, commonsense (reminiscent of Wellington's), all recalled his English background, and all contributed to his powers as an outstanding colonial administrator. His manner of speaking, as his way of living, was all strongly English. Even in his taste for exotic palaces, he recalled the fashionable English tastes of his youth, when the *ton* had circled round the Prince Regent in the Pavilion which Humphry Repton had conceived at Brighton, 'in the Hindoo-Gothic style', where domes and minarets, incongruous but beautiful, gleamed, rain-washed, under inclement skies. Now, at Aloupkha, Voronzov sounded the same note of exoticism, merged with the Gothic; only now, it was less incongruously placed on glowing Crimean shores which seemed, like the tea-cup vistas, to be some fabled land, radiant and improbable.

Even so, there were critics: that peculiar character, Laurence Oliphant, travelling about Southern Russia in 1850, condemned Aloupkha for its admixture of styles. 'It is difficult to decide whether the building before us bears most resemblance to the stronghold of the Black Douglas, or the Palace of the Great Mogul. . . .'

As architect, Count Voronzov employed an Englishman, Edward Blore, who worked for both King William IV and Queen Victoria, and whose Gothic revivals included portions of Lambeth Palace and Windsor Castle. Together they chose the site, rising one hundred and fifty feet, sheer above the Black Sea. A special greenish stone was used. It was quarried in the Urals, and cost vast sums to transport. When, later, the Tzar Alexander II built his own Crimean palace at Livadia, he had wished to use the same substance, but his architect soon disillusioned him. 'Even your Majesty cannot afford that!' he said, and the Tzar had to be content with marble. There was a Wedgewood drawing-room, an Empire salon and a sombre library recalling that of an Oxford college.

The gardens were no less varied in style. There were formal parterres, English flower-beds, and an immense botanic garden where the rarest vegetation flourished. Everywhere, under a drooping willow, in the shadow of a colonnade, or beside a pool, were sad little graves, where marble tombs and tiny sarcophagi marked the passing of some much-loved animal. The Voronzov family adored them; generation by generation they mourned lost cats, cherished dogs, parrots, squirrels, or chargers, all laid to rest, at last, in the splendour befitting Voronzov pets. Dominating everything, stood two lofty cypress trees. They had been planted by the Empress Catherine and Potemkin on their journey to her southern domains. From these two trees were grafted all the many cypress groves and alleys which came, a hundred years later, to be so typical of the Crimean landscape.

Aloupkha had been a drain, even on the limitless Voronzov fortune. When it was completed, Count Voronzov ordered all the bills to be presented to him. They filled several large leather trunks, and were placed in his study, where behind locked doors, he went through every item. No one ever knew the exact amount they represented. Every bill was paid—but the Count burned all the papers and receipts which told of his outlay. It had been a sort of folly—a massive folly, the only touch of fantasy, in a whole life of stern purpose; a life which had led him from a youth battling against Napoleon to an old age pitted against Shamyl, on the battlefields of the Caucasus.

18

Dargo

Men, they are the first and best instrument of war.
DRAGOMIROV

Count Voronzov's early years of military service enabled him to judge
the conduct of the Caucasian wars shrewdly. He was no mere civil
administrator, however powerful, but by origin a soldier and tactician
who had, long ago, foreseen the cumulative disasters of the campaigns.
On several occasions he had had the courage to tell Nicholas that his
system of directing the war from St. Petersburg was responsible for
many failures. He had never underestimated Shamyl as an enemy, and
he had openly criticized many of the Russian generals—Grabbé and
Niedhardt in particular.

General Niedhardt cuts a sorry figure in the great gallery of Caucasian commanders. He had been Governor of Moscow for some time,
and it would have been better for the Army of the South if he had not
returned to active service. He was a Germanic pedant, 'only great
in small matters', constitutionally incapable of commanding the Caucasian fronts. He was indecisive, and weighed down by the unrealistic programme outlined for him by the Tzar. Towards the end of
1843, Niedhardt received orders from Nicholas 'to enter the mountains
of Daghestan and defeat and scatter all Shamyl's hordes, destroy all
his military institutions; to take possession of all the most important
points in the mountains, and fortify hose whose retention may seem
necessary'. The Army of the Caucasus was to be immediately reinforced,
the General was told: twenty-six battalions, four regiments of Cossacks,
and forty big guns, as well as filling up the ranks already on the spot by
twenty-two thousand time-expired men and freshly trained recruits.
'As to your plan of action, the War Minister will send you full instructions,' wrote the Tzar. 'It will be for you to accept these views
wholly, or in part, but remembering always that from such gigantic
means I expect corresponding results.' He ended by saying that in no
circumstances did he, the Tzar, intend to leave the reinforcements now
entrusted to Niedhardt, in the Caucasus, beyond the month of December 1844. In short, Niedhardt was to win the war within the year.

Niedhardt was unable to command, or delegate to his brilliant and eager younger officers. Moreover, each campaign was hampered by peremptory orders and counter-orders issuing from the Winter Palace, which plunged the Caucasian commanders into confusion and despair. Occasionally, a minor engagement was victoriously undertaken, without adhering to the main plan. In June, the summer's campaign in Daghestan was opened by young General Passek who, with only one thousand four hundred men, led a desperate attack in person, killing with his own hand two of Shamyl's most faithful Naibs, and gaining a decisive victory over a massed force of Murids, at Ghillee. Russian prestige was raised by this, and Shamyl, in consequence, lost numbers of tribesmen who decided to throw in their lot with the Russians. All through the summer, the Russians continued successful minor engagements, but were, overall, no nearer a decisive victory. Moreover, they suffered what could be considered a major defeat by the loss of Daniel Beg, Sultan of Elisou, that puissant native ruler, rich, proud and cunning, who had so many years earlier, sworn allegiance to the Russians, to become a major-general in the Russian army.

Daniel Beg was finally goaded beyond endurance by General Niedhardt who, inexplicably, set himself up to remove the Sultan's powers over his people, and even sent an officer to his capital, in order to find some pretext which could serve as grounds to abolish Daniel Beg's authority. The Sultan, who had been a loyal vassal to the Russian Crown (although his family had been rulers long before the Romanovs), now tore off the Russian uniform he had worn with pride and, wrapping himself in a bourka, fled to the mountains, sought out Shamyl, became his ally, and secured for him the support of whole provinces in southern Daghestan. Nothing could have been more detrimental to Russian prestige, and Niedhardt alone was to blame. Although there was never any love lost between Daniel Beg and Shamyl the latter knew how to subjugate his personal feelings, where the furtherance of Muridism was concerned, and he welcomed Daniel Beg with a show of warmth. The Sultan was always inclined to treat Shamyl with aristocratic patronage: he belonged to that conservative land-owning group of native rulers, Begs or Khans, generally of remote Tartar origin, who mistrusted Shamyl's radical tenets. Nevertheless, he thought it expedient to surround his own change of colours with something of the Imam's religious aura. Before announcing his change of heart, he was careful to immure himself in the mosque for a day and night of prayer. He emerged, carrying the Koran, to tell his people: 'I have known all of earthly glory that a man may wish. But now, having perceived the Truth, I cast off this world, and dedicate myself to Allah, whose first Prophet was Mahommed, and whose second is Shamyl!'

Daniel Beg's defection from the Russian ranks was disastrous to their prestige, and Neidhardt's conduct towards the Sultan was considered to be the cause: but it was only one of so many blunders. A short while later, he failed to execute a carefully laid plan by which Shamyl was enclosed in a defile and could have been, with the flower of his army, annihilated there. Neidhardt gave the order to attack a few hours too late: Shamyl managed to escape from the trap, and even to harass and account for a large number of Russian troops during his retreat. General Niedhardt was recalled in ignominy. He returned to Moscow where, shortly afterwards, he died, a broken man.

No one had imagined that his successor would be Count Voronzov. The army themselves had cherished a hope that the old lion, Yermolov, might be called out of his retirement, to the scenes of his former victories. The capital and the Court believed that the War Minister, Tchernitchev, would take command himself. Voronzov did not seem a likely choice: he was sixty-three, and was said to be out of favour with the Tzar for his independent spirit and the manner in which he sometimes spoke his mind to his sovereign. In Odessa, it was believed he was surrounded by spies, and that his staff, and servants even, reported regularly to the Winter Palace, on his every word. Yet it was he whom Nicholas chose. Moreover, he invested him with an authority never granted any other subject, since that with which Catherine the Great had invested Potemkin. Nicholas created Voronzov Viceroy of the whole of Southern Russia, a domain stretching from the Bukovina, on the west, to the Caspian, on the east; from the Caucasian mountains to the Turkish and Persian frontiers. The Royal ukase appointed him, not only Viceroy of this vast province, but Commander-in-Chief of the whole forces serving in the Caucasus, answerable to no man but the Tzar. This last and astounding investiture of power was obtained by Voronzov himself, who refused to accept the responsibilities entrusted to him, unless he were freed from all foreign interference, from St. Petersburg staff officers, or the War Ministers who had rendered every Caucasian general's task insupportable. However, Voronzov had still to reckon with the Tzar. But even here, confronting the dread autocrat, he insisted on the abolition of the Commission of the Caucasus, and any but the most generalized directives, from the Tzar alone. Nicholas now acquiesced meekly enough. He recognized Voronzov's abilities, and was beginning to see Shamyl in a far more formidable light than hitherto.

But no sooner had Voronzov taken up his command, than a series of dispatches began to arrive from the Winter Palace, each one urging a course of action unacceptable to the Commander-in-Chief. His army, wrote the Tzar, was to move deep into Daghestan and subdue the various centres of resistance there, without more ado. Voronzov and his staff passed from irritation to discouragement, so that soon Voronzov was writing: 'I dare not hope great success from our enterprise; but, of course, I will do all I can to execute the Emperor's desires, and justify his confidence.' A number of minor engagements ensued, which, while accounting for small casualties on both sides, were in no way decisive. J. F. Baddeley, in his *Conquest of the Caucasus*, analyses the following expedition, the Dargo expedition, with his customary clarity:

Shamyl [he says], as usual, based his strategy on a complete and masterly appreciation of all conditions affecting either himself or his foe. He knew that, as Argoutinsky (a Russian officer) had pointed out, the Russians, in present circumstances, could penetrate the mountains, but could not maintain themselves there. He also knew that he had no earthly chance of beating such an army as this in the open, nor even of harassing it seriously on the outward march, while men and horses were fresh, munitions plentiful, and supplies adequate. His opportunity would come later or when Nature, his great ally, had done her work, and the invaders, worn with toil, weak from privation, uninspirited by successes in the field, would have to face the homeward march over the barren mountains of Daghestan or through the forests of Itchkeria. Then, indeed, he would let loose on them his mobile hordes, break down the roads in front of them, seize every opportunity of cutting off front or rear guard, of throwing the centre with its weary baggage train and lengthy line of wounded into confusion, and give the men no rest by day or night. At best they would succeed in fighting their way back to their base on the Soulak or Soundja, but he would take care it would be in such a plight as would lower them in their own eyes, and in the eyes of every native from the Caspian to the Black Sea, from the Terek to the Persian frontier. Meanwhile, he would show just enough force to lure them on.

This Shamyl did. On June 3, 1845, the Russian army, under Voronzov's supreme command, moved out from their headquarters in the pacified regions of Vnezapnaya. They planned to attack and take the pass between Salatau and Goumbet, thus to descend on Andi Gates, another pass which Shamyl was expected to defend strongly, as it led to the aôul of Andi, 'that nest' as the Tzar described it, controlling an inner area of Daghestan, which centred round Dargo, the Imam's headquarters.

Passek, leading six divisions, stormed the pass, but found it practically undefended, and it fell to the Russians easily enough. On the morning of the 6th, Passek, with characteristic impetuosity, continued his forward thrust, without waiting instructions from Voronzov. Arriving at Zounou-Mir, ten miles farther on, he found himself isolated; abruptly, as so often in the Caucasus, the weather changed. Summer sun gave place to winter cold, snow, frost and cutting winds. For five days the troops were without shelter or provisions. Frost-bite attacked four hundred and fifty of them, and five hundred horses died. On the 12th, the weather changed, the sun shone again, and Voronzov was able to join Passek and prepare for the attack on Andi Gates. But Shamyl, too wise to court failure, set fire to Andi and all the surrounding aôuls, and retreated in good order, forcing the population of the sacked aôuls to join him. On the 14th, the Russians took possession of the smoking ruins. Although Shamyl had escaped, the passes were taken. So far the campaign was moving according to the Tzar's plan. The delighted Emperor wrote to Voronzov: 'God has crowned you and your heroic troops with deserved success, and shown once more that nothing can ever stop the Russians—the Orthodox Russians—when with firm reliance they go where their Tzar bids them.'

God and Tzar! The two were ever interwoven, in his mind.

Dargo lay over the mountains—ten miles away. But no one who had not seen and experienced the difficulties of Caucasian warfare could know what those ten miles represented in effort and danger. Nevertheless, the Tzar commanded, and it was for Voronzov to obey. It would be, he knew, a signal victory if he could take it before winter set in and immobilized both Russians and Murids alike. Still, he had his doubts. He wrote to the War Minister: 'If the orders I received to take the offensive, this year, before resuming the construction of the Tchetchen advanced line (for as soon as the troops were not engaged in active combat, they had to construct roads and forts) were at variance with my own opinions, as they are with those of all the local generals, I should carry them out with the same zeal; but——' and here he began to outline a number of problems which confronted him. One of the greatest problems in the Caucasus was the lack of roads, communications, or supply bases. The Russians would have been well advised to have proceeded slowly, first constructing their means of transport, and in so doing, winning the support of local tribes, as they did in parts of Tchetchnia, where the agricultural communities were the first to profit by roads and the ensuing trade. But the Autocrat of All the Russias was only concerned with an immediate victory—with Shamyl's head, and an end to the ceaseless drain of manpower and money which the Caucasus demanded; Voronzov knew he must execute his orders as best he could, at whatever cost.

By virtue of his great name, he gathered round him an illustrious force. Besides an army of ten thousand, his staff and personal suite was composed of such noble personages as Prince Alexander of Hesse-Darmstadt, Prince Wittgenstein and the Prince of Warsaw (sons of the great generals); the Princes Bariatinsky and Orbeliani, and many more scions of the great Russian families. But few of them, save

Orbeliani and Bariatinsky, were accustomed to Caucasian warfare—though his generals, Lüders, Klugenau, Passek, and others, had all been tried by years of this harsh campaigning.

Like the Commander-in-Chief, the generals were each surrounded by a resplendent staff, and all the 'pomp and circumstance of glorious war'. Voronzov's flag was red and white—the family colours—his personal guard were Kurds, in splendid and barbaric costumes; 'Shocking ruffians!' Lady Shiel found them, watching a troop of cavalry pass her caravan. All the same, we sense her appreciation: '*Most* manly, with sinewy, wild looks. They move in a compact body, at a half walk, half trot, making great way, their spears are held aloft, with a black tuft dangling. In front are the chiefs, beside them, the kettle-drums, beating with vast energy.' Even Voronzov's lesser officers had large numbers of guards, body-servants, grooms and cooks, making the movements of the army a considerable undertaking. Gone were the days when officers and men slept wrapped in their bourkas, or dug into *zemliankas*—underground huts—nourished on army biscuits heated in warm water.

This sybaritic train moved laboriously over the mountains, and since the comforts took up so much space, far too few essential provisions arrived. One English traveller, Captain Wilbraham, calling on two of the Emperor's aides-de-camp, Count Vasiltchikov and Colonel Catinin, at Staff Headquarters, found them engaged in 'the serious occupation of the toilette, and I must confess that I have never seen more luxury displayed in that department than by these Petersburg Guardees. Their dressing-cases, of English manufacture, were fitted with jug and basin of solid silver, and their dressing-gowns almost shamed me, who had but just arrived from the land of silks and kashmeres. They were both handsome, agreeable men, more French than Russian in manner.' It is clear that to the Englishman, Russians in general were regarded as Asiatics—barbarians.

Voronzov or 'The Accursed One', as he was to the Murids, waited at Andi Gates, nearly three weeks, for the necessary accumulation of food-supplies to follow from Vnezapnaya. He could not proceed without them, for he found that Shamyl had razed the surrounding country. As for horse-fodder, the scorching July suns had burned up the grass, so that the horses were worse off than the men. On the 18th a large force was dispatched towards Botlikh, and the lake of Ardjiam, but returned, having failed to engage the enemy, and succeeded only in destroying a few dozen trout in the icy green depths of the lake. Wags dubbed the whole affair *l'expedition détruite*, and in camp, that night, there was a good deal of banter, to the sound of popping corks, as they drank to victory, in champagne.

Progress was very slow across the passes, which were proving, even in summer, almost impassable. In some places the column had to turn about and find other, less precipitous paths through lower and longer tracts of hill country. But on July 4, Voronzov's tent, its six-tailed Bashaw's standards hardly stirring in the summer air, was pitched within ten miles of Dargo. He had decided to move on the aôul. The latest dispatch received from the Winter Palace showed how impatient the royal taskmaster was now becoming. July—August—perhaps September—there were less than three months of fighting weather left. Snow settled on the mountains by October; there was no time to dally. Although Voronzov knew he had only a few days' supplies and rations left, and that the next sumpter wagons could not arrive before the 10th, he made his fatal decision. He would attack, but send back a part of his force to bring up the supplies to his advancing line, as soon as possible.

Very early on the morning of the 6th, a renegade native numbered among Voronzov's personal bodyguard, crept to the tent where his favourite charger was picketed, and mounting it, galloped right across the astonished lines, making off to the mountains, to warn Shamyl of the imminent attack. Nevertheless, the army marched, and by noon, were within five miles of Dargo. While they halted, preparatory to the attack, the men ate, rested, prayed, and turned their eyes far away to the north, to where, across the hostile ranges of the Tchetchen mountains, and the flash of silver that was the Terek, winding through the plains, forty versts distant, they could see a streak of blue on the horizon—'Russia, Holy Russia, Mother Russia, upon which many now looked for the last time.'

The path to Dargo lay along a narrow steep crest, or ridge, sometimes only a few feet wide. Shamyl had barred this path, at intervals, by a series of giant tree-trunks, their branches interlaced, and forming the most effective obstacle to any oncomers. As the Russians advanced, and stopped short to negotiate these barriers, they were shot down, one after the other, by hidden sharp-shooters. Changing their tactics, the Murids next allowed a large force to proceed, unchallenged, before cutting them off, and reopening the attack on the following troops. Now confusion deepened: a number of officers, among them General Lüders and Voronzov himself, found themselves trapped, exposed to heavy fire. 'A mountain gun was brought up, and turned sideways, to sweep the wooded ravine on the right flank whence the shots came thickest; but after the second discharge, every man serving it was killed or severely wounded; it was manned again, and in a few minutes the result was the same. For a brief space of time, the gun stood alone, but for the dead and dying around it: no one dared to cross the neck of land under fire.' At this juncture, General Fok made his way to the gun and loaded it himself, but before he could fire it, fell, mortally wounded. Voronzov now sent a Georgian militia and some Cossacks to attack the woods from where the fire was coming. 'And in a few minutes, we were as safe on the road as at home,' says one of the eye-witnesses.

Once again, Shamyl was employing his evasive, delaying tactics. His men simply vanished—the woods appeared empty, beyond a suicide-band of human targets, left there to draw the Russians' fire, and to put up a show of resistance. They died to a man; but then, the Murids were expendable: it was the first tenet of their faith. Shamyl was watching the battle from a mountain-top, telescope to eye, surrounded by his Naibs, all awaiting his commands. He had ridden out from Dargo with a small force, to observe the battle's progress. The main body of his troops were left behind, concentrated round the aôul. When he saw the size and importance of the approaching Russian force, he rode back to Dargo, giving orders that the aôul was to be fired. All crops were razed, and once more, Shamyl fell back, luring the Russians on, ever deeper into the stony wastes that were his fortress.

When the Russians reached the still smoking ruins of Dargo, they discovered the quarters which had been occupied by a number of Russian deserters who had gone over to Shamyl some time before. They had decorated the walls with crude sketches and inscriptions, generally of a gross nature, and directed at the Tzar, in person. As night fell, the Russians could hear these deserters, over the river, in Shamyl's camp, out of gun-shot reach, playing, most impudently, Russian marches and tattoos, with the regimental drums they had seized in battle. Shamyl had placed four guns on the bluffs above the river, and as their fire 'caused considerable annoyance', a column was sent out to rout them. General Labeentsiev led the attack, which seemed entirely successful. After a token fight, the enemy retired, the guns were seized, and the Russians, watching from their base camp, applauded this triumph. But, as they watched, once again, they saw victory turned to defeat. The way back lay through maize fields, surrounded by rising ground and woods. From behind each tree and stone, sprang a furious enemy. The Russians died where they stood, unable even to fire back at their jack-in-the-box adversaries. The remnants of the column struggled into camp, with the loss of one hundred and eighty-seven men. That night the enemy retrieved two of their guns, and reoccupied their positions, and once again, the deserters were heard drumming their infernal tattoo.

From that moment, a curious gloom descended on the army, pervading all ranks. 'It was not the sight of nearly two hundred killed and wounded; we were used to that kind of thing: but the conviction that the sacrifice was in vain depressed us all.' The Lioubinsky regiment, who had lost their Colonel, had bayoneted some captured mountaineers they believed to have fired the fatal shots. Not content with that, they now cut off their heads, and garnished their pikes with these barbaric trophies. The Tousheen contingent, fighting with the Russians, and celebrated for their valour, came back to camp with numbers of hacked-off Murid hands, their customary practice, but one which, somehow, did not raise the spirit of the army. 'The ceaseless chanting of the funeral service by the Orthodox priests, and volley firing, as the bodies were lowered into their graves, deepened the general feeling of depression, besides telling Shamyl the number of the killed; moreover, powder was none too plentiful. Orders were given to bury the dead in silence.'

On the evening of the 9th, rockets flamed into the sky, beyond the forests, from where the army had fought its way so hard; this was the signal, telling the arrival of the supply convoy to the original point of departure. But now it was seen they could never get through, traverse either the barricaded ridge, or combat Shamyl's hidden fire, and a disastrous decision was taken. It was decided, although Klugenau opposed it with violence, that, since the whole force could neither retreat, now, nor go forward without supplies, and since the provisions were for all the units, each one should send back half its strength, to bring in its own share. A column, led by Klugenau, with the fiery Passek in command of the advance guard, and brought up in the rear by Victoroff, a veteran general but an equally impetuous fighter, now set off, four thousand strong, a heterogeneous lot, unaccustomed to close fighting, and composed of various sections of the army, unmounted Cossacks, sappers, infantry and so forth. Passek, with two battalions of the Kabardinsky regiment, dashed back to the terrible ridge, on the morning of the 10th, and was followed by Klugenau. Together they fought their way through the barriers which had been replaced and strengthened by Shamyl's men. Presently, as before, the forward troops became separated from the centre, the centre from the rear. The enemy swarmed in between, firing from behind every stone, and from the trees above.

Whenever confusion broke among the exposed Russian columns, the Murid sprang out on them, materializing, as usual, from nowhere, to finish them off with kindjal and shashka. General Victoroff was killed, along with a large number of officers. The wounded now hampered the column tragically. General Klugenau decided it would be impossible to withdraw again across that death-trap ridge, and that he would do better to make his way out, north, abandoning all thought of supplies, and leaving Voronzov to fight his way on to Gherzel. However, Passek persuaded him to rejoin Voronzov, and a daring young ensign undertook to carry a message to the Commander-in-Chief. The column was to start on its return journey at dawn, on the 11th. Voronzov, believing that contact had been made with the supply column, received the news with joy, and even promoted the ensign.

Three cannon shots told Voronzov that Klugenau and Passek had started; in the grey half-light of an overcast summer dawn, those at Dargo could see the puffs of smoke rising above the trees in a regular line, showing the slow progress of the column as once more it fought its way back along the ridge. Passek, again commanding the advance guard, found the barriers renewed all the way: on reaching the narrow neck where, on each occasion, Russian losses had been so heavy, the path was blocked by a breastwork of felled trees, to which had been lashed the stripped and mutilated bodies of the Russians who had fallen there, the day before. While they were trying to surmount this ghastly barrier, slipping in blood, clambering over their dead comrades, a hail of bullets fell on them from smaller barriers set at each side, and a little farther on. It was a massacre. The Russians were falling back in confusion, when a company of the Lioubinsky regiment under Valkhovsky, a green young guardsman fresh from St. Petersburg, stormed the right-hand breastwork, but the boy fell dead, and the men retreated again. Passek led his men on the left-hand defences but fell mortally wounded. 'Farewell, my valiant brigade!' were his last words. 'After that, the men broke in disorder; though individual men showed the utmost bravery.'

By now, unaware of the carnage, the main body, detailed to collect the supplies, had arrived, encumbered by an ever increasing number of wounded. Klugenau led companies to the attack repeatedly, like any ordinary captain, and somehow, in spite of a ceaseless fire, the column progressed, in twos and threes, straggling, struggling, dying. . . . The Murids' fire never ceased, and from time to time they dashed in among the Russians, cutting down wounded and dying along with the rest. At the extreme rear, the Kabardinsky regiment maintained a strict discipline, and when their ammunition gave out, formed square, and stood waiting for the final onslaught. Klugenau, when all his staff had fallen, was seen, sitting his charger, miraculously preserved, pale, stern, but calm, looking, in his light grey uniform, riddled with shot 'like the statue of the commander in Don Juan'. Passek's body was tied into a hollow sheet of bark, and dragged along, sledge-wise by his devoted men, sliding and slipping in the mud and blood. He was glimpsed, his face blood-stained but peaceful. Later, his body was lost: in a moment of panic, the bark-coffin was pushed over the edge of a ravine, never to be seen again. It is said that the Murids found it, and cut off the head, displaying it for many months as their proudest trophy; but this has never been proved.

Thus perished General Passek, 'bravest of the brave, whose name alone was worth whole battalions'.

II

Yet there had been a time—almost all of his short life, in fact, when the name of Passek spelled disgrace to the world of courtiers, police spies and toadies. Passek's family background was typical of its moment. He came of that unsung band of martyrs whose lives were systematically crushed or deformed by the persecutions of the State. Siberia was peopled with such families, who sprang up, and were mown down, throughout nineteenth-century Russia. Herzen calls them the aristocracy of misfortune. They were, too, quite unlike the popular conception of persecuted Slavs, who, in literature and legend were generally represented as passively suffering whatever fate decreed, and quite immobile, either incapable or unwilling to work. They were idealists, intellectuals, patriots, whose independence of spirit was never destroyed. 'Their faces,' says Herzen, 'were eloquent of that dignity which misfortune lays, not upon every sufferer, but on the faces of those who have known how to bear it.'

Passek's father had been seized in the reign of Paul I, and in consequence of someone's treachery, flung into the fortress of Schlüsselberg, from there to be exiled to Siberia. In prison, he fell in love with the daughter of a garrison officer. She returned his love, and accompanied him to his exile. Their life was terrible; but poverty, cold, hunger, grinding work—none of these things broke them. 'They brought up a family of young lions; the father educated them by his example,' says Herzen; 'the mother, by her self-sacrifice and tender care. . . . Alexander I brought back thousands of those exiled by his insane father, Paul I. But Passek was overlooked. He might have claimed part of an inheritance which had now passed into other hands: it was those other hands which kept him in Siberia.'

There, often lacking the necessities of life, the young lions grew up to a tradition of idealism, patriotism and hope. . . . 'Yes—why be afraid of words,' says Herzen, 'they were a family of heroes. What they had all born for one another, what they had done for the family was incredible, and always with head held high, not in the least crushed. . . . In Siberia the three sisters had only one old pair of shoes between them; they used to keep them for going out, by turns, so that strangers should not see the extremity of their need.'

In 1826 they received the long-desired permit to return to Moscow. But the pardon did not include a restitution of property. It was winter, but they set out at once, full of hope. The journey, partly on foot and without warm clothes, should have killed them, yet they survived, reaching Moscow at the moment of the Tzar's coronation. The ancient city was *en fête*; processions and junketing greeted them as they wandered, happy, but homeless, through the flag-decked streets. But misfortune would not let them go so easily.

Now they discovered that their property remained confiscated and there was no means of regaining their modest fortune. The two elder girls drew up a petition, begging the Tzar to examine their case. When they stepped quietly forward from the crowd and tried to present it to him, he brushed them aside, his dread pewter stare went over their heads, in haughty indifference. They were seized by the police, and suffered many indignities, before being released—to starve. Disillusioned, at last, their father died. Somehow, the mother kept the family together, and the elder sons worked their way through university. They were idealists, brilliant, and eager. One found employment in the Admiralty, another in the Engineers; with the extra money they made, giving lessons in mathematics and history at night, they contrived to educate their younger brothers.

At last it seemed they had overcome their misfortunes, and Herzen was among this group of fiery would-be reformers who used to gather round their simple table, plunged into those timeless discussions in which the young indulge everywhere, before life has taught them silence. Of such were the Petrashevsky group, of which Dostoievsky was one—young students who were condemned as criminals for their idealism, and who were sentenced to death, led out to die on the gallows, wearing their shrouds, before this 'salutary lesson' was transmuted to penal servitude in Siberia. We hear Herzen's voice, again: 'May the rule of Nicholas be damned for ever and ever. Amen.'

Within a few years, the three eldest Passek brothers were dead. Poverty and persecution was ever their lot. Vadim, the historian, was offered a chair at Kharkov University, only to have it snatched from him. The State intervened. A Siberian background—a dangerous liberal—it was not for such as he! For seven years he struggled on, trying, like his father before him, to support his wife and children—to raise another brood of young lions, living on watered broth, turning his hand to any work he could find. He had kept his convictions, 'but he kept them like a warrior, who will not let the sword drop out of his hand, though he knows he is wounded to death', says Herzen. In 1842 he died of tuberculosis. A few months later, his elder brother died, wasted by a similar life of endeavour and persecution.

The third brother Diomid was that youthful general 'whose name alone was worth battalions'. It did not seem strange, to him, to fight for a country from which he had received nothing but ill. He still believed in the tradition of service—to his country and his own ideals. He made a brilliant army career, without any of the privilege and string-pulling which advanced so many of the Guards officers. He was adored by his men, and revered by the Caucasians for his bravery. Of all the family, he alone met a fitting death. As long as the Caucasian wars are remembered, he will be recalled as one of its greatest soldiers.

III

To return to the battle of Dargo: Voronzov sat outside his tent, now stripped of all its trappings, its writing desk, its gold-mounted *nécessaire de toilette*—even the Bashaws' six-tailed standard; he was in conference with his staff-officers, an unshaven, haggard group. All the men who could be spared had been sent back to rescue the supply column: orderlies and grooms had been issued with rifles and joined the column, so that the officers were left to tend their own horses, and generally to look after themselves. They were no longer exigeant: everyone now realized the true situation. Faced with annihilation, few of them cared if their boots were muddy, their supper meagre. There were graver issues to be faced. All that evening the priests were busy, confessing both the dying and the living. At midnight, the rescue column returned in triumph: they had succeeded in reaching the remnants of the supply column, and now brought them back with them, to Dargo, under cover of darkness.

But of the provisions for which all this terrible sacrifice had been made, little or nothing reached Voronzov: whole wagons had been tipped over the ravines, or abandoned in the mud. The Commander-in-Chief was now left with half his forces—five thousand bayonets, many wounded, practically nothing to eat, very little ammunition, and a triumphant enemy closing in. Gherzel was forty-one versts away. His position was hopeless, unless he could send word to General Freitag, at Grozny, to come to the rescue. Five separate messengers were sent out, to make their way through the twilight world of dense forests, which lay between themselves and Grozny. Voronzov warned Freitag of his desperate straits, and urged him to concentrate a relief column on the road to Gherzel, thus arresting the inevitable massacre which awaited Voronzov's men once they moved forward. Shamyl was only waiting now for this moment, when he would have the whole force at his mercy, weakened to breaking point, and without supplies. No one of Voronzov's staff, or army, believed the messengers would reach Freitag, or that he could get to them in time. All were now convinced they would perish, to a man. And, as among the Murids, who faced the end with their dirge-like chants and death-songs, the Russians now sang, their deep, melancholy voices united in the sombre chants of the Orthodox Church.

Shamyl, Imam of Daghestan
Portrait by Thomas Horscheldt, 1859

The aôul of Tindi. *By courtesy of the Royal Geographical Society*

The siege of an aôul by Russian troops

Murids fording a river. *Drawing by Prince Gagarin*

Dancing the Lesghinka

Prince Alexander Bariatinsky as a young man
Artist unknown; reproduced by permission of Prince Alexis Sherbatov

Prince Michael Voronzov
Portrait by Sir Thomas Lawrence

Position of the Caucasus

SEA OF AZOV

Kertch

Taman

CRIMEA

Anapa

Novorossisk

KOUBAN COSSACK REGIMENT

Stavropol

Ehaterenodar

Kisslovo

BLACK SEA

ABKHAZIA

Soukhoum Kalé

R Ingour

MINGR

Redout Kalé

Poti

PASHALI

Batoum

T

Trebizond

R Tchorok

U

PAS

Eryeroum

PA

.... Boundaries of Countries

–·–·–·– Boundaries of Khanates
& Pashaliks

– – – – – Cossack Line

·········· Advanced Cossack Line

············ Georgian Road

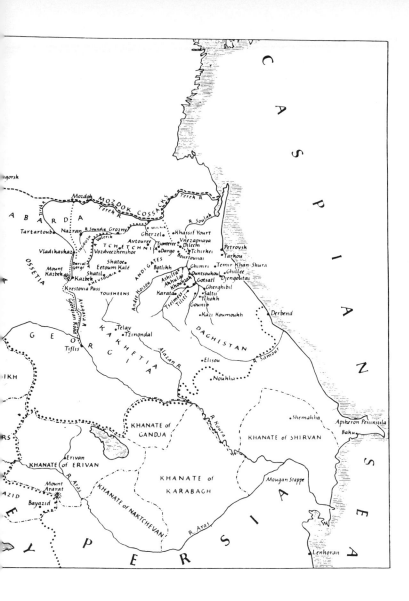

The Caucasus in the late eighteenth and the nineteenth centuries

Mahommed Emin

Daniel Beg, Sultan of Elisou,
Tiflis, 1859

Hadji Mourad at the aôul of Ghimri. *Drawing by Prince Gagarin, 1851*

Above, left: Khazi Mahommed,
Kalouga, 1860

Above, right: Djemmal-Eddin.
St. Petersburg, 1854

Right: A noblewoman of
Daghestan

The Winter Palace

Top, left: Mosque of Khounzak. *Drawing by Prince Gagarin*

Below, left: A Tchetchen aôul

The Emperor Alexander II

Shamyl, Imam of Daghestan, 1859

Shamyl's second daughter, Fatimat,
Kalouga, 1861

Mahommed Kamil,
Constantinople, 1918

Khazi Mahommed, his second wife,
Habibette, and daughter Nafisette,
Kalouga, 1865

Mahommed Sheffi and his second
wife, Meriam, Kazan, 1886

Shamyl and his sons Khazi Mahommed and Mahommed Sheffi

Left: Photograph taken immediately after the surrender, St.
Petersburg, October 1859

Below: The last photograph,
Kiev, 1869

When, earlier, Voronzov had written to Freitag, telling him of his proposed march on Gherzel, Freitag had replied: 'It is no secret, among the Tchetchens, that Your Excellency intends to come down to the plains from Dargo. "We have not yet begun to fight the Russians," they say. "Let them go where they will, we know where to attack them." And indeed they do know; in the forests all the advantages are on their side, and they understand well how to make the most of them. . . . On the downward march in the forests, you will meet with such difficulties, such opposition, as probably you do not anticipate. I will not attempt to prove that this operation is well-nigh impossible. Your losses will be enormous. You will find the Tchetchens know how to fight (rather than withdraw) when necessary.' Freitag went on, with considerable courage, to say that he considered Voronzov's campaign a mistake. 'Allow me to say, simply, you are being deceived. However successful your movements, they will have no influence on the ultimate subjugation of Tchetchnia.'

Too late, Freitag's words must have echoed in Voronzov's ears, terribly, beside the groans of the dying. Too late to draw back, they must go on, to Gherzel, there to be relieved by Freitag, or to perish. It was no longer a question of winning over, or impressing the Tchetchens, as of fighting for their honour; their lives seemed lost. The Commander-in-Chief is reported to have shed bitter tears.

On the 12th preparations were made for the march. At dawn, on the 13th, they moved forward, painfully slow, for there were an enormous number of wounded, and even the strongest men were now weakened by lack of sleep, for Shamyl's fire harassed them by day and night. On the 14th, a fearful fight took place at Issa Yourt, but although the mountaineers fought ferociously, the Russians succeeded in gaining and keeping a position on the left bank of the Askai. Eighty men were killed and seven officers: among them three brothers, Georgian princes, who expired in each other's arms, leaving the Georgian militia leaderless, so that the Russian officers, trying to command them, with no knowledge of their language, caused terrible confusion. Another three hundred wounded were added to the overloaded wagons. Among them was that same love-crossed Captain Allbrandt who had executed so many dangerous missions without finding the death he sought. Even now, he only lost an arm, and was seen, sitting quietly puffing his pipe, while it was amputated. He was not prevailed upon to take his place in the wagon until he had fainted twice from loss of blood.

All through the 15th and 16th, Voronzov's men fought their way by inches, step by step, finding barriers, traps and ambushes awaiting them in the forest. In the hand-to-hand fighting, the columns became broken, artillery was left uncovered, sappers were cut off and surrounded, while, wherever the wounded lay, the Murids rushed among them, finishing them off with sword thrusts. Now there were more than two thousand five hundred wounded, and few were able to both fight and scout; even the Apsheron regiment began to show signs of demoralization. At one point, four hundred men lay down and refused to move. 'General Beliavsky turned on them, raging: "It it possible there's not one honest man left amongst you, to die with his General?" At which a handful of the Apsheron men sprang up, the rest followed, and another barrier was taken heroically.'

On the 17th, Voronzov realized he could go no farther. His men were starving, staggering with weakness. For three days, they had had nothing to eat but a few grains of maize found in the nearby fields. The artillery had hardly a round left to answer Shamyl's bombardment. No one knew whether the messenger had succeeded in reaching Freitag. The uncertainty was terrible. The Commander-in-Chief's son, Count Simon, had been cut off at Andi Gates, and his father, realizing the hopeless nature of the fight, dispatched a renegade native to get through to him, warning him of the approaching end, and ordering him to make good his escape. But the messenger had crawled back to camp, terribly maimed. At last one of the Avar chieftains who had submitted to Russian rule some time before, volunteered to carry the message and succeeded, so that Count Simon and his troop reached Khassif Yourt safely. But this his father could not know, at the time.

On the 18th, Voronzov issued an order of the day: 'About ourselves we need not bother; we can always make good our way. Our main care must be to get our sick and wounded through; that is our duty as Christians, and God will help us fulfil it.' Once again, the Commander-in-Chief was seen to shed bitter tears.

When we try to assess the Dargo campaign, like so much else of Caucasian warfare, it must be remembered that the sources are always Russian: memoirs and military archives. These present the campaigns in the most heroic terms, and with a strong Russian bias. The only Murid voice is that of Mahommed Tahir, Shamyl's secretary, who recorded the accounts of Shamyl and his Naibs and other eye-witnesses, as well as spies and prisoners, among the Russians. But these Arabic chronicles, written in an archaic and elliptical style, sometimes shed a rather different light. The truth probably lies somewhere between the two view-points. The character of Voronzov, for example, is presented quite otherwise than in the Russian eulogies.

At Dargo, in his old age, even the Russians cannot convince us of his generalship: too many blunders are apparent. Through Tahir's chronicle he emerges as a tired, overwrought figure who made decisions, reversed them, plunged into follies, and was no longer able to command. This is the only logical explanation for much of the Dargo campaign. According to Tahir, the Field-Marshal, while sending his troops to wanton death was also overcome with remorse, and frequently burst into tears, appalled at the holocaust. In the last, desperate days, he is even alleged to have been making his escape 'carried in a steel-plated box, on the back of Colonel Prince Orbeliani', who, learning that Freitag's relief column was sighted, hurriedly returned the Commander-in-Chief to base. The truth of this statement cannot be vouched for; but I give it as an example of that other side which always exists, and of which we see so little, in the records of the Caucasian wars.

On the sixth day since leaving Dargo, the troops had only fifty rounds of shot left. The guns were without ammunition. There was still no sign from Freitag, and the Murids were all around, watching, waiting to pounce with cat-like enjoyment. At dusk, it was believed they would attack in the night, and that no man would be left to see the morning. Suddenly, through the trees, there sounded the muffled boom of a cannon—three shots, signal of Freitag's approach. All five messengers had got through. The first one had reached Freitag on the night of the 15th–16th, and he had not waited for more, but set out, riding one hundred and sixty versts in two days, collecting forces as he rode till, in the evening of the 18th, his advance guard, firing their cannon, came within sight of Voronzov's beleaguered camp. Next day, they escorted the exhausted army into Gherzel without more opposition, while, once more, the Commander-in-Chief was overcome with emotion. By some miracle, the remnants of the Russian forces had escaped. Inexplicably, Shamyl's men vanished into the mountains or faded into the forest depths before coming into range of Freitag's fire. This sudden, mysterious slackening of the Murid grip was never explained by the Russian sources: but undoubtedly Mahommed Tahir's chronicles give us the true reason. Shamyl had received news that Fatimat was dying and calling for him. At first he had hardened his heart, and stayed in the thick of the battle. But when, on the 17th, it seemed the whole Russian force was surrounded, and too weakened to resist further, he had allowed himself to be persuaded by his Naibs. They had urged him to go to her: they knew the depth of his love. It was only a matter of hours now, they said, before Voronzov capitulated. They did not know of the messenger sent to Freitag. Nor would they have believed he could make the dash from Grozny to Gherzel in time. The Imam must go to his wife they said: his orders would be executed faithfully. Shamyl, listening to his heart, allowed himself to be persuaded, and accompanied by one Naib, he rode day and night across the mountains, reaching Fatimat in time to hold her in his arms when she died. Two days later, he rode back to the battle, to find his victory turned to dust and ashes. Freitag had relieved the beleaguered Russians, and they had slipped through the Murid trap: even so, he knew that some-where among his ranks there had been treachery. His orders had not been executed: the Naibs had remained immobile, when they could have struck. With Freitag's arrival, it was too late. A great victory had turned into one more indecisive, costly battle. From now on, Shamyl looked on his Naibs with a growing suspicion.

Shamyl always knew when to conserve his strength, as he knew when to attack, and had no false pride about retreating. Having measured Freitag's force, he gave orders to disperse. His men vanished into the mountains, or faded into the forest depths, before coming into range of Freitag's bullets. But not before he had turned on his Naibs, casti-gating them, as he lashed himself, for having let the enemy slip through their fingers. Accustomed as he was to the mountains, and even with his way of covering great distances at top speed, he had not imagined messengers could reach Freitag, or that the General could make the dash from Grozny to Gherzel in so short a space of time. From now on, he looked on the Russians with a new respect, based not so much on their force, as their spirit, and their growing skill in guerilla warfare.

A last tragic postscript to the whole Dargo campaign was to be found in the final retreat to Gherzel. Once again, the heroic Kabardin-sky regiment made up the rearguard, and, with the usual incompetence in the top echelons, was somehow overlooked, left behind, to be wiped out by Shamyl's retreating men. Only three survivors returned to base. Out of Voronzov's glittering array, ten thousand strong, three generals were killed, two hundred officers, and three thousand five hundred and thirty-three men killed and wounded. Of the Kourinsky regiment, only twenty-four men survived. Alas! for the six horse-tail standards of the Commander-in-Chief, the Kurdish uniforms, the gold lace, and all the 'pomp and circumstance of glorious war'. They were left strewn about the rocks, among the quiet dead, moujiks and Most High Excellencies, while the mountain eagles and the birds of prey circled overhead.

> In the heat of noonday, in the vale of Daghestan . . .
> With a bullet in my heart, I lie . . .

So sang the soldiers, and the village choirs, and all the people, for a century to come, remembering the disasters and bravery of Dargo. I have described the expedition in some detail, for it was typical of many, many years of Caucasian warfare: heartbreaking, indecisive, wanton, heroic.

The Tzar, loyally supporting the man of his choice, decided that Voronzov's escape constituted a major victory. He created him Prince, and wrote on the margin of the Commander-in-Chief's report of the expedition: 'Read with the greatest interest, and with respect for the fine courage of my troops.' No doubt it made splendid reading for the Autocrat sitting in his green-walled study overlooking the Fortress of Peter and Paul. He was always deeply interested in military matters, and after all, this whole expedition into Daghestan had been, in the first place, his idea.

19

Treachery

They shall scoff at the kings, and the princes shall be a scorn unto them: They shall deride every stronghold.

HABAKKUK I

In 1846, Shamyl, Imam ul' Azam—the Great Imam as he was now known—decided to launch his long-cherished invasion of Kabarda. It was a most audacious scheme. Kabarda lies in the centre, or heart, of the Caucasus. To the east, a line running from Vladikavkaz to the Caspian was held by Shamyl; to the west, from the Kouban to the Black Sea was similarly his. But between lay Kabarda, severing his two territories. Once unified, they would become a solid block of opposition, cutting the main Russian supply lines, straddling the whole Caucasian isthmus, from east to west, and isolating the Russians in the east. Moreover, once contact had been established with the Tcherkess tribes, who had been skulking inland since the Russians occupied their coastline, the Infidels could then be attacked from the rear, pushed back into the Black Sea, or across the Persian frontier.

Kabarda was inhabited by a notably fiery race who lived feudally, but which had, however, submitted to Russian rule in 1822, and had remained, if not hostile to Shamyl, at least, unhelpful. But of late, they had shown signs of dissatisfaction with the Russians; an increasing tension prevailed, and Shamyl believed the moment was ripe for them to rise in revolt, and join with him. For some years Shamyl had contemplated this attack, and now, hardened by the thought of his son's captivity, and encouraged by numerous overtures from the princely Kabardan rulers (who were at last becoming convinced of his might, and the holy nature of his war), he began to assemble a vast horde of Murids preparatory to launching the campaign. In April 1846, the Russian spies reported a massing of the Murids in Tchetchnia, although where they would strike was not known. 'Every hostile movement was known to the opposing side almost as soon as initiated; its progress watched and reported daily, if not hourly', says Baddeley. 'The Russians, holding exterior lines, could seldom hope to conceal their designs; the concentration of their troops at any given point indicated pretty clearly the object in view. But with Shamyl it was otherwise. Completely surrounded by hostile territory, *but acting from within*, he could gather his forces and threaten the enemy in more directions than one, leaving them in doubt, up to the last moment, as to where the blow would fall. . . . Having puzzled his antagonists, and completed his own preparations, he could choose where to strike, in accordance with the defensive measures they had seen fit to adopt.' Thus, his forces standing to arms in Tchetchnia, no one knew where he would strike, Russian headquarters in Daghestan seeming most likely.

When the huge concentration of Murid hordes was reported to Prince Voronzov, he was convinced Shamyl was preparing to raid Temir-Khan-Shura and the Caspian ports, although some of his generals and notably General Freitag, believed otherwise. It will be remembered that the Tzar had ordered the return of large numbers of troops, by the end of 1844: the mediocre General Neidhardt had been quite unequal to his responsibilities, with or without the reinforcements Nicholas had so grudgingly assigned him, in 1843. These troops had overstayed their term considerably, and now were on the eve of departure. Even Prince Voronzov dared not oppose the orders from St. Petersburg on this issue: but it is the measure of that courage, intuition and dispatch which characterized some of his generals, that Freitag now dared take the responsibility of retaining the troops against the Tzar's orders. Events were to prove this defiance fully justified. Shamyl's forces were now concentrated in Western Tchetchnia, at Shalee. On March 13, riding at the head of his troops, and surrounded by a forest of lances, he crossed the Argoun river and headed for Kabarda. Now his plan was clear, and the Russians rushed all their available men to Grozny. Freitag reckoned that to enter Kabarda, Shamyl must cross the Terek at the ford of Tartartoub, for, any farther to the south, a large Russian garrison at Vladikavkaz would menace his crossing. The desolate rock landscape of Tartartoub still echoed with historic battles. Here Tamerlane defeated Toktamuish; here, beside the lonely minaret, Mansour Bey was captured by Potemkin's troops, in 1785. Here, Murids and Russians now met in another terrible struggle.

Freitag had sent messengers as far as Tiflis, demanding reinforcements. Troops were ordered to join him, by forced marches, across mountainous country, from all points of the compass. Voronzov realized that if Kabarda was lost, Russian prestige would decline dangerously among the mountaineers. Even the more remote tribes of the Asiatic steppes would be affected, and Shamyl's absolute ascendency be assured throughout the whole Caucasus. He gave his orders: all available forces to march at once. Bugles rang out; barracks and stables filled with scurrying figures. Field-guns and ammunition-

wagons and baggage-trains began to move out of Shemakha, heading
west, accompanied by the usual lines of plodding, stoic men. The
officers, on their fine mounts, seemed elated at the prospect of some
action. Life in a garrison town became insufferably tedious. There
might be a little sport on the way: pheasants were plentiful; so were
buck. Together, they discussed rounding up some of the magnificent
Kabarda horses; some brood mares, perhaps. The Shaloukh breed—
generally a dappled grey—from around Tartartoub were considered
the finest. Thus, said the officers, the expedition might prove worthwhile from all points of view.

By March 18, Russians and mountaineers had come face to face in
several indecisive skirmishes, and Shamyl had succeeded in repelling
several attacks. Now he ordered the evacuation of a number of aôuls
which lay in the line of battle, and the inhabitants, crowded into slow
moving arbas, drawn by oxen, piled with household goods, wailing
children and old people, and followed by their flocks of goats and cattle,
were being herded along the roads under pressure from the Murids,
and swept by Freitag's fire. Shamyl's plan was to enter Kabarda, cross
the province, rousing the people as he went, and with their aid, hold
the Russians while he linked forces with the tribes on the west, in
Abkhazia, Suanetia, and along the Black Sea coast. Thus his dream of
cutting the Caucasus in two would be realized. He planned to seize the
gorge of Darial and the vitally important Georgian Military Highway,
while counting on the Galgais and other tribes round about to support
him. Then, controlling the only road, by which both men and supplies
must come from either north or south, Kabarda would be his, and the
Russian armies trapped.

But the audacity of this plan was equalled by the daring with which
Freitag, now combining the courage of despair with brilliant intuitive
strategy, dogged Shamyl: march by march, following, harrying, never
letting him pause, never letting the Kabardians doubt that a force
equal to Shamyl's followed like a retribution. In spite of the dangers of
penetrating ever deeper into an alien territory, almost unprepared, and
unsustained by supplies or reinforcements, Freitag believed it the only
possible way to check the Kabardians from joining Shamyl. Should this
happen, he knew no battles, no amount of men and guns, could dislodge Shamyl from his stranglehold.

Thus, every mile that Shamyl advanced, Freitag followed. No
sooner had the Imam negotiated with the chieftains than they saw, hot
on his heels, the Russian army, in appearance, a mighty one. They
could not know that Freitag marched alone, almost cut off, and with
little hope of reinforcements, that his march was a last desperate bluff.
They began to waver. Shamyl had bargained with them; in return for
their support he undertook to destroy every Russian fort along the

Terek and across the country; together they would push back the Infidel invaders beyond their frontiers, and together, they would rule Kabarda according to Moslem traditions. Yet when the chieftains saw that the Russians were commanded by Freitag, a general they had learned, in bitterness to fear and respect, their weapons dropped from their hands, and they seemed transfixed. Thus the whole splendid daring of Shamyl's plan was lost. Each force, Murid and Kabardian, waited, and was interdependent on the other. Neither could act alone: without Kabarda's support, Shamyl was powerless to destroy the Russian posts along the Terek; without these forts falling, the Kabardians could not rise. Shamyl had not counted on Freitag's obstinate pursuit, and for the first time, he began to doubt his ability to win the Kabardians. So the first fruits of his daring were lost. Each day brought Russian reinforcements nearer, lessening his chances of success. He decided to push on to the west, to gain the support of the Balkar, or Tartar tribes who, together with the Trans-Kouban peoples, might still influence the Kabardians to join together in common hatred of the Russians.

As Shamyl rode west, as inscrutable as ever, displaying neither his thoughts nor his fears, Voronzov, at Shemakha, now thoroughly alarmed, set out for Vladikavkaz, bringing with him all the available men he could collect en route. On the 25th, Shamyl received news that his Naib, Nour Ali, had not been able to take, or even reach, the Darial defile, and with it, the Georgian Military Highway, and had been obliged to retreat in disorder. The Russians at Vladikavkaz had not anticipated any threat of their forts at Darial, or the route itself; they had not enough troops to resist a major attack. But while they waited in a state of indecision, it happened that General Gourko, lately chief-of-staff to Voronzov, on his way back to Moscow, and believing his term of Caucasian service was over, arrived at Vladikavkaz. When he heard of Shamyl's approach, and the reported threat to Darial, he immediately took command, sent messages back to Tiflis (written in French, as a precaution, lest they should be intercepted by the tribesmen) demanding heavy reinforcements, at once. He then reorganized the garrison, sent all available men to guard the Military Highway and hold the defile, and generally had so galvanic an effect upon Vladikavkaz, that Nour Ali's scouts reported the hopelessness of their position, and the Murids retreated, without having come to grips.

This news, together with the knowledge that the Russians were converging on Kabarda from all over the Caucasus was a heavy blow to Shamyl. Although it had not, basically, lost him the support of the tribes (for one and all had scarcely believed so daring a plan could be carried through), he sensed, now, that the Russians were beginning to prove themselves in partisan fighting, in flexibility and speed, as well as in pitched battles. He sensed, too, their limitless reserves, and their spirit, as stubborn as his own. He knew that the Kabarda invasion had failed: he must return to his more limited, but still powerful, partisan tactics, and local forays. But he never wasted time in mourning; let the women wail and lament. His part was action. He turned back, making for the Terek, his cavalry streaming after him, as they raced across the foothills, towards fresh battlefields and further struggles. That his Kabardian enterprise had failed was evident, yet so great was his prestige, that no one among his followers doubted but that he would have succeeded, had it not been for the Kabardians' lack of co-operation. Russian initiative, Russian daring, received little or no acknowledgement from the Caucasians. They were well aware of the sophistry, the cynicism, by which Russia laid claim to Kabarda. According to Moscow and St. Petersburg, since Ivan the Terrible had married the daughter of a Kabardian prince, Russia could lay claim to the province; then, an expedition undertaken by the Russians, in 1717, against the Khan of Khiva, had for commander a Kabardian prince. This proved the Russians and Kabardians were age-old allies. . . . Such syllogisms merely served to bewilder the tribes and to increase Shamyl's prestige.

II

But Shamyl himself now knew the nature of his enemy, knew, as he lay in camp, wrapped in his bourka, watching the stars which sparkled in the cold darkness of the spring night, that he could not hope to maintain, forever, his stand against this enemy, without outside aid. From time to time he had bolstered the spirits of his Naibs by reminding them of the help which, presently, would be forthcoming in quantity, from both Britain and Turkey. He was, he said, already in correspondence with both Queen Victoria, and the Sultan. Perhaps, too, even though the Kabardians had failed him, there might be a spark of independence still left among the Krim Tartars, living such supine lives, along the groves that fringed the Black Sea coast. But though, in principle, he had the sympathy of the Krim Khans, it was clear he could no longer count on their active support.

Unlike the Christian Georgians, their sympathies were with his opposition to the Infidel, but these Krim Tartars had become a passive people, becalmed in the legends of their past. Even though there were many links between the Caucasus and the Crimea, the Khanate was now irrevocably subdued. It had always been their tradition to send their princes, as children, to be educated in some noble household of Circassia or Daghestan. There they learned the arts of arms and chivalry and acquired something of that imcomparable horsemanship for which the Caucasians were celebrated. All over the Caucasus and Asia

Minor, a mountain education was considered the finest. There was no greater compliment than to say of some young man that he appeared to have been brought up in the mountains; 'polish comes from the city—wisdom from the hills', is an ancient saying in the Caucasus. Thus, many of the Khans and nobles of Little Tartary were known personally to Shamyl, the Avar noble of Daghestan: but they could not help him. Their struggle was done; he must fight alone.

Shamyl had never succeeded in welding the Circassian (or Tcherkess) tribes into a force upon which he could count. They loathed the Russians, and fought them, but their help was sporadic, and weakened by inter-tribal disputes. Abkhaz set on Oubikh; Adighe fought both. All of them, from the Murid view-point, were indifferent Moslems. The abnegations of the Shariat were not for them. They clung to their own Adats, or traditional laws. And their clan system of prince and vassals was also opposed to the fundamentally democratic principles of Muridism.

Shamyl had first sent a representative there in 1843; in 1850 he sent another, stronger man, the Naib Mahommed Emin. This crafty individual played one tribe off against another, enforced his rule with terrible severity, instigating massacres in the name of discipline, while accepting bribes, to line his pocket. Moreover, he married no less than seven Circassian beauties, some of whom were from princely families, and whom he left languishing in his harem. Gradually he turned all Circassia against him. When the Turks sent Sefir Bey to unite the tribes against Russian aggression, the two rivals fought a personal battle, and the support of a unified Circassia was lost to Shamyl forever.

British support, however, was another matter. Shamyl was aware that the English regarded Russian proximity to the North-West Frontier provinces as a threat of invasion, nothing less. Therefore, he believed that they shared a common aim, to halt Russia's eastward expansion. He looked to England for aid, both moral and physical, and although Britain's conduct with regard to Afghanistan and the Afghan wars had caused the most deplorable repercussions in Asia, Shamyl knew the value of British support. He was aware, as was all Asia, of the exact nature of English demands in Afghanistan, how on the pretext of chastising the rulers of Kandahar and Kabul, who were charged with harassing English commerce, Her Majesty's Government had decided to seize both these rich provinces and incorporate them in her Indian Empire, which, under pressure from the merchant companies, showed insatiable greed. Some Russian agents had overstepped their trading rights in Afghanistan, by offering, for commercial concessions, to give Russian support against England's ally, the King of Lahore. They also offered to place the King of Kandahar under Persian protection (so that the Shah could obtain his dream of annexing Herat), at which Lord Melbourne flew into a violent rage, and on the spot, ordered an expedition to Afghanistan, to annex them for Britain. He considered, Her Majesty's Government considered, the Russian agents' manœuvres nothing less than the prelude to the Russian occupation of Afghanistan—to Russia's designs on India. In short, to Russia behaving precisely as England had been doing for centuries. . . . Countess Nesselrode had been right . . . The simple fact of Russia's being a great power showed the most *insufferable* lack of delicacy.

Yet in spite of Britain's unsavoury reputation in Central Asia, in spite of Lord Auckland's obstinate ineptitude in his conduct of Indian affairs, the inertia and the oblique manœuvres of the government, balancing trade and power, treating both Dost Mahommed and Shah Soudja with cynical indifference, the English still retained a legendary reputation for justice.

Perhaps it was won individually, rather than collectively, not so much by governments, as by men such as Connolly, Nicholson, Eldred Pottinger, the hero of Herat, or young Lieutenant Wyburd, and many more, unsung. These men were understood by the Asiatics, for their particular blend of bravery and spiritual force was in the tradition of Eastern heroes. They were both feared, and revered. Their legend travelled with the caravans, and was known from the marble courts of Oudhe to the nomad camps of Uzbekistan.

Legends of British Might through Right reached the Caucasus too. It seemed quite logical, to Shamyl, that the English might come to his aid. He therefore addressed his plea for British support to Queen Victoria. She was the figure-head: she stood for Justice, just as, some years later, Garibaldi's name echoed round the world, the synonym of Liberty.

In his memoirs, Prince Peter Kropotkin, the reformer, recalls that Russian peasants were convinced the longed-for abolition of serfdom would only be brought about by Garibaldi. They did not know where Italy was, they had never heard of Rome, but Garibaldi's name shone for them, in the darkness. 'Nothing will be done unless Garibaldi comes,' sighed one of the Prince's own serfs, discussing the approaching, but much-delayed Emancipation Bill. And to Shamyl and all the Caucasian tribes, Queen Victoria was known as a defender of the faith. Theirs—hers? It did not signify; a champion of the oppressed. Shamyl addressed his letters to her in a glow of confidence. This was, perhaps, rather naïve; after all, Britain's annexation of India, and other territories, could have been viewed as a ruthless conquest. It all depended whether you were conqueror or conquered. It was unlikely that the British would really understand the view-point of an invaded people. They had acquired the habit of invading; although they brought quinine and bishops in the wake of their guns, they were still, basically, conquerors. To anyone more sophisticated than Shamyl, it must have been evident that the British would temporize, cynically.

But Shamyl knew nothing of European ways, or Western politics. He had not learned to temporize, or compromise, either. He had never left the mountains of Daghestan; he came of a race of men who lived and died by the dagger, and whose first principle was to defend their land. He was the mighty Imam, whose Murids fought for Allah, against the Infidel. Ghazavat! Their war was holy, was just: thus the letters to Queen Victoria.

There is no telling if these Turco-Tartar scripts ever reached the Royal breakfast table, though I like to think they did. Perhaps the Prince Consort intervened, before Victoria, still sometimes inclined to impetuosity, could be embroiled. Rebels, however useful strategically, were never really *bien vue* by the Palace, even rebels who were also such great religious leaders as the Imam Shamyl was said to be: even when his letters were signed by eighty or more cäids, magistrates, and the most venerable and respected mollahs. Somehow, these Caucasian leaders did not wholly inspire sympathy . . . They were so very violent. . . . Positively savage, in some respects. . . . And then, those harems . . . So *unnecessary*. . .

For years, O honoured Queen [wrote Shamyl], we have been at war against Russia, our invader. Every year we must defend ourselves against the invader's fresh armies which pour into our valleys. Our resistance is stubborn, altogether we are obliged, in winter, to send our wives and children far away, to seek safety in the forests, where they have nothing, no food, no refuge against the severe cold. Yet we are resigned. It is Allah's will. He ordained that we should suffer to defend our land. But England must know of this—of our ceaseless struggle against Russia . . . We beseech you, we urge you, O Queen, to bring us aid.

It will be seen that Shamyl, with infinite delicacy, refrained from stressing the religious nature of his struggle, of the battle between Cross and Crescent. Perhaps he had heard of the warmth with which Victoria supported various missionary movements. He was hoping for arms, and soldiers, rather than bibles, or bishops. The Queen was known to favour romantic leaders of lost causes (perhaps her Stuart blood responded). Kossouth and Garibaldi were both inflaming Britain, during the 'fifties, when they visited London, and were warmly received by all classes of society. The Queen shared Europe's mistrust of Russia. She thought the Tzar overweeningly ambitious . . . his son, the Tzarevitch Alexander—that had been another matter. He had visited her in 1839. She had not been married then. . . . They had danced the mazurka together. 'Such a merry time', she recorded in her journal, quite taken with the tall, elegant, if rather sheep-faced boy. 'Looks rather livid,' said Lord Melbourne dismissing the Heir to All the Russias with his usual pithiness.

We feel he would have been more impressed by Shamyl.

In October 1846, *The Times* reported: 'Shamyl, Imam of Daghestan is believed to be still holding out in the hills north of Khounzak. A force of some 4000 Russian regulars and Cossack cavalry, under the command of General Gourko, are closing in, but rebel reinforcements led by the chiefs, Tenguz the Wolf, and the Lion of Shepsuk, are flocking down from the mountains to harass the Russian lines. The campaign is likely to continue throughout the coming winter, in the most severe conditions. . . .'

As time went by, Shamyl and his dread band were becoming a matter of the liveliest concern among a wide section of the British public. When the Circassian tribes dispatch a delegation to London in the 'fifties, they received an enthusiastic welcome. Their request for support in obtaining autonomy, as an escape from Russian oppression, interested the Queen, who commanded a report on the whole matter. Khousht Hadji Hassan Haidar was received by the Prime Minister, 'and a number of influential persons in political circles'. In Hyde Park, he addressed large crowds, who gathered under the trees to watch this exotic figure, quite carried away by his fiery eye and splendid costume. On learning of the birth of a Royal child (perhaps Princess Beatrice?), Khousht flung a whole purseful of gold coins among the crowd, amid cheers and cries of *Bravo Circassia! For he's a jolly good fellow!* But quite apart from Circassian eloquence or generosity, it was generally seen that ultimately, the Caucasus must be crushed by the sheer might of Russian arms. And then . . . the road was open to India. Something must be done.

Shamyl was the hero of the hour. Public meetings were, as ever, a relief to pent-up feelings; but the Government remained non-committal. 'England does not relish the notion of having Russian neighbours [in India], but is it in her power to put a stop to it?' asked one newspaper. There were rallies, where enthusiastic crowds vowed to support Shamyl's courageous solitary stand against Russian aggression. The Midlands, in particular, took the matter to heart. No doubt the cotton industry saw India with particular clarity. A meeting held in the Mechanics Institute of one Yorkshire town was typical: its robust tone would have raised Shamyl's hopes again; perhaps it was as well he never heard of it, for it came to nothing. After a number of rousing speeches which were greeted warmly, a Mr. Pickles moved the following Resolution: 'That this meeting views with alarm the continuous efforts on the part of Russia to subdue the Caucasian people, and to annex to herself a territory which would give her a position dangerous to India.'

Mr. Levi Driver and Mr. Jonas Wells seconded the resolution to boy-
cott Russia. It was carried unanimously, and a memorandum was
addressed to Parliament.

Gradually, more and more voices joined the chorus: Count Zamoiski,
a Polish nobleman who devoted himself to fanning flames of hatred
against Russia, his country's oppressor, dwelt on his efforts to acquaint
Europe with Russia's imperialistic designs. He described himself as
having spent twenty years on the road, going between London and
Warsaw. Other compatriots, as we have seen, took a more direct line,
and found their way across the Carpathians to the Caucasus, to fight
beside Shamyl.

While Russian aggression was denounced up and down the country,
from patriotic and humanitarian platforms, and silver collections were
held 'for those poor brave Caucasians', the Foreign Office, less emotion-
ally involved, was watching Shamyl attentively, from afar. The press
had found an excellent new peg on which to hang their threadbare
clichés. And it was always worth while to berate the government for
inertia.

> The world will no doubt, for a certain time, continue to be an object
> of contention between Absolutism and Liberty. . . . But how can
> Liberty expect to achieve a final triumph if it recoils from a contact
> with its Adversary? [said those journals which urged immediate
> action]. Let the English resolutely declare themselves the generous
> defenders of liberty, and their moral influence will overwhelm the
> brutal forces of the Russian Empire.

And so on: clichés change little over the years; their echoes boom down
the centuries in every language: sententious, empty phrases.

In vain did journalists and travellers return from the Caucasus
to denounce British apathy and paint a graphic picture of Russia's
designs on Britain's Indian possessions. ' "India" sounds as welcome to
the ears of a Cossack as the merry peal announcing his marriage does to
the impatient bridegroom. I have often seen these fellows caper like so
many half-crazy dervishes at the mere pretension of a *prospect* of marching to the land of pearls and diamonds,' writes one such traveller. His
patriotic and picturesque fervour mounting, he goes on: 'Above all, at
every hazard, Caucasia should be preserved independent. That stronghold, with its inaccessible defiles and manly inhabitants offers a *pied à
terre* of more value to England than Turkey herself, with her indolent
effendis and servile rajahs' (here the East India Company idiom creeps
in, insidiously). 'In Caucasia, we might at any time, and for a trifling
expense, owing to the war-like disposition of the people, equip 20,000,
or more, of the bravest troops in the universe, capable of carrying fire
and sword (should such an extreme measure become necessary) on to

the very gates of Moscow!' In vain the pen raced over the page with such a flourish, with so much eloquence.

The apprehensive English, recalling the recent catastrophes in Afghanistan, raised more funds, and founded Circassian Committees to organize the expedition of arms and volunteers. About sixty English, French, Hungarian and Polish 'volunteer freedom fighters' were shipped out, while Captain Bell was gun-running energetically to the Black Sea. Reports assured British supporters that 'The Caucasus has now received 9 cannon with 30,000 rounds, 150 revolvers and 3,400 rifles'.

But it was too little, too late. In vain Shamyl tried to interpret the arrival of such supplies, and a handful of Indian Army officers who seeped through the North West Frontier provinces, via Persia, and whose mission was to acquaint his troops with modern artillery methods, as Queen Victoria's direct response to his letters. Nothing official was ever forthcoming, either from the Queen, or her Government.

The full implications of the Caucasian campaign were never fully grasped by England. When, in 1854, the Crimean War broke out, and almost all Russia's forces were deployed to the Crimea, the moment would have been ripe to make amends for past negligences; to come out, at last, into the open and support Shamyl: thus he might have established his supremacy, and held the Caucasus as the independent state England so much desired, strategically. 'Had England sent an army into the Caucasus, at that moment, after the fall of Sebastopol, Shamyl would have been counted our ally. . . . *Shamyl, the Avar!*' Thus one English army tactician, writing years later of missed opportunities in the English and Russian struggle for Asian supremacy, and obviously torn between military tactics, and a certain deep-seated mistrust of 'foreigners' as allies; especially Avars, about whom one knew so little....

But, one romantically-minded English committee threw caution to the winds, and dispatched a flag to Shamyl. It was composed of three stars, for Circassia, Georgia and Daghestan (firmly ignoring the fact that Georgia had ceded to Russia a number of years earlier). If the piece of bunting ever reached Shamyl's aôul, from where his own black banners were spreading their eagle-like shadows across the mountains, he probably found the gesture, if empty, at least gratifying. It was that moral support he had craved so long.

20

Hadji Mourad

And hate, with them, is limitless as love.   LERMONTOV

Shamyl was able to retreat, as he attacked—without losing faith in himself. Nor did he lose face in the eyes of the tribesmen—it was all part of the ebb and flow of battle. Thus certain tribesmen were able to leave him, were able to go over to Russia, and then go back to the Imam once more, without being considered turncoats. There were several examples of such pliancy, and when they were combined, as they generally were, with an extreme courage and daring, no voice was raised to call them traitorous. We have seen how Daniel Beg, Sultan of Elisou, born a mountaineer, pledged allegiance to the Russians, and wore their uniform. Yet, when angered by General Niedhardt, he broke with them, abandoned all the glitter of the Viceregal court, the honey of civilization, to join Shamyl, who accepted him in honour.

Another, who obtained glory, or rather, power, in alternate camps, was a young Tchetchen, Bata Shanourgov who, having been found homeless and orphaned after the storming of an aôul, by Baron Rosen, was adopted by him, and grew up to serve the Russians as a favoured interpreter. But his vanity being still unappeased, he deserted to Shamyl, who, finding his knowledge of Russian and Russian army organization invaluable, indulged him even more. To placate his greed for power, he appointed him ruler of the Greater Tchetchnia, but Bata was still unsatisfied, and abusing Shamyl's trust, began levying heavier and heavier taxes on the aôuls under his rule. Shamyl never tolerated personal graft. He removed Bata from office; at which the petulant changeling fled the mountains and made once more for the Russian lines. He must have been born under the most fortunate of all stars— that of mediocrity; knowing no heights, he knew no depths, and was for ever cushioned in easiness. The Russians welcomed him back warmly. There were no recriminations: he was immediately given the rank of captain, and made governor of Kachkalykov (the Russianized version of the local Kachalyk), where his abuses of power were studiously ignored by the Russian administrators—although Bariatinsky always distrusted him. Thus, his small horizons bounded by personal triumphs and gains, he continued to prosper, becoming, by some courtier's alchemy, a prime favourite with each succeeding Russian commander-in-chief.

*   *   *

Hadji Mourad was another of these veering figures—the word turn-coat has an ugly ring, and could never be applied to such a man. He was Shamyl's greatest Naib, his most valued lieutenant, one of the most haunting and extraordinary characters in all the gallery of Caucasian heroes. His life and death have been immortalized by Tolstoy. He was an heroic figure. In the words of Voronzov, 'desperately brave'.

It was Hadji Mourad who, as has been told, killed Hamzad Beg, in the mosque at Khounzak in 1834, when he and his brother, foster-brothers to the Khan of Avaria's sons, and, after his death, protégés of his widow, Pakkou-Bekkhé, had avenged the slaughter of her sons. Hadji Mourad and his brother had been the dark shadowy figures who, that fatal Friday, had hurled themselves on Khazi Mollah and sheathed their kindjals in his flesh. Hadji Mourad had escaped, but his brother Osman had died, falling beside the body of the hated Hamzad Beg. It was, in part, due to Hadji Mourad's influence that Shamyl met with such unexpected resistance at Khounzak when he succeeded Hamzad Beg, as third Imam. Hadji Mourad could not forget the whole series of crimes which the rise of Muridism had caused. Besides Hamzad Beg's murder of the two elder princes, there was Shamyl's wanton slaughter of the little Prince Boulatch, and finally, the decapitation of Pakkou-Bekkhé, besides a legion of nameless, lesser victims. Hadji Mourad went about the mountains, feeding the flames of hatred and vengeance which smouldered among the people. It would be wiser to look north, he said: Russia could be their salvation; only beside so powerful an ally could they now hope to resist the tides of Muridism. The Shamkhal of Tarkou had sworn allegiance, and lo! his people prospered. Their lands were not devastated by wars, and their commerce flourished: so did that of the Avarians who were governed by the Khan of Mektoulee, another local ruler who had gone over to Russia. Just as Russia could be a terrible foe, so it could be an all-powerful ally, said Hadji Mourad.

But he was not entirely disinterested. His counsels were, in part, actuated by personal motives of ambition and revenge. He loathed and was jealous of Akhmet, Khan of Mektoulee, his sworn enemy, who had long ago determined on his downfall, for what reasons we do not know. In this climate of violence, hatreds flared up, an organic part of the land, like the naphtha sources—and as inextinguishable. Perhaps the feud was begun over a woman, or a falcon, or a horse: over some imagined slight, or a boyish battle. In any case, as grown men, Hadji Mourad and Akhmet Khan were enemies. The Khan envied Hadji Mourad's reputation for bravery, while Hadji Mourad resented the eminence and power bestowed on Akhmet by the Russians. Just as the Russians cynically exploited the local vendettas, in order to weaken the enemy's ranks, so, sometimes, the mountaineers, too, used the Russians to further their own personal ambitions and schemes, jockeying for power through and round the Viceregal Court.

Hadji Mourad's horror of Murid despotism was only equalled by his loathing for Akhmet Khan. By allying himself to Russia, he now saw a way to make a stand against both Shamyl and his Murids, and also to obtain for himself the power and glory that might, in time, place him above the detested Akhmet Khan. He saw himself ruling a province—holding it, at last, against both Murids and Russians. True, the price of his glory would mean temporarily accepting the Infidels: but believing that the ends justified the means, that whatever the political manœuvres, his faith remained his own, something untouched, within himself, he now resolved to vow allegiance to the Great White Tzar—the Padishah of Russia, and his Sirdar, Voronzov.

There was something childlike in Hadji Mourad's nature, a sort of innocence, which is apparent, beside the savagery, in the portrait, said to be taken from life, by Prince Gargarin, one of the series of many wonderful drawings he made when serving in the Caucasus, between 1840–55. Thus, while Shamyl could foster religious fanaticism to further his political aims, Hadji Mourad could set aside his faith to obtain power. Yet both were, in essence, profoundly pious Moslems. In his *Religions et Philosophies de l'Asie Centrale*, Gobineau writes: 'If we separate religious doctrine from political necessity, which often acts in its name, there is no religion more tolerant, one might say, in matters of faith than Islam.' Both Shamyl and Hadji Mourad could make this separa-tion.

When Akhmet Khan learned of Hadji Mourad's new allegiance, he wasted no time planning his rival's ruin. He knew what might be the consequence for himself, if Hadji Mourad gained the Russians' confi-dence, proved himself, and was given power. He knew the measure of Hadji Mourad's daring, his qualities of leadership, and the influence he already wielded among both the nobles and people of Daghestan. He ordered his horse and, accompanied by a suite of noukkers, pages and guards, set out for Tiflis, where, seeking an audience with the Viceroy, he denounced Hadji Mourad as a spy, a most dangerous man, playing a double game and, in reality, Shamyl's Naib. Voronzov smiled his pale, thin, courtier's smile. He thanked the Khan for his solicitude. . . . It was most thoughtful . . . most loyal. . . . Yet neither he nor his officers were convinced. No doubt they knew of the blood-feud between the two men: no doubt they preferred to believe in Hadji Mourad's sincerity. They too knew his mettle, his extraordinary daring, and the influence he wielded in the mountains. He was a most valuable asset.

Akhmet Khan saw that he had been precipitate, and he did not press the matter. He dined in state off gold plate at the Viceroy's table, accepted a handsome watch from one of the generals, and refreshed himself by some evenings among the dazzling, unveiled Russian ladies of Tiflis. He found their top-like gyrations in the waltz even more stimulating than the static, though unmistakably inviting postures of dancers in his own harem. He returned to Avaria, apparently in the best of spirits. Vengeance could wait—but he presently contrived that Major Lazareff, commanding the Russian division at Khounzak, should also hear a number of alarming rumours concerning Hadji Mourad's secret ties with Shamyl. He foxily arranged that a whole series of incriminating admissions should now materialize, all from apparently unrelated sources, all of them systematically destroying the Russian confidence in Hadji Mourad.

At last, Major Lazareff became thoroughly uneasy, and reported matters to General Klugenau, who decided to place Hadji Mourad under arrest forthwith. He was to be seized, sent to Temir-Khan-Shura for investigation, and shot, if he attempted to escape. Of all people, he allowed the order to be executed by none other than Akhmet Khan, who arrested his rival with glee, and had him chained to one of the big Russian guns which fortified his capital. He did not conceal his triumphant happiness in this turn of affairs, and for ten days, the bewildered and outraged Hadji Mourad was kept thus. While he raged, demanded justice, the right to be heard, to see his wife and sons (to whom he was passionately devoted, a weakness which was, at last, to bring about his end), the Russians sent messengers to Tiflis, announcing their captive. Prince Voronzov wasted no time in replying that either way, captive or ally, Hadji Mourad was of the first importance, and he was to be brought, under heavy escort, at once, to General Staff Headquarters.

It was winter. Thick snow blocked the passes and blanketed the wild gorges. The officer and forty-five men of the Apsheron regiment, detailed to escort Hadji Mourad to the Russian headquarters, set out on a leaden-skied morning, dragging their boots laboriously from one deep snow-drift to the next. It had been snowing for over a week.

In such weather the Caucasian mountains appear great pyramids of black rock where the glaciers spill down from the peaks to merge with the snow-drifts of the lower slopes. There is no sign of life, except for a few ravens circling over the empty sheep-pens. Cattle and men are all huddled into the half-buried saklias, from which sluggish spirals of smoke hang on the still, icy air.

When Hadji Mourad and his guards set out, the main road through the pass to Temir-Khan-Shura was blocked, and the only bridge for fifteen miles had collapsed, under an avalanche of snow and rocks, a few days earlier. It was a scene of supreme desolation. The convoy took a mountain path, by way of the aôul of Boutsro. Here the path ran beside a precipice; it was so narrow that the men were obliged to edge along in single file, and even then, to hug the cliff face above them. From the watch-towers of the distant aôuls, the mountaineers observed them, balefully. Might they perish, all of them, Infidel dogs—yellow-haired pigs, marching off Allah's warrior, Hadji Mourad! This was what came of going over to the Russians. . . . Was it better to stay with Shamyl? Either way led to disaster. They strained their eyes to follow the dark thread of dots that was slowly disappearing round the mountainside. When the last dot had vanished, and only whiteness and cold emptiness was left, they pulled their bourkas round them, and went to the mosque to pray.

Hadji Mourad walked like a prince, although his hands were tied. His black lambskin papakh descended low over his face, merging with the arc of his brows; his shaggy bourka mounted to his chin, merging with his short-clipped red beard. He went sure-footed, stepping cat-like beside the precipices. This was his native terrain. But his guards, shivering in their wretchedly thin grey overcoats, plodding along in their clumsy boots, stumbled and reeled away from the awful depths below. At each stumble, a shower of small rocks were dislodged, and pitched down the ravine falling out of sight sickeningly. No place, here, in such a war, for queasy stomachs or giddy heads.

In all the cumulative disasters which the military historians and memoirs recount of these Caucasian wars, of its privations and sufferings and horrors, no one mentions the agonies of vertigo. This must have made many men long for the release of death, as they went into battle on the edge of precipices, or were forced to scale a perpendicular rock face, or cross chasms spanned by a single insecurely-lashed tree trunk. This was still warfare conducted on classic, heroic lines. Welfare officers were unheard of. Army doctors did their best, with a tourniquet and a hacksaw. The long-haired, long-bearded, black-robed priests were sometimes there, to comfort the dying. But the living had only the drum, or a ration of vodka, to raise their spirits. The modern conception of psychological tests, to gauge the men's individual aptitudes, or inhibitions, was unimaginable. Psychopathic cases, neuroses, or allergies, were unknown. Orders were given, were executed, and nothing—not even so straightforward a failing as vertigo was admitted.

So Hadji Mourad marched along the precipice edge, and his guards struggled on as best they could. At last the path became so dangerous, the men stumbling so repeatedly, that the officer in charge ordered a rope should be tied round Hadji Mourad's waist, that incredibly narrow waist which was the distinguishing mark of Caucasian men. The soldiers immediately preceding and following him were to hold the rope: this way, stumbling or no, the men were in full control of their prisoner. Thus, the officer; thus too, the men, lulled to a false complacency by their bound captive. But as the file reached the highest, most precipitous ledge, Hadji Mourad suddenly turned on his captors. Seizing the rope in his bound hands, he wrenched it free from the astonished soldiers and hurled himself headlong into the abyss, dragging one of the guards after him. The sound of their fall echoed across the ravines and peaks; stones pelted after them, rocks thundered down, out of sight, until, at last, all was still. The soldiers strained their eyes, but could see neither man. There was no means of searching for the bodies of either prisoner or guard. It was God's will! They crossed themselves, fatalistically.

The men's mood lightened as they went on their way. They sang the traditional airs of their homeland, their voices muffled by the snow-flakes that now began to fall. They were singing of the sweethearts they had left in Holy Russia—in the great flat hinterland that was Riazan, or Smolensk, Novgorod, or the Ukraine, where the horizons were one with the sky, and the mildest slope was counted a hill; where the sun-flowers grew ten feet high, but a mountain or a precipice was unknown. The convoy was descending, now, towards the valley. The men looked forward to a warm evening round the fire, in barracks, with more songs and vodka. But their officer, already dreading the censure his carelessness would provoke at G.H.Q., was overcast. His prisoner *must* have died . . . He *could* not have escaped—could not have survived . . . Yet . . . what if he still lived? ('These men don't seem to know when to die . . . They have not the slightest idea of propriety. . .') The troop arrived in Temir-Khan-Shura, the officer reported the incident, suffered the inevitable reprimands, and, at last, Hadji Mourad was written off, as dead.

But the truth was quite otherwise: he had counted on the snow to break his fall, and he had fallen into a snowdrift. One leg was shattered, some ribs broken, and his skull cracked open. The soldier had died outright. Perhaps it was as well, for he would have found no help among the mountaineers. For good measure, Hadji Mourad cut the dead soldier's throat, and then lay hidden till nightfall when he contrived to crawl to a sheep-farm belonging to the aôul of Mansokha. Here he was hidden for some weeks—long enough for him to make up his mind. If the Russians could be so lacking in faith—could chain an ally to a gun, and arrest him on suspicion, on the word of an enemy, alone, then he had been wrong to throw in his lot with them. He would return to his people—to the mountains—to Allah!—and to Allah's prophet on earth, Shamyl.

Before the winter of 1840–1 was over, Hadji Mourad had recovered from his fall (although his shattered leg caused him to limp, ever after) and made peace with Shamyl. This is his letter to the Imam:

> I am torn by the ingratitude of those whom I made powerful. I who governed Avaria for their benefit, am now a fugitive in my own country. Allah crushes me with the weight of his anger because I aided the Russians against the warriors of his faith. I desert my false friends to turn to you—my implacable enemy. Accept my arm and my vengeance. You learned its worth when I fought against you at Khounzak. Will you try it once more, now that I offer to fight *beside* you?

One eagle had recognized another; Shamyl replied:

> Allah spares those he needs, and guides them in the right path. . . . Thou hast marched in the shadows, and thou hast come back into the light! Our doors are open—our hands outstretched to welcome you. Allah reveals himself to us in signs. The words of the Prophet are accomplished in thy person. When the believer stumbles, God himself supports him. In truth, time is not far distant when the double-headed black eagle of the Tzar will burn beneath the Crescent of Islam.

Both these letters were incorporated in a proclamation which Shamyl distributed throughout Daghestan, while creating Hadji Mourad his first Naib, Governor of Tselmess, in the neighbourhood of Khounzak. It was a master stroke; those of the population who had begun to waver, now rose in arms to follow Hadji Mourad. Being ever sensible to feats of daring as well as persecutions at the hands of the Russians, he represented, for them, a doubly heroic figure, and they rallied in force. Hadji Mourad set about inflaming the farthest aôuls, undermining Russian influence throughout the mountains, and naturally, that of his arch enemy, Akhmet Khan of Mektoulee.

The Russians' treachery, or loss of faith, had cost them dear. The mountains were in a ferment; raiding parties swooped on fortress and outpost and garrison town alike, with incredible audacity. Presently, a former ally, Kibit Magoma of Tilitl, left the Russians, taking with him a number of tribes, all of whom joined Hadji Mourad. Within a few months, Shamyl's power, like his frontiers, had trebled. Tiflis knew itself menaced, and the agitated Russian commanders sent north for large reinforcements. After Shamyl, Hadji Mourad now represented the Russians' most deadly foe.

General Klugenau, who had always recognized Hadji Mourad's strength, both as ally, or enemy, made a series of overtures to regain his confidence, but was met with flat refusals even to treat with the Russians. G.H.Q. became extremely uneasy. General Golovine wrote: 'We have never had so dangerous and savage an enemy as Shamyl... He has surrounded himself by blind executants of his will. .... Inevitable death awaits all who draw down upon themselves the faintest suspicion of wishing to overthrow his rule. .... Hostages are slaughtered without mercy. .... The suppression of this terrible despotism must be our first consideration.' But, in spite of the Russian awareness, little was achieved. Daily skirmishing merged into major operations; neither were, in general, successful against such an enemy, fighting from such a land.

For the next five years, Hadji Mourad continued as the glory, under Allah! of Shamyl's forces. Battle by battle, he won the greater admiration and trust of Murids and Shamyl alike. His exploits are recalled to this day. To the Russians he was known as the Red Devil; he wore a crimson tcherkesska, his beard was red, his whole legend steeped in blood and daring. It was Hadji Mourad who first shoed his horse backwards, and thus throwing his pursuers off his tracks, achieved a brilliant series of raids which went unchallenged. He who surprised the garrison at Djengoutai, and under their very noses, with the streets full of soldiers, made off with the widow of Akhmet Khan, his old enemy. However, his daring sometimes overreached itself. The Khanum had been installed as his concubine—but beside being the widow of an enemy, she was the step-mother-in-law of Daniel Beg, that Sultan of Elisou who had returned to the Murid ranks after some years of allegiance to Russia. Shamyl did not wish to alienate him. Therefore he ordered Hadji Mourad to free his captive immediately. This Hadji Mourad did with a bad grace, for the lady was very beautiful. The affair rankled, breeding bad blood all round.

Hadji Mourad's audacity and savagery reached its apogee in his raid on Temir-Khan-Shura, headquarters of the Russian forces in Daghestan. He had learned there was to be a ball at the home of Colonel Prince Orbeliani, the Commanding Officer; he therefore decided to surprise the troops, and was even planning to pounce on the dancers as they revelled. He had never witnessed one of these western diversions; nor was he, at that time, familiar with any of the garrison towns built by the Russians. It was a dark, starless night, when he and his men leapt the barricades and galloped past the astonished sentries; Hadji Mourad, not unnaturally, led the way to the largest, most brightly lit building he could see; but this turned out to be the military hospital, where the patients barricaded themselves in their wards, and prepared to fight. By now, the sentries had given the alarm, and the garrison rushed to the rescue, the officers dashing out of the ballroom, brandishing their swords, leaving their partners, and the astonished band, in the middle of a mazurka. Hadji Mourad and his men were forced to fly, but as they had reversed their horses' shoes, they got away and, although hotly pursued, were not tracked to their mountain hide-out.

In all this violent evening's work, only one man had been killed, a hospital orderly; but Hadji Mourad's name had now assumed ogre-like dimensions, and the legend spread that he had killed off all the wounded in the hospital, and cut up their flesh into shashliks, and left the roasted and skewered titbits strewn about the long kitchen tables, so that when the Russians returned, they would think the Murids had been surprised at their dinner, and fled, leaving the shish-kebabs, which, of course, the Russians finished up, unaware that they were devouring the flesh of their own comrades. This gruesome story obtained much credence among the Russians; and although the General Staff, and Viceroy, and the Tzar himself, knew it to be false, no one denied it very vigorously, for Hadji Mourad was a figure whose every exploit turned into a legend. It would be better if he could be detested, rather than admired; but it was obvious—such desperate daring won the ungrudging admiration of the Russian soldiers and mountaineers alike.

In 1850, Hadji Mourad penetrated eastern Georgia, and slaughtered the whole garrison of Barbaratminskaya, and a few months later, with five hundred horsemen, he made another of his sudden night raids on the rich aôul of Bouinakh, killed the Sheik, brother of the Shamkal of Tarkou, in his own bed, and carried off his wife and children. With his shrieking captives flung across their saddle bows, the Red Devil and his men rode a hundred miles in a day and a night and, shaking off all pursuers, escaped to join Shamyl in the mountains, with these valuable hostages, for whose return Shamyl was able to obtain large sums of money which went to purchase new rifles, ammunition, and other materials of war which they needed desperately.

Such a man as Hadji Mourad, such a partisan fighter, one so reck-lessly brave, inspired not only admiration, but jealousy too, even among the Murids. Where once his enemies and rivals had calum-niated him to the Russians, now there were others who denounced him to Shamyl. These denunciations confirmed the Imam's fundamental misgivings. Hadji Mourad was becoming too powerful, too arrogant. If Shamyl were to be killed, there was no doubt who would set himself up as the Murid's new leader. In 1851 Shamyl proclaimed his second son, Khazi Mahommed, his heir; it was twelve years since Djemmal-Eddin had been forced from him, at Akhulgo. Twelve years of bitter-ness; he had never succeeded in obtaining any hostage of sufficient weight to be used as a bargaining point: (not even Prince Ellico

Orbeliani, who faced a firing squad coolly, but would not speak of ransom). He had come to believe, at last, that he would never see his eldest son again. Thus, he proclaimed Khazi Mahommed his successor. When Hadji Mourad heard this he was enraged. 'The sword will decide who will succeed—only the sword!' he said. Shamyl, learning of his Naib's insolence, deprived him of his rank, and ordered him to return all his war booty. But Hadji Mourad, who was then lording it over the aôul of Batlindge, replied: 'All that I have I got with my sword' Let Shamyl come and get it with his sword!' This was mutiny, and Shamyl set out to subdue his arrogant lieutenant. But before they could come to grips, a group of powerful mollahs intervened, and persuaded the two men to come to terms: above all things, inter-tribal wars would have weakened the Murids' force. Thus Shamyl and Hadji Mourad agreed, for the present, to put aside their personal quarrel.

But Shamyl knew he could now never rely on Hadji Mourad and he convoked a secret meeting of his Naibs where Hadji Mourad was condemned to death as a traitor. Just as, once it had not suited the Russians to believe what they had heard against Hadji Mourad, so, now, it suited Shamyl's book to give credence to stories of Hadji Mourad's treachery. Yes, he must be killed, agreed the Naibs who never questioned their Imam.

Nevertheless, one unknown Naib acted with independence, and warned Hadji Mourad just in time. Once again, Hadji Mourad felt the same sharp sense of bewilderment and anger, as when the Russians had turned on him. But now, he gave his enemies no time to chain him to a gun. He fled, accompanied by four of his most devoted Murids, and, making his way by night to the nearest Russian fortress, gave himself up to the commander, Colonel Prince Simon Voronzov, the Viceroy's son.

Tolstoy has left us an account of Hadji Mourad's life, and end, told in his own marvellous manner, at once detailed and simple. He obtained many of his facts from the military archives, and Hadji Mourad's own story of his life, which was taken down by Count Loris Melikov—one of Voronzov's staff officers, who spoke Tartar fluently, and thus was able to record everything that Hadji Mourad recounted.

It is interesting to note how, in his writings of the Caucasus, Tolstoy constantly uses the words 'bright', 'merry', 'calm' to describe the mountaineers, Hadji Mourad and his men, in particular. A bright smiling face; a calm, intent look, for Hadji Mourad; a merry voice, a sort of healthy tranquillity, for the young mountaineers. Again and again he insists on this almost innocent gaiety, or the good spirits (no doubt born of an untroubled conscience and a perfect liver), till we sense the simple, animal magnetism of these men, so far from the cynical and over-sophisticated Russian officers. Or, for that matter, the dark force of Shamyl who broods behind everything, a mysterious and satanic majesty enthroned among his mountain peaks.

Prince Simon Voronzov was delighted to acquire, in so effortless a manner, so splendid a prize, and he dispatched Hadji Mourad to Tiflis without delay. Arrived in the capital, he was made much of, while being, in fact, thoroughly mistrusted. The Viceroy patronized him, in his cold, urbane manner. An interpreter and aide-de-camp were detailed to his service, and a phaeton, horses and grooms, were placed at his disposal. It was a gilded cage. The drawing-room sycophants who circled round the Viceregal Court, peered at the virile, creature, who seemed to look over, and through them as he gazed out, with his wide, dark, inscrutable eyes. For them, he was a sort of raree-show, and they stared unashamedly. For the first time, Hadji Mourad found himself among all the lavish tricklings of the West: the staff-officers in their brilliant uniforms, their women crinolined and curled, sidled round him, preening, displaying their bosoms, asking him if he liked what he saw—themselves, a ball, a dinner party, the opera. . . . To them, this legendary partisan leader was a wild animal they would tame by pats. But the silent, dignified figure never seemed awkward or at a loss, nor any nearer to being snared by their seductions. He placed his hands on his heart and bowed, in the ritual manner, and spoke in the traditional Moslem metaphors. But it was plain, his thoughts were elsewhere. Even the Italian Opera had not held him. He had watched most of the first act with an unblinking stare, and then quietly stalked out, every eye riveted on him, so that the Viceroy, in the Royal box, and even the soprano, achieving a high C, felt their thunders stolen.

No, it was not like this at home, he agreed politely, his inscrutable black eyes with their curious air of childlike candour surveying the glittering salons of the Viceroy's palace. It was a magnificent setting for the Voronzov pomp, with its marble colonnades, its gigantic chandeliers and gilded furniture. Wherever Hadji Mourad looked, he saw knots of whispering women, or officers, talking together in low tones, and always, he knew, they were talking about him. He was treated as an honoured guest, they said, but both he and they knew he was a captive. It was a kind of protective custody, said Voronzov, when Hadji Mourad began to ask for liberty, for means to take arms against Shamyl. In vain he begged the Viceroy to give him men and guns. He would guarantee to raise all Daghestan against the Murids, he said. In vain he asked to be allowed to go to Tselmess, where Shamyl was holding his wife and children prisoners. . . . He was consumed with anxiety on their behalf. He knew how Shamyl treated his prisoners. . . . Day after day, he was put off with small-talk, and vague promises. Soon, next week . . . said the aides-de-camp, steering him away from the Viceroy's study. . . . Surely Hadji

Mourad could see that this period of enforced inactivity—this protective custody was, in fact, saving him from Shamyl's vengeance? Just a little more patience, said the interpreter. . . . Everything would turn out all right. A big new offensive was being planned against Shamyl, and then Hadji Mourad would have his chance. He would be given a regiment to lead. He would be able to settle his score with the Imam, in person. But nothing was said about rescuing his family: day after day Hadji Mourad's fire was damped down by small-talk and procrastination. Day after day, the limping figure would arrive at the palace, to wait in dark dignity in the Viceroy's antechamber and, day after day, see every minor official and petty government clerk obtain an audience, while he, the raging fighter, the man of daring, waited . . . not knowing the fate of his family, and whether as it was said, Shamyl had put out his son's eyes.

II

In a letter dated December 23, 1851, Tolstoy, in the Caucasus, writes to his brother, Sergei, in the North: 'If you want to boast of news from the Caucasus, you may announce that the second personage after Shamyl, a certain Hadji Mourad, has just surrendered to the Russian government. He was the finest warrior and horseman in all Tchetchnia, yet he committed this baseness.' By which it will be seen that Tolstoy, not only in his later, considered account of Hadji Mourad, but in his immediate, intimate correspondence, found it base for an Avar naib to go over to the Russians, rather than the act of enlightened humility that it appeared to most of his contemporaries; they saw the mountaineers as savages who could only come to salvation by way of the Viceregal throne. Through Tolstoy's eyes, as through the accounts of contemporary travellers, we see this sophisticated society imposing their petty protocol and St. Petersburg refinements, on a wild land, a free people, their mundane chatter, like the rattle of the tea-cups and the shuffling of cards, sounding a gnat-like, yet insistent hum, over the gun-fire from the mountains. Tolstoy, intoxicated by his new-found vistas of reality of nature (and Marinka, the Cossack girl who embodied all nature to him), wrote of the world he had escaped, in terms of loathing.

> They rise before me, instead of my cabin, my forest, my love, those drawing-rooms, those women with pomaded hair, through which the false locks appear, those unnaturally lisping lips, those concealed and distorted limbs and the prattle of the salons which pretends to be conversation. . . . Those dull faces, those rich, marriageable girls: 'That's all right—but don't come too near me, even though I am a rich marriageable girl!' All that sitting down and changing places; that impudent pairing of people, that never-ending gossip and

hypocrisy; those rules—to this one your hand, to that one a nod and with that one a chat, and, finally, that eternal ennui, deep in the blood, passing from generation to generation.

So the salons of Tiflis must have seemed to Hadji Mourad, too, as he stood silently, amidst the Viceroy's guests. Throughout the long evenings, his eyes were always fixed on the windows where, between the looped crimson brocade curtains, the mountain tops could be glimpsed, dark and menacing, looming above the steep-rising streets of Tiflis. Somewhere in those mountains, in a fetid pit, ten feet deep, his son was rotting, perhaps blinded and forgotten. In some mountain aôul, his family were held as Shamyl's hostages, their fate hanging by a thread, while he must sit at the Viceroy's table, sampling soufflés and delicacies which sent the rest of the guests into ecstasies. Yet, if he were to exchange this for the promised protection of Shamyl . . .? He mistrusted the successive letters which Shamyl still continued to send him, offering pardon, reinstatement with honours, and all the rest. Shamyl showed himself very eager to have his first Naib beside him once more. Too eager, thought Hadji Mourad: would he, Hadji Mourad, return to the Murid ranks, only to find his family already slaughtered, and his own death decreed? Sometimes, at nightfall, a cloaked figure crept to G.H.Q., there to report on doings in Daghestan, where Hadji Mourad's loyal followers had promised to mass, with the intent to raid Shamyl's aôul, and rescue Hadji Mourad's family.

'Let them,' said Voronzov's staff officers cynically. 'Let them do our work for us: even if they fail to kill *him* (as they always referred to Shamyl) there will be great losses on both sides: so many Tartars the less. *Tant mieux!*' And they shrugged their epauletted shoulders, and sat dealing the cards, drinking hock and seltzer. But nothing positive materialized; and Hadji Mourad knew Shamyl's terrible threats had intimidated even his—Hadji Mourad's—own Avars. He was cornered, for he could not convince the Russians of his sincerity. Given the chance once more, given men and arms and trust, he pleaded, he could raid Shamyl's aôul, and raise all Daghestan to his own standard. 'Let him go? Give him men and arms? Ridiculous; a hare-brained scheme,' said the staff officers, and there was agreement in Voronzov's pale eyes, when, once again, the tiresome subject of Hadji Mourad arose. Some were for putting him out of sight and mind, in Siberia. Some wanted him imprisoned, under lock and key, in Tiflis: some resented the largesse with which he was treated: some were stung by the barbs of jealousy, seeing the excitement he aroused, and the way in which he intrigued their women. This romantic-looking creature was both to be pitied and feared, a mixture quite irresistible to the fair sex. So Hadji Mourad remained carefully guarded, a show-piece in the Viceregal suite, his dark eyes looking through and beyond them all, to the faraway mountains, while the ladies followed him with sighing glances; and December gave place to January and then early spring, and still nothing was done.

III

The Voronzovs lived in enormous state. After the Imperial family, they were the first in all the land, and were honoured but not always liked, accordingly. Envy tinged the attitude of most of the aristocracy; but the Voronzovs were loved by the people, who accepted their superiority, and did not feel resentful, as did the nobility, when they were compelled to stand in their presence, leave the room after them, and sit well below them at table. The Voronzov *train de vie* was royal, whether in the capital, at Tiflis or Odessa, where the palace, built in the Russian Empire style, by Zaharoff, architect of the celebrated Admiralty, had the finest parquet in all Russia. Three hundred lackeys, dressed in the crimson and white Voronzov livery, ministered to wants. Their daily dinners were banquets of twenty or more courses, and never set for less than fifty guests; though they did not go so far as Prince Youssoupov, who regaled his guests with a ballet of several hundred serf girls who performed in the nude. Perhaps the Viceroy's English upbringing had dampened his native, more lavish, sense of hospitality. However, at the Viceregal Palace (which every soldier, on or off duty had to salute, as he passed by) the Voronzovs did their utmost to make their guests feel at ease—particularly the native rulers who had sworn allegiance—the Shamkals and Begs, and even the wilder, less reliable ones, such as Hadji Mourad.

The Princess, whose charms, at fifty, were scarcely less than at twenty-five, when, it was recalled, Pushkin loved her to distraction, had a soft and charming manner and was constantly on the alert to launch new topics of conversation when long awkward silences fell, as they frequently did, in such a polyglot society, the generals sitting red-faced and awkward, beside inarticulate Georgian beauties, and the local rulers only able to utter their own outlandish syllables. An American traveller left us his account of one such evening, which began by Prince Kotchubey discussing local problems in a most confidential tone: 'These Circassians,' he said, 'are just like your American Indians—as untamable and uncivilized—only *extermination* would keep them quiet . . . or, if they came under Russian rule, the only safe policy would be to employ their wild and warlike tastes against others.'

The Princess Eliza Voronzov is described minutely, as having languid blue eyes and a brilliant complexion, her dark chestnut hair looped in heavy swags, each side of her delicate face (her age was put at thirty-five, or thereabouts). He goes on to say that a curled ostrich plume and an enormous pearl pendant adorned her head, and her necklace was of huge turquoises and diamonds—perhaps part of the Potemkin inheritance. The salon (all crimson brocade) to which she led her guests after dinner, was like the dinner-table, decorated with sumptuous flower and fruit arrangements, pyramids of tropical blooms, set in gold and crystal epergnes, or in rare Chinese dishes. A resident painter was kept fully occupied, arranging new each day a series of still-lifes, throughout the house; this being a most imaginative extension of the feudal custom which kept resident astronomers, theologians, or apothecaries about the place. When all the guests were assembled in the salon, the Princess clapped her hands and called for her *tchibouque*, an Oriental habit which astounded and outraged her American visitor. An elaborately dressed dwarf, with huge moustachios, a page of the presence, brought her the pipe; but after a few graceful puffs the Princess put down the amber mouthpiece, and concentrated all her attention on a small pet, a wild little creature, rather like a flying fox that scampered across the parquet, ignoring the fine company, and sat chattering in her lap as she fed it grapes. While the younger officers stamped their spurred boots in a mazurka, and the Georgians followed suit with one of their undulating dances, the Prince drew his more favoured guests into his library, showing them some of the *objets de vertu* with which his palaces overflowed. The Prince was apt to confound his visitors by turning abruptly from the fine arts, to speak with knowledge with passion, even, of the new stratas of coal he was developing in Imeretia; or he would show them specimens of cotton with which he was experimenting in Guriel. 'Not so good as American,' he said regretfully, but went on to describe the excellence of Imertian coal: it was being used on the Black Sea steamers, and in the Turkish frontier forts too, where timber was scarce, he explained, and his guests tried to display a suitable interest in the problems of army stoves; it was easier to rhapsodize over Benvenuto Cellini goblets.

They made a splendid showing, these Voronzov treasures. Alas! Aloupkha and the other Viceregal palaces shared the fate of most of the great houses during the Revolution.

'Why dost thou build thy hall, son of the wingèd days? Thou lookest from thy towers today: yet a few years, and the blast of the desert comes and it howls in thy empty courts.'

But all such violence lay more than seventy years away, well into the next century. Meanwhile, only a few days ahead lay the terrible and heroic death which awaited Hadji Mourad. That strong body which stood so proudly among the guests, was soon to lie headless in a forest clearing, plugged with lead, slashed with sabres, while that unbowed head was to be stuffed into a sack and dispatched to St. Petersburg.

* * *

At last Hadji Mourad realized Voronzov's polite procrastination was deliberate, a diplomatic technique for evading the issue. When General Argoutinsky would arrive in Tiflis—in the summer—there might be discussions as to a large scale attack in which Hadji Mourad could take part; but the latter now resolved to have done with Russian half-promises, and the stifling life of Tiflis. He requested to be allowed to live at Noukkha, a small Moslem town nearby, where it would be easier for him to negotiate with his own Avar followers, he said, and easier too, to devote his empty hours to the prayer and meditation which alone could support him in his terrible plight. From what, to Hadji Mourad, was the greatest crisis in his life, with his family as hostages, their lives balanced against his faith in the Russians, was, to the Russians only, one of many political manœuvres. The Viceroy was becoming bored with the grave figure who had haunted his Palace, and so gave him permission to leave. He was accompanied by five Murid henchmen, and a small guard of Cossacks commanded by two officers, who were lodged in the same house as Hadji Mourad and his men. It was hard by the mosque and Hadji Mourad spent most of his time there, in prayer. The news which the Daghestan tribesmen brought him was not encouraging. No one dared to raid Vedin, Shamyl's aôul, where Hadji Mourad's family were imprisoned. The Imam had proclaimed he would inflict terrible tortures on anyone who raised a hand to help them. No one knew what had befallen Hadji Mourad's son.

Suddenly Hadji Mourad's mind was made up. Prayer had failed: prayers to Allah, and to the White Tzar's Sirdar alike had remained unanswered. The time for action had come. He would escape from his captors, make his way to Vedin, gathering his supporters on the way, and breaking through Shamyl's cordon, surprise the aôul in one of his celebrated dashes. He would carry off the prisoners, or he would die in the attempt. No life, no power, no favours, were to be measured against the lives of those he loved so profoundly. Speaking the guttural Tchetchen dialect which ran little risk of being understood by the guards picketed in the yard below his window, Hadji Mourad outlined his plan to his followers, and they spent the rest of the night priming their pistols and sharpening their kindjals. Before dawn, they prayed. At the first pale break of day, Hadji Mourad sent word to the duty officer, saying he wished to ride out. No mountaineer can be kept without some appearance of liberty of movement, unless he is chained. The officer was accustomed to Hadji Mourad's daily rides, and merely ordered a guard of five men to accompany them. The horses were saddled by the grumbling, yawning Cossacks and the little band trotted out of town, the sound of the horses' hooves muffled by the heavy morning mists into which they vanished. Hadji Mourad was leading, and spurred his horse to a canter, increasing his pace, as his men followed, until, suddenly, they were racing towards the distant mountains, crouched low over their horses' necks. The eagles had flown.

A Russian sergeant who had imagined himself in charge of the expedition hollered to them to stop: he spurred his horse, and began gaining on them. Now he knew they were making off. This was no early morning ride, but a planned escape. He felt for his pistol, shouting to his men to follow. As he drew level with Hadji Mourad, the mountaineer turned and, quietly aiming, shot the Russian through the heart. When the Cossacks reached their dead comrade, the five Murids wheeled suddenly, and charged at them, hacking at them with their shashkas, ripping them up, before the astonished men could defend themselves. As the riders fell from their saddles, they were trampled by their horses which stampeded and slipped in the blood that spurted everywhere. Having taken the dying Russians' rounds of ammunition, the Murids made off towards the distant line of mountains now emerging, splendid and remote, from the low-lying mists which still hung across the valley.

At Noukkha, the alarm had been given by frightened peasants who had come running into the town with stories of the fight. The duty officer wished himself dead: that such a prisoner would escape, from beneath his nose, would cost him his commission, if not his life. He preferred not to think of how he would inform the Viceroy. After sitting, head in hands, and contemplating a suicide letter to his wife, he became completely unnerved and, ordering his carriage, drove into Tiflis at breakneck speed, to hasten his own end. But Colonel Korganov, commanding the town, was a man of different mettle, and knowing that the defiles into the mountains were heavily guarded, he set out, with a large body of men, to track down the fugitives. He reckoned he would overtake them in the foothills; and this he did.

The Caucasians had lost much valuable time, floundering in a bog of rice fields, so that by the time they had got their horses clear, it was high noon, and they were no longer sheltered by the mists. All around, the brilliant light sparkled on the valley and mountains, revealing every tree and rock and stream with dangerous clarity. Hadji Mourad judged it more prudent to lie hidden in a nearby coppice, until nightfall, when they could gain the mountains unperceived. But while they hobbled their horses, and performed their ritual mid-day ablutions and prayers (every Murid carried a ewer of water in his pack, for this sole

purpose, for to miss the ritual was the unthinkable), Colonel Korganov's troop had met an old man who had told of seeing five Murid
horsemen entering a little wood. . . . It was one of those seemingly
chance encounters which yet changes history. Had Hadji Mourad
escaped, he might have met and defeated Shamyl, and the bloodshed
of the Caucasian wars been shortened by several years; the months of
anguished captivity endured by the two Princesses, which in turn was
to bring about the sad fate of Djemmal-Eddin, who paid for their
liberty with his life, also might have been avoided.

But fate led the old man down the road, to be questioned by Kar-
ganov's interpreters, and, within an hour, the troops had surrounded
the coppice, and Hadji Mourad and his five men were trapped and
outnumbered, a hundred to one. The game was up, and they knew it.
But not one of them spoke of surrender. While the Russian officers were
shouting to them to lay down their arms, they set about making their
last stand. Neither they nor their horses would be taken alive. In the
traditional manner of their kind, they slit their horses' windpipes, and
making a rampart of their bodies, dug themselves a trench with their
kindjals. Now the Russians were creeping nearer and beginning to fire.
Shot was answered by shot. The Caucasians had a reputation for deadly
marksmanship, especially if they could rest their guns on the twisted twig
tripod they generally used. Now they fired sparingly, from across their
saddle-bows; as long as their ammunition lasted each bullet accounted
for a man, and the Russians fell back.

Presently the Russians were joined by a number of renegade tribesmen who, learning of the battle, came slinking down from the hills, like
jackals eager for the kill: Hadji Mourad had been their terror for years.
Among them was the son of his old enemy, Akhmet Khan of Mektoulee. More demands for surrender were again answered by shots. As
the five hundred attackers closed in, they could hear the Murids intoning their ritual death-chant, mournful and glorious. Hadji Mourad and
his men unsheathed their shashkas; their ammunition was almost gone,
but they still had their steel. Two of the Murids were shot, and died
quietly, beside their leader. A bullet hit Hadji Mourad in the shoulder,
and he stuffed the wound with cotton from the padded lining of his
beshmet. Another bullet pierced his side, and again he plugged the
wound with cotton. Here is Tolstoy's wonderful description of the end:

> The wound in the side was fatal, and he felt that he was dying.
> Memories and pictures succeeded one another with extraordinary
> rapidity in his imagination. Now he saw the powerful Abu Noutzal
> Khan, dagger in hand, and holding up his severed cheek as he rushed
> at his foe; then he saw the weak, pale old Voronzov with his cunning
> white face, and heard his soft voice; then he saw his son Yusuf, his
> wife Sofiate, and the pale red-bearded face of his enemy Shamyl,

with its half-closed eyes. All these images passed through his mind without evoking any feeling within him—neither pity, nor anger, nor any kind of desire: everything seemed so insignificant in comparison with what was beginning, or had already begun, within him.

Yet his strong body continued the thing he had commenced. Gathering together his last strength, he rose from behind the bank, fired his pistol at a man who was just running towards him, and hit him. The man fell. Then Hadji Mourad got out of the ditch and limping heavily, went dagger in hand straight at the foe. Some shots cracked and he reeled and fell. Several militiamen with triumphant shrieks rushed towards the fallen body. But the body that seemed to be dead suddenly moved. First, the uncovered, bleeding, shaven head rose; then the body, with hands holding to the trunk of a tree. He seemed so terrible, that those who were running towards him stopped short. But suddenly a shudder passed through him, he staggered away from the tree and fell on his face . . . He did not move, but still he felt.

He lay, with his still bright eyes staring up at the morning sky, until young Akhmet Khan hacked off the head, and the rest gathered around, to stab and kick the body lying in its blood on the trampled grass. Where it was buried, no one can say.

The Viceroy had passed some disagreeable moments, since he had learned of Hadji Mourad's break-away. It would have been really very unpleasant trying to explain to the Emperor. . . . However, it had all turned out for the best, and Voronzov, ever chivalrous to a fallen enemy, pronounced a valedictory tribute: 'Thus on April 24, 1852, Hadji Mourad died, as he had lived, desperately brave. His ambition equalled his courage, and to that there was no bound.'

As to the head, Voronzov displayed it in the military hospital at Tiflis, 'to reassure the public'. Later it was embalmed, making a battle trophy entirely worthy to be laid at the Emperor's feet.

21

The North

A time to get and a time to lose; a time to keep and a time to cast away. A time to love and a time to hate; a time of war and a time of peace. ECCLESIASTES

Thirteen years had passed since Shamyl's son, Djemmal-Eddin, was brought to St. Petersburg as a wild little captive. Those thirteen years had seen his father's rise, phoenix-like, from the ashes of Akhulgo, to straddle the Caucasus, a colossus against whom successive waves of Russian troops had been flung, only to fall back; had seen, too, the captive child change from a savage eaglet into a quiet, reflective young officer, Cornet Prince Djemmal-Eddin Shamyl, passionately devoted to his adopted country, and, above all, to the Tzar, on whom he had centred all the loyalty and idealism of his nature. He had come to consider himself a Russian; his whole past was forgotten; he no longer remembered the Caucasus, his father, his family, the language they spoke, or his childhood in the aôul. Somewhere, in a vague dream-like past, he still recalled the mosques, and the ritual of his faith. No one had tried to convert him to the Orthodox Church; in matters of religion, he had simply been left alone. It is probable that the Tzar calculated his hostage would be more useful to him as a Moslem, when the day came for him to fulfil that destiny for which he, the Tzar, had shaped him. Nicholas envisaged Djemmal-Eddin as his mouthpiece in the Caucasus, bringing enlightenment to the subdued mountaineers, and easing the ultimate imposition of Russian rule.

Although Shamyl, by now, had become a household word in the North, an ogre into whose voracious maw many thousands of Ivans, Selifans and Grischas vanished, every year, never to return, he had remained an heroic figure too, so that Djemmal-Eddin still retained a certain remote, impersonal pride in his origins. But it was not the seething pride of l'Aiglon, fostered by frustration, forever craving his father's inheritance, suffering a solitary, bitter imprisonment among aliens. Djemmal-Eddin's whole outlook, beliefs and interests were now one with Russia: he saw through the eyes of the young Guards' officers about the Court, among whom he had grown up. Their convictions and hopes had become his own. He shared their belief that the Caucasus must come under Russian rule—that to become part of the Empire would be a glorious consummation. Every fresh battle, every act of barbarism reported from the Caucasus was not the work of his own race, or the orders of his own father—but the terrible price of this just war. He did not blame the mountaineers for their resistance: he even admired it, impartially, but he longed for them to learn what true civilization could mean—what this other, Western world represented in its essence. He believed that Russian rule would bring peace, justice and prosperity to the mountaineers. He had passed his military examinations brilliantly; but the Tzar, who had appointed him one of the Imperial Escort, would not countenance his fighting against the people of his origin. He had other plans for him. Later, when the bloodshed was over, Djemmal-Eddin would have his place there. As Shamyl's son and the Tzar's pawn he would make a perfect Viceroy.

It was with this end in view, no doubt, that Nicholas is said to have crushed an idyll between Djemmal-Eddin and a Russian princess. The young man had been supposed to be much in love. He had asked the Tzar's permission to marry. But the Tzar had been perfectly frank, perfectly cynical.

'You may have as many women as you wish: but do not think of marriage. Certainly not with a Russian woman.' He was adamant. The boy must be kept free to marry some local ruler's daughter. It would ensure his acceptance among the tribes. Thus, forever a pawn and a prisoner, Djemmal-Eddin found his love, like his whole life, sacrificed to the interests of other people. But he did not complain: his devotion to the Tzar remained unshaken. He was posted to the Grand Duke Michael's regiment of Uhlans stationed in Warsaw, dividing his time between the Viceregal Court at Warsaw, and the Winter Palace. Thus, his life appeared as empty as that of all the rest of his comrades. Though perhaps it was not. Djemmal-Eddin, besides being an intriguing figure at Court, showed a studious side; he spoke several languages, studied astronomy, was musical, and liked to paint. Added to these accomplishments, he rode magnificently, like all Caucasians: but unlike them, his handsome dark features had a curiously dreamy expression: gentleness had replaced the harsh bearing of the Avars. He seems to have achieved a rare balance of popularity, being not only the *coqueluche des dames*, but regarded with affection and respect by all his fellow officers. Unlike many of the Asiatic princes who came to Court, he seldom wore native dress, eschewing even the tcherkesska, which made every man look so dashing, preferring the Russian uniform, as if symbolizing his total conversion to the West. Only his large mournful, rather questioning dark eyes, set slanted in high cheekbones, and his black hair, that densely dark glossy hair of the Asiatics, which seems plumage rather than hair, still told of his origins.

Since the Emperor's first love was for everything military, he always favoured his Guards' officers. There were the Chevaliers Gardes, and the Gardes à Cheval—the Life Guards and the Horse Guards. Some regiments were recruited for their great height; some for their cast of countenance, such as the Kurnos Regiment, where every man was snub-nosed. It had been founded by the Emperor Paul I, to be a multiple reflection of his snub-nosed self. The Preobrajensky Footguards were the first regiment in all Russia, having been begun for, rather than by, Peter the Great, when he was a boy, in the village of Preobrajensky, near Moscow. At first they had been considered in the nature of living toys—real live soldiers for the boy to play with: but, over the century, they had grown into the first and finest regiment. Their barracks were in Millionnaya, beside the Winter Palace, and were joined to the Royal residences, both the Winter Palace and the Hermitage, by a galleried bridge, spanning the Winter Canal. It had been built for them, as a reward for their unwavering loyalty during the Dekabrist Rising. There were Uhlan regiments quartered farther afield, around the Champ de Mars, a vast parade ground where the troops were perpetually drilling, marching and manœuvring. 'Petersburg looks like a row of barracks', wrote the Tzarina when she first went there as a young German Princess. But how opulent, these barracks; enormous palaces, adorned with colonnades, peristyles, and baroque plaster-work, which housed the Cadets Corps School, the Horse Guards Manège, the Pavlovsky Barracks, or the Artillery Headquarters. These and many other military establishments were all grandiose. The whole city was, before all else, a luxurious armed camp punctuated by triumphal arches, and monuments to great generals, or the fallen. The uniformed inhabitants were to be seen, for the most part, marching, parading, presenting arms, saluting and being saluted. The jingle of spurs and the beat of drums, like the metronome step of the sentries and the thunderous gun-salutes, sounded by day and night.

To belong to the privileged military hierarchy was the sum total of a young man's life. To remain in the country, on the family estates, was impossibly provincial—bailiff's work; to enter the Foreign Office, or one of the Ministries, was *bien vu*, but it did not carry the prestige of an army career. Intellectual life, if taken beyond the University gates, was unthinkable; and in 1839, the Tzar's iron hand descended on Kiev, to suppress the University of St. Vladimir, where the faint stirring of a liberal conscience among the students had been condemned as dangerous revolutionary tendencies. The Tzar had not forgotten the Dekabrists. Indeed, he never was to forget them. Day and night, the military overcoat he had worn when he rode out to confront them remained beside him in his rooms at the Winter Palace, and it was on his bed when he lay dying.

From the memoirs of Prince Peter Kropotkin, the revolutionist, we read of the young, aristocratic pupils in the Corps des Pages—the Eton of military schools—where an atmosphere of rigid military discipline was softened by a number of privileges and worldly distractions. The boys shared something of the life of the capital, going regularly to the opera, and to Court. St. Petersburg was then divided, says the Prince, into two camps, of Italian and French opera, duels being fought over their respective merits. The Corps des Pages were given boxes, into which they crammed, wearing their resplendent gold-laced uniforms. Somehow, the opera was becoming linked with the radical movement, says the Prince; the revolutionary recitatives in *I Puritani* and *William Tell* were always met with storms of applause, not strictly according to their musical rendering.

Russian opera, as it is known today, those wonderful, purely national works such as *Kitej*, *Boris Goudenov*, *Russalka*, *Evgueni Oniegin*, or *Prince Igor*, were yet to be written, ten and twenty years ahead, but already germinating in the minds of their future composers: young Rimsky Korsakov, about to begin his life as a naval cadet; Mussorgsky, a Guards' cadet, already playing the piano gracefully to a circle of admiring young ladies—but no hint, yet, of those great arias by which Boris lives and dies. Dargomyjsky, depressed by the failure of his first opera, *Esmeralda*, in 1847, but working, doggedly, on *Russalka*, which he only completed in 1855. Tchaikovsky, a nervous child, struggling against parental discouragement (they considered music had an unhealthy influence) and without teachers, improvising, dedicating a waltz to his governess, and entering, unwillingly, the School of Jurisprudence in 1852. Borodin, studying chemistry and science, at the Academy of Medicine and Surgery, but also concentrating on the art of the fugue, attending practice meetings of an amateur string quartet, trudging seven miles on foot, slushing through mud and snow, for he had no money to hire a droshky. *Prince Igor* was only published posthumously, in 1888. Musically, the early 'fifties in Russia were a moment of transition. Glinka's *A Life for the Tzar*, so much enjoyed by Nicholas, was already becoming a trifle outmoded among some of the fledgling intelligentsia.

Djemmal-Eddin, unlike Prince Kropotkin, did not criticize the monarchy or the régime, nor did he fall under the spell of machinery for improving factory conditions, and the workers' lives, as did the Prince. To him, Russia was all wonderful, and civilization was in full flower, here and now, in St. Petersburg. He did not know, nor would he have believed Turgeniev's summing-up, looking back across Europe, to his homeland, from the vantage-point of a Parisian salon: 'The trouble with us Russians', wrote Turgeniev, 'is that the Tartar is so close behind us. We are a semi-barbarous people still. We put Parisian kid-gloves on our hands instead of washing them. At one moment we bow and utter polite phrases, and the next, flog our servants.'

The Ministry of Public Instruction had lately created a number of local schools and new chairs at the universities; they were for Oriental languages. At Kazan, a chair of Chinese, Armenian, Arab, Persian, Turco-Tartar and Mongol was inaugurated, 'to instruct the proposed governors and administrators' of these remote regions. The merchants had always known how to get along in their own language of roubles, tea, pelts and barter; but these new university chairs indicated the Government's colonial intentions, and the Tzar's convictions of his country's civilizing mission; even so, none of the *jeunesse dorée* applied themselves to such useful Oriental studies. That was left to the less privileged civil servants. There was, however, an exception at Court. The Tzar's son, Constantine, showed a penchant for learning, for Orientalism in particular. His special passion was for everything Turkish—principally for planning a Turkish conquest: it was as if he believed himself to be predestined. His name may have fostered this belief: Constantine, the Russian, ruling over a new Byzantium risen from the ashes of the Moslem Empire. It was an age-old Russian prophecy, and the cherished dream of all his Romanov forebears. It was perhaps with this in mind that the Tzar's personal escort were recruited entirely from among the Asiatic princes and nobles. Therefore, to wear one of the exotic uniforms was much admired, as it was to have the intriguing slant-eyed features of the Mongol and Circassian Princes, or to be a Shamkal, or an Emir—a suitably tamed mountain eagle. Or, like Djemmal-Eddin, to be surrounded by a romantic aura, at once dramatic and mysterious—a wild hostage, who had grown up to become one with the West. But fashionable St. Petersburg stopped there. The profound roots of Orientalism, the cultures, beliefs and languages of the East were ignored. The Caucasians, like the Persians and the Turks, were a people whom it had been a habit to fight since the beginning of the century. One day they would be conquered. That was all.

Meanwhile the young St. Petersburg aristocrats, Djemmal-Eddin among them, continued in the extravagant manner of their kind, card-playing, steeplechasing, love-making, and keeping the regimental tailors busy with the exigencies of their uniforms, which were particularly splendid: 'a red, tight-fitting tunic with gold braid, for the Court balls, a green one with blue trousers, for the town balls, a green military frockcoat, for dinners and calls; for service, a white cloth tunic with gold braid, top boots coming up to the knees, and a gold-plated cuirass and helmet: on the crest of the helmet, an Imperial eagle' was *de rigueur* for the Hussars. For the Guards' officers, in attendance at the Court balls, knee breeches of white cloth, silk stockings, buckled shoes, dress sword and a tricorn hat, black for the Infantry, white for the Cavalry.

Nor were the other regiments behind in splendour. Mess dinners were particularly elaborate. French chefs of each regiment vied with one another to produce masterpieces. Tokay was the fashionable drink and imported at great expense from Hungary. 'Sterlet' (each fish of considerable value) 'was boiled down in champagne to make a soup.' Such flamboyance was greatly admired. So the round of pleasures went: dining, dancing, supping, visiting the gypsy cabarets, the opera, the French and Italian theatres, and the ballet. To keep a ballerina as mistress was as essential as to have two or three thoroughbreds, and a fine equipage.

In St. Petersburg, everything was on a giant scale, as if to match the Emperor's own towering stature and pride. The classic and rococo perspectives hardly breathed of Europe—by their scale alone, they told of Asia's infinity. Yet, sometimes, behind the noble Italianate façade, reminders of Muscovite roots were glimpsed. The severe Anitchkov Palace, a prison-cage of masonry, was suddenly confounded by the gilded cupolas of its chapel, thrusting up from behind its high walls, soaring like some legendary Russian fire-bird, glittering and exotic, recalling the ancient Slav capital which Pushkin loved as 'golden-headed Moscow'. But for the most part, St. Petersburg had already fulfilled the destiny its founder, Peter the Great, had decreed: it had opened a window into the West, and, to its inhabitants, appeared a Western capital, even if conceived in such exaggerated terms that, to more western European eyes, it still appeared entirely strange, and wholly Slav.

The great houses were each almost as vast, as sumptuous as the Royal Palaces. The Voronzov Palace, overlooking the Neva, was painted the family colours, crimson and white. The Tauride Palace was a rich blue; some were lilac, or salmon: the Youssoupov Palace was reflected, a shimmer of yellow, along the Fontanka Canal. The Winter Palace had been originally coloured pistachio green, its pillars white and gold; but later, it had been repainted a heavy maroon red. Liveried lackeys and clumsy ragged serfs swarmed over the courtyards and pillared entrance halls of every fine town house, running messages, fetching wood or water, gossiping, thieving, spying, lying, quarrelling among themselves, devoted or hostile, treacherous or loyal, according to their kind. But never indifferent. Russian servants were always deeply involved with their masters, their lives bound up with, and absorbed by the families they served.

For the Court and nobility, it was a curious way of life; a round of supper parties and balls began about midnight, and lasted until the small hours: the general time for visits was 11 p.m., when a caller might learn the hostess was not yet up. The ladies, who dined at home about six o'clock, often retired to bed, 'to rest their complexions' before emerging, radiant, at midnight. Supper was the favourite meal, never served before 2 a.m. The evening seldom broke up before 4 a.m., so that the city remained shuttered and still until long after the late winter's dawn broke, between nine and ten in the morning. Save for the errand-boys, milk vendors and soldiers, few people were abroad before ten-thirty. Yet those few who were, could see one lighted window in the Winter Palace, the green-shaded lamp which burned there was the Emperor's study. He began his day's work at 5 a.m. The mounds of State papers and military dispatches (mostly pertaining to the Caucasian campaigns), which arrived daily to be piled before him, scarcely seemed diminished after a whole morning's work.

Like his Court, the Tzar spent his afternoon driving about the city: it was fashionable to race a sleigh along the quays, or to the Islands, before the short winter's afternoon darkened. But, unlike his people, the Emperor returned, not to dally, to prepare for the evening's festivities, but to his desk, to receive his ministers again. For his aides-de-camp, this austere time-table was exigent in the extreme, and many of them had to abandon all hope of living the social life of their caste. But for those outside the Emperor's entourage, or the exuberant guardsmen of Djemmal-Eddin's circle, the round of diversions never ceased. The child who had been born in an aôul of Daghestan no longer recalled the *djighitovkas*, which were all the Caucasians knew of festivities. He had become one of the fêted St. Petersburg élite; the malachite and gold salons of the Winter Palace his natural habitat, his lot, not that of ordinary mortals, but rather, it seemed, roses, roses, all the way.

With the first heavy snows, usually at the beginning of November, the whole city was transformed into a white sparkling world, curiously hushed, where the long, beautiful perspectives were sprinkled with diamond-dust frost, shimmering over the gilded cupolas, making the city appear a gigantic, iridescent Christmas bauble, a snowstorm paper-weight world of its own, enclosed, unreal, remote. A hundred thousand sleighs and sledges flew over the smooth white tracks. *Poidi!* Make way! the traditional cry of the *isvostchik*, or coachman, was as peculiar to the city as the gondoliers' call is to Venice. These isvostchik in their hugely padded overcoats stood like grotesque wooden toys, rigid arms outstretched, reins grasped in fur-mittened paws, their beards frozen stiff with icicles. . . . *Poidi!* Make way! . . . But now they too have made way for another age. The last of them were still to be seen in provincial Russia, in the early nineteen-thirties: I recall riding behind one of these figures, and being overturned, pitched clear of the decrepit droshky, to the tune of a hundred lamentations, addressed to God (at that time, rather *mal vu* in Russia), but by then the isvostchik had outlived his own moment in time—and was already as picturesque, as archaic, as any ikon.

When the waters of the Neva became one vast ice-flow, its dark steely surface supported whole battalions marching on parade; trotting races were held upon it; strings of lamps stretched from one shore to the other, and bright coloured groups of skaters, swirling around, to the strains of the latest Viennese waltz. Here and there, the ice was dotted by encampments of Lapps, who came down from the Arctic each year, with their reindeer, to trade furs. They set up their tents within sight of the Winter Palace, but lived quite unmoved by the proximity of such urban splendours, and could be seen fishing through deep holes pierced in the ice.

Such was the look of the city: its sounds, above the silence of the snows, were the melancholy chants of the moujik cart drivers—and bells. Bells of all kinds, the great bronze tongues of the cathedrals, and the jingling, tinkling, silvery bells of the sleighs dashing over the ice. Indoors, the soft hum of the samovar, the deeper purr of the *pechi*—the big porcelain stove round which every house, every room centred. All autumn long, there was the rumbling and creaking of carts, an endless procession of slow-moving carts trundling in from the dark forests ringing the city, bringing in wood without which St. Petersburg would have perished, and which was stacked, roof-high, in each courtyard. A wood famine would have been a major disaster. Deforestation was already threatened, but nothing more was done about it. The rich fanned themselves in their glowing drawing-rooms, and the poor, their feet wrapped in birch-bark and rags, waited their turn for a place on the smoking hot ledge above the stove at the inn, where they could sweat away their miseries for a few kopeks. Temperatures were very low; twenty degrees below freezing-point was usual. Double windows kept the houses suffocatingly hot: there was much anaemia and tuberculosis in consequence.

The arrow-straight four mile length of the Nevski Prospekt sped towards the cruel wastes of the north: but on its way it was lined with cathedrals and palaces, hotels, restaurants, and shops, and the dark, yet glittering depths of the Gostinii Dvor, the huge bazaar, a conglomeration of merchandise, ramshackle wooden booths filled with furs, French silks, old clothes, salted fish, diamonds, stolen goods, pickles, Oriental cashmeres and wooden toys. Here, the bearded merchants, lumbering in their padded caftans, lived in a world of their own, talking shop, weights and measures, and food. Their pleasures were simple: women —some sly-eyed peasant girl, if their massive wives had begun to pall; the marriages of their sons and daughters, and food, those rich, interminable meals of the merchant classes, washed down by great draughts of tea, or *kvass*. Every booth was strewn with the husks of the dried sun-flower seed they ate incessantly: every counter had a wad of grubby rouble-notes and receipts, weighted down by a saucerful of salted cucumbers. They were shrewd business men, though not all of them could read or write: the bead-strung abacus of the East was their calculating machine. Their wares were, for the most part, advertised by crudely drawn signs, which spoke to an illiterate public. The merchants and their families were not received by the *beau monde*, though occasionally some desperate young aristocrat, hounded by his creditors, took a merchant's daughter to wife, had his bills paid, and treated her badly for the rest of his life. Society usually found it easy enough to overlook the *mésalliance*—so long as they did not have to know the wife; so the husband returned to his own world, and the wife returned to hers, living in the indolent Oriental manner of her ancestors: overeating, sleeping late, exchanging confidences with her servants, lolling all day in a shift, stretched on a sofa, her pet cat beside her, a serf-girl tickling the soles of her feet with a goose-feather, to induce sleep.

Once a year, on New Year's Day, the Winter Palace threw open its great doors to the whole population. The Tzar and the Imperial family received the people—peasants, merchants, clergy, beggars, all were free to stampede into the marble ballrooms, to stare and wonder and jostle the Grand Dukes, the beggars' greasy caftans pressed against the bemedalled tunics of the Chevaliers Gardes, and the crimson velvet, ermine-lined Court dress worn by the ladies-in-waiting. Though foreign visitors were astounded, both the Court and the crowds felt that this ceremony expressed democracy in its fullest sense. Only the Palace lackeys detested the custom, sulking as they presided over the extravagant buffet, scowling as they watched the ragged crowd clawing for caviar and sorbets, served on gold plate.

Magnificence reached its apogee at the Court Balls, to which the invited elect drove in their great gilded state coaches, accompanied by out-riders and preceded by runners, carrying flambeaux (a custom which continued until the turn of the century, and was only abandoned finally because of the unwieldy nature of the vehicles, causing indescribable confusion in the Palace courtyards, as they tried to manœuvre). These courtyards were each centred by a curious looking iron structure resembling a bandstand. They held enormous log fires which were replenished all through the night, and beside which the half-frozen coachmen stood, drinking hot *sbiten*—a ginger and honey mixture, while the horses were walked around, treadmill fashion, heavily blanketed, their breath steaming out in frozen puffs on the arctic air.

At the Palace, the liveries of the servants were almost as resplendent as the uniforms of the guests. The Empress was always followed by her negro pages, figures from Scheherezade's palace, turbaned and plumed, with enormous baggy trousers, while the Court Runners or messengers posted about the Palace wore feathered tricorn hats dating from the eighteenth century. All the members of the Imperial family were surrounded by their own suite, pages, ladies-in-waiting, chamberlains and aides-de-camp: the Grand Maître de la Cour, who, at the time of which I write, was the crumbling old Count Ribeaupierre, had begun as page to the Empress Catherine II and lived on solely for the intricacies of Court etiquette; he had been known to criticize even the Emperor, for what he considered a lapse in protocol. The Emperor, towering above his guests, a god-like figure, always opened the ball by dancing a polonaise; the Tzarina, who adored dancing, joined the two thousand guests who swarmed on to the shining expanses of parquet and danced uninterruptedly till dawn.

Thirty thousand candles shone from the huge crystal chandeliers, or were arranged spirally round the jasper pillars bordering the ballroom, and glittered over the fabulous jewels of this most lavish Court. 'One could literally trample on diamonds', wrote Horace Vernet. . . . 'One walked on pearls and rubies. It must be seen to be believed.' Even in 1553, an English visitor to the Court of Ivan the Terrible wrote home, 'I never heard nor saw people so sumptuous'. The Russian approach to jewels was wholly Oriental, totally lacking in restraint. Necklaces spilled down to their waists, great shimmering rivières of diamonds, whole hawsers of pearls, and saucer-sized brooches were set with rubies and emeralds as big as pigeon's eggs.

All around the ballroom were lesser salons of equal splendour; flowery groves for whispered rendezvous, or political intrigue; a malachite salon where favoured guests were received by the Tzarina; rotundas, *salles d'armes*, and an Arab room full of Moorish conceits, reserved for card-play. The state stairway was lined with immobile figures, Guards in splendid uniforms, standing to attention like Musée Grévin figures of servitude and loyalty. Everywhere gigantic mirrors reflected the brilliance; the jewels sparkled and shimmered as their wearers spun and dipped to the music of innumerable violins. Whole regiments of aides-de-camp bowed before numberless ranks of *dames du palais*, and leading them on to the floor, began the polonaise, with all its fierce stamping, wooing pantomime of conquest and submission. Among them, Djemmal-Eddin, dashing down the parquet, stamping his spurred boots before one of the Smolny beauties—youngest of the Tzarina's ladies, perhaps one of the beautiful Georgian princesses who were sent north to acquire Western polish and grace the Court with their languid loveliness. The mirrors reflected a fabulous world—world without end, it must have seemed to Djemmal-Eddin, bemused and enmeshed within it.

But outside, the night, the dread cold, those bundles of rags that dozed, crouched in doorways and died of hunger and exposure: all those miles of nothingness extending across all the Russias to the Arctic, to China, to Siberia—or to the Caucasian battlefield.

II

With the killing of Hadji Mourad, Shamyl was aware that the first shadow of defeat had fallen across his mountains. Although his former Naib had turned against him and was counted as an enemy, he had represented an influence only second to that of the Imam; Shamyl had been thinking of freeing his hostages with a view to securing, once more, Hadji Mourad's support. Now it was too late. The fact of his death at Russian hands had done much to gain the respect of the tribes. The Great White Sirdar had killed Hadji Mourad! Had cut off his head! *Aie! Aie!* He must be a mighty warrior! They bowed submissively, and a number of Daghestani aôuls went over to the Russians without more ado. A few fanatic bands vowed vengeance and joined Shamyl's men, but it was becoming increasingly apparent, now, that the Russians were gaining territory, prestige and support. They were learning the technique of guerilla warfare, coming to know the mountain terrain better: and their resources of men and money were poured into the struggle with the assurance that only limitless resources can give. They would win, and they knew it—in five years, in ten years, in half a century: it did not much matter when, or how. The Tzar's earlier sense of frustration, of humiliation at being baulked by a few savage tribes, had given place to a kind of inverted pride. The more savage and predatory the tribesmen, the longer the struggle, the more terrible the cost, the more importance and glory his armies assumed, in his eyes. Lives were cheap, and there was plenty of time.

But Shamyl, foreseeing the end, bitterly, foreseeing the destruction of his armies and territories, was still determined to make the Infidel pay.

The following account, by General Tornau, of one desperate defence, by Tchetchens, of their aôul, is typical of many such terrible engagements. An aôul had been stormed, and all that remained were three saklias, from which a band of desperate tribesmen were making their last stand. They were surrounded and vastly outnumbered, and when the Russian sappers succeeded in climbing over the roof-tops, and throwing lighted grenades down the wide chimneys, it was supposed they would be smoked out, at last. Not so.

Volkovsky, the commander, was sorry for the brave creatures and ordered his interpreter to tell them that if they would lay down their arms, he would spare their lives, and give them the right to be exchanged for Russian prisoners. . . . The defenders listened to the proposal, conferred together, and then a half-naked Tchetchen, black with smoke came out, made a short speech, followed by a volley from all the loopholes. What he said was this: 'The only grace we ask of the Russians is to let our families know we died as we lived, refusing submission to any foreign yoke.'

Orders were now given to fire the saklias from all sides. The sun had set, and the picture of destruction and ruin was lighted only by the red glow of the flames. The Tchetchens, firmly resolved to die, set up their death-song, loud at first, but sinking lower and lower as their numbers diminished under the influence of fire and smoke. However, death by fire is a terrible agony, such as all had not strength to bear. There was a flash; a bullet whistled past our ears, and brandishing his sword, a Tchetchen dashed straight at us. Artarshtchikov let the raging desperado come within ten paces, quietly took aim, and put a bullet in his bare breast. The Tchetchen sprang high in the air, fell, rose again to his feet, stretched himself to his full length, and bending slowly forward, fell dead on his native soil. Five minutes later the scene was repeated; another sprang out, fired his gun, and brandishing his sword, broke through two lines of sharp-shooters, to fall bayoneted by the third. The burning saklias began to fall asunder, scattering sparks on the trampled garden. . . . Not one Tchetchen was taken alive; seventy-two men ended their lives in the flames!

The last act of the bloody drama was played out; night covered the scene. Each one had done his duty according to his conscience; the chief actors had gone their way into eternity: the rest, together with the mere spectators, with hearts like lead, sought the refuge of their tents; and maybe more than one, in the depth of his being, asked himself, why must such things be? Is there no room for all on this earth without distinction of speech and faith?

Shamyl, his faith like his pride, remained firm: he meant to prolong the struggle until there was no one left to fight, not one man, woman or child. Was he still avenging an outraged Allah, or had a purely personal desperation now crept into his resistance? Outwardly, he remained the same great and terrible figure, his pale face inscrutable, framed in its dark beard, scarlet with henna, vivid against his sombre black bourka, and huge chieftain's turban. His slit-eyes still glittered as he surveyed his threatened mountain kingdom. And he still indulged, most successfully, in those theatrical effects, which maintained so much of his legend. While relying on thunder-storms, heavenly bodies and other natural phenomena to produce what he described as direct answers to prayer, he sometimes organized a theatrical coup which never failed to impress the mountaineers. Here is a contemporary account of one such manœuvre.

A great attack was to be made on a Russian encampment. When the morning came, Shamyl caused it to be reported that he was dead, but that in dying, he had left word that they, his followers, should not fail to carry out his plans, and that his spirit would be with them accordingly. They went, disheartened to the place of the battle. Shamyl watched them from afar, and on the instant when he saw they wavered, he descended from the mountains, and as his white charger came sweeping over the plains, all thought it bore his ghost, and the cry of *Shamyl! Shamyl!* rang along the battlelines, above the sounds of the strife, and electrified every heart; but when his bright sabre, like lightning, was seen cleaving the enemy, his hosts became invincible; they fought like madmen and were victorious.

No matter how heavy the odds, Shamyl always knew how to reach his warriors; his rhetoric too always inspired them to fresh feats of valour. 'If we are not victorious, let the slaughter we make of those Christian dogs atone fully for our defeat' was now the usual tone of his address before battle. And, on the eve, he would say: 'We sleep tonight as beneath the veil which, lifting, reveals to us the glories of our Prophet's abode in Paradise; and tomorrow, when we fight in his name, be sure that wherever you see floating the black banner of your chief, there will be Allah, and know that his defence is swift and strong.'

'Mashallah!' answered the Naibs and Murids, gathered before the mosque, from which Shamyl habitually addressed his forces. 'Mashallah! In the name of God!' The cry broke from the crowds and echoed round the bare hills, to rumble like faraway thunders, across the vast and empty valleys, while the sound of women wailing for their doomed men was lost in the turmoil of an army on the move.

III

Although Shamyl's word was still absolute, his whole system of government was such that he could not altogether ignore the wishes of his Naibs, or the chieftains allied to him. Sometimes their demands forced him to act against his own convictions. When, in 1852 his Naibs denounced Daoudilaou of Tchokh, one of the Imam's most devoted followers, and celebrated throughout the Caucasus as the finest sword-smith and jeweller, even Shamyl was unable to defend him. He was accused of treachery; the evidence, supplied by his enemies, seemed conclusive, and he was exiled to one of the most inaccessible aôuls, Tchitil, 'the aôul without sun'. It was used largely as a place of banishment. It clung high on the mountainside, overshadowed by two great peaks, so that its inhabitants lived in a perpetual twilight. The sun only reached it in summer, in one spot, and for a short while. Then the women would rush into the patch of sunlight, to weave, or mend, something they could not see to do in their dark, unlit houses.

To this grim aôul Daoudilaou, his wife, baby son Fazil, and eight-year-old daughter Kistaman were sent. Very early one morning they had been torn from their home without warning: Daoudilaou's wife had been combing her dark hair when the guards came. She was dragged out, the comb still in her hand. They had no money, no belongings, with which to start again. But Kistaman set about teaching Arabic and the Koran to the children: her father had insisted on a very strict education; now her learning served them well. For every lesson she was paid in food. Thus, the family were enabled to eat. Gradually they established themselves, and Daoudilaou again produced his wonderful swords. In the Caucasus, an armourer is never without work. But the unjust exile and disgrace, continued for another two years. No word came from Shamyl or Khazi Mahommed, his son, both of whom, Daoudilaou believed, would try to clear him.

One winter day in 1855, as the dark clouds hung over the peaks, and snow lay deep, there was a sound of gun-fire. It echoed ominously, and the people knew the Russians must be somewhere in the valleys, far below. But they were unlikely to try and reach the aôul through such snowdrifts. That night, three hooded figures, wrapped in bourkas, knocked on Daoudilaou's door, asking for him; Kistaman admitted them; her father was out. They asked for food and shelter; one of them was wounded, he was young and handsome but his manner was imperious, which Kistaman resented. As she dressed his wound, he asked her name, and when she told him, he said he found it a very ugly one. At which she lost her temper and replied: 'Such insolence! Who do you think you are? The Naib Khazi Mahommed?'

The stranger laughed: he seemed to enjoy her spirit. When Daoudilaou returned, the two men flung themselves into each other's arms. It was Khazi Mahommed himself. The young Naib of Karaty had escaped a Russian trap while trying to reach 'the aôul without sun'. He had wanted to tell Daoudilaou to have patience; he was not forgotten, and before long his name would be cleared, his calumniators subdued, and his exile ended. When at last Daoudilaou was freed, it was due to Khazi Mahommed's secret efforts. This episode was to have a profound effect on Khazi Mahommed's later life.

IV

Sometimes Shamyl still wrested a victory, but more often now the battles went to the Russians. Even so, the Imam himself emerged unscathed from the carnage, never faint-hearted, and always ready to re-form, and attack again. He still knew the country better than his enemy, still used its natural defences as his own, and was still aided by numbers of Polish and Russian deserters, who trained and directed his meagre batteries, which, from unassailable mountain vantage points, still accounted for terrible losses among the enemy.

But one battle was won by Voronzov's cunning; pure foxiness, instead

of military strategy. The battle had gone against the Russians, and
when night came, after terrible slaughter on both sides, the Murids had
entrenched themselves at Saltee, in great strength; they intended to
finish off the remaining Russians at dawn, before reinforcements could
arrive. But during the night, Voronvoz sent a small party to dam and
divert the stream which ran beside the Murid camp. It was a simple,
but ingenious piece of strategy, and it was entirely effective. Left without water to drink, and, above all, left without water with which to
perform their ritual ablutions, the Murids lost the day. The garrison of
Saltee put up a most desperate resistance, one which was unequalled in
the Murid Wars, except, perhaps, by that of Akhulgo, or Tchokh, but
at last, after a bombardment of big mortars, which continued all day,
the trapped Murids knew themselves beaten, and were given the order
to make their get-away, or die fighting. No one was to be taken alive.

At dusk, the main body of fugitives, carrying with them their
banners, one pathetic home-made cannon, an affair of wood and
leather of a type they had constructed and used before obtaining a few
captured guns, were intercepted in a defile below the aôul, where a
Russian company, under Major Count Orhelm, put them to death
there and then. The few stragglers who were found escaping singly, or
in pairs, fought desperately, but were bayoneted. The valleys swarmed
with riderless horses, quietly cropping the scrub, or whinnying for those
masters who would never return to gallop them over the hills.
Shamyl and a handful of Murids had fought their way to a rock above
the aôul, and from there, had escaped to the heights. 'As they wound
their way high up along the edge of the mountain, the moon burst out
from a dark cloud, and Shamyl, on his black charger, bearing the
banner of the Prophet, was seen by the Russians far below. His bright
steel coat of mail glittered in the light, and he seemed a spirit resting
half-way between heaven and earth; his sacred standard waved amid
the clouds, and his noble animal, fearless as its rider, had advanced to
the very brink of the rock, waiting, motionless, among the faithful few
that had so signally escaped death. . . . And now this discomfited band
filed along the summits of these great barriers they thought no enemy
could ever pass, or dare assail, and looking down on the distant and
diminutive mosque and minaret, and the fatal rivulet still glistening in
the moonlight like a silver thread, all were silent as the shadows about
them. But as each one reached the highest ledge, where Shamyl had
paused, each one drew rein, and paused, too, giving a last prayer of
farewell to the graves of his fallen comrades in the valley below; then,
turning his horse's head, followed his chieftain to those caverns and
distant haunts of the mountains which were still their own.'

They had lost Saltee; they were losing battle after battle. But the
Russians were still not masters of the Caucasus.

22

Bariatinsky

*In my cradle lay the marching route for
the whole of my life.*   HEINE

And now, the towering figure of Field-Marshal Prince Alexander
Bariatinsky limps across the Greater Tchetchnia and stands confronting
Shamyl. This northern giant was a strange character, a mixture of
discipline and dissolute living, one of the greatest generals, Voronzov's
successor as Viceroy, and Shamyl's conqueror. He was a Petersburg
Lothario who forswore all the adulation and privilege of Court life, as
the Tzarievitch's closest friend, to return to the Caucasus, where he had
first won glory, banished there in disgrace as a very young man in 1833.
In 1851, he was appointed commander of the Left Flank, and began
to win, battle by battle, those victories which were to culminate in
Shamyl's final surrender.

Prince Bariatinsky was born in 1815. A few days after his birth, a
horoscope, believed to have been cast by a Masonic lodge, was left,
mysteriously, on the steps of the house. It foretold his life of victories,
of triumphs in the East, and it also warned him of the supreme powers
and responsibilities that would be his, emphasizing that his true great-
ness would lie in, and through, his mercy towards the fallen. All this
was prophetic. But the horoscope does not seem to have foreseen the
drama brought about by the Field-Marshal's love for the wife of one of
his staff officers: it was to cost Bariatinsky his Viceroyship, thus depriv-
ing not only the Caucasus of his enlightened rule, but Russia of his
vision and grasp of international politics. As to the Prince himself, it
condemned him to a declining life of exile and regret.

To return to his splendid morning: he belonged to that small but
puissant aristocracy of Europe, which, encompassed by the Almanach
de Gotha, dictated the terms of war and peace between that world
which they divided between themselves. They intermarried, loved,
duelled, schemed, visited, manœuvred and out-manœuvred each other
ceaselessly. But it was all among gentlemen. They had measured each
other long, long ago and knew they would all abide by the rules. The

old Prince Simon Voronzov, writing to Count Stroganov (who succeeded him as Ambassador to London), spoke of the more regrettable consequences of Napoleon's victories as being the sort of thing which always arose when one dealt with parvenus.

Prince Bariatinsky's mother had been a Princess Seyn-Wittgenstein, daughter of the German Ambassador to St. Petersburg. His grandmother, the Princess of Holstein Beck, a first cousin of the Tzar Peter III. Prince Alexander was the eldest son; he and his three brothers, the Princes Vladimir, Anatole and Victor, spent much of their youth at the Courts of Vienna and Berlin. There was, in Prince Alexander, a marked Germanic strain—an exactitude, a concentration, and a total absence of that mysticism so typical of *l'âme slave*. Like Voronzov, his education had made him international, disciplined, and worldly; yet, like Voronzov, he remained, first of all, a great Russian nationalist.

His father had drawn up a most minute educational schedule for his first-born son. Since the Prince was so remarkable a man, so great a general, whose tactics at last subdued the Caucasus, let us follow his early training in some detail. His father, like Prince Voronzov, was an Anglophile; he believed in a severe, but well-balanced, education. Until the age of five, the child was to be left to women. The next two years were to harden his body: cold baths, gymnastics, fencing and riding unbroken horses. At seven, learning: languages, with especial emphasis on Russian, which few of the Russian aristocracy then bothered to speak correctly; French, German, Italian and English were followed by Latin, Greek, and Arabic; poetry, elocution, mathematics, engineering, experimental agriculture and carpentry were added; these last, to give him a practical bent. After some years of such intensive studies, the young Prince left Russia for five years of travel, all over Europe, accompanied by a troop of tutors, a doctor, a chemist, a botanist and a mechanic, the better to appreciate every aspect of the lands in which he found himself. The same pedagogic entourage next accompanied him on a tour of his homeland—two years across European and Asiatic Russia. His exigent parent had further stipulated that his son, on attaining manhood, should occupy himself with the welfare of his serfs and estates; these were at Ivanovskoye, in southern central Russia, in the province of Kursk. Later he might enter the Ministry of the Interior, or of Finance, but was under no circumstances to embrace a military, diplomatic, or Court career. Such was his father's last will and testament, bequeathing everything to his eldest son. But the young Prince decided otherwise. At the age of sixteen, under the spell of a dashing Guards' officer friend, he decided to enter the army. In vain his widowed mother pleaded with him to continue at the Moscow University. No tears or threats availed. He was the eldest son: he had inherited the title, the power and the glory. He would choose his own life. At last the family quarrel reached the ears of the Empress, who supported him, appointing him to her own regiment, the Chevaliers Gardes. In 1831, he was an established figure among the *jeunesse dorée* of the capital. At eighteen, he was notorious for his good looks and dissipation. He was immensely tall, 'a Bogatyr figure', who subjugated all the ladies as much by his scandalous aura as his enormous wealth and historic title. (The Bariatinskys were the only noble family directly related to the Romanovs.) His dissipation became the talk of St. Petersburg, ranking only second in interest to that of the Grand Dukes, yet the strictly watched Tzarievitch was his closest friend; and Bariatinsky was one of the Royal party visiting the young Queen Victoria at Windsor in 1838, where he was admitted (as a temporary member) to several of the most select London clubs.

Although no doubt his visit was conducted in circumstances of unimpeachable propriety, upon his return to St. Petersburg a wild life was resumed, and since his military studies were always relegated to the background, Bariatinsky was presently disgraced, by failing to pass the required examinations. Posted to a slightly less elegant regiment, the Gatchina Cuirassiers, he continued his spectacular *train de vie*, scandal piling upon scandal, until the Emperor at last showed his awful displeasure, telling the young Prince he must reform. At which Bariatinsky, flying to extremes, asked to be sent to the Caucasus. The Tzarievitch begged him not to go; so did the Empress, who had an especial weakness for him. All the Grand Dukes were inconsolable; as to Princess 'Ollie', the Tzar's favourite daughter, she was sick for love of the young Prince. But he did not return her devotion. On the contrary, he was passionately enamoured of an Austrian princess; but being thwarted in this love, and having no wish to be cornered by a Royal alliance, he turned towards the Caucasus with that sense of gratitude which so many others shared. Its great peaks offered escape—forgetfulness—another way of life. The Tzar had been displeased by the young Bariatinsky's conduct, and uneasy as to the sort of influence he exercised over the Tzarievitch. It could lead to trouble . . . He arranged that Bariatinsky should be transferred, at once, to serve under Veliaminov, with a regiment of Black Sea Cossacks.

'Tell the Emperor that though I may be wicked, I can also be loyal', wrote young Bariatinsky to his friends at Court. He was not yet twenty when he proved his mettle, fighting a most spectacular engagement against the tribes, last survivor of a cornered band. Terribly wounded, he had fought on single-handed, for which he was promoted and given a gold sabre by the Tzar, who, like all his Court, now welcomed back the reinstated young hero sent home from the front to recuperate. His advancement was rapid: for the next fifteen years he went between the Caucasian front and the capital, alternately fighting, being wounded, recovering, and returning to fight once more; and ever, eluding marriage.

In 1848 he had been given leave to go abroad, to convalesce at one of the German spas. But passing through Warsaw, from where Field-Marshal Prince Paskiévitch was about to set out to suppress the Hungarian risings, he could not resist the Prince's offer to join him. The offer had been made rather in the manner of one sportsman proposing some rather good rough shooting to another. Bariatinsky found military life far more to his taste than idling at a spa, and he spent some weeks on active service, again covering himself with glory.

II

At this time, the dedicated Russian officers, whether serving in the Caucasus or not, usually found some means of keeping their hand in. There were so many frontiers to be defended; so many hostile tribes to subdue; so many local insurrections to quell. And in 1849, a large number of regiments were suddenly ordered west, to defend the tottering Hapsburg dynasty against Hungarian revolutionaries—desperadoes —or so the alarmed courts of Berlin and Vienna believed them to be. From 1848 to 1849, the monarchists of Europe trembled. Riots swept Paris. There was revolution in Vienna and Berlin. In September 1848, Kossuth was proclaimed dictator of Hungary, and the whole ferment of central European politics broke loose. (Beyond the perimeter of battle, Thackeray published *The Book of Snobs*; the Pre-Raphaelite brotherhood was formed, and gold was discovered in California. And—less dramatic, but as heroic—the Chartist Riots shook England's complacency.)

With the new year, Hungary declared independence from Austrian rule. The young Emperor Franz-Joseph quailed. His generals had proved quite incapable of stemming the fiery tide. In France, King Louis-Philippe had abdicated and Rome was declared a Republic, under Mazzini.

The trumpet had sounded.

Franz-Joseph turned towards the one man whom he believed strong enough to restore order. He appealed to the Tzar Nicholas—the policeman of Europe—to save the Hapsburg throne. No cause could have been more dear to the Tzar, for he believed profoundly in the divine right of kings. Every throne that trembled menaced his own. He acted swiftly. One hundred and fifty thousand men, led by a Cossack regiment and commanded once again by Paskiévitch, marched westwards overnight. (Some regiments were even taken straight from the parade-ground, without any proper equipment, so urgent did Nicholas consider the Hungarian crisis.)

Until now, the magnificent fighting qualities of the Magyars had repelled and overcome all Austria's might. They out-generalled them, and out-fought them. They were fighting for something in which they believed passionately—their freedom from the Austrian yoke. But when the limitless Russian forces poured in, they were overwhelmed and sank beneath the sheer weight of numbers, bearing out Stendhal's definition of the art of war: 'It simply consists in seeing to it that you have two soldiers on the battlefield to every one of the enemy.' The Hungarian forts which had resisted every Austrian assault were battered into submission by Russian cannon; the men impaled on Russian bayonets. *Hungary lies at your Majesty's feet*, wired Paskiévitch, echoing earlier announcements of victory over other rebellious peoples, also achieved by weight of numbers.

Thus the Hapsburg throne was secured for a number of years to come, lasting, indeed, a year or two longer than that of the Romanovs. As to Russia's timely aid—it was soon forgotten. The Crimean War presently revealed that Franz-Joseph's protestations of eternal gratitude were empty phrases: he did not come to the aid of Nicholas at that crucial hour: in fact, he was to turn against him.

III

In 1847, Bariatinsky had been responsible for launching a series of successful attacks against Shamyl, and in 1848, after the taking of Gherghibil, he was made a major-general of the Tzar's retinue: the Court wanted him back among them—alive. Better a live courtier than a dead general, they said, and set about finding him a bride. At thirty-five, limping and scarred, he was even more irresistible to women, but his amours had been at last brought to a standstill by the wife of one of his officers. It was a fatal passion, encompassing, at last, his ruin; but first there were many years of intrigue and dalliance, power and glory.

After a period of hard fighting, and more ill-health (for wounds, coupled with gout, legacy of his youthful debauches, laid him low from time to time), the Prince was once more in St. Petersburg. But he indicated that he had no intention of marrying into the Court, or living any life other than a rigorous military one. He made over all his properties to his brother, and the better to kill any lingering thoughts that he was a *parti*, grew shaggy side-whiskers, cut short his romantic curls, wore a rather shabby uniform (although plastered in medals and the most enviable orders) and affected even more of a limp than his many wounds had left him. But the ladies were not deceived; he was still the most fascinating creature, at all costs to be snared. However, the Prince was seldom seen about town, spending most of his time studying books concerning the Caucasus, and working with the Tzar's staff officers, analysing and correcting past campaigns. He criticized

Yermolov's tactics; above all, the General's frequent breaks in fighting. He agreed with Veliaminov that the Caucasus could be likened to a gigantic fortress, only to be stormed by continual assault. He was, the Court at last perceived, a dedicated soldier and a most obstinate man.

In 1847, the Tzar had appointed him, on Voronzov's request, to command the Kabardinsky regiment, and to direct the fighting of the Left Flank. At last Bariatinsky was obtaining the recognition and positions of responsibility he had wished. From now on he was to live entirely in, and for, the Caucasus. It was the consummation of his dreams. Nevertheless, he decided to make his life in the south one of magnificence. A whole fleet of boats flying the Bariatinsky colours, blue and yellow, took him down the Volga, surrounded by all the trappings of a great prince: his bloodstock, his cellar, his library, pianos, silver dinner ser ices, chefs and a hundred other luxuries. He intended to raise the whole tone and style of his regiment.

The men awaited their new chief with impatience; with apprehension, too. He was known to be worldly, haughty and distant; no one was admitted to his intimacy, although he was a generous host. Above all, he was a merciless disciplinarian, before whose frown the most seasoned soldiers trembled. Every detail of regimental administration was known to him. Now, the wide range of his education came into play, and the sumpters and the engineers, the grooms and the cashiers, like the sappers and priests, staff officers or doctors, all found him a tireless, eagle-eyed chief. Any man could come to him, at any time, for he removed all the barriers which surrounded former commanders. Administrative injustices were quelled, and the whole tone of his regiment was raised. Every evening he held court in his tent, or at his headquarters, where his lavish hospitality conjured an atmosphere of unimaginable luxury. He was a curious mixture of generosity and harshness. Like Voronzov, he made the gestures of a great seigneur.— When the regiment was found lacking in certain equipment, he provided it from his own pocket. Yet he intimidated most people, displaying an arrogance which was inbred, involuntary. Tolstoy, in his journals, during his period of military service in the Caucasus, writes: 'I made the Prince's acquaintance during a raid under his command, in which I took part, in 1851, and afterwards, spent a day with him, in a fortress. . . . Undoubtedly I am gaining little amusement from the acquaintance, for you will understand the footing on which a subaltern stands towards his general.' And again, writing of the Olympian figure, and the shades of social grading which ruled the army, he describes an apothecary's assistant—a Pole, reduced to the ranks for some political misdemeanour: 'A most entertaining creature. I am sure Prince Bariatinsky never imagined that he could ever stand side by side with an apothecary's assistant, but so it is, for Nicolenka is on a very good footing here—both the commander and the officers all love and respect him.'

By the early 'fifties, Prince Bariatinsky was appointed commander-in-chief of the Left Flank, and his full stature as fighter, tactician and administrator was recognized unreservedly. Though as a man—as a Lothario—there were sometimes mutterings of criticism. Not every husband was as blind as Prince Simon Voronzov, or Bariatinsky's staff-captain, the easy-going Davidov. The frequent presence at the General's camp of either the Princess Marie Voronzov, or Madame Davidova still occasioned comment. The latter, born the Princess Elizabeth Orbeliani, was descended from the feudal princes of Erbil, in the Persian province of Iraq. She was a diminutive little creature, as darkly beautiful as a Persian miniature. She was, besides, possessive and audacious. . . . People shrugged. . . . If the husband did not object—nor the Tzar— nor the Viceroy. . . . Well, then? A few allusions to Mars and Venus generally closed the subject gracefully, till it was reopened by further gossip. Though no doubt the Prince (unaware of the future) would have subscribed to the views expressed by the proud Russian lady who said, 'None but *low* people can be affected by scandal, inasmuch as censure can only proceed from superiors.'

The Prince, as a threat to domestic bliss, raised the liveliest apprehensions. Tolstoy records a conversation with his friend Gorchakov, who had confided in him that 'the mere thought of Bariatinsky shatters all my dreams of married happiness. This man is so brilliant in every respect, possesses so many external qualities superior to mine, that I cannot but imagine that my wife might, one day, prefer him to myself. Just to think of this robs me of the peace and contentment, worse still, of the self-confidence and pride which are the essential attributes of love between men and wife.' Tolstoy tried to be consoling, but there is no doubt Bariatinsky inspired as much terror among husbands, as he did among the tribesmen.

IV

During the winter of 1851 and the spring of 1852, the Russians embarked on what might be regarded as the final conquest of the Tchetchnia, beginning with a large-scale attack based from the fortress of Vozdivzhensky. Bariatinsky, as commander, was employing new, encircling tactics. By a series of outflanking manœuvres, then new in Caucasian warfare where direct head-on battle had been usual, with appalling loss of life, he was now able to achieve victories while reducing his losses of men. There were other strategies, too—Bariatinsky's highly-coloured personality appealed to the mountaineers, and he knew how to play on them. His sense of theatre, of dramatic self-presentation almost equalled Shamyl's. Upon one occasion, having subdued a large body of Tchetchens, with terrible fighting on both sides, he accepted their surrender, and then, giving them back their swords, dismissed his own men, and ordered the Tchetchens to guard him while he slept.

His slumbers, like his labours, were all directed to one end—mastery of the Caucasus. Besides his personal methods of impressing the tribesmen, he inaugurated a more elaborate spy-system, and set about restoring and reorganizing the conquered aôuls. This was conducted in such a manner that the mountaineers soon believed they had little to fear from their conquerors, being helped to rebuild their homes, while their farm-lands and cattle were replenished. The civil administration was confided to locally elected rulers, not necessarily the mollahs. This new system of local government was headed by Colonel Bartolomei, a distinguished Orientalist who had had much experience of Moslem communities.

Bariatinsky's clemency was the outcome of his theories regarding the conduct of the Caucasian wars; but, perhaps, too, he recalled the mysterious horoscope which had foretold his greatest glories would be achieved through mercy. Even in the matter of hard fighting, of raiding, and punitive expeditions, Bariatinsky's new approach was to be seen. 'It had been the custom to rush the aôuls by night when, taken by surprise, the women and children had no time to escape, and the horrors that ensued under cover of darkness, when the Russian soldiers made their way by twos and threes, into the houses, were such as no official narrator dared to describe', writes J. F. Baddeley. Under Bariatinsky, the villages were still, it is true, approached and surprised by night, 'but'—here Mr. Baddeley quotes from the Russian military archives—'they were first bombarded. The inhabitants, roused by the firing, ran out from their houses, and the contest that followed, in the streets or outskirts of the aôuls, was an open, honest fight. The women and children and helpless old men were no longer ruthlessly slaughtered on their own hearths; they were taken prisoners under the eyes of the Russian leaders, as soon as the village was in our hands; if, as in some of the saklias, the defence continued, these were battered down by artillery fire, or taken by storm, and this was always accompanied by less loss in men than the former system under which the troops penetrated, two or three at a time, into unknown, half-lighted, or even wholly unlighted, houses. And the morale of the soldiers improved.'

Prince Bariatinsky's next reforms were concentrated on the land itself—the battle terrain. By constructing a series of bridges across the chasms of the Mitchik gorge, he opened up the high plateaux of the Tchetchnia, so that, in winter or summer, an army on the march could cross directly, without the former agonizing series of descents and ascents. During this time he also began a systematic clearing of the great forests from which the Murids had been able to fight, and win, so many battles. Stroke by stroke, the Russian axes felled the trees, clearing the scrub and tangled vegetation, destroying at each blow the Murids' defence bastions. Timber had always been Shamyl's greatest natural resource and he treasured it accordingly, imposing very heavy fines on any man found cutting wood for his own purposes: sometimes, the culprit was hung from a high beech tree and left to rot, awful warning to other, would-be timber thieves.

Prince Bariatinsky's legion of woodcutters were defended by whole regiments of artillery, and Shamyl's men could never get within fighting distance. Their own few guns were hopelessly outranged; volunteers for hand-to-hand fighting were shot down as they advanced. There was nothing Shamyl could do. Far above the forests, from high on the mountains, standing in bitter immobility, he watched his doom approach; his telescope was fixed on the clearings far below, where the tiny ant-like figures could be seen, their axes catching a gleam of sunlight, as they raised them, to fell the great trees, his allies, brought low, as one day he too must be.

23

Madame Drancy

*There are no moments in our life that are without
consequence or significance for the future. Mektoub!
It is written.*   ISABELLE EBERHARDT

It is through the eyes of a French woman, a small, sharp, insignificant
French governess, that we are able to see Shamyl at first hand, in his
aôul, surrounded by his wives and children, holding his councils of
war, riding out to battle or returning to woo his youngest wife; it is
through her eyes—far from objective, in their evaluation, however, for
she was the Iman's prisoner—that we learn something of his daily life
during the last years of his glory, from July 1854 to March 1855. Since
the abortive meeting with General Klugenau, in 1837, no one outside
of the Murid ranks had ever seen Shamyl face to face, save certain
prisoners as he passed sentence, or that Mozdok merchant, Shouanete's
cousin, who was allowed to visit her in 1848.

Shamyl had become an abstraction of enmity, a force of nature
mysteriously directing his campaigns from the unattainable summits of
his mountains. He had become a myth, and the Russian soldiers now
shared the Murid view that he was not as other men. 'He' was there,
somewhere among those dark peaks, watching them, by day and night.
'He' was indestructible, rising after each defeat, to fall on them again.

But now, a matter-of-fact Frenchwoman appears on the scene to
pierce the veils of mystery surrounding Shamyl the Avar. Anna Drancy
steps forward, a neatly dressed, brisk figure, unpacking her rather
shabby calfskin portmanteau at a second-class Tiflis hotel, and, a year
later, no longer so neat or so brisk, arriving at the Imam's aôul by a
strange and circuitous route.

She was born in Paris, in 1822. Her parents, François and Louise
Lemaire, were petty-bourgeois stock, and they lived in a tall grey house
in the Rue des Acacias. A portrait of her at eighteen shows us a pertly
pretty girl, in a bare-shouldered lace dress, with ribbons and a fan.
She glances out enquiringly, her head held sideways, her bird-bright
eyes full of audacity. By 1843 she had married a 'limonadier', or seller

of soft-drinks, who also worked as a chef and restaurant-keeper, Jean-Baptiste Auguste Drancy. Two years later the couple separated. A son had been born in 1843, and Anna, her husband having left her, returned to live with her parents. But eight years later, seeking independence and, perhaps, adventure too, she decided to set up a business in Tiflis. Why she chose so remote a place we do not know. Her grandsons told me they believed she had gone there to open a French library. She was, they said, energetic, courageous, and *très fine*.

There were no bookshops in Tiflis in the late 'forties, and only one house with bookshelves, says a visitor. But perhaps Anna had heard how French literature was all the rage there, although the importation of French journals and newspapers was subject to heavy Russian censorship. Foreign newspapers were not generally allowed. In 1839, the French Consul was only permitted to receive the *Journal des Débats* on the condition it was never shown to any Russian subject. If the news it printed were considered offensive by the censor, the copy was confiscated, or the passage in question snipped out. One local paper and the *Petersburg Gazette* were all that was officially obtainable (though the reader may recall that Shamyl contrived to obtain a number of foreign and Russian newspapers, and have them read to him by his interpreters).

Nevertheless, some foreigners did settle and prosper in Tiflis, usually opening bonnet shops, or restaurants. So, for one reason or another, adventure or commerce, Madame Drancy packed up, put her child to school in England, at Stockton, where the mayor was a family friend, and set off eastwards—one woman against the fates.

II

Even as late as the 1850's travellers who journeyed to the Caucasus took their lives in their hands: the mountain brigands, the lawlessness and ferocity of 'the Tartars', in general, beside the battles which had raged for so long, made any journey a desperate undertaking. Moreover, nature took a hand, and showed herself at her most menacing. Avalanches lunged down from the mountains, blocking the only road through the Darial Pass, for as much as three months at a time. Heavy snow-storms blocked the way, and as they melted, raged down to swell the rivers and carry away the bridges. Those more prudent travellers who attempted the longer coast approach by way of Constantinople and the Black Sea, often found themselves in as great a danger, from shipwreck, or the threat of marauding bands of Tcherkess, who although driven inland by the Russians' seizure of the coast, still lurked balefully, and were in the habit of putting out in small boats to attack them under cover of darkness, or lay in wait, along the shores, for boats beset by submerged rocks, thick mists and other hazards. Ships which went aground were not always sighted and protected by a Russian man o'-war. Then, by means of signal fires, they would hope to attract the attention of the Cossack patrols, who would encamp on the shore to prevent attack by tribesmen. The Tcherkess were watching from all along the chain of mountains which dominate the coast, and ever ready to gallop down and snatch their prize from under the Russians' noses. Mr. Ditson, an American traveller—the first of his race to visit the Caucasus, he claims—spent an uneasy night on board a grounded vessel which lay off the coast, near Novorossisk, in 1850: he feared the Black Sea might whip up one of its sudden storms and dash them, literally, on to the waiting daggers of the Tcherkess.

In the morning Mr. Ditson peered through a telescope at his would-be assassins with a sort of morbid fascination—that of the rabbit for the snake. He found them a handsome lot, 'tall, splendidly formed men. Each had his gun swung on his back, and a silver-mounted knife hanging at his belt. Their long drab, well-fitting frocks, their black, fur-bordered caps, their glittering arms, their stately carriage, gave them an extremely interesting appearance. But when, presently, a transport ship came to our relief, and anchored not far from us, not a Circassian was to be seen. When hope of plunder ceased, they sprang into their saddles, each one taking the path which led to his own valley or cliff.'

Novorossisk had been taken by the Russians in 1838, and besides the soldiers, had a population of one thousand, almost all of them fugitives from justice, felons, runaway serfs, and escaped murderers. The Emperor, with a view to colonizing his new territories, had published an ukase pardoning, unequivocally, all who would settle there. Thus, a scarcely less cut-throat lot surrounded the traveller who was congratulating himself on his escape from the Tartars.

Beside the exotic and the dramatic aspects of this land, there were other, sullen aspects. One large body of water inland was known as the Putrid Sea; its stagnant, foul-smelling waters were dreaded by man and beast alike; fevers bred there, and were carried far afield. . . . Along the Caspian, too, were noxious marshes, brackish wastes where only poisonous insects throve—scorpions, and a species of bed-bug which fell on the passing caravans, and whose bite was sometimes fatal. The Caspian, like the Black Sea, could show a sinister side, and storms would whip across its expanses, suddenly and violently. Just as the Black Sea earned its name less for its dark, inky-blue colour than for its malevolent moods, so the Caspian was held to be possessed by a Grey Spirit. 'At moments an unnatural stillness fell—the sun's rays were withdrawn. Sea and sky became one dull grey, the cypresses looked, more than ever, sombre and funereal, and the croak of the frogs sounded harsher and more dismal. The wind whistled across the hills, and the jackals, fancying that the sun had set, began their nightly howling, creeping stealthily among the orange trees.'

Whether Madame Drancy reached Tiflis overland, or by boat by the Black Sea, we do not know; but by the end of 1852 she had arrived there, and was occupied with some kind of commercial enterprise. By midsummer 1853, relations between Russia and France were becoming strained. The first rumblings of the Crimean War were to be heard, though the conflict was not to break out for another nine months—on April 3, 1854. But whatever Anna Drancy's business, it did not prosper. If it were a French library, then she must have discovered the increasing difficulty of importing books from France, to say nothing of the conditions of transport within the Russian frontiers. Nor did she have much help from the French Consul, a Monsieur de Berrère, who took sick leave about now, and seems to have been too occupied with his health to have taken any active part in Consular administration. His assistant, a Monsieur Steyert, later stated that his chief had sent no reports or information to his government since early in 1851. In February 1854, the French Ministry of Foreign Affairs informed the Consulate of a rupture between the French and Russian governments. In May, the sickly Monsieur de Berrère rose from the *chaise-longue*, and closed the Consulate. It remained shut until 1856; French citizens who remained in Tiflis were marooned. During the war, their interests were handled from St. Petersburg by the Bavarian Minister; and it was through the Bavarian Foreign Office, via Munich, that occasional letters from Madame Drancy reached her anxious family in Paris.

The Crimean War was particularly tragic since it was, in the first place, unnecessary: the governments concerned were each activated by a fevered bellicosity—war for war's sake, their quarrels based on the most unreal motives. Suddenly, the descendants of those Crusaders who fought with St. Louis and Richard Cœur de Lion found themselves fighting beside the age-old Mahommedan foe, dying to defend a Moslem country which for almost a thousand years Europe had been trying to drive from the Christian continent. It did not make sense. But some English Russophobes, Lord Palmerston and Sir Stratford Canning in particular, derived great satisfaction from the thought that Russia, the bugbear, was being beaten down at last, on no matter what pretext. Ever since the defeat of Napoleon, Russia's voice had been heard too loud: first the Tzar Alexander, lording it over the Congress of Vienna, and now this Nicholas, whom they considered insufferably interfering. His nickname, 'the policeman of Europe', irked them, too; English statesmen were wont to regard policemanship as their own prerogative, whether in Europe or Asia. As to Napoleon III—the Bonaparte upstart as he was regarded by most Royal Houses—he was frankly delighted to dispatch his ill-equipped army to the Crimea; it distracted the French people from governmental shortcomings at home. Besides, it was a splendid means of paying back the Tzar's patronage. The manner in which Nicholas had snubbed Louis-Napoleon had not been forgotten: the bilious-looking little Frenchman still writhed when he recalled the occasion, his accession to the Imperial throne, and how he had sent out the customary letters, monarch to monarch, circularizing all the European courts, addressing each ruler in the traditional format, *Sire et cher cousin*. But Nicholas, the Romanov, had not deigned to consider a Bonaparte of equal blood, and in replying, he rather pointedly omitted *cher cousin*.

During the spring and summer of 1854, the Caucasus was a clearing house for troops and war supplies which were being rushed south to the Crimea to stem the massing of English, French and Turkish armies who now threatened Russia all along her southern frontiers. The more domestic issues of the Murid Wars were almost halted; a token force, under General Réad, still held the mountaineers at bay, but no major engagements took place, only being resumed in all their force, at the end of the Crimean War, when the defeated Russian army, a heroic remnant, returned stoically to get on with the local campaigns. There can be no explanation for Shamyl's apparent apathy during the Crimean War, save that his forces were now depleted and lacked supplies, and he was too weakened to take advantage of the moment. For him, the Crimean campaign was six years too late. Nor did Russia's foes, the English or the Turks, seize this strategic moment to bolster him, and, fighting beside him, gain the whole Caucasus.

When the Sultan Abdul Medjid asked Shamyl how many men he could put into the field, Shamyl admitted that his resources were drained, and that beyond harassing the Russians, he could not undertake any large-scale offensive. But since Shamyl's devotion to the cause of Islam was unquestioned, the Sultan, anticipating victory, nominated him Viceroy of Georgia, a fine title, but of little practical value. Had the allies now launched an offensive on Tiflis, from Kars, they would have been joined, in the east, by many of the Tcherkess; by cutting off the Crimean peninsula from the rest of Russia, and aided by Shamyl, they could have blocked the supplies from the north, controlled the ports, and thus finished off the Crimean War in a matter of weeks, and with Russian forces out of the Caucasus too, the whole aspect of near Eastern politics would have been changed for a century to come.

But the exhortations of military observers still fell on deaf ears: all the travellers' tales and warnings, all the promptings failed to penetrate the minds of either the Ministers of War or the generals in command. 'Had England sent an army into the Caucasus, even after the fall of Sebastopol, Shamyl would have been our ally—Shamyl the Avar!'

But just as Shamyl failed to seize his chance, so the Allied command failed to support the Caucasian tribes who were ranged beside them as enemies of Russia.

III

The climate of war was usual to Tiflis: the Georgians, like all the people of the Caucasus, were born to the sound of gunfire, and the clash of steel. Their own battles against the Turks and Persians had merged into the Murid Wars, so that the further tension of the Crimean War, running concurrently with Shamyl's steady depredations on the Georgian lowlands, seemed no more than daily life. The men of the Georgian aristocracy were officers in the Russian army, and now considered themselves wholly Russian: the women, less easily westernized, still wore the national dress, though they were given to such anachronisms as French corsets and parasols; the noblest families all sent their daughters to St. Petersburg, to be educated at the Smolny Institute, and to become, later, one of the bevy of gazelle-like young creatures who were invited to Court, as ladies-in-waiting to the Tzarina, or, perhaps, to catch the eye of one of the Grand Dukes . . .

Among the most beautiful and distinguished of the Georgian princesses at Court, during the seasons of 1846 and 1848, were the two grand-daughters of George XII, last King of Georgia. Her Serene Highness the Princess Anna, and her younger sister, the Princess Varvara, were both princesses of Georgia, in their own right, this title having a royal connotation, far above and apart from the term 'Georgian Princess' of which there were legion. Both had been appointed ladies-in-waiting to the Tzarina, and had spent some time, fêted and courted, as belles of St. Petersburg society, before they married two handsome young Georgian princes (both serving in the Russian army) and returned to Georgia, to live between their family estates and Tiflis. The Princess Anna married Prince David Tchavtchavadzé, and the Princess Varvara married Prince Ellico Orbeliani; but not to live happily ever afterwards. In 1854, the shadows were already gathering round them. At first they had lived the luxurious life of their kind, among the huge, sprawling families of Georgia, among children, grandparents, nephews, nieces and great-aunts, generation upon generation, all surrounded by cohorts of devoted family servants, all swarming about the rambling, untidy, family houses. They did not hanker unduly after life in St. Petersburg: both were absorbed by their children and their responsibilities, and running the family estates which were their charge, during their husband's absence at the front. But early in 1854, Prince Orbeliani was killed, fighting the Turks, at Oğuzlu, leaving his young widow with a three-months'-old baby. Their elder son had died almost the same day as his father, and they had been buried together. Now, the Princess Varvara's life was centred round the baby Prince George, all that was left of her happiness.

Colonel Prince Ellico Orbeliani had lived and died as a warrior, like his father before him. Both had been in the Russian army; both had been prisoners of the Murids. In 1842, Prince Ellico had been Shamyl's captive, kept in one of the dread prison pits for eight months, and his bravery and dignity had much impressed the Imam, who had hoped to exchange him against his son, Djemmal-Eddin. But the Prince had refused to discuss the matter and after some months of obstinacy, Shamyl had consigned him to the prison pit, from where he was dragged, almost dead, four months later. But still he refused to bargain for his freedom with another man's life. Exasperated, the Naibs told him he must die—but that he could choose his manner of death: Shamyl had granted him this supreme favour, as a mark of esteem for his courage. 'Any death that frees me from being your prisoner would be welcome,' was the reply. The Prince was placed against the wall, and a firing squad was summoned. But Shamyl was watching, unseen, behind a chink in the wall. As the soldiers took aim, he appeared, ordering them away.

'Ellico,' said the Imam. 'They told me you were a brave man: they did not lie. I watched you face death. I shall ask nothing more of you than your word you will not try to escape.' The Prince gave his word, and lived in liberty among the Murids, until, at last, he was exchanged against some of the Imam's men; at which he had at once returned to the battle. Although of the highest courage, he was not, it seems, distinguished for his generalship.

His young widow (she was only twenty-five) spent her days and nights in prayer, was seen no more in Tiflis society, and joined her grief to that of her brother-in-law, Prince David Tchavtchavadzé's elder sister Nina, widow of Griboyedov, who had been slaughtered by the Persian mob storming the Russian Legation at Teheran in 1828. She had remained inconsolable all these twenty-six years, living among her Tchavtchavadzé relatives, still dressed in crêpe, and rather aloof from life.

These two bereaved ladies were often to be found at Princess Anna's house. Here they prayed, played with the children (Princess Anna had five), and followed the Caucasian War with gloomy foreboding. Would the bloodshed never end? Every puff of smoke in the mountains told of some wounding, some death; every bulletin from St. Petersburg, or the Porte, spoke of the approaching Crimean war, when thousands of men would die, horribly, and thousands of widows would mourn—as they.

During the early part of the year, Madame Drancy came to realize she could not continue in Tiflis. Her business had failed. She could not stay on in Russia now that the country was clearly heading towards war with France, and she had no choice but to return to her homeland; but just at the moment of her departure, fate intervened. It is impossible to believe that these seemingly chance encounters are not part of some vast predestined pattern. 'There are no moments of our life that are without consequence or significance for the future. . . . Mektoub! It is written,' noted Isabelle Eberhardt, plunged into Islam, her own destiny leading her a strange dance before fulfilling the pattern fate had decreed for her. So it was with Madame Drancy. The Tchavtchavadzé had been needing a French governess for their two elder daughters, but the growing tensions of the international situation had made it impossible for them to obtain one of these commodities—for so French governesses and tutors were regarded by the Russian aristocrats. They offered the post to Madame Drancy, who accepted, thankfully, and so became one of the Tchavtchavadzé household, sharing with them their fantastic adventure.

IV

French preceptors occupied a singular position in Russian households. Whatever the barriers of geography, politics or language which isolated Russia from the rest of Europe, large numbers of French tutors found their way there during the eighteenth and nineteenth centuries, and were followed by an invasion of English nannies. Both occupied a remarkable place in the westernization of the country. The tutors may be said to have had a profound effect on Russian education and culture, sophisticating and Gallicizing their little charges just as the nannies Anglicized them, superimposed discipline, plain foods and punctuality on these basically tempestuous babies: though neither tutors nor nannies appear to have been able to achieve more than purely superficial effects of logic and order. As soon as their charges grew up, numbers of them were to be found blowing out their brains over some imagined slight; breakfasting at midnight, sobbing away whole afternoons sustained by pickled herrings, gambling or drinking for forty-eight hours on end, or galloping across the steppes in furious charges against fate. *Soudba! Toska!* Fate! Spleen!

French tutors, and even English nannies, were no match for the Slav soul.

Nevertheless, for two hundred years, French tutors were all the rage: nobody ranked as fashionable if they did not boast at least one such foreign import. As each family emerged from medieval background, cut their beards, wore knee-breeches instead of the long padded and fur-edged caftans of tradition, they were very conscious of their backwardness. 'We Russians still have the Middle Ages on our shoulders,' they said. As late as the beginning of the eighteenth century, Russian women had gone veiled; the Tzarina and the Grand Duchesses living in harem seclusion, in that part of the Kremlin known as the Terem, 'behind twenty-seven locks', undefiled by the sight of any man but the Tzar. But once emancipated by Peter the Great's bracing methods, his nobles began to crave the daring sophistication imparted by the presence of a French preceptor. By the end of the eighteenth century, a number of French émigré aristocrats who had fled the Terror, arrived in Russia to make their living as best they could: as music masters, soldiers, or tutors. Sometimes there were deceptions. One enterprising Finn contrived to pass himself off as French, and was employed for over a year by a rather naïve provincial nobleman, who was under the impression that the Finnish phrases his children were acquiring were the purest Parisian French. Sometimes the most exceptional tutors were found: Marat's brother taught in the aristocratic lycée at Tzarskoe-Selo. While the Tzar Alexander I was schooled by Laharpe, his younger brother Nicholas had an adored Scottish nurse, the beautiful Miss Lyons, and one Russian family, the Raimanovs, claimed the Irish pianist, John Field, 'Russian Field', as their children's music-master. They rescued him from a dypsomaniac's death in a Neapolitan hospital, where he had drifted after declining in popularity in St. Petersburg. His playing and his lessons (Glinka was one of his pupils), and above all his Nocturnes—a title and form which were his invention—were all the rage. The silvery cadences of his music were to float out across the snows, lingering in the birchwoods and lilac thickets, until, at last, they crossed the frontier, and reached the Polish village of Zelazowa-Wola, where they were to leave their echoes, forever, in the heart of a delicate-looking boy, the young Frederick Chopin. We can imagine how fugitive and lovely sounded the music that the dying Field played on the Raimanov's school-room piano. It was his swansong, heard only by his benefactors. A few months after his return to Russia he was dead.

Often, the life of a foreign tutor in Russia was dangerous. They were treated with an odd mixture of contempt, cruelty and envy, too. These men, their employers felt, however lacking in the roaring appetites and vigour of the North, had other qualities. . . . They had travelled—had crossed frontiers, knew Europe. . . . Nevertheless, they were the butt of masters and serfs alike. Practical jokes, horsewhipping, shooting or hanging (as in the case of the Pushkins' tutor) being their lot when they failed to please. Or sometimes, when they pleased too well. Some of them, young, handsome and unfortunate, were the object of the liveliest competition among the ladies; not only their romantic young pupils, but the lady of the house, the aunts, the cousins, companions, and housemaids, too. All these women were herded together on the big estates, embedded in snow for five months of the year, and remote from everything but passion. The household which Turgeniev sketches in *A Month in the Country* is such a one—fading beauty, preoccupied husband, faithful friend, shy tutor and awakening girl. All the ingredients for suffering; but when we transfer these ingredients to a more robust setting—some Moscow merchant's domain, or that of an arrogant Prince who brooks no competition in his serail—then we sometimes find the tutor strung up at the gates, or run through in cold blood.

Wretched breed! Shabby, exiled, alone . . . Neither welcome in the salon or the servants' hall, yet sometimes fatally welcome in the alcôve. Instructing their charges in irregular verbs, classifying the unused library, occasionally accompanying Madame on a sleigh-ride; playing cribbage with the grandmother, duets with the cousins. . . . Tip-toeing from the attic bedroom to one on the first floor. . . . This was the tutor's life—and, sometimes, his death, too.

V

Madame Drancy accepted the Tchavtchavadzés' offer with alacrity. She had not relished the idea of returning to her parents, where the double failure of both her marriage and her business would now place her in a most humiliating position. But suddenly cornered, in an alien country with no means of support and no especial qualifications, she found herself demanded and respected—a French governess. She snatched at her chance, and so moved another step nearer to Shamyl's aôul.

By April, when the Crimean War was declared, she had settled into her new life. As a member of the Tchavtchavadzé household, she was protected from the embarrassments suffered by other aliens who found themselves isolated in an enemy country: although it must be recorded that the status and treatment of aliens was the object of the Emperor Nicholas' positively fastidious delicacy. At the outbreak of war he had issued a proclamation, assuring them of his protection, and calling on his subjects to maintain their ancient reputation for hospitality . . . The English residents in Russia were unanimous in their statements that 'what was, before the war, indifference or toleration, now became the most studied attention'. Moreover, Mr. Grey, the British chaplain to an English factory in Moscow, who had been told they must no longer pray for the confusion of H.M. Queen Victoria's enemies, refused to accept this chauvinistic attitude and referred the whole matter to the Emperor Nicholas. The Tzar at once telegraphed his sympathy, ordering that Mr. Grey should be free to pray for his sovereign's victory without any considerations as to who those enemies might be. Even if the Tzar's personal esteem for Queen Victoria and her country were apparent here, while the French were ever regarded coldly, with mistrust and scorn, individually French aliens were not persecuted.

Madame Drancy seems to have become an excellent governess, strict, but not repressive to her young pupils, and well-liked, though not, perhaps, really loved by the household. These full-blown, fiery, the Georgian aristocrats were always to remain, at heart, strangers to self-contained, sharp, bourgeois Frenchwoman. Even the terrible ordeal which they were to share, as Shamyl's prisoners, does not appear to have brought them really close, although all of them behaved towards each other with exemplary courtesy and loyalty, in the most trying circumstances.

At the end of June, Tiflis sweltered under a tropic sun, and the Princess Anna decided on her annual withdrawal to Tzinondali, the family estates in Kakhetia, about eighty miles north-east of Tiflis. Her husband, Colonel Prince David, had lately been appointed to command the local militia in Kakhetia, which stood ready to supplement the Lesghien Cordon, or line of forts, upon which the Russians relied to repel any Murid invasions of the lowlands. The forts were widely spaced and, sometimes, marauding bands of mountaineers were able to carry out an audacious raid and retreat, unscathed; though, generally, they were met and held by the militia, and a furious battle would ensue. When the Princess announced her forthcoming departure, there was some opposition in Tiflis. General Réad, the military governor, refused to sanction it, and the garrison called it foolhardy. One Russian colonel, looking dramatic, presented Madame Drancy with a dagger, urging her to learn how to handle it before facing the dangers of the countryside. She accepted it gracefully, and putting it among her souvenirs thought it would make a nice paper-knife.

But Prince David agreed to his wife's plan. The Lesghien Cordon was very strong. He himself would be on duty in the neighbourhood, and able to keep an eye on Tzinondali, he said. His estate, being on the right side of the river, the side farthest from the mountains, was doubly protected, first by the Lesghien Cordon—the line of forts that ran parallel with the river, immediately facing the mountains and standing between them and the unprotected lowlands; and then, the Alazan was a racing deep river, almost impossible to cross at this point. Where it narrowed, running into shallows, was immediately below the Russian forts. Therefore, the Tchavtchavadzés had always felt comparatively secure at Tzinondali, and this year even less uneasy than before. Shamyl was believed to be in bad shape, in the mountains, since his regular supplies of arms from Turkey were no longer coming through, the Ottoman armies now having need of every round of ammunition themselves.

Therefore, the Princess went placidly on with her preparations for leaving Tiflis. She was to be accompanied by Madame Drancy, a number of domestics, the Princess Orbeliani and her baby son, Prince George, and a niece, Princess Nina Baratoff, a beautiful young creature of seventeen. There was also the Princess Tinia, a garrulous old lady of nearly eighty, one of Prince David's many aunts. His sister, Princess Nina Griboyedova, did not accompany them, but taking the third Tchavtchavadzé child, Elena, also left Tiflis, to spend a few weeks with her cousin, the Princess of Mingrelia, who had also fled the heat and dust of the town for her country estates.

On June 18, the cavalcade set out. Twelve servants accompanied the family; the carriages were followed by arbas, heavy two-wheeled ox-carts used through Asia, loaded with samovars, bedding, supplies of groceries, saucepans and ikons. All these luxuries were considered necessities. Conditions of life, like travel, were primitive to the point of barbarism, unless combated by the most extensive agglomeration of comforts. Travellers generally found the posting-houses supplied a room; but no more. If there was a wash-basin, there was no water or towels. (We read of a Russian officer who, having obtained a small tumbler of cold water at the inn, surprised an English fellow-traveller by rinsing his mouth out, holding the water in it long enough to warm it, then, spitting it into his cupped hands, washed them, his face and neck, and dried them on a grubby bandana, explaining his toilette was *à l'Anglaise*.)

Nor were the inns more accommodating in the matter of food. If a skrawny chicken was at last obtained, there would be no dish to cook it in. Beds were usually benches, with a straw-stuffed mattress, or none. Bed-linen was unknown. As to plumbing—then a rare item in the most luxurious houses outside the capital, there was, we are told, no W.C. south of Pskov. The stable-yard, among the tethered pack-mules and camels, had to serve most Caucasian travellers. Travelling light was unknown, and people carried all they needed with them, down to the last candle, setting up a home around themselves at each night stop. And when Princess Tchavtchavadzé had the baggage carts loaded she was ensuring not only a comfortable journey, but that the three summer months she planned to spend at Tzinondali should continue the luxurious life she led in Tiflis.

Tzinondali was very isolated, seven miles from the nearest small town, Telav, and two days' hard riding from Tiflis. But the great Georgian country houses were quite self-supporting, raising their own cattle and making their own bread and wine. Swarms of domestics, carpenters, grooms, gardeners, farm-hands, dairy-maids and scullions centred devotedly round the pivot-point of the Prince and Princess. It was a patriarchal life, at once luxurious and simple.

Tzinondali was one of the most celebrated beauty spots in all Georgia. During the life-time of Prince David's father, the Prince Alexander, it had been a meeting place for writers and poets—the old Prince himself was a celebrated poet. Lermontov had stayed at Tzinondali while writing his *Demon*. The colonnaded white house with its big courtyard and terraced gardens was set beside a ravine, below which ran a small tributary of the Alazanl. All around, were groves of trees, orchards and vineyards and the exotic vegetation of Asia which astonished Madame Drancy. Across the river, the foothills of the mountains rose steeply to merge with great snow peaks. From afar, seen from the rich lowlands of Kakhetia, they did not seem terrible or menacing as they did to those who trespassed on them, but rather some poetic cloud-land which glowed, a pearly rose, at sunrise and sunset. Tzinondali was the soft breathing south: nothing of the harsh Caucasus here. Groves of trees encircled the house, and at evening the nightingales sang from their depths; by day the bees hummed over the rose-garden, and from the busy kitchen quarters came sounds of a never-ceasing activity, forks beating up eggs, milk-churns being rolled across a tiled floor, knives being sharpened, dishes being scoured, the authoritative tones of the head cook. Sometimes, above the smell of hay and summer flowers that surrounded the house came pungent wafts of some unnamable spice, the drenching sweetness of rose-leaf jam, or the pervading, bitter-burnt smell of green peppers roasting slowly on a hot stove, the smell which above all others epitomizes the Near East to the traveller.

At the end of the garden there was a little gazebo overlooking the valley. Here, in the long hot summer afternoons, a huge silver samovar presiding, the ladies drank tea, and received other princely families who rode over from their neighbouring estates. Prince David was often able to return home, bringing with him some fellow officers, to dine, or celebrate a local victory over some skirmishing mountaineers. Every day, the two Princesses walked together in the gardens, indulging in those long maternal conversations peculiar to mothers everywhere. Princess Anna, the elder, was very dark, with the long-nosed, classic features of her race. Her heavy brows almost met, giving her magnificent dark eyes a rather stern expression. Her black hair was coiled in a huge chignon, to which a gauze veil was attached with large diamond pins. Princess Varvara was as dark as her sister, but hers was a softer beauty. She was petite, where her sister was statuesque. Now, as they paced up and down the terrace, Princess Anna walked imperiously, her head held high, her voice firm and insistent, while her sister seemed to droop within her heavy widow's weeds. Her head was bent, her voice a low murmur, her thoughts far away, at the Orbeliani family chapel where, beside the tomb of her husband and child, the Armenian monks kept a perpetual vigil she would have liked to share.

Beside the twining vines which covered the private chapel, the little Marie and Salomé struggled with French verbs under the vigilant eye of Madame Drancy, while the younger children and the babies were dandled and petted by a regiment of peasant nurses headed by the majestic centenarian head-nurse, Maria Gaideli, who had been with the Tchavtchavadzé family, rearing each successive generation, since her first charge, Prince Gersevan, had grown up to become Georgian Ambassador to the Court of Catherine the Great. Ever since, she had ruled the Tchavtchavadzé children, and even now, Prince David (a grandson of Prince Gersevan) deferred to her in matters of a domestic nature. Now, leaning on a stick, her wizened old face peered lovingly at her four latest babies, Tamar, aged four, Alexander, eighteen months old, Lydia, four months old, and their cousin, the seven months' old Prince George Orbeliani.

Only the Princess Nina Baratoff seemed left out of life at Tzinondali, too young for her aunts, too old for her cousins. She had just returned to Tiflis from St. Petersburg, where her gazelle-like beauty had been most remarked at Court. Her head was quite turned, and now she was inclined to be sulky. Her aunts thought she must be in love; but she was not communicative, and sat staring out, morosely, across the empty sweep of countryside, remembering the brilliant life she had barely glimpsed at St. Petersburg, between leaving the Smolny Institute and her abrupt recall to Tiflis. Her father, who had lately lost his fortune, was paralysed; when her mother died, the family decided she must return home. There was no money to launch her on St. Petersburg society; to marry her off without a dowry was difficult, too. In any case, she returned to Tiflis to brood, feeling ill-used by fate, bored by provincial society, and fancying her beauty wasted, her youth slipping from her. Perhaps she was dreaming of some dashing officer, one of the Tzar's aides-de-camp, a young Grand Duke, or one of the many young men who partnered her at the Court balls, and with whom she flirted, racing along the pink granite quays in a troika, darting sly inviting glances over her little sable muff.

24

Tzinondali

*Their horses are swifter than the leopards, and are
more fierce than the evening wolves; and their horsemen
shall spread themselves; and their horsemen shall come
from afar; they shall fly as the eagle that hasteth to eat.*

HABAKKUK I

At the beginning of July, the countryside was alive with rumours that
Shamyl in person was descending from the mountains and planning
an attack on Telav. But rains had so swollen the Alazan that Princess
Anna was not alarmed, knowing it was almost impossible to cross it at
any point now. Moreover, she had received word from her husband,
absent with his militia, saying that his fortress had been attacked by a
large number of Lesghiens, but that they had been beaten back with
heavy losses. He would be at Tzinondali within the next few days, he
wrote; meanwhile, there was no cause for uneasiness. (What the Prince
had meant to say was that his wife should not be uneasy on his behalf:
unhappily the Princess read it otherwise—that she herself was in no
immediate danger.) But next day, in the hills, across the Alazan, the
crops could be seen burning and smoking, fired in the night by the
mountaineers. It was evident that they had come down from the
mountains and meant to attack somewhere along the Lesghien Cordon.

Still the Princess did not feel Tzinondali was threatened. Although
the mountaineers were age-old enemies of low-land Georgia, there
had been no instance of any large body of them crossing the Alazan
since the beginning of the century, when Omar, Khan of Avaria, at the
head of twenty thousand Lesghiens, had marched to within sixty miles
of Tiflis before being checked. Their lesser raids were always concentrated on some fort or village. The Princess argued that an isolated
country house and handful of women and children were no especial
prize for them. Besides, her husband's letter had been so reassuring.
Therefore, beyond posting a few servants as guards she took no further
precaution, although both the steward of the estate, and the Natzvala,
or head man of the village, implored her to leave immediately. They

urged her to take refuge in the woods, where, in the past, the peasants had often succeeded in escaping Lesghien raids, lying hidden in the dense thickets. But the Princess, who was of a passionately maternal nature, was now wholly absorbed by the demands of the youngest, four-month-old baby, whom she was nursing herself. She seemed becalmed in some passive, sensuous world of her own, a realm of animal content, where only she and the baby existed. She did not want to be disturbed; voices from the outside world only reached her in muffled whispers. So she did nothing.

All through the night, gunfire could be heard across the river, but next day, the firing was only intermittent, and seemed to come from very far away. The weather was cloudless, burning hot, the sun shimmering in shifting mirages across the vineyards. The whole family, with the exception of Princess Anna, who was asleep, went to church to render thanks for the repulse of the mountaineers. On their way back to the house they were met by a villager saying that one force of Lesghiens had succeeded in crossing the Alazan, but had been halted by a strong body of militia. However, the man was not believed. Alarmist talk—the peasants were beginning to panic, said the Princess Orbeliani, while the old Princess Tinia, who exacted the obedience and respect which old age is always accorded in the East, positively forbade any member of the party to mention it to Princess Anna. And the same summary attitude was adopted towards one of the peasants, who reeled into the courtyard an hour later, his clothing singed by bullets. He had been down to the river to reconnoitre, and some hidden sharpshooters from the other side had fired on him: he was sure the Lesghiens meant trouble. But as he was known for a drunkard, no one paid any attention to him, and he fell asleep, snoring, in the kitchen.

That afternoon a stranger limped up to the house and asked shelter for the night. His clothes streamed with water, for he had managed to cross the Alazan at the ford of Tognia, thus escaping a band of Lesghiens on the far bank, he told them. Since the swollen rain-fed rivers of late June had now subsided a little under the present torrid suns, his statement was not questioned. He added that he was a merchant, on his way to Telav. Hospitality is a sacred law in the Caucasus: he was given food, dry clothes and a place to sleep. But later that night the servants saw him loading a gun, and they told the Princess. She forced herself out of her maternal preoccupations, and issued firearms to the menservants, ordering them to patrol the estate. But they were tired; after a heavy supper, two of the guards fell asleep. The third was engaged in chaffing a nursery-maid, when the sound of a single shot rang out in the silent evening. At the same moment, the stranger was seen making for the woods. Once in their shelter it was impossible to catch him. But now his presence in the house was understood. He was a Lesghien spy; he had fired his gun as a signal. But what it told, no one knew. At last, the Princess Anna was awake to the dangers of their position, and she decided to leave for Tiflis at dawn. The servants were ordered to fetch the big trunks and to start packing at once.

Throughout history, in moments of danger, we find the same recurrent obsession with trivialities and worldly possessions which seizes the threatened, holding them in thrall until their doom is encompassed. Marie Antoinette, safely on the road to Varennes, dawdled fatally, picking wild flowers, and throwing away her life with every bloom she gathered. So we find the Princess, at this last moment when escape was still possible, concerned over the niceties of packing. Had she seized her children and led the household to the woods, they might still have escaped. But while the servants dragged out the cumbersome trunks, she stood over them supervising the disposal of her valuables. Two *pavoskas*, light carriages which can travel fast, were ordered to be got ready, and a messenger was sent off to inform Prince David of their departure. The Princess and all the family went to bed early.

It was a still oppressive night. Only the nightingales sang rapturously in the trees. Madame Drancy could not sleep, and went out into the garden. She was haunted by premonitions of danger. She would have taken refuge in the woods herself, but considered it her duty to remain beside her employers. An enormous moon swam overhead, lighting the garden and the whole vast range of mountains. Across the Alazan, fires could still be seen burning among the ravaged villages, and the yelping cries of the jackals echoed in the hills, a mocking sound. Under its dense arbour of vines, the little chapel door stood open, and Madame Drancy could see a pin-point of light, ruby red, glowing from the lamp before the ikon. She went towards it, and sinking on her knees, prayed for protection.

As she turned back towards the house, a tall figure stepped from the shadows and crossed the courtyard, making no sound. The man did not see Madame Drancy, who stood paralysed with fear: he might have been one of the Princesses' servants—Madame Drancy did not know them all; but something in his bearing, his dark, intent face and stealthy tread told her he was not. As he disappeared she saw that a gun was slung across his back. She rushed towards the house. On reaching the terrace she saw with horror that below, in the ravine, the stream was flowing much less rapidly after the long hot day. Two men were leading their horses along the bank, searching for a place to cross. The moonlight glanced over their weapons. They were Tchetchen scouts.

Madame Drancy burst into Princess Anna's bedroom. The Princess was sleeping, but she woke calmly and began to dress, ordering the children to be wakened and fed. The household was roused, and soon the whole place was a scene of scuttling confusion, orders and counter-orders, candlelight and huge shifting shadows. Madame Drancy hurriedly crammed a few possessions into a small bag, and placed some old letters and a keepsake, entwined locks of hair, in her corsets. Mindful of her responsibilities as a governess, she also packed a French grammar and a pious book entitled *Dieu est Amour*.

In the greying dawn some villagers arrived with stories of Shamyl himself marching on Telav. The servant-girls were by now on the verge of hysterics and had to be calmed by a brew of tea. Their inefficiency caused the loss of another hour, for, wailing and shuddering as they recounted to each other the terrors of capture by the mountaineers, they had not packed in a manner Princess Anna expected, and some of the trunks had to be re-packed. It was eight o'clock, the sun high and strong in the brilliant blue sky when the last strong-box was placed in the pavoska. The children were jumping about excitedly, tugging at Madame Drancy's skirts, when a cry sounded from beyond the garden: 'God save us! The Tartars!' A shot rang out, and the voice choked and was heard no more. There was the sound of galloping horses, men shouting, a terrible tumult sweeping down on the old house. The shrieking servants scattered in all directions. The Princesses and Madame Drancy seized the children and fled inside the house, followed by the nurses, some maids, and the old Princess Tinia, who even now could not believe that disaster had overtaken them. 'They would not dare!' she kept muttering angrily. Princess Anna, imagining that the Lesghiens were raiding the house to loot its treasures, decided they had better barricade themselves in an attic, where she thought it unlikely the mountaineers would think of looking for anything of value.

She did not realize that she, her sister and their children were the treasures Shamyl sought—the only hostages of sufficient value to enable him to bargain at last—at long last—for the return of Djemmal-Eddin, his son. She had no idea that this raid on Tzinondali was the consummation of long years of scheming, of hopes deferred. Looking round the dusty, low-ceilinged attic at the frightened faces of her family and servants, she burst into tears. 'God forgive me! Why did I wait so long? You could all have been saved. . . .' She knew what indignities and terrors, if not death, awaited them, were they to be discovered.

By now, 'the Tartars', the dread horde, had entered the house and could be heard below, smashing down doors, ripping curtains, and thumping wildly on the piano. Their guttural cries, mingled with the sounds of broken glass and china, mounted to the attic where the maid-servants were on their knees, praying noisily for deliverance. In vain the Princess urged them to be silent: at each fresh uproar, their wailing began again. The old Princess Tinia seemed stunned and repeatedly ordered them to go downstairs to rescue a tea service she especially cherished, The older children, now terrified, were calmed by Madame Drancy, while the Princess Orbeliani was occupied with the babies. The ancient nurse Maria Gaideli was trembling convulsively, and had set up the traditional wailing of grief-stricken Georgians. It was now impossible to hope their presence in the attic would not be discovered. From the tiny windows Madame Drancy could see the gardens overrun by ferocious-looking turbaned riders, their horses trampling the parterres. The dried up river-bed was now a pathway leading to the house, a path along which hundreds of horsemen galloped, pouring down from the hills, their savage cries ripping the morning air. As they rode into the courtyard, they brandished their shaskas over their heads, and reining their mounts up on to their haunches, whirled them round and round, while the animals snorted and plunged viciously.

Now the Tchetchens had discovered the stairs leading to the attic, and were swarming up them, battering on the door. Inside, everyone was kneeling, crossing themselves. At last the door broke with a shattering impact. The tribesmen burst in, their cries of triumph mingling with the wailing of the maids and the shrieking of the children. The Tchetchens sprang on the women. A savage figure grabbed Madame Drancy, and ignoring the stairs leapt down the whole flight, to the hall below. One after the other, the Princesses, their children and women were seized or flung down the stairs, which suddenly splintered and gave way under the weight of so many rushing figures. As the prisoners reached the main hall the Tchetchens began fighting among themselves for their prey. The women were passed from hand to hand, the tribesmen's heavy shashkas flashing over their heads. It was quite useless for Madame Drancy to try and disengage herself, shrieking that she was a French citizen—that they would regret what they were doing—they fought over her in a way which would have been most gratifying, had she been reading of it, safely in bed, in the Rue des Acacias. She fell to the lot of a turbaned monster, as she was later to describe him, who dragged her out into the courtyard and ordered her by gestures, and in some uncouth tongue, to hold two horses. Her clothes were torn off her, leaving her in her stays, her chemise, a petticoat, and a pair of kid boots from the Rue de Rivoli. When she tried to escape, the monster grinned sardonically and cut her across the shoulders with a heavy whip. Scarlet in the face with rage and humiliation, Madame Drancy realized there was nothing she could do but obey.

The whole courtyard was in an uproar: men and horses, shrieking women, the pavoskas overturned, their horses cut from the traces and stampeding in terror, children trampled underfoot, the packages and trunks ripped open, their contents flung everywhere. On the steps, a little apart from the rest, crouched the old nurse, wailing, cursing a God that had let her live to see such a day. The little Marie and

Salomé were each being strapped to the saddles of a couple of wild Tchetchen riders. The Princess Orbeliani and her niece, Nina Baratoff, were nowhere to be seen, nor were the Princes Alexander and George. Princess Anna was lying on the ground, apparently unconscious, the baby Lydia still clasped close. Her dress had been torn off; one slipper had fallen from her foot, which was bleeding from a terrible wound, caused by a nail which had driven itself deep into the flesh. Her black hair flowed round her, where she lay; two magnificent diamond earrings still glittered in her ears, till a Lesghien wrenched them from her. She raised her head and looked wildly round her. 'The children— the children,' she cried, seeing Madame Drancy, and fell back, unconscious. At this moment, Madame Drancy was astonished to see the young Princess Nina Baratoff, mounted on a splendid horse, in no way molested, her clothing, her veil and all her jewels untouched, being led through the courtyard by an elegantly clad young Tchetchen who seemed less savage than the rest. At the same moment, the old Princess Tinia appeared, quite naked, her white hair falling in wisps on her shoulders. Her arms extended to heaven, she was praying for death, and a release from such indignities.

Now that the Princesses Tchavtchavadzé and Orbeliani were their captives the tribesmen could concentrate on pillaging the house. They broke the silver plates in their eagerness to cram them into their saddlebags. Sugar, coffee and tea were equally prized. Diamond brooches were trampled into the earth, pearl necklaces ground under the horses' hooves. Pots of face cream and pommades for the hair were tried out as edible delicacies—likewise the chalks that Madame Drancy had used for the schoolroom blackboard. The scene, at once horrible and grotesque, reached its climax when a band of swarthy Lesghiens burst out from the house wearing the children's flower wreathed summer hats.

While Madame Drancy fought down a hysterical desire to laugh, her captor returned and made her mount his horse. One by one the Tchavtchavadzé household rode out from Tzinondali, each behind a Murid horseman. Only the Princess Anna was on foot, the baby Lydia clutched to her, one arm bound to the stirrup of her captor, who evidently enjoyed seeing her suffer. So they set out, crossed the stream, while the Princess strove to keep the baby's head out of the water as she stumbled.

Reaching the other bank, they were joined by a number of Tchetchens who had rounded up the cattle of the village and were now driving them towards the mountains. It was high noon, and the sun beat down mercilessly: the dust rose in suffocating clouds as the frightened cattle stampeded around them, a surging and bellowing sea of horns and hooves menaced the terrified prisoners. Not one of them now hoped for mercy. All of them prayed for death.

25

The Great Aôul

'Tis the clime of the East, 'tis the land of the sun.
Can he smile on such things as his children have done?

LORD BYRON

News of the Princesses' capture did not reach Tiflis for more than two weeks. When it did, the public were outraged. No details were known, so that neither the civil nor military authorities could decide what steps should be taken to rescue them. No one knew where they were; but two Georgian officers of the Imperial Guard at once volunteered to try and reach Shamyl's aôul in the mountains, and discuss terms for liberating his captives. General Réad, as Commander-in-Chief of the Armies in the Caucasus, refused to sanction the project. He wrote to the Princesses' father, then in Moscow, in terms of the most florid grief, informing him of the disaster which had overtaken his daughters. 'It has pleased Heaven to allow the mountaineers to make a successful incursion into Kakhetia. In spite of all possible human foresight,' wrote the General (not entirely accurately), 'your daughter and grandchildren are the victims of this marauding expedition.' He went on to say that all hope of obtaining their liberation was not yet lost.

No one, naturally, informed Madame Drancy's parents of her disappearance. Their first news of the disaster only reached Paris two months later, when a letter they had sent to their daughter was returned to the Rue des Acacias unopened; scrawled across it: *'Returned to sender owing to assassination of addressee.'* At the same time, newspapers all over Europe were publishing blood-curdling accounts of the raid on Tzinondali, dwelling with morbid relish on the probable fate of the Princesses and their household. According to the tone of the paper the capture was variously represented: as a social disaster, 'Princesses of the Blood Royal, Ladies-in-waiting to the Tzarina, prisoners of barbaric tribesmen.' Or politically, 'Savagery in Russian territory: French citizen abducted.' Or with a religious bias, as from Constantinople, 'Shamyl Imam, Viceroy of Georgia, has made a successful sortie into territory seized by the Infidel invaders, and is holding a Christian

322

family as hostages, against the return of his son Djemmal-Eddin torn from him by the Infidels, and brought up in the Christian faith, since 1838.' While the penny press, seeking sensation by numbers, spoke first of forty noble Russian families taken prisoner by Shamyl, who menaced Tiflis itself; and later, of Shamyl, the Lion of Daghestan, at the head of fifteen thousand Caucasians, seizing more than eight hundred of the Georgian nobility and holding them captive in the mountains, all bound together and dying of slow starvation.

* * *

Meanwhile, what was happening to Colonel Prince David Tchav-tchavadzé during those first fateful days of July? He had left his house a few days before the attack. On July 1 he was inspecting the defences of Hando, a frontier village. On July 2 he returned to Shildi, and was dining late with Captain Prince Ratiev, who commanded the garrison, when a scout galloped into camp, dusty and exhausted. He had ridden hard from Pohali Tower, the most advanced of the Russian outposts, and well up into the foothills below Shamyl's mountains. It was always a dangerous post, and now it had been raided, and was occupied by the Lesghiens; the mountaineers were believed to be converging on Shildi, to wipe out the fort, said the scout. The Prince left at once to strengthen the defenceless villages around Shildi and to post his men at various vantage-points and ambushes along the way. All next day and night the Georgians waited for the attack, but there was no sign of the tribes-men, and the golden, smiling landscape of Kakhetia lay basking in the sun. Early on the morning of July 3 Shildi was attacked, the houses fired and a violent but irregular conflict raged for some hours, before the tribesmen were repulsed. At midnight they attacked again in force, but now reinforcements had arrived with several field guns, and the enemy was repulsed with heavy losses. It was at this point that the Prince wrote the unfortunately worded letter to his wife, telling her there was no cause for alarm.

But next day more scouts arrived, telling the Prince that a large body of horsemen, Lesghiens, Tchetchens and Avars, were thundering down from the mountains, led by their Naibs; they were pouring down like a mighty stream, a raging torrent, threatening the lowlands, said the scouts. They were heading for the Alazan. 'He'—Shamyl had come down from the Great Aôul, to watch the battle. The Prince was now thoroughly alarmed for his family and ordered four companies to march towards the spot where he believed the tribesmen would try to ford the river. He was at the head of the column, and had scarcely left Shildi when one of his men broke rank and rushed to his side, crying, 'Look, Prince! Look!' The Prince rose in his stirrups and saw, far away across the woods, flames and columns of smoke rising from five or six villages, Tzinondali among them. He was too late. The Lesghiens had crossed the Alazan, and were already in the defenceless lowlands. He ordered his men to march to the first ford, and to gain the right bank at all costs. But at the point where they reached the river, the water was churning and raging through the rocks and was impassable. They would either have to lose time going far out of their way downstream to the shallower water where the marauders must have crossed, or lie in wait for their return, hoping to intercept them as they made for the mountains.

The Prince was now faced with a fearful decision: his first impulse was to rush to Tzinondali, to defend his family. But as a soldier his duty lay elsewhere. Military discipline prevailed. He made the sign of the cross in the direction of Tzinondali, confided his family to God's care and ordered his men to wait in ambush for the return of the tribesmen. He was still hoping that his household had escaped, and had taken to the woods. For the house itself he held no hopes. It must have been sacked. All that day, from noon till six o'clock, the Prince and his men lay in wait: their ambush was well chosen, and the few small bands of Lesghiens who appeared were surprised and killed in a matter of moments; but still there was no sign of the main body of Murids.

At dusk, another small party of tribesmen was ambushed and dispatched. According to Caucasian custom, the marauders' heads, and the booty found in their saddle-bags, were brought by the Prince's men, and laid at his feet, battle trophies. The last sinking rays of a blood-red sun lit up the heap of plunder, the freshly decapitated heads and a number of objects, among which the Prince recognized belongings from the dining-room, bedrooms and nurseries at Tzinondali.

While he was debating what to do next—for he knew that any attempts to rescue his family might prove fatal, since the mountaineers preferred to slaughter their prisoners than risk losing them—a messenger arrived from Shildi where Prince Ratiev was being heavily attacked, and seeking help. The Prince sent some of his men off towards the mountains, by the hill of Kontzhi, a narrow defile through which it was thought the tribesmen must pass; they were ordered to hold them there at all costs. The Prince and the rest of his men returned to Shildi, where they arrived in time to turn the attack.

At nine that night, word came from Captain Hitrovo who commanded the small expedition to the hill of Kontzhi: the enemy had been intercepted returning from Tzinondali, wrote the Captain; they carried much booty, and a number of prisoners from the surrounding villages. But being met with a volley of Russian fire, there had been a skirmish, in which some tribesmen and prisoners were killed, and a few of the prisoners rescued. The main body of horsemen had made off into the hills. He said nothing about the Tchavtchavadzé family.

Next morning, the Prince sent men to the hill of Kontzhi to collect the bodies of the fallen. Some of these men were the Prince's own serfs. Among the corpses and debris of the fight, they found the body of a baby, wrapped in a lace shawl. It was the little Lydia. The men decided to keep this terrible discovery from the Prince, and two of them were detached to carry the dead child to the village of Tzinondali which, though sacked, was only partially burned. The Church of St. George had escaped, and here they buried the baby. Thinking it best to spare their leader, his men still did not disclose the true state of affairs to the Prince. It was only on July 6 that the danger seemed abated enough for the Prince David to leave his post, and go to investigate the fate of his own home. Accompanied by two officers and fifteen men who had volunteered to accompany him, the Prince set out. In spite of very fast currents, they swam their horses across the Alazan without loss, and reached Tzinondali at dusk.

The blackened ruins of the house still smouldered. All around was desolation and death. Bodies lay about the courtyard, or sprawled across the steps. The overturned pavoskas still lay before the door. The stables were empty and the cattle had been driven from the pastures. On the edge of the woods they found the old nurse; she was tied to a tree and quite distraught. She remembered the building of the house as the most important event of her childhood; she had grown up in its shade and shared all its glories. Now she was wailing a funeral chant, her voice discordant with age and grief. All around her, in the boxwood thickets, the nightingales sang on, rapturously.

II

When the Princesses and Madame Drancy rode out from Tzinondali as captives, they rode into a region of suffering and fear. Each of them were taken in charge by their original captor who, in each case, appeared to regard them as his own property, for whom he would receive handsome rewards, on delivery to the Imam. But each tribesman knew the rank and significance of his captive, and although behaving in a most brutal manner, no one assaulted them. They addressed the Princess Anna as Khancha—wife of the Khan David. In spite of her appearance, half-naked, stumbling and bound, they showed their admiration; and when she asked for her children to be brought to her, they refused to believe that so young and beautiful a woman could be the mother of five. Their own women were old at thirty. At this time, the Princesses had not realized the difference between Tchetchen and Lesghien tribesmen. They were all 'Tartars' to the Georgians. But the Princesses were to find out, to their cost, that while their present captors were for the most part Tchetchens, the élite of Shamyl's troops, the Lesghiens were of a far more savage nature, insensible to pity, '*des gens durs*' as Madame Drancy described them. All the mountaineers, however, showed a bewildering mixture of brutality and kindness. Thus, a man who later procured sugar for the starving baby Alexander, beat the nurse cruelly, dragging her by one arm for some distance, as his horse galloped over the rough country.

The Princess Anna, who was now in great pain from her foot, still held herself proudly, arrogantly, even. Her black hair fell over her shoulders, covering her like a cloak. She was a king's granddaughter, and she still moved with an air of majesty which impressed the tribesmen. The Princess Orbeliani had lost her veils; her hair, too, fell about her shoulders, but she still wore her black dress. As the widow of Ellico Orbelinani, the great warrior, she was the object of especial veneration and curiosity among the mountaineers. Her husband's courage was remembered by all of them, and they crowded round to see his wife, and to touch the little Alexander, his son; with a clumsy kindness, they tried to console her, telling her they knew her husband was still alive —was a prisoner of the Turks, as he had been their prisoner—but not dead, not such a hero! The Princess stood in their midst, dishevelled and exhausted, their captive; yet she held court: the memory of her husband's bravery had crowned her, in their eyes, and she managed to smile for them.

The young Princess Nina had endured least, although she had ridden all the way with her arms pinioned behind her, for she was a vigorous and healthy creature who had resisted her captors energetically. The gold and pearl embroidered velvet *katiba* which she wore impressed them as much as her youthful beauty, and apart from falling from her horse in crossing the Alazan, to be rescued from drowning and plunging horses' hooves by her captor who was holding the other end of the rope with which her arms were bound, she had not suffered greatly. Fished ashore, gasping, but still beautiful, she was now strapped to the croup of a Tchetchen cavalier's saddle, and sent on again, still escorted by the young Tchetchen noble, who never left her side, and appeared quite overcome by her beauty. But he was all respect.

Not so Madame Drancy's captor, a Lesghien desperado, who lashed her bare shoulders if she did not obey him; who taunted her for her obvious terror of the horses and the mountain paths, and when they dismounted at last to sleep in a dismal swamp-like spot, spread his bourka and urged her to share his couch. This honour she refused vituperatively, informing him (in French) that she was not accustomed to receiving such offers from strangers. But the proprieties were quite lost on him. When he discovered that the gold chain she still wore round her neck was hung with holy medals, he mistook them for money and began searching her in a most impudent manner. His great paws soon discovered the love-letters and the locket of hair tucked in her corset, so that captive and captor were to be seen struggling savagely. It was dark, and the medals fell on the grass, never to be found again; at which the Lesghien took his whip and beat her soundly. Yet Madame Drancy's shrewish French fury remained undaunted, and she gave him a lot of trouble, all the way. At one halt the draggled, but still spirited Frenchwoman was the object of further interest. Another fierce-looking creature, his face darkened with smears of gunpowder, leant forward and pulled her to his side. Madame Drancy was paralysed with terror.

'Does this one know how to make shirts?' demanded the Lesghien, speaking broken Georgian. One of the Tzinondali servants, showing, even here and now, that spite which family servants always seem to display towards governesses, especially foreign ones, replied that she could, indeed, sew.

'Then I'll give three roubles for her,' said the Lesghien, hauling her up on to his horse, at which Princess Orbeliani, with great presence of mind, rushed forward, crying that the lady was the wife of a famous French general—that she too would be ransomed, and must be treated with due deference. None of the men, even the Naibs, had heard of France. They doubted its existence and suspected that this spitfire foreigner would not be worth much. Madame Drancy was only rescued from her would-be purchaser by the return of her first captor, who snatched her away in violent rage; the two men were about to draw their kindjals and rush on each other when a Naib intervened. 'For Shamyl Imam!' he roared. The men fell back and the march was resumed. But Madame Drancy was a most determined woman. She had gone to Tiflis to better her lot. Things had not turned out at all as she had expected. Yet, as the days went by, she was making up her mind to better even such a lot as this. 'I thought of Gaston, my child, and my old mother, and I resolved to spend three years, *surely the utmost that could be necessary*, in teaching one of these vile monsters the French language, so that he could understand me, and help me to escape, to return to my dear native land.' By which we see that Madame Drancy, besides being optimistic, was oddly unrealistic for a Frenchwoman.

As the party approached the hill of Kontzhi, they were unaware that the Russian troops were waiting for them in the defile. The fine Kabarda horses were cantering along at an easy pace, the trembling prisoners clinging to their captors, still surrounded by the cattle which were driven along with them towards the uplands. Princess Anna, who was now so weak she could not stand, was riding behind one of the Naib leaders. As they entered the defile they formed into close order, the Tchetchen guards first, then those carrying the prisoners, and lastly more guards, pack-horses with the loot, and the herds of cattle. Suddenly, all was turmoil, rearing horses, shouting men and screaming women. They were met with volley upon volley of musket fire—from where, by whom, none knew. The advance guard lost a number of men, and some of the prisoners were also killed—by Russian bullets. The Tchetchens immediately wheeled and took flight, followed by volleys of Russian fire. Princess Anna's captor, whose horse was particularly powerful, headed the retreat, racing over the rough country at a break-neck speed. The Princess was obliged to hold on to her captor's belt with one hand; for her other arm clutched the baby. Bullets whined past them as they rode, and looking round, the Princess saw a riderless horse gallop past, bearing on its saddle a torn black skirt, which she took to be that of her sister whom, she imagined, had been shot and had fallen from her horse. The exhausted Princess felt her arms numbing, and knew that she too would fall, if she could not make the Tchetchen stop, and either tie her child to her, or attach her to his saddle. But although she was now shrieking her entreaties, he seemed not to hear and galloped on. Twice her numbed arm slipped and the baby almost fell. The Tchetchens galloped, faster and faster, towards the shelter of their mountains, and the Princess still clutched the wailing baby by one foot; with each bound the little creature was swung to and fro, dashed first against the stirrup and then against the horse's flank. But the Tchetchens would not draw rein for the sake of a baby. Another few minutes and the Princess's numbed fingers loosened. The baby fell to the ground, its cries drowned by the mother's shrieks. Still the Naib rode on, followed by the whole troop of Tchetchens, who galloped their horses over the tiny body without knowing, or caring. As they rode, they laughed and shouted to each other: Allah was great! They had looted Tzinondali, seized the hostages and now escaped a Russian trap. *La Allah illa Allahi!* Presently the whole cavalcade had disappeared into the rocky passes of the foothills, leaving only a few riderless horses and some bodies strewn about the valley. Among them the baby which Prince David's men were to discover next morning.

When they reached the Tower of Pohali, the Russian outpost which, it will be recalled, had lately fallen into Shamyl's hands, the Princess Anna began to question everyone about the fate of the baby Lydia. In her weakness, she imagined the child had escaped death and must have been found by the rest of the troop. She did not know that they had ridden on, over the body. Princess Orbeliani, who had seen the rush of horsemen that followed, did not dare tell her sister. Only hope seemed to sustain the Princess now.

Shamyl himself was at the Tower of Pohali, accompanied by his second son, Khazi Mahommed, who had organized the raid on Tzinondali. The Imam had come down from the mountains to watch the series of attacks his men were launching all along the Lesghien line and the Tower was surrounded by his massed troops, ten thousand of them. As the captives were led through their ranks, the men seemed turned to stone. Only the wind flapped at the black banners, or a dangling, severed head spun slowly on its rope. It was the first time most of the Murids had seen unveiled women—Georgians, at that: they seemed transfixed. Then, they began to shout, raucous wild cries, as terrifying to the captives as their savage appearance, heightened by faces blackened with gunpowder, a measure to prevent sun and snow burns. Involuntarily, the women covered their faces with their hands. Had it not been for their officers, the men would have fallen on the prisoners as spoils of war. But Shamyl's Naibs rode up and down the ranks, shashka in hand, and the prisoners entered the Tower of Pohali unmolested.

Almost at once, Khazi Mahommed came in person to inspect the prisoners, accompanied by his suite of Naibs. Shamyl's second son, his heir, was Naib of Goulali and governor of Karaty, where he had lived when not at the wars. He was loved and respected by both people and Naibs, for although obeying his father implicitly, he was less harsh. Shamyl's dread reputation was beginning to work against him, and there were whispers that Khazi Mahommed would make a better chieftain. He was, besides, one of the Murids' ablest commanders. Young, handsome, powerful, beloved, this was his glowing noon-tide. Everywhere he went he was fêted, and the aôuls watched for his coming. *O Khazi Mahommed, may your path be strewn with pearls, and every wish come true*, sang the women, as they gathered round.

The Caucasians composed songs for every occasion: songs for waking, for sleeping, for victories and defeats. After a terrible battle, when Khazi Mahommed had been forced to retreat, riding desperately, to reach the shelter of the mountains, he had at last fallen asleep across his saddle. At dawn, a scout brought news of the Russians' approach. The Murids gathered round him, to rouse him with a song.

> Sleep no more, Khazi Mahommed,
> Sleeping is done.
> The Russians are on us.
> The war to be won.

So the young Naib awoke, and led them to battle again. His courage was celebrated: 'fighting in the front line was his hobby,' as his descendants were to tell me.

Now he stood over the Princesses, tall, narrow-waisted, a typical

Caucasian delikan; his handsome hawk-features and half-closed eyes very like his father's; his pale, rather set face was framed in a small curling reddish beard; he wore his tcherkesska elegantly, and the prisoners remarked a supremely natural grace. He bowed to each of the Princesses and enquired, courteously enough, after their well-being, promising that warm food and some clothing should be provided at once. He also promised that a search would be made for the baby Lydia. His father the Imam would see them later, he said, and bowing again, making the ritual Moslem salutation, hand on heart, brow and lips, he left. Presently a bundle of assorted rags and odd clothing was brought in, together with a sackful of left-foot shoes, which were of little use to anyone. The Princess Anna covered her nakedness in a baggy pair of chalvari, or Turkish trousers, a shawl round her shoulders, while Madame Drancy was buttoned into a coachman's coat which, however, was presently torn from her, leaving her once more in her chemise. The rest of the servants rummaged in the bundles and were provided with a few rags with which to cover themselves, partially at least.

While the prisoners huddled together, too exhausted to cry, a Naib entered.

'Shamyl Imam asks for the Khancha Anna,' he said.

'What does he want?' demanded the Princess.

'To speak with her,' answered the Naib.

'Then let him come here,' said the Princess. 'I will not go to him.'

'He is the Imam ul Azam—Allah's Prophet on earth,' said the Naib in awed tones.

'And I am a Princess of Georgia,' was the haughty reply.

The Naib turned on his heel, his face incredulous. No woman—or man—of his race would have dared to oppose the Imam.

Prostrating himself before Shamyl, he told him, in a whisper, of the captive's arrogance.

For some moments the Imam remained silent, his half-closed eyes expressionless, then a smile flickered across the pale face; flickered, and was gone. 'So be it,' he said. 'Take them all to Dargo-Vedin. I will see her there. It is better so. Allah is wise.'

Next morning, before resuming their journey, the prisoners were visited by some Naibs who spoke Russian, among them Daniel Beg, Sultan of Elisou, who ordered them to write to their relatives in Tiflis informing them of their situation, and telling them to raise the ransom money without delay. The Princess Anna's black eyes glittered dangerously. 'Assassins! Thieves!' she raged. 'I will never obey you!' But, at last, her sister thought it more prudent to comply with their captors, and she wrote to General Réad: 'We and the whole family are in captivity. We are alive, but in want of everything. Come to our assistance, and inform our relatives of our situation. Address us to Shamyl's camp, at Dargo-Vedin.'

The captives were led out, and given fresh horses and fresh guards too. Now, about to start out for the Great Aôul, they found their escort would be composed of Lesghiens. Now, the difference between Tchetchen and Lesghien was fully realized. The Tchetchens, however ferocious, were Shamyl's picked troops, whereas the Lesghiens were his soldiers of the line, and immediately they made their captives aware of their brutality, their hatred for their Infidel victims.

* * *

For many days and nights the prisoners were driven on, ever higher in the mountains, reaching wilder, more impassable country at each march, struggling up tracks so steep that those who rode were often made to dismount to save the horses, of which the Murids were very careful. Below yawned crevasses so fearful that some servants flung themselves down, overcome by vertigo. Their food consisted of a few pieces of almost uneatable dried meat, or *koumeli*, an unappetizing mixture of rough millet flour which the mountaineers moisten with water and knead till it becomes a sort of dough. Yet it seemed to satisfy the Lesghiens, who marched whole days on such fare, occasionally supplemented by a handful of rhododendron leaves, which were evidently regarded as particularly sustaining. On one occasion, the Princess Anna contrived to barter away her last diamond ring for a lump of bread and a mutton-bone, which all the family gnawed in turn, without, however, appeasing their hunger. On another occasion, the hooks and eyes of Princess Orbeliani's dress proved as valuable as any diamonds, procuring onions and apricots in exchange. One of the Lesghiens gave Madame Drancy an apple: 'I know you Georgians are used to eating every day,' he said, watching her curiously.

Gradually, terror and suffering overcame hunger, and the prisoners scarcely cared whether they lived or died, starved or ate. But Princess Nina, who had learned that Shamyl knew of her family's straitened circumstances, their inability to raise a ransom, was convinced her captivity would be brief, and therefore she was less downcast than the rest, and even showed a healthy appetite. Madame Drancy, too, managed to eat whatever could be found (no doubt recalling with anguish the *pot au feu* of the Rue des Acacias). The children had now recovered sufficiently to amuse themselves imitating the Murids at prayer. They had plenty of opportunities for observing them, for several times a day they performed their rituals, oblivious of all else, swaying and chanting, facing the East, invoking Allah, and prostrating themselves devoutly.

As the little band pressed on, day by day, never knowing where the day's march would end, or how, struggling knee-deep in mud, or crawling hand over hand up sheer ravines before descending again to torrid almost impenetrable brush, through which the captors were obliged to hack a path with their shashkas, they were sometimes joined by other weary, wounded groups: Georgians and Armenians who had been seized from the villages around Tzinondali, and who were also being marched to Dargo-Vedin.

By now, fever and dysentery were further reducing the captives. At last, some could go no farther and were left to die. Some were finished off mercifully by a dagger thrust. The children, often separated from their mothers, shrieked with terror and hunger. Little George Orbeliani was still with his wet nurse and so far had not come to any harm: but the baby Alexander Tchavtchavadzé, who was carried by a scullery-maid, was barely kept alive on handfuls of snow, which she fed him as they staggered over the passes. When at last he was returned to his mother, he was unconscious, his jaws clenched, his face livid. The baby of one of the serfs so exasperated the Lesghiens by its howls that its head was dashed to pieces against the rocks and its body flung down the ravine; at which the mother shrieked so terribly, she was dispatched with a knife. The Princesses were in terror that the crying of their own children would end in a similar way. But the Lesghiens were kinder to the bawling three-year-old Princess Tamara, merely stuffing her head-first into a saddle-bag, from where her stifled cries gradually stopped, and she slept soundly. Salomé, a fiery child, never ceased re-viling her captors, menacing them and striking at them with her tiny fists, which seemed to amuse them. The little Marie, of a more timid nature, had cried bitterly at first, but when one of the Murids gave her an apple she ate the fruit and ended by chattering gaily with a serf child from Tzinondali, like herself a prisoner. Mercifully, the full horrors of this situation were not apparent to the children; the most ghastly trophies, severed heads, or the woman's hand (obviously that of a Georgian captive, for a gold wedding-band was on one finger) which dangled from Madame Drancy's saddle, did not seem to disturb them. But the Frenchwoman could not turn her eyes away from the horrible object and was nauseated every time it flapped against her.

This ghastly journey was punctuated by a series of river crossings, each more alarming than the last. Sometimes the prisoners had one hand tied to the stirrup and were made to swim the icy torrents beside the horses, sometimes they had to cross a chasm, bridged by a single felled tree, so that every step was a torture. At one point Madame Drancy would have preferred death and sank down, too exhausted, too terrified to advance. The Lesghiens motioned her to hold on to the horse, flung a cloak over her head and, giving her a cut over the shoulders with their whips, sent her on. Another time, wobbling across a narrow tree-bridge, the unfortunate Madame Drancy lost her footing and was only rescued, hanging head-down, by a Murid who grabbed her by her boots, the same long-suffering footwear that had been purchased in the Rue de Rivoli—a whole world away.

Sometimes the cortège wound through low, steamy valleys, filled with unfamiliar exotic vegetation, where the stony paths blistered their bleeding feet. Madame Drancy still wore her boots, but had lost almost all else: at one river-crossing her petticoat had been dragged off by the force of the current and she struggled up on to the dry land in her corsets and a muslin chemise which clung to her with such effect that at last her captors were constrained to cover her in a bourka. Useless to order their women prisoners to veil their faces—to give them lengths of coarse linen and tell them to cover their heads—most of them were by now almost naked, their bodies still fatally provocative to the ascetic Murids, although torn by brambles, cut by whips, bruised and alternately scorched brown by noonday suns and blue and mottled by the snows through which they floundered crossing the high passes.

The way to the Great Aôul was long—but their captors deliberately took them by the most circuitous paths, climbing deviously to bewilder them and throw them off the true route. After two weeks they were so exhausted and starved, the children so ill, their spirits so low, that they could hardly distinguish day from night, east from west. It was a timeless journey into fear, each painful step taking them farther from hope, or help.

They had been told that throughout Shamyl's domain, no woman was allowed to remain a widow for longer than three months, a measure designed to keep up a population decimated by perpetual warfare, and they now envisaged themselves compelled to enter some Murid's harem. What they had seen of the aôuls had not been encouraging—bleak eyries from which a hostile population issued to stare at them. The mountaineers watched them balefully, Russian Khanums, wives of Infidel Princes, enemy women; they were curious to know what their Imam would decree for captives of such importance. Their ransom money was bound to be very big, said their guards. Meanwhile, they must not be harmed. 'For Shamyl Imam!' cried their captors, and the crowds stepped back sullenly.

At one point, the Princess Anna seemed near death. She was gripped by a violent ague, was at times delirious, and her wounded foot had begun to fester, so that much of the time she had to be carried. She was further exhausted by the fact that she was trying to nurse not only little Alexander, but the baby of one of her serfs, whose mother had died on the journey. She scarcely seemed to notice what went on around her, or to feel the wound in her lacerated foot. She still prayed that some miracle would restore the lost Lydia to her, and every time they encountered a band of Tchetchens, she would stagger forward to question them. Had they seen the baby Princess? Was she left behind in some aôul? The men could tell her nothing, and none of the captives dared to disclose the truth, for fear the distracted mother would lose her mind.

Towards the end of their journey, they were becoming resigned to their lot, submitting to, rather than raging against, what they believed to be the Divine Will. The country through which they passed was now of a fabulous beauty, with cascades pouring from high rocks, frothing between banks of tropical flowers and huge ferns. Herds of fine cattle were grazing in the fields, and the terraced rocks were ridged with green lines of vineyards. One lofty peak was topped by a single gigantic tree which, 'springing from an unattainable height, rose majestically into the air far above every other thing'. So beautiful was this land that the captives' spirits began to revive in spite of themselves; their sufferings were forgotten: their hunger, wounds, the dreadful scenes they had witnessed, their filthy ragged condition, the children's verminous heads—for by now the nights they had spent in rat-infested stables and granaries had brought vermin to add to their discomforts —all these things were forgotten; and when they halted at noon, the Princesses wandered about picking nosegays of flowers for the children who were of course quite uninterested, far preferring to watch the Lesghiens skinning and roasting a wild boar they had shot.

It was decided by their captors that a halt of two or three days should be made in this agreeable spot. The Lesghiens were waiting for messengers to tell them of Shamyl's arrival at the Great Aôul. It would be unseemly, the prisoners learned, for them to be taken there before the Imam's return. And such is the natural ebullience and resistance of human nature, that the whole party now began positively to enjoy themselves. The mere fact of repose in this serene setting, took on the quality of some holiday outing. When they were joined by a party of Lesghiens who had also been at Tzinondali and were seen to be wearing some of the silver knives and forks engraved with the Tchavtchavadzé arms stuck in their belts beside their kindjals, the Princesses could not restrain hysterical laughter, thus mystifying their captors. The sight of one Naib walking majestically under the patch of shade afforded by Madame Drancy's parasol, a fringed, ivory-handled toy, which a page held over his head, in the Oriental manner reserved for persons of distinction, was irresistibly comic to the prisoners. But soon tension returned. As they broke camp and began to climb again, the skies clouded over, becoming leaden and sullen; they were lashed by rain hurled slantwise across their path, and icy winds howled down from the dark peaks. Snow-drifts lay late in the high passes, and there were still avalanches and tracks sheeted with ice as late as July. The mountains loomed above them menacingly. Again the mountains! Again those hostile regions where they dragged themselves laboriously from waist-high snow-drifts. However high they climbed, the great peaks were always above them, scowling, implacable. All their suffering seemed to come from these mountains.

One night, when they halted outside an aôul, the Princesses could hear, across the flat roof-tops, the plaintive songs of their own Georgia. The songs came and went, faintly, fitfully, carried on the gusts of wind that swept round the aôul. The singer was some unknown and forgotten prisoner, a soldier long since written off as dead, who had never been ransomed and would never again see the darling lowlands of his home. His songs seemed echoes of a lost paradise, and the captives sobbed themselves to sleep once more.

When they were a day's march from the Great Aôul, the party was met by a small band of horsemen who conferred with the guards and presently gave each woman a square of black silk, which they were instructed to wear covering their entire heads. No Avar woman of consequence could appear in public, or before the Imam, without being veiled. Women were not considered worthy of gazing direct on the Imam. Through the dark folds, the Princesses could still see quite well, but the whole scene now appeared even more overcast and sinister, the shadows darker, the mountains more forbidding, and every cloud an approaching thunderstorm.

It was dusk when they climbed the steep approaches to Dargo-Vedin, on the last mile of their journey. They had been on the move for a month, and were tattered, skeletal figures, almost unrecognizable from that household at Tzinondali which they had once been. The Great Aôul scarcely showed against the surrounding rocks, but a few spirals of smoke mounted and hung like a pall above the flat roofs. As the cavalcade drew near, a number of ravens rose in cawing flight to circle overhead, a dark presage to the blackest moment of the captives' lives. All of them were shivering with terror, exhaustion and cold, the children crying, the servants wailing. The rain sleeted down, and rolling clouds closed in from the mountain tops, blotting out the minaret and the stone watch-towers. They came to a high stockade, pierced by iron-bound gates. Before it stood a group of tall, black-cloaked Tchetchens whose towering black lambskin caps made them appear gigantic figures of doom. The gates creaked open, and the captives were led into a large courtyard, walled with roughly piled stones and clay, with a wooden gallery running around three sides. There was a great bustle of men and horses, and some veiled, trousered women scuttled into low doorways beneath the galleries. Each door was hung with curtains that stirred uneasily in the gusts of wind, and it seemed that the women were peeping out furtively. The torchlight flickered over this sombre scene, reflecting in puddles of mud and piercing the gathering darkness, glinted on the silver-mounted pistols and heavy weapons which the guards wore. Beyond the circle of light, and barely visible in the gloom, the Princesses were suddenly aware of a tall figure, dressed in a long white cloak, standing aloof on a balcony over-hanging the courtyard. He seemed to be regarding them intently. Abruptly he raised his hand and a stillness fell over the scene. Even the children stopped crying, surprised by the sudden hush. 'Allah is Great!' said the white-cloaked figure, and turning, disappeared in the darkness. It was Shamyl the Avar, the dread Chieftain, the Lion of Daghestan. As the heavy door-bolts were shut behind them, the captives knew that now they were hostages in his seraglio.

Part Three

26

A Captivity

*How shall we sing the Lord's song in a strange
land?*   PSALM CXXXVII

In an account of the prisoners' life in the aôul, published after their
release by a Tiflis newspaper *Kavkas*, we learn that 'the first evening
was taken up with introductions', a phrase giving an oddly social glow
to a moment that was, in fact, overcast with forebodings. But from the
first, Shamyl had ordered that his captives were to be respected as his
own wives. When their sufferings during the journey were made known
to him, he expressed his awful displeasure. That the captives should
have continued to suffer was not as much his fault as that they were
civilized women bred to other conditions, to whom the discomforts and
privations of the aôul were a severe strain. Daniel Beg, Sultan of Elisou,
who had been uneasy at the terrible state in which he found the captives
at the Tower of Pohali, had asked Shamyl to let them be held prisoners
at his own home. Having lived among the Russians for so long, he knew
their mode of life. But Shamyl refused: he would not risk such valuable hostages anywhere but in his own seraglio; besides, they were to be
treated like his own family. What more could any woman ask? So the
prisoners entered the Great Aôul, to live there for eight months, from
midsummer 1854 through the terrible winter months, and on until the
spring of 1855.

When they were led inside the quarters allotted to them, one of the
cell-like rooms opening on to the main courtyard, they were confronted
by a low-ceilinged, white-washed room lit by an unglazed window 'no
bigger than a pocket-handkerchief—about a quarter of a square yard'.
They measured the room by pacing it: 'eighteen shoes long and twelve
broad'. Here, the two Princesses, the children, Madame Drancy, and
most of the Tzinondali servants—making in all twenty-three persons,
were to live, eat and sleep as best they could. The Princesses were determined to sacrifice their own comfort in order to keep their household

339

around them, for they knew that once they were separated there would be little hope of ever finding them again, and once dispatched to other aôuls, they would be lost forever. Therefore all of them remained together, in conditions of suffocating heat and discomfort. There was no furniture: felt mats covered the floor and on high shelves, running round the walls, were stacked bundles of rather frowzy bedding, quilts and pillows stuffed with flax. Their belongings were presently augmented by a few battered casseroles, a tea-pot, some glasses and a loaf of sugar. The women of the aôul pressed in curiously, to further overcrowd the room, their children already making shy overtures to the little Princesses; but they fell back awed with the arrival of Shamyl's two elder wives, Zaïdate and Shouanete, who welcomed them formally, and presented some sweet-meats from Tollet, the best confectioner of Tiflis.

Conversation was difficult, for in all the seraglio only Shouanete, the converted Christian girl, remembered a little Russian from her childhood in Mozdok. Whereas Zaïdate plainly scorned and disliked the Giaours, Shouanete at once showed a warmth which touched the captives. She was not strictly pretty but glowed with a soft grace and kindness. Throughout their captivity, their welfare was her first care, and she never ceased to share with them the few luxuries and privileges her rank commanded. It was always Shouanete who tried to soften Zaïdate's harshness, and to intercede for them with the Imam. Zaïdate, who enjoyed and abused her position as first wife, wielded supreme power over the seraglio, but not over Shamyl, who had married her out of politic reasons and plainly preferred Shouanete, 'the Pearl', while earnestly endeavouring to observe the tenets of the Koran, and show no favouritism. Zaïdate was small, thin, shrewish, aquiline featured, with a pock-marked face, and a sly malicious smile. But even her victims, the Princesses, granted her grace, her high-bred delicate hands and feet.

Behind these two ladies, the captives observed a dazzlingly pretty young creature, coquettishly dressed, wearing the same long linen tunic and Turkish trousers as the others, but with brighter colours and gayer veils. She appeared to be about eighteen; her small upturned nose was impudent; her large eyes a clear grey. Moreover, her beautifully shaped mouth was flanked by two deep dimples. Her whole appearance was different from the rest of the dark mountain women. This was Aminette, a Kist, Shamyl's third wife. She had been captured in a raid, at the age of three, and brought up in Shamyl's household beside his children; Djemmal-Eddin had been her first playmate, but when he had been surrendered at Akhulgo, she had transferred her affections to his brother, Khazi Mahommed, two years her senior, whom she had grown up to love passionately.

When she was sixteen their idyll ended. Her beauty was so striking that the Imam took her as his third wife. His son married Kherimat, the daughter of Daniel Beg, a union dictated on the Imam's side by political motives. He mistrusted Kherimat, but an alliance with her father was wise. In any case, Khazi Mahommed had fallen desperately in love with her. Her early years, spent in Tiflis, during the term of her father's allegiance to the Russians, had turned her into a most sophisticated coquette. She was ambitious, too, and determined to marry the Imam's heir. Her blend of Asiatic beauty and Western seductions dazzled her young husband as much as it exasperated her father-in-law. Whenever Kherimat arrived from Karaty to visit the Great Aôul, she rode in on a wave of perfume, her veils of gold gauze fastened with jewelled pins, her brocaded cloak lined with sable, at which Shouanete and Zaïdate could not restrain their envious glances. The Imam's rigid views on personal adornment rankled, even with the loving Shouanete. Sometimes Kherimat's extravagance so enraged Shamyl that he would seize her baggage and burn it. At which she would pretend to weep, knowing that she had many more fineries at Karaty; and Khazi Mahommed would be more enslaved than ever by her pretended sobs; but Aminette would rush into her room and bolt the door, crying herself to sleep for love of her step-son.

But of all of this the prisoners only became aware by degrees. At first they were too exhausted, too alarmed as to their fate to look beyond the four damp-stained walls of their room. They flung themselves down on the stale-smelling mattresses and tried to sleep. All night the children wailed fretfully. Outside the footsteps of the sentries sounded, coming and going. Far away across the mountains, the jackals yelped and were answered by a dog in the valley. At dawn the muezzin's cry roused them from their uneasy sleep, and they rose, shivering and draggled, to face this new phase of their captivity.

At noon they were informed by Shamyl's steward, Hadjio, a most important person in the aôul, that the Imam intended to visit them that afternoon. The steward was a handsome, gaunt man, black-eyed and black-bearded; but his eagle features belied the curiously gentle consideration he was always to show towards the prisoners. He ordered them to veil themselves, and a chair was placed in the gallery, outside their door, for the Imam would not cross their threshold. The interview was conducted by means of two interpreters, Shah Abbas, an Armenian, and Indris, a Russian deserter to whom the Princesses took an instant dislike, and not without cause, for they were to discover how dependent they were upon him, and how often his personal spite was to misrepresent both their statements and the communications they wrote, or received, regarding their release. Shamyl was an imposing figure, seated on the shabby wooden chair as if it were a throne, and flanked by his bodyguard and chief executioner—a touch of bravura not lost on the captives.

He fixed them with his strange scimitar-slit eyes. 'They say, Varvara, you are the wife of Ellico. He was my prisoner: a noble, brave man, who never deceived me. Understand me—I abhor trickery. Nothing bad will befall you, if you do not try to deceive me. The Russian Sultan took my son away from me, and no matter how often I have offered prisoners of distinction in exchange, he has never given back my son. . . . They say, Anna and Varvara, that you are the granddaughters of the Sultan of Georgia. You therefore are fit persons to write to the Russian Sultan: let him return me Djemmal-Eddin, and I will free you on the hour. My people also demand a ransom. I will treat with your families on that subject later.'

When the interpreter had translated these words, the Princesses felt themselves lost: money might be raised; but how could they hope the Tzar would ever countenance the return of his protégé Djemmal-Eddin; how expect the elegant and fêted young aide-de-camp they had known in St. Petersburg to return to these wilds he had left so young? The walls of the aôul seemed to close in implacably, and Shamyl continued:

'I hold letters addressed to you; I have had them translated to me. But one letter is neither in Russian, nor Georgian, nor Tartar. Understand me, you will neither receive nor send anything which I cannot read. Allah counsels man to prudence. I follow Allah's word. . . . What is this strange language? Why do you employ such a script? Do you seek to trick me?' So saying, he tore the letter in pieces, and as it fluttered to the ground Madame Drancy was able to recognize, with anguish, her mother's handwriting. . . . Choked with tears of homesickness, she turned away. The Princess Anna was so enraged by Shamyl's lecture that she rushed forward, forgetting all the protocol of the seraglio, and pushing aside her veil, glared at the Imam, hurling a most undiplomatic reply at the tyrant.

'You need not threaten us. We have no intention of tricking you. Our rank and our education forbids us to lie. You can rely on our word. But we cannot be responsible for letters others send us. With us is a foreigner, a Frenchwoman—another of your innocent victims. The letter you destroyed was probably addressed to her.'

Shamyl's face remained impassive during this tirade, but his heavy-lidded eyes scrutinized the Princess from head to foot. Then he rose, majestically. 'So be it,' he said. 'Conduct yourself well, and you have nothing to fear. You shall have those letters which I have read. But never forget—all deceit is an offence against Allah and his servant Shamyl. The first time I find you plotting to escape, or to deceive me, I shall have you killed. To cut off heads is my right—my duty, as

Imam.' He turned and stalked away, followed by his suite. In the silence that fell, Madame Drancy's sobs sounded shrill and loud.

* * *

In their suffocating room, the captives sank into a melancholy which nothing could dispel. Even the arrival of a parcel from their relatives in Tiflis, containing a few necessities—soap, combs, towels and such, only raised their spirits briefly. Beyond stating that they were alive and well they were not allowed to communicate with their families, save on the subject of the ransom.

The health of the little Alexander now began to cause them apprehension. The journey had nearly killed him. He was teething, and screamed convulsively, so that each fit seemed as if it would destroy him. Shamyl loved children, and every day the captives' children were brought to his rooms, where he played with them, petting them and allowing them every liberty. No matter how great his preoccupations, whether the wars went well or ill, he always had time for them. They seemed to understand each other, in some universal language, the children clambering about him, shouting and laughing, so that, hearing the uproar, the Princesses trembled for their audacity. But the children always returned happy and over-excited, carrying the fruit and lollipops he crammed into their fists. He was especially solicitous for the baby Alexander's health: in vain he fetched celebrated medicine-men from his farthest provinces; in vain he procured rare herbs, or had him wrapped in the skin of a freshly slaughtered sheep—generally regarded as an infallible cure; the baby did not thrive, and lay wailing on the Imam's knee. But whether his concern was for the sick child, or for Princess Anna's child—or for so valuable a hostage, no one could say. The airless heat of the overcrowded room where they all slept was weakening the baby more and more; at last Princess Anna obtained Shamyl's permission for him to sleep outside, under the gallery, watched by a nurse; at which he began to mend, slowly.

The lack of ventilation and exercise gradually exhausted both their minds and health. Shamyl had decreed that none of them were to leave their room (indeed, to ensure the privacy and honour of his captives, he himself was scrupulous never to cross the courtyard before their door, always choosing the far side of the quadrangle). But during those first sultry months, they had been allowed to sit outside at night, when Shamyl had retired to rest, or to mount on to the flat roof under cover of darkness, there to taste the fresh mountain air, and watch the starlight glitter over the distant peaks. For some time this was their only solace. Under the vast dark vault of heaven, the unhappy women felt soothed and sustained.

Gradually their listlessness was overcome, and they began to observe the life around them, the customs and characteristics of the seraglio and its inmates. Besides Shamyl's three wives already described, there were his daughters, Nafisette, aged thirteen, and Fatimat, aged ten, gentle creatures, with their father's strange, slit-eyes. Their half-sister, the little nine-year-old Nadjavat, was Zaïdate's child, very pretty, but crippled, her legs being quite twisted. Shamyl was devoted to her, and carried her about with him, indulging her: even when she once set fire to the seraglio, she was not punished. About a month after the arrival of the prisoners, the number of children was augmented by the birth of a daughter to Shouanete; all her others had died in infancy. Zaïdate had produced no more children since the birth of Nadjavat and longed for a son, thus to strengthen her position with Shamyl. It was soon apparent to the prisoners that while Shouanete cared only for Shamyl, pining if he was absent, paling if gun-fire was heard afar, blushing like a bride when he returned, Zaïdate cared most for power. While Zaïdate was berating the slaves, harassing the household and generally giving the whole seraglio the sharp edge of her tongue, Shouanete was seated in her cushioned room, a samovar humming beside her, as she listened for Shamyl's footstep.

The Imam's youngest son, Mahommed Sheffi, a boy of fifteen, handsome, good-natured and exuberant, was seldom seen by the captives, as he was training to ride and shoot in a manner befitting Shamyl's son. His elder brother, Khazi Mahommed, was considered the finest horseman in all the mountains, second only to the Imam, whose marksmanship he was said to rival. Thus the boy felt he was unworthy and was forever practising, riding out from the seraglio at all hours, his horses' hooves clattering over the cobbles, while the crack of his rifle echoed back across the great walls of the rock, and the ravens rose and circled in flight.

Shamyl's mother-in-law, Bahou, grandmother of his children by Fatimat, also lived in the seraglio, enjoying great respect: she was an animated old lady, who liked nothing more than to make the bread for the whole seraglio. (Unfortunately it was made in the Caucasian manner, with an outer layer of thick grease, covering the crust. This so nauseated the captives, that they never became accustomed to it, and were obliged to pare off crust and grease, leaving a much diminished loaf which they then soaked in water and hung up to dry, until the reek of grease had subsided.) The seraglio also housed a malicious middle-aged Tartar woman, Hadji Rebel, the governess to Shamyl's daughters, who lost no time making herself disagreeable to the Giaours, with a sanctified air, as if executing Allah's wishes. There were besides, Nana, the mother of Aminette, and Batchoum who, being the wife of Shamyl's old tutor, the Mollah Jamul u'din, was

Zaïdate's stepmother; she was only a few years older than Zaïdate, and of a remarkable beauty. She was gentle and self-effacing, but Zaïdate detested her, making her feel an intruder, and she was seldom seen. The rest of the household consisted of Ilita, the steward Hadjio's wife, a managing woman who kept her husband under her thumb and was generally occupied in the storeroom; Labazan, the Imam's cook, Bey Mourza, his personal servant, and Selim, his arms-bearer and body-guard, who were also lodged within the confines of the seraglio (which in the East represents the main body of the house, as opposed to the harem, a specific portion strictly reserved for the women); while a number of guards, grooms and other servants lived outside the gates.

The seraglio, or inner court, was centred around Shamyl's own quarters, a separate building composed of three small rooms, adjoining a little mosque. The women's quarters, those of his wives and children and the prisoners, ran all around the court and opened on to the gallery. The entrance gate was flanked by the treasury, and a reception room, or selamlik, where Shamyl received his guests and conducted the affairs of his army and provinces; for he was as great a legislator as warrior. The rest of the seraglio was screened from these rooms by a partition, or high wooden paling jutting across the court-yard, and from behind which the women peeped through the chinks at the coming and going of the outside world. They were not allowed to pass this barrier, and the captives presently named it 'the wall of jealousy'. A bakery, store-room, stables and well completed the seraglio, making it a self-supporting unit within the outer aôul.

For eight months this was the prisoners' entire world, its stone walls and ramshackle wooden cells their whole horizon, the monotonous hours of the day and night only marked by the cry of the muezzin. There was nothing to do, and nowhere to go. But as time went by, they began to take pleasure in the visits of Shamyl's wives, and as they began to understand each other better, Shouanete to remember the Russian of her childhood and the captives to pick up a little of the Tchetchen dialect, they were drawn, in spite of themselves, into the life around them. When Shamyl rode out to battle, they felt for Shouanete in her anxiety; when he returned with pieces of silk for his wives, and there was not enough left for Aminette, they understood her frustration, and shared her impudent glee when, one night, she rushed to hide in their room, keeping the great Imam waiting before her door like some boyish suitor. At last, receiving no answer to his knocks, tired and cold, the Lion of Daghestan pocketed the key left in her door (the Princesses noted with amazement that he did not let himself in), and thus, locking out the errant Aminette, stood hidden in the shadows waiting for her return. But Aminette, watching through a crack in the Princesses' door, stifled her laughter and announced she would not go back. After a long wait, endured with the patience and humility of the most ardent lover, the bitter cold at last drove Shamyl back to his own quarters, and he crossed the courtyard looking dispirited. But what was, to Aminette, a prank, was to the prisoners a matter of life and death. None of them had forgotten the executioner's axe; all of them could imagine their fate, if Shamyl discovered they had abetted Aminette, or seen him off his guard, and they did not breathe freely for some time after this nocturnal episode.

Even the detestable Zaïdate assumed a human quality when she confided her problems to them. She feared she had become sterile. None of the local herbs had helped her. Could the Princesses write to Tiflis and obtain some new medicines for her? This they did, Shamyl's messengers taking the letters and returning with the drugs, and advice from the doctor. As long as Zaïdate was following the cure, she was agreeable to the captives, sending them extra delicacies and the best food available—a most welcome change from the usual diet of bread and goat's cheese. But after a while, finding the drugs were of no use to her, their food was once again meagre and unappetizing, and would no doubt have continued that way, had not Shamyl, returning from one of his military sorties, come in person to inspect the fireplace he had ordered to be repaired in their room. During his visit, he observed a saucepan of dingy-looking onion water which passed for soup and was the captives' only nourishment that day. At which he flew into a violent rage, sent for Zaïdate and lashed her with his tongue, so that she wept before him. A few minutes later, Shouanete arrived, beaming, followed by Hadjio, bringing them meat, rice, butter and tea (the kind generally used by the Caucasians: a sort of heavy compote of tea-leaves mixed with sheep's blood and formed into square bricks, which melted when put into hot water). For once the prisoners were able to eat their fill and so felt at peace with the world—even with Zaïdate.

But not for long. She was forever tormenting them, demanding to know how much money their families could raise—assuring them of the awful fate that awaited them if the ransom did not materialize; or she would taunt them: 'Your husband cannot love you greatly,' she would tell the Princess Anna, 'otherwise he would have liberated you long ago.' Or again: 'Today, we spoke with a man who had been at Tzinondali. He was amazed at such splendours, that so much riches could belong to one man. . . . How strange that your ransom has not yet been raised.' She would then speak of the large sum which the prisoners learned had been set, not by Shamyl, but by the People's Council, a body which even he could not gainsay. Shouanete could do nothing to persuade her husband to lower the sum; for himself he only wanted his son back; but the people demanded money in exchange for the prisoners.

Shamyl was, in a sense, himself a prisoner. For all his autocratic rule, he could not go against the will of his people, in this respect, for he would have risked losing the support of his most puissant Naibs, all of whom regarded the Princesses as a unique means of obtaining the money needed for arms and to repair the devastation which was a regular part of Russian tactics. The mountaineers were convinced that no sum would be too exorbitant to demand from such a princely family. They could not understand that the Tchavtchavadzés' wealth lay in land, rather than actual money. Nor could they understand that the papers and deeds found among Princess Orbeliani's things were her husband's will and title-deeds to the estate which was entailed, only to be inherited by the baby George upon his majority. The Princess explained it all laboriously; but Zaïdate had her answer ready. 'In that case, your son will remain here until he is of age, and can realize the estates. But do not worry. Our mountain air is keen. He will grow up big and strong.' At which Princess Varvara burst into tears, and Zaïdate went away looking satisfied.

Three months had gone by, and November brought little change, except that summer had given way to autumn storms. Low-rolling dark clouds hung over the aôul, blotting out the mountains for days at a time. Rainstorms flooded down, leaking through the roofs and cascading down the narrow paths. The courtyard was knee-deep in mud in some places, while an icy film of damp settled on the walls; a never-ending wind moaned through the aôul, flapping at the doors, dislodging the tiles on the roof and nagging at the captives' nerves. Their tattered garments were quite insufficient, and their fireplace smoked intolerably. Their situation now aroused pity among some of the *karaaouls*, or seraglio guards, who waited on Shamyl's guests (mollahs, governors of his provinces and his Naibs who ate in the reception room beside the gates) so that they never failed to reserve a few scraps for the Princesses, a piece of meat, or some fruit for the children. Gradually the prisoners came to a curious sort of understanding of the mountaineers; though they had beaten and harassed them so brutally on the journey, this was out of fear that any delay risked their being rescued by the Russians. The children felt no fear of any of them. The babies, Alexander and George, soon became used to these swarthy, fierce men who came to fetch them to Shamyl, and would be carried off crowing happily.

If fate had been cruel to the Princesses, how much more cruel to the wretched Madame Drancy; she was a foreigner, with no hope of ransom, or of anyone to be interested in her lot; she was of no account politically, or personally, to the Murids. She could speak neither Russian nor Georgian, let alone any of the Tartar dialects, so that every word spoken among the captives had to be translated into French by the Princesses, if she were not to remain shut out from their last refuge —talk. The smallest thing was of interest now: the shape of the clouds, the flight of a bird, glimpsed through the tiny square of window; even the habits of insects which crept from the walls were all events for discussion. One book—the *Imitation de Jésus-Christ* had reached them from Tiflis—Shamyl being reassured as to its sacred nature had allowed it to pass. With this, Madame Drancy instructed Marie and Salomé in French reading, while she and the Princesses derived consolation from its sermons, which dwelt on the patience with which the true Christian carries his cross. Madame Drancy tells us that the Princess Orbeliani ever set a pious example, but that neither she, Madame Drancy, nor the Princess Anna, could refrain from bitter complaints. The French-woman would creep into a corner, there to cry, unperceived, recalling her homeland and her mother.

'Crying for your mother?' asked one of the wives, finding her sobbing. 'But you don't need a mother any more, Frenchwoman—you are not a child.'

'These women are not like us,' says Madame Drancy. 'For them maternal love diminishes rapidly, as the child grows up. Neither mother nor child are deeply attached, once the child has no more physical dependence on the mother.' The monotony and mischief-making petti-ness of the daily life in the harem, so stifling to the captives, was not so to the wives, and they were genuinely astonished at the captives' sufferings. They considered them blest, and signally honoured, to be lodged in the Imam's own seraglio. Shouanete alone recalled some-thing of another life beyond the mountains, and she was always asking the prisoners to tell her more about European ways. Sometimes she spoke of the bonnets and cloaks she recalled seeing the Russian women wear, at Mozdok. 'I am happy here,' she said, 'so happy, and yet—sometimes—I cannot help regretting——' She stopped short.

'Regretting?' asked the Princess.

'Regretting that Shamyl *will not* permit us to dress better,' she replied, and changed the conversation, firmly.

The Princesses had received word from Prince David and General Réad that everything possible was being done to free them. Beyond that they knew nothing, save that the sum of money demanded was astronomic, and seemed as impossible to achieve as Djemmal-Eddin's return. They told their captors flatly that such a sum could never be raised. But financial computations were generally something the mountaineers could not grasp. They wanted money—not for them-selves, but to restore the ruined aôuls and pastures of the community. Every time the Naibs suggested the Princesses should write personally to the Tzar, they refused. 'Our captivity is the fault of my careless-ness,' said the Princess Anna; 'I would die rather than approach the Emperor with my troubles—especially now, when the Crimean cam-paign absorbs his whole mind.' One day Zaïdate bustled into their room carrying an old copy of the *Russki Invalid*, a St. Petersburg paper, and pointed out a marked paragraph which Indris had translated to her. It told of a very large sum which had been granted by the British government for some special purpose.

'There you are!' said Zaïdate triumphantly. 'You see, such big sums of money *do* exist. If the Khancha of England can pay millions, so can the Khancha of Russia. You were her ladies-in-waiting. She will pay, if you ask her.'

'Why should she? *She* is not your prisoner,' replied the Princess Anna, who still refused to write to the Winter Palace.

As the weeks dragged by, it seemed they had never known any other life. They remembered, with a remote impersonal clarity, their house in Tiflis, receptions at the Voronzov Palace, the shining busy kitchen at Tzinondali, with its great churns of cream, the cool cellar with the vats of their own Kakhetia wines. Seated on the floor in the cramped dark room, they exchanged memories: Madame Drancy told them of Paris, of rain gleaming on the *pavé*, reflecting the glowing balloon-like gas-globes of the Place de la Concorde; of willows overhanging the Seine; of theatres along the boulevards, restaurants and shops. She would fall silent, recalling the Rue des Acacias, her brief bitter life with Jean-Baptiste, and her child in England. She did not speak of them; they would not be of interest to Princesses of Georgia. Then the Princesses would relate their girlhood in St. Petersburg—their lives at the Smolny Convent, and how they came to Court, as the youngest ladies-in-waiting; how they wore the diamond badge of office; how gracious the Empress was; how handsome the Emperor; how fabulous the great Court balls at the Winter Palace . . . And then, perhaps, they would recall Djemmal-Eddin, the dark handsome young aide-de-camp, always a pace or two behind the Tzar, whose favourite he was, and how, when he danced the mazurka, even the musicians missed a beat, watching his dashing grace. Madame Drancy must have seen that they remembered him as a young god, favoured, happy, beloved, one with his adopted country. How could they ever hope he would leave all this?

II

In all the detailed accounts of life in Shamyl's aôul, left by both Madame Drancy and the Princesses, no mention is ever made of one vital aspect of daily life. Sanitation is ignored: a veil of modesty is drawn over what must have been, perhaps, the most terrible aspect of their captivity. All these women and children were cooped up in one small room, in sickness and in health. We are told they were never allowed to leave it for the first few months. A copper ewer and basin was probably all that was provided for the ablutions of twenty-two bodies. For the rest, it is unlikely that the aôul possessed the primitive but efficient water-closets which are still to be seen in the medieval harem quarters of the Sultan's palace, Topkapu Serai, nor the steam-baths which, in varying degrees of luxury, are found all over Turkey. And even if there were such comforts, were they allowed to leave their prison? In the sketches and plans of the Imam's seraglio which were published in a Tiflis news-paper after their release, the Princesses were exact in their detailed placing of each room, of the well, stables and such; but there is no trace of any bath-house, or latrine. Was this accurate, or an omission due to overwhelming delicacy? Are we to suppose there was, at least, some sort of outhouse attached to each room, as in the manner of those special eyries perched over ravines, found in the Balkan monasteries? Or was their captivity made more hideous by a total lack of privacy and hygiene? We shall never know: even the foundations of the Great Aôul are now destroyed; the restless mountain wind sweeps across the plateau where once it stood; there is no one left alive who can recall such trivial yet obsessive details. The conventions of the age in which the Princesses lived closed round their letters and journals; loneliness and fear, despair, hunger and dirt are described in detail. But the body's functions and the chamber pot are resolutely ignored, and we are left wondering, shuddering.

III

Now it was December. Outside their small window the snow fell softly: inside, the smoking chimney still filled the room with a pall of acrid, whitish smoke from the *kizyak*, cakes of dried cow-dung and straw used for fuel. The servants, rocking backwards and forwards, solaced themselves with interminable wailing chants, which they improvised according to their mood. Sometimes they were moving; at other times, they irritated the already frayed nerves of Madame Drancy, who also found the children's habit of copying the mollah's chants almost unbearable. In vain she tried to teach them *Cadet Roussel*. They preferred *La Allah illa Allahi*.

'O! what have we lived to see?' wailed the servants, shrill in their grief. 'The flower and light of our Kakhetia have fallen into the hands of the hated Lesghiens! What are our sufferings beside theirs? Let us pray for our Princesses and their children. With them perish all the beauty and hope of our land.' None of which was calculated to raise the spirits, and, presently, they would send word to Aminette, asking her to join them. The giddy little creature generally contrived to dispel their gloom. She had become attached to the Princess Nina, finding in her a companion of her own age. Together, they devised new ways to tease Hadjio. They had discovered that, as a devout Moslem, the steward regarded the touch of a Giaour would defile him. Therefore, egged on by Aminette, the Princess Nina would find a dozen ways to brush up against him in the courtyard, bump into him in the stables, or touch his hand as he brought in their provisions. At each defiling contact he was obliged to perform a series of purifying ablutions, seven times over. At which the two girls would rush away across the courtyard, stifling their laughter, and even Shouanete looked reproving.

Aminette possessed a lovely voice, clear and soft, with nothing of that nasal tone so typical of Eastern singers. The captives' greatest pleasure was to listen when she sang her plaintive Asiatic airs. Such melodies seem to share something of the Brazilian (or Portuguese) Modinhas which Beckford describes as 'languid, interrupted measures, as if the breath was gone with excess of rapture and the soul panting to meet the kindred soul. . . .'

When Khazi Mahommed returned to the Great Aôul, Aminette could not conceal her joy, and sang, bird-like, her eyes shining as she flitted about (Aminette always ran, never walked), preparing his quarters, stealing her husband's embroidered pistol-holsters to copy them for his son, sitting beside the Princesses for hours at a time, sewing feverishly; but Khazi Mahommed received her gifts carelessly, soon passing them on to Mahommed Sheffi. When he rode away again, he was a splendid figure, at once foppish and harsh, mounted on a white horse with a scarlet saddle, his yellow shoes thrust through gold-inlaid stirrups (for his wife's taste for luxury had begun to corrupt and embolden him, against his father's wishes). With a clatter of hooves and steel he was gone, and all the women pressed to the 'wall of jealousy' to watch him out of sight. Only Aminette fled to her room to hide her tears.

She too had begun as a captive; she was so lonely, she said. Zaïdate tormented her, Shouanete was all kindness, but much older, while Napicette and Nafisette were children, so that she lived a solitary life in spite of her position.

'And your husband?' asked the Princess Anna curiously.

'The Imam! Somehow I cannot get used to being his wife. . . . When I am in his presence I am almost afraid to breathe.'

She had never known the West; the dandified men, softened by civilization, were unknown to her. Unlike the Princess Anna, she was not aware of Shamyl's magnetic force, his fascination. She did not tell them, but they knew, that her heart still longed for Khazi Mahommed. Sometimes she would leave them abruptly and, drawing her veils about her face, climb on to the roof of the seraglio, where she would gaze out, long and fixedly, across the mountains, far away, to Karaty, the province where he lived as governor; and she would sing, as if to charm him to her side again.

As the life of the aôul became their own, and seemed to be all they had ever known, the captives discovered new values. A walk, which Shouanete arranged for them—the only one they were permitted to take in all their captivity—assumed enormous proportions, becoming an expedition. But after half an hour, going through the narrow steep ways of the aôul, they begged to be taken back. The unaccustomed air and exercise was too much for them. Each month, when the new moon appeared, a fragile crescent glimmering in the greenish evening skies, all the women assembled in the courtyard to pray. Their cries and chants rang through the air piercingly, redoubling as their ardours mounted, and they beat their breasts and sobbed with exhaltation. Only Zaïdate and Shouanete were allowed to pray with the Imam: a rug was placed on the balcony outside his rooms, and he knelt, barefooted, his two wives, also barefooted, kneeling a pace or two behind him. Aminette was debarred from the honour so long as she remained childless.

Once, during Shamyl's absence from the Great Aôul, Aminette offered to show them his rooms. Bluebeard's apartments! The captives struggled against terror and curiosity; the latter winning. But the Imam's rooms were not rewarding. A great number of books and manuscripts lined the walls, which were white-washed, and some Caucasian rugs covered the floor, while a collection of arms, kindjals and pistols hung beside the hooded chimney-piece. The captives crept away, feeling cheated, although they had long known the austere nature of Shamyl's life.

In general, he rose at dawn, to pray. At seven, he drank tea, and ate a little white bread, this meal being brought him by Shouanete. From then, until one o'clock, he worked, received his Naibs, and went over reports from his provinces or battlefields. His mid-day meal, always brought him by both Shouanete and Zaïdate, was simple: a pilaff, and some raisins, or a little goat's cheese. The rest of the day was spent in meditation and prayer, or in theological discussions with the Mollah Jamul u'din. Sometimes Indris or Shah Abbas read the foreign journals to him, and most days, the children were brought to see him at dusk. At nine, he ate a frugal supper alone. At eleven, he went to bed, choosing, in strict rotation, a week at a time, his different wives. But after seven nights with one or the other, he always devoted twenty-four hours to solitary purifying prayers. On Friday, his whole day was spent in the mosque.

Such was the rigorously simple tenor of Shamyl's life in the Great Aôul.

When he rode out to battle he was a heroic figure, and the prisoners, in spite of themselves, were profoundly impressed by the sight of him, sitting his horse so superbly, as it caracoled about the courtyard, eager to be gone. As always, he was simply dressed; while his horse was caparisoned in crimson leather, he wore a sober black tcherkesska, his drab cloak lined with black fur, the silver inlay on his weapons his only adornment (for to the strictest Moslem sects gold ornaments are forbidden), his dark, henna-stained orange beard the only note of colour. While the whole seraglio gathered in the courtyard to receive his blessing, he always paid a last visit to the old Bahou who, as mother of the dead Fatimat, remained very dear to him.

When it was known that the Imam was leaving the Great Aôul, whether to survey his domains, lead his troops, or preach the Tarikat, gloom descended on the seraglio. Zaïdate and Shouanete supervised the packing of provisions, tested his saddle and bridle, primed his pistols and inspected his bourkas and clothes minutely. No one else was trusted to do this.

He never left without calling together all the servants, beggars and poor of the aôul, to whom he distributed money and cotton cloth, telling them their prayers were acceptable to Allah, and that they should pray for him. Then, all assembled before his door, they made their farewells, the children, now joined by the little Tchavtchavadzés, clinging to him, howling dismally. The captives observed that he often seemed reluctant to leave; he would sigh and look around with an air of regret. Then, shaking off his melancholy, he would vault into the saddle and setting his horse at the gates, thunder out at a gallop. The aôul was surrounded by three separate walls or bastions, each pierced by a low portal barely high enough for a rider to pass under, even when crouched over his horse's neck. But Shamyl never slackened his pace; as he approached each gate, he swung himself low over the horse's side, and at once rose again to stand in the stirrups, flinging himself down again only a second before reaching the next gate. It was the most dashing display of horsemanship the hostages had ever seen. They watched him, open-mouthed, as he sped away into the distance, followed by his Murids, their banners streaming from their lances, the echo of their battle-chant borne faintly on the wind. The women, prisoners and wives alike, watched him out of sight in silence—then, as the gates were closed, the heavy bars and bolts clamped in place, an air of desolation descended on the seraglio. Shouanete retired to pray for her lord and master's safety, while Aminette rushed to the roof, to catch a last glimpse of the cavalcade, as it disappeared over the farthest pass, into a world of freedom she had never known. Zaïdate immediately put on a collection of finery that she treasured but never dared to wear in Shamyl's presence, and even had the bad taste to flaunt some of the diamonds looted from Tzinondali. The prisoners went back to their room, amazed to find that, contrary to feeling relieved or freer without the dreaded Imam's presence, they felt more abandoned and insecure. They had discovered that Shamyl was no ogre, but a just, honourable man acting according to his beliefs, and within his means, careful of their well-being. He was a gaoler who never deliberately persecuted them, or permitted the malicious abuses which Zaïdate's jealousy and Hadji-Rebel's meanness inflicted on them during his absence.

The prisoners had no means of telling how the wars went, any more than the progress or otherwise of their own affairs. Sometimes, judging by Shouanete's pale, tear-stained face, they guessed at a Murid defeat, but dared not ask. 'I cannot understand what men seek. Why do they go to war when they might remain peaceably at home with their own families?' sighed Shouanete; while Zaïdate, with her thin smile, told the Princesses not to hope for rescue, under any circumstances. She was plainly jealous of the Princess Anna. It was rumoured that if no ransom was forthcoming, the captives might be distributed among the Naibs; but she believed Shamyl would keep the Princess Anna for himself.

'Don't imagine you will better yourselves, or go free, if Shamyl should be killed,' she said, one dark winter's day, as the sound of gun-fire reverberated around the mountains. 'We have our orders. If he should be killed, we are to cut your throats.'

'And we would far rather die, than live here for the rest of our lives,' the Princesses assured her tartly. At which Indriss accused them of not being co-operative in the matter of their ransoms, and when the Princesses replied that under *no* circumstances would they beg either from the Emperor or Prince Voronzov, Zaïdate flew into a rage, still finding the ransom no nearer. 'How *dare* you defy the Imam's wishes? You, a prisoner! How is it you do not fear him?'

The Princess replied she feared no one but God.

'Unheard of impudence!' screamed Zaïdate. 'The Imam is a saint!'

'How dare you disobey his Holy command!' shouted Hadji-Rebel, edging into the scene.

'Holy he may be,' rejoined the Princess, 'but he cannot give me back my dead child.' At which a frightful uproar broke out, the Princess ordering Hadji-Rebel out of the room, and the Tartar governness shoving and pinching the hostages until she was at last led away by Shouanete, who begged the Princesses to be more guarded in their speech.

On one occasion Zaïdate slyly suggested to the Princess Anna that the Russian government would probably be pleased to pay their ransom, in token of her husband's outstanding bravery during a recent engagement. But the Princess was not to be caught. She did not display the slightest curiosity, thus balking Zaïdate's desire to withhold any information she might ask. 'With us,' said the Princess, 'only cowards are remarked. It is impossible to distinguish bravery—for all are brave.'

After which, Zaïdate saw to it that their food was worse than usual, sending it to them rancid, or filled with weevils; while the window-pane, now broken, was not repaired. The icy mountain air poured into the room; moreover, the children had by now all caught severe colds, from running about the courtyard barefooted in the snow. Yet so stifling was the room at night, they could not endure to stuff up the window with rags or oiled paper such as the wives used, and which darkened their quarters to a lugubrious twilight.

They were now terribly emaciated and weakened. Princess Anna's lovely hair had fallen out in handfuls, and she had begun to cough alarmingly. Her health was a matter of acute concern to the prisoners, not only on her own account, but because, by Murid tenets, any child orphaned while a captive was Allah's own, and therefore to be brought up in the Moslem faith. Were the Princess to die, Marie, Salomé and Alexander would have been taken from them on the hour. But for her child, the Princess Orbeliani would have preferred to die; to find, in death, the husband she had lost in life. Only the young Princess Nina still retained a glow of youth and hope. Her friendship with Aminette flourished: by now Aminette had learned to speak some Georgian. Together the two girls discussed their emotions; Aminette's love for her step-son, and Princess Nina's Tiflis flirtations, while the Princess described the luxuries of civilization by the hour. The Princess Nina, sighing neither for a faraway child, like Madame Drancy, nor remembering a husband, dead or alive, as did her aunts, pined for mere abstractions—luxury, gaiety, the world. Her chief anxiety seemed to be that she might never taste the glories her aunts had known at Court, as ladies-in-waiting.

When Hadji-Rebel told her that, in any case, even if the Imam's terms were met, and all the rest were liberated, she, the Princess Nina, was to be kept in the Great Aôul, to become Djemmal-Eddin's bride, her shrieks of fury and terror rang through the seraglio, even overcoming the muezzin who, at that moment, was sounding his piercing evening call to prayer from the minaret which rose above the surrounding roofs. 'Marry that monster's son? I would sooner die! You are all torturers! I will throw myself down the well rather than stay among you another hour.' She rushed sobbing to her aunts, who were alarmed to find the whole seraglio aroused by the uproar, and crowding into their room. They were led by Hadji-Rebel, flaming with indignation, hurling threats and imprecations at the young princess, and menacing her with her fists. 'Ungrateful girl! Insolent Giaour! How dare you speak of Shamyl thus? How dare you refuse his son? Remember you are the Imam's slave and instead of selling you, he has sheltered you in his own home, keeping you pure as a lily. You are not worthy to marry his son. Djemmal-Eddin is a prince—all the beauties of Circassia would give their eyes to become his bride. Don't think you'll get him after this! You'll be lucky if Shamyl gives you to a Naib. . . . You'll see. . . .' All the women were now shouting at each other, and the Princesses' servants could hardly be restrained from attacking their captors. Calm was only restored when the Princess Orbeliani tactfully explained that her niece could not endure the prospect of changing her religion, and would rather die than adopt the Moslem faith. Religious convictions, however misguided, were understood in the seraglio, and the captives were left in peace. Nevertheless, the incident was not forgotten. Even Shouanete seemed offended at the Princess Nina's outburst. It was evident that Shamyl was indeed sacred to them—a supreme being, above all earthly criticism. For a long while after, the captives were shunned, seeing none of the wives.

Discussing the affair, the Princesses voiced their uneasiness. Could this intention explain the curious way their niece had been spared the humiliations and rough treatment of the journey? While they walked, she rode; her clothes, even her jewels remained untouched; her captors almost obsequious. This was undoubtedly on Shamyl's orders. His spies must have informed him, when he was planning his raid, of Princess Nina's presence in Tzinondali, and of her youth and beauty. Shamyl was known to select Christian or captive women from other races for his brides; this choice probably being designed not so much to bring fresh blood into the race as to avoid, both for himself and his sons, the complications which might arise from marrying into a Naib's family. (Kherimat was an exception, and even so, as Daniel Beg's daughter, Shamyl found her less amenable than he liked.) Now he must think of suitable wives for Djemmal-Eddin, and presently, Mahommet Sheffi. Perhaps for himself, too. The Prophet sanctioned four. Shouanete and Zaïdate were no longer very young, and Aminette had given him no children. . . . Therefore the Princess Nina would be an excellent choice for Djemmal-Eddin. She was a western woman, such as he had known in St. Petersburg, and such a marriage would mitigate the strangeness of his return. All this was supposition, yet not altogether improbable, and the more the Princesses discussed it, the more apprehensive they felt.

From time to time, they were subjected to a curious inspection which they never understood. It was always the same. Hadjio would arrive, without warning, telling them that some 'unknown persons' were at Dargo-Vedin, and were asking to see them. The first time, the Princesses were plunged into a violent state of agitation, imagining that it was one of their family, or a representative, come to treat on the matter of the ransom. They were led to the gates, where all the inmates of the seraglio were gathered, in two lines, the women muffled in their veils. The gates were at last thrown open, and outside, they saw a strange figure, his face enveloped in a black cloth, cut with two eye-slits, through which he regarded them intently. No word was spoken; the captives and the mysterious hooded figure stared at each other for a few moments, and then the gates were closed. This curious interview was repeated several times, but the Princesses never discovered its significance. They believed they were being displayed to emissaries or deputies from distant provinces, who wished to be assured that they were still alive, and that the large ransom which they represented, and on which the people in general had a claim, was still under discussion.

*   *   *

Two days before Christmas, according to the captives' reckoning, Shamyl returned from his campaigns overcast, throwing a pall over the whole seraglio. It was evident the battles were going badly for him. He was in no mood to listen to the small talk and back-biting of his women, the increasing tension between Zaïdate and the captives, or Aminette's burning sense of injustice over her treatment at the hands of the other two wives. The Kist girl was becoming more and more rebellious. Amber *tespyehs*, or lengths of satin sent as offerings to the Imam's harem, were apportioned between the elder wives, and Aminette was generally overlooked. But when Khazi Mahommed returned from the battlefield soon after his father, limping from a wound in the leg, and also in a sombre mood, Aminette forgot everything else, and was as usual in transports of happiness to be near him. It seems that during one particularly violent scene with Zaïdate, she had threatened to run away from the seraglio to Khazi Mahommed's home at Karaty, unless Shamyl intervened to ensure better treatment for her. At which Shamyl, immediately informed by Zaïdate of Aminette's infatuation, but, inscrutable as ever, spoke kindly to her, even saying he would no longer detain her if she wished to return to her native land. After four years of marriage she was still childless, and sooner or later, he knew he must divorce her, or face the charge of indulging a merely carnal passion— something the austere tenets of Muridism could not sanction. Their basically democratic principles allowed the people to criticize and even condemn their Imam—were he ever to give them just cause: but, in the personal conduct of his life, Shamyl was above reproach.

Aminette naïvely refused the offer of freedom: she had no intention of forfeiting her chance to see Khazi Mahommed from time to time. But she congratulated herself on having asserted her rights and achieved a better standing in the harem. She did not know that Shamyl, the great Imam, could be jealous of his son, or that he had already determined

her future. She did not wish her freedom? Very well, she should stay—
for the present. But never again should she be with Khazi Mahommed.
He was ordered back to the battle-front overnight. Never again was the
love-sick Aminette to be near her handsome step-son. Now she wept
beside the captives, or sitting alone on the roof she would gaze out across
the mountains, brooding over her lost love.

The Princesses were further saddened, during the winter, by the loss
of their servants, who were removed and placed in the outer aôul,
without any further means of communication. This was brought about
circuitously. One of the young Georgian girls, Pelago, had been ransomed, and was to leave the next day. But Hadji-Rebel and Zaïdate
insisted that three large sacks of sugar must be added to the ransom
money. This rapacious pair were in the habit of extorting money or re-
saleable goods from the less important prisoners, whom they could
approach unknown to Shamyl. They would see to it that the victims,
generally those kept outside the seraglio, in the ordinary prisons of the
aôul, were left half-starved, so that their relatives, receiving heartbreaking accounts of their sufferings, usually managed to raise some
money. It might not be a large sum, for they were for the most part
poor, but even the most modest amounts were acceptable to Hadji-
Rebel and Zaïdate, who, like Lord Byron, held that ready money
resembled Aladdin's lamp in its power to work all kinds of agreeable
magic.

When Pelago learned of the further demands, knowing that sugar
was a costly luxury and that her family had given all they could, she
lost heart and hung herself. Shamyl's cook, Labazan, happened to be
passing the granary at that moment, and was in time to cut her down.

She was dragged insensible before Shamyl. The Imam took pity on
her, and being convinced that no more could be added to her ransom,
and that in any case Hadji-Rebel and Zaïdate had acted wrongly and
without his consent, he gave Pelago her freedom. But he kept her little
sister, Eva. And, exasperated with the ceaseless dramas and quarrelling
of the women, he now decreed that all the Princesses' household were
to be removed from the seraglio. Only Madame Drancy and the wet-
nurse for the Orbeliani baby remained. Although this, at last, gave the
Princesses more room, air and privacy, they were haunted by fears
for the safety of their servants who now had no one to defend them
against all kinds of privations and harsh treatment.

In this atmosphere of apprehension and melancholy, the winter
dragged by, and the first pale spring sunshine came without bringing
any change in the prisoner's lot, nor any fresh hope.

27

A Sacrifice

God hath pre-ordained five things on his servants, the duration of life, their actions, their dwelling places, their travels and their portions.   ARAB SAYING

The same pale sunshine of this January of 1855 shone wanly on St. Petersburg, barely piercing the white mists which shrouded the city and hung over the canals, so that the delicate wrought-iron bridges spanning them appeared floating in a limbo land of vapours, from which figures emerged briefly, only to disappear again. The whole city seemed oppressed, apprehensive; with each courier from the Crimea came worse news. Battle after battle was being lost. One by one the forts fell, the heroic garrisons died, ravaged by cholera as much as by the fire of the nations ranged against them. Treachery and defeat were in the air. There were no more fêtes at the Winter Palace. The great façade remained unlit, its courtyards almost deserted, save for the coming and going of the couriers. In the green-walled study overlooking the Neva the Tzar paced up and down in anguish. His world had fallen about him. All the mighty empire he had held—in trust to God, he believed —was crumbling. 'As each bad report came in,' wrote his personal physician, Dr. Mandt, 'he was completely shattered. Tears streamed from his eyes, his sufferings were inhuman. . . .' For him, a beaten army was the bitterest blow. The hope of reforming the legislation along more liberal lines—of reducing corruption and internal strife—these things were of no account to him. In his eyes, everything began and ended with military might. He had aged terribly, in the last few months. The majestic carriage was bowed; the thinning grey hair was no longer pomaded and brushed forward in an artful manner. He had done with artifice. His sunken eyes stared out from a greenish face. The spectre of his former glory, like the former invincible might of his armies, haunted him. He could not believe that, one by one, France, England, and now Austria, were ranged beside the Turks. Austria openly espoused the Turkish cause (forgetting her indebtedness to Russia in the matter of the Tzar's intervention, in 1848, to suppress the patriot Magyar risings) and demanded the retreat of all Russian troops, under threat of war, from Austrian territory along the Danube, the Tzar knew himself finally betrayed. He turned the young Emperor Franz-Joseph's portrait to the wall, *Du Undankbarer* (ingrate) written across it in his florid hand-writing.

The Russian people, too, were becoming hostile. His enthusiasm for the just cause of the war, as he believed it to be—'for the altar of Christ to be raised, once more, under the Holy dome of Saint Sophia'—was not shared by his people—not even by his former idolators in reactionary Court circles. The moujiks, whose centuries of serfdom had rendered resigned, or passive, trudged off to war fatalistically, dying stoically, just as they had done for centuries. But with this difference: now they muttered—a low resentful muttering, which was gathering momentum, whether in war, or peace, and which was never to be silenced until, half a century later, it swelled into the mighty roar of revolution. Once, these oppressed and simple people had died for Mother Russia—for her defence or glory. Now they were dying for another man's beliefs—that man the Emperor, their 'Little Father' whose autocratic harshness had at last alienated them. They no longer felt themselves his children—they knew they were his slaves, and awaited the hour of their deliverance.

The army was restive. They still fought heroically, but they were betrayed by governmental mismanagement and corruption. Constantin de Grunwald tells us: 'Nicholas' methods of government had produced a profound demoralization of the administration. Under an outward appearance of perfect order, corruption had gradually gained even the highest spheres. The equipment of the army, with its highly polished buttons, was to be found more defective than ever. Weapons were old-fashioned, the health service inadequate. The Commissariat had neither stocks of provisions nor means of transport.' Communications were poor, or non-existent. The railway did not run farther south than Moscow. The roads, such as they were, were waist-high in mud, or snow-drifts, for more than half the year. Cannon balls were carried laboriously from province to province, on slow-moving carts, all across the country to Sebastopol. Yet, as one general said: 'Cannon balls are dumb: only the bayonet speaks.' And now there were not enough trained men to hold the bayonets.

Field-Marshal Paskiévitch, the Supreme Commander, was over seventy, and when he was retired, to give place to Menchikov, things were no better. 'There is not an army in Europe where the death-rate is as high as in the Russian army', wrote Barante, the French Ambassador, some time before this fatal war. The terrible discipline, the long marches, the poor clothing and intense cold, all sapped the men's morale: at last, many of them lay down to die gladly. Now, the Navy too was humiliated: it could not make a stand before the British fleet, and soon was heroically scuttled, off Sebastopol, to create a barrier across the roadsteads. Meanwhile, British ships were everywhere, bombarding Odessa, off the coast of Finland, attacking the north Pacific ports, and even sailing to Cronstadt, within sight of St. Petersburg: yet the English admiral's boast, that he would fête Queen Victoria's birthday in the Winter Palace, did not rouse the Russian people from their fatalistic apathy. Although Nicholas now prepared to defend Moscow, with the glorious echoes of 1812 still sounding in his ears, his people remained inert. During this winter the Tzar had been living at the gloomy palace of Gatchina, removed, if only by a few miles, from the hostile and malicious eyes of his subjects which followed his every move. The palace had stood empty for many years; a few suites of rooms were hurriedly prepared, and there the Royal family and their entourage camped uncomfortably.

Gatchina had the appearance of a fortress; its main hall was known as the Arsenal. Yet it was now a fortress without power; a dilapidated reminder of former might. 'The Tzar's appearance rends one's heart', wrote one of the ladies-in-waiting. The all-puissant autocrat had vanished, to be replaced by a worn-out man of fifty-eight, disillusioned with himself as much as with events. For hours at a time, after receiving dispatches from the front, he would roam through the pine-woods which encircled the palace, a solitary bowed figure, dark against the snow. He could neither sleep nor rest. All through the night he could be heard, pacing the corridors, backwards and forwards, or stumbling through the unlit halls to reach the chapel, there to pray for strength.

In February 1855, Lord Palmerston became England's Prime Minister. He was a violent Russophobe, and John Bright voiced a widespread bitterness over the causes and conduct of the Crimean War, when he spoke of fifty thousand Englishmen dying, to put Palmerston in office. The Tzar knew that now, however he sacrificed his pride, there was no further hope of coming to terms. England, France, Turkey, Austria, Italy—even pygmy Sicily were all ranged against him. Along the Nevsky, and among the slums, in the vodka cellars, as in the drawing-rooms, there was talk of abdication. 'I have failed in my duty to God, and my country,' said Nicholas, feeling himself abandoned by both.

But in Warsaw there was one young heart that still remained loyal, still loved him faithfully and saw him as the apotheosis of glory and enlightenment. Djemmal-Eddin was stationed in the Polish capital. Most of his regiment, the Vladimirski Lancers, had been detached to the south Crimean front; only a token force remained behind to patrol the uneasy city. Again and again Djemmal-Eddin's request to be sent on active service, either in the Caucasus or the Crimea was refused. The Tzar's scruples would not permit him to use the changeling he had grown to love in the service of a country which was not, by birth, his own.

In this Western capital, Djemmal-Eddin and the other Russian officers moved among the Polish nobility on outwardly easy terms. The patriot risings of the 'thirties were past; those of the 'sixties were yet to come. At this moment the tensions were barely apparent, however much they seethed below the surface, however much the successive Russian governors ensconced at the Zamek, or castle, abused their power, imposing their arrogance everywhere. They would hear no petitions unless spoken in Russian; trials were often conducted without interpreters, or any proper representation for the Polish prisoners. One of the most loathed governors was 'Hanging' Mouraviev, who cynically divided the human race—and his family, some of whom were revolutionaries—into those who were hanged and those who hanged.

Russia held Poland in an iron grip. 'The Poles will never be free as long as we live in fetters . . . as long as autocracy rules us by the Grace of God', wrote Prince Wiazemski. Behind the two countries lay centuries of bitterness. Both were at fault. In the words of Constantin de Grunwald:

> While the Poles under the sway of an impassioned and sorrowful patriotism, have not feared to distort the truth in order to get the sympathy of the world for a cause they felt sacred, the Russians, on their side, disdaining public opinion, have done hardly anything to establish the truth and defend a point of view which was different, but also justifiable. The facts, nevertheless, are very simple: branches of the great Slav tree, the Russian people and the Polish people, have, since their distant origins each followed different evolutions, and this makes them antagonistic to each other, involves them in cruel struggles and clashing interests and creates a real incompatibility of temperament.

Peter the Great regarded Poland as a protectorate. Catherine II made Poniatovski, her ex-lover, King. Her grandson Alexander I, overflowing with humanitarian beliefs, determined to redress the wrongs inspired by his ancestors, and in 1815, again in Monsieur de Grunwald's words: 'Poland experienced a miraculous revival. . . . But soon, the Poles had to make a sacrifice for the greater benefit of Europe, and show in this way their gratitude to the allies for having freed them from Napoleon's bondage.' Poland was dismembered. Galicia remained with Austria, Posnania went to Prussia, while Russia took Lithuania and the Ukraine; the Romanovs ruled over Poland once more. By 1855 years of abuse and increasing severity had hardened both the hatred of each nation for the other. Gradually Nicholas came to feel a personal antipathy for the Poles, which at last overcame his first chivalrous instincts to uphold his dead brother's reforms. He never forgot how many Poles there had been among the Dekabrists, and his spies kept him well informed as to the numbers of secret societies which flourished in Poland. When the revolt of 1830 flamed out, Nicholas, with his customary mixture of nobility and cold calculation, urged his troops to feel no hatred for the Poles, 'our blood brothers'; after which a brief, but terrible war followed. Field-Marshal Paskiévitch, whom Nicholas, in a flush of military infatuation, always addressed as his 'Colonel-Father', took command. On August 18, after desperate fighting, he made his entry into the capital, from where, on September 8, he dispatched a message: *Warsaw is at the feet of your Majesty*. Poland was incorporated into the Russian Empire, and all independent institutions were suppressed.

By the time Djemmal-Eddin was stationed there, twenty-five years later, Poland was completely subdued. Although conscription (into the Russian army, by means of drawing lots) had been abolished, there were plans to revive it, and when some years later they did so, it was in a manner designed to rob the country of its best men. Arbitrary powers of selection enabled the authorities to choose only the men from the towns, this being, as Lord Napier wrote to the Foreign Office, 'intended to make a clean sweep of the revolutionary youth of Poland, to shut up the most dangerous and energetic spirits within the restraints of the Russian army—a plan to kidnap the opposition and carry it off to Siberia or the Caucasus'.

But this aspect of Russian rule had not penetrated Djemmal-Eddin's consciousness. He knew Poland only a brief while, in the years of enforced order, of outward calm. To him Russia was all-glorious. Its might was won by right; it conquered only to bestow enlightenment— in Poland, as in the Caucasus, and he would gladly have laid down his life for Holy Russia.

Warsaw was beautiful and elegant, like its women, who were considered the most fascinating of all Europe. Canaletto's nephew, Bellotto, who painted much in the manner of his uncle's Venetian perspectives, shows us precise vistas of old houses and palaces set in parks, with ornamental fountains and narrow streets dotted with little carriages. The great palaces, the Potockis', the Zamoiski's Palais Bleu, or the lovely little classical palace of Lazienki were as elegant, though conceived in less barbarically splendid terms than anything in St. Petersburg. The nobles lived on their vast estates in feudal magnificence. For the moment they bowed beneath the Russians' yoke, seldom spoke of politics, and contented themselves with the pleasures their ancestors had known; drinking, hunting, riding across the marshy plains where herds of wild horses roamed. They had forsworn their brocaded caftans, shaven polls and huge drooping moustaches of their forebears, but life in the country did not change greatly. There was a mosque in Cracow, and Tartar colonies at Troki and Vilno. But Warsaw was linked with the West, regarding itself as wholly European, one with the West which Djemmal-Eddin naïvely believed Russia to represent. Railway lines ran to Paris. Theatres gave all the latest plays from France and Germany. Polish couturières rivalled those of Paris. Travellers arrived from Vienna, Rome, or London. It was very cosmopolitan compared to St. Petersburg. People going through to Russia were always regarded by the Poles as going into exile, threatened with unspeakable dangers and discomforts all along their route. They were always urged to take large supplies of foodstuffs, ready cash, medicines and other necessities, rather in the manner in which those in Russia departed for an even wilder destination—Siberia, or the Caucasus. Or indeed, as some Americans travel today facing the rigours of other, less comfortable continents.

As each fresh bulletin from the Crimean front reached Warsaw, the Poles could barely conceal their satisfaction. There were more rumours of abdication: of Austrian troops marching on to St. Petersburg, and Djemmal-Eddin fretted to be beside the man whom others were now beginning to desert. On a December day of black frost, the summons came. The Tzar wished to see him: for what reason the messenger could not say. Lieutenant Prince Djemmal-Eddin Shamyl was to proceed to St. Petersburg at once. He left on the hour.

In the Winter Palace, the Tzar's drawn face stared from the window across the frozen Neva to where, through a gathering snow-storm, he could see the shadowy outline of the Peter and Paul fortress. Once it had represented might—the prison where his enemies rotted. But now he saw it as the tomb of his ancestors. Many of the Romanovs were buried there, and the Tzar envied them their peace. His equerries were sorting the mass of papers on his desk—dispatches from the Crimea, chiefly, and the conduct of the Caucasian campaigns hardly seemed to count now beside the mounting tide of disaster stemming from the Crimea. Once he had read General Réad's account of the sack of Tzinondali with shocked interest; he recalled the beautiful Georgian princesses who had been his wife's ladies-in-waiting, and he had followed their husbands' military careers closely. But lately, disasters of such magnitude had overwhelmed him that the whole affair had slipped his mind. Now he had received the most urgent requests from the Viceroy, Prince Voronzov, General Réad and Prince Bariatinsky; all these three mighty Caucasian officers were compelled to admit they could neither rescue the Princesses, nor treat with Shamyl. After receiving a last desperate appeal from Prince David, they had decided to approach the Emperor, something neither the Prince, nor the captives dared to do. Only the Emperor—only Djemmal-Eddin could save them now. Even if the money could be raised, it was of no avail without the return of Shamyl's son: moreover the renegade spies brought rumours that the Imam was tiring of the whole matter, and if nothing was settled soon, he would probably distribute the Princesses and their women among his Naibs, as spoils of war. Christian women abandoned to Moslem lusts! The Tzar was at last roused.

Thus, in the dusk of this snowy afternoon, he waited for Djemmal-Eddin's arrival. He had grown to regard him as a son. In many ways he was far more satisfactory than Nicholas' own sons: the Tzar and his ward shared the same devotion to duty. Moreover, the young Caucasian had a studious mind, was a disciplined officer, and was never involved in scandals, like the profligate Grand Dukes, nor did he retain intractably savage streaks as most of the other Asiatic Princes. The Tzar foresaw what his chivalrous response would be, now that he was faced with this decision—he foresaw too, the tragic destiny which would close around him, among his native mountains.

'Do not give me your answer now,' said the Emperor. 'Go away and reflect on the sacrifice that is asked from you.' His face softened, and he laid his hand on the young man's shoulder. 'Come back in two days, when your mind is made up.'

'Sire,' replied Djemmal-Eddin. 'Shamyl's son and your ward does not need two days to decide where his duty lies. I will go back at once. The two days you offer me shall be for my farewells.' He knelt before the Tzar, who blessed him and then embraced him like the son he felt him to be.

'Go then; try always to do good among your father's people, and never forget your true country—Russia, which made you a civilized man.'

They were never to meet again. Each went the way of duty. Djemmal-Eddin was to enter his prison; and at that same moment the Tzar was to die—a self-willed death, the only means of bringing peace to his unhappy country—the peace for which his pride could not allow him to sue.

28

A Farewell

Weep ye not for the dead, neither bemoan him; but
weep sore for him that goeth away: for he shall return
no more.   JEREMIAH XXII

On January 4, 1855, in the bitter cold of dawn, a troika, accompanied by a small escort of Cossacks, set out from St. Petersburg, heading south for Moscow. It was the first stage of Djemmal-Eddin's return
to the Caucasus. The young man sitting there, muffled in a heavy fur
pelisse and bearskin rugs, stared about him, hungrily, noting it all, the
great marble palaces, the classic perspectives—seeing it all for the last
time. The streets were empty and shuttered; but as they reached the
poorer quarters, a few raucous snatches of song and chinks of light came
from the vodka shops which still did a brisk trade with all-night
revellers, or early customers fortifying themselves for the day to come.
At the city limits, the guards lifted the black and white striped barriers
to let them pass. There was none of the usual long-drawn inspection of
papers, for these were Cossacks of the Imperial escort, and they carried
an *ordre de mission*, signed by the Tzar himself. It was snowing heavily
and the little cavalcade was soon lost to view in the spinning whiteness
into which they galloped. After some days, Moscow, 'golden-headed
Moscow', lifted its glittering domes and crowns from the snows;
Kolomna, Riazan, Kozlov: small provincial towns, lost villages, empty
provinces, all lying still under their winter cover; Voronej, Peter the
Great's ship-yard for his Don fleet; Novo-Tcherkassk, headquarters of
the Don Cossacks.

All along the route, news of Djemmal-Eddin's coming, of the circumstances of his journey, had preceded him, mysteriously, and everywhere a hero's welcome awaited him. At Rostov on Don the skies
lightened, but snow still covered the ground until, as they raced onwards towards the south, a barren land emerged. The last snow melted,
and coarse grass steppes dotted with lonely Cossack outposts stretched
as far as the eye could see. The smooth running troika was exchanged
for a tarantass which rattled and plunged across country. Now the wind

366

blew keen, and the mountains rose abruptly up out of the distance, a dark jagged line stretching across the horizon; the giant peaks of the Caucasus; the wall dividing Europe and Asia; the barrier that Djemmal-Eddin must now pass, to go back into that forgotten world of barbarism.

At last the little cavalcade came within shadow of the mountains, plodding now across marshes or fording streams. It was a landscape of desolation. Reeds growing tall as a man bordered rivers that wound sluggishly towards the coast. From faraway, a strange barque could be seen approaching. It drifted listlessly with the current. Only its mast could be glimpsed above the reeds, appearing and disappearing through the banks of low-lying mist that hung over the water. A large bell was tied to the masthead, and clanged monotonously, echoing in a melancholy fashion. When the barque came into view, it was seen that there were no oarsmen, no one at the tiller, which was lashed. The mast was in the form of a rough crucifix, and to it was nailed a dead man. The barque sidled past them slowly, veering aimlessly.

'That's how they punish, hereabouts,' said one of the Cossacks. 'But what had he done—was he a murderer?' asked Djemmal-Eddin. The Cossack grinned, showing a pack of yellowing teeth. 'Most likely he was a lowland tribesman, come over to us, as a spy, and fool enough to get caught . . . he'll drift for weeks; but there'll only be bones left when he reaches the sea. The vultures follow the rafts for miles. They know the sound of the bell. . . .'

Long after the mast-top was lost to sight in the reeds, the bell sounded across the marshes, dinning its terrible message in Djemmal-Eddin's ears.

This was the world into which he had been born. This was the world which he must now call his. These ruthless mountains which loomed dark as the vultures' wings were now his home.

At the beginning of February, the cavalcade rattled into Vladikavkaz, where Prince David had arrived from Tiflis and was waiting to welcome Djemmal-Eddin. For the rest of Djemmal-Eddin's time among the Russians he shared quarters with the Prince, living the last of that life of liberty and civilization which had become his own. During the final weeks of negotiation, while Shamyl still posed a number of lesser conditions which delayed the exchange by another month, Djemmal-Eddin was fêted everywhere. Both his brother officers and the inhabitants of the garrison-towns between Vladikavkaz and Tiflis gave suppers and receptions in his honour. It was at once a triumphal progress, and in a sense, a calvary. Djemmal-Eddin gave himself up, fully knowing what awaited him, and what a price he must pay to free the Princesses whom he remembered so long ago, in that brilliant world of Tzarskoe-Selo. He fully realized what they must have suffered, as prisoners, for only he had known both the Court life and that of the aôuls. The primitive conditions and the fanatic warrior-communities of Daghestan still lingered in his mind, like some half-forgotten nightmare. But he never dwelled on his fate, and waved aside all the eulogies, as he did Prince David's gratitude. Only once the Prince came on him, pale and downcast, sitting surrounded by books, in the Commanding Officer's library. He spoke, almost as if to himself:

'How strange is a man's fate! I was only seven[1] when I was taken from the half-savage aôuls to receive a human understanding and education; and at the very hour when I begin to appreciate the advantages of learning and am ready with all my heart and soul, to apply myself, fate flings me back into the midst of ignorance, where I shall probably forget all I learned, and go backwards, like a crab.'

Djemmal-Eddin's baggage consisted largely of books, atlases, paper, drawing-materials and paints, bulwarks of civilization behind which he hoped to make a stand. Prince David said he had never seen a Musselman with so little of the Tartar about him, who was so completely Europeanized, and had such Russian views, feelings and habits as Shamyl's son. The irony of the situation was only equalled by its pathos, and the Prince's joy was almost overshadowed by the anguish he felt for Djemmal-Eddin's lot. Above all, the Prince and all his fellow-officers admired the manner in which the young man refused to be lionized or pitied, 'abstaining, throughout, from appearing in the interesting and romantic character of deliverer'. But that he was, and so he appeared to everyone. The ladies were particularly moved by his sad fate. He was so handsome, so tragic. He danced so well! He wore his uniform with such elegance! Shamyl's son, the Tzar's aide-de-camp, the hero of the hour! they fluttered around, their eyes misty. At Hassiff Yourt there was a ball in his honour; it was to be the last that Djemmal-Eddin ever knew. As he waltzed with the local beauties, the candle-light glowing over their ringlets and muslins, and the gold-laced uniforms of the officers, the strains of the Aurora waltz filtered through the windows to where, hidden in the oleander bushes, the Lesghien spies crouched, watching it all. Amongst them Younouss and two other Naibs who had known Djemmal-Eddin as a child, and were now sent by Shamyl to ascertain if it were really he who had come back.

The Naibs returned to the Great Aôul with long faces. Yes, they felt sure it was indeed the Imam's son: but lost to Allah! Dancing— embracing half-naked Giaour women, drinking wine, smoking cigars. . . . A lost soul. They went to the mosque to pray for his deliverence. Zaïdate pursed her thin lips, saying that no good could come of all this. Better a larger ransom than such a son, she said, hissing like one of the serpents on the steppes of Moughan.

[1] Djemmal-Eddin was in fact eight, two months before he was taken hostage.

II

'Today,' wrote the Princess Anna to her husband who, with Djemmal-Eddin, was now with the garrison at Hassiff Yourt, 'they were going to distribute us among the Naibs. We thought we were lost; but Khazi Mahommed and the Mollah asked Shamyl to send messengers to you for the last time.' She went on to implore the Prince to save them from this dreadful fate. 'What is to be done?' she wrote. 'It seems as if it were not God's will we should see each other again, in this world. I know you have not spared yourself any effort to save us; but it is impossible to reason with these people. It is impossible to convince them you cannot collect a larger sum, or that what you already offer is not your own, but has been borrowed or begged from others. May God bless you and give you strength. I can add no more.' The Princess was not yet aware that Djemmal-Eddin had agreed to return, but had been told that a further sum demanded by Shamyl was now the stumbling block. These fresh demands were, in fact, as irksome to Shamyl as to Prince David; but they were imposed by the rapacity of the Naibs. However much he longed for his son, however gladly he would have given up his prisoners in exchange, he could not now overrule the whole of his Murid forces who, for the first time, realized their power and were determined to extract the utmost benefit from their valuable hostages.

The messenger who brought the Prince his wife's letter also brought one from the Imam. 'I thank you for keeping your word respecting my son,' wrote Shamyl to Prince David; 'but this cannot end the negotiations. You must know that besides my son I require a million roubles, and one hundred and fifty of my Murids whom you now hold prisoner. Do not bargain with me. I will take no less. If you do not comply, I have resolved to distribute your family among the different aôuls. This would have been done already, but for my son Khazi Mahommed, who prevailed upon me to offer you one last chance to add to the paltry forty thousand roubles you originally offered me.' These fresh demands were due to the Murids having discovered that Prince Tchavtchavadzé's sister had married none other than the Prince of Mingrelia;—it was a hereditary title which, although bestowing honours and, indeed suzerainty over the whole province of Mingrelia, did not imply wealth as the Murids believed.

The Prince was thunderstruck, but managed to keep an appearance of calm before the Imam's messengers. Forty thousand roubles was all the family had been able to raise, and neither the High Command, nor the Tzar could be expected to pay out Government funds to swell the Murid coffers. The Princesses, like so many less distinguished prisoners, would have to be abandoned. Prince David now lost all hope, and turning back to Shamyl's agents, spoke in a voice choked with rage.

'I shall not reply to your Imam any more. You can tell him from me that, long ago, on the banks of the Alazan, I took an eternal farewell of my family. I can only trust them now to God's mercy. These are my last words. If, by Saturday, you do not bring me the solemn acceptance of my offer, I swear by the Creator that on that day I will leave Hassiff Yourt and take Djemmal-Eddin with me. You may follow me a thousand versts, and beg me to return, but I will not. And you may do what you like with my family. They will no longer be mine. I shall have renounced them. Tell your Imam that I have always been grateful to him for the manner in which he has respected my family, but if he carries out his threat of sending them to the aôuls, from the moment they cross the threshold of his seraglio, I renounce them. If they are made the slaves of your Naibs, I shall no longer recognize my wife as my wife, nor my daughters as my daughters. This is as true as that I am standing here before you. And if, after I have fulfilled my threat, Shamyl could offer to give me back my family for nothing, together with all the treasures he possesses, I swear by God that I will not receive them back.'

The Murids listened with stony faces and then bowing, begged the Prince to write his ultimatum to Shamyl.

'No,' replied the Prince. 'I will not write another line. I am sorry I have wasted so much paper on a man who consistently breaks his word.'

The Murids then asked the Prince to give them a week more to permit Shamyl's considered answer. The Prince brushed them aside and was about to leave the room, when they called him back.

'There is another way . . .' they said after some hesitation. 'The Imam would agree to let your family go, in exchange for his son and forty thousand roubles. . . . But, in that case, Princess Orbeliani and her son must remain. Her release would be a matter for later negotiation. . . .'

The Prince now lost all self-control and flung himself at the messengers, but was fortunately restrained by Prince Bagration, Djemmal-Eddin and some other officers present at the interview. 'Not only will I not leave my sister-in-law,' stormed the Prince, 'but I will not even allow the youngest of my servants' children to be detained.'

Hassan, one of Shamyl's emissaries, who acted as interpreter, turned to Djemmal-Eddin, who was now almost as infuriated as the Prince. 'Do not be upset,' he said. 'This is the mountaineer's way. . . . But it will end well.' At these words Djemmal-Eddin turned scarlet with rage and humiliation.

'*I* am not upset,' he replied. 'What do *I* have to be upset over? You know well enough at what age I was taken from Akhulgo. I am no longer an Avar. *You* were one of those who gave me up to the Russians! I have forgotten everyone and everything in my native land. I do not return there with any joy. . . . I would go back to Russia tomorrow, if circumstances only permitted it. . . .' Prince Bagration seized Djemmal-Eddin by the shoulders, trying to check his rash words. 'Be careful what you say!' he cried. 'You risk everything if you anger them more. . . .'

'The devil take them,' shouted Djemmal-Eddin, now trembling with fury. 'Am I to stand on ceremony with them? Am I to grovel?' he cried, reaching for his revolver. With the same alacrity the Murids grasped their kindjals. Both were atavistic gestures: mountain man had met mountain man, and already the salons of St. Petersburg were very far away. The messengers were hurried from the room, and the officers endeavoured to calm Prince David and Djemmal-Eddin.

It was decided that Isaac Gramoff, the Armenian interpreter who had been present at all the negotiations, should make one more attempt to convince Shamyl of the Prince's intentions. Gramoff was an astute Armenian serving with the Russian army. He was admirably suited to his delicate task, for he had lived among the various mountain tribes since childhood, speaking their dialects as well as Russian and German. He was attached to the staff of Prince Gregory Orbeliani, and had at once offered his services on behalf of the Prince's sister-in-law Princess Varvara. Gramoff has left detailed accounts of his interview with the Lion of Daghestan.

The first time he reached the Imam's camp, he was told that Shamyl had already announced his arrival, saying he had had a dream, in which he saw Prince Orbeliani's interpreter advancing towards him with good news from his son. But Gramoff was aware of Shamyl's excellent spy system, and realized this was only an example of the Imam's technique for fostering his legend as prophet and seer. On another occasion, riding beside the Imam, as he headed for the Great Aôul, Gramoff was able to observe his remarkable self-mastery, and the skill with which he concealed what was passing in his mind. Across the mountains there was the sound of heavy gun-fire, and later Gramoff learned that the Murids had lost a battle and retreated with many losses. But Shamyl ignored the gun-fire, showing neither annoyance nor anxiety: as he and the interpreter rode he cunningly began diverting his companion from thoughts of battle. He pointed to a horse with a couple of saddle-bags slung across its back.

'Isai Bey,' he said. 'You see that horse? He carries the whole of my baggage—all that I need, to live, or die. And yet I am Imam of Daghestan—commander of all my armies. With you, every ensign carries more. That is why your columns are so long and straggling—which is not very desirable on a march.'

A few miles farther on the artillery fire became louder and more frequent. With the same inscrutable face, Shamyl stopped, listened attentively, and then, as expressionless as ever, asking Gramoff many leading questions about international politics and the Crimean War, resumed his journey. Presently a messenger galloped up from the direction of the battle. He gave Shamyl a dispatch scrawled on a crumpled piece of paper. The Imam read it smiling, and appeared delighted; he congratulated his guard on the victory which had just been gained over the Russians. Taking his sword he handed it to the messenger: 'Thank Eski-Naib for his bravery and give him this shashka in token of my great satisfaction at his news,' he said. And riding on, he resumed his conversation with Gramoff. Although Gramoff believed the message to have been, in fact, telling of defeat, he marvelled that Shamyl could have such command over himself as to maintain this piece of play-acting without showing the slightest trace of uneasiness.

* * *

On the occasion of the final, decisive interview with Shamyl, Gramoff reached the Great Aôul at sunset and was kept cooling his heels till the next evening, when he was ushered into Shamyl's room, where a solemn conclave was assembled. Daniel Beg, Ker-Effendi, and the elder Naibs were grouped around the Imam, while twenty Murids were ranged along the walls, ten a side, the tallow candles casting gigantic shadows behind them.

The conclave was opened by the customary flowery exchanges, Gramoff bowing and turning his phrases in the complimentary manner Oriental protocol demanded, Shamyl replying in a similar vein. Then abruptly, his face changed: the tawny cat's-eyes darkened, the mouth hardened. 'Isai Bey,' he said, 'great personages always begin their speeches with pleasantry, and later come to matters of import. We have followed this system. Now to business. Is Prince Tchavtchavadzé trifling with me, or no? Until now, he has done nothing but feed me sweet letters. . . . It would be better to write less and do more. He is my enemy. He must understand I do not trifle with him.' His face suddenly appeared terrible in its ferocity, and Gramoff shuddered with the fanatic hatred it expressed. It required all his delicacy and intuition to convince the Murids that the million roubles they demanded was utterly beyond realization. Gramoff was certain none of them realized what a million represented. 'Let me tell you,' he said, 'that if you were given a million grains of rice to count, and all of you set to counting them, by day and by night, and were not allowed to eat until you had finished your task, all of you would die of hunger long before. . . .'

The negotiations dragged on, and Gramoff observed that the Naibs held fiercely to their demands, so that Shamyl was unable to back down. At last he broke up the meeting, saying that it was his hour for prayer, and Gramoff realized nothing would be achieved unless he obtained a private audience; accordingly he manœuvred to obtain this. Next night Gramoff was led stealthily to the Imam's rooms, and it was evident that Shamyl, too, was anxious to escape the vigilance of his Naibs. Now the two men could speak freely.

'In my place,' said the wily Gramoff, 'I should be content with the glory of the whole affair. It will not be a small thing to be able to boast that you, as it were by force of arms, compelled the Russians to restore your son, whom the Great White Sultan treasured as his own. The whole world will hear of it; it will be printed in all the newspapers that you have gained this great triumph over the Russians.'

'But it will be as well to receive the money, also,' said Shamyl with a sly smile. Gramoff again insisted on the impossibility of offering more than forty thousand roubles. At last Shamyl seemed convinced; he sighed, and, standing up, held out his hand to Gramoff.

'So be it. I shall try to finish everything with my people as soon as possible. You know that without them I can do nothing. I hope and pray for a just conclusion. Go back to Hassiff Yourt and await my reply. See that my son is not surrounded by ill-intentioned persons who might persuade him not to return to me. Serve me, too, in this affair, and let purity guide you in all your actions, so that Allah smiles on you. Farewell.'

There were three days to go before the fatal Saturday set by Prince David. No word came from Shamyl, and it can be imagined in what a frame of mind the Prince and his fellow officers waited through Wednesday, Thursday and Friday, when Gramoff returned without a positive answer. The days and nights dragged by. A hush hung over the garrison, broken only by the sound of cannon-fire a long way off, for local engagements and skirmishings between the Cossacks and the mountaineers went on ceaselessly.

The Princesses had by now learned of Djemmal-Eddin's self-sacrifice; but their joyous hopes of freedom were short-lived for they were next told of the Murids' further demands. Zaïdate was in her most tormenting mood. 'We have just heard that Prince David has received a much larger sum than that which he offers for your ransom. He is trying to keep some back. But we are not to be duped.' At which, the Princess Anna, who had born the brunt of a prolonged series of threats and promises, fell to the ground insensible.

'Your sister is dying,' said Zaïdate to Princess Varvara. 'It is all the same to us, now, whether we keep her or let her go: she could go at once if you consented to remain behind, with your child as hostage, till the million is paid.'

The Princess replied that she was quite resigned to staying if it would free the rest of the prisoners, but that a million roubles could never be raised in any case. 'A million roubles—do you know what a million roubles represents? I doubt if you could count up to a thousand . . .' said the exasperated Princess. Zaïdate did not deign to reply, but later that day Hadjio was observed sitting in a corner of the courtyard before an enormous heap of dried beans, sorting them feverishly. In reply to the Princess's question, he said that Zaïdate had ordered him to count out a million.

So the arguments continued, day in, day out, the nagging of Zaïdate telling on the captives as much as the lamentable state of weakness to which they were now reduced by eight months of captivity and hopes deferred. It was at this point that the Princess Anna dispatched her last desperate appeal to her husband which, as has been related, caused him to offer his ultimatum to Shamyl.

When the emissaries returned to the Great Aôul with the Prince's reply, their arrival was known throughout the seraglio; there was an air of excitement and bustle, but the Princesses dared not ask for news and remained in a state of anguish, until Hadjio took pity on them, saying that although the Prince had replied with inconceivable arrogance towards the Imam, he, Hadjio, had the impression Shamyl was not displeased. Boldness and decision were ever a quality he admired. 'Last night,' said the steward, 'Isaac Gramoff talked long with the Imam. I believe your affairs are now taking a favourable turn.' He went on to explain that the venerated Jamul u'din was espousing their cause and was even now closeted with Shamyl, discussing how best to arrange the matter to the satisfaction of everyone concerned.

That night, the Princesses received a visit from the Mollah Jamul u'din, who questioned them at length on the deadlock. Being at last convinced that not another kopek could be raised, whether they stayed or left, he rose abruptly, seeming satisfied, promising them that all would end well. 'Shamyl, though a man of great decision, is still my son. I shall speak with him.'

'But what if his subjects will not accept a smaller ransom? We are told they value money far more than Shamyl does,' said Princess Anna.

'There is one way of convincing the people,' replied Jamul u'din, a smile at once kindly and foxy lighting his wrinkled old face. 'But what that way is I cannot tell you yet. Before long, you may have discovered it.' On this mysterious note he left the prisoners.

The plan which Shamyl and the Mollah had devised was admirable: it saved Shamyl's face, avoided his appearing to climb down in his demands and yet, in the name of Allah, overcame the people's greed. Far up the mountains, in a cave, lived a celebrated anchorite, who had removed himself from all human contact some years earlier, to live in holy contemplation and solitude. Shamyl now had him brought to the Great Aôul, and lodged him in his own room. News of this spread across the mountains and the people began to assemble in large numbers before the gates, awaiting the oracle. Shamyl had proclaimed that the question of the prisoners' liberation would be finally settled by the anchorite. 'Even I, your Imam, am not worthy to decide this matter lest it be said I cared only for the return of my dearly-loved son,' he said.

The holy visitor now preached to the people from Shamyl's balcony. Through the chinks in their door the prisoners could see him. Between his speeches he prayed, 'giving to his body the grinding, circular movements of a pestle and mortar', singing in a piercing voice, '*Astafiour! Alafiour, Allah!*' While those around him on the balcony, Shamyl, Khazi Mahommed, Jamul u'din and the most distinguished Naibs, sang in chorus, '*La Allah illa Allahi!*' their deep guttural tones as contra-basso to the anchorite's shrill cries. All of them executed the same swaying, circular movements, both chants and movements becoming more and more rapid until at last, achieving a state of ecstasy, their cries became a deep wolf-like baying, their bodies spinning in the top-like gyrations —the zikr—of the dervish sects.

Day and night these religious exercises rang through the aôul, till Madame Drancy's self-control almost snapped, '*Assez! Assez de ces prières!*' she shouted, stopping her ears. The children, however, were delighted, and now copied the prayers with deafening accuracy, so that, both in their room and outside, the captives heard nothing but *La Allah illa Allahi!* The wet-nurse pursed her lips, saying: 'Is it possible, Madame, that their God will accept such prayers? Ours would not.'

Although the Mollah Jamul u'din had raised their hopes again, they did not have much faith in the anchorite's influence on the Murids. Yet so strongly was he venerated, that gradually he began to impose what he described as Allah's will—in reality, Shamyl's—upon them. He spoke at enormous length on abstinence, on the vanity of worldly possessions, on the dangerous effects of riches upon the soul, and how the greedy were debarred from any hope of entering Mahommed's paradise. So the days passed, the prisoners sitting together, their hands over their ears, the people listening open-mouthed to the anchorite. Sometimes Shamyl added his own picturesque style of exhortation:

'Money is grass,' he told them. 'Money withers and is gone. We must not serve money, but Allah!' And all the while, though the Princesses did not know it at the time, he was preparing the last details of the exchange. Already, large numbers of his soldier-captives had been dispatched to cut a rough road from the Great Aôul, down to the banks of the river Mitchik, where Shamyl had decided the exchange should take place. Yet the theatrical effects, the tension and mounting ecstasy of the prayer-meetings were maintained until the last, so that there was not one Murid, not one tribesman, who was not finally convinced that by renouncing the million roubles, he was in fact saving his own soul. *The world is a carcass and he who seeks it a dog.*

On Friday the anchorite redoubled his ecstatic prayers, joined by enormous crowds who thronged the courtyard and surged around the outer walls like a mighty tide. Shamyl spent the whole day in the mosque, while his wives remained invisible, at prayer in their rooms. On Saturday evening, the captives heard running footsteps approach their door. Hadjio stood on the threshold, his dark face shining, shouting, waving his arms wildly. 'Go! Go quickly! You are free!'

Shouanete appeared behind him, laughing and crying at the same time. She flung herself into the Princess Varvara's arms. 'Shamyl has freed you,' she cried. 'It is over.' Turning to the weeping Madame Drancy, she said: 'Don't cry, Frenchwoman. You too will go home. You will find your son and your mother. You will be happy again. All days are not days of mourning, all life is not tears. . . .' But Madame Drancy's brief hour of drama, of consequence, was drawing to a close. Ahead lay liberty—but little else, save tears and mourning and memories.

III

Thursday, March 11, was the day set by Shamyl for the exchange. Thursday was his favourite day, one he always chose for momentous undertakings. The six days which remained of the prisoners' life in the aôul were occupied with preparations and leave-takings. The whole seraglio came to congratulate them. Only Zaïdate seemed sour. However, she seized the last chance to profit at their expense, and sent word that if they wished to buy back any of the things taken from Tzinondali, they could come to her room and inspect them. The Princesses found a number of people, all seated on cushions, drinking tea and behaving with great formality. Kherimat had arrived the day before, for she particularly wished to see the Princesses. She was, as always, extravagantly dressed and beautifully mannered. In the middle of the room lay a heap of plate and jewels, most of it terribly damaged. Some of the loveliest heirlooms, such as the diamond and enamel bouquet, given by Catherine the Great to Prince David's grandmother when Ambassadress at St. Petersburg, was in twisted fragments. Among the wreckage, there was a pretty little bracelet which had belonged to Salomé. Mahommed Sheffi at once took it to give it back to the child, but Zaïdate snatched it from him, speaking very sharply. When the Princess Orbeliani discovered a box of her trinkets, containing some rings which had belonged to her husband, she made the mistake of rejoicing at her discovery. At which Zaïdate took the box away, and contrived to slip the rings up her sleeve. The Princesses now refused to buy anything whatever, and the meeting broke up in coldness.

Shouanete gave another, happier farewell-party, decorating her room with fine rugs, and serving tea in the inlaid silver goblets reserved for great occasions. She was feverish and ill, coughing as she lay beside the fire, wrapped in a fur-lined shouba. She too had one of the Princesses' rings, a fine diamond which Shamyl had given her, but here they felt no sense of resentment. She wore it on her brow, hung on a ribbon, sparkling between the loops of her chestnut hair. 'Soon you will be gone,' she said, tears running down her cheeks. 'And I—never! You will forget us. When you are at home once more, you will live as before. . . . But I . . . We have become fond of you. You occupied and interested us. . . .' She sighed, and they knew that, even in spite of her love for Shamyl, there were moments when she recalled her family and Christian origin and was bitterly lonely in the aôul. Now, for the last time, she was with friends from the outside world, and could not hide her sense of loss. The Princesses prepared her poultices, while the rest of the party sewed a little chalma, or turban, as a farewell present for the Orbeliani baby. 'Do not forget,' said Zaïdate, 'with what kindness you were treated—how much was done to alleviate your sufferings.'

'We shall certainly not forget those who have been kind to us,' replied Princess Anna.

The night before their departure a gloom hung over the whole seraglio. Even the captives dreaded their parting with Shouanete and Aminette. They were astonished to find how much the life of the aôul had become their own and they watched the final preparations for their journey with a curious sense of loss. Shouanete had insisted on getting up, to supervise the packing of provisions. Hadjio was saddling the Imam's horses and paying particular attention to a magnificent white stallion with a black star on its forehead, which was destined for Djemmal-Eddin. The Murids' black banners and the green banner of the Prophet were placed on Shamyl's balcony, ready for the standard bearers. As the Princesses crossed the courtyard, to say farewell to the old Bahou, she came out to meet them, to thank them. 'For through you,' she said, 'I shall see once more, before I die, my lost and favourite grandson.' Beside her, staring up earnestly from face to face, stood a little Georgian girl, Thecla, child of one of the dead prisoners, who belonged to no one and whom no one had ransomed. The Princesses had tried to arrange that she left with them, but this Shamyl had refused: probably she was destined to become the wife of one of his family—Mahommed Sheffi, perhaps. The Princess looked at the abandoned child through her tears. Making the sign of the cross over her, she said: 'If you should grow up here, never forget you are a Georgian, and whenever you have an opportunity, help the Christians.' The little girl stared wonderingly and then hid herself behind Bahou's wide trousers. She was too young to realize her fate.

By dawn the arbas were already at the gates, loaded with foodstuffs, rugs and a samovar; for the journey was to take a day and a night. The Princesses observed that horses instead of oxen were in the shafts, and the coachmen and postilions were dressed like Russian coachmen, their wild Tartar faces staring out oddly from their unaccustomed outfits. It was evident that Shamyl intended to make a fine showing on the banks of the Mitchik.

The last moment had come, and there was nothing to say. The Princesses bowed politely to Zaïdate, shook hands with Kherimat and the rest of the seraglio, and then embraced and kissed Shouanete; all were now crying. 'Do not forget me,' sobbed Shouanete. Aminette could not restrain her grief, and broke from the group. Wrapping herself in her cloak she rushed on to the roof-top, from where she could watch her friends to the last turn of the road.

As the Princesses drove through the Great Aôul, they were surrounded by a large military escort, a whole division of Shamyl's troops, led by Khazi Mahommed, in white; another by Mahommed Sheffi, in blue. The arbas creaked along the rough stone way, and they saw through the heavy veils they were once more commanded to wear, that the flat roof-tops, watch-towers and balconies were crowded with people, silently waving them farewell. Above the silence a wailing chant arose, swelled, and sank again. But it was to sound in the Princesses' hearts for evermore.

'*O! You who know what we suffer here, do not forget us in your prayers.*' It was the voices of those other Georgian captives, soldiers and people of no consequence, who had not been ransomed, and would never again see their homeland.

29

An Exchange

I am become a stranger unto my brethren, and a stranger unto my mother's children. PSALM LXIX

While, in the Caucasus, the last details of the exchange were being settled, St. Petersburg was thunderstruck to learn the Tzar was dying. He did not wish to live any longer. If death would not come to him, he would go to meet it. He had a severe cold, but insisted on going out to review a regiment leaving for the front. He wore no overcoat, and his physician cautioned him. 'Thank you, doctor. You have done your duty in warning me. Now leave me to do mine,' was his answer.

He was abdicating from life, as his pride could not allow him to abdicate from the throne. He lay dying, on the simple iron camp-bed, in his study at the Winter Palace. Paralysis of the lungs had set in, and he suffered dreadfully: but he remained conscious, calling for the friends and companions of his hey-day. All through the night the last farewells continued. Outside his suite, the echoing halls were crowded with silent ranks of courtiers. At five o'clock in the morning he dictated a telegram of farewell to Moscow—to his ancient 'golden-headed' capital. Some grenadiers were brought to his bedside that they might carry his farewell to their comrades. The army, above all, the heroic defenders of Sebastopol were remembered. He had all the Guards' regiments brought to the Palace so that they could swear allegiance to his son, as soon as he was dead. There was to be no repetition of the confusion and dangers that surrounded his own accession. Even the last echoes of the Dekabristi must be stilled. . . . 'The long night was drawing to a close when young Menchikov arrived bringing dispatches from Sebastopol. The Emperor was told, but said: "Those things no longer concern me. Let him give them to my son," ' recorded one of the ladies-in-waiting in her journal. Now, neither the Crimean battlefields, nor those of the Caucasus were of importance; least of all the Caucasus, for while the Crimean War represented a national, defensive movement, the Caucasian campaigns had always been a matter of personal pride, or aggrandizement—the Tzar's might thwarted by Shamyl, a

379

mountaineer. But now everything was fading, dwindling, vanishing. . . .
All the Russias, from Finland to the Caucasus. . . . Just before the end,
he regained the old, firm tones. Turning to the Tzarievitch, he made
an energetic movement of his hand, as if grasping something. 'Hold
all! Hold all!' he cried. They were his last words.

March 11, the day set by Shamyl for the exchange, was also that of
the Tzar's funeral. The procession took two hours to cross the city, and
all the way, brilliant sunshine glittered on the gold baldachin above the
coffin which was draped in cloth of gold and surmounted by the regalia.
'But even the Tzar is put to bed at last, with a shovel,' said the peasants
who had crowded into the city to watch the procession. The streets
were thronged with whispering crowds. Everywhere, there were
rumours of the Tzar's suicide: he had taken poison, he had commanded
his doctors to give him a fatal drug; he had been poisoned by his
enemies. . . . It was not a natural death, they said. The body began
to rot and turn black before it was cold. Drenched in perfumes, the
smell of putrefaction still overwhelmed every one at the lying-in-state.
Young Prince Peter Kropotkin, the future revolutionary, one of the
Corps des Pages who stood guard, was sickened by the ghastly ordeal.

II

The same day, March 11, dawned brilliant in the Caucasus too. The
sun rose, warm as summer, to glitter on the river Mitchik where, on
each side, the Russian and Murid troops were advancing to await the
arrival of the Princesses and Djemmal-Eddin. Shamyl had chosen the
meeting-place with his usual caution. His own territory—the Greater
Tchetchnia—sloped down to the water's edge abruptly, so that he had
the shelter of bluffs and wooded hills. Across the river, on the plains of
Koumuik, the Russian terrain lay flat and exposed for several miles
and could be raked by Shamyl's fire. Even at this last moment there
had been difficulties. Shamyl had stipulated that the money should be
paid in silver, which had not been easy to collect. A number of Murids
had been sent to Hassiff Yourt to count out the thirty-five thousand
roubles before having them placed in sealed bags. (The remaining five
thousand were to be paid in gold.) Hadjio was one of the counters and
had to admit that had it been a million he would have been lost. As
it was, the count took twenty-four hours. It was remarked that the
Murids were extraordinarily careful, checking and re-checking the
roubles in piles of ten. They were suspicious that the Russians might
intentionally give them more than the agreed sum, in order to cause a
dispute during the exchange, which would thus provide an excuse to
start fighting.

On Wednesday night the garrison of Kourinsk, a fort near the Mitchik, was holding a farewell dinner in honour of Djemmal-Eddin. Baron Nicolai, the Commander-in-Chief (whose wife was one of Prince David's numerous sisters), Prince Bagration, and their suites, and several other high-ranking officers, had arrived to be present at the exchange, when a Tchetchen messenger was announced. Prince David started to his feet, fearing that something had again gone wrong. 'Is it possible there can be even more changes or new conditions?' he asked. 'Why not?' replied Djemmal-Eddin, an edge of cynicism in his voice. 'They gave you their word on the Shariat, and now perhaps they want to act according to the Adat.' (The Shariat, it will be recalled, was the Murid book of sacred laws as imposed by Shamyl; the Adat, their traditional laws and customs.) The officers all observed the bitterness in Djemmal-Eddin's tone, the pale, drawn sadness of his face, and they realized, once again, the cruel fate that was now to separate him, forever, from all he held dear.

When news of the Tzar's death reached the Caucasus, Djemmal-Eddin received it in silence. He asked for no details, but shut himself in his room to mourn the man to whom he had been devoted. When the troops had assembled to take the oath of allegiance to their new Tzar, Djemmal-Eddin had been the first to raise his hand. Even for those few days left to him, he wished to be one with the country that had become his own.

Shamyl's messenger had come to the fort to request that Gramoff be sent to him at once, to receive his last instructions regarding the conduct of the exchange. It was a densely dark, starless night, and bitterly cold in the hills. Gramoff lost his way and only reached the Murid camp at Maior-Toup, Shamyl's last outpost, in the small hours. He found the Imam in his tent, half-reclining among cushions and carpets, before a blazing fire; beside him slept his inseparable old friend Ker Effendi. The Imam was counting the amber beads of his tespych. He was in an excellent mood and called for tea. 'Be quick,' he said. '*My* Isak Bey has been nearly frozen on the road.' The mighty warrior looked strangely leonine, as if he might begin to purr with contentment. 'Tomorrow is a great day for us,' he said. 'Tomorrow we shall be at peace with the Russians. There must be no foul play. I want to tell you that according to our customs, a father ought not to go and meet his son; but I shall do so for two reasons: to escort my honoured guests, the Princesses, and also to prevent all chances of disorder during the exchange. As soon as it is light, I shall call my men together and forbid them to step beyond the appointed boundary. You can answer for the Russians too?' Gramoff assured him of their good faith, and transmitted a request from Prince David that the mountaineers should refrain from the firing and powder-play which was their usual expression of joy; this, said the Prince, was necessary to avoid all possibilities of misunderstanding and disorder.

Shamyl agreed, but added: 'Is there no likelihood of your troops rejoicing and firing, too?' Gramoff told him of the Emperor's death, and how there could be no rejoicing for six months.

Shamyl had not heard of the Tzar's death and remained silent for some moments, no doubt evoking the memory of his powerful enemy and all he had heard of him. 'For such a great Sultan, six years would not be too long,' he said. 'But a great man should have a great son. How is his successor, the Prince Alexander?' Although Gramoff described the new Tzar in glowing terms, it was obvious Shamyl's mind was elsewhere. A short silence fell, and then he began to speak of the subject nearest his heart. 'What of *my* son? Is he well? . . . I am told he does not know a word of Tartar.'

'But you must not find fault with him for that,' said Gramoff. 'He has lived so long in Russia.'

Shamyl's face softened. 'Believe me, I shall not; only let him come back to me.'

He sat gazing at the fire with narrowed eyes. He did not speak for a long while. 'You do not wish to sleep, Imam?' asked Gramoff, who was nodding with fatigue. 'No. Not tonight,' replied the Imam. 'I cannot sleep for thinking of my son. May Allah grant the affair is terminated without treachery.'

So the night passed, and at dawn Shamyl went to address his Naibs while Gramoff, having visited the Princesses' tent and found them already dressed and impatient to be off, galloped back to Kourinsk with the Imam's last instructions.

'They shall leave at the first cry of the mollah,' Shamyl had said. The sun had risen to gild the whole scene, shining gloriously, and the Princesses and their household were again seated in the lumbering arbas, their veils over their faces, moving slowly towards the Mitchik. They had become grotesque figures during their captivity, skeleton-thin, bundled into an assortment of ragged fur *shoubas*, coarse linen tunics and draggled Asiatic garments. Behind and around them rode seven thousand Murids, all intoning their sacred chants. From time to time, Khazi Mahommed galloped up to see if all was well. (The day before, one of the carts had overturned, and Madame Drancy had been pitched down a ravine, to be rescued, considerably bruised and shaken.) As they drove, they noticed that one of the coachmen was singing a plaintive folk-song in Russian. 'You are Russian, then?' asked the Princess Varvara in some astonishment. A pair of blue Slav eyes stared back at her sombrely from beneath the Caucasian papakh. 'I no longer know,' replied the man. He was a deserter who had thrown in his lot with the tribesmen many years before.

Now a gathering horde of riders began to appear from all sides, galloping down the mountainside, emerging from the woods and leaping the chasms to join them. Their cries of *Shamyl! . . . Shamyl Imam!* echoed across the hills, telling his approach. These were the élite of his army, the Avar and Tchetchen nobles, his chief Naibs and picked cavalry: 'A brilliant cortège,' says Madame Drancy. 'Their tcherkesskas were sewn with silver lace, orders and decorations; their arms resplendent, their turbans magnificent, their cloaks fur-lined, their horses pure-bred. . . .' In short, nothing was lacking to form an impressive spectacle. In their midst rode Shamyl, 'his fine and noble face literally shining with joy'. Although he was their captor, the cause of all their miseries, both Madame Drancy and the Princesses were always conscious of his nobility, his largeness of nature, never seeing him as a barbarous murderer, or religious impostor, as did those who knew him less well. A Prussian officer who has left his memoir of the exchange, quoted the Princesses as saying: 'the mountaineers are not human beings—they are wild beasts', when, in fact, the Princesses had said: 'They are human beings and have human sentiments, but they do not happen to be civilized.'

Shamyl approached the arbas to bid farewell to his captives; one by one the children were lifted out and placed in his arms. The Imam embraced them lovingly, bowed ceremoniously to the Princesses and rode back to his Naibs. As the arbas gained the brow of the hill, Hadjio cantered alongside, pointing his whip. 'Look! There is the Russian army!'

The words galvanized the captives, who all stood up, nearly upsetting the arbas. Straining their eyes, they could see far away on the hill facing them, a long cordon of men and horses and guns. The sun glittered on the column and, as it advanced, they could distinguish the pennons and banners fluttering gaily.

The Caucasians, too, stared avidly at the column. The hated Giaour! But today there must be no bloodshed. They fingered their guns longingly. As the distance between the two armies diminished, the Princesses were surrounded by Lesghien cavalry with drawn swords; there must be no risk of being taken by surprise. On a small knoll, to the side, Madame Drancy noted Shamyl, enthroned in state, beneath a large yellow parasol and surrounded by his Naibs. From time to time he surveyed the Russians through a telescope. On his right sat Daniel Beg; on his left, Ker Effendi and the Mollah Jamul u'din. Behind them, in absolute silence, stood the cavalry, five thousand strong, their banners closing round, like the wings of some giant black bird, at once menacing and protective.

Across the river, the Russians had halted and were taking up positions, infantry and artillery in the centre, cavalry on the flanks. The officers were grouped around the Commander-in-Chief, Baron

Nicolai, and all of them were now training their field-glasses on the
Murid ranks, eager to see the legendary Shamyl. Djemmal-Eddin stood
a little way apart, the glasses held to his eyes for a long time, straining
to see that other world which was now claiming him. But the distance
was too great; all that could be picked out were the dark banners.
It was a halcyon morning; a radiance shimmered over the countryside. Beyond the hills where the Murids were assembled, glittered the
towering snow peaks, dazzling against the blue.

The point of meeting was to be a lone tree, standing half-way
between the two positions. Now a horseman dashed out from Shamyl's
ranks and galloped to the tree; rearing his horse, he waved a pennon.
It was the signal for the exchange. Now the arbas were led towards the
ford, accompanied by Khazi Mahommed, Mahommed Sheffi and
thirty-five Tchetchen guards. Only the sound of creaking wheels broke
the perfect stillness. From across the ford, the prisoners could see a
small body of horsemen coming towards them: it was Djemmal-Eddin,
Prince Tchavtchavadzé, some officers, and the stipulated thirty-five
soldiers with carts containing the bags of silver and sixteen Lesghien
prisoners—their ransom. As the two groups drew near, the Prince
could see the women huddled together, but as they were all veiled, he
could not distinguish his wife from the rest. Suddenly a childish voice
shrilled out: 'Look, Mamma! There is Papa on a white horse!' It was
Salomé, waving delightedly. Hadjio now took the little Alexander and
carried him to his father; the other Murids galloped over with the rest
of the children, who hung round their father's neck. The Prince was
about to go towards the arbas, when Khazi Mahommed rode across
his path. He looked pale and ill at ease, but bowed with his customary
grace.

'My father, the Imam, charges me to tell you that he took as much
care of your family as if they hàd been his own. What they suffered was
not our intention, but rather arose from our ignorance how to treat
such noble ladies, and from our lack of means. My father bids you
know they are returned to you pure as the lilies, sheltered from all eyes,
like the gazelles of the desert.'

The Prince could not reply. Anger, joy and vengeance filled his heart.
He bowed. Meanwhile, Djemmal-Eddin, wearing Russian uniform,
had ridden forward to embrace his brother, and was now taking leave
of the Russian officers. Baron Nicolai presented him with his own sword.
'Don't cut down any of our people with it,' he said jovially, trying to
raise Djemmal-Eddin's spirits.

'Neither ours, nor theirs,' replied Djemmal-Eddin in a voice choked
with emotion, clinging, even at this last moment, to his adopted country.
As he rode forward the Princesses threw back their veils, the better to
see their deliverer. He drew rein beside them, staring long and

earnestly. But not a word was said. It was as if the prisoners were turned to stone. All the gratitude and relief they felt remained unspoken: no words would come. Tears rolled down Princess Varvara's thin cheeks, as she looked on the man who had been the Tzar's favourite, the dashing figure whom the whole Court had found so romantic.

III

This dramatic scene in its strange setting of massed armies and great mountain backdrop, had everything required to lure the biographer from the strict path of exactitude. How tempting, here, to luxuriate in one of those dramas which often lurk beneath the surface of history. The situation is tragic enough in itself; yet how can we refuse, at this point, to be influenced by the voices of Lermontov, Bestoujev Marlinsky, and all those romantic writers whose flights of imagination still vibrate through the Caucasus—through the mountains they made a setting for their tales of love, heroism and sacrifice? Perhaps, one day, a new poem will be added to Caucasian lore, and Djemmal-Eddin will take his place beside Thamar and Ammalat Beg, Ismael and Sara and the Prisoner of the Caucasus. It will tell of Djemmal-Eddin's love for the Princess, whom he had known at Court, how this love, more than anything else, had steeled him to this sacrifice. Djemmal-Eddin is a figure predestined to tragedy. Long ago, he had been torn from his people to remake his life in another world. Did he forswear this life, which had become his own, to save the lives of his father's prisoners, but above all, to save the life of the woman he loved? Only by returning to the mountains himself could he free her. Yet in going back he lost his last chance of winning her. Or, double, treble, tragic imbroglio—did the Princess Varvara love another? Did Djemmal-Eddin learn of this and still immolate himself, as a supreme gesture of devotion? Was the Princess Varvara when they met at the Mitchik, going towards a new life, and a lover's arms? Her known devotion to her dead husband confounds this utterly, but it would have been in the true tradition of nineteenth century romanticism. All the ingredients are there; hopeless love, true love, love denied, love achieved through the sacrifice of another . . . a pathetic episode, its minor cadences as typical of its age as the music of Schumann sounding faintly through an autumn twilight . . . a plaintive, imagined melody, which might have sounded beyond the thunders of established fact.

IV

It is due to the accounts left by Gramoff and a Prussian officer attached to Baron Nicolai's staff, that we have two eye-witness accounts of Djemmal-Eddin's return to his father. The Prussian published his account, *Ein Besuch bei Schamyl*, in Berlin a few months later; but some of its statements, such as those concerning Shamyl's treatment of prisoners, are wildly distorted and quite at variance with the Princesses' own accounts. His description of the exchange, however, tallies with that of Gramoff. Both of them describe the scene in detail, but since the Prussian officer was new to the Caucasus, the drama and strangeness of the scene made a far greater impact on him, sharpening his vision acutely. He was one of the officers who rode out with Djemmal-Eddin. Here is his description:

A dip in the land concealed the mountaineers for some moments, and then, suddenly—we were face to face. Never shall I forget the sensation which their first appearance caused in me. All the poetical ideas which had been formed in Europe about Shamyl and his followers, the fallacy of which my three years sojourn here has sufficiently proved to me, seemed more than justified by reality. At the head of the troop who were slowly advancing rode a young man, very slender, with a pale, immobile face. His entirely white appearance—he was mounted on a beautiful white horse, wore a white tunic and a white fur papakh, gave me a disagreeable impression—an impression much strengthened by his affected manner and studied gestures. Behind him in two ranks came his thirty-two followers, all Murids, splendidly equipped, mounted and armed. There was a grace in their proud bearing which was enhanced by a dash of half-savage wildness. They carried their long guns cocked, and resting on the right [thigh. Their stern dark faces and wiry forms, the richness of their arms, glittering with gold and silver, the beauty of their fiery little horses, combined with the background of forests and mountains, offered a *coup d'œil*, the like of which I never saw before, or since.

He then describes the Prince's reunion with his children, Djemmal-Eddin's halt beside the arbas, the meeting of the two brothers and their advance towards Shamyl's lines.

Our march was thus. Sixteen Murids preceded us. Then came Djemmal-Eddin and Khazi Mahommed, between a Russian officer and a Naib. Then a troop of Cossacks, and again the Murids, bringing up the rear. But order only lasted a few moments. . . . As we approached the river, great numbers of tribesmen galloped down and pressed around us to meet Djemmal-Eddin, trying to kiss his hand, the hem of his tunic, his boots. . . . He submitted very quietly, only endeavouring more and more strenuously to keep me and the Russian officer beside him, for he knew he could not be answerable for what might happen to us, were we to become separated by this dense fanatic crowd. Once or twice, when confusion threatened, he gave way to strong words and gestures—though the former were not understood, as he only spoke in Russian; but the force of his gestures made an impression, and the mob drew back in submission and respect.

Now Gramoff takes up the tale, telling us that Hadjio, the steward, arrived to greet the Imam's son, and to present him with a magnificent tcherkasska, explaining that the Imam did not wish to see his son in anything but native dress. Gramoff translated the message, but Djemmal-Eddin frowned, appearing put-out.

'What an extraordinary idea,' he said. 'How can I change clothes here, in front of everyone. . . . Why, I can be seen by the Princesses. . . .' It was plain that he felt humiliated. And it is curious to note that, even here in the far Caucasus, at this supreme moment of drama and tragedy, standards of mid-nineteenth century modesty prevailed.

'Your father's wishes are law,' said Gramoff. 'You will learn that no one disobeys the Imam—no one.' The Murids closed around in a compact circle; Djemmal-Eddin dismounted and began to take off his Russian uniform.

There were Murids of all ages [says the Prussian officer], marked with shot-wounds and sabre-cuts; their dress was tolerably uniform, simple and in good taste, their splendid weapons richly inlaid. Besides these stately figures, there were crowds of wretched halfstarved creatures of the lower orders who, whenever they got in the way of the Murids, were recklessly ridden over, or treated to heavy lashes of their whips. They gazed at the Russian officers with avid curiosity, but no hatred. My English saddle with pistols in its holsters —and above all, my eye-glass—fascinated them. After some hesitation one or two came up and touched the eye-glass which at that time I was using. It naturally fell down, and they drew back in terror, thinking they had poked out my eye. The percussion locks of my pistols were an entire novelty to the Murids—their guns being only provided with flints. One of the Naibs clapped me on the back with familiarity and informed me, through the interpreter, that though to-day we were friends, when next we would meet, our only communication would be that of gun and sabre. 'The sooner the better,' I replied. . . .

And we sensed that to this arrogant Prussian, the Caucasian wars, with all their fury and idealism and lost endeavour, were merely excellent shooting—a blood-sport, to be enjoyed in picturesque surroundings.

When Djemmal-Eddin had changed his clothes, so that not a boot or spur or a handkerchief remained of his Russian past, the circle broke, and he rode out to meet his father. He was transformed. His long dark tcherkesska was ornamented by superb arms; his mount, the white stallion with the black star blaze, caracoled across the grass, the sunlight playing over the crimson and gold chaprak. Under the heavy white lambskin papakh, Djemmal-Eddin's pale face was turned resolutely towards his father. As he approached, a wild cry burst from the mountaineers and they surged forward, all semblance of order gone. The Prussian officer was almost unseated, his terrified horse plunging and neighing; across a sea of savage faces he saw the Russians struggling to regain Djemmal-Eddin's side. The young man had reined back his horse and was refusing to go farther without his escort. At last the Naibs succeeded in imposing order, and Djemmal-Eddin dismounted, to cross the last few hundred yards on foot. He gave his left hand to the Prussian officer, his right to one of the Russians.

> The close proximity of the dreaded Imam began to produce its effect. A stillness as of death succeeded the deafening clamour: the mob had fallen back. Thousands of devouring eyes were upon us as we walked slowly forward. Djemmal-Eddin's hand trembled violently in mine.

Shamyl remained seated cross-legged on his carpets, while his son bowed and knelt before him. Then all the Imam's impassivity vanished. He embraced Djemmal-Eddin, tears streaming down his face. Now, before both the Russians and his Murids, he sobbed unrestrainedly. At last he spoke: 'I thank Allah for preserving my son, and the Tzar for permitting his return,' he said. Then, observing the Russian officers standing near, he asked Gramoff who they were. On being told they were Baron Nicolai's aides-de-camp, and his son's escort, he bowed. 'I thank them too. Today, my opinion of the Russians is changed.'

The moment had now come for the Russians to leave. It was noticed that Djemmal-Eddin seemed to falter. His fellow officers took leave of him in the traditional manner, embracing him with a triple kiss. Djemmal-Eddin's dark gentle eyes filled with tears, and he was unable to hide his emotion. At which Shamyl, anxious to avoid the bad impression which might be caused among his followers, seeing his son's grief at parting with the Giaours, turned towards his Murids saying: 'These were my son's dearest friends.'

He was plainly impatient for the Giaours to depart—to be left alone with his son, whom already, in his heart, he was beginning to reproach for having forgotten his native tongue. He foresaw that his son's reconversion to Avar life was going to present many difficulties. But then he remembered thankfully, that Shouanete, 'the Pearl', had recovered her forgotten Russian when talking with the Princesses. She would be the interpreter, until the years of Russian bondage were expurged from Djemmal-Eddin's mind. Allah was great!

Shamyl took leave of the officers with extreme courtesy and thanked Gramoff for his services. 'Today I have no gift worthy of the occasion, though I shall send you something I hope you will accept.' (Later, a magnificent watch, set in diamonds, reached Gramoff at Temir-Khan-Shura.) 'But remember this, Isai Beg, that my children and all my family will ever acknowledge your services: if you or any of your relatives should fall into our hands, know that they will instantly be freed. This I say in the presence of my chief Naibs.' Behind him the silent ranks of cavalry were ranged, in absolute stillness, their dark faces intent.

The radiant morning had meanwhile clouded over, becoming grey and overcast. A chill wind sprang up, soughing in the trees and ruffling the horses' manes. Shamyl called for his bourka and then, putting his arm around his son's shoulders, led him towards the Naibs. As their banners dipped in salute, Djemmal-Eddin was observed to cast a final long look back towards the Russian lines. '*La Allah illa Allahi!*' cried the Murids; very faint on the breeze sounded the strains of a military band playing Russian national airs—drowned out by the harsh and exultant voices of Djemmal-Eddin's countrymen: '*Shamyl Imam!* There is none but Shamyl!' they cried.

30

A Defeat

I had brothers whom I looked upon as coats of chain mail. Lo! They have become mine enemies. I counted them as sharp arrows—such indeed they were, but arrows that have pierced my heart.

SHAMYL—QUOTING AN UNIDENTIFIED

ARAB POET

Yours kill ours—ours kill yours! This had been the cry which Murids and Russians hurled at each other for thirty years, while drum-beats and death-chants rang round the mountains in never-ending echoes. For thirty years the serpent-coils of hatred had locked them in mortal combat. Now the Murid grip was loosening. Shamyl and his Naibs remained as fanatic as ever, and many Naibs still drank 'the sherbet of martyrdom', but the bulk of the people were no longer behind them. They were exhausted. The Murid creed was too demanding; their faith no longer inspired a new generation which had grown up in the shadows of this sombre creed. Faced with a life-time of suffering, whole tribes began to cede over to the Russians. Once they had followed Shamyl blindly, at whatever cost, for as Gobineau says in his *Religions et Philosophies dans l'Asie Centrale*: 'The whole meaning of man's existence is to meet God. Anyone who can advance him along his way must therefore be followed regardless of what orders he may give.' This had been the explanation of that strange blend of fanaticism and passivity which characterized the Murids. But, as once it had been written that Shamyl should be their victorious leader, so now, it was written that the Infidel should conquer.

Three things brought about Shamyl's defeat. The cumulative force of Russian arms, which at the end of the Crimean War was concentrated in the Caucasus; the leadership of Prince Bariatinsky, who was appointed supreme commander in place of the old ailing Voronzov; above all, Shamyl's cause was lost by internal dissensions. The many different tribes had, from time to time, weakened his ranks by fighting among themselves. But now, their internal dissensions grew, and spreading like forest fires, swept across his territories with devastating speed. Overnight, whole aôuls and provinces went over to the Infidels. Exhausted by Shamyl's demands, they gave themselves up and were placed under Russian protection against his reprisals. Terror had always been his strongest weapon: it was ever the guiding force in Asiatic warfare. Now Bariatinsky's clemency was proving a stronger weapon. The tribes feared Russian guns—but not Russian vengeance. They had discovered their enemy to be terrible in battle, but magnanimous in conquest. So they ceded over in their thousands, leaving Shamyl and his remaining Murids isolated, a diminishing force, withdrawing each day farther into the high mountains.

Change was in the air. All was new. New times, a new Tzar, new generals and a new concept of conquest. What Yermolov's force and Voronzov's might had not been able to accomplish, Bariatinsky was now achieving by a more humanitarian approach. We have seen something of his administrative methods, as brilliantly conceived and executed as his military tactics, when commanding the Left Flank in 1848. Now he approached his zenith, unhampered by any criticism from the Winter Palace. The new Tzar Alexander II, who was thirty-seven at the time of his accession, had been the companion of his childhood and youth, and they were to remain united all their lives, the Tzar defending him against all the attacks which his unorthodox approach to both the problem of the Caucasus and the conduct of his private life exposed him. As long as Nicholas I had lived, Bariatinsky's detractors were sure of moral support from the throne. The Tzar felt as they: the Prince was a brilliant soldier, and as such could serve the Empire; yet too much power must not be given to a man whose whole youth and personal life was tarnished by scandal. But in 1855 Nicholas died.

His son was of a very different type. He was, first of all, benign, an adjective never applied to the Autocrat of all the Russias. His gentle, if rather bulging blue eyes radiated kindness. He detested force and had inherited none of his father's impassioned militarism. Reports of the wounded soldiers' sufferings during the Crimea had so tormented him that he had with difficulty been restrained from offering himself in the capacity of a hospital orderly. When in the south, soon after his accession, he had seen the graves of one hundred thousand soldiers; it was perhaps this more than all else which influenced him to accept peace terms without prolonging the struggle. All around him the Court and the Ministers opposed him, dwelling on the shamefulness of defeat. But not for nothing was he the pupil of Joukovsky. Another formative influence had been that of his aunt, the Grand Duchess Elena Pavlovna, a liberal and profoundly cultivated woman whose palace was always the centre of an advanced society wholly foreign to the traditions of the Winter Palace.

The new Tzar openly advocated a Constitution, and the liberation of the serfs; thus he was mistrusted in some circles. He began by lesser reforms: the abolition of capital punishment, measures to reduce graft and the abuses of local administration. He abolished the detested system of military colonies, with a promise that no recruits should be levied for the following four years. Flogging was next prescribed, in spite of the Archbishop of Moscow, who opposed this measure with passion, saying it was approved by the Holy Scriptures. By 1857, the ceremony of releasing certain prisoners from the fortress of Peter and Paul, traditionally held on the Emperor's birthday, had to be abandoned, there being no prisoners left. The whole country was released from the despotic grip in which it had writhed for years, although this increased freedom saw also the growth of secret societies, impatient bands of nihilists and revolutionaries, who served as an excuse for the brutalities of a secret police which, in the name of public safety, gave themselves up to terrible abuses of power. *Zemstvos*, or political assemblies, were established, to prepare the way for self-government and a Constitution. However, the new Tzar, although inclined to that woolly-headed sentimentalism of which his critics accused him, saw his country clearly enough, telling Milioutine, *à propos* the Constitution, that he did not believe Russia—as a body, both nobles and people— had yet acquired the qualities needed for self-government.

*   *   *

In the Caucasus the old order was changing fast. Voronzov was worn out by the many high offices and campaigns which had been his whole life. He had been weakening for some while, and a succession of cures in Germany had been unavailing. Now he stepped aside, making room for the new order. But the empty procession of his last days were cheered by the presence of a little granddaughter, Elizabeth, child of his only daughter Sophie, Countess Shouvaloff. One by one, all his sons had died. Simon and his butterfly wife (whom Bariatinsky had loved briefly) remained childless. Prince Simon died before his father, and at last the sole heir to all the Voronzov glories was this small child in a frilled pinafore, prattling to her grandfather, walking beside him down the long alleés of Aloupkha, where he had withdrawn.

Upon Voronzov's resignation, Mouraviev had been appointed as acting Commander-in-Chief: but this precipitated a crisis at staff-headquarters where Bariatinsky, in command of the Left Flank, had become too puissant to accept orders from any newcomer whose views were diametrically opposed to his own. He already saw himself as the

supreme commander, and when he realized that none of his recommendations were followed, and that the war was, once again, to be need-
lessly protracted, he asked to be transferred. He was at once appointed
to the new Tzar's suite, a move he had no doubt foreseen. Now the two
friends were together constantly, Bariatinsky advising, discussing and
dissecting the whole conduct of the Caucasian campaigns from the
Winter Palace itself. Thus he was able to win over the Tzar to his own
views. Soon the monarch was completely indoctrinated. Alexander
loved him as a friend and believed in him as a general. Overruling all
administrative and Court opposition, he next appointed Bariatinsky as
Commander of the Special Caucasus Corps, and acting Viceroy; moreover, he decreed that he was to retain all the privileges and supreme
powers accorded Voronzov.

St. Petersburg fumed: it was irresponsible favouritism; he was too
young! His dissipated youth was recalled in detail; and then, there was
that continuing, unfortunate infatuation for Madame Davidova. Was
the Viceroy proposing to flaunt his mistress—still the acknowledged wife
of one of his officers—at the Viceregal Palace? In 1852 she had borne him
a daughter. Even so the scandal had not separated them. Indeed the
Tzar, then Tzariévitch, had been quite open in his support; the child
had been legally adopted by her great grandparents, Prince and Princess
Paul Orbeliani, thus making her aunt to her own mother. Madame
Davidova's father was Prince Dimitri Orbeliani, but he had died and
his father, Prince Paul, adopted Tebro. *Most* irregular, said Prince
Bariatinsky's enemies.

She was a singularly lovely child, the little Princess Tebro. It had
been rather a delicate matter explaining Tebro's presence in the elderly
Orbeliani household. They said she was the child of a Georgian priest
killed when Shamyl sacked a village near Telav. She had been found
crying in the ruins, sole survivor of the raid, they said. . . . But no one
could explain why the Emperor took so close an interest in her, nor
why he loaded the priest's child with benefits.

Colonel Vladimir Davidov remains an enigmatic figure. Perhaps he
had reached an understanding with Bariatinsky, who may have preferred a mistress to a wife; perhaps rapid promotion and favours made
the life of a *mari complaisant* acceptable to the Colonel. Perhaps he
had other interests, or was just biding his time until revenge was really
worthwhile. In contemporary memoirs he is usually mentioned *en pas-
sent*; a lean, silent man, almost, one might say, a skeleton at the feast,
remaining in the background at all the Viceregal functions. Occasionally
he was persuaded to talk about his noble French relatives, the Duchesse
de Gramont among them; or to display a curious stone which he
possessed, a talisman, or cure for poison, well-known in this part of the
world, and which enthralled visitors, among them Alexander Dumas.

Such stones generally belonged to the princely Persian and Georgian families and were handed down from father to son. They were about the size of a plover's egg, of spongy substance and dull bluish colour, bruised with black. Yet this unprepossessing looking object possessed the powers of life and death. In the case of a snake bite, or that of a scorpion, mostly fatal in these regions, the stone was rubbed over the wound, at which it changed colour, becoming a livid grey as it absorbed the venom. On being placed in a saucer of milk it disgorged its poison and assumed its original colour.

A traveller, passing through the Caucasus at this time, described a dinner-party at the Prince's summer chalet in the mountains at Burjan. The Prince's own band was playing, and the whole atmosphere was one of great luxury—of frivolity, even. We learn that Field-Marshal Prince Bariatinsky, 'now the second personage of rank in Russia, was a splendid figure, about six foot three inches in height, well-built, with a superb carriage. He seemed about forty, had light brown hair and a high massive forehead which shelved upward, narrower at the top than at the brow. His eyes were blue-grey, with a stern commanding expression.' At one end of the table two chairs were placed side by side. The Prince sat in one, and beside him sat the beautiful Madame Davidova, adopting a rather proprietary air (in keeping with her sobriquet, 'La Maréchale'). Later there was an expedition to a ruined monastery, the Prince's band still accompanying the party, the Prince now surrounded by a bevy of beauties and gallant officers, 'feet tripping lightly in the gay mazurka, over the graves of the monks'. A huge swing or roundabout had been erected, to further the fun. The traveller eyed it rather censoriously, remarking it looked more like a gallows; but then, this was the Caucasus—where dalliance was always in the nature of an interlude.

Meanwhile, all-glorious, all-powerful, Bariatinsky ruled as a god. The whole army rejoiced in his return—dandy officers and hoary troopers alike. The tribes, too, knew him as a chivalrous foe; they began to believe in a peace which might be obtained without loss of honour. This was no Infidel tyrant sent to oppress them by Nicholas the hated Sultan of the North, but rather their own tried enemy, baptized by Caucasian fire, twice pierced by their own bullets, a worthy foe, a worthy conqueror, even, if Allah now willed they should be conquered.

Bariatinsky's supreme powers gave him the means to reform the army, develop and administer the new territories his soldiers won, and to conclude the war as rapidly as possible. Great projects and achievements lay before him. But there were only four years of power left to him. Since he was a man of both vision and action, his plans were no sooner conceived than set in motion, so that most of his vast projects were realized during those few years. First, more troops were posted to the Caucasus. They poured down from the north in uncounted numbers; next, Milioutine, a particularly brilliant soldier (he was later to earn the odium of the Court for his partial democratization of the Guards' regiments), was appointed his second-in-command. These two ardent reformers—iconoclasts, said their detractors—together with Prince Alexander Gagarin and General Yevdokimov, set about the final conquest of the Caucasus. Their first care was to redistribute their forces. Formerly, the armies of the field had often been under orders from headquarters far removed from the scene of action. These headquarters in turn were dependent on the decisions of the Viceroy, in Tiflis, if not the Tzar, or War Ministry, far away in St. Petersburg.

Bariatinsky re-divided the Armies of the South into five separate armies, each under a chief invested with full powers within his district. Three of these five now began to close in on Shamyl. The Army of the Left Flank, under Yevdokimov, stood facing the Tchetchnia. The pre-Caspian Army, under Prince Gregory Orbeliani, descended on Daghestan and the Caspian coast areas. The Army of the Lesghien Line, under Baron Vrevsky, was based to the south-east of the main chain of mountains. All three now began methodically to assault the last Murid strongholds. And, for the first time, the Russian troops were using rifles. (It will be recalled that the Tzar Nicholas had been violently opposed to this innovation, insisting on flint-locks throughout his reign.)

Bariatinsky's earlier methods of clearing the forests were continued, so that the mountaineers were forced to fight in the open, or to retreat farther into the barren hills. Gradually they found themselves pitted against an enemy with whom they could never come to grips. In the words of Bariatinsky: 'Fighting implies some sort of equality, and so long as they could fight, the mountaineers had no thought of submission. But when, time after time, they found that, in fact, they could never come to blows, their weapons fell from their hands. Beaten, they would have gathered again on the morrow. Circumvented and forced to disperse without fighting, they began to come in next day to offer their submission.' Once it had been the Russians who could not fight, or win, or even reach the Murids in the forests; now the situation was reversed. Even the mountains were being brought low by bridges, and long-range artillery fire and dynamite. Then, too, Prince Bariatinsky's presence had a galvanic effect upon the Russian troops, who had become stagnant in the long years of monotonous and indecisive fighting. He inspired his men by his own vast horizons. He spoke to them of Asiatic conquest beyond the Caspian, of commercial relations and political influences which would spread across Asia: of railways which would traverse the dreaded desert wastes, of the riches and glory

that would be Russia's—all of which had depended on the first step—
that of Shamyl's absolute submission. His regiments felt themselves
part of his vast enterprise, and all of their former disillusion vanished.

Tolstoy records the boredom and disillusion which had become
habitual. Two officers are talking; the newcomer asks the seasoned
campaigner why he stays on:

> Because I feel myself even more incapable of returning to Russia!
> And as to how I came here—it is supposed to be enough just to be
> in the Caucasus, to be overwhelmed with rewards. . . . It is one of
> those legends engendered by men like Passek, and such. From afar,
> everything seemed to be waiting for us, mountains and marvels. . . .
> But, in fact, I have been here two years, fought through two cam-
> paigns and received absolutely nothing for my pains.

Now the increasing number of renegade tribes were providing civil
labour for the army, and serving as guides and spies. Corruption, too,
played its part in the conquest. Alcohol and bribes were powerful
weapons in Russian hands, something they knew how to exploit to the
full, like flattery and theatrical effects. Voronzov had been magnificent,
but not flamboyant. He had lacked something of those histrionic
abilities which characterized both his precedessor, Yermolov, and his
successor, Bariatinsky. Perhaps he was too much of an English Milord
for the tribesmen. Perhaps his early schooling had left him too restrained to deal effectively with the Asiatics. Those same playing-fields
of Eton upon which the battle of Waterloo was said to be won, might
also account for Voronzov's failure to win over the tribesmen. Roaring,
posturing Yermolov had known how to make himself a legend, as
did Shamyl, with his aura of mystery and heavenly portents. Neither
they nor Bariatinsky ever despised theatrical effects.

Bariatinsky, with his great height, his fair hair and boyard appearance, his mixture of *grand seigneur, bon viveur* and stern warrior, travelled
about the Caucasus, planning his victorious campaigns and holding
court with equal panache. Just as Shamyl was always accompanied
by his executioner, so Bariatinsky was accompanied by a treasurer,
bestowing lakhs of gold or precious stones on co-operative chieftains.
Medals awarded for valour were not cast in the Russian pattern of a
cross, which might have caused offence to the Moslem recipients, but
were, instead, engraved with a star.

Shamyl, watching with growing despair, continued with his usual
courage. But he would not give up. Not till the last aôul, the last peak
was wrested from him, and the ultimate victory had been as costly to
Russia as he could make it. He too offered rewards, though his coffers
could never compete with the Russians. Besides bestowing medals, he
was now forced to make some concessions, to abandon his former

standards of Muridic austerity, and to promise the most unexpected rewards. At the siege of one particularly significant Russian fort in the Tchetchnia, where the garrison had made a desperate resistance lasting more than a week, and where the Colonel's daughter was known to be beside her father, Shamyl went so far as to promise her to the first Naib who planted his banner on the walls. As the Archduke Charles of Austria had written to Paskiévitch, '*il faut transiger avec les principes*'. Such practical cynicism penetrated even to the Caucasus, in times of stress.

But nothing, neither medals nor oratory, nor the promise of Colonels' daughters stopped the mass desertions and treacheries which ravaged Shamyl's armies and began to gain among the people too. His concessions came too late. Demoralization was rapid. When the Kabardians ceded, to be followed by the Ossetes, forming a pro-Russian block in the very heart of the Caucasus, only the tribes on the extreme east and west remained loyal. Sometimes they were again heartened by some lesser victory—a carefully staged ambush into which a whole body of Russians would stumble and perish. Shamyl's key-posts were defended only by those who had taken the ten-fold Murid oath, to die rather than yield. But such fanatics were rarer with each battle. The heroism of whole populations, as at Akhulgo, became a memory . . . 'I had brothers whom I looked upon as coats of chain mail . . .' Shamyl counted himself blessed, now, if one skirmish turned in his favour.

An ever-growing fatalistic acceptance of defeat, rather than a lack of courage, now enfeebled the Caucasian peoples. They still resisted, but with passive bravery. The storming of Gherghebil exemplifies this passivity. The Russians had attacked the aôul, which was defended with ferocity. The roofs had been taken off and replaced by brushwood so that the Russians, storming forward, fell through the traps, to be impaled on the Murid pikes. It seemed as if the battle would go to the Murids, but cholera had broken out among the ranks defending the lower bastions. The men were so weakened, most of them dying at their posts, that a breach was made in the outer defences and, once again, successive waves of Russians advanced, this time not to be caught by the brushwood traps. The remaining Murids did not go out to meet them, as once, but, as in so many instances during the last years of the struggle, they awaited the end fatalistically. 'Between the bursts of gunfire the Russians could hear their death chant rising, as from an open grave.'

There were many such graves during the winter of 1857–8, in each one another of Shamyl's hopes lay buried. Inch by inch he was driven back into the high peaks of the Tchetchnia. His position might be likened to that of the North American Indians who fought the white man's invasion hopelessly. Like the Apaches, he retreated to the mountains, his hunting ground, crops and timber taken from him, his laboriously cultivated food no sooner raised than destroyed; his people forever withdrawing into more barren country; no means of subsistence left now but what could be raised by raiding tactics which were repaid by severe punitive measures.

All through the years Shamyl still resisted a negotiated peace, although Bariatinsky sent emissaries, and Daniel Beg implored to be allowed to treat with his former allies. Shamyl was now short of men. As always, Turkish aid promised much, but proved meagre. In desperation, clumsy home-made wood and leather cannons had been tried out, only to burst, killing the gun-crew where they stood. This had been the idea of Mahommed Hidatli, his chief of artillery, who was convinced that thick wood and iron hoops, and many layers of buffalo hide, would be strong enough to resist the explosion. Shamyl had been sceptical, saying: 'It will not work—and I value your head too much. You will be blown to pieces. Besides we do not wish the Russians to make jest of us.' At last their desperate need overcame all scruples, and the guns were tried out, but soon abandoned.

Now, as both guns and ammunition became scarce, they sometimes drove an iron nail through the bullet, fixing its head into the cartridge, thus forming a deadly missile, for the reinforced cartridge inflicted a fatal wound. An ordinary bullet, passing through healthy flesh, often left the warrior little the worse: now, every bullet must account for a life.

But by the end of 1857, all the lower Tchetchnia was in Russian hands: the eastern part of Daghestan had fallen, while the forces of the Lesghien line had succeeded in crossing the main chain and were concentrating on the hitherto impenetrable Deedo country.

*   *   *

In February 1858, a Tartar messenger galloped into Hassiff Yourt asking to see the Commandant—'In the name of Shamyl Imam.' He was brought before Colonel Prince Mirsky and explained that Djemmal-Eddin was desperately ill in the mountains, that no local medicines could help him; Shamyl, knowing his son's trust in the Russians, and the Russians' love for his son, begged that suitable drugs should be sent to him. That Shamyl, the proud vengeful father, should at last send such a message told of Djemmal-Eddin's desperate need. No word had ever reached his friends in Russia, neither the Imperial Family, nor his fellow officers, since that March day in 1855, on the banks of the Mitchik. Silence had closed around him, and all the enquiries and communications had been brought to a standstill before the black rocks beyond which—somewhere—he languished. The garrison's best doctor,

Piotrovsky, having questioned the messenger on Djemmal-Eddin's symptoms, which he diagnosed as those of consumption, prepared a case of drugs. Prince Mirsky also sent word that if a doctor was required one would be sent—on certain conditions. The messenger remained mute to all the questions as to Djemmal-Eddin's whereabouts and rode away as soon as the medicines were stowed in his saddle-bags. Even the local garrison had not been able to discover anything about Djemmal-Eddin's situation, although there were occasional scraps of information to be gleaned from Tartar spies.

It seemed he had been sent to live at Karaty, beside his brother Khazi Mahommed: the two young men got on well together. Karaty was celebrated for the beauty of its women; the Imam's son was treated in a princely fashion. His father planned to give him the daughter of the celebrated Naib Talgik to wife. *Aie! Yie!* said the spies: she was graceful as a young poplar tree. Allah be praised, he was a fortunate young man; as the Imam's heir he wanted for nothing. And indeed, Shamyl presently insisted on his son's marriage to the daughter of a Tcherkess prince. Djemmal-Eddin obeyed, but refused to live with her, and so, at last, was permitted to withdraw into his final solitude.

II

Early in May, the sentries at Hassiff Yourt saw a small cloud of dust approaching along the sun-baked white road leading down from the mountains. As it drew near, a Tartar horseman emerged, to gallop in, grey with dust, his inexpressive face showing traces of strain. It was the same messenger who had ridden down some months earlier. Again he was taken before the Colonel. Djemmal-Eddin's condition was worsening rapidly, he said. Shamyl implored the Russians to send a doctor without delay: he would agree to any conditions. Dr. Piotrovsky volunteered to go, and three Naibs were demanded by Prince Mirsky as hostage during his absence. Shamyl had anticipated such a request and five Naibs were waiting, hidden in the hills, for a signal. The requisite number of shots being fired, all five of them appeared, seeming to materialize out of the ground, their horses streaking into the town at a great pace. Three remained at the fort, two escorted the doctor on the first stage of his journey into Shamyl's kingdom.

It was a terrible ordeal which took nearly a week, traversing the same kind of savage gorges, inaccessible plateaux and chasms that both the Princesses and the Armenian merchant, Shouanete's cousin, had endured. Each day the doctor grew more exhausted, more uneasy. Each day his guides were changed for others, silent, ferocious-looking tribesmen, with whom he could hold no communication. Sometimes passing through an aôul, his guides became his guards, protecting him by their drawn swords from the fury of the people, who crowded round menacingly. Giaour! The hated Infidel! Their dark features were carved in lines of hatred. The fifth day they reached the summit of Goumbet and following the great crenellated chain, could see, to the north and west, the whole gigantic line of the Caucasus and, to the east, the pale glitter of the Caspian. They continued to climb, one summit succeeding another, the path following goat tracks, mounting and descending; at last, before a vertical descent which was lost to view below them, too steep for horse or mule, they turned their mounts loose, leaving them cropping at the dry tufted herbs, and plunged downwards on foot. For five hours, grasping at rocks and skeletal bushes, they inched their way, the doctor not daring to look down, overcome with nausea and terror, pouring with sweat and trembling —but there was no turning back. At last the nightmare was over and, gaining the foot of the mountain, the doctor found himself on a plateau which, in itself, rose giddily far above the surrounding peaks. A group of gigantic rocks confronted him—Andi Gates, entrance to the inner, hidden aôul of Soul-Kadi, where Djemmal-Eddin lay.

The doctor, now almost fainting, flung himself on the ground and wept. But his guides jerked him to his feet, indicating that he must hurry on. They pressed forward through the great rock portals, but the doctor could no longer control his muscles and shook convulsively. Another hour's march brought them to their destination. Night had fallen, as they went through the narrow stone alleys. It appeared to be a large aôul with many two-storied houses, but no one was abroad. Except for the barking of dogs, silence hung over the place, like the thin wraiths of mist which drifted over the roofs and around the minaret. A sentry was marching up and down outside the house where Djemmal-Eddin lived. The Naib in charge received the doctor with evident satisfaction and led him straight to Djemmal-Eddin's room. By the light of a tallow candle, the doctor saw the young man to be asleep on a small army cot. Across the room another bed had been prepared, indicating that the doctor had been expected. These two truckle-beds were the only trace of the West. It was a small poor room, almost empty: there were no books, no comforts, nothing to recall St. Petersburg. The candle-light flickered over the white-washed walls and glinted on a brass samovar, a gun, and a fine inlaid sword hung on the wall— perhaps that same sword which Baron Nicolai had given Djemmal-Eddin on parting, at the Mitchik. The wavering shadow cast by the Naib followed him as he moved stealthily about, placing the doctor's bag on his bed and bending over Djemmal-Eddin, who still slept, his young, emaciated face a mask of sadness. The doctor let him sleep on, and flung himself down on the truckle-bed. One look at his patient had told him that there was little to be done that night, or any time now, but bring him echoes of the world for which he was pining away. Dr. Piotrovsky stayed three days; but there were no medicines, no treatments he could prescribe: life—the life he had accepted, was killing Djemmal-Eddin. He seemed overjoyed to see the doctor—to talk Russian once more, to speak of that faraway, longed-for world. His sunken eyes glowed briefly, as he recalled people and places he would never see again. *They* were reality—this was a dream. He did not complain, but only by describing his life among the Murids, the doctor knew how terrible were the terms imposed—all unknowingly by Shamyl. At first Djemmal-Eddin had been sent on a tour of his father's territories; but he had not been able to stomach some Caucasian interpretations of justice; nor had he been able to hide his despair at the continuation of the war. His father would hear no talk of peace terms; or indeed, any talk of the world beyond the mountains: civilization, science, the arts, history . . . they were all taboo. At last, he forbade Djemmal-Eddin to discuss the conduct of the war, or to speak of his life in Russia. For some months he had kept his son beside him in the seraglio, at the Great Aôul, where a succession of mollahs had instructed him, by day and night, in the principles and practices of Muridism. There had been endless theological discussions, five *namez* each day, and all the other observances expected of the Imam's son. But in spite of Shouanete's loving kindness, he had not shown real aptitude in recovering his knowledge of the Ma'arul-matz language. He had not been quick to adapt to the food, the houses, or the climate. Life in the aôul had seemed as hard to him as to the Princesses, said Zaïdate tartly, voicing Shamyl's unspoken thoughts.

All the Imam's joy at his son's return was clouded as he realized his heir had been lost to him forever, at Akhulgo. A Russian had returned —no son, but a prisoner, who hid his heart from his father and seemed to live apart, immersed in some secret, unapproachable world of memories. In vain Shamyl sent him out hunting with Khazi Mahommed: the brothers would gallop across the uplands, their falcons on their wrists—but when they returned Khazi Mahommed (who admired his brother as a being from another world) would tell of how Djemmal-Eddin would loose his falcon and then rein up his horse and stare, long and hungrily, across the mountains, north, to where Russia lay. . . . In vain Shamyl spoke to him of glory, of his inheritance, of the mountains and aôuls that trembled before him, of Allah's orders; of the dishonour of accepting Russian peace terms; Djemmal-Eddin remained mute. In vain Shamyl sent for the most beautiful slaves, Circassians, the gazelle-like creatures who fetched such high prices in the harems of Constantinople. Djemmal-Eddin would have none of them. In vain Aminette sang to him, fetching her little tambourine and chanting in that clear bird-like voice that had delighted the Princesses. He smiled gently; but his soul was listening to other strains: Chopin, as he had heard it played in Polish salons; some Viennese waltz that was all the rage in St. Petersburg ballrooms. . . . The echoes of a Russian soldier's song . . . *A Life for the Tzar* . . . In vain the delikans from all the surrounding aôuls assembled at Dargo-Vedin to hold djighitovkas in his honour. He rode with them, equalling them by his daring marksmanship. And then the ring of giant peaks would fade, as he recalled the ornate pillared length of the Horse-Guards' *manège*, and he would fling himself out of the saddle, and seek the quiet of Shouanete's room. Outside, the feasting continued: sheep roasted whole, the courtyards still running with the blood of ceremonial slaughter, while the dancers stamped and sidled in the wild rhythms of this lesghinka.

Seated beside Shouanete, Djemmal-Eddin often spoke of the Princesses. And sometimes, alone with his brothers, Khazi Mahommed and the young Mahommed Sheffi, he would respond to their eager questioning, and describe that other world he had known: Petersburg—Moscow; the Russian Nianyia who had come to be like a mother to him during those first months in the Tschukin house; his training in the Corps de Pages, military studies, his life as the Tzar's aide-de-camp. . . . The Great White Sultan himself. . . . Unimaginable wonders and splendours; railway trains and telegraphic communications; Court balls; the charm and wit of Russian women; Polish beauties; the opera and ballet. . . . And then Khazi Mahommed would fetch a little musical-box that he had contrived to have brought from Tiflis, unknown to Shamyl. They kept it hidden under their pillows, for such distractions were Shaitan's own, said the Imam, who had become increasingly opposed to any diversions, particularly those which smacked of the West. He used to quote the Moslem proverb; *this world is a carcass, and they who seek it are dogs.* Yet the musical-box was such a gaily painted little object, of Swiss make, embellished with a naïve picture of the Lake of Lucerne; it seemed the essence of innocence. The brothers would sit together, cross-legged on cushions in Djemmal-Eddin's room, shutters clamped across the low-set windows, listening to the tiny tinklings, Khazi Mahommed's muscular brown fingers turning the handle round and round. . . . *The Skater's Waltz, the Gondoliers' Song.* . . . Wafts of perfume, the flutter of fans and ringlets and bonnet-strings rose around them, as once again Djemmal-Eddin recounted the pleasures of that other world, and Mahommed Sheffi listened, shining-eyed and spell-bound, while Khazi Mahommed leant forward, his hawk-like face intent, puzzled. He could imagine no other life but that of battle and the mountains, but he too had fallen under his brother's spell. Such wisdom, such experience! Kherimat had watched him from behind her veils and told her husband that he was a true Russian—all that was best in that mysterious race.

Khazi Mahommed had wanted to learn about the books, pictures and maps which were strewn about Djemmal-Eddin's room, but soon these were all confiscated, along with a Bible that had, for Shamyl, come to represent an intangible force standing between his son and his return to the Moslem fold. While in Russia, Djemmal-Eddin had not been subjected to any proselytizing, retaining, in principle, his Moslem faith; yet an ikon had become one of his most treasured possessions. The Naibs began to mutter ominously. None of them sensed that, rather than a change of faith, this might represent a souvenir of some friend whom he would never see again. A farewell love-token, perhaps.

Djemmal-Eddin's loneliness was deepened by the suspicion and fanaticism which surrounded him. He had begun to build a European house, but it had to be abandoned. The people gathered angrily, saying it was in the shape of a cross. What else could you expect, with a Giaour in their midst? Shamyl was no longer strong enough to override his followers. Again Djemmal-Eddin had to be sacrificed. Nothing—nothing must be left to remind him of that hated, humiliating past. No letters might be received or sent. Nor was he allowed to read the foreign newspapers by which Shamyl's interpreters still kept him informed as to outside events. Any attempts on Djemmal-Eddin's part to speak of peace were met angrily. At last Shamyl gave up visiting his son, and forbade the brothers to see him. In any case, being hard-pressed, he and Khazi Mahommed and Mahommed Sheffi too were needed at the battle front. Djemmal-Eddin's isolation was complete.

Soon, he was too weak to go riding, and sat silently on the flat roof-top of his brother's house, his eyes fixed on the far hills under their canopy of clouds. He loved roses: they alone seemed to assuage his melancholy, and his bare room was filled with the great, sweet-smelling yellow blooms of Daghestan. Even the most fanatic Murids could not grudge him that solace. The Prophet, too, had loved roses.

As the wars took on a more desperate aspect, and Bariatinsky pressed them increasingly, both Shamyl and Khazi Mahommed were in the field, leading their respective armies, fighting their last battles. Young Mahommed Sheffi, too, had now taken his place at the head of a troop of Murids, leading them in furious sorties. But as a fighter he was never of the same calibre as his father, or Khazi Mahommed; nor did he share their mystical fervour. He was a pleasant, rather ordinary young man, who stood in awe of his father, but was not cast in the same heroic mould. Only Khazi Mahommed loved and served his father with an absolute and unquestioning devotion in all things, living and dying in his shadow.

Shamyl would not risk a second capture of Djemmal-Eddin, and so when the Great Aôul was threatened he sent him to live at Soul-Kadi. There behind the dark rock gates of Andi he would be safe. There nothing could touch him. So, under close guard, the young man lived, quite alone now, with neither friends nor family, awaiting his only escape—in death. It was not long in coming. In the stifling July evenings he liked to be carried out to lie on the terraced roof. The people of Karaty strewed it with roses. Too late, they were trying to show their sympathy for the Imam's lonely son. There, on the night of July 12, 1858, among the roses, Djemmal-Eddin died. Shamyl had lost his son for the second time.

III

The year 1859 dawned bleakly for Shamyl. The three Russian armies were closing in, remorselessly. Now he could hardly hold them at bay. One by one his forts fell. On January 15, he was tricked by news of a vast Russian column setting out to besiege the heavily defended aôul of Akhtouree. But this was a ruse on the part of Bariatinsky and Yevdokimov. Even the columns were unaware of their destination, marching all night through snowdrifts so deep that the cavalry had to trample a path for them. At dawn they had reached the defile of the Argoun—thirty versts west of Akhtouree, their supposed objective. The defile was a key position, hitherto regarded as impregnable: the terrain was such that one column took seven hours to march less than five miles through the gorge. But having penetrated and burned every aôul within reach, the Russian columns straddled the confluents of the river Shato Argoun, holding the high land between, thus establishing a spearhead into the last foothills leading to Shamyl's lair, the plateau of Vedin. Shamyl, hearing of the column's counter-move too late, rushed to the attack, only to be forced to retreat. When, some days later, he learned that the whole defile had fallen to the Russians, he is reported to have wept. The end was very near now, and he knew it.

All through February, the Russians were occupied clearing the defile of its giant trees: clearing the way for their supplies and cannon. Their axes were recent importations from England; but Shamyl's longed-for arms never materialized. Some of the beech trees were nearly three hundred feet in height and thirty and forty feet in girth, and resisted all axes, having to be blown up. But gradually a huge path was opened; a path clearing through forest and hill, leading towards Vedin; gullies and chasms were again bridged, now guarded by cannon so that the Murids could never approach to destroy them. Frustrated in every attempt to attack, they retreated into the last cover left them, 'swarming in the tangled forests and gullies which stretched for ten miles, and where no enemy had ever yet penetrated'. The Murids worked day and night, to stem the inexorable Russian advance, constructing traps, earthworks and ambushes. But there was no stemming

Bariatinsky. His whole life as a soldier had been leading to this campaign; at last he was putting into execution all his long-cherished plans; presently the Russian troops had cut their way through the Murids' last line of natural defences. By July, Khazi Mahommed, commanding the Greater and Lesser Varanda area, saw, one by one, the aôuls fall, the land occupied, and the people submit passively.

While the three Russian armies were converging on one of Shamyl's forts, Éetoum Kalé (subsequently known as Yevdokimovsky), the people of Nazran, who had long ago submitted to Russia, suddenly revolted against what they considered harsh and predatory measures. Their complaints were not altogether unjustified, for the Russian administration had decided to move large numbers of Ingoush tribesmen from their straggling aôuls into concentrated settlements, easier to control. This aroused violent opposition, and presently developed into open revolt. The Ingoushi dispatched messengers to beg for Shamyl's aid, while they set about slaughtering the token Russian force at Nazran. All Shamyl's old vigour, courage and daring responded to this appeal and, showing magnanimity instead of vengeance, he made his last offensive. At the head of four thousand horsemen he descended on the plains, directly under Yevdokimov's fire, only to be defeated at Atchkoi and forced to withdraw across the Argoun. The alarm signals from the garrison at Nazran had been heard, and reinforcements were rushed to the spot. The rising was suppressed ruthlessly, and without reference to Bariatinsky, who opposed savage reprisals.

By the early summer of 1859, the Russians had completed their subjugation of all approaches to Shamyl's last stronghold.

But before Vedin itself fell, the Imam managed to have his wives and household evacuated to the forests, where they lay in hiding until he could send for them. Kherimat was not among them. A few days before, a letter from her father, Daniel Beg, had been smuggled into the aôul. 'Leave them', he wrote. 'The game is up. Bariatinsky is closing in. Come over to us.'

It had suited Kherimat to be the great Imam's daughter-in-law just so long as he was powerful. Now, she chose to follow her father's traitorous path and she made her get-away one black night of storm. Khazi Mahommed was fighting far off at the time, and did not learn of her treachery for some while.

There remains from this tragic moment a tiny square of yellowing paper, a letter, sent by Khazi Mahommed to his faithless wife. It has survived, where most of the battle-orders have perished. Khazi Mahommed learned of Kherimat's flight some time later, but he still loved her desperately, and all his anguish is in the few words he bribed a spy to take her, behind the Russian lines.

'My little Kherimat, how could you do this to me?' was all he wrote; but perhaps it pierced even her worthless heart, for after her death, it was found among her belongings.

It was chiefly Yevdokimov's strategies and achievements which brought about Shamyl's final defeat. The Tzar now raised him to the rank of Count; to the mountaineers he had long been known as 'the Three-Eyed One', in token of a deep puckered wound, where a bullet had gone clear through his head, from left to right, yet leaving his reason and sight unimpaired. The sobriquet was also earned by virtue of his vigilant, all-seeing sixth sense, which made him so outstanding among the Russian commanders. A faded photograph, one of those browning *carte-de-visites* which are displayed in the Military Museum at Moscow, show a square-faced, chunky man, standing to attention, staring earnestly, a huge drooping moustache falling over a formidable jaw, his paunch plastered with decorations. Here is Bariatinsky's summing-up of this great general, in a dispatch to the Tzar:

> Yevdokimov never once gave the enemy a chance of fighting where they meant to, and where the advantage might have been with them. . . . Shamyl's strongest positions fell, at last, almost without resistance, as a result of well-planned movements alone. In contrast to earlier engagements, such as Akhulgo and others, the sieges of which were to cost us many thousands and were often unsuccessful in their outcome, the capture of Vedin, where Shamyl had concentrated all his means for a desperate resistance, cost us no more than twenty-six killed and wounded.

In June, Dargo-Vedin fell. The terrible fastness where the Princesses and Madame Drancy had been incarcerated crumbled at last beneath the Russian guns. Its defence had been stubborn, but at last shells had breached the outer walls, toppling the minaret, and levelling the whole seraglio to dust. The fortress-aôul of Tchokh surrendered on July 24 and four days later Kibit Magoma deserted over to the Russians; as gauge of his good faith he led them to storm Tilitl, where Bariatinsky, now making a triumphal progress, welcomed and fawned-upon, was pleased to dine at the traitor's house. Now the last Avar aôuls fell around Shamyl like card houses. Even Daniel Beg had surrendered his fortress of Irib and thrown himself once more on Russian mercy, finding them again indulgent. By the end of July, Bariatinsky left his headquarters to join Yevdokimov in his camp at Vedin, from where they planned their final assault.

Shamyl was known to be preparing to make a last stand at Gounib, on the desolate rock-plateaux of his native Daghestan. He had chosen it well. It had been his terrain—the birthplace of Muridism, and here he and his few remaining faithful Murids would die fighting. Before the Russians introduced their long-range guns, it had been considered unassailable—'the Gibraltar of the Caucasus'. It stood alone, isolated from the surrounding mountains, rising sheer from the valleys below, a thousand or more feet high. The summit was hollowed out like a deep shell, covered with grass which afforded excellent pasturage for sheep and horses; this shell was protected from enemy fire by high rock scarps edging it all round. There were freshwater springs, and on one side the cliff face was broken into a series of flat, rock-edged terraces, again protected from bullets, but where patches of grain and fruit flourished. Moreover, one or two seams of coal were found in the rocks, so that with the exception of materials for making gunpowder and lead, for bullets, Gounib supplied everything needed to withstand an attack.

Even so, a considerable garrison was needed—some thousands, to defend it at all points, from Yevdokimov's massed attack which Shamyl knew he must meet. With the four hundred men—last remnants of Murid might, all that he could now muster, it was doomed. But 'he who thinks of the consequences will never be brave'. Neither Shamyl nor his remaining Naibs ever contemplated surrender. They would make their last stand for Allah, for freedom, at Gounib. It was written!

Shamyl had gathered round him his whole family, his sons, wives and daughters: he did not care to risk the women's chance of survival, were they to go into hiding in the mountains that were now over-run by Russian troops, or the renegade tribes who would have snatched at the chance to slaughter Shamyl's wives, presenting their heads to the Russians, their new masters, as triumphant proof of their loyalty. Making their way over the mountains to Gounib, Shamyl and his band had been attacked and plundered by marauding tribesmen: all their baggage had been taken: they could not even defend themselves properly—their few rounds of ammunition had to be kept to use against the Russians.

*   *   *

It was August 24. For the last time, Shamyl led his followers to prayer. As the long summer evening faded, the voice of the muezzin floated down to the valley, to where the Russian lines were formed, a vast army of men, tents and guns. From each scarp of the rock, the Murids could see similar camps, east, west, north and south. They were completely encircled; Bariatinsky had decided to launch the final assault the following morning; August 25 was the Emperor's birthday. The fall of Gounib—Shamyl's submission—would be a fitting gift. It appealed to his sense of theatre.

The morning dawned stifling hot and still, with a thick mist rising from the valley. Behind this cover, the Russians mustered for the attack. Wreathed in vapours, in drifts of milky mist, they were able to bring up their guns and scale the first plateau unperceived. Shamyl had expected to stand a long siege, and this over-whelming mass attack took him by surprise. The Naib Ali Kadi had betrayed him, selling his gatehouse, so that the Russians poured in. A hundred Murids, outnumbered ten to one, fought desperately and all perished, unable to stem the oncoming tide of Russians. At one bastion, a handful of Murids leapt out on the Apsheron regiment, women among them; all fought furiously, dying on the Russian bayonets. Bariatinsky had given orders that Shamyl was to be taken alive, if possible. Shamyl had retreated to the aôul with his sons, and was preparing to die as he had lived—for Allah. Twice, Bariatinsky halted the fighting and sent envoys to demand his surrender. Each time, he was met with a furious refusal. The third time Bariatinsky sent his ultimatum—unconditional surrender, or the immediate bombardment of the whole aôul, and with it the death of every living soul. For the first time, Shamyl hesitated. Had he been alone, with his sons and Murids only, there is no doubt he would have chosen to die thus. But he was surrounded by his wives and children, and the wives and children of his faithful followers. Never before, save at Akhulgo, had he had to consider their safety. . . . His battles had always (save at Dargo, when Fatimat lay dying) been fought unencumbered by emotional considerations.

During these last terrible moments, no one had dared to speak to him of surrender. Such talk had always been punishable by death. At last the remaining Naibs persuaded Khazi Mahommed that he alone could broach the subject. They sent him to the mosque where Shamyl was praying. Twice Khazi Mahommed joined his father and knelt beside him, yet each time he found himself unable to speak. The third time, when he went back, Shamyl looked at him with a sad smile.

'I know why you have come. You, like all the rest, wish me to surrender. So be it.'

It was as if, at last, the Great Imam was conquered—not by the weight of Russian arms, but by love—love for his family and remaining followers.

The Russians sent Colonel Lazareff to negotiate: he was an Armenian who had served with the Russians for many years, but he was known to Shamyl personally, and was respected by the Caucasians, for his bravery and justice. He possessed the astuteness of all his race. Now he bowed before the Imam, and with a most insidious mixture of respect and authority, urged him to surrender, promising him that his own life, that of all his family, and the entire garrison would be spared, and that an honourable peace would be at once concluded. The last battle was lost, was nobly lost, he said. Mektoub! It was as Allah willed. Allah had willed that for thirty years Shamyl, his servant, should oppose the Russians. All things were with Allah. Now it was written that Shamyl should cede to the White Sultan.

'Shamyl had failed because it was no longer possible for him to succeed', wrote J. F. Baddeley. And such was the Imam's fatalistic acceptance, at last, of his defeat. His pale set face showed no emotion as he mounted his horse and rode out towards the Russian lines. He was followed by fifty Murids, all that remained of those mighty hordes whom he had led, so gloriously, for so long. They were a ragged lot, their faces smeared with blood and gunpowder, but they still carried their black banners defiantly, reining in their proud-stepping horses behind their chief.

Prince Bariatinsky awaited his fallen enemy with an equally impassive face. He was seated on a small stone, in the shade of a birch copse, surrounded by his staff. Although Shamyl had asked that none of the renegade tribesmen, and those who had betrayed him, to join the Russians, should witness his submission, they were all crowded there, exulting, gloating; among them, Mahommed Emin, Bata, Ali Kadi, Kibit Magoma and Daniel Beg, and it is to Bariatinsky's eternal shame that he allowed this.

As Shamyl rode out from the gates of Gounib a hush fell; only the jingle of bridle and bit sounded. The Russian army stood to attention, watching the advancing figure. 'He', their dread enemy, the legendary Imam, the Lion of Daghestan, who had resisted them and their fathers before them. 'He', whom no man among them had seen face to face since Klugenau's meeting at Ghimree in 1837, was now about to surrender. The Caucasus, that mighty fortress, 'whose walls were gigantic peaks, whose trenches chasms', had fallen. They broke into wild cheers. Shamyl flushed, and when he saw the renegade chiefs he began to wheel his horse back towards the aôul. Better death than dishonour. But Lazareff, showing his usual astuteness, galloped back to intercept him.

'Imam! They cheer you as a great chief—as a valiant warrior!' he said. 'Show them you can be as lion-hearted in the hour of defeat as in all your years of victory.' It was well put. Shamyl drew rein, seemed to hesitate for a moment and then, his face calm, proud and as inscrutable as ever, he went forward towards submission. . . . As he dismounted, some Russian officers made as if to disarm him. But he thrust them aside imperiously, with such an air of authority that they fell back. He walked slowly on, to where the Field-Marshal, Prince Bariatinsky, awaited him. Bariatinsky told him that he, personally, would answer for the safety of all the Imam's family, but that Shamyl's own fate must depend on the Emperor's will. Shamyl stood with bowed head, seeming not to hear the words. Then he slowly unbuckled his shashka, a magnificent weapon, the curve of its dark blade damascened in gold. Bowing, 'with a gesture at once noble and humble', he offered it to Bariatinsky.

'I would not allow my sword to be touched by unknown or unworthy hands,' he said. 'I give it up to you, Sirdar, since you have conquered myself and my army.'

The slit-eyes were raised, for a moment, to fix Bariatinsky with a piercing regard. Bowing again, he turned away, a captive. Shamyl, Warrior and Imam of Daghestan, was no more. Only 'God's poor pilgrim', as he was to describe himself, remained. Only the scars of eighteen wounds were left to show for his life's work.

*   *   *

Sixty years later, in 1918, an officer in the Chevaliers-Gardes, was fighting beside the Ural Cossacks, against the Red forces, battling for possession of the Orenburg-Tashkent railway line. He was badly wounded and taken prisoner. At the point of a gun, the Tartar commander ordered him to give up his weapons. Bitterly, the officer handed over his sword, a magnificent damascened shashka, part of his grandfather's collection; this particular weapon had been presented to him by Field-Marshal Bariatinsky. The young man had taken it to the wars, keeping it throughout the campaigns. It was Shamyl's sword—his 'sabre of Paradise'.

Where is it now? In that moment of battle, it is unlikely that it was preserved, or even recognized. Perhaps it lay among a heap of surrendered steel, or was melted down; or, for the sake of its workmanship, classified, and later placed in a museum,—'a fine example of Caucasian armourers' work'. Or did it fight its way south, out of the country, to become part of a tarnished clutter in the Great Bazaar in Istanbul? Was it at last bought by some romantically minded traveller and does it now adorn some dining-room, among the antlers, foxes' masks, duelling pistols and other trophies of a gentleman's life?

31

Another World

After all the evils I have done you, you do not tear me to pieces, but welcome me, and I am overwhelmed.

SHAMYL TO THE RUSSIANS

The Tzar Alexander II's idealistic nature is exemplified by his generous treatment of Shamyl, his prisoner. Although his father, the Emperor Nicholas, generally showed a certain chivalry in his dealings with a fallen enemy—always providing it was a military, rather than political foe—it is unlikely that Nicholas would have displayed such marked magnanimity as his son was to do. Caucasian resistance had ever been a thorn in his flesh, something which he felt was aimed at him personally, a reflection on his might, and Shamyl, 'this obstinate man', had aroused his personal ire. But Alexander abhorred bloodshed, had no inflated sense of majesty, and had absorbed Bariatinsky's views on the Caucasus. He regarded Shamyl, not as a personal enemy, but as a great leader of heroic stature: he was impatient to meet him, and ordered that he be sent north immediately. His orders were categoric: the Imam was to be treated with every mark of respect and to be presented to any of the military commanders, noble personages or prelates he might encounter on his journey through Russia. Moreover, all officers at each town or garrison (where Shamyl was to be lodged in the Governor's own house), were to present their respects in full dress, orders and decorations. He was to visit Moscow and St. Petersburg, so that he might have the occasion to see something of the cities, institutions and Court, before settling in one or other of the provinces. The Tzar himself would personally supervise the question of his future establishment, his suite, and allowances.

But of all this Shamyl was unaware when he was led away from Gounib, God's poor pilgrim and Bariatinsky's captive. As he rode off, surrounded by squadrons of Cossacks, the mountainside burst asunder, thousands of his people issuing from every crack and gully to see him pass for the last time, running beside him, kissing the hem of his tcher kesska. But Shamyl seemed unaware of what went on around him, his

411

eyes half-closed, staring their curious inward stare, his face graven, 'recalling polished ice, covering the surface of a fathomless lake'.

It is only in captivity, during the last years, that we are able to splinter that ice, and to know something of Shamyl the man, without the barriers of terror or awe which surrounded his legend. Even so, between the memoirs left by those who came to know him well at this time, whether Captain Runovsky, or Madame Chichagova, or the manuscript written by his secretary Mahommed Tahir (now in the Asiatic Museum in Leningrad), there are gaps—vast stretches where no dates fit, where facts are missing, and much has been overlooked. This is in part due to Shamyl's own unwillingness to speak of himself. 'I am unworthy of interest,' he would say when Runovsky questioned him. 'I was Allah's mouthpiece. Now I am but a poor pilgrim.' Madame Chichagova simply states that she forgot to write down many of the interesting things which Shamyl recounted about his life. So the biographer returns, baulked, to the mass of small-scale details which chronicle these last years. Even so, with a sense of adventure and gratitude; until now, Shamyl has remained a figure of mystery, but these details have the cumulative effect of bringing him before us with a curious veracity, and he emerges from the provincial drawing-rooms more clearly than from the battlefields, or aôuls. At last, the man is seen at close quarters, with all his sense of irony, his credulity, pathos and essential dignity. He is no longer the posturing ogre nor the inspired leader, but a great and simple human being, conducting himself as nobly in failure as in success. This last domestic phase was, nevertheless, to him, one of violent challenge, of adaptation, and new, bewildering values.

Speaking years later of his surrender at Gounib, he described his feelings of despair and resignation. He had expected no mercy and waited for Bariatinsky to revile him, 'as a beaten dog'. He had been prepared to die, there and then, by his own kindjal. But the Field-Marshal's measured terms had left him nonplussed and, finding himself treated with honour, he had given up his sword in token of his honourable submission. All the same, his fanatic Moslem nature could not imagine mercy, in such circumstances. He was convinced that he would be killed, his sons and Naibs with him, and that his path now led to the place of execution.

When Colonel Lazareff had entered the aôul to take Khazi Mahommed and the remaining Naibs, he had been greeted by convulsive scenes of grief: the wives and children, Naibs and warriors alike, had all prostrated themselves, begging for Shamyl's life. Their own was of no further consequence. Lazareff reunited them with the Imam, in his tent, at which the sobbing and wailing had redoubled. Next day, Shamyl's family was removed to Temir-Khan-Shura; but the dreaded captivity had been transformed into a sort of treat outing, by the charm and tact of the officer in charge, a young lieutenant Dimitri Astouroff, who was able to speak Turco-Tartar, kept them well supplied with sweets, and even purchased a musical-box for them. This sympathetic treatment won them over completely; even the grief-stricken Shouanete dried her eyes, and Zaïdate was at her most affable. They called him 'our Dimitro-Dimitro', and positively doted on him when he arranged for them to have beautiful new dresses made. All of them were ragged and unkempt after the last months of fighting and retreating across the mountains, and Shamyl, too, now found himself at the military tailors, being fitted for a tcherkesska instead of the anticipated shroud.

On September 3, he left Daghestan for ever. Accompanied by Khazi Mahommed and a small suite of Naibs and servants, an interpreter, and Colonel Bogoslavsky, the adjutant appointed to have charge of him, he headed north. For the moment, young Mahommed Sheffi was to remain with the rest of the family at Temir-Khan-Shura; and so, in the pale mists of an autumnal dawn, Shamyl set out. Baron Wrangel, the Commander-in-Chief, had placed his own carriage at his disposal and came to see him on his way, with a ceremonious leave-taking. To the west the great chain of mountains towered above the low-rolling clouds. Sometimes they were completely hidden and then, as if emerging to look their last on the man who had been born among them and fought for them so long, they would show themselves in all their majesty, shining in a farewell salute, before shrouding themselves once more. Shamyl did not look up at them; nor did he look back; but it was observed that he followed the winding route by means of a small pocket-compass; each time the needle veered east his face darkened, and he braced himself for a Siberian martyrdom.

But now, as they descended towards the foothills, a most extraordinary change occurred. The journey began to take on the character of a triumphal progress. At each stop, news of his coming had preceded him, and eager crowds awaited him, turning each changing of horses into a fête. At Kourtoumkali, the garrison wives from Petrovsk had ridden over to greet him with garlands: these women whose husbands and brothers and sons had lived, or died, fighting him, gave him laurels. At Cherveleniiya, a comfortable hooded travelling-carriage was awaiting him. It had stood there, in the posting-house yard, for three months. Bariatinsky had ordered it in June; he had always been certain of his victory, and determined to ensure the welfare of his future prisoner. It was typical of the Field-Marshal's absolute faith in his powers, and his foresight and attention to the smallest detail.

All the way, Shamyl was given a hero's welcome. The soldiers who had fought against him so long and bitterly crowded around him, their officers preparing banquets in his honour. He remained aloof, but was visibly gratified. As for the Naibs, they appeared stunned. At Mozdok, numbers of carriages and riders came out to meet him and escort him into the town, where cheering crowds lined the streets. Even so, Shamyl still considered this was a protracted journey to the scaffold. At Stavropol, crowds ran after his carriage, cheering, or stood in silent admiration before the house where he lodged. The park was illuminated in his honour, a choir sang specially composed anthems and that night, amid bursts of fireworks, there was a ball at the railway station.

This choice of locale recalls the surprising Swiss habit (persisting to this day) of identifying gaiety with the railway. Indeed it is quite customary to find the inhabitants of a small town seeking distraction on Sunday evenings or fête days, seated along the platforms, litsening to the station band, or supping at the *buffet de la gare*, in preference to other restaurants. However, in Russia, the high standards of railway buffet food was generally conceded by even the most carping travellers. There, instead of the stale buns and strong tea upon which passive Britons travelled, the most delicious foods abounded, tureens of steaming bortsch, cream-soaked blinis and caviar. Though perhaps it was not always wise to look too closely. I recall a Russian friend whose childhood was passed in a remote province where, when the bi-weekly train was signalled and the station sprang to life, the waiters would straighten their aprons, flick over the plates, and give the open-faced caviar sandwiches a quick last lick, to make them glisten appetizingly.

But to Shamyl, the unimaginable strangeness of the railway station must, in itself, food or festivities apart, have seemed dazzling. With what amazement he must have seen, for the first time, a train, an engine. . . . None of the Murids could believe their eyes. Stavropol was a metropolis after Temir-Khan-Shura, and Sodom and Gomorrah beside the Great Aôul. 'Is it possible that St. Petersburg is even greater?' asked Khazi Mahommed, voicing the wonder all of them felt confronted by the fringes of civilization.

On September 13, they reached Kharkov, where an aide-de-camp of the Tzar's was awaiting them. His Imperial Majesty was reviewing his troops on manœuvres nearby and wished Shamyl to proceed there at once, to be presented to him. When the mountaineers were told they might keep their weapons in the presence of the Great White Sultan, they could not believe their ears, when Colonel Bogoslavsky expanded on Christian beliefs, the forgiveness of enemies, charity, and such, they looked bewildered. Shamyl listened attentively, but said nothing, retreating into his inward, trance-like stare. The meeting of Tzar and Imam took place at a parade of honour—amid the fluttering pennons of the Lancers, the blare of military bands and the eddies of dust raised by the Cossacks as they charged. The Tzar exerted himself to make Shamyl feel honoured rather than humiliated. We are told that Shamyl rode to meet his conqueror looking his old impressive self dressed in a long white tcherkesska, the chieftain's huge chalma on his head, his bearing calm and proud.

'I am very happy that you are here in Russia,' said the Tzar. 'I wish it could have happened sooner. You will not regret it. I shall look after your interests and we shall be friends,' he said, embracing him, while for his part Shamyl met the defiling touch of the Infidel without shrinking. From this moment all his apprehensions vanished. The Tzar kept him by his side, discussing the manœuvres in a man-to-man fashion most soothing to the vanquished Imam's susceptibilities, and he also insisted that Shamyl should ride with him when he reviewed the cavalry; moreover he told the Imam how astonished he was that even Bariatin-sky's army had been able to storm Gounib. 'Such a fortress—I thought it quite impregnable.' Before the day was out, Shamyl felt the last bitterness of defeat fall from him. This new life in Russia, this too was Allah's purpose. If his path had led him from Gounib to St. Petersburg, it was written, and he would bow to Allah's will.

The triumphal tenor of the tour continued, and everywhere there were the same scenes of enthusiasm, of artless joy at the coming of a hero, rather than a fallen foe. In Moscow, Shamyl was shown the splendours of the Kremlin, and the fabulous collection of Crown jewels. But he preferred Peter the Great's seven-league top-boots, clasping them to him and plying the interpreter with questions about the Great White Tzar's heroic ancestor. The Moscow visit reached its peak by a meeting with old General Yermolov, growling and pacing his room, still living in the afterglow of his great days. Both warriors were overjoyed and set to discussing their battles. Next night, the Bolshoi Theatre was illumin-ated, the huge pillared portico blazing, as Shamyl and his entourage drove up for a gala performance. *Les Näiades* was on the programme; a balletic fantasy where the ballerinas enacted a pathetic story of unre-quited love; it affected the mountaineers profoundly, and they all sobbed. The following morning Khazi Mahommed, who was of a deeply sentimental nature, was still so carried away by the theatrical illusion that he asked to be allowed to walk beside the stream where one dancer had perished so gracefully. He said she looked like Kherimat. . . .

On September 26, a month and a day after the fall of Gounib, they reached St. Petersburg. News of Shamyl's triumphal progress, his grandeur and heroic stature, had preceded him, so that scenes of even wilder enthusiasm awaited him as he stepped from the train. That, too, had been a major experience; travelling by train was something, he said, to which no language could do justice—certainly not the Turco Tartar or Avarian tongues.

It was a grey, drizzling, autumn day, the gutters choked with mud and dead leaves, the cobblestones greasy and wet. The sombre city seemed to rise from a miasma. The whole Znaminski Square, in front of the station, with its hotels, droshkys, and yellowing trees, was packed with an enormous crowd which surged up the Nevsky to converge there, awaiting Shamyl's arrival. When at last he appeared, he was greeted with wild cheering and cries of welcome. He stood silently on the steps, receiving the ovation with bowed head. His Naibs stood a pace behind him, on each side, sinister, effigy figures in their black bourkas and high black papakhs, their arms crossed on their chests, their eyes downcast in the manner prescribed by Caucasian etiquette, in deference to the Imam's rank.

Shamyl was to stay at the Znaminski Hotel while in the capital; and there he was to meet Captain Runovsky, the officer appointed to be his adjutant, in charge of his household at Kalouga, which, it had now been decided, was to be his future place of residence. Runovsky was a most fortunate choice; he spoke several Tartar dialects, knew the Caucasus, and was of a lively and sympathetic nature. Moreover, he was prepared to appreciate his opportunity to live close to the great Imam.

He has left an account of his years with Shamyl from which both he and his charges emerge in a most pleasing light. For that first meeting he had been ordered to present himself at the hotel at 10 a.m. But by midday, he was still cooling his heels in the hall. There was no sign of the party. They had left early that morning, accompanied by Colonel Bogoslavsky, on the invitation of one of the Grand Dukes, to review the fleet at Krondstadt, said the manager, who was at once delighted and despairing at the enormous publicity caused by Shamyl's presence in his hotel. As he spoke, the crowds were invading the dining-rooms, filling the entrance-hall and corridors, swarming upstairs, rattling door-handles and peeping through keyholes, in their determination to catch a glimpse of the legendary Shamyl. The trail of their muddy boots across the parquet began to exasperate the manager. Runovsky resigned himself, and sat down to await his future, reflecting how odd the turns of fate; that he, who had fought in the Caucasus, and always imagined that one day he might fall into Shamyl's hands, as a prisoner, was now appointed to control his household.

About four o'clock, as the early autumn dusk was closing in, Runovsky heard the tumult of an approaching multitude. From the windows he could see a small group fighting their way towards the hotel; in the middle he glimpsed some turbans, and bearded swarthy faces. . . . 'Bravo Shamyl . . . Here he is!' cried the crowd, sweeping into the already overcrowded hall, drowning the manager's protests and trying to follow Shamyl upstairs.

At last Runovsky reached the Imam's room, and the introductions were made by the interpreter. Shamyl, says Runovsky, was sitting on a sofa and appeared exhausted by his day's sight-seeing. But gratified, too: he had never seen a battleship before; besides he was delighted at the honour shown him by the Grand Duke and the naval officers. Runovsky diagnosed his pleasure as being not so much that of gratified vanity at his ovation, but, rather, a deep happiness that these Infidel strangers, too, valued his virtues as much as his own people did. 'All this was written on his noble, grave face,' says Runovsky, who had immediately fallen under the Imam's spell.

'Your boys are pleased to see me a prisoner, but they do not wish me harm,' said Shamyl, peering through the lace curtains, watching the cheering mob outside. 'With us, it would be different. Our boys would have stoned me—killed me. I shall write to the Caucasus and tell them to change their ways—to forbid our former violence: they will obey me still, I think,' he added, rather wistfully.

Tea was brought and Shamyl settled down to talk with Runovsky; on learning that he had served nineteen years in the Caucasus, the whole party beamed: a soldier like themselves. . . .

'You will be my friend,' said Shamyl, crushing Runovsky's hand in a steel grip. Khazi Mahommed followed suit, and the Naibs, who still stood to attention each side of Shamyl, allowed themselves to relax a trifle, while conversation turned on military matters, though rather haltingly, as the interpreter was now absent, and Runovsky had to confess that his Caucasian dialects had become rusty; at which they clucked their tongues disapprovingly. When he told them that his name was Apollon, they found it impossible to pronounce. Afilon was as near as Shamyl ever got (but then, in all his eleven years' captivity, he only mastered one phrase: '*Zdrastvouitie!* How do you do!') 'I never heard such a name before,' he said. 'Here in Russia everyone seems to be called Nicholas. In the Caucasus we always called all our prisoners Ivan. It saved a lot of trouble.'

He next enquired as to Runovsky's rank and, sitting cross-legged on the sofa, fingering his beads, began reeling off the Russian army ranks with obvious relish. He had taken prisoners from every grade—private to general, but he seemed more familiar with the higher ranks which, he explained, was because of his pourparlers. He spoke of many commanders by name, recalling their methods of fighting and individual strategies, as if they were physical attributes. When he spoke of Passek his face took on a mournful cast. 'So great a fighter should not have died at Dargo; he should have had many more battles before him. . . .' Fighting was still life to Shamyl.

For the next week, Runovsky accompanied the mountaineers everywhere; to the photographers, where Monsieur Denier, darting out from under a black velvet cloth, was all praise for Shamyl's absolute stillness. While Khazi Mahommed and the Naibs were posing, Shamyl picked up a volume of *Keepsakes*; he stared intently at the valentine wreaths, clasped hands, and water-colours of dewy-eyed damsels; but on finding photographs from the Dresden Art Gallery, he became rigid, poring over a statue of Jesus Christ. 'Who is this?' he asked in a voice hoarse with excitement. When Runovsky told him, he kissed the picture. 'Your Saviour,' he said. 'I too shall pray to him, for I now know he has taught you many beautiful things . . . And perhaps he will bring good fortune,' he added naïvely.

At dinner, I observed he knew how to use a knife and fork [wrote Runovsky], though they were annoying to the others, even to Khazi Mahommed. Only Shamyl was deft, as if familiar, which I believe he was not. Sometimes he took a rib of lamb in his fingers, but he ate as he moved—with a natural elegance. The Murids made desperate efforts to catch mayonnaise on their forks, but found it quite unmanageable. At first, they were angry, but presently they guzzled happily, licking their fingers, leaving their forks severely alone. Shamyl looked at them with a slight air of superiority and made a few deprecating remarks on their clumsiness. He seemed to enjoy our Russian dishes, though eating only chicken, fish and lamb, of course; sometimes he discussed a dish most knowledgeably; but the rest seemed indifferent, only finding the food tolerable, because the meat had been prepared, and the animal slaughtered, in the ritual manner prescribed by their faith. The Murid Taoush, a rather villainous-looking fellow, was relegated to this task.

Beside Taoush, Shamyl's suite consisted of Omar, a cheerful, stocky young Tchetchen who had been aide-de-camp to Khazi Mahommed; a secretary, besides Hadjio his steward-secretary, who had been beside him for so many years, two interpreters (Mustafa the butler and Labazan, the faithful cook followed later) and the Naib Hadji-Harito, one of Shamyl's youngest generals, who figures largely in the memoirs; another Naib, Abdul Mahommed, and a strange Afghan dervish, Hai Roulah, who shared the Imam's captivity for some years, but about whom we know nothing. Runovsky describes him as the most interesting of creatures, 'the personification of harem gossip, deserving a detailed description, which I shall give later'. But, as with the Naib Abdul, another mysterious figure, he arouses our curiosity only to leave us unsatisfied.

After dinner, Shamyl sat reading a collection of rare Oriental manuscripts he had been loaned by the University, but his studies were constantly interrupted by a stream of callers. No request for an audience was refused. Bogoslavsky would have turned down most of them, but a man had only to say he had served in the Caucasus, for Shamyl to admit him. There was an awkward moment when one visitor brought the picture of a terribly wounded, naked man with shaven head, lying beside a smoking saklia. It was Khazi Mollah, the first Imam of Daghestan, said the visitor, a very rare and valuable picture of his death at Ghimri; as such, he believed it would interest Shamyl. The Imam examined it carefully, his face expressionless. Then, with a withdrawn air, he dismissed both picture and caller. 'Not Khazi Mollah,' he said tersely. The Murids glowered, and the visitor, palpably alarmed, retreated, his hopes for the authenticity of the picture dashed, and seeming now more concerned for his life. Runovsky observed the terror which Shamyl could still inspire, without any display of force. Suddenly the captive in the hotel had given place to the dread Imam, and a chill wind from the mountains seemed to blow across the room.

When the photographs arrived from Deniers, everyone was entranced. They were excellent. The Naibs kept holding them up beside each other, and Shamyl, comparing them with the original. 'Aie! Imam! Imam!' they exulted; each had one of their leader, and Shamyl said he would like to send one of himself and Khazi Mahommed to the family at Temir-Khan-Shura, which was done. 'All this while crowds surrounded the hotel, and stood outside our doors, in the corridor, so that to reach the stairs sometimes took us ten minutes', writes Runovsky. The big Znaminsky square was filled, day and night; the crowds were packed together like so many grains of caviar, waiting to catch a glimpse of the hero. Every time he appeared they cheered. 'God bless you! Stay with us!' they shouted, watching him enter his carriage. The days of sight-seeing continued; visits to the fortress of Peter and Paul, conversations with the leading Oriental scholars, a tour of the Winter Palace and the Engineering Palace (scene of the mad Tzar Paul's murder), now the Sappers' School. Here a solemn reception was held, and Shamyl pored over technical exhibits and models of fortifications. A spiral staircase particularly pleased him. He had had the same idea, he said, for defence in the hills, but it had proved altogether too complicated for his limited means. Everything to do with the army interested him. Visiting the barracks, he examined the accoutrements minutely. Blankets and pillows astonished him, like the cleanliness and order. 'Such luxury for a soldier?' he asked. 'Mine would stifle in such surroundings. But then I was poor. I could give them little. They came to me as my guests, to fight beside me. I gave them what I could.'

The Zoological Gardens produced the liveliest reactions. He had not imagined such animals could be. He shook hands with the monkeys over and over again, laughing delightedly, and saying he must describe them in a letter to his family. 'Do you know who they are?' he asked Bogoslavsky, who replied that they were apes.

'Yes. But before?' said Shamyl—'before, they were Jews, and when they angered God, he caused them to turn into monkeys. So it is written in our Book,' he declared with conviction, and no argument could shake him.

He had never seen lobsters or cray-fish, and picked one up, to examine it, his face expressing disgust. When the creature nipped him, he flung it down, but continued to watch it, avidly. When he saw its crawling, sideways gait, he shuddered. 'So must Shaitan look,' he said, fearfully. When Bogoslavsky explained that they made excellent eating, he faltered: the hero of a thousand battles paled, the body that was riddled with eighteen sword-thrusts recoiled. 'For Giaours, perhaps,' he said. 'But not for me.'

The day before the departure for Kalouga, Runovsky went to the Naibs' room, to see how they were progressing with their packing. The small room, with its prim beds and white porcelain stove, seemed to throb with a strange savage life. Hai Roulah was praying, rocking backwards and forwards, chanting shrilly; the floor was spread with bundles and chemodan, small trunks; Taoush and Hadji-Harito began wrestling, rolling over and over, venting their pent-up animal spirits, laughing and singing noisy secular songs, a counterpart to their companions' prayers. Taoush was a truculent-looking individual. But Hadji was very handsome, of the fine-drawn typical Caucasian cast. He had a hawk-like profile, a small dark beard, beautiful teeth, and bright enquiring eyes fringed by very long lashes, of which he was well aware. He smiled more often than the rest, and had a way with him which was already working havoc on the hotel chambermaids. Runovsky foresaw that he would settle easily into Western ways. Now Hadji-Harito was busy, taking clean linen out of the trunks, sorting and arranging, folding and winding the long white muslin strips which were used for Shamyl's turbans. He next inspected all the boots. 'Yaman! Bad!' he said, squatting among them, finding some worn through. He showed them to Khazi Mahommed, who was lying on his bed, looking bored and sulky. He was balancing an unsheathed shashka on one finger, a dangerous game. He took the boots and whistled through his teeth, throwing them up and catching them, crashing them against the ceiling with the force of each throw. 'Aie! Yie! Capitan,' he said. 'Boots gone.' Then he sank back moodily, beginning to play with his sword again. He was like a caged tiger: his harsh face had never softened, or shown interest or pleasure, as Shamyl, or the other Murids. He bitterly resented his present position, and the fatalistic calm with which his father now accepted his surrender. He was not generally liked in Russia, being considered a sinister figure; but Runovsky, ever understanding, came to like and esteem him. He discovered that he raged, not only for freedom, for battle, but for his wife too. He spoke a few words of Russian, which served him well enough. 'Your wife in Caucasus?' he asked. 'Mine gone. Must come. My wife bring! Father's many wife too. Bring children. All come. Yes?'

Runovsky promised this should presently be done.

'Quick!' said Khazi Mahommed, his eyes sparked with furious desire, thinking of Kherimat, the lovely, the seductive, so far away, and perhaps already won back to the West and to some western man she had known in her father's house, before her marriage. When Kherimat had deserted the family at Dargo-Vedin, she had been pleased to live among the Russians again. But as soon as she learned that Shamyl was not to be killed, that he had, in fact, gone to St. Petersburg as an honoured captive, she made up her mind life would be more rewarding in the capital, and she set about reinstating herself with the family. She made several calls on Shamyl's wives, at Temir-Khan-Shura, enquiring solicitously after their well-being. Next, a series of pathetic, longing letters to Khazi Mahommed soon won his forgiveness. But Shamyl thought his son well rid of her, and refused to have her sent north with the rest of his household. It was only after some time, when he saw Khazi Mahommed's misery, that he relented, and promised that she too should come. Meanwhile Khazi Mahommed believed he would never see his wife again, and he fretted, seeming withdrawn and dour.

Runovsky lingered in the room, watching the Murids curiously. Their sinewy force seemed utterly incongruous, cooped up in the hotel. Their harsh guttural voices and violent movements were as noisy as their singing, which Runovsky feared would disturb the occupants of nearby rooms. Abdul Mahommed was ill; he had caught a chill, and lay shivering on his bed, covered by a Russian army shouba. His dark, expressive face, at once sinister and attractive, seemed to simmer with a magnetic force. 'He was a figure out of a novel,' says Runovsky, who was much intrigued by the manner in which he remained aloof from the rest, who ignored him, following their Imam's lead. Both Shamyl and his son showed a marked coldness to the handsome young Naib Runovsky scented some strange drama. But what? Why was he among this chosen band around Shamyl? Had he been the Imam's choice? Had he been sent by Bariatinsky, fearing his dangerous powers of leadership which might cause trouble if he stayed? Had he set himself up to be Shamyl's successor? Did the Imam condemn him for disloyalty? 'I am resolved to learn the Avar language,' notes Runovsky. But we never learn any more about Abdul Mahommed; he remains mysterious, emerging from the Caucasian peaks, briefly, to lie shivering in a hotel bedroom in St. Petersburg, a silhouette, not even the hero of a novelette.

The St. Petersburg visit wound up with a gala evening at the ballet. Shamyl was now becoming accustomed to the theatre—he had heard several Italian operas, and neither he nor his Murids had been able to restrain their tears at some of the more pathetic arias. On this particular night, they saw two ballets particularly suited to them: *La Peri*, which had first been performed by Grisi, tells of a Sultan who loves Zulma, his slave, and says he will renounce all other wives for her. Now, seated on a gilt chair, framed in the splendour of an Imperial box, Shamyl sat watching the curtain rise: *Act One—A harem*. . . . The scene opened on posturing odalisques, fountains and divans. Shamyl nodded complacent approval. 'Thus it is, in the great harems,' he said. And Khazi Mahommed concurred. As the coryphées tripped forward, pointing their toes classically, but striking the most abandoned poses in the *Pas des Odalisques*, he produced his telescope, the same little telescope through which he had watched so much terrible and decisive warfare. At first he appeared to be coldly appraising the dancers, who fawned round the Sultan as he slept. At this Bogoslavsky asked him how he liked it. Shamyl turned lazy half-shut eyes on the Colonel, and with an edge of irony in his voice, replied:

'The Prophet promised us to see such houris in Paradise—but only in Paradise; I am fortunate to have seen them here, on earth.' 'Which,' says Runovsky, 'was not quite sincere, since his earlier remarks showed that he was familiar with the harems maintained by the more extravagant Caucasian chieftains.'

When the Sultan woke from his sleep, refreshed, to woo Zelma with a leaping dance expressing his love, Shamyl stiffened, frowned, and began muttering angrily. When he understood that the Sultan was wooing the slave, he lowered the telescope and laughed sardonically. Suddenly Runovsky saw the cruel, terrible mask by which he was known to so many. That a Sultan should demean himself thus! That the Giaours should believe such goings-on among the Moslem Princes! He moved his chair, and did not look at the stage again, till the end, when he applauded very coldly.

The next ballet (it seems to have been either *Katerina*, or *La Révolte au Sérail*, for both were in the repertoire of the Imperial ballet, at this time) dealt with an Amazon battalion, a hundred and fifty armed girls, who deployed, marched and counter-marched, and destroyed a bridge across a ravine, all *sur les pointes*. The Murids followed every step, breathlessly. When the cardboard bridge was demolished by the glittering silver-paper axes, they looked at each other, spellbound. The whole drama of mountain warfare was there, cardboard or no. Shamyl kept his telescope glued to his eyes, shifting from one to the other, seeing, perhaps, those other Amazons who had defended Akhulgo; or Pakkou-Bekké, sword in hand, defying him at Khounzak; visions of the mighty mountains he had failed to hold; Kazbek, looming dark against the 'wolf's tail', that first brush of grey which lightens the sky before dawn, and for which the hunter, and the fighter wait. Of Dargo, and

Ghimri, and Gounib, and the road to defeat—to the crimson velvet
chair in the Imperial box. . . . When the curtain fell, and they descended the marble stairway, Bogoslavsky asked if he thought the
Amazons had fought as well as they danced. Shamyl smiled, irony
again lighting the half-closed eyes. 'Yes, truly. Had I such a regiment,
Gounib would never have fallen,' he replied.

*   *   *

Next morning, the whole party left for Kalouga: a pullman carriage
had been reserved on the train, and Shamyl was conducted through the
waiting crowds, to take up his place at the window. The platform was
thronged with the usual, enthusiastic mob, through which the regular
passengers could not pass, so that chaotic scenes took place as the time
of the departure drew near, and numbers of third-class passengers,
laden with bundles and samovars, fought vainly to reach the train.
Shamyl stood at the carriage window, hand on heart, bowing ceremoniously. So great was the enthusiasm and the confusion, that the departure was delayed for half an hour. At last the whistle sounded, and
agitated officials stepped back, waving and bowing. The train steamed
out while Shamyl was still addressing the cheering crowds in Arabic,
which Bogoslavsky and the interpreter were trying to render, above the
uproar. 'Tell them my feelings are as deep as my wounds,' said Shamyl.
'Tell them their attentions give me such happiness as I have not had
since the liberation of Dargo. . . .'

It always came back to battles, to the pulse of Caucasian life.

32

An Acceptance

And he says much, who says evening . . .
HUGO VON HOFMANNSTHAL

In victory, Russia showed the same largesse towards Shamyl that France had displayed towards another surrendered rebel leader, the Algerian chieftain Abd-el-Kadir, who had been treated royally, living at the château of Amboise in terms of luxurious exile, while Shamyl was sent to Kalouga where his life, if not as regal as that of Abd-el-Kadir, was certainly luxurious after standards of living in the aôuls. It was decided that a suitable house should be found for him and his family. Meantime he was lodged at the Hotel Coulon.

Kalouga lay to the south of Moscow. It was the heart of the Russian provinces, typical of many hundreds of such small, self-contained townships. Little wooden houses with peeping double windows, half-buried in winter, when the snow was banked deep around them, alternated with a rather more lofty architecture; comfortable, stucco houses, adorned with carved wood decorations, laurel wreaths and lyres; sometimes an impressive classical portico had been added, looking a size too large for the façade it adorned. The quiet streets were lined with acacia trees, and tumble-down fences divided the garden plots that surrounded the houses. The broad reaches of the river Oka ran beside the town, and a range of humpy hills broke the monotony of the surrounding countryside. Thirty-five ornate Byzantine-domed churches, a convent, barracks, arsenal, a bishopric, the seat of the government of the province, a club for the nobility, and a large tanning industry made up its resources. The population was about fifty-five thousand; its way of life placid, or stagnant, according to individual reaction.

From this distance, we can have no conception of the degree of placidity, or stagnation, which prevailed in the Russian provinces at this time. News of the outside world was filtered through a government censorship which operated first on the newspapers of Moscow or St. Petersburg. These arrived two or three days late, to be read and re-read for many weeks, in the local cafés, or passed around from hand to hand, as they were inherited by less fortunate citizens from the wealthier few who were subscribers. There were no telephones; tele-grams were generally reserved for catastrophic announcements; radio and cinema were undreamed of. There was no theatre at Kalouga. Entertainment was generally interpreted as supper-parties, dances, a conjurer, or concerts given by amateur music-societies, who often maintained a brilliantly high standard.

Kalouga received Shamyl with enthusiasm. He came among them as a legend, from an unimaginable world of violence and colour. He must be asked to dine! And so we have the surprising picture of the Lion of Daghestan and his Murids launched on the tide of provincial society, shepherded to balls and receptions by the delightful Runovsky. The Captain had taken over from Bogoslavsky with some misgivings, for he saw how attached Shamyl had become to his first adjutant. When the Colonel left, Shamyl had stood in the street in the sharp cold of a November night, without a shouba, muttering prayers and blessings on his departing friend. He watched the carriage out of sight, and then returned to his room to pray. Later, he presented himself at Runovsky's door, accompanied by his interpreter (that same Gramoff who had served him so well over the matter of his son's exchange). He plunged into a long speech, and in the Asiatic manner, reached his true subject by a series of elliptical approaches.

'When God orphans a child, he often replaces the mother by a nianyia,' he said. 'This nianyia feeds him, cares for him and defends him. If a child is clean and gay, everyone praises his nianyia. But if the child be dirty, or ill-behaved, they blame, not him, but the nianyia, for her neglect. I am an old man [he was sixty-three], but here I am alone in a strange land, knowing neither your language or customs, so I believe I am no longer Shamyl, the Imam, but, by God's will, have become that helpless and humble child who needs a nianyia. The Tzar has appointed you as my adjutant—but I believe Allah sent you to be my nianyia. Now I ask you to love me as good nianyias usually love their charges, and I promise you that I shall love you both as a grateful child, and as Shamyl loves a man who is good to him.'

Runovsky was naturally quite won over by this disarming speech, replying: 'I shall love you, not because I am ordered to do so, but because I respect you greatly.' Shamyl's face softened, irradiating a sudden warmth.

'When I saw you first,' he said, 'I told Khazi Mahommed, that is a good man—a man we can trust . . . Shamyl never yet made a mistake in appraising a man upon whom he had looked for a long time. *Yakshé!* It is good!' he said. Runovsky had lived among Moslems enough to know that once their trust was given, it was for life; he knew Shamyl had attached himself devotedly to Bogoslavsky, and had feared his replacement might be resented. Now the bond of this new friendship (which was to last unshaken until Shamyl's death) was sealed with another crushing handshake.

Nevertheless, the Imam pined for Bogoslavsky; at first he could not believe that anyone else could be so *sympathique*; his despondency was increased by his separation from his family, and his passionate wish to prove to the Tzar, his feelings of gratitude, his truly changed outlook. His usual five *namez*, or ritual prayers, were increased to nine each day, but still his gloomy apathy was apparent: he scarcely touched his food, and seemed to live in a shadowed world of his own. Runovsky consulted the Naibs on how best to raise his spirits. Hadji-Harito recommended music. 'The Imam loves it. In the aôul he could not allow himself time to listen, but here . . . Later he will enjoy visits, meeting people—but much later . . . Music will lighten his sadness at once.'

Runovsky arranged for a 'fizgarmonia' to be brought from Moscow. This was a kind of harmonium, a small organ-like instrument worked with pedals, such as still lingers in parish halls and vestries, for choir practice. Shamyl was entranced, listening with unblinking attention for hours on end. He would examine its mechanism minutely, touching it reverently. Runovsky asked him why he had forbidden music in the aôuls.

'Because I had so few warriors compared to your Russian millions,' he replied. 'It was thus with tobacco and wine and dancing, too. I did not forbid them because I thought them sinful, but for their effect on my men. I feared they could exchange a night watch for a woman's arms—that they would forget the music of battle for the songs their mistresses sang.'

But even the siren strains of the fizgarmonia could not altogether dispel Shamyl's depression when he spoke of his absent family. He confided in Runovsky that he feared Shouanete might now be won back to Christianity.

'And if she were . . . Would you still want her for your wife?'

Shamyl seemed perturbed: almost reluctantly, he agreed he would.

Later Hadji told Runovsky he believed Shamyl would like nothing better than to hear Zaïdate had been converted, as this would give him the excuse to divorce her. Hadji spoke of Kherimat's elegance and charm in lyrical terms: 'Such beauty does not exist anywhere else—not in St. Petersburg, Moscow or Kharkov,' he said, his black eyes glittering. 'Khazi Mahommed saw all the unveiled beauties in your theatre. . . . I, too; but never was there such a rose as Kherimat.' Runovsky asked him how he knew, since Caucasian noble-women were always veiled. 'Ah! in Shamyl's seraglio they are—but Kherimat is not always

there . . . Outside the aôul we can, and do, often see women unveiled,'
he replied with a slyly triumphant air. Later, Runovsky was to find
Shamyl's young Naib living a life of positive debauch (according to
Murid tenets) among the Kalouga belles; but that was yet to come. At
present they were all living in monastic seclusion. A sort of class-room
atmosphere prevailed, as they gathered around the table in the hotel
suite, eating their simple meals, learning some elementary Russian, and
occasionally visiting either the commandant at the barracks, or the
Governor.

Winter had come, and with it the little town took on an air of
snugness, each house tucked into the deep snow. The gold crosses on the
churches shone bright under leaden skies; the pink or yellow painted
stucco houses warmed the streets by their glow, reflected on the snow
piled up before the doors. Kalouga possessed one remarkable building;
a covered market. It still stands, edged on to the street by arcaded
booths dating from the seventeenth century. They are elaborately
crenellated, with machicolations and balustrades, recalling the Tartar-
Italianate architecture of the Moscow Kremlin.

Under the avenues of bare trees, Shamyl and his suite sometimes
walked, still marvelling at all they saw. The passers-by uncovered
respectfully as the strange band ventured into the dark booths where
the merchants crouched among the stores, peering into lighted windows
of the houses with childlike curiosity, watching the faces, the carriages,
the life around them. The Tzar followed Shamyl's daily life closely—
regular reports being sent him by Runovsky, who also sent reports to
Bariatinsky, in the Caucasus. Presently, the Tzar offered a carriage and
pair, and several blood horses for the exiles to ride—a gesture which
delighted them.

The town beggars had soon discovered Shamyl's generosity, and
would swarm around him every time he went out. Runovsky had to
adopt stern measures to preserve Shamyl's allowance from being distributed right and left. This yearly grant was an ample one, but Shamyl
had no sense of money values. Or perhaps he had: when Runovsky
found him giving away as much as ten roubles at a time, he suggested
kopeks instead of roubles. 'They will abuse your kindness and drink it
all away,' Runovsky warned him. Shamyl asked what ten kopeks would
buy. When he was told, he laughed. 'If I give alms, it is to help the
beggar. . . . Ten kopeks will not help him. . . . He asks for my aid, and
I must give it. Our Book—the Koran—says so. Your Bible says so too.
Yakshé! It is good! Many good things are written in your Book.'

He was studying the Bible; in the Archbishop's library he had discovered a copy of the Gospels in Arabic, and now began to take their
teachings to heart. One day Runovsky discovered that, upon Shamyl's
orders, Hadji walked up and down outside the hotel each day after

dinner, stopping anyone he thought poor, to give them alms in the Imam's name. This practice was soon known to every drunk or tramp in the town. Runovsky came upon Hadji standing among a crowd of them, his left arm behind his back, holding a purse between his strong white teeth, taking out money with his right hand. The beggars were jostling him with out-stretched hands.

'*Tokhta! Tokhta!* Stop it, brothers!' cried Hadji, beating them back vigorously, as they snatched at the money.

'What on earth were you doing?' asked Runovsky, as the crowd slunk away.

'I give money on Imam's orders,' replied Hadji. 'Shamyl says: "Give with your right hand, so your left hand sees not." . . .' Thus were the Scriptures interpreted by the Murids.

From time to time, soldiers who had been Shamyl's prisoners, came to see him. They seemed to bear no resentment. On his side, as a mark of special esteem, he would sometimes show them his wounds. Among these soldiers were some who had been kept as working prisoners, at the Great Aôul, and who had often been detailed to take or fetch Shamyl's children back from visits to the old Jamul u'din's house. The children had got on well with the Russian soldiers, and Shamyl invited them all to return to see his family, as soon as they should reach Kalouga.

During the first winter months, before the rest of the family arrived, Shamyl spent most of his time in prayer. He needed little sleep and often prayed or meditated all night. He kept to the time-table he had known in the mountains in the winter, retiring to bed, or his room, at seven each evening. After he had gone, Hadji would come to Runovsky with a paper and pencil, eager to learn Russian; he would draw little pictures of what he had seen, and ask questions, or he would describe life in the aôuls. 'This is the way we made gunpowder' . . . 'Here are our guns' . . . Then he would sigh and say: 'In those days we saw things differently. What was black there, is white here. Once, if even Khazi Mahommed had done wrong, Shamyl himself would have decapitated him. And we loved and honoured him for his ipmartiality. But now we learn to be forgiving. It is all very confusing.'

When thieves attempted to steal one of the blood horses presented by the Tzar, the Naibs' indignation knew no bounds. They rushed for their shashkas, and Omar, bristling with steel, primed his pistol, determined to slay the villains. Runovsky had the greatest difficulty in persuading them to leave vengeance to the law. Dispassionate, third party justice was something quite alien to them. Besides, they felt it a personal reflection on their sense of gratitude, *vis-à-vis* the Tzar, if they stood by while the law caught and chastised the thieves. . . . It was indeed very confusing, sighed Hadji, turning back to his Russian phrase-book.

In three months he had become quite fluent, speaking an engaging kind of pigeon-Russian, which served well enough to obtain him all the favours he sought. He would creep out at night for some 'midnight kind admittance', without any of the other Murids being aware of his absence. 'Your ladies give me jam,' he told Runovsky, who never asked him to elaborate on this odd statement. No doubt the sweets he obtained were doubly delicious for being stolen. The snares of the devil had begun to claim him from the first, and he showed a certain scepticism for the Shariat's pronouncements, one of which, denouncing the crime of going to any place where there were unveiled women, maintained that not only would the sinner forfeit paradise, but that the roof would fall in and crush sinner and temptress alike. In St. Petersburg, returning from a reception held after a performance of the opera, where both guests and singers (all unveiled) had been presented to Shamyl and his suite, Hadji had made a very heretical remark, saying: 'Well, glory to Allah! In spite of our having been to a forbidden paradise and meeting a hundred unveiled houris, the roof did *not* fall in—and here we are, safe and sound.' Shamyl said nothing, but gave him a very searching look, at which Hadji seemed to shrink. For some time after that, he gave up thinking of Western divisions, and spent his time reading 'The Book' and trying to show Shamyl (to whom he was profoundly attached) that he knew he had gone too far.

But as time went by, Hadji again turned towards the seductions of the West, letting his hair grow beneath his turban, and sporting fine batiste handkerchiefs and a crimson silk undershirt, barely concealed by his old woollen tcherkesska. Runovsky supposed his nocturnal absences accounted for the change. He realized Hadji's adventures were due as much to the encouragement and enterprise of the local ladies, as to the young Naib's own daring. Shamyl did not seem aware of the change. Once, at dinner, overpowering wafts of eau de cologne floated across the table from the Lothario's immaculate person. Shamyl sniffed suspiciously, while Hadji grew red and then paled. 'What is that smell?' asked the Imam ominously. Hadji said he thought it might be the gravy; but Runovsky rushed to the rescue, saying he had tipped too much scent on his handkerchief, and would the Imam pardon such carelessness? After which Hadji became his devoted slave.

Khazi Mahommed still remained aloof from the rest—a sombre figure, brooding over lost battles and his absent wife; but gradually he too came under the spell of Runovsky kindness, and the hospitality and deference of the Kalougans. They were anxious to celebrate Shamyl's presence among them, and now he received and accepted a number of invitations to visit the leading citizens. Their hospitality did not spring from what Alexander Herzen, speaking of provincial life, describes as 'the geniality of desperate boredom', but was rather the expression of their genuine desire to do him honour.

Now, for the first time since his arrival in Russia, Shamyl saw something of the well-to-do bourgeois life, and ordinary people, rather than glimpses of Court and official life, which he had seen in St. Petersburg. His first visit was to the home of the commanding officer of the garrison, Colonel Yeropkin, where the Marshal of Nobility made a flowery speech: 'We see a hero in our midst . . . We are happy and proud . . .' Shamyl replied through his interpreter, and spoke with emotion . . . 'After all the evils I have done you, you do not tear me to pieces, but welcome me, and I am overcome.' The guests crowded around him, eager to make him feel at ease. The ice was broken; driving home, he asked Runovsky if the visit had really gone off well. 'I conducted myself fittingly? I was well received? Would others receive me so well?' On being reassured that he would be welcomed everywhere, he glowed. 'Then I shall go and call—at night, since you tell me there is usually music then. I wish to know them better.'

He now began to attend a series of local soirées. 'A splendid figure of sober elegance, in a dark brown tcherkesska', enthroned on a sofa, holding court, flanked by his Naibs in their towering fur caps, and still striking their ritual pose, arms folded, eyes downcast. (Though, as soon as he left, those who were able to linger flung themselves into Western diversions, eating ice-cream, watching the dancing or card games. Hadji-Harito was particularly bold in his advances towards the West, and lost no time in learning to waltz.)

None of the Murids were able to appreciate the elegance of the crinoline. 'Is she truly so fat?' they would ask, seeing some bell-shaped figure sweep past. 'Will she wear it on the day of judgement?' they demanded. 'Well, if you wear your shashkas and kindjals, she will probably wear her crinoline,' replied Runovsky, who was acquiring the Murid habit of reducing everything to terms of battle. 'But those are our weapons,' said the Murids indignantly. To which Runovsky replied that the crinoline might sometimes be considered as an even more dangerous weapon. But his sally was not appreciated.

Shamyl always asked to see his host's children, and they responded to him at once, crowding round and fighting to climb on his knee. It was then fashionable to have part of the drawing-room converted into a winter garden, or aviary, stocked with tropical plants and rare birds. Shamyl loved these birds, and would beckon to them, at which they would fly to him as if mesmerized, perching on his hand, and hovering ecstatically. In short, he was an unequivocal success, and the local society outdid themselves to do him honour, hiring string bands, liveried flunkies, and those elaborately tiered, silver *épergnes* which lent such tone to every buffet. Perhaps the most outstanding feature of provincial festivities at this time was THE PINEAPPLE. This exotic rarity was always referred to in capitals, and was hired out by the evening, along with the little gilt chairs. Caterers invested in one at the beginning of the winter: it was a costly importation, preserved throughout the season by being embedded in snow when not in use. The hours it spent, each night adorning a different buffet, hardly began to thaw it, and it remained nobly inviolate, from November to March, when at last the caterer and his family were able to get at it.

So, in a sense, Shamyl might be said to have occupied a place akin to the pineapple—he was an exotic rarity who, by his presence alone, imparted glory and a festive air to any gathering. But after a while the late hours began to tire him; and he found the women's low necklines rather disturbing too. 'Are not the ladies cold?' he asked almost timidly. The Book had many severe things to say about such temptations, he told Runovsky.

'What do you feel when you see such lovely faces and such naked bosoms?' he asked, and went on to say that low necks and tight trousers, such as the dancers wore, could only lead to temptation and sin— especially for the women.

'You think them weaker—more imperfect than men?' asked Runosvky.

'Allah meant them to be weaker,' said the Imam. 'That is why he bade them obey men in all things. Does not your Book, too, say Man is Master?'

Runovsky replied that the Bible did indeed consider man as stronger, but that was why he must defend woman, protect her from rough work, treat her as his helpmeet. Shamyl seemed sceptical. 'What work can she do? Bring up his children, keep his house, and by her love make life sweeter for him. But she can never become his equal,' he said firmly.

Runovsky suggested that it depended on the woman: that in some cases she might prove a higher type, or even supersede him. This was purest heresy to Oriental ears, and Shamyl frowned. When Runovsky added that, in any case, woman must keep her own sense of dignity, Shamyl expressed doubts that she could, if she wore such *decolletéés.* When Runovsky reminded him of the Caucasian custom of putting the guest to sleep with the host's daughter, Shamyl corrected him. 'In my Daghestan, when an honoured guest arrives, he sleeps in the same room with the girl. It is a sign of especial esteem and confidence. The guest may woo her—caress her, even, but if he importunes her too rashly, she leaves him. "You are no man, you cannot restrain yourself," she says, and the whole aôul laughs him to scorn.'

When Runovsky remarked that it seemed an unnecessarily severe test, Shamyl adroitly switched the conversation, dwelling on the Shariat's methods of dealing with social crimes. Adultery was punished by stoning to death; fornication (among the unmarried) merely merited a hundred lashes. . . . Runovsky again said he thought such sentences far too harsh . . . 'But I suppose this severity suppresses the crimes entirely?'

'Oh, no!' replied Shamyl. 'Strange to say, I believe such things happen more often there than here.' His heavy-lidded eyes ranged over the ballroom, observing the dancers' flying feet, the diamonds sparkling on the women's bare panting bosoms, and the ardent faces of their partners. . . . 'Strange,' he muttered. 'Very strange.' Soon after, he took his leave, going back to pray and meditate.

*   *   *

When a celebrated French conjurer arrived in Kalouga, Runovsky decided such innocent entertainment would be perfect for his charges. However, when the Imam learned that female acrobats (in tights) were also on the bill, he refused to attend, at which the Naibs' faces fell pathetically. At last it was arranged for the conjurer to come to the hotel, alone, and go through his repertoire privately. Everything went off splendidly, though when Monsieur Guery was told he was to perform before the great Shamyl, he suffered an attack of nerves. He had been in the Caucasus years before and had never forgotten the terror Shamyl's name had inspired at this time. He had been in Daghestan, performing for the Russian army, and had nearly fallen into a Murid ambush. When Shamyl came quietly into the room, wearing a long *khalat*, or Oriental dressing-gown, looking the picture of domestic benevolence, the conjurer trembled convulsively, confronted by the dread figure. But he pulled himself together and began a series of wonderful tricks which flabbergasted everyone. Shamyl was determined to resist the magic, and tried to examine some of the props, which Monsieur Guery refused. But on catching the fiery eye, and hearing the thunderous tone: 'Give!' he hastened to comply. Shamyl soon discovered the false bottom to a box and other devices, and looked very pleased with himself. 'Once I should have cut off his head for this,' he remarked. But the conjurer got his own back by producing a bunch of feathers from Hadji-Harito's nose. Shamyl and the Naibs could not fathom this, and laughed hysterically, tears pouring down their swarthy cheeks. For years to come, Shamyl would suddenly burst out laughing, remembering the trick, saying: 'Why did I see this? Now I can no longer pray properly. Every time I begin my *namez* I see that bunch of feathers and Hadji's nose, and I start to laugh!'

II

A pretty, old, two-storied house was finally chosen for Shamyl. It was known as the Soukhotine House, on Ranievsky Street, and was surrounded by acacia trees and flowering bushes. A small mosque was now built in the garden, and the stables and outhouses lodged the servants, and coachman and watchmen, who were recruited from among the Tartar soldiers of the local garrison. When it was known that the family would be arriving some time in January, Shamyl spent many anxious hours selecting the wall-papers and furnishings for his wives' rooms. He was insistent that no silk should be used anywhere. It was an emblem of the abhorred luxury. But agreeable colours and patterns, soft textures, comfort—luxury, by Caucasian standards—he now accepted gratefully. A solid silver table-service had been chosen by the Russians; but this he had refused. Wooden spoons or a hunting knife had done well enough in the Caucasus. At last the simplest silver-plate was arrived at as a compromise. The Imam's refusal of all luxury impressed his captors greatly.

His own room was simple green and white—with white *takhtas*, or divans, and bookshelves to house his library, which was already on its way north. Green was his favourite colour, and he took a great fancy to a card-table topped with baize; he did not play cards, but the table stood beside his divan. A large armchair, of eighteenth-century formal style, upholstered in green tapestry, and a small writing-desk, set between the windows, completed the furnishings. At prayer-time, Shamyl knelt on his own Caucasian prayer-rug, which went with him everywhere. Generally the furnishings of the house were simple, retaining a strongly Oriental flavour. Shouanete's room had white divans and curtains, and a pretty wall-paper of pink oak-leaves on a black ground; for her bedroom, Shamyl chose a blue and white striped paper and a large double bedstead, with a hair mattress that must have seemed particularly inviting after Caucasian furnishings. Zaïdate's rooms were furnished exactly the same with divans and a green and white paper in the bedroom, and yellow in the sitting-room. The rooms reserved for Khazi Mahommed and Kherimat were similar, though Khazi Mahommed asked for nothing but European furniture here, knowing this would please his wife. One large room, on the first floor, was reserved for family gatherings; this was wholly Oriental: takhtas ran all around the walls; there were no mirrors or pictures, or any decoration, save two fine rugs. When the whole house was ready, Shamyl inspected it from cellar to attic, and was overjoyed. 'In all Kalouga there is no finer house,' he said. 'Allah has found me the haven I need for my family.' Indeed his enthusiasm went so far as to persuade him that the landscape of Kalouga resembled the Caucasus—the lowlands of Tchetchnia, and he would sit at the window, looking across the green fields, smiling. 'Kop Tchetchen!' he would say, quite blinded by his wish to adapt himself.

In January, four months after Shamyl's surrender, his library reached him in Kalouga. Several large, unwieldy bundles were brought to the house: the priceless manuscripts and holy books were tied up in Daghestani rugs, which had protected them on the long journey. Hadjio, the steward, having now acquired the Russian viewpoint on money, tipped the coachman who brought them, a mere twenty-kopek piece. But when Shamyl learned that the coachman spoke of passing the family on the way—that they were, in fact, only two or three stages behind him, he had the man fetched back. For such a piece of news he must be given gold, he said.

'That day, during dinner, we were told Mahommed Sheffi, as the advance guard of the party, would be arriving within the hour', writes Runovsky. 'Shamyl could not conceal his excitement; he jumped up, went to the head of the stairs, and then changed his mind, returning to the table, trying to assume an expression of complete indifference. But he could eat no more, and was obviously listening for the sound of wheels. At last, hearing the carriage drive up, and Sheffi's footstep on the stairs, he hurried to meet him—something a Moslem father generally considers undignified, we are told. A ceremonial greeting followed. Sheffi silently approached his father, kissed his hand and, with downcast eyes, waited on the threshold for Shamyl to invite him inside, and to question him.'

According to Eastern etiquette, it would be improper for two men to speak publicly of their women: if absolutely essential, an oblique reference could be made, but no direct questions could be asked, or answered. Therefore, although Shamyl was burning with curiosity to know exactly how many of his household, and which of his wives and children had been dispatched, he was constrained to approach the matter in his usual elliptical fashion, Mahommed Sheffi taking his cue accordingly. 'Has the cold been very severe?' asked the Imam.

'Not so severe that *Shouanete* suffered too much,' replied Sheffi, thus assuring his father of the Pearl's approach. Then, circuitously, listing the household, he went on to say that the warm clothing provided for *Nafisette*, *Sofiate*, *Fatimat* and *Nadjavat* had protected them along the way. Bahou had been interested in all she had seen, he said; *Zaïdate*,— and here his sharp slit-eyes seemed to read his father's thoughts— *Zaïdate* was not too exhausted by the strain of organizing and directing the packing. He did not mention Aminette, and Runovsky discovered later she had been divorced by the Imam, some time earlier.

Since the Princesses' sojourn in the Great Aôul, Shamyl's family had been enlarged by the addition of two sons-in-law. His daughter Fatimat had married one of Zaïdate's younger brothers, Abdurrahim, while Nafisette had married another brother, Abdurrahman, thus rendering the family ramifications ever more involved. Several babies had been born, including another daughter, to Zaïdate; and some had died, Shouanete's babies being regularly still-born, or dying in infancy; but the family party and domestics now arriving brought the total of the Kalouga household up to thirty-four persons. Mahommed Sheffi was now married to the daughter of the Naib Enkau Hadjio, but their first child had died just before the surrender of Gounib. Sheffi was twenty, 'handsome, very tall and well-built, but heavy, which spoiled his natural Caucasian grace', says Runovsky. His lively gesticulations and ebullience, when not confronted by his father who subdued him, recalled Khazi Mahommed's affected manner, but he was of a far lighter, more sociable nature, and obviously enraptured by all he saw of the West.

When Shamyl had assured himself that his whole household had been sent north, he ordered Sheffi to offer up prayers of thanksgiving, at which the young man kicked off his red slippers and set to praying noisily, gabbling through the prayers, the quicker to inspect the marvellous, exciting Russian house in which his father lived.

At dusk, the household was alerted that the caravan was approaching. Runovsky saddled a horse and galloped to meet them. Across the river he could see the long cortège, winding its way, laboriously. The lanterns reflected, bobbing, in the dark still waters of the Oka. Khazi Mahommed had gone south to fetch them, and now headed the procession, riding in an open *kibitka* with Abdurrahim, his brother-in-law. The rest were in coaches, mounted on sleighs. One particularly elephantine vehicle, looking like a tightly curtained Noah's Ark, contained all the women save Zaïdate who, claiming the first wife's honours, insisted on travelling in separate state. The bad roads, deeply rutted and iced over, made their progress laborious, and the caravan spread out for a mile in length. When the Noah's Ark stuck in a pot-hole, Runovsky went to help the outriders free it; the curtains parted and a very pretty woman's face looked down at him, smiling. But seeing the crowd of moujiks and coachmen below, the face disappeared, to be replaced by that of a pretty little girl: this was Sofiate, Runovsky later learned; the smiling beauty, her mother Shouanete, whom he never saw again unveiled. Runovsky hung about, trying to catch a glimpse of Zaïdate, but her carriage windows were curtained and shut fast. Even from the closed carriages, wailing complaints issued, mingled with groans and lamentations. The journey had been very hard; the carriages were breaking up fast, and the ladies quite exhausted by the ordeal. Kherimat in particular, it seemed, was prostrated, and Khazi Mahommed was very anxious on her behalf. When at last they reached the house, and were conducted inside, so many shapeless bundles of veiling and drapery, they fell back before such unimaginable luxury. '*Vallah! Thamassa!* Praise be! We have arrived safely,' they exclaimed, staring around in amazement at the big white porcelain stoves, fingering the curtains, while the children began sliding across the polished parquet floors.

Shamyl was awaiting them, as etiquette prescribed, in the reception-room. Runovsky followed them upstairs, curious to see the reunion. The Imam was seated on the divan, fingering his tespyeh. First he received the men of the party, each with the same ceremony he had accorded Mahommed Sheffi. Then it was the women's turn. 'Is it you, Nafisette—is it you, Fatimat?' he asked his daughters, for all the bundles looked alike, and none of them could unveil before strangers; while those who were married could only lift their veils for their husbands. The children were greeted, one by one, and then his daughter-in-law, Kherimat, to whom he showed a marked coldness. Turning towards his two wives, Shamyl motioned to the rest of the family to leave him. The door shut on their meeting. Runovsky asked Hadji if he believed Shamyl would show any preference between the two women. Hadji shrugged. 'He loves Shouanete best, but Zaïdate is his first wife,' he said. 'She is clever; she knows every duty and right of woman, according to the Koran; she will never let the Imam's feelings for Shouanete usurp one shred of her position.'

A few days after her arrival, Shouanete wrote to her brother in Mozdok: 'The great White Tzar is generous to us. I cannot express our gratitude for the comfort here, the care that has been taken of our Gospodin (master); we want for nothing, thanks to the Tzar, for whom we pray, and for whom we should like you, too, to pray.' She signed the letter: 'Shouanete (who is in need of God's mercy) wife of the poor pilgrim Shamyl.'

For the first month after their arrival, the women were never seen; but they were heard, chanting their prayers, the clock round. They had vowed themselves to a month of prayer and fasting, should they ever be reunited with the Imam. At last Runovsky came to know them well, as their friend and confidant; but he never saw any of them unveiled: he speaks of the incredible beauty and elegance of their feet and ankles. 'Only Caucasians have such delicate bones,' he notes, recognizing each of them by a turn of the ankle, or an individual manner of applying henna to their heels. Perhaps it was as well they remained mysterious figures—even Kherimat might have proved disappointing. 'In the tents are hidden many beautiful women: beautiful beneath their veils. Yet lift a veil, and you will see your mother's mother,' wrote Sa'adi, voicing the age-old cry of disillusion.

Shamyl's women were always well enough dressed (he preferred them to wear only white, or black), but their jewellery was limited to a few gold coins. All the rest (the diamonds from Tzinondali, we imagine) had been seized by renegade tribesmen, pressing home their advantage, when the women were hiding in the hills prior to the fall of Gounib.

Yet presently it transpired that even at this dark hour, Zaïdate had contrived to conceal one or two fine pieces in her *chalvari*, or trousers. She had kept them hidden from the rest of the family till, at last, vanity overcoming discretion, she had flaunted them when the Kalougan ladies came to call in state. The Russian ladies themselves were glitteringly bedecked, which aroused the wives' and daughters' sharpest envy; but this was as nothing beside their fury when they saw that Zaïdate, too, was resplendent. Even Shouanete raged. It was not that she minded being without jewels, she sobbed, but that Zaïdate had been so unfair—and would be able to parade before 'Our Gospodin' in all her finery, while she had nothing. . . . The whole house rang with their cries, so that Shamyl retreated to the mosque, and Runovsky was at a loss how to calm them, diamonds being quite beyond his budget.

Gradually be became identified with the household; 'our house'— 'with us', he writes, sharing all their joys and sorrows, assisting at their religious ceremonies, their confidant, tutor, and the arbitrator of every dispute. They called him 'Our Dear', and loved him as he loved and understood them.

He watched over them anxiously, for he feared their health would not withstand the damp northern climate; and he knew, too, that one day, his appointment would come to an end; that the authorities would transfer him elsewhere, and he dreaded to think of how his family might fare in other hands.

Even his watchfulness could not always avoid awkward scenes, when some tactless visitor, either deliberately or carelessly, launched a topic, or let fall some remark wounding to the Imam. Colonel Zaharin, a young officer at this time, later described his first meeting with Shamyl when a good deal of ill-feeling was brought about by the tactlessness of a fellow-officer.

'I arrived in Kalouga', writes Zaharin, 'and presented myself to the commanding officer, Colonel Yeropkin, who told me of Shamyl's presence in the town. "You know all officers, including generals, are ordered to make an official visit to him—Bariatinsky's orders," said the Colonel.' There had been an unfortunate incident, not long before, when an arrogant high-ranking Russian officer had expected Shamyl to call on him. Neither would lower themselves to make the first move. At last the General was compelled to obey orders: but with an ill grace. He was determined to make the Imam aware of the honour. Shamyl fixed him with an awful eye. 'You—' he said, 'I had half-a-dozen of your kind as my prisoners.' The meeting was not a success.

On the day appointed for Zaharin's call, he was joined by several more officers. Together, they drove to the house on Ranievsky Street.

They were resplendent in full dress, gold-laced and glorious, their spurs and swords jingling, their white kid gloves impeccable. They were shown into the simple reception-room. 'There we found several more officers, also passing through Kalouga, and waiting for an audience. . . . Captain Runovsky and the interpreter joined us, warning us that when the Imam spoke to us, we must reply briefly and clearly. We heard footsteps descending the stair, and the door opened to reveal a very tall athletic figure. His huge square beard was dark red, his half-shut eyes green and very bright, his thick eyebrows looked unfriendly, menacing even; though his face was worn and tired. He wore a large white turban and a short touloup of sheepskin, unbuttoned, over a green beshmet; his shoes were soft leather. He greeted us courteously, but unsmiling. The presentations began; he shook hands with each of us. Then, still silent, he seated himself on the divan. "Imam wishes you to sit," said Gramoff. Only then, I noticed several Tartars who had entered behind him, dressed in very rich tcherkesskas, fine weapons and tall papakhs, who ranged themselves each side of him, standing rigidly. The Imam addressed a few words to each of us. Conversation was laboured. When my turn came, I said that my friends envied me my chance to meet Shamyl. The Imam's face lit up with a strange, sad smile: he asked me where I came from. "Tchembar," I replied, "near to Lermontov's grave."

' "Lermontov? I have heard of him: he wrote of my Caucasus," he said (remembering, perhaps, how the poet, transported by patriotic fervour, had predicted the conquered Caucasians would come to say, proudly, "We may truly be slaves—but enslaved by Russia,—Ruler of the Universe").

'When it was Lieutenant Orloff's turn, Shamyl asked him for what he had been given the St. George's Cross.

' "For storming the aôul of Kitouri, where we captured the Naib Magomoi," was the swaggering reply.'

Once more, it was apparent that Shamyl, the tired, ageing captive, could still, when he chose, become the dread Imam. His whole face darkened to a harsh scowl, as he sprang to his feet with that same force of a steel spring uncoiling that had been remarked so many years ago at his meeting with Klugenau. 'His suite which, until now, had stood like statues, began to shift uneasily. . . . A shiver ran through them, and I saw Runovsky grow pale', writes Zaharin. 'Shamyl repeated, twice, a sentence in which the name of Magamoi recurred. Gramoff spoke: "Imam says Naib Magamoi was only taken when he was dead. What you say is false. No Naib ever surrendered."

'Shamyl dismissed the audience, looking through us. As he stalked out, Runovsky attacked Orloff. "How *could* you say such a thing to Shamyl? How *dared* you?" Orloff tried to wriggle out, citing dispatches of the engagement which, to make the action seem more glorious, reported that the Naib had been taken prisoner. Only later, when the official reports were published, was it proved that Magamoi had been found dead in a tower which he had defended to his last breath.'

33

An End

When Allah hath ordained a creature to die in a particular place, he causeth his wants to direct him to that place. MAHOMMED

The years of exile slipped by, and the strange household became part of Kalouga's daily life, sometimes surprisingly adapted to the West, and sometimes uncompromisingly Asiatic. Shamyl's absolute acceptance of his life puzzled Runovsky, who found no traces of bitterness or regret in the Imam's attitude. Perhaps he believed the spirit in which he accepted defeat was also a means of self-purification, of sacrifice to Allah, like any of his battles. It was also his fate—Mektoub—and he accepted it, unquestioningly, as he accepted the bad climate, or some ill-prepared dish. When, on one occasion, the food being thoroughly unappetizing, Runovsky sent for the cook and complained, Shamyl told him it was a sin to complain. Runovsky countered that it was a sin to cook so badly.

'Yes,' replied Shamyl: 'but for that, God will punish him. In the Book it is written that man must never show displeasure at anything whatever. . . . Therefore I am generally satisfied. I have few wants, and, when necessary, can always forget my habits—even the habits of a lifetime,' he added, looking around the European dining-room. Runovsky did not remind him that he used to flog and punish his people for the slightest misdemeanours and travel about his realm accompanied by an executioner.

Recalling the ruthless manner in which he had suppressed the Tadbourtzi tribes (who were, in fact, the dregs of the Caucasus, an unprincipled, savage and dishonest lot) Shamyl said: 'I was cruel and merciless—but you would have been the same. You Russians should thank me, for having, in small measure, tamed them. Before Allah, I am not ashamed to answer for what I did to those robbers and murderers.'

But once, when he was reminded of the terrible conditions in which he had often kept his Russian prisoners, half-naked and in pits, he looked around the comfortable room, the well-stocked dining-table, and sighed: 'I knew no better, then,' he replied. When they reminded him of twenty-two prisoners who had tried to escape, being put to death, he replied: '*We* did not kill them; it was Prince Voronzov who killed them by planning their rescue. In war, prisoners cannot be permitted to escape.'

And so, withdrawing ever farther into a world of prayer and meditation, Shamyl seemed content. He neither intrigued, nor repined—a lesson to dethroned rulers everywhere. When they asked him if he regretted leaving the Caucasus, he replied: 'The Caucasus is now here, in Kalouga.' All the same, he remained humble at heart, signing his letters *the serf of Allah.*

The town had become accustomed to the little mosque, half-hidden among the trees and shrubs of the garden; no one now remarked the monotonous chanted prayers issuing from the small barred windows, at dawn and noon and sunset, or at the rising of each new moon, the long-drawn-out, strange, yelping cries of the women's prayers. No one turned round to stare any more when the wives, desperately emancipated, drove about, still heavily veiled, but shopping, or walking beside the river, in the pale sunshine of a northern summer. The younger men had at last followed Hadji's lead and become familiar figures strolling through the streets and attending all the parties they could. Even the farouche Khazi Mahommed had been partially won over, though he never learned to speak more than broken Russian. All of them began now to crave latitude, though it was still necessary to conceal their longings from Shamyl's strict eye. His life of violence and achievement was over; he could not understand how bitterly the exile and tiny horizons weighed on the younger members of his household. His own horizons were limitless, for he was already turning towards another world. But for his sons and Naibs it was a life of frustration and monotony. Inactivity, after the ferocious pace of their former life; calls instead of raids; drives instead of the wild gallops they had known; a little shooting in season—a partridge or hare—after the lifetime of gun-fire and cold steel they had savoured.

Even the civilization they found so alluring was, in the end, but another cage. The religious observances and meditations which pre-occupied Shamyl no longer held them, and they lived dispossessed, in a void, where no force, reality, or conviction remained—a temperate zone—where only their complete devotion to Shamyl still counted. Sometimes they escaped, for a few hours, to the Sobranié, or Club, where the wild strains of the lesghinka resounded as the Naibs performed their traditional dances. But when Ramadan arrived, all of them willingly forswore these small distractions, to pore over the Book, passing their days and nights in prayer and fasting, and in ritual observances led by Shamyl, who was still their Prophet, Allah's Shadow on

Earth, for whom they would all have died, in battle, as in fact they were dying, by inches, sharing his kind captivity.

He was adamant in his refusal of all luxury. When the Tzar presented him with a solid gold tea-service, he sent it away. But Mahommed Sheffi was seduced by its glory, and decided to keep it for his own use, concealed in his room. Khazi Mahommed, who stood beside his father in all things, was profoundly shocked at this display of filial disobedience and corruption. After a struggle of conscience, he told the Imam. Shamyl ordered Sheffi to bring him the tea-set, and, still terrible in his wrath, ground the soft gold to pieces beneath his feet. The women, too, sometimes showed signs of corruption. In secret, they had obtained some lengths of satin and were busy concocting new dresses for a forthcoming Moslem celebration. Unfortunately they too were discovered. The Imam ripped the finery into shreds with his own kindjal. 'None of my women shall wear satin until every woman in every aôul of Daghestan can do likewise,' he said.

There were still occasions when Shamyl emerged from his meditations to take part in the Russian scene. A number of distinguished visitors were regularly received, 'Shamyl always adapting his conversation to the interests or nature of his visitor,' notes Runovsky. Festivals such as Easter or Christmas delighted him: he had wished to attend Mass at the Orthodox cathedral, but the clergy had been unco-operative. *No one* might enter the church wearing a hat—and to them, a turban was such. Since Shamyl's faith denied him the right to remove the turban, the project had to be dropped. But more secular manifestation, Easter rabbits, and the gaily coloured, painted eggs of Russian tradition entranced him. He said the red ones tasted best, but made quite a collection of all kinds, lining them up on the little card-table, and turning them over, admiring the crude stencilled patterns with childish wonder, playing with them long after spring had given place to summer. Sometimes he was invited to attend manœuvres, or official celebrations in Moscow or St. Petersburg. The Tzar was ever conscious of his responsibilities towards his illustrious captive, always treating him as an honoured guest, and showering him with delicate attentions as if he could never make up to him for the loss of his liberty. When he learned that the Imam would not accept luxuries such as the gold tea-set, he arranged that the finest, hand-embroidered household linen should replace the existing things at Kalouga. Every piece was embroidered with the Imam's initials. And whenever Shamyl and his sons came to dine at the Winter Palace, the Tzar was always careful to order a brand-new service of both cutlery and china, so that his guests need not fear defilement by touching objects formerly used by Infidels. Once, carried away by Shamyl's interest in Sulieman the Magnificent's sword, displayed in a museum, the Tzar seized it off the wall, presented it to his mysterious and wonderful friend, and waved aside all the protests of the outraged curator. This time, Shamyl accepted the present happily, though it must have seemed a poor exchange for that sword he had surrendered to Bariatinsky.

At the wedding of the Tzarievitch to the Princess Dagmar of Denmark in 1866, Shamyl's noble bearing was much remarked. The bride had bent to kiss his hand; she was radiant, in lace and jewels, and Shamyl had at once saluted her with a graceful verse, '*Eyouh El Dagmar! Rodat el anwar!*' in which he likened her to a garden of radiant delights. The Tzar was particularly pleased, and made a great deal of it to the foreign embassies and visiting dignitaries. He always found the Imam irresistible. It was at this wedding that Shamyl made his famous speech ending:

> Let everyone know this: to the end of his days, the old Shamyl will regret that he is not able to live again thus to dedicate his whole life to the service of the White Tzar.

Was this hypocrisy, or was it merely an Oriental figure of speech— and only meant to be taken as such? Given his life again would he have accepted Russian domination? This is entirely improbable, and unlike any facet of his character, fighting as he did, for thirty years, for the liberty of his land. But we must take his words as an expression of his genuine gratitude for the Tzar's maganimity; also, perhaps, his wish to stress, in terms understandable to the West, that no bitterness remained, that whatever he may have once felt towards the Giaours,—his personal liking for both the Tzar and Bariatinsky was unshakable.

Shamyl had been both grieved and bewildered by the fact that scandal could overthrow so great a figure as Bariatinsky. Whereas Voronzov had always been able to steer between the shoals of private passions and public life, Bariatinsky was less astute. His liaison with Madame Davidova had lasted a number of years, in a most convenient atmosphere of harmony, abetted by her husband's complacence. Yet suddenly, in 1861 after years of silence, Colonel Davidov instituted divorce proceedings against his wife, named the Viceroy as co-respondent, and challenged him to a duel. But the Viceroy, embodying the Emperor, could neither accept the challenge, nor be cited as a co-respondent, and was forced to resign.

The scandal shook even the easy-going Court of Alexander II; nor could the Tzar avert the catastrophe of Bariatinsky's departure. Accompanied by his mistress, he left Tiflis in a rather furtive manner by night. Supposedly, he went alone to a German spa. 'Ill-health', said the newspapers, but everyone knew the truth. 'La Maréchale', as Madame Davidova was dubbed, was not liked in Tiflis. She had been too beautiful, too powerful, for too long. But lately her influence over the

Prince had begun to decline: he was finding romantic interests else-where. Then, suddenly, the scandal broke, and forced his hand. I have sometimes wondered if the Colonel's repudiation of the liaison he so long tolerated was not devotion to his wife's interests. Perhaps he and Madame Davidova had decided on it together, a piece of strategy which quite out-manœuvred the Field-Marshal, whose newer conquests had now to be abandoned, leaving Madame Davidova in sole possession.

Prince Bariatinsky often invited Shamyl and his sons to visit him in Moscow, or on his estates at Ivanovskoye, and they accepted joyfully. 'Our Field-Marshal' they called him with touching pride. It was to whom they had surrendered. Only he had been worthy of Shamyl's sword. When Bariatinsky had left the Caucasus he had spent much time at Ivanovskoye. Shamyl had originally been placed in Bariatinsky's custody, although as long as the Field-Marshal had been in the Caucasus their meetings were dependent upon Bariatinsky's visits to Moscow or St. Petersburg. But Kalouga was only a few days' ride from Ivanovskoye. In a new wing added to the old classically-porticoed white house, a suite of rooms was always kept ready for the Imam's frequent visits. The rooms were elegantly furnished in the pale golden birchwood pieces—*le style Empire* then so typical of the fine Russian houses. The windows of Shamyl's suite overlooked a vast park and a lake. Here the two Caucasian giants walked together by the hour, happy to recapture their heroic past, discussing the techniques and strategies of Caucasian warfare in an atmosphere of mutual esteem.

Mahommed Sheffi wrote to friends in Temir-Khan-Shura, describing the marvels of Russian life in rhapsodic terms: 'In Moscow, I saw many wonderful things such as my late brother Djemmal-Eddin used to recount, but which I could never quite believe. One must know science to describe them. I had better be silent: but if only Allah fulfils my wish to learn properly, I shall be able to tell you of these things in the fullness of time.' It was remarked that Khazi Mahommed still re-mained rather withdrawn during these visits. He had never arrived at his father's state of fatalism, nor could he adjust with such humility. For him, defeat in battle still rankled as a personal failure. He was particularly embittered, about this time, by the loss of the adored Kherimat. The climate had brought on galloping consumption, and she died in his arms; his last and dearest treasure.

His passionate love for her was never reciprocated. By nature she was fickle and calculating. It had been good to marry the Imam's heir, ruler of Karaty, but later, when she was sequestered in the provinces, neither a free Russian woman nor a Caucasian Khanum, his love had not been enough: she grew restive and tried to solace herself with dangerous flirtations among the young Naibs. Perhaps it was as well she died before the thrust of a kindjal avenged her husband's honour.

No veneer of civilization would have restrained the drama that must have followed, had she continued on her wanton way.

A year later, Nafisette, Shamyl's favourite daughter, also died of consumption. One by one, the less robust members of the household were succumbing to their northern exile. Some were buried in Kalouga, but the bodies of both Nafisette and Kherimat were sent back to the Caucasus, to lie among the mountains, at Ghimri, where the people wept, saying: 'It was not thus we imagined Shamyl's family would return among us.' Of the thirty-four persons who made up Shamyl's entourage over the eleven years of his captivity, seventeen died, victims of the climate, among whom were included the babies who were either still-born, or died in infancy. However, a son Mahommed Kâmil, was born to Zaïdate. The photographs show us a costive-looking little creature, in a rather Fauntleroy outfit: no doubt he was the adored Benjamin of the household. Najavat, the crippled, had been miraculously cured by the Russian doctors. 'A djinn came to see her, put her to sleep; and lo, without pain, her twisted legs were straightened', wrote Abdurrahim. The Mollah Jamul u'din had made the long journey from the Caucasus to Kalouga, alarmed at local reports that Shamyl was kept in terrible conditions, and even tortured. The devoted old man decided to share his sufferings; but on seeing the agreeable nature of the Imam's captivity, he returned to the mountains reassured, and rather bewildered by all he had seen.

II

After Kherimat's death, Khazi Mahommed had been inconsolable; and developing consumption himself, seemed about to die. But Shamyl still thought along patriarchal lines. Neither exile, grief, nor illness must be allowed to destroy the family. There must be more sons. Khazi Mahommed was sent to the Crimea to regain his health, so that he could marry again.

At first he had refused; he still raged for the lost Kherimat. But at last he gave way, on one condition: he would marry Kistaman, the daughter of Daoudilaou of Tchokh, or no one. He reminded his father of the injustice done to Daoudilaou his friend, so long ago, when he had been exiled to 'the aôul without sun'. This marriage, he said, would at last right the wrong, would clear forever the doubts which still surrounded Daoudilaou's name. Perhaps, too, Khazi Mahommed had not forgotten the sharp-tongued little creature whose name he had found so ugly.

Messengers were sent to Tchokh, demanding Kistaman's hand, and her father was overjoyed. Not so his daughter. She refused, furiously, reminding her father of their cruel exile, the years of injustice. But at last her father persuaded her: it would clear his name, and then, he reminded her, it was due to Khazi Mahommed's intervention that they were at last released. But perhaps Kistaman, too, had not forgotten the handsome young Naib of Karaty. She made the long journey to Kalouga accompanied by her young brother, Mahommed Fazil, and in February 1863 married Khazi Mahommed, whom she loved consumingly for the rest of her days. He re-named her Habibette—the beloved.

She was not beautiful, but her grace and charm and brilliant mind won over everyone who knew her. Shamyl loved her from the first. She was very devout, and sometimes told him to his face that it was sacrilegious to call himself Allah's Second Prophet on Earth. Not only the family, but the Imperial family and the Bariatinskys fell under her spell. 'La Maréchale' sent the most affectionate letters and diamond bracelets to 'dear Princess Shamyl'. The Field-Marshal arranged for her brother to be placed in a military academy at St. Petersburg; the Tzarina showered her with splendid gifts, worldly delights. . . . Habibette preferred to study languages (she spoke six) and to write verses. The jewels were put away: when the Tzarina gave her one of her favourite necklaces, five rows of enormous amethysts and pearls, she hung it, bauble-wise, over the cradle of her baby daughter, Nafisette, who was born in 1864. Gradually, Habibette's presence came to transform Khazi Mahommed, and he seemed almost serene in his exile, forgetting, or putting away, the bitter memories of defeat and death.

III

In 1866, Shamyl, both his elder sons, and the Naib Hadji Harito and Abdurrahman took the oath of allegiance to the Tzar. The ceremony took place in the Salle de Noblesse at Kalouga before a large gathering. Shamyl had not been asked, or expected, to do this, but it had long been his wish to prove his loyalty and devotion to the man whom he had come to regard as his true friend. Khazi Mahommed had not wanted to take the oath, but as long as his father lived he followed him in all things. In 1862, Mahommed Sheffi (who had never been able to resist the fascination of everything Russian, particularly the dashing uniforms worn by the Lancer regiments to which his brother Djemmal-Eddin had belonged) was accepted into the Russian army. It was a remarkable gauge of the Tzar's faith in his total conversion that, in 1865, he was sent back to the Caucasus to select 'Tartar' cavalry for the Tzar's squadron of Life-Guards. The tribes descended from the mountains *en masse*, when they learned that Shamyl's son had come back among them. However, Sheffi refused to treat with them, and having chosen the 'Tartar' troops, he returned north, to become one of the Imperial Escort.

One of the aspects of Russian army life which most impressed British military observers at this time, was the absolute equality with which the Asiatics were incorporated into the army. As Russia's Asiatic conquests increased, so more and more 'Tartars' were recruited—both soldiers of the line and princes and khans; 'Mohammedan and Christian officers are intermingled, the senior commanding the junior in every case, and no limit being placed on the promotion of the Mussulman soldier. This Russian system differs greatly from that of the Indian army, in so much as, while in our army no native can command a European, in the Russian no distinction whatever is made.' The writer goes on to say that this is, however, a very safe measure, since in the Army of the South, Moslem troops were in a proportion of five to fifty, whereas in India, the European was as one in a thousand to the population.

Shamyl was living in Russia at a time when great administrative changes were taking place. The Manifesto of Emancipation (of the Serfs) was published in February 1861 (the year in which Civil War broke out in America, over the same issue). Although to Shamyl everything Russian seemed marvellous, he was particularly interested in the electoral system. He was able to observe at close quarters the workings of the Zemstvo (local administrative bodies formed to conduct regional affairs) spending whole days, sitting cross-legged on the platform, flanked as usual by the impassive Naibs in their effigy-like poses, the interpreter working feverishly to keep them abreast of each speech. The system of balloting was incomprehensible to Shamyl; he could not believe it indicated the people's true wishes, and he examined the ballot-boxes very carefully, perhaps recalling the conjurer's trickeries.

Among his new Russian friends, he was especially attached to the Tschukin family, and when it seemed likely that Feodor Tschukin would be elected Marshal of Nobility for the district, Shamyl became very anxious on his behalf. He could scarcely contain himself during the balloting, going from voter to voter, fixing each man with his compelling gaze, as if trying to force them to vote for his friend. No doubt he would have preferred to have settled it quickly at the point of a kindjal. Like Hadji, he still found the restraints of civilization puzzling at times.

It had been this same Tschukin family with whom Djemmal-Eddin lived during his first years as a hostage. The eldest son had been his closest friend, and later they were in the same regiment together. The family nianyia was that same kind peasant woman who had loved and cared for the little boy, and taught him his first words of Russian. Sometimes she came to call on Shamyl, stumping up the stairs to the reception-room, to share a glass of tea with the majestic Imam, her round, red-apple face puckered in grief, as they talked together of their lost boy. Tschukin often brought officers who had known Djemmal-Eddin well to visit Shamyl; and when they left, he would sit, staring that curious inward-turning gaze, looking back at emptiness and remorse. One day Runovsky asked him what was his considered opinion of Russia, now that he had seen the biggest cities, and lived among the people for several years.

'Now I know why my son died,' he replied. The laconic remark was accompanied by a look of infinite melancholy, as if he knew himself to blame for Djemmal-Eddin's death.

As long as Runovsky remained, the exiles were loved and spared every possible humiliation or misunderstanding. But in 1862, the dreaded separation came, and 'Our Dear' was replaced by a man whose very presence poisoned the air. Colonel Przhetzlavski, the new adjutant, was of Polish origin, intriguing, cruel and malicious, and how he came to be appointed cannot be explained, unless it was through the machinations of Shamyl's enemies at Court, or in the War Ministry, who were jealous of the favours shown him by the Emperor. He must have had many enemies scattered throughout Russia; an escaped prisoner, perhaps, or the father of an officer who had died in the Murid prison pits, who was vowed to vengeance and now saw his chance: but what remains inexplicable is that the Tzar was unaware of the persecutions Shamyl endured for so long.

In every way Przhetzlavski sought to destroy Shamyl's peace of mind. He patronized him, taunted him, restricted him, interfered with the administration of the household, spied on the family, offended the women, was harsh with the Tartar servants, and at last made so much mischief by his allegations and calumnies, that some of the Kalougans who had formerly showed themselves all friendliness towards the Imam now boycotted him. The Pole's first overt act of hostility was when Shamyl refused to sign, or authorize a manuscript which Przhetlavski had concocted, part translation and part falsification, on the three great Imams of Daghestan: Khazi Mollah, Hamzad Beg and Shamyl, together with an interpretation of the Murid doctrines. Shamyl found this document inaccurate and in bad taste, and repudiated it. From that moment on, Przhetzlavski was actuated by a furious personal spite, never missing an occasion to vent his fury on the defenceless exiles. In his reports to the War Ministry, he insisted that Shamyl was never satisfied with his treatment, and grumbled incessantly over the insufficiency of his allowance. He also condemned the Imam for underpaying the domestics, and hoarding: an absurd statement, since Shamyl was quite unaware of the value of money, leaving all transactions to Hadjio, and was, in any case, of a nature that never counted the cost—in effort, time, or money.

Shamyl bore these persecutions uncomplaining for two years, never speaking of them, even to Bariatinsky; but at last he was unable to endure them any more, he applied to the Governor of Kalouga to arrange for a new adjutant to be appointed. Although a Lieutenant Simenov was sent, he had no sooner reached Kalouga than, by means of some mysterious pressure applied by Przhetzlavski, he returned to St. Petersburg with a letter, purporting to be from Shamyl, asking for Przhetlavski to remain. For two more years the hateful presence brooded over the house, at one point involving Shamyl in a most delicate matter of Russo-Polish politics. Like all Poles, Przhetzlavski was adept at turning everything to political account. After the suppression of the Polish risings in 1863, he often spoke to Shamyl of the sufferings of the mutineers, trying to rouse the Imam's sympathies, describing in vivid colours the persecutions to which they were subjected by the Russians. Knowing on what good terms Shamyl stood with Alexander II, he suggested that the Tzar was not aware of the true situation and that it would be of great service to both the wretched Poles, and the Tzar himself, if Shamyl would intercede for them.

Shamyl remained silent and refused to commit himself. But Przhetzlavski returned to the attack with a most impertinent letter to the Tzar, written in Shamyl's name, which he asked the Imam to sign; there were two texts, one in Russian, the other in Arabic. Shamyl read the latter, frowning ominously:

'Your Majesty has treated Daghestan and others mildly. But when it comes to the Poles, they are cruelly abused. I, Shamyl, beseech your Majesty to show them the clemency you showed the Caucasians.'

Shamyl spoke politely, but with suppressed anger. 'I beg you, Colonel, not to come to me with this matter. I would not dare to trouble the Tzar over something which does not concern me.' When Przhetlavski saw that Shamyl was adamant, he became alarmed, and extracted a promise that the Imam would never speak of the letter to anyone. Shamyl kept his word, and it was only thirty years later that Mahommed Sheffi told the whole story to Zaharin, from whose book this account is taken.

The Pole, being unable to coerce Shamyl, now began to persecute him systematically, distorting his every move, accusing him of intriguing against Russia; endeavouring to have him removed to Vyatka, in Siberia, and, when Shamyl applied for permission to make a pilgrimage to Mecca, even insinuating that he was preparing a coup in the Near East.

There had been a mass exodus of the Tcherkess peoples to Turkey in 1864, when they had been finally overwhelmed by the weight of Russian arms. For the five years following Shamyl's submission they had continued their own opposition to Russia, for they had been considerably aided by both the Sultan and foreign powers, whose agents swarmed about the coastal areas to such a degree that General Raievsky, commanding the Russian forces, ordered his decrees and manifestos to be circulated in French as well as Russian and Arabic, to avoid any possible misunderstandings. The wars, revolts and intrigues of the Tcherkess are a study in themselves, and cannot occupy here the space they merit. Suffice it to say that having fought apart from Shamyl, and never, after the earlier years of his struggle, and Mahommed Emin's ambiguous leadership, been closely allied to him, they too were at last outnumbered, betrayed and crushed.

Mahommed Emin had continued his treacheries, passing over to the Russians, during one of the most critical battles, to hand over Circassian military secrets. For this he was rewarded by a handsome pension, and was dispatched for safety to Turkey, living under his new friends' protection, in the Russian Embassy. But he was hunted down by the Circassians, determined on vengeance, and was forced to live hidden in the Anatolian hinterland for many years, until, having lost his mind, he was of no more account.

When the Russians finally crushed, and occupied Circassia, the tribes fled to Turkey, where the Sultan offered them asylum. Some of the first had put to sea in mahones (cynically provided by the Russian authorities) which proved unseaworthy, and sank while still in sight of the Circassian coast. The Sultan was horror-struck, and saying 'Their elder brothers are my elder brothers, and their younger brothers my younger brothers' he now provided a fleet to take off his co-religionists, and so the great exodus began.

More than three hundred thousand are said to have left their native land, and as each man departed, he fired his gun three times, as a farewell salute to the mountains, while the great peaks gave back the shots in rolling, thunderous echoes.

* * *

'Przhetzlavski never allowed Shamyl to forget he was a captive', wrote Zaharin, reminding his readers that once a Moslem is grateful, nothing will shake his loyalty. Shamyl remained unswerving in his feelings towards Alexander II—his captor, but his friend too—and if to be loyal meant enduring Przhetzlavski, then he would do so. He would ask no favours, nor bother the Tzar with his own troubles.

It was probably due to Przhetzlavski's calumnies that in 1868 the Tzar refused Shamyl's request to go to Mecca, for he replied that at present conditions in the Caucasus were too unsettled (in fact, the Imam was still regarded as a potential danger). Shamyl wrote to

Bariatinsky: 'I am ashamed before you and his Imperial Majesty, and regret having spoken of my desire, which, truly, is only the desire of every pious Moslem. I would not have raised the matter, had I known the Caucasus was still not completely pacified.' Being sure of his own loyalty, he could not imagine others might doubt him. In 1869, his old enemy Daniel Beg had been pensioned off, and allowed to settle in Turkey. Yet Shamyl was still refused Mecca. Poor Pilgrim of Allah! His life was draining away in bitterness. Those who saw him at this time describe him as having aged terribly, his face livid, his breath coming in short gasps. Sometimes the old wounds still troubled him. He was becoming noticeably weaker, and suffered recurrent fainting fits, to which he had always been subject, but which once he had used to further his miraculous legend, and which now he merely accepted as an infirmity rather than a divine visitation. Runovsky diagnosed them as part cataleptic, part nervous exhaustion. . . . 'It is in the mountains that the eagles dwell', and in the valleys that they die.

The entire household was now suffering from homesickness. They craved the wind of freedom, the air from the mountains. The Murids had become gloomy and liverish; the women were wasting away. Sometimes they would wander to the bluffs above the Oka, and sit there for hours, gazing out over the fields to the horizon, straining their eyes for the mountains they would never see again. The ceaseless dinning of church bells depressed them. Ding-dong, sounded the Giaour bells, infinitely melancholy to the captives. Shamyl tried to comfort them. 'They say Hakkân—Hakkâ—From God—to God!' he said, and the household were sustained by the thought that, perhaps, God was here, in Kalouga, too. But provincial life was suffocating them; everything was on so small a scale. Orel, Tula, Koursk, Jmérinka. . . . Little townships, tiny stations where railway lines branched off to smaller townlets; to infinity. . . . But who went there, for what purpose? Who lived there, was snowed up there . . . died there? For what—for whom? Thus the household; yet knowing that for them Shamyl's presence would always be reason enough, and that no exile could be so harsh as separation from him.

Only Hadji-Harito remained unchanged, gay, saucy, more dashing and elegant than ever, preoccupied with his amorous conquests and devising ways to maintain the giddy round he enjoyed, without displeasing Shamyl. Being a Murid, however, he had to make some show of observing the strict rulings of the Shariat. While Shamyl was growing more and more preoccupied by thoughts of another world, Hadji was increasingly obsessed by this one, and ever on the look-out for a means to justify his social cravings. He would dwell on the wonderful warmth of the Kalougans, and on their basically harmless custom of calling on each other in the evenings—especially on fête days. 'If we refuse to go,'

he would say, 'we should be sowing suspicion that we scorn them—
that we do not value their golden hearts.' Of course, he continued, they
understood that the Imam was in ill-health—they made exceptions for
those who were genuinely indisposed. All the same, it might be more
civil if he, Hadji, were to go and present the Imam's apologies in
person. And Shamyl, anxious to give no cause for offence to such
kindly neighbours, agreed. And thus, on the appointed night, Hadji
would set out, reeking of Rose de Bengale, a debonair figure, his
copper watch-chain now rarefied to gold, and wearing a ring composed
of a heart pierced by an arrow. At which the rest of the Murids looked
censorious, or envious, according to their temperaments.

Shamyl continued to dissemble his loathing of Przhetzlavski, though
whenever he saw him, his face contracted and he turned away. At last
he formally requested the Governor of Kalouga to hear his complaints
before a tribunal: the Governor, the Vice-Governor, the Marshal of
Nobility, and Major-General Chichagov, were assembled to hear the
charges. Shamyl was categoric in his repudiation of all Przhetzlavski's
calumnies. But he kept his word, and never told of the letter regarding
Polish affairs. He had spoken with restraint and dignity; but at last his
whole fury exploded. Once again, Shamyl, Prophet and Imam, the
Lion of Daghestan, rose up before them, in all his dark force, 'flames
darting from his eyes' . . . 'When I see him, my sight is blurred, blood
rushes to my head, I feel I shall kill him—or myself. This man appears
before me as an evil spirit, who prevents me from praying, and who
haunts my house, sowing discord among my family. Now that I am old,
my only desire is to lead a monastic life and to approach God worthily.
I do not want to feel hatred for any man. And I am grieved when he
blackens me before the people of Kalouga, who were my friends, and
who now visit me seldom, although my doors are always open to them.
I love the Tzar; I have never complained; if such letters exist, then they
have been forged! I ask, in justice, that this man be removed before
I die.'

Przhetzlavski was dismissed, in ignominy, to be replaced by Major-
General Chichagov, an appointment which delighted both the Caucasian household and the Chichagov family. From 1866 until 1869, when
Chichagov died, Shamyl lived in harmony with his new guardian.
Sometimes he would arrive at his house, to spend half the night there,
talking. 'In spite of eighteen sword thrusts,' says Madame Chichagova,
'his carriage was superb—like that of some demi-god, at once majestic
and graceful.'

But his health was failing fast; he would lie on cushions spread beside
the stove, his face drawn, but smiling, as he played with the Chichagov
babies. When the moon rose, he would leave them, shutting himself in
the General's study, where he would pray, kneeling on a white sheet,

which was always kept ready for him. Then he would return to take up the conversation again. He would discuss astronomy with the General, or ask him to explain the atlas; or he would talk of old battles, and Caucasian legends; of the prophecy that one day a great power would arise in the West—to humble the Padishah of Moscow. . . . And another, which holds that the Ottoman Empire will at last be brought to dust by a power 'from beyond the north wind'. . . Of the pre-existence of souls. According to Ayishah, Mahommed stated that souls, before they were united with bodies, were like assembled armies, waiting to be dispersed and sent into the bodies of mankind.

We have known Shamyl only as a man of action—of few words: yet now the time for action was over, and he sometimes spoke at length, recounting his wonderful life, while Madame Chichagova listened spell-bound—and forgot to write most of it down. However, she had long conversations with the wives, which followed more accepted lines: babies, husbands. . . . On the subject of polygamy Madame Chichagova was very severe.

'We Christians think it quite impossible for a man to love several women at once,' she said. At which Zaïdate sighed longingly, saying: 'How fortunate you are to be the only wife.' But Shouanete took up the attack: 'I too was once a Christian,' she said. 'I know that Christian husbands do have several wives—only secret ones.'

However, Madame Chichagova had the last word. 'If that were true,' she said indignantly, 'we should have no happy marriages . . . which is *not* so.' And the wives did not pursue the delicate subject further.

When Major-General Chichagov died suddenly, in 1869, Shamyl was the first to reach the widow's side, trying to console and sustain her. 'He came and sat with me,' she writes, 'sharing my grief, weeping with me.' 'Now we have lost everything,' he said, thinking of the seventeen whom death had stolen from him: his daughter, babies, followers, servants, all were dying; Kalouga had become a graveyard.

In October he left for Kiev. Bariatinsky, who watched over his old enemy from afar, obtained permission for him to move south. There, for a few months, amid the gold-starred domes of the monasteries, 'the Jerusalem of Russia', and under radiant southern skies, the household regained something of their health and spirits. But it was only a last interlude. Shamyl knew he had not much longer to live. In March 1870 he obtained the Tzar's permission to go to Mecca. He was seventy-four, and had written explaining that he had a premonition of death. Even so, the authorities had been exceptionally strict, and refused to allow either Khazi Mahommed or Mahommed Sheffi to accompany him.

Hadji-Harito, although the most devoted of followers, decided against going to Mecca. It was not that he chose to linger among the seductions of Kalouga, but he yearned increasingly for the Caucasus. When the Russians offered him the rulership (under the Viceroy) of the district of Ountkratl, he accepted, packed his silk shirts and gewgaws, and shaking off the clinging white arms of his Kalougan conquests, returned to his homeland.

And so, surrounded by his women and children and the remaining Naibs, Shamyl set out on his pilgrimage.

IV

They had skirted the Caucasus, embarking at Anapa for Constantinople. Shamyl had been childishly pleased to send a farewell telegram 'by drawn thread' as he described the wires, to friends at Temir-Khan-Shura. It would take two hours to get there, they told him. But he remembered how the caravans had taken two months and marvelled. On arrival at Constantinople enormous crowds thronged the water-front, prostrating themselves, or cheering wildly, giving him a royal welcome. The Russian Embassy invited the party to stay there, but Shamyl refused, saying that on Turkish soil he was the guest of the Padishah. The Sultan Abdul Aziz received him in great state, and in the shimmering pearl-encrusted halls of Dolmabagtche the Sublime Porte bowed low before Allah's Second Prophet on Earth, while the crowds followed him wherever he went, kissing the ground he had trodden on his way to the mosque.

The Sultan offered him a choice of palaces, but none of these were acceptable to his austere tastes. How much more deeply the ageing warrior must have felt his exile, here, among the perfumed alcoves and voluptuous corruption of the Osmanli Court, than among the hardy Russians at Kalouga. Faith apart, the tenor of life at the Porte was wholly alien to him. The Sultan had feared Shamyl, as one whose overwhelming popularity might threaten the Osmanli throne. 'They told me you were a bandit,' he said. 'No more than you,' replied Shamyl, with a sly smile, and asked him why his often-promised aid had never materialized. All the same, the Sultan had been quick to profit by the Imam's presence, asking him to go to Cairo, to mediate in a bitter dispute between Turkey and Egypt. Shamyl undertook this mission, and brought it to a triumphant conclusion. His argument, that the Giaours would rejoice at dissension between the Faithful carried the day. On the way back, there had been one of those dramatic moments whereby the legend of Shamyl's mysterious powers were always fostered. A fearful storm had broken, and the ship seemed lost. Shamyl (not insensible to such a role, perhaps) promised to calm the tempest. He wrote some cabbalistic letters on a piece of paper, pronounced a few words, and flung the paper into the raging seas, which almost immediately subsided.

During Shamyl's absence, his family had waited in the big house at Koska, in the aristocratic Akserai quarter, which Shamyl had accepted from the Sultan. It was an old, fifty-roomed Turkish house, shaded by gigantic plane trees and with its own mosque; a factor which had decided Shamyl in its favour. A constant flow of Caucasian exiles, gathered in the vast selamlik, recalling their mountains and the days of battle. Their mournful chants came to be handed down among Shamyl's descendants, cradle songs, by which each new child was lulled.

> O mountains of Gounib, O soldiers of Shamyl,
> Shamyl's citadel was full of warriors,
> Yet it has fallen, fallen forever . . .

When Shamyl returned, the whole caravanserai moved eastwards, to Mecca. Here, in the holiest of cities, sacred to the glory of the Prophet, Shamyl's legend and magnetism was such that when he appeared, it was as if a mighty force passed through the streets, drawing all the people to him. When he went to pray, the mosques became so overcrowded that at last the Turkish police (Mecca being under the jurisdiction of the Porte) could not control the crowds and at last allotted Shamyl special hours for his devotions, behind locked doors, or at night, while most of the Faithful slept.

So the last months of his life were spent, as he wished, in prayer. He was far from the mountains, but he was no longer an exile. The black stone of the Qua'abah was the heart and soul of Moslem belief: Mecca was a province of paradise, the pilgrimage and rituals the fulfilment and crown to his whole life of high endeavour. The battle was done; the pilgrimage nearing its end. Allah's Prophet upon Earth was nearing home.

From Mecca Shamyl wrote to the Grand Duke Michael, then Viceroy of the Caucasus:

> So, at last I am come to the place for which I yearned, and I shall ever bless you for your aid. Now I suffer a number of illnesses, and lie abed. I believe I shall soon leave this world. Therefore I humbly ask your Imperial Highness to take care of my family and my Murids, showing them the kindness you have always shown me. I rejoice that you are granting that my sons may come to me here, and have given them money for the journey. Your benevolence is that of God towards the Prophet Job. I can never repay you: I can only tell you, once more, of my profound gratitude. May Allah protect you always.
> [He signed himself] 'the ill and very ancient pilgrim, Shamyl'.

Towards the end of 1870 his strength was failing rapidly. He had left

Mecca for El Medina, the 'thrice holy city of the Blessed Valley', 'the beautiful, the green', sacred to the Prophet, where he had lived and prayed and died. His burial place, and that of his family, is in the cemetery of Djánet El Bakir, hard by. And, as if Nature herself wished to render homage to the Prophet, the black basalt rocks have given place to groves of date palms where doves flash through the dappled shade, and streams water orchards of apricots and pomegranate. Amid this green and pleasant land the domes and minarets of the Five Mosques point the way to the shining turquoise dome of the Prophet's tomb.

O Man! Here is a lovely portion of God's creation: then stand before it and learn to love the perfections of thy Supreme Friend, says the Arab poet, describing the beauty of El Medina.

There Shamyl lived in the house of the Sheik Akhmed el Roufai; gone were the striped wall-papers, the green-topped card-table, the fizgarmonia, and the big white porcelain stoves. The household had returned to their original way of living: cushions on a straw-matted floor, and little else. Like their 'Gospodin', they wished to approach God worthily, attuning themselves to the sacred aura of Medina without worldly or western distractions.

It was a time of sadness, of preparation: the shadow of partings had fallen on them. The terrible heat took its toll. The household would have liked to return to the temperate Bosphorus, but Shamyl, sensing his end was near, wished to remain at Medina. All the time, he was hoping to be joined by Khazi Mahommed: he could not believe the Russians would detain his sons, now. Late in 1870 Sofiate, Shouanete's daughter, died. Soon after, Zaïdate succumbed at Taif, in the hills, where she had gone to escape the heat. Of his wives, only Shouanete remained beside Shamyl; of his sons, only the little Kâmil. In Turkey, Nadjavat had married Daoud the Tcherkess, son of the traitor Mahommed Emin. He had broken with his father and come over to Shamyl, following him in his exile, and was now one of the diminished household at Medina.

Shamyl was writing to Russia with increasing urgency now, for his elder sons to join him: Had not the Prophet said: 'take your son there, and if you have no son, your servant.' But the new year came, and still the Russians withheld permission for their departure. Shamyl expected them hourly. He refused to believe the Tzar, his friend, would not understand. Perhaps the matter never reached the Tzar, for he seems to have been unaware that Shamyl was sinking. Bariatinsky was probably travelling abroad at the time, so that the matter was left to petty bureaucrats. Khazi Mahommed did not wish to discourage his father, and wrote that he would be with him very soon . . . he would be leaving in a few days. . . . But the time passed, and no permit was forthcoming. At last, he broke all the years of silence and discipline, and forcing an interview with the authorities, threatened to escape, to kill them, or himself, if he was not allowed to leave at once. His violence roused them. They hoped that one day he would be persuaded to return to the Caucasus as their representative; the whole country would have lived peaceably under his rule, so they ceded, with a bad grace. He could go to Mecca; but Habibette and the baby must remain, as hostages, against his return. Nor was Mahommed Sheffi allowed to go: but then he had never been so close to his father. He was one of the Imperial Escort in St. Petersburg. For good or ill, he had thrown in his lot with Russia. Habibette's grief was terrible, for she believed she would never see her husband again. Once outside Russia such a man was unlikely to walk meekly back into the trap.

From Constantinople Khazi Mahommed pressed on, east, but the desert route was cut by Arab bandits, and some more days were lost in ambush. At last, reaching Mecca, he went to perform the ritual prayer which every newcomer must make at the Qua'abah. As he knelt before the Black Stone, a ragged, green-turbaned old dervish came to stand beside him. Rocking backwards and forwards he began to exhort the pilgrims to pray: 'O ye faithful, pray now for the great soul of the Imam Shamyl!'

It was thus that Khazi Mahommed learned of his father's death. How the old dervish knew Shamyl had died the night before has never been discovered, for El Medina lay twelve days' march across the desert. Khazi Mahommed set out, that same day, walking barefooted on the stones, as if expiating a crime. Russian procrastination had lost him his last meeting with his father. He never forgot or forgave.

In January, Shamyl had decided to return to Mecca. He desired to make one more pilgrimage to the Qua'abah. He was very weak, and could no longer ride, but they placed him in a litter—a *takhtrawan*, one of the ceremonial red and gold camel litters, tufted with ostrich plumes and gaily curtained, which were generally used by persons of quality traversing the stony wastes surrounding the Holy City. The first night of the journey, as they advanced slowly to the measured pad of the camels, the family and the Naibs walking beside the litter, a camel stumbled, and the straps broke. Shamyl was pitched forward and so badly hurt that to go farther was impossible. *When God hath ordained a creature to die in a particular place he causeth his wants to direct him to that place.* The caravan turned back to El Medina, their laments echoing across the rocks.

In the house of Sheik Akhmed el Roufai, Shamyl, Imam ul'Azem, lay in a small room overlooking the Prophet's Tomb: but his bed was placed facing the door. Each time it opened he thought it would be

Khazi Mahommed, returning to him at last. He continued to believe in Russia's benevolence, and wrote one more letter to the Grand Duke Michael:

'My last request is that you will make it possible for all the members of my family to gather in one place after my death, lest they become like a flock of sheep left in the steppes without a shepherd.'

On February 4, 1871 (25 Zil Kaida 1287 of the Hejira), just before the Maghreb, or evening prayer, Shamyl roused himself. At the last, all his old force sounded once more. 'Allah! Allah!' he cried exultantly, and then the strange, half-shut eyes closed forever.

He was buried in the cemetery of Djánet El Bakir, his tomb becoming a place of pilgrimage for the pious. Today, there is no trace of the splendid monument, for Ibn' Saud's disciples have razed all such glories. But northwards, far away in the Caucasus, the mountains are still crowned by the ruins of Ghimri, Akhulgo, the Great Aôul, and Gounib. The mountains are his monument.

Epilogue

I

The great Caucasian drama was played out—its hero vanished, but lesser figures lingered on. Let us follow them into the shadows. Khazi Mahommed assumed leadership, and now all his pent-up bitterness was unleashed. He had been born and bred to hate the Infidel invaders. Fighting had been his whole life's pattern. He could not share his father's gratitude, or fatalism. The battle must be renewed, and he, the dispossessed but 'undoubted Chieftain of Daghestan under Allah', would renew the struggle from Turkish soil. An oath taken under duress—and to the Giaours—was not binding. He led the family back to Constantinople, to the great house at Koska.

On the return voyage, Nadjavat's husband Daoud sickened and died of typhoid. The captain ordered his body to be buried at sea. But Nadjavat, distracted with love and grief, had defied him, and posted two Lesghien guards at the cabin door. They had stood there with drawn kindjals till the boat reached Beyrout, where the interment at last took place. After which Nadjavat locked herself in the cabin where her husband had died, and there, before the ship reached Constantinople, gave birth to his child.

*   *   *

In 1874, Napoleon Ney was at Yildiz Kiosque, one of the royal palaces, where he noted 'a handsome young man, none other than Shamyl's son. He was dressed in Lesghien costume, with tcherkesska and papakh. As aide-de-camp to the Sultan, he accompanied him everywhere, was among the Generals and high dignitaries of state at the Selamlik (or *levée*) and was treated with the utmost deference.'

As the late Imam's son, escaped from Russian captivity, Khazi Mahommed was sure of a welcome. When the Sultan paced down the ranks of courtiers curved into that slavish obeisance prescribed by protocol, he saw a taut figure, towering above the rest, one hand held to his gigantic papakh in a military salute. This was Khazi Mahommed, a soldier, who never stooped to become a courtier. Caucasian loyalty and courage had long been known in Turkey. The Sultan created him a Pasha of the Ottoman Empire, Commander of one of his regiments, and 'Roumeli Beyler bey'—one of the highest civil appointments of the Empire. With these splendid titles came many emoluments. Materially, Khazi Mahommed, 'Mehmet Pasha' to the Turks, flourished. At

Koska he lived lavishly, yet retained that essential simplicity which his father's code imposed. His wealth was used largely to support a *train de vie* which permitted the house to be a kind of Caucasian caravanserai where exiled Murids, fallen chieftains, dignitaries of the Sultan's court and spiritual leaders came from all over the Moslem world. Even old enemies came there, sometimes, in a spirit of abnegation. Mahommed Emin, who had lost Shamyl his cause among the Circassians, strayed there, crazed with guilt, recoiling from some imaginary vengeance, and shrieking for mercy. Khazi Mahommed had been proclaimed fourth Imam in 1873, and while remaining a military figure, he was now invested with a growing spiritual force. No one found it strange that the fiery figure wearing the tcherkesṣka and the Sultan's arms should enter the mosque at Koska, there to lead the household in prayer.

At Koska, Habibette (at last released by the Russians) presided over the harem quarters. Here her little daughter Nafisette had died, in 1873, and now there was another, Emiré Nafisette. Births, deaths, marriages, days of mourning and fête days were all celebrated at Koska. The Caucasians came there to die, to give birth, to seek refuge. Here Sheffi sometimes came to visit his brothers and sisters. To Koska came Habibette's young brother, Mahommed Fazil Daghestani (or Daghestanli as he became known in Turkey). He left the Russian military academy to follow his sister to Constantinople, and to become Khazi Mahommed's inseparable friend. He too rose rapidly in the Sultan's service, being appointed Commandant of the Imperial Guard and like his brother-in-law, a Pasha, covered in honours. Thus these two Caucasian exiles occupied key positions in the Ottoman Empire, and enjoyed the Sultan's entire confidence.

In 1876 the Sultan Abdul Aziz had been deposed, and died soon afterwards, probably by his own hand. His nephew Murad succeeded, and was likewise deposed, for 'mental instability'. He was replaced by his younger brother, who became the Sultan Abdul Hamid II. But each successive Padishah maintained the same cordial relations with the Imam's family.

At Koska, Shouanete died. She could have returned to her Christian relatives at Mozdok, but for her there was no other family or faith than Shamyl's. For six years after his death, 'the Pearl' lingered on, desolate and withdrawn, looking out through the lattices on a life she no longer lived, until at last, in 1876, death freed her. Whether at the end she returned, in her heart, to the Christian faith, we do not know. It would have been very hard for her to die in the belief that she could not rejoin Shamyl in Mahommed's verdant Paradise.

* * *

The Circassian exodus to Turkey, in 1864, had been swelled by numbers of still rebellious mountain people from Tchetchnia and Daghestan. Pockets of resistance had remained long after Gounib fell, but now the Russians decided to crush any further opposition with terrible severity. The mountaineers were rounded up and brought down from the hills, to be dispersed about the lowlands at the point of a gun. However, they no more wished to exchange their aôuls for farms than to submit to the Giaours. They joined the Circassians, to take refuge under Moslem rule in Turkey. Much later, it was alleged that some of their leaders had been in Russian pay, obtaining so much a head for every Caucasian they enticed away. It suited the Russians to repopulate the emptied land with their own, more amenable Cossack settlers. Once again, England was said to have had a hand in the game, encouraging the Sultan to take them in. A body of fanatic Moslem fighters could do much to strengthen the Ottoman Empire against the reviving threat of Russian domination.

After the Crimean disaster Russia might have seemed crushed, but this was not the case. Lord Stratford de Redcliffe, 'the Great Elchi' whose life of power politics had centred round the Bosphorus and the Black Sea, wrote to Lord Clarendon in a prophetic vein: 'Nicholas' Russia is to all appearances on its knees, but the Russia of nature is still in its growth, shorn of its most forward branches, but capable of shooting into greater luxuriance at no distant period'.

A wave of panslavism now began to reshape Russia's foreign policy. The romanticized Slavophilism of an earlier Russia was giving place to the most positive, nationalistic fervour, fostered by mass emotion and the powers of the clergy, then at their zenith.

Meanwhile, the numbers of Circassians and Caucasians who had fled to Turkey had been dispersed about Asia Minor—a large colony at Adabazar; in Rumania, in the Dobrudja, and in Bulgaria; but little provision had been made for them, beyond imposing them on the local communities. Together with the Bashibazouks (irregular troops) whom the Turks employed to police their subjugated provinces, many of the Circassians now set up a reign of brigandage, suppressing every sign of independence with savagery. At last a series of atrocities in Christian Bulgaria aroused Europe's collective conscience and Mr. Gladstone's denunciations thundered through the House of Commons. The British Ambassador to the Porte, Sir Henry Elliot, admitted that Britain had been upholding 'Turkey, . . . a nation we know to be semi-civilized'. Disraeli struck a cynical note, and spoke of those Circassians who had taken so large a share of Bulgarian plunder as being settlers who had a great stake in the country. . . . Still, British interests in the Near East had to be maintained; to go to war with Turkey over this issue would have been unwise.

It was left to the Russians to defend the Christians, their co-religionists. In April 1877, Russia declared war on Turkey.

*   *   *

Now Khazi Mahommed sprang to life again. In the Sultan's suite, he had been a caged tiger beside the Sweet Waters of Asia, but at last the years of inactivity were over. Once more it was given him to lead an army of the Faithful against the Russian Giaours. He was created Commander of a Daghestani regiment, and at the head of a force levied from the exiled populations (who were overjoyed to exchange what they regarded as petty bloodshed for real warfare) Khazi Mahommed marched east, to where, beyond Kars, the Russians were massing.

Another force was led by his brother-in-law, Mahommed Fazil Daghestanli Pasha; the two Caucasians had sent emissaries into Daghestan to raise a revolt there, but the Russians had countered swiftly with terrible measures, the leaders being sent to Siberia in chains, or hung. Habibette's father, Daoudilaou of Tchokh was among the suspects, and had been poisoned. Thus Khazi Mahommed and Mahommed Fazil fought not only the abhorred Infidels, but the murderers of so many of their own blood.

Khazi Mahommed's five thousand cavalry were irregulars and poorly equipped. They were further disorganized by a lack of supplies: no food, no ammunition reached them, and cholera broke out. If Khazi Mahommed's messengers got back to base, no help was forthcoming. Treachery had lost Shamyl so many battles: it was to lose his son this one. The unique position of trust that he—the Caucasian—enjoyed close to the Sultan was not lost on the Turkish courtiers, and his enemies seized their chance. Still Khazi Mahommed fought, as he had always fought, impetuously, bravely. But standing before the Russian-held fortress of Beyazit, his demands for surrender were met with a bitter answer. Captain Stokovitch replied:

'Shamyl's son should have learned by now that Russia does not know how to surrender forts—only how to take them.'

The war continued for another year, but once again Russia's manpower and fighting qualities prevailed. In July, the battle of the Shipka Pass opened the way to Constantinople. From bases in Rumania the Russian army moved forward implacably. On January 31, 1878, the Porte sued for peace.

The whole map of the Balkans was changed. The treaty of San Stefano, dictated by Russia, was a moderate settlement which had freed the Christian minorities, though leaving Turkey far too weakened to suit the rest of Europe. The sick man of Europe *must* be propped up; *must* still represent a bulwark against Russian designs. A combined

assault of European plenipotentiaries headed by Bismarck, Disraeli and
Andrassy contrived a second treaty—that of Berlin. The map of the
Balkans was changed once more—now largely to suit the rest of
Europe, the original causes of the war being (as so often in the first
flush of peace) rather overlooked.

Many of the great Caucasian Dispersion now found themselves
absorbed into autonomous states, while some were under Russian rule
or influence again. Some remained in Turkey; among them, Khazi
Mahommed and Mahommed Fazil Daghestanli.

Yet such was the magic which Khazi Mahommed's name still held
for the Caucasus, that the Russians still tried every means to tempt him
to return there as their Viceroy. (Mahommed Sheffi, for all his loyalty,
counted for little among the tribesmen.) Had Khazi Mahommed consented to go back, the whole Caucasus would have been won over, and
followed him blindly. But he refused every overture. Nevertheless, for
many years the Russian Government continued the same allowance his
father had been given. The money was paid in to the Russian Embassy
in Constantinople, where it mounted, lying year after year, untouched.

*   *   *

In 1880 Khazi Mahommed and Mahommed Fazil Daghestanli were
at last brought low by the machinations of their numerous enemies.
They—the Caucasians—had enjoyed the Sultan's confidence for too
long. Late one night Deli Fuad Pasha, an unscrupulous, intriguing
character, came to Koska to ask Khazi Mahommed's support in a pro-
jected *coup d'état* by which the Sultan would be deposed, and the young,
'progressive' party put in power. Khazi Mahommed refused, saying he
had sworn fidelity to the Sultan. Mahommed Fazil followed suit, and
all Deli Fuad's persuasions could not move them. But fearful that they
might denounce him to the Sultan, he rushed to Yildiz Palace, and
accused them of the very plot he himself had instigated. So deeply was
the Sultan steeped in intrigue and counter intrigue that he allowed himself to be turned against his two most loyal followers. He sent for
Khazi Mahommed, telling him cruelly that the threatened *coup d'état*
had been averted without recourse to neither the seven thousand men
under his command, nor the Imperial Guard, under Mahommed
Fazil's orders.

'How am I to trust you, when you did not warn me of Deli Fuad's
plot?' asked the Sultan. To which Khazi Mahommed replied:

'Sire, I am a soldier, not a spy.' Abdul Hamid was now too deeply
sunk in the quagmire of intrigue: spies seemed more natural to him than
guards. He decided to gain the support of his wavering court at the
price of removing the two Caucasians.

Thus Khazi Mahommed and Mahommed Fazil Daghestanli were banished for ever from Constantinople. Their last request was that they might share their exile. But the Sultan feared their combined force, once it was not directed upon his defence. Khazi Mahommed was sent to languish in Medina; Mahommed Fazil to Baghdad. They were never allowed to meet again. Even Fazil's yearly requests to make the Hadj were refused: Mecca was too close to Medina. Although the Sultan feared and thwarted Mahommed Fazil, to the Bedouins and Kurdish tribes he became a hero, and presently, weary of Turkish rule, they offered him the crown of Iraq. But he refused, still feeling himself bound to the Sultan.

The youngest of Fazil's twelve children is known, today, throughout the world, as Major-General Khazi-Mahommed Daghestanli, who as Deputy Chief-of-Staff for the army of Iraq, was, in 1958, condemned to death, and who, in spite of the intervention of Queen Elizabeth, President Eisenhower and Nehru, is still imprisoned as I write this, his fate as uncertain as the tempo of Middle Eastern politics.

* * *

In exile, Khazi Mahommed's last years were lit by the devotion of Habibette. Not that she was a cloying slave. When they left Constantinople for Medina, their caravan was attacked in the desert by marauding tribes. She had been ordered to shelter in the *shugdūf*, or camel-litter. But having commended her child to Allah and veiled her face, she leapt down to fight beside her husband, firing a pistol and thrusting savagely with her kindjal. . . 'I know how to use a dagger, I was born in the Caucasus. . . .'

That was to be Khazi Mahommed's last fight. Gradually exile wore away his fiery spirit. He lost hope, realizing that he would never again go into battle, for the Caucasus or for the Sultan. Like his father before him, he turned towards prayer and meditation. Like Shamyl, he too became head of one section of the Nakshibandyié dervishes. To the people of Medina, he was 'father of the poor'. Over the years, his harsh face had become gentle, his tcherkesska exchanged for the mollah's robes, his weapons sheathed, forever. But at Báiram, when fireworks lit the skies, and the cannons thundered, he would climb to the roof top, and watch the puffs of smoke, listening to their roar with a tragic intensity. For him, it was the music of the spheres.

On September 27, 1902, Khazi Mahommed lay dying, watched over by the anguished Habibette. 'There must be no tears for God's will,' he told her, and died calling for Mahommed Fazil, who had not been allowed to share his second and bitterest exile. Khazi Mahommed was buried beside his father at Djánet el Bakir. Habibette turned her face to the wall. Three months later, she too was dead.

II

When Voronzov relinquished his Viceroyship in 1856 he was seventy-seven. His last public appearance was in Moscow, at the coronation of Alexander II, where he stood, a ghostly but still arrogant figure, weighed down by the diamond orders and decorations of a superbly successful life. Beside him stood his wife, the Princess Elizabeth. They were the embodiment of earthly glory.

Three months later the Prince died. His widow lived on for more than another quarter of a century, a survival from another age. Her childhood had been watched over by Great Catherine. She had been loved by Pushkin, had queened it over all Southern Russia. She had lived through so much of Caucasian history, and known so many of its giants. So many Caucasian heroes had dined at her table. . . . Gun-fire had always sounded behind the waltzes in her ballroom.

She lived on, an old lady at last, dressed in black and given over to good works. She was adored in Odessa, where she chose to remain and where she founded hospitals and almshouses for other, less fortunate old ladies. When she died, in 1883, she was buried beside her husband, in the cathedral at Odessa. During the revolution, when the cathedral was pulled down, the Voronzov vaults (along with the tombs of some Archbishops) were broken open, and the remains of this most illustrious family consigned to a communal grave.

Today, in the U.S.S.R., his memory is respected as a great Russian administrator, though he is also condemned for being feudal. His statue still dominates the Odessa waterfront; the Apollo-like figure stands splendid in cloak and uniform, although Pushkin's lines 'half ignoramus, half fool . . .' were chiselled on the plinth by the first fervent revolutionaries. The marble countenance still wears its cold half-smile of supreme indifference, staring out loftily, over those domains he ruled and enriched for Russia.

Fifty years after Prince Voronzov's death another Voronzov returned to rule the Caucasus with the same splendour. The gypsy's prediction had come true. The princely house had dwindled. Only the Viceroy's grand-daughter remained. The little Elizabeth who had prattled to her grandfather, in his last days, inherited all the titles and properties. Moreover, a strange fate was to bring her back to the Caucasus as Vice-reine. She had married a distant cousin, Count Voronzov-Daschkov, who, in 1905, was appointed Viceroy. 'He reigns—but she rules,' they said in Tiflis, tracing her grandfather in her haughty features, her absolute conviction of rulership. Those early years beside the great old man had formed her in the Voronzov mould: as Vicereine (and earlier at the Court of Alexander III, where she had been *Premiere Dame de Cour*), she wielded supreme power, for the good of the State, as she saw it, and as her grandfather and great-grandfather had done before her.

The cypress trees which Potemkin and the Empress Catherine had planted at Aloupkha had grown very tall, dark sentinels towering over the beautiful landscape. They had shaded her childhood, and were there when she returned as Vicereine; and they still stood, when, in her old age, the Bolsheviks arrested her. She had been imprisoned, and found it very disrespectful that other people were led out to be shot before she was.

'My name and my rank should have entitled me to go first,' she said. It was almost an anti-climax when she was released.

Soon, the Voronzov Palace was requisitioned, to become the House of the Pioneers, and a museum. The Theatre of the Georgian Nobility, where in her childhood Hadji Mourad had created such a stir, became the National People's Theatre. One by one the statues of her family were defaced or pulled down, to be replaced by newer demi-gods.

The Countess died in Wiesbaden in 1924. But the great cypress trees remained, soaring above Aloupkha for another twenty years, to tower over Roosevelt and Churchill and Stalin the Georgian, when they met there for the Yalta Conference.

III

The shadow of Shamyl's black banners reached across Europe to shadow a small French provincial town, La Feuillie, where Anna Drancy had found genteel employment. Her health had been shattered by what she had undergone in the Caucasus. After the exchange at the Mitchik, Madame Drancy had accompanied her *nobles protectrices*, as she describes them, back to Tiflis, where the whole town was *en fête* to welcome them. Madame Drancy found herself a heroine, and believed her troubles at an end. When the Princesses left for Moscow, to visit their mother, the widowed Princess Anastasia of Georgia, the French-woman again accompanied them. On the occasion of the Tzar's birth-day, a Te Deum was held in the cathedral. Madame Drancy was present, and carried away by emotion, longed to fling herself at the Tzar's feet, crying '*Merci! Merci!* How can I thank you—my saviour?' quite overlooking the fact that it was, before all, Djemmal-Eddin to whom she owed her release.

Soon afterwards she left for Paris, only to learn her mother had died. Her husband had disappeared, and now she found herself unaided, with her child to support. In 1857, assisted by a cousin, Edouard

Merlieux, she published a memoir, *Souvenirs d'une Française, Captive de Shamyl*, but the whole episode had become out-of-date. There was no love story; the writing was dry: sales were disappointing. Suddenly, she found herself a ghost, in a grey land, with nothing left to hope for. All the violence and terror and colour of that other life she had known and hated, had vanished; yet, curiously, it had been *life*. Now, anxieties replaced terrors, and respectability was all. Now it rained constantly, the steady downpour of northern Europe, so that her whole world was seen from under a dark cotton umbrella. Her *nobles protectrices* seem to have dropped her. There are no indications that they ever corresponded, or cared what happened to her.

At last, she was appointed post-mistress of a village in the department of Eure, exchanging the sound of those wild sorties when the Murids had leapt the walls of the Great Aôul, for the sedate trot of carriage horses approaching the village. She was only forty-two, but her whole self had been used up in that strange episode she had lived as Shamyl's prisoner.

In 1864 she died. Her grandsons are still living, very old gentlemen, who speak of her with pride, as a splendid mother, who struggled, alone, to bring up their father. They seem far less impressed by the extraordinary adventure she lived as Shamyl's prisoner—the only western woman who had ever entered the Great Aôul.

Yet those who trace the vast sweep of the Caucasian wars can never overlook her. The portrait of Shamyl and his Murids which she has left remains a remarkable document.

IV

When Alexander Dumas questioned the Princess Anna Tchavtchavadzé about her captivity, some years later, she referred him to Madame Drancy's book. 'She was always so exact,' said the Princess, turning her enormous black eyes on the impressionable Frenchman.

But was she not, perhaps, looking beyond him, recalling that other, strange, compelling gaze, 'the veiled eyes of a lion at gaze'—those of Shamyl the tyrant, who in spite of everything, she could not hate; and whom, perhaps, she loved.

There is a tradition in the Shamyl family that they had not been indifferent to each other: that the fiery Princess and the Chieftain of Daghestan had lived an unspoken idyll. She had returned to her family, to her marriage, in a curiously withdrawn spirit. Prince David shared the Georgian nobles' preoccupation with acquiring Western ways, but it lost them their original force: and a woman of Princess Anna's temperament must have been aware of the change.

Dumas sensed, but could not define, the Princess's air of melancholy.

He described her as a Niobe figure; rich, noble, 'a beloved wife, a fecund mother . . .' yet something baffled him. He supposed she was still steeped in the tragic loss of her baby, trampled to death by the Murid cavalry. When she spoke of their capture, of their life in the aôul, she broke into tears. Perhaps she mourned, too, another unavowed loss.

Her niece, Tamara Grigorievna, Princess of Georgia, remembered her well. 'Aunt Anna was small, and rather severe,' she told me. 'She did not like to speak of the adventure.' Indeed, it does not seem to have occupied much space in their busy overcrowded family life, soon becoming a vague legend.

I found the Princess very old and tired, living in a little apartment overlooking the chimney stacks and television aerials of New York. 'When I used to stay with Aunt Anna during my holidays, I did not listen much to family histories . . . it all seemed rather unreal. . . . Aunt Varvara, my Orbeliani aunt died in 1884, but I remember, she was softer, more approachable than Aunt Anna. . . . She didn't talk about Shamyl either—or if she did, I have forgotten . . . it was all so long ago. . . .'

V

As to the Tchavtchavadzé children, they soon forgot the whole affair. A vague remembrance of their friend, the Imam, faded; even the raucous dervish prayers they had loved to imitate dwindled to a faint echo . . . some adventure-game they had once played. . . .

In 1920 the Bolshevik revolution raced southwards, engulfing the princely families on its way. At Tzinondali, in the house which Prince David had rebuilt on the ruins left by the Murid raid, an old widowed lady was still living, where she had spent her whole life, cultivating its vineyards, and cherishing her estates. She remained unmoved by the approaching storm and was only persuaded by her children to leave with them for Turkey at the eleventh hour. This was the Princess Marie who had once studied French verbs with Madame Drancy, under the vine-wreathed arbour, that fatal summer of 1854. But on reaching Batoum she changed her mind and, deaf to all entreaties, returned to Tzinondali. The Georgian Communists respected her so much (her husband had come of a celebrated family of topers, something the Georgians always revered) that they commandeered a special train to take her back. A month later, she was dead. Tzinondali became a collective enterprise. Today, as the Sovkhoz vineyard of Tzinondali, it produces the finest wines in all Russia.

In 1945, after the fall of Berlin, the officers of the Red Army toasted their victory over the Nazis in wines from Tzinondali. Such a truly great victory was worthy of Russia's finest wine.

VI

The Naib Hadji-Harito's end was violent, his blood shed for Russia. When he returned to the Caucasus as Russian-appointed Naib of Ount-kratl, he no longer believed everything could be settled by the sword, and for some while he endeavoured to rule peaceably. The savage population thought their new ruler given over to fripperies, and misjudging him for a fop, resisted every effort of conciliation, continuing to harry and terrorize the province. At last their ringleaders were handed over to the Russian authorities, to be tried according to law. If Hadji-Harito had met them on their own terms, in hot blood, knifed them or shot them down, they would have found him just and strong; but that he adopted *legal* measures was his death-warrant.

The people bided their time, and had not long to wait.

Hadji-Harito was in the habit of riding across his territory, with his escort, to hold courts of enquiry at the outlying aôuls. On a night of tempest he took shelter in a mountain saklia. It was the chance his enemies had been waiting for. He had time to draw the bolts and barricade the tiny window before the attack. His escort had fled but for some hours he held off his enemies, firing through the chinks, each bullet dispatching a man. When at last a silence fell, the tribesmen knew his last bullet was gone, and they set light to the saklia, to smoke him out.

Hadji-Harito had come back to spread enlightenment, but nothing had changed; only now he, Hadji-Harito, was the enemy, and they stabbed him to death.

His assasssins were captured and tried, being sentenced to Siberia. In Kalouga, the women he had loved, those who had 'given him jam' in his own strange phrase, probably remembered the swaggering ways of their Moslem lover long after they had forgotten the great Imam.

VII

Field-Marshal Prince Bariatinsky's years of wandering began when he left the Caucasus in 1862, toppled from the Viceregal pedestal by scandal. The wreckage of such a career was not the happiest foundation for any marriage. That world that Bariatinsky had, in great measure, created in the Caucasus cannot have been well lost for love. He was at his zenith, and forty-five years old in 1862, when he was relieved of all his posts except that which he held in the Council of Empire. In Brussels, he married Madame Davidova, thus conferring on her that title by which she had so long been known—la Maréchale. They spent their honeymoon at a watering place in the south of England, which to some must have seemed just retribution.

Alexander II expressed his friendship in terms of solid gold swords encrusted in uncut diamonds, and the life tenancy of Skierniewice Castle, once the residence of the Kings of Poland. The Tzar still sought his advice in matters of state, often over the heads of his ministers; but there is no doubt that the fatal conduct of affairs in Circassia, leading to the exodus of 1864, would never have occurred had Bariatinsky remained in office.

The procession of half-lived hours—days—years—began to destroy the great Field-Marshal as they had destroyed Shamyl. But while the Imam, many years his senior, was withdrawing into a world of fatalistic contemplation, Bariatinsky, at fifty, was still raging with life: a conqueror with nothing to conquer. He had known a consuming passion for Madame Davidova: and he had married her; but it is doubtful whether human relationships, especially passions, can take first place—particularly as a substitute for a vocation such as Bariatinsky's Caucasian career had been.

He turned to morphia: at first, it stilled the pain of his old wounds, but soon, it stilled regrets, and even ennui. In the fashion of their age, the Bariatinskys were regular visitors to spas, Plombières, Ems, Baden-Baden. As their carriage rolled along, under the trees of the Lichtentaler Allee, the crowds could see that la Maréchal's small dark face had now assumed a rather fretful cast. As to the Field-Marshal, although he had lately been made honorary Colonel-in-Chief of the Prussian Hussars, he appeared turned to stone.

When the Russo-Turkish war broke out in 1877, the Tzar asked Bariatinsky to return and lead the Russian armies once more. However the Prince was now too ill; he was dying by inches, not 'as souls like his should die, in the hot clasp of victory', but like some mighty tree, rotting from within. Nevertheless, all that summer of 1878 he was back in St. Petersburg, working on plans to counter the war which he believed would develop from the Balkan issue.

Later that year his health worsened. He travelled back to Geneva, to consult a specialist, but it seemed too much effort to return to Skierniewice or Ivanovsky. He lay in bed, his face turned towards the mountains, those snowy Alps which, beside the mountains of the Caucasus, must have seemed like sugar-topped toys.

His mind was still on Russian affairs, foreign policy in particular, and he dictated a number of memoranda to the Tzar. He had always been against intervention in the Austro-Hungarian war, just as he had advocated the dismemberment of Austria, in spite of his Austrian blood and his attachment to the country. He was, first of all, a great Russian, dedicated to the interests of his country, and those of his friend—the Emperor. Above all, Bariatinsky criticized Russian policy in the Balkans; one day, he prophesied, this would lead to a world war.

And thirty-five years later, at Sarajevo, he was proved right. The force and stature of Prince Bariatinsky has not yet been properly assessed. He died before his time, with only one aspect of his genius—that of the great soldier—realized.

On a chill afternoon, in February 1879, Bariatinsky suddenly sprang up with all his old vigour.

'By God! If I'm to die, I'll die on my feet,' he cried, and fell back, dead.

In his will he ordered all his papers and correspondence to be sealed, for the next fifty years. In 1918, the Bariatinsky house was burned to the ground; thus perished what must have been unique sources on the Caucasian conquest. Although perhaps they are not lost. Even in the rage of revolution, the Bolsheviks showed a remarkable acumen in preserving documents and papers that might be of historic value. It is likely that the Bariatinsky papers, and many others, were removed, before all the rest was pillaged or destroyed, and are now among the extraordinary collection of documents and diplomatic sources in the Soviet archives, awaiting their historians.

While grandiloquent Voronzov monuments abounded in the Caucasus, Bariatinsky's greatest triumph was commemorated by one simple stone. At Gounib, where Shamyl surrendered to him, a small boulder remains to mark the exact place; today, it is roofed over by a pavilion. Here the conqueror sat, receiving the Imam's sword. The laconic inscription—BARIATINSKY—was ordered by the Prince himself. He would have no pompous phrases. Perhaps he had not altogether relished his rôle as Shamyl's conqueror.

VIII

The Tzar Alexander II, 'the Tzar Liberator', survived his dearest friend by two years: but for some time now it had been clear that he was doomed. The Nihilists and the mob—the Dark People—had marked him down. All the reforms he had tried to achieve had not won them over, and had only succeeded in alienating the nobles. Bombs found their way into the Winter Palace, or were discovered wherever the Tzar went. His sole comfort was the Princess Catherine Dolgoruky, who, seventeen years earlier, as an infatuated school-girl, had become his mistress, to live only for him. When the Tzarina died, in 1880, they were able to marry morganatically, and the Tzar created her Princess Yurievkskaya. He intended to recognize her, and their three children, publicly, although he was opposed by the Imperial family and almost the entire Court.

There was another, equally unpopular announcement he also wished to make. He had drawn up a plan for a Constitution. All these centuries Russia had been without either a Parliamentary representation or a

Constitution: everything had hinged on the will of one man—the Tzar. Now the ukase was signed, and only awaited publication.

On March 31, 1881, the Tzar was driving beside the Catherine Canal, when terrorist bombs exploded round him. He was dragged back to the Winter Palace, horribly mangled, and expired an hour later. The ukase granting a Constitution, which was to have been made public next day, was destroyed immediately by those Ministers who believed their action to be in the interests of the new Tzar—and no doubt, of themselves, too.

Alexander II's outlook was truly liberal. Yet he had never been appreciated by his people. He had tried to advance them, but they countered with bombs.

A curious blight had hung over him all his life. It had been noticeable even in his cradle. The Empress Elizabeth, wife of his uncle, Alexander I, noted in her journal that the new baby had 'a most pathetic little look'. Although he never acquired the stature of tragedy, he remains a haunting figure.

IX

In 1889, during the reign of Alexander III, two Russian officers, veterans of the Caucasian wars, were walking through the park at Kisslovodsk. They were discussing the heroic past. One was General Potto, who had written a history of the Caucasian campaigns; the other was that Zaharin, whose accounts of Shamyl, in Kalouga, have already been given. General Potto indicated a Herculean figure who was approaching them:

'Here is someone who can tell you more than anyone else about the Caucasus,' he said, and introduced Zaharin to Mahommed Sheffi. Thirty-eight years had passed since their last meeting. Shamyl's third son had been hardly more than a boy; now he was a heavy, very tall, middle-aged man, still athletic in build, with a short reddish beard. He spoke Russian fluently, but not very grammatically. He thanked Zaharin for the article he had written on Shamyl a year or so earlier. It was all perfectly true, he said: no lies, no distortions, such as the Pole Przhetzlavski had published.

Mahommed Sheffi had remained in the Russian army, reaching the rank of Major-General. During the Russo-Turkish war of 1877, Alexander II had refused to use him against men of his own faith—against his own brother, moreover. 'Wait until there is a war with the Prussians, then you shall go and fight for us,' he said.

Whenever Mahommed Sheffi returned to the Caucasus, news of his arrival spread across the mountains, and the tribes flocked down to see him, to catch a glimpse of Shamyl's son. They never ventured to speak to him, nor did he ever stop and talk with them: it was as if he wished to stress his break with the past: while for their part, they wished to show the feelings they still held towards Shamyl's kin. There had been a legend in the mountains, that on the night of Shamyl's death a strange light was seen in the sky. An old shepherd, speaking thirty years later to J. F. Baddeley, said: 'I was out by night watching my sheep. All at once the sky grew bright as fire and red as blood. I was afraid. Long after they told us the great Imam had died that night.'

Besides Sheffi, only Abdurrahman, his brother-in-law, had remained in Russia. He had a small pension and lived quietly in the Caucasus, on his estate at Kazi-koumoukh. He had stayed in the Russian army long enough to obtain the rank of Lieutenant-Colonel, but was now given over to theological studies.

After the death of his first wife, Mahommed Sheffi had consoled himself among the aristocracy of St. Petersburg. As one of the Imperial Escort, and Shamyl's son, he was considered irresistible. The glittering slit-eyes and the superb horsemanship quite compensated for the lost waistline. But gradually his sun began to decline. He was no longer in the immediate circle of the Court, for upon the accession of Alexander III, the Imperial Escort, recruited from among the Asiatic nobles, had been suppressed, almost overnight; their last appearance being at the funeral of Alexander II. They were replaced by Kuban Cossacks, in whom the Tzar's reactionary advisers felt more confidence.

Mahommed Sheffi withdrew to Kazan, where he presently married the daughter of Akhmet Ayagoff, a Tartar mourza, or Prince. There had been Tartar colonies in Kazan ever since the passing of the Golden Horde, and their strange and exotic city now became Sheffi's headquarters. Meriam, his second wife, was frivolous, considerably younger, and he doted on her.

Mahommed Sheffi had gone very far, in spirit, from the Great Aôul of his childhood. He still visited his family, though he never stayed in the house at Koska. The Russian Embassy became his headquarters; sometimes he arrived in a yacht lent him by the Tzar. To the end Alexander II showered his benefits on the Imam's family. When in St. Petersburg, Sheffi stayed at an officers' club. Sometimes he travelled abroad, to Vienna or Paris. And once, staying there with a Russian friend, Count K., he found himself billed as a fairground attraction. *Le Figaro* announced that no less a person than the celebrated Mahommed Sheffi, son of the great Caucasian leader, 'THE MUCH-WOUNDED HERO OF A THOUSAND BATTLES, THE DEATH-DEFYING RIDER WHO ESCAPED MIRACULOUSLY FROM GOUNIB, WILL PERFORM A NUMBER OF EQUESTRIAN FEATS, TOGETHER WITH A DISPLAY OF SWORDMAN-SHIP. NIGHTLY, 8 P.M. PRICE OF ADMISSION: I FRANC'. Once more, the Murid banners seemed to stir, a ghostly flapping, drowned by the blaring music of the roundabouts.

Mahommed Sheffi flew into a terrible rage, and seizing his kindjal rushed bellowing along the boulevards. Confronted by the true Mahommed Sheffi, the impostor, an Armenian, told a string of lies, trembled and tried to wriggle out of Mahommed Sheffi's grip, which was not relinquished until the police arrived.

Zaharin's last meeting with Mahommed Sheffi was in 1901. Shamyl's son was then over sixty. 'He seemed ill, and alone, and was living in a modest room at an officers' club.' Another Tzar was on the throne now; the young Nicholas II, great-grandson of that Nicholas whom Mahommed Sheffi had been brought up to fight, did not display any of the characteristics of his gigantic forebears. He was entirely absorbed by his own world of domestic felicity and dominated by his wife. Occasionally, affairs of State impinged, but were, as much as possible, kept at a distance. It is unlikely that he concerned himself over living links with more heroic ages.

Mahommed Sheffi and Zaharin spoke of the Boer war, then raging, and of the unequal struggle between Boer guerillas and the might of British arms. The nature of the struggle recalled the Caucasian wars. Zaharin remarked on the sympathy and admiration which the whole world felt for the Boers.

'But fifty years ago, father fought without even a sigh of sympathy from anyone,' replied Mahommed Sheffi sadly. Towards the end, his letters to Khazi Mahommed revealed his regrets; he realized that he had betrayed his heritage.

He died in 1904, in Russia, the land which had become his own, but which was to show his descendants so harsh a face. His two daughters Fatimat and Nafisette married, successively, Mahommed Dakhodaiev, a Communist engineer who disappeared in one of the purges after 1920. Sheffi's son, Zahed, also married the daughter of a Tartar, Baibekoff, and became head of a press department of the Ministry of the Interior, at St. Petersburg. He took an active part in the overthrow of the Tzarist régime, but was arrested by the Bolsheviks in 1924, and nothing is known of his fate. Nor is anything known of his three children. It is believed that Mansour, an engineer, died in a German concentration camp. Sofiate has vanished. There is no trace of the youngest, who was born in 1908, and bore the name of Khazi Mahommed.

X

Although the old house at Koska is no more, Shamyl's last descendants still live in Turkey. Mahommed Kâmil lived out his life there, for ever planning for the day when he could lead the exiled Caucasians back to their mountains, and during the Russian Revolution he was among the many who made a last stand in the Caucasus. For him, it was a first stand—his first sight of those great peaks which had been wrested from his father. His young son Säid had accompanied him: but once again Russia's arms—Bolshevik, now—conquered, and they were driven back to Turkey. Mahommed Kâmil died there in 1951. Säid and his two sisters live in the Fatih quarter, where, in an impersonally modern setting, the Murid's black banners still seem to dominate everything, as they did in the time of the Shariat. Today, throughout the Near and Far East, the Imam Säid Shamyl is known as one of the most dynamic figures of the Pan-Islamic movement. Yet, wherever his travels take him, I believe he holds first to the family ideal, the exile's dream of a return to their mountain birthright.

* * *

At Besiktas, in an old house beside the Bosphorus, I found the grandchildren of Khazi Mahommed. And just as the family names are preserved from one generation to another, so the family features persist: the same high-set, compelling slit-eyes, and the long, proud faces recur, unmistakably. Even Djemmal-Eddin's rather different cast of countenance, with its melancholy, enquiring gaze, recurs in the last generation.

Their mother was Khazi Mahommed's daughter, Emiré Nafisette. At Medina, in 1888, when she was fifteen, she married the Sheik ul Harem, or Military Governor, Field-Marshal Chapli Bereketuko Osman Ferid Pasha. He was of Circassian origin, an Adighe, and thirty years her senior. As a young exile from Russian aggression in 1870, he had been presented to Shamyl, who was then *en route* for Mecca; he had glimpsed the Imam's daughter Sofiate, and decided that he would marry her, or no one. But she had seemed inaccessible, her father too illustrious to be approached. And then, she had died. Nevertheless, no other woman would do, and the romantic young soldier remained unmarried until, eighteen years later, he encountered the Imam's grand-daughter. It was among their surviving children (they had eleven) that I pieced together the fragments of knowledge I had gathered from so many sources—from Russian military archives, Mahommed Tahir's Arabic chronicle, and from the recollections of many human links. Above all, from the family. Some of them recalled Khazi Mahommed. All of them had known the Murid battle chants as their lullabies: from their mother, they had learned the closely woven texture of their Caucasian background as no biographer could know it.

In their lofty rooms overhanging the Bosphorus, I found faded daguerreotypes—including the only known portrait of Djemmal-Eddin—family documents, battle orders, Shamyl's black tespyh; a high, padded Caucasian saddle, the shashkas and kindjals these mighty warriors had used—Caucasian wrack, cast up on a softer strand. Here, at last, listening as they spoke of their Caucasus, as they sang the melancholy chants of Daghestan, I consummated my years of research in so many different countries, among so many dusty archives.

XI

In Russia, during the last forty years, evaluations of Shamyl and the Murid movement have undergone a number of violent changes, reflecting various shades of party opinion and larger political issues too. Like place names, these differed with the years. The town of Vladikavkaz, as it was under Tzarist rule (and which had been originally the Ossete village of Zaloutch, later the village of Terek-kala), became known after the Revolution as Ordzhonikidze, after a People's Hero; but under Beria, it was named Dzau-Dzhi-Kau; and post-Beria, reverted to Ordzhonikidze, while Temir-Khan-Shura became Bouynaksh. And official re-appraisals of Shamyl have ranged from nuance to *volte-face*, these changes being admirably assessed in E. Walter's and Z. Laqueux's collection of articles: *The Middle East in Transition.*

Tzarist Russia saw Shamyl in heroic terms, one whose courage they magnified, if that were possible, in order to heighten the achievement of defeating him. For the first Bolsheviki he remained a hero; he had fought against feudal Tzarist oppression. Besides, Karl Marx had found him a great democrat; ideologically a forerunner of Communism. In 1930 the Party handbook stated that 'although Shamyl was leader of a religious movement, this in no way diminished his progressive significance. Even in conditions of developed capitalist society the class struggle often takes forms which conceal its content.'

Until the end of the war Shamyl remained the prototype of a People's Hero. The epic war years, Stalingrad, and the final assault on Berlin, had left no time for the finer shades of party evaluations. But afterwards, in 1947, Shamyl and the Murid movement were attacked as being ultra reactionary—the expression of militant Islam.

In opposing the Tzarist régime, Shamyl had, unfortunately, shed *Russian* blood. This was difficult to condone. During the war, it had been expedient to glorify all former feats of arms, irrespective of the fact they had been achieved under Tzarist rule, often in support of imperialistic designs. Thus Shamyl, fighting Russian troops, pitting himself against Mother Russia, automatically became an enemy. (Even so, travellers passing through the aôuls of Daghestan often encountered the

Imam's photograph usually turned to the wall—not so much for any political significance, however, as for the Moslem injunction against portraiture.)

Behind all the denunciations a note of anxiety sounds, as if some hard core of resistance had once more formed in the mountains. The mass deportations of various Caucasian tribes, in the immediate postwar period, proves the degree of alarm with which the government viewed the 'conquered' Caucasus. But had they ever been truly conquered? They had, at best, acquiesced: but essentially, they had withstood all their invaders, Tzarist troops, Cossack settlers, Revolutionaries, Red Armies, White Armies (which made their last heroic stand there), Bolshevik rule, Nazi invasion, and even, in some measure, Soviet dictation too. This was so much resented by certain tribes that they misguidedly imagined they might be better off under the Germans, and went so far as to favour Hitler's overtures.

Throughout the century since Shamyl had surrendered, an element of resistance had always remained in the mountains, to rise up and fight—to shelter outlaws, fugitives from Tzarist rule—or any other rule. From 1905 onwards, the Caucasus had become a breeding ground for revolutionaries and counter-revolutionaries. It was the headquarters of the Trans-Caucasian Activists, a group headed by the young Stalin, and their wild raids recalled the exploits of the abreks of another age. In 1907 Stalin, then known as Josef Djugashvili, had thrown the bomb which heralded a most audacious bank robbery, undertaken in broad daylight, in the main thoroughfare of Tiflis, and under the noses of the Cossack guards. The stolen money was designed to swell the party funds, and set up yet more printing presses. The Caucasus was the centre for Bolshevik propaganda. Their presses were hidden in Tiflis cellars or in mountain saklias, turning out millions of inflammatory pamphlets. Local prisons had a strange way of being unable to contain their Caucasian prisoners for any length of time. Once an escape was made, every mountain and valley concealed and defended the prisoner. Resistance there was always a whole way of life. It was to win over this spirit of independence, to cajole the Daghestani to join forces with the Bolsheviks, rather than with General Deniekin, that Lenin had dispatched a number of Shamyl's banners and trophies from the museums of Moscow to be placed in the custody of the people of Daghestan. However much the mountaineers resisted their latest invaders or the Bolsheviks, they loathed above all the Cossacks, they had never forgotten the wounds and humiliations of the Murid Wars. In 1919 at Gounib yet another terrible battle raged. One hundred and sixty Cossacks were hurled from the bridge at Saltee to perish as once the mountaineers had done.

After the war, in 1944, it was found expedient to disperse a number of truculent minority groups from the Caucasus. The autonomous re-public of the Tchetchens, who had collaborated with the Nazis, and been dangerously restive under the Soviets (one revolt breaking out in 1930, and another in 1941), were rounded up and sent to labour camps or exile settlements in Central Asia. Twenty-four hours later, the entire Tchetchen people were gone. The empty regions were soon re-peopled with more docile Russians from Orel and Koursk, though they prob-ably did not relish their enforced change of locale any more than the Tchetchens, struggling to adjust elsewhere. In this mass dispersal, seven whole nations were removed. The collaborationist Krim Tartars were re-settled in the Ukraine, while some Ukrainians were sent to Alma-Ata, capital of the Kazakh republic.

Since Stalin's death there has been yet another change in the official viewpoint on Caucasian minorities, and what is described as 'the Shamyl question'. The Soviet Union ranks as the fourth Moslem power; it would be impolitic to alienate Moslems within and without the frontiers of U.S.S.R. by continued hostility towards Shamyl, Murid-ism and Moslem minorities. Shamyl is no longer accused of having been an agent of British capitalism, or denounced as 'an Oriental-theocratic-feudal-monarchistic, despotic, military-religious ruler'. He has become the Lion of Daghestan, once more.

Today, the dispersed Caucasians are being replaced in their aôuls and valleys; historical works on the Murid movement, which had been withdrawn from the libraries, are returned to the shelves, and books presenting Shamyl in a sympathetic light are again in evidence. Im-portant conferences and debates, both in Daghestan and Moscow, have re-established him, though the *anti-Tzarist* rather than *anti-Russian* nature of his struggle is stressed. In his homeland, the Daghestani Ministry of Culture has restored a number of Shamyl's exhibits to the local museum. In one corner stand some of his banners, rather dejected looking rags. But the shadow of their former might reaches out, beyond the museum, beyond the little town, to the mountains, from where, all his life, Shamyl fought for freedom.

Genealogical Notes
on Shamyl and his wives
and children

Shamyl, third Imam of Daghestan. b. Ghimri 1796. d. Medina 1871. Son of Dengau an Avar of Ghimri and Bahou-Messadou. Both were of noble descent.

Fatimat. Shamyl's first wife. b. Ountsoukoul 1810. d. Alousind 1845. Daughter of Abdul Aziz, a celebrated surgeon. Three sons, two daughters:
1 Djemmal-Eddin.
2 Khazi Mahommed.
3 Mahommed Sheffi.
4 Nafisette.
5 Fatimat.

Djavarat. Shamyl's second wife. b. Ghimri 1821. d. Akhulgo 1839. One son:
Säid: died in infancy.

Zaïdate. Shamyl's third wife. b. Kazi-koumoukh 1823. d. Medina 1870. Daughter of Mollah Jamul u'din, Shamyl's spiritual teacher and descendant of the Prophet. Two daughters, one son:
1 Nadjavat.
2 Bahou-Messadou.
3 Mahommed Kâmil.

Shouanete. Shamyl's fourth wife (The Pearl). b. Mozdok 1825. d. Constantinople 1876. A Christian captive, converted to the Moslem faith. One daughter:
Sofiate.

Aminette. Shamyl's fifth wife: a Kist (Tchetchen). b. 1835. Divorced 1858. No children.

FAMILY: IN ALPHABETICAL ORDER

Bahou-Messadou. Shamyl's fifth daughter (by Zaïdate). b. Dargo-Vedin 1856. d. Constantinople 1875.

Djemmal-Eddin. Shamyl's eldest son (by Fatimat). b. Ghimri June 15, 1831. d. Karaty July 12, 1858. Taken as hostage by the Russians 1839. Returned to the Caucasus 1856.

Fatimat. Shamyl's second daughter (by Fatimat). b. Dargo-Vedin 1843. d. Medina 1871. Married Abdurrahim, son of Mollah Jamul u'din.

Kamil. (Mahommed.) Shamyl's fifth son (by Zaïdate). b. Kalouga 1861. d. Istanbul January 18, 1951. Married Nebihé. Four children: Säid, Nadjia, Nadjavat, all living in Turkey; Jamul u'din died in Damascus.

Khazi Mahommed. Shamyl's second son (by Fatimat). b. Ghimri April 1833. d. Medina September 27, 1902. Proclaimed the Imam's heir 1851. Married, in 1851, Kherimat. No children. Second wife: Kistaman (Habibette). First child, Nafisette, b. Kalouga 1864, d. Constantinople 1873. Second child, Emiré Nafisette, b. Constantinople 1873, d. Istanbul November 2, 1950. She married, in 1888, Field-Marshal Chapli Bereketuko Osman Ferid Pasha, Sheik ul Harem, Governor General of Medina. Eleven children, of whom five survive.

Kherimat. Khazi Mahommed's first wife. b. Tiflis 1835. d. Kalouga 1861. Daughter of Daniel Beg, Sultan of Elisou.

Kistaman. (Habibette.) Khazi Mahommed's second wife, whom he married 1863. b. Tchokh 1844. d. Medina 1903. Daughter of Daoudilaou of Tchokh, the most famous swordsmith and metal worker in the Caucasus.

Mahommed Sheffi. Shamyl's third son (by Fatimat). b. Baiyan 1839. d. Piatigorsk 1904. Married first, Aminette, daughter of the Naib Enkaou Hadjio. Second wife, Meriem, daughter of Akhmet Ayagoff, a Tartar Mirza (or Prince) of Kazan. Two daughters and one son, Mahommed Säid, d. Moscow 1924.

Nadjavat. Shamyl's third daughter (by Zaïdate). b. Dargo-Vedin 1846. d. Constantinople 1874. Married Daoud the Tcherkess, son of Mahommed Emin. One daughter died in infancy.

Nafisette. Shamyl's eldest daughter (by Fatimat). b. Dargo-Vedin 1842. d. Kalouga 1862. Married Abdurrahman, son of the Mollah Jamul u'din. Their daughter died in Constantinople 1874.

Sofiate. Shamyl's fourth daughter (by Shouanete). b. Dargo-Vedin 1855. d. Medina 1870.

Author's Note

Much of my material derives from nineteenth-century Russian military sources, where Caucasian names are Russified as part of the process of colonization. Thus, the Caucasian Kachkalyk becomes Kachkalykov. This is understandable—but the fact that it is ethnographically incorrect and must forever rankle among Caucasians is equally understandable.

Generally, I have tried to follow those spellings which seemed to me most suitable, though I did not attempt to unify them, since in both Russian and Caucasian place names, I have used a spelling which approximates to the sound. Chechnia, the customary English spelling, does not risk being pronounced 'kecknia', if written Tchetchnia. In the name Khazi Mohammed, Khazi seems to me closer to the Arabic sound, than the classic Ghazi: the phonetic Voronzov replaces the more usual Worontzov, while the names Chichagova and Davidova are the feminine gender of the family names Chichagov and Davidov.

In the complications of Shamyl's household, Mahommed being attached to so many names, besides two generations of Fatimats and Nafisettes, Hadjios and Hadjis, Abdurrahmins, Abdurrahmans, etc., etc. to make the uninitiated reader reel, I have sometimes taken the liberty of spelling the same name in two ways to differentiate between two persons. Thus Shamyl's son is Djemmal-Eddin; but the Mollah after whom he was named, is called by the alternative spelling Jamul u'din. Hadjio, the steward, might be confused with the young Naib of the same name were not the latter known here as Hadjio Harito. The prefix Mahommed is sometimes rendered Magoma, Magomet or Magomoi, as in certain sources, to facilitate identification.

As to the use of the word Circassian for Caucasian—a confusion which is constantly found in a number of nineteenth-century English sources, and therefore occurs in quotations. I would remind the reader that while the term 'Caucasian' applies to all tribes of the Caucasus, 'Circassian' is specific to the peoples of the Circassia and 'Tcherkess' is the Russian version of the same name. Again 'Tartar' is often loosely used by the Russians to describe the tribes of far different origins; locally the term 'Tartar' is held to mean those of Turkic or Mongol origin.

L. B.

Bibliography

ABERCROMBY, J. *A Trip through the Eastern Caucasus.* London 1889.

ALLEN, W. E. D. *A History of the Georgian People.* London 1932.

ALLEN, W. E. D. and MURATOFF, P. *Caucasian Battlefields.* Cambridge 1953.

ARBERRY, A. J. *An Introduction to the History of Sufism.* London 1943.

BADDELEY, John F. *The Russian Conquest of the Caucasus.* London 1908.
The Rugged Flanks of the Caucasus. 2 vols. Oxford 1940.

BALLEYDIER, Alphonse. *Histoire de l'Empereur Nicolas.* Paris 1857.

BECHHOFER-ROBERTS, Carl Eric. *In Denikin's Russia and the Caucasus, 1919–1920.* London 1921.

BELL, J. S. *Journal of a residence in Circassia, 1837–39.* 2 vols. London 1840.

BENCKENDORF, Count Constantin de. *Souvenirs intime d'une Campagne au Caucase, 1854.* Paris 1858.

BODENSLADT, Frederic. *Les Peuples du Caucase et leur querre d'indépendance contre la Russie.* Paris 1859.

BOHUSZ, Sciestrzencewicz. *Histoire de la Tauride.* 2 vols. Paris 1800.

BRAYLEY HODGETTS, E. A. *The Court of Russia in the Nineteenth Century.* London 1908.

BROCKELMANN, Carl. *History of the Islamic People.* New York 1947.

BROWN, Edward Granville. *A Year among the Persians, 1887–8.* London 1893.

BUXTON, Harold. *Russian Rule in the Caucase.* London 1914.

Cambridge History of British Foreign Relations (The). Cambridge 1923.

CUNYNGHAME, Sir Arthur. *Travels in the Eastern Caucasus, etc.* London 1872.

CUSTINE, Astolphe de. *La Russie en 1839.* Paris 1843.

CZARTORYSKI, Prince Adam. *Mémoires.* Paris 1887.

DEPPING, G. *Shamyl, le Prophète du Caucase.* Paris 1854.

DITSON, George Leighton. *Circassia; or, a Tour to the Caucasus.* New York 1850.

DUMAS, Alexandre. *Impressions de voyage.* Paris 1868.

Ein besuch bei Shamyl—Brief eines Preussen. Berlin 1855.

FLORINSKY, Michael. *Russia: a History and an Interpretation.* 2 vols. New York 1953.

FONTON, V. *La Russie dans l'Asie Mineure.* Paris 1840.

FRESHFIELD, Douglas. *Travels in the Central Caucasus and Bashan.* London 1869.

GAGARIN, Prince Grigorii Grigorievitch. *Le Caucase Pittoresque, dessiné d'après nature par le Prince G. G. Gagarin (texte par le Comte Ernest Stackelberg).* Paris 1847.

GAUTIER, Théophile. *Voyage en Russie.* Paris 1867.

GOBINEAU, Count Joseph Arthur de. *Souvenirs de Voyage.* Paris 1872.
Les Religions et les Philosophies dans l'Asie Centrale. Paris 1865.

GOLOVIN, Ivan. *La Russie depuis Alexandre le Bien-Intentionné.* Paris 1859.

GROUSSET, R. *L'Empire des Steppes.* Paris 1938.

GRUNWALD, Constantin de. *Trois siècles de diplomatie russe.* Paris 1945.
Tsar Nicholas I. Paris 1952.
HAXTHAUSEN, Baron von. *The Tribes of the Caucasus.* London 1835.
The Russian Empire. 2 vols. London 1856.
HERZEN, Alexander. *Du développement des idées révolutionnaires en Russie.* Paris 1851.
Mémoirs. 6 vols. London 1924.
HOMMAIRE DE HELL, Mme Adèle. *Lettres et Mémoires, après la prétendue traduction du Prince P. P. Wiusemsky, forme fragmentaire.* Paris 1887.
HOMMAIRE DE HELL, Adèle and Xavier. *Travels in the steppes of the Caspian Sea, the Crimea, the Caucasus, etc.* London 1847.
HOMMAIRE DE HELL, Xavier. *Voyage dans les steppes du midi de la Russie.* 3 vols. Paris 1844.
Les steppes de la mer Caspienne. Le Caucase, la Crimée et la Russie méridionale, historique et scientifique. Paris 1843–5.
JESSE, William. *Notes of a Half-Pay in search of health.* London 1841.
LACROIX, P. *Histoire de la vie et du règne de Nicholas I.* Paris 1865.
LAMMENS, H. *Islam. Beliefs and Institutions.* London 1929.
LANG, David. *The last years of the Georgian Monarchy.* New York 1857.
LAQUEUR, Walter Z. (ed.). *The Middle East in Transition.* New York 1958.
LERMONTOV, M. *A Hero of Our Times* (trans. E. and C. Paul). London 1940.
LOFTUS, Lord Augustus. *Diplomatic Reminiscences.* London 1929.
MARLINSKY, Alexander. *(Bestoujev) Esquisses Circassiennes—Esquisses sur le Caucase.* Paris 1854.
MARNIER, X. *Du Danube au Caucase. Voyages et littérature.* Paris 1854.
Mémoire de la Province du Shirvan en forme de lettre adressée, au Père Fleuriau—Lettres édifiantes. Lyon 1819.
MEREJKOVSKY, D. *Eternels Compagnions de route.* Paris 1949.
MERLIEUX, Edouard. *Souvenirs d'une Française captive de Shamyl.* Paris 1857.
MILTON MACKIE, J. *Life of Shamyl.* Boston 1856.
MONTPEREUX, F. Dubois de. *Voyage autour du Caucase, chez les Tcherkess, Abkhases, et, en Armenie, Géorgie et le Crimée.* 6 vols. Paris 1839.
MORELL, J. R. *Russia and England. Their strength and weakness.* New York 1854.
MOUNSEY, H. A. *A journey through the Caucasus and interior of Persia.* London 1872.
MOURIER, J. *La Mingrélie.* Paris 1883.
OHSSON, C. d'. *Des peuplades du Caucase.* Paris 1828.
OLIPHANT, Laurence. *The Russians Shores of the Black Sea.* London 1854.
The Trans-Caucasian campaign of the Turkish Army under Omer Pasha (1806–1871). Edinburgh and London 1856.
ORSOLLE, E. *Le Caucase et la Perse.* Paris 1828.
PALÉOLOGUE, G. Maurice. *La Russie des Tzars pendant la Grande Guerre.* Paris 1922–3.
The Tragic Romance of Alexander II. London 1926.
Revelations of Russia in 1846. (Anon.) 2 vols. London 1846.
ROUX, C. *Alexandre II. Gorchakoff et Napoléon III.* Paris 1913.
RUMBOLD, Horace. *Recollections of a diplomat.* 2 vols. London 1902.
SALA, G. A. *Journey due North.* London 1858.
SCHLEGEL, C. W. Friedrich von. *The Philosophy of History.* 2 vols. London 1835.

Bibliography 487

SHEIL, Lady. *Life and Manners in Persia.* London 1856.
SKRINE, F. H. *The Expansion of Russia, 1815–1900.* Cambridge 1904.
SOLOGUB, A. V. A. *Au bord de la Néva.* Paris 1856.
SPENCER, Capt. *Turkey, Russia, Black Sea and Circassia.* London 1854.
    Travel in Western Caucasus in 1836. London 1838.
    Turkey and Russia. London 1854.
SUMMER, B. H. *Russia and the Balkans, 1870–1880.* Oxford 1937.
SYKES, Sir Percy. *A History of Persia.* 2 vols. London 1921.
THIELMANN, Max von. *Journey in the Caucasus. Persia and Turkey in Asia.* London 1875.
TOLSTOY, Alexandra. *Léon Tolstoi, mon père.* Paris 1956.
TOLSTOY, Leo. *Ivan Ilych and Hadji Mourad.* Oxford 1935.
    The Diaries of Leo Tolstoy, 1847–52. London 1917.
URQUHART, D. *Progress and Present Position of Russia in the East.* London 1838.
USSHER, John. *Journey from London to Persepolis.* London 1855.
VASSILI, Count Paul. *Behind the veil of the Russian Court.* London 1914.
VERDEREVSKY, M. *The captivity of two Russian Princesses* (trans. H. Sutherland Edwards). London 1857.
VERNET, Horace. *Lettres intime pendant son voyage en Russie, 1842–1843.* Paris 1856.
WAGNER, Frederick. *Schamyl and Circassia.* London 1854.
WAGNER, Maurice. *Travels in Persia, Georgia and Kurdistan.* 3 vols. London 1856.
WALISZEWSHIK. *Autour d'un trône. Catherine II de Russie.* Paris 1897.
WARDROP, Oliver. *The Kingdom of Georgia.* London 1888.
WILBRAHAM, Capt. Richard. *Travels in the Trans-Caucasian Provinces of Russia.* London 1839.
WOHL, Janka. *Souvenirs d'une compatriote.* Paris 1887.
WOLFF, Reverend Joseph. *Narration of a mission to Bokhara (1843–1845).* London 1846.
WRANGEL, Baron W. *Memoirs, 1847–1920.* London 1927.

SPECIAL SOURCES AND PERIODICALS

Bibliographia Kavkaza. Vol. I. St. Petersburg 1874–6.
CONSTITUTIONS; ELECTORAL LAWS AND TREATIES, in Near and Middle-East. New York 1947.
CROZIERS QUARTERLY, 1944.
THE ENCYCLOPEDIA OF ISLAM. London 1913–34.
FRAZERS MAGAZINE. January 1873.
IZVESTIA. October 14, 1939.
KAVKAZKI JOURNAL, Tiflis, Nos. 72–6.
MINISTERE DES AFFAIRES ÉTRANGÈRES. Correspondance Commerciale, Tiflis, 1842–71, Tome III. Correspondance Politique, Russie, Vol. 211, 1854.
LE MONDE SLAVE. 1925–6.
LE PAYS. September 9, 1854; October 4, 1854.

REVUE DES DEUX MONDES. December 15, 1865.
REVUE LITTERAIRE ÉTRANGÈRE. January 1854.
THE SOVIET ENCYCLOPEDIA, 2nd edn. Moscow 1949–58.
L'UNIVERS. September 8, 1854; September 10, 1854; September 11, 1854.
Voprossi Istorii, No. 7. 1956.

RUSSIAN SOURCES

Adati Kavkazkhi Gortzev. Adats of the Caucasian Tribe of Gortzev. F. Leonto-
vitch. Odessa 1883.
Akti Sobranniyie Kavkazkoy Arkheografitcheskoi Komissii (Papers of the Archeo-
grafical Commission of the Caucasus). Tiflis.
Arkhiv Voronzov (The Voronzov Archives). Moscow 1870–95.
BOGDANOV, D. P. *Pamiat o Shamyle v Kalouga* (Recollections of Shamyl in
Kalouga). Istoriitcheski Vestnik. St. Petersburg 1913.
BRUCKNER, A. *Smert Pavla I* (Death of Paul I). Moscow 1909.
CHICHAGOVA, M. N. *Shamyl na Kavkazie ii v Roussii* (Shamyl in the Caucasus in
Russia). St. Petersburg 1889.
GORCHAKOV, N. *Vtorjenie Shamyla v Kabardou 1848* (Shamyl's intrusion into
Kabarda). Kavkazkii Sbornik. Tiflis 1879.
Kavkasky Sbornik (Caucasian Chronicles). Vols. VIII–X. St. Petersburg 1887–9.
KAZEM BEK. *Muridism ii Shamyl* (Muridisim and Shamyl). Rousskoye Slovo.
St. Petersburg 1859.
Kerimat neviestka Shamyla (Kherimat, Shamyl's daughter-in-law). Istorichesskii
Vestnik. Vol. 121.
Lermontov, M. Y. Akademia Naouk, U.S.S.R. Leningrad 1953.
Narodi Dagestana (People of Daghestan). Akademia Naouk, U.S.S.R. Moscow
1955.
Novir Mir (New World). Vol. 33. No. 2. Moscow 1957.
Pamyatnaiya Knizka Dagestanskoi oblasti (Journals of the Daghestan province).
Temir-Khan-Shura 1895.
POTTO, GENERAL V. A. *Yermolova v Dagestan* (Yermolov's campaigns in
Daghestan). Rousskaia Starine (Old Russia). Vol. XXIV. Moscow 1879.
PRZHETZLAVSKI, P. G. *Shamyl ii ego semya a Kalougye 1863–1865* (Shamyl and his
family in Kalouga). Rousskaia Starina. St. Petersburg 1877.
RUNOVSKY, A. *Zapicki Shamyla* (Notes on Shamyl). St. Petersburg 1861.
TAHIRA, MOHAMMED AL KARAHI. *Khronika* (Chronicles, concerning the wars
of Daghestan in the time of Shamyl). Translated from the Arabic.
Akademia Naouk, U.S.S.R. 1941.
Voprossi Istorii No. 7 (Questions of History). Moscow 1956.
ZAHARIN, I. N. *Kavkaz ii ego geroii* (The Caucasus and its Heroes). St. Peters-
burg 1902.
   Vstretchi ii vospominanyia (Encounters and Recollections). St. Petersburg
   1903.

Index